P9-DVG-265

DARK ALLIANCE

DARK ALLIANCE

The CIA, the CONTRAS, and the CRACK COCAINE EXPLOSION

GARY WEBB

SEVEN STORIES PRESS
New York

A Seven Stories Press First Edition

In the U.K.:
Turnaround Publisher Services Ltd., Unit 3, Olympia Trading Estate, Coburg Road, Wood Green, London N22 6TZ U.K.

In Canada:
Hushion House, 36 Northline Road, Toronto, Ontario M4B 3E2, Canada

Library of Congress Cataloging-in-Publication Data

Webb, Gary.
Dark alliance: the CIA, the contras, and the crack cocaine explosion / Gary Webb.
p. cm.
ISBN 1-888363-68-1
1. Crack (Drug)—California—Los Angeles. 2. Cocaine habit—California—Los Angeles. 3. Counterrevolutionaries—Nicaragua. 4. United States. Central Intelligence Agency. I. Title.
HV5833.L67W43 1998
363.45'09794—dc21 97-52612
CIP

9 8 7 6 5 4 3 2 1

Book design by Cindy LaBreacht

Seven Stories Press
140 Watts Street
New York, NY 10013

Printed in the U.S.A.

TO SUE, WITH LOVE AND THANKS

Contents

Foreword

BY CONGRESSWOMAN MAXINE WATERS

The night that I read the "Dark Alliance" series, I was so alarmed, that I literally sat straight up in bed, poring over every word. I reflected on the many meetings I attended throughout South Central Los Angeles during the 1980s, when I constantly asked, "Where are all the drugs coming from?" I asked myself that night whether it was possible for such a vast amount of drugs to be smuggled into any district under the noses of the community leaders, police, sheriff's department, FBI, DEA and other law enforcement agencies.

I decided to investigate the allegations. I met with Ricky Ross, Alan Fenster, Mike Ruppert, Celerino Castillo, Jerry Guzetta, and visited the L.A. Sheriff's Department. My investigation took me to Nicaragua where I interviewed Enrique Miranda Jaime in prison, and I met with the head of Sandinista intelligence Tomas Borge. I had the opportunity to question Contra leaders Adolfo Calero and Edén Pastora in a Senate investigative hearing, which was meant to be perfunctory, until I arrived to ask questions based on the vast knowledge I had gathered in my investigation. I forced Calero to admit he had a relationship with the CIA through the United States Embassy, where he directed USAID funds to community groups and organizations.

The time I spent investigating the allegations of the "Dark Alliance" series led me to the undeniable conclusion that the CIA, DEA, DIA, and FBI knew about drug trafficking in South Central Los Angeles. They were either part of the trafficking or turned a blind eye to it, in an effort to fund the Contra war. I am convinced that drug money played an important role in the Contra war and that drug money was used by both sides.

The saddest part of these revelations is the wrecked lives and lost possibilities of so many people who got caught up in selling drugs, went to prison, ended up addicted, dead, or walking zombies from drugs.

It may take time, but I am convinced that history is going to record that Gary Webb wrote the truth. The establishment refused to give Gary Webb the credit that he deserved. They teamed up in an effort to destroy the story—and very nearly succeeded.

There are a few of us who congratulate Gary for his honesty and courage. We will not let this story end until the naysayers and opponents are forced to apologize for their reckless and irresponsible attacks on Gary Webb.

The editors of the *San Jose Mercury News* did not have the strength to withstand the attacks, so they abandoned Gary Webb, despite their knowledge that Gary was working on further documentation to substantiate the allegations of the series.

This book completely and absolutely confirms Gary Webb's devastating series. This book is the final chapter on this sordid tale and brings to light one of the worst official abuses in our nation's history. We all owe Gary Webb a debt of gratitude for his brave work.

Acknowledgments

I am forever indebted to my friend and colleague Georg Hodel, who helped me chase this epic through Central America at immeasurable risk to both himself and his family in Nicaragua. His persistence, his wisdom, and his courage were a constant inspiration, and a melancholy reminder of just how far from the path of righteousness corporate American journalism has wandered.

Another journalist to whom I owe a special debt is Nick Schou of *O.C. Weekly*, who put the *L.A. Times* to shame with his reporting, and was very generous with his time and his discoveries. Pam Kramer of the *San Jose Mercury News* Los Angeles bureau was a joy to work with as well, being smarter (and braver) than almost every other reporter I know.

In the 1980s and early '90s, a number of journalists began unearthing parts of this skeleton bone by bone. My investigative predecessors are also owed thanks, not only for their thoughts and their files but for their courageous work in helping to bring this story to light: Tony Avirgan, Brian Barger, Dennis Bernstein, Alexander Cockburn, Leslie Cockburn, Sally Denton, Brian Donovan, Guillermo Fernández, Martha Honey, Peter Kornbluh, Jonathan Kwitny, Jonathan Marshall, John McPhaul, Jefferson Morley, Roger Morris, Micah Morrison, Robert Parry, Seth Rosenfeld, Peter Dale Scott, Josiah Thompson, Douglas Vaughan, and David Umhoefer. Patriots all.

Thanks much to David Paynter and Elizabeth Lockwood of the National Archives in College Park, Maryland, who unfailingly answered my Freedom of Information Act (FOIA) requests within ten days and patiently searched the Walsh databases for needles in haystacks. I am also grateful to the many cheerful librarians at the California State Library's Government Publications Section in Sacramento, particularly senior librarian Deborah Weber, who taught me the wonders of the FBIS microfiche.

John Mattes, Jack Blum, and Jon Winer of the Kerry Committee staff were extraordinarily helpful, and one day, I am sure, they will be hailed for the remarkable service they rendered to the American public under very trying circumstances.

The efforts of my agent, Flip Brophy, are much appreciated, though I'm sure her self-esteem will never recover from the torrent of rejections. I am also beholden to my fearless publisher, Dan Simon, and the folks at Seven Stories Press for their faith and patience.

Finally, I would never have been able to write this book and survive these past few years without the love, support, and understanding of my wife, Sue, and our children, Ian, Eric, and Christine. You're the best.

—G.W.
Sacramento, March 1998

Author's Note

This, sadly, is a true story. It is based upon a controversial series I wrote for the *San Jose Mercury News* in the summer of 1996 about the origins of the crack plague in South Central Los Angeles.

Unlike other books that purport to tell the inside story of America's most futile war (*Kings of Cocaine* by Guy Gugliotta and Jeff Leen and *Desperados* by Elaine Shannon spring to mind), *Dark Alliance* was not written with the assistance, cooperation, or encouragement of the U.S. Drug Enforcement Administration or any federal law enforcement agency.

In fact, the opposite is true. Every Freedom of Information Act request I filed was rejected on national security or privacy grounds, was ignored, or was responded to with documents so heavily censored they must have been the source of much hilarity down at the FOIA offices. The sole exception was the National Archives and Records Administration.

Dark Alliance does not propound a conspiracy theory; there is nothing theoretical about history. In this case, it is undeniable that a wildly successful conspiracy to import cocaine existed for many years, and that innumerable American citizens—most of them poor and black—paid an enormous price as a result.

This book was written for them, so that they may know upon what altars their communities were sacrificed.

—G.W.

Cast of Characters

The Contras

THE FUERZA DEMOCRÁTICA NICARAGÜENSE (FDN)

BERMÚDEZ, ENRIQUE—"Commandante 380," the supreme military commander of the FDN. Former military attaché for the Somoza regime in Washington. Hired by the CIA in 1980 to reassemble Somoza's scattered brigades into a fighting force. Close friend of the Meneses family. Reportedly trafficked in arms and cocaine with Norwin Meneses. Murdered in Managua in 1991, a slaying that has never been solved.

CALERO, ADOLFO—Longtime CIA agent, former manager of the Coca-Cola bottling plant in Managua. Selected by the CIA in 1983 to lead its political wing. Worked closely with Oliver North. Met with Norwin Meneses several times during the years Meneses was selling drugs for the Contras. Now a member of the Nicaraguan Assembly.

PEÑA, RENATO—Spokesman for the FDN branch in San Francisco and one of Norwin Meneses's cocaine dealers. Admitted hauling millions in drug profits from San Francisco to Los Angeles for delivery to the Contras during the early 1980s. Convicted of cocaine trafficking in 1985.

SÁNCHEZ, FERNANDO—Former Nicaraguan ambassador to Guatemala, and the FDN's representative in that country during the war. Identified by the FBI in 1982 as one of the cocaine suppliers to the Contra drug operation in San Francisco. Brother of FDN founder Aristides Sánchez.

SÁNCHEZ, ARISTIDES—Wealthy landowner under Somoza who became the head of supplies and logistics for the FDN. Also went on the CIA payroll in the early 1980s as an aide to Enrique Bermúdez. Allegedly served as the conduit for cocaine money flowing from the Meneses drug ring in California in the early 1980s. Died in Miami in 1993.

UNION DEMOCRÁTICA NICARAGÜENSE—FUERZA ARMADA RESISTENCIA NICARAGÜENSES (UDN-FARN)

AVILES, FRANCISCO—U.S.-educated Nicaraguan lawyer and CIA asset who worked closely with the CIA in Costa Rica in the 1980s, funneling CIA and U.S. government funds to various Contra organizations. Brother-in-law of top Meneses cocaine trafficker Horacio Pereira. Directly involved in the San Francisco Frogman case in 1983, though never accused or charged with cocaine trafficking. In 1998 Aviles was working for the Nicaraguan government.

CABEZAS, CARLOS—While not a member of UDN-FARN, Cabezas supported it through his cocaine sales in San Francisco in the early 1980s. As a U.S. government witness, he testified that his drug profits were going to Contra organizations in Costa Rica. He pleaded guilty to drug charges in 1984 and served several years in prison. He is now practicing law in Managua.

CHAMORRO, EDMUNDO—Second in command to his brother, Fernando. Implicated in cocaine trafficking with the Meneses organization during Costa Rican police investigation in 1985, but never charged. Close ties to the CIA, according to a DEA report. Current whereabouts unknown.

CHAMORRO, FERNANDO "EL NEGRO"—Commander of the UDN-FARN, which was based in Costa Rica during most of the war. An alcoholic whose army was teeming with Cuban-American drug traffickers, terrorists, and assorted other ne'er-do-wells. While working for the CIA, he was approached by Norwin Meneses and asked to haul cocaine to the United States from Costa Rica, but he was never directly implicated in cocaine trafficking. Died in Nicaragua in the early 1990s. (Fernando and Edmundo were only distantly related to the influential Chamorro clan that included martyred newspaper editor Pedro Joaquin Chamorro.)

RAPPACCIOLI, VICENTE—CIA asset based in Costa Rica. One of the leaders of UDN-FARN and related Contra support groups. Directly involved in 1983 Frogman cocaine case, but never charged. He reportedly died in the early 1990s.

ZAVALA, JULIO—Major cocaine trafficker in San Francisco Bay Area during early 1980s, and top-ranking U.S.-based member of UDN-FARN. Recruited Carlos Cabezas into Contra drug ring. Convicted of cocaine trafficking in 1984, he now reportedly works as an informant for the FBI.

ALIANZA REVOLUCIONARIA DEMOCRÁTICA (ARDE)

AGUADO, MARCOS—CIA-trained pilot, business associate, and reputed drug-trafficking partner of Norwin Meneses. Aguado got ARDE commander Edén Pastora involved with Colombian drug traffickers. Accused of cocaine trafficking in Costa Rica, he fled to El Salvador, where he assumed a high-ranking position with the Salvadoran Air Force. Implicated but never charged in Meneses's 1991 cocaine bust in Nicaragua. Currently in San Salvador.

GONZÁLEZ, SEBASTIAN "GUACHAN"—CIA asset who was heavily involved in drug trafficking in Panama and Costa Rica. Close to Manuel Noriega. Suspected of involvement in the beheading of Contra supporter Hugo Spadafora, shortly before Spadafora was to make information about Noriega's drug involvement public. González is a close friend of Norwin Meneses and, according to the CIA, was a fellow cocaine trafficker during the Contra war. Now living in Panama.

PASTORA, EDÉN—**"Commandante Zero."** Former Sandinista war hero. Recruited by CIA officer Dewey Clarridge in 1981 to assume command of the Southern Front Contra armies based in Costa Rica. Longtime friend of Danilo Blandón, from whom he received money, vehicles, and rent-free lodging. Eventually broke with CIA and was accused by the agency of consorting with drug traffickers. Ran for Nicaraguan president in 1996.

The Investigators

CASTILLO, CELERINO—Decorated Vietnam War veteran, former Texas policeman, and former DEA agent assigned to El Salvador and Guatemala during mid-1980s. Discovered Contra cocaine trafficking at Ilopango Air Force Base in El Salvador and began reporting it. Subsequently subjected to numerous internal DEA investigations and forced to retire on disability in early 1990s. Currently lives in Texas.

GORDON, THOMAS—Veteran Los Angeles County narcotics investigator. As a sergeant for the L.A. County Sheriff's Office in 1986, Gordon led the investigation into and obtained the search warrants for Danilo Blandón's drug operation. After his retirement, he was indicted by the Justice Department and accused of failing to report stolen drug money as income. Convicted on income tax charges. Currently lives in San Dimas, California.

GUZZETTA, JERRY—Bell, California, police department's sole narcotics investigator. Began the investigation that led to the arrests of Danilo and Chepita Blandón in 1986. Subsequently subjected to internal affairs investigation involving missing cocaine from evidence locker, but never charged. Retired in early 1990s and lives in Los Angeles area.

JUAREZ, ROBERT—Veteran L.A. County Sheriff's Office narcotics officer who raided Ronald Lister's house in 1986 and reported finding Contra and CIA-related material there. Juarez, regarded as one of the department's best undercover operatives, was subsequently indicted by the Justice Department and convicted of stealing cocaine money. He lives in Los Angeles.

KELSO, JOSEPH—Former CIA operative and undercover Customs informant. Kelso pleaded guilty to attempting to buy Harpoon missiles for the Iraqis in the early 1980s. Investigated allegations of the involvement of DEA agents in cocaine trafficking in Costa Rica during Contra war. Was beaten and threatened with death by DEA agents, deported, and arrested for probation violation upon his return to the United States. Now working somewhere in Arizona.

POLAK, STEVE—Longtime Los Angeles Police Department narcotics investigator. One of the founders of the Freeway Rick Task Force. Subsequently indicted on federal charges of corruption, income tax evasion, and civil rights violations. Pleaded guilty to misdemeanor civil rights violations and retired. Lives in Los Angeles.

The CIA and Fellow Travelers

CLARRIDGE, DUANE "DEWEY"—Former chief of the CIA's Latin American Division from 1981 to 1984. Oversaw creation of Contra project and recruited many of its leaders. Indicted in 1991 on seven counts of perjury and providing false information to Congress during the Iran-Contra scandal. Pardoned before trial by ex-CIA director George Bush.

FERNÁNDEZ, JOSEPH—CIA station chief in Costa Rica from 1984 to 1986. Integral part of Oliver North's illegal Contra resupply operation. Responsible for pushing Edén Pastora out as commander of Contra forces in Costa Rica and promoting Fernando Chamorro and his Cuban-American legion, which included terrorists and drug traffickers. Indicted in 1989 on four counts of providing false information to Congress during the Iran-Contra scandal. The case was dropped when the U.S. attorney general refused to declassify evidence needed in the case. Fernández now works with Oliver North at North's publicly traded company, Guardian Technologies, which sells security consulting services and body armor.

FIERS, ALAN JR.—Took over Contra project in 1984 from Dewey Clarridge. Admitted having information on drug trafficking through Ilopango Air Force Base in El Salvador and also had knowledge of Contra drug dealing in Costa Rica. Pleaded guilty to withholding information from Congress during Iran-Contra scandal. Later pardoned by George Bush. Now works in Washington as government relations specialist.

"GÓMEZ, IVAN"—Pseudonym of Venezuelan CIA contract agent who handled logistics on the Southern Front for the Contras during the war. Identified by Carlos Cabezas as the conduit for drug money from the Meneses organization in San Francisco to the Contras in Costa Rica. "Gómez" denied it in an interview with the CIA. Married former girlfriend of Meneses lieutenant Marcos Aguado and is reportedly living in Spain.

HULL, JOHN—Indiana farmer who was CIA liaison to the Contras in Costa Rica. Hull's ranch was reportedly the site of numerous drug transshipments, an allegation he has long denied. Hull worked closely with suspected drug traffickers Marcos Aguado and Dagoberto Nuñez on Contra projects in Costa Rica. He was indicted in 1989 on drug trafficking and murder charges there and fled the country with the assistance of the Costa Rican DEA office. The drug charges were later dropped, but he was permanently forbidden reentry into Costa Rica. Hull is currently living in Indiana.

NIEVES, ROBERT "THE SNOWMAN"—Head of DEA office in Costa Rica while Meneses and Dagoberto Nuñez were working as informants there. Meneses identified Nieves as his control agent. While he was DEA attaché in Costa Rica, the DEA office was alleged by Costa Rican officials to be involved in drug trafficking and protecting cocaine labs in Contra war zones, charges that were never proven. Nieves went on to become the head of all DEA operations internationally and resigned in 1995. He works for Oliver North and Joe Fernández in the security business and is a frequently cited drug expert for network television news.

NUÑEZ, DAGOBERTO—Cuban Bay of Pigs veteran and CIA-DEA operative suspected of cocaine trafficking in Costa Rica. Worked closely with North's illegal Contra resupply operation and helped U.S. government funnel money to the Contras there. Helped John Hull escape from Costa Rica. Reportedly runs a cellular telephone dealership in San José, Costa Rica.

OWEN, ROBERT—Former prep school counselor in Los Angeles who became a key CIA operative in Costa Rica for Oliver North and Joe Fernández. Owen served as a go-between, or "cutout," for the agency's dealings with the Cuban-American drug dealers assisting the Contras on the Southern Front. Intervened in the Kelso case and destroyed alleged evidence of DEA involvement with cocaine trafficking. Reportedly working as a teacher in Florida.

SEAL, BARRY—Major drug trafficker in southern United States in early 1980s. Became CIA-DEA operative in 1984 White House attempt to entrap Sandinista leaders in cocaine bust. Reportedly flew weapons for the Contras and returned to the States with cocaine. Murdered in New Orleans in 1986 by Colombian hit men.

The Crack Dealers

BROWN, LEROY "CHICO"—Corner Pocket Crip and major Compton crack dealer with the Patrick Johnson organization. Became involved with Ricky Ross as a business partner in early 1990s. Pleaded guilty to drug charges in San Diego in 1996 and is serving an eleven-year sentence.

NEWELL, OLLIE "BIG LOC"—Ricky Ross's childhood friend and partner in what would eventually become South Central L.A.'s largest crack distribution network in the early to mid-1980s. Convicted of drug charges in Indiana in late 1980s and released from prison in 1997. Now living in Los Angeles.

ROSS, "FREEWAY" RICKY—Leader of South Central's first major crack distribution ring. In the space of four years Ross went from selling fractions of an ounce to shipping multimillion-dollar cocaine shipments across America. Convicted of cocaine trafficking in 1996, he is currently serving life without the possibility of parole.

The Meneses Organization

CORÑEJO, RAFAEL—Distributor for Norwin Meneses in San Francisco Bay Area since mid-1970s. His territory stretched all the way to Portland, Oregon. Arrested, tortured, and jailed by Manuel Noriega's men in 1977 while he was smuggling cocaine through Panama for Norwin. Convicted of income tax evasion in San Francisco in 1985. Indicted and jailed for cocaine trafficking in 1992; convicted and sentenced to thirty years in 1996.

MENESES, EDMUNDO—Former Nicaraguan ambassador to Guatemala, former general in Nicaraguan National Guard, former chief of police in Managua, all before Somoza's fall. Norwin's brother and main protector. Probable CIA asset. Graduate of U.S. Army School of the Americas. Assassinated in Guatemala in 1978 by guerrillas shortly before Somoza's overthrow.

MENESES, GUILLERMO—Nephew of Norwin. Handled cocaine distribution for Meneses family in Bay Area and Los Angeles in the early 1990s. Targeted by FBI in Corñejo investigation but never charged.

MENESES, JAIME—Nephew of Norwin and son of Jaime Meneses Sr. Involved in cocaine trafficking in San Francisco Bay Area since late 1970s. Became a crack addict in the late 1980s and dropped from view.

MENESES, JAIRO—Nephew of Norwin and son of Edmundo Meneses. Involved in cocaine trafficking in San Francisco Bay Area since late 1970s. Arrested and jailed in 1985. Reportedly rearrested on cocaine charges in the early 1990s.

MENESES, NORWIN "EL PERICO"—The King of Drugs. Leader of the Meneses organization. Believed to have been the Cali cartel's representative in Nicaragua. Drug trafficker since early 1970s. Lived in United States from 1979 to 1985. Close connections to Cuban anti-Communist movement. Worked for the Contras as a recruiter, arms supplier, and benefactor during the entire war. Worked with DEA from 1985 to 1991. Indicted in the States in 1989 on drug charges but never arrested. Arrested and jailed in Nicaragua in 1991, sentenced to twelve years in prison.

MIRANDA, ENRIQUE—Former Sandinista intelligence officer, CIA asset, DEA informant, and right-hand man to Norwin Meneses from 1989 to

1991. Part of supersecret Sandinista dirty-tricks unit inside the Interior Ministry. Testified against Meneses in Nicaragua in 1992 and reportedly targeted for death by the drug lord as a result. Miranda "escaped" from prison in 1995 and was recaptured in Miami in 1996, where he was kidnapped by the FBI, allegedly for the escape, and put on a plane back to Nicaragua.

PEREIRA, HORACIO—Friend and business partner of Norwin Meneses in prewar Nicaragua. Joined him in exile in Costa Rica where he become one of Meneses's top cocaine dealers there. Identified by FBI in 1982 as source of cocaine for Frogman drug ring in San Francisco. Conduit of drug funds from Meneses operation in Bay Area to Contras in Costa Rica and Honduras. Convicted of cocaine trafficking in Costa Rica in 1986 and escaped. Meneses says he was murdered in Guatemala in the early 1990s.

SÁNCHEZ, TROILO—Brother of FDN officials Aristides and Fernando Sánchez. Business partner of Meneses in prewar Nicaragua and in Costa Rican exile during the 1980s. Flew for the CIA in Nicaragua in the 1960s. Identified by FBI in 1982 as source of cocaine for Frogman ring in San Francisco. Arrested on drug charges in Costa Rica in mid-1980s but acquitted. Recovered drug addict. Now lives in Nicaragua.

VIGIL, FRANK—Former Nicaraguan advertising executive and longtime business partner of Norwin Meneses in prewar Managua and in Costa Rican exile. In the 1980s he worked in Mexican political campaigns and was in business with the Venezuelan government in Florida. Suspected of selling cocaine for the Contras in Los Angeles in early 1980s. Indicted by Nicaraguan government in 1991 on cocaine charges with Meneses but was acquitted. Now lives in Managua.

The Blandón Organization

BLANDÓN, DANILO "CHANCHIN"—Head of multiton cocaine distribution ring in Los Angeles from 1981 to 1991. First major trafficker to make inroads into South Central Los Angeles in early 1980s, providing the street gangs with their first direct connection to the Colombian cocaine cartels. Longtime supplier to Freeway Rick Ross. Worked as part of Meneses organization, but struck out on his own in 1985. Founded FDN chapter in Los Angeles. Arrested and convicted of cocaine trafficking in 1992 and became DEA informant. Now divides his time between San Diego and Managua.

BLANDÓN, CHEPITA—Danilo Blandón's wife. Identified by the DEA as being closely involved in the trafficking activities of her husband. Arrested and jailed in 1992 but charges were dropped when Danilo agreed to become a DEA informant. Was made a naturalized United States citizen as a result of his cooperation.

CORRALES, HENRY—Cocaine distributor for Blandón in Los Angeles in early 1980s. One of Freeway Ricky Ross's first suppliers. Left the States in mid-1980s for Honduras. Current whereabouts unknown.

GUERRA, SERGIO—Mexican millionaire and owner of lucrative parking lot on Mexican border near Tijuana. Money launderer for Blandón in California and Florida. Business partner with Blandón in several used car lots. Convicted of money-laundering charges in early 1990s and sentenced to jail. Deported to Mexico, where he is reported to be living.

LISTER, RONALD JAY—Ex-police detective who served as a money launderer, security adviser, and mule for Blandón in the mid-1980s. Involved in arms deals with the Contras and security work for Salvadoran politicians and Iranian exiles. Has worked as FBI, DEA, and local police informant. Convicted of drug trafficking in late 1980s and sent to prison. Released in 1996. Current whereabouts unknown.

MORENO, APARICIO—Colombian supplier to both Blandón and Meneses organizations during the Contra war. Reported ties to the FDN and CIA. Implicated in drug trafficking in Guatemala in 1988 in connection with top CIA agent there. Current whereabouts unknown.

MURILLO, ORLANDO—Chepita Blandón's uncle and suspected money launderer for Blandón organization. Economist who served on the board of Nicaragua's Central Bank before the revolution and managed many of the Somoza family businesses. Managua representative of Swiss Bank Corp. and Citizens and Southern Bank before the war. Became an investment banker in Florida while in exile. Elected to the Nicaraguan Assembly in 1996 and announced his resignation during an interview with the author and Georg Hodel. Though long suspected by the DEA of money laundering, he was never charged with a crime in the United States.

TORRES, JACINTO AND EDGAR "THE TREES"—Longtime friends and sometime rivals of Blandón in the cocaine business. Related by marriage to ex-Medellín cartel boss Pablo Escobar. Jacinto was convicted of drug charges in 1986. Both became DEA informants in early 1990s after conviction on cocaine charges.

Every government is run by liars and
nothing they say should be believed.

—I. F. STONE, 1907–1989

PART ONE

"It was like they didn't want to know"

When I came to work in the sprawling newsroom of the *Cleveland Plain Dealer* in the early 1980s, I was assigned to share a computer terminal with a tall middle-aged reporter with a long, virtually unpronounceable Polish name. To save time, people called him Tom A.

To me, arriving from a small daily in Kentucky, Tom A. was the epitome of the hard-boiled big-city newspaperman. The city officials he wrote about and the editors who mangled his copy were "fuckinjerks." A question prompting an affirmative response would elicit "fuckin-a-tweetie" instead of "yes." And when his phone rang he would say, "It's the Big One," before picking up the receiver.

No matter how many times I heard that, I always laughed. The Big One was the reporter's holy grail—the tip that led you from the daily morass of press conferences and cop calls on to the trail of The Biggest Story You'd Ever Write, the one that would turn the rest of your career into an anticlimax. I never knew if it was cynicism or optimism that made him say it, but deep inside, I thought he was jinxing himself.

The Big One, I believed, would be like a bullet with your name on it. You'd never hear it coming. And almost a decade later, long after Tom A., the *Plain Dealer*, and I had parted company, that's precisely how it happened. I didn't even take the call.

It manifested itself as a pink While You Were Out message slip left on my desk in July 1995, bearing an unusual and unfamiliar name: Coral Marie Talavera Baca.

There was no message, just a number, somewhere in the East Bay.

I called, but there was no answer, so I put the message aside. If I have time, I told myself, I'll try again later.

Several days later an identical message slip appeared. Its twin was still sitting on a pile of papers at the edge of my desk.

This time Coral Marie Talavera Baca was home.

"I saw the story you did a couple weeks ago," she began. "The one about the drug seizure laws. I thought you did a good job."

"Thanks a lot," I said, and I meant it. She was the first reader who'd called about that story, a front-page piece in the *San Jose Mercury News* about a convicted cocaine trafficker who, without any formal legal training, had beaten the U.S. Justice Department in court three straight times and was on the verge of flushing the government's multibillion-dollar asset forfeiture program right down the toilet. The inmate, a lifer, had argued that losing your property *and* going to jail was like being punished twice for the same crime—double jeopardy—and seventeen judges from the Ninth Circuit Court of Appeals agreed with him. (Faced with the prospect of setting thousands of dopers free or returning billions in seized property, the U.S. Supreme Court would later overturn two of its own rulings in order to kill off the inmate's suit.)

"You didn't just give the government's side of it," she continued. "The other stories I read about the case were like, 'Omigod, they're going to let drug dealers out of jail. Isn't this terrible?'"

I asked what I could do for her.

"My boyfriend is in a situation like that," she said, "and I thought it might make a good follow-up story for you. What the government has done to him is unbelievable."

"Your boyfriend?"

"He's in prison right now on cocaine trafficking charges. He's been in jail for three years."

"How much more time has he got?"

"Well, that's just it," she said. "He's never been brought to trial. He's done three years already, and he's never been convicted of anything."

"He must have waived his speedy trial rights," I said.

"No, none of them have," she said. "There are about five or six guys who were indicted with him, and most of them are still waiting to be tried, too. They want to go to trial because they think it's a bullshit case. Rafael keeps writing letters to the judge and the prosecutor, saying, you know, try me or let me go."

"Rafael's your boyfriend?"

"Yes. Rafael Corñejo."

"He's Colombian?"

"No, Nicaraguan. But he's lived in the Bay Area since he was like two or something."

It's interesting, I thought, but not the kind of story likely to excite my editors. Some drug dealers don't like being in jail? Oh.

"What's the connection to the forfeiture story?" I asked.

Rafael, she explained, had been a very successful "businessman," and the government, under the asset forfeiture program, had seized and sold his automobiles, his houses, and his businesses, emptied his bank accounts, and left him without enough money to hire a lawyer. He had a court-appointed lawyer, Coral said, who was getting paid by the hour and didn't seem to care how long the case took.

"Rafael had the most gorgeous house out in Lafayette, and the government sold it for next to nothing. Now what happens if he's acquitted? He spends three or four years in jail for a crime he didn't commit, and when he gets out, someone else is living in his house. I mean, what kind of a country is this? I think it would make a good story."

It might, I told her, if I hadn't done it half a dozen times already. Two years earlier, I'd written a series for the *Mercury* called "The Forfeiture Racket," about the police in California busting into private homes and taking furniture, televisions, Nintendo games, belt buckles, welfare checks, snow tires, and loose change under the guise of cracking down on drug traffickers. Many times they'd never file charges, or the charges would be dropped once the victims signed over the loot.

The series created such an outcry that the California legislature had abolished the forfeiture program a few weeks later. But I knew what I would hear if I pitched Coral's story to my editors: We've done that already. And that was what I told her.

She was not dissuaded.

"There's something about Rafael's case that I don't think you would have ever done before," she persisted. "One of the government's witnesses is a guy who used to work with the CIA selling drugs. Tons of it."

"What now?" I wasn't sure I'd heard correctly.

"The CIA. He used to work for them or something. He's a Nicaraguan too. Rafael knows him, he can tell you. He told me the guy had admitted bringing four tons of cocaine into the country. Four tons! And if that's what he's admitted to, you can imagine how much it really was. And now he's back working for the government again."

I put down my pen. She'd sounded so rational. Where did this CIA stuff come from? In seventeen years of investigative reporting, I had ended up doubting the credibility of every person who ever called me with a tip about the CIA.

I flashed on Eddie Johnson, a conspiracy theorist who would come bopping into the *Kentucky Post*'s newsroom every so often with amazing tales of intrigue and corruption. Interviewing Eddie was one of the rites of passage at the *Post*. Someone would invariably send him over to the newest reporter on the staff to see how long it took the rookie to figure out he was spinning his wheels.

Suddenly I remembered who I was talking to—a cocaine dealer's moll.

That explained it.

"Oh, the CIA. Well, you're right. I've never done any stories about the CIA. I don't run across them too often here in Sacramento. See, I mostly cover *state* government—"

"You probably think I'm crazy, right?"

"No, no," I assured her. "You know, could be true, who's to say? When it comes to the CIA, stranger things have happened."

There was a short silence, and I could hear her exhale sharply.

"How dare you treat me like I'm an idiot," she said evenly. "You don't even know me. I work for a law firm. I've copied every single piece of paper that's been filed in Rafael's case and I can document everything I'm telling you. You can ask Rafael, and he can tell you himself. What's so hard about coming over and at least taking a look at this stuff?"

"That's a fair question," I allowed. Now, what was my answer? Because I lied and I do think you're crazy? Or because I'm too lazy to get up and chase a story that appears to have a one-in-a-thousand chance of being true?

"You say you can document this?"

"Absolutely. I have all the files here at home. You're welcome to look at all of it if you want. And Rafael can tell you—" In the background a child began yowling. "Oh, Sierra! Just a minute, will you? That's my daughter. She just fell down."

The phone thunked on the other end, and I heard footsteps retreating into the distance.

Well, that's a promising sign, I thought. Were she a raving dope fiend, they wouldn't let her raise an infant. She came back on, bouncing the sobbing toddler. I asked her where she lived.

"Oakland. But Rafael's got a court date in San Francisco coming up in a couple weeks. Why don't I meet you at the courthouse? That way you can sit in on the hearing, and if you're interested we could get lunch or something and talk."

That cinched it. Now the worst that could happen was lunch in San Francisco in mid-July, away from the phones and the editors. And, who knows, there was an off chance she was telling the truth.

"Okay, fine," I said. "But bring some of those records with you, okay? I can look through them while I'm sitting there in court."

She laughed. "You don't trust me, do you? You probably get a lot of calls like this."

"Not many like this," I said.

Flipping on my computer, I logged into the Dialog database, which contains full-text electronic versions of millions of newspaper and magazine stories, property records, legal filings, you name it. If you've ever been written about or done something significant in court, chances are Dialog will find you.

Okay. Let's see if Rafael Corñejo even exists.

A message flashed on the screen: "Your search has retrieved 11 documents. Display?" So far so good.

I called up the most recent one, a newspaper story that had appeared a year before in the *San Francisco Chronicle*. My eyes widened.

"4 Indicted in Prison Breakout Plot—Pleasanton Inmates Planned to Leave in Copter, Prosecutors Say."

I quickly scanned the story. Son of a bitch.

> Four inmates were indicted yesterday in connection with a bold plan to escape from the federal lockup in Pleasanton using plastic explosives and a helicopter that would have taken them to a cargo ship at sea. The group also considered killing a guard if their keepers tried to thwart the escape, prosecutors contend.
>
> Rafael Corñejo, 39, of Lafayette, an alleged cocaine kingpin with reputed ties to Nicaraguan drug traffickers and Panamanian money launderers, was among those indicted for conspiracy to escape.

The story called Corñejo "a longtime drug dealer who was convicted in 1977 of cocaine trafficking in Panama. He also has served time in a U.S. prison for tax evasion. He owns several homes and commercial properties in the Bay Area."

This sure sounds like the same guy, I thought. I scrolled down to the next hit, a *San Francisco Examiner* story.

> The four men were charged with planning to use C-4 plastic explosives to blow out a prison window and with making a 9-inch "shank" that could be used to cut a guard's "guts out" if he tried to block their run to the prison yard. Once in the yard, they allegedly would be picked up by a helicopter and flown to a Panamanian cargo ship in the Pacific, federal officials said.

The remaining stories described Corñejo's arrest and indictment in 1992, the result of an eighteen-month FBI investigation. Suspected drug kingpin. Head of a large cocaine distribution ring on the West Coast. Allegedly involved in a major cocaine pipeline that ran from Cali, Colombia, to several West Coast cities. Importing millions of dollars worth of cocaine via San Diego and Los Angeles to the Bay Area.

That's some boyfriend she's got there, I mused. The newspaper stories make him sound like Al Capone. And he wants to sit down and have a chat? That'll be the day.

When I pushed open the doors to the vast courtroom in the San Francisco federal courthouse a few weeks later, I found a scene from *Miami Vice.*

To my left, a dark-suited army of federal agents and prosecutors huddled around a long, polished wooden table, looking grim and talking in low voices. On the right, an array of long-haired, expensively attired defense attorneys were whispering to a group of long-haired, angry-looking Hispanics—their clients. The judge had not yet arrived.

I had no idea what Coral Baca looked like, so I scanned the faces in the courtroom, trying to pick out a woman who could be a drug kingpin's girlfriend. She found me first.

"You must be Gary," said a voice behind me.

I turned, and for an instant all I saw was cleavage and jewelry. She looked to be in her mid-twenties. Dark hair. Bright red lipstick. Long legs. Short skirt. Dressed to accentuate her positive attributes. I could barely speak.

"You're Coral?"

She tossed her hair and smiled. "Pleased to meet you." She stuck out a hand with a giant diamond on it, and I shook it weakly.

We sat down in the row of seats behind the prosecutors' table, and I glanced at her again. That boyfriend of hers must be going nuts.

"How did you know it was me?" I asked.

"I was looking for someone who looked like a reporter. I saw you with a notebook in your back pocket and figured—"

"That obvious, is it?" I pulled out the notepad and got out a pen. "Why don't you fill me in on who's who here?"

She pointed out Rafael, a short handsome Latino with a strong jaw and long, wavy hair parted in the middle. He swiveled in his chair, looked right at us, and seemed perturbed. Coral waved, and he whirled back around without acknowledging her.

"He doesn't look very happy," I observed.

"He doesn't like seeing me with other men."

"Uh, why was he trying to break out of jail?" I asked.

"He wasn't. He was getting ready to make bail, and they didn't want to let him out, so they trumped up these phony escape charges. Now, because he's under indictment for escape, he isn't eligible for bail anymore."

The escape charges were in fact the product of an unsubstantiated accusation by a fellow inmate, a convicted swindler. They were later thrown out of court on grounds of prosecutorial misconduct, and Corñejo's prosecutor, Assistant U.S. Attorney David Hall, was referred to the Justice Department for investigation by federal judge Saundra Brown Armstrong.

(In a *San Francisco Daily Recorder* story about the misconduct charge, it was noted that "it is not the first time that Hall has been under such scrutiny. While serving with the Department of Justice in Texas, the Office of Professional Responsibility reviewed Hall after an informant accused Hall of approving drug smuggling into the U.S.... Hall said the office found no merit in the charge.")

Coral pointed out Hall, a large blond man with broad features.

"Who are the rest of those people?" I asked.

"The two men standing over there are the FBI agents on the case. The woman is Hall's boss, Teresa Canepa. She's the bitch who's got it in for Rafael."

As Coral was pointing everyone out, the FBI agents whispered to each other and then tapped Hall on the shoulder. All three turned and looked at me.

"What's with them?"

"They probably think you're my hit man." She smiled, and the agents frowned back. "Oh, they just hate me. I called the cops on them once, you know."

I looked at her. "You called the cops on the FBI."

"Well, they were lurking around outside my house after dark. They could have been rapists or something. How was I supposed to know?"

I glanced back over at the federal table and saw that the entire group had now turned to stare. I was certainly making a lot of friends.

"Can we go out in the hall and talk for a minute?" I asked her.

We sat on a bench just outside the door. I told her I needed to get case numbers so I could ask for the court files. And, by the way, did she bring those documents she'd mentioned?

She reached into her briefcase and brought out a stack an inch thick. "I've got three bankers' boxes full back at home, and you're welcome to see all of it, but this is the stuff I was telling you about concerning the witness."

I flipped through the documents. Most of them were federal law enforcement reports, DEA-6s and FBI 302s, every page bearing big black letters that said, "MAY NOT BE REPRODUCED—PROPERTY OF U.S. GOVERNMENT." At the bottom of the stack was a transcript of some sort. I pulled it out.

"Grand Jury for the Northern District of California, Grand Jury Number 93-5 Grand Jury Inv. No. 9301035. Reporter's Transcript of Proceedings. Testimony of Oscar Danilo Blandón. February 3, 1994."

I whistled. "Federal grand jury transcripts? I'm impressed. Where'd you get these?"

"The government turned them over under discovery. Dave Hall did. I heard he really got reamed out by the DEA when they found out about all the stuff he gave us."

I looked through the transcript and saw parts that had been blacked out.

"Who did this?"

"That's how we got it. Rafael's lawyer is asking for a clean copy. As you'll see, they also cut out a bunch of stuff on the DEA-6s. There's a hearing on his motion coming up."

I skimmed the thirty-nine-page transcript. Whatever else this Blandón fellow may have been, he was pretty much the way Coral had described him. A big-time trafficker who'd dealt dope for many years; started out dealing for the Contras, a right-wing Nicaraguan guerrilla army, in Los Angeles. He'd used drug money to buy trucks and supplies. At some point after Ronald Reagan got into power, the CIA had decided his services as a fund-raiser were no longer required, and he stayed in the drug business for himself.

What made the story so compelling was that he was appearing before the grand jury as a U.S. government witness. He wasn't under investigation. He wasn't trying to beat a rap. He was there as a witness for the prosecution, which meant that the U.S. Justice Department was vouching for him.

But who was the grand jury investigating? Every time the testimony led in that direction, words—mostly names—were blacked out.

"Who is this family they keep asking him about?"

"Rafael says it's Meneses. Norwin Meneses and his nephews. Have you heard of them?"

"Nope."

"Norwin is one of the biggest traffickers on the West Coast. When Rafael got arrested, that's who the FBI and the IRS wanted to talk to him about. Rafael has known [Norwin and his nephews] for years. Since the Seventies, I think. The government is apparently using Blandón to get to Meneses."

Inside, I heard the bailiff calling the court to order, and we returned to the courtroom. During the hearing, I kept trying to recall where I had heard about this Contra-cocaine business before. Had I read it in a book? Seen it on television? It bothered me. I believed that I had a better-than-average knowledge of the civil war in Nicaragua, having religiously followed the Iran-Contra hearings on television. I would videotape them while I was at work and watch them late into the night, marvelling the next morning at how wretchedly the newspapers were covering the story.

Like most Americans, I knew the Contras had been a creation of the CIA, the darlings of the Reagan Right, made up largely of the vanquished followers of deposed Nicaraguan dictator Anastasio Somoza and his brutal army, the National Guard. But drug trafficking? Surely, I thought, if there had been some concrete evidence, it would have stuck in my mind. Maybe I was confusing it with something else.

During a break, I went to the restroom and bumped into Assistant U.S. Attorney Hall. Just in case he and the FBI really did think I was Coral's hit man, I introduced myself as a reporter. Hall eyed me cautiously.

"Why would the *Mercury News* be interested in this case?" he asked. "You should have been here two years ago. This is old stuff now."

I considered tap dancing around his question. Normally I didn't tell people what I was working on, because then they didn't know what not to say. But I decided to hit Hall with it head-on and see what kind of reaction I got. It would probably be the last thing he'd expect to hear.

"I'm not really doing a story on this case. I'm looking into one of the witnesses. A man named Blandón. Am I pronouncing the name correctly?"

Hall appeared surprised. "What about him?"

"About his selling cocaine for the Contras."

Hall leaned back slightly, folded his arms, and gave me a quizzical smile. "Who have you been talking to?"

"Actually, I've been reading. And I was curious to know what you made of his testimony about selling drugs for the Contras in L.A. Did you believe him?"

"Well, yeah, but I don't know how you could absolutely confirm it. I mean, I don't know what to tell you," he said with a slight laugh. "The CIA won't tell me anything."

I jotted down his remark. "Oh, you've asked them?"

"Yeah, but I never heard anything back. Not that I expected to. But that's all ancient history. You're really doing a story about that?"

"I don't know if I'm doing a story at all," I said. "At this point, I'm just trying to see if there is one. Do you know where Blandón is these days?"

"Not a clue."

That couldn't be true, I thought. How could he *not* know? He was one of the witnesses against Rafael Corñejo. "From what I heard," I told him, "he's a pretty significant witness in your case here. He hasn't disappeared, has he? He is going to testify?"

Hall's friendly demeanor changed. "We're not at all certain about that."

When I got back to Sacramento, I called my editor at the main office in San Jose, Dawn Garcia, and filled her in on the day's events. Dawn was a former investigative reporter from the *San Francisco Chronicle* and had been the *Mercury*'s state editor for several years, overseeing our bureaus in Los Angeles, San Francisco, and Sacramento. We had a good working relationship and had broken a number of award-winning stories. Unlike many editors I'd worked with, Dawn could size up a story's news value fairly quickly.

I read her several portions of Blandón's grand jury testimony.

"Weren't there some stories about this back in the 1980s?" she asked.

"See, that's what I thought. I remember something, but I can't place the source."

"Maybe the Iran-Contra hearings?"

"I don't think so," I said. "I followed those hearings pretty closely. I don't remember anything about drug trafficking."

(Dawn's memory, it turned out, was better than mine. During one part of Oliver North's congressional testimony in July 1987, two men from Baltimore had jumped up in the audience with a large banner reading, "Ask about the cocaine smuggling." The men began shouting questions—"What about the cocaine dealing that the U.S. is paying for? Why don't you ask questions about drug deliveries?"—as they were dragged from the room by the police.)

"So, what do you think?" she asked, editorese for "Is there a story here and how long will it take to get it?"

"I don't know. I'd like to spend a little time looking into it at least. Hell, if his testimony is true, it could be a pretty good story. The Contras were selling coke in L.A.? I've never heard that one before."

She mulled it over for a moment before agreeing. "It's not like there's a lot going on in Sacramento right now," she said. That was true enough. The sun-baked state capital was entering its summertime siesta, when triple-digit temperatures sent solons adjourning happily to mountain or seashore locales.

With any luck, I was about to join them.

"I need to go down to San Diego for a couple days," I said. "Blandón testified that he was arrested down there in '92 for conspiracy, so there's probably a court file somewhere. He may be living down there, for all I know. Probably the quickest way to find out if what he was saying is true is to find him."

Dawn okayed the trip, and a few days later I was in balmy San Diego, squinting at microfiche in the clerk's office of the U.S. District Court. I found Blandón's case file within a few minutes.

He and six others, including his wife, had been secretly indicted May 5, 1992, for conspiring to distribute cocaine. He'd been buying wholesale quantities from suppliers and reselling it to other wholesalers. Way up on the food chain. According to the indictment, he'd been a trafficker for ten years, had clients nationwide, and had bragged on tape of selling other L.A. dealers between two and four tons of cocaine.

He was such a big-timer that the judge had ordered him and his wife held in jail without bail because they posed "a threat to the health and moral fiber of the community."

The file contained a transcript of a detention hearing, held to determine if the couple should be released on bail. Blandón's prosecutor, Assistant U.S. Attorney L. J. O'Neale, brought out his best ammo to persuade the judge to keep the couple locked up until trial. "Mr. Blandón's family was closely associated with the Somoza government that was overthrown in 1979," O'Neale said. Blandón had been partners with a Jairo Meneses in 764 kilos of cocaine that had been seized in Nicaragua in 1991, O'Neale claimed, and he also owned hotels and casinos in

Nicaragua with Meneses. He had a house in Costa Rica. He had a business in Mexico, relatives in Spain, phony addresses all over the United States, and "unlimited access to money."

"He is a large-scale cocaine trafficker and has been for a long time," O'Neale argued. Given the amount of cocaine he'd sold, O'Neale said, Blandón's minimum mandatory punishment was "off the charts"—life plus a $4 million fine—giving him plenty of incentive to flee the country.

Blandón's lawyer, Brad Brunon, confirmed the couple's close ties to Somoza and produced a photo of them at a wedding reception with *El Presidente* and his spouse. That just showed what fine families they were from, he said. The accusations in Nicaragua against Blandón, Brunon argued, were "politically motivated because of Mr. Blandón's activities with the Contras in the early 1980s."

Damn, here it is again. His own lawyer says he was working for the Contras.

Brunon argued that the government had no case against his client, and no right to keep him in jail until the trial. "There is not the first kilogram of cocaine that had been seized in this case," Brunon said. "What you have are accusations from a series of informants." But the judge didn't see it that way. While allowing Chepita to post bond, he ordered Danilo held without bail.

From the docket sheet, I could see that the case had never gone to trial. Everyone had pleaded out, starting with Blandón. Five months after his arrest, he pleaded guilty to conspiracy, and the charges against his wife were dropped. After that, his fugitive codefendants were quickly arrested and pleaded guilty. But they all received extremely short sentences. One was even put on unsupervised probation.

I didn't get it. If O'Neale had such a rock-solid case against a major drug-trafficking ring, why were they let off so easily? People did more time for burglary. Even Blandón, the ringleader, only got forty-eight months, and from the docket sheet it appeared that was later cut almost in half.

As I read on, I realized that Blandón was already back on the streets—totally unsupervised. No parole. Free as a bird. He'd walked out of jail September 19, 1994, on the arm of an INS agent, Robert Tellez. He'd done twenty-eight months for ten years of cocaine trafficking.

The last page of the file told me why. It was a motion filed by U.S. Attorney O'Neale, asking the court to unseal Blandón's plea agreement and a couple of internal Justice Department memorandums. "During the course of this case, defendant Oscar Danilo Blandón cooperated with and rendered substantial assistance to the United States," O'Neale wrote. At the government's request, his jail sentence had been secretly cut twice. O'Neale then persuaded the judge to let Blandón out of jail completely, telling the court he was needed as a full-time paid informant for the U.S. Department of Justice. Since he'd be undercover, O'Neale wrote, he couldn't very well have probation agents checking up on him. He was released on unsupervised probation.

All of this information had once been secret, I noticed, but since Blandón was going to testify in a case in northern California (the Corñejo case, I presumed), O'Neale had to have the plea agreement and all the records relating to his sentence reductions unsealed and turned over to defense counsel.

I walked back to my hotel convinced that I was on the right track. Now there were two separate sources saying—in court—that Blandón was involved with the Contras and had been selling large amounts of cocaine in Los Angeles. And when the government finally had a chance to put him away forever, it had opened up the cell doors and let him walk. I needed to find Blandón. I had a million questions only he could answer.

I began calling the defense attorneys involved in the 1992 conspiracy case, hoping one of them would know what had become of him. I struck out with every call. One of the lawyers was out of town. The rest of them remembered next to nothing about the case or their clients. "It was all over so quickly I barely had time to open a file," one said. The consensus was that once Blandón flipped, his compadres scrambled to get the best deal they could, and no one prepared for trial. Discovery had been minimal.

But one thing wasn't clear. What had the government gotten out of the deal that was worth giving Blandón and his crew such an easy ride? O'Neale claimed he'd given information about a murder in the Bay Area, but from what I could see from his DEA and FBI interviews, he'd merely told the government that the man had been murdered—something the police already knew.

Back in Sacramento, I did some checking on the targets of the 1994 grand jury investigation—the Meneses family—and again Coral's description proved accurate, perhaps even understated. I found a 1991 story from the *San Francisco Chronicle* and a 1986 *San Francisco Examiner* piece that strongly suggested that Meneses, too, had been dealing cocaine for the Contras during the 1980s. One of the stories described him as the "king of cocaine in Nicaragua" and the Cali cartel's representative there. The *Chronicle* story mentioned that a U.S. Senate investigation had run across him in connection with the Contras and allegations of cocaine smuggling.

That must have been where I heard about this Contra drug stuff before, I decided. A congressional hearing.

At the California State Library's Government Publications Section, I scoured the CSI indices, which catalog congressional hearings by topic and witness name. Meneses wasn't listed, but there had been a series of hearings back in 1987 and 1988, I saw, dealing with the issue of the Contras and cocaine: a subcommittee of the Senate Foreign Relations Committee, chaired by Senator John Kerry of Massachusetts.

For the next six days I sat with rolls of dimes at a microfiche printer in the quiet wood-paneled recesses of the library, reading and copying many of the 1,100 pages of transcripts and exhibits of the Kerry Committee hearings, growing more astounded each day. The committee's investigators had uncovered direct links between drug dealers and the Contras. They'd gotten into BCCI years before anyone knew what that banking scandal even was. They'd found evidence of Manuel Noriega's involvement with drugs—years before the invasion. Many of the Kerry Committee witnesses, I noted, later became U.S. Justice Department witnesses against Noriega.

Kerry and his staff had taken videotaped depositions from Contra leaders who acknowledged receiving drug profits, with the apparent knowledge of the CIA. The drug dealers had admitted—under oath—giving money to the Contras, and had passed polygraph tests. The pilots had admitted flying weapons down and cocaine and marijuana back, landing in at least one instance at Homestead Air Force Base in Florida. The exhibits included U.S. Customs reports, FBI reports, internal Justice Department memos. It almost knocked me off my chair.

It was all there in black and white. Blandón's testimony about selling cocaine for the Contras in L.A. wasn't some improbable fantasy. This could have actually happened.

I called Jack Blum, the Washington, D.C., attorney who'd headed the Kerry investigation, and he confirmed that Norwin Meneses had been an early target. But the Justice Department, he said, had stonewalled the committee's requests for information and he had finally given up trying to obtain the records, moving on to other, more productive areas. "There was a lot of weird stuff going on out on the West Coast, but after our experiences with Justice...we mainly concentrated on the cocaine coming into the East."

"Why is it that I can barely remember this?" I asked. "I mean, I read the papers every day."

"It wasn't in the papers, for the most part. We laid it all out, and we were trashed," Blum said. "I've got to tell you, there's a real problem with the press in this town. We were totally hit by the leadership of the administration and much of the congressional leadership. They simply turned around and said, 'These people are crazy. Their witnesses are full of shit. They're a bunch of drug dealers, drug addicts, don't listen to them.' And they dumped all over us. It came from every direction and every corner. We were even dumped on by the Iran-Contra Committee. They wouldn't touch this issue with a ten-foot pole."

"There had to have been some reporters who followed this," I protested. "Maybe I'm naive, but this seems like a huge story to me."

Blum barked a laugh. "Well, it's nice to hear someone finally say that, even if it is ten years later. But what happened was, our credibility was questioned, and we were personally trashed. The administration and some people in Congress tried to make us look like crazies, and to some degree it worked. I remember having conversations with reporters in which they would say, 'Well, the administration says this is all wrong.' And I'd say, 'Look, the guy is going to testify to X, Y, and Z. Why don't you cover the fucking hearing instead of coming to me with what the administration says?' And they'd say, 'Well, the guy is a drug dealer. Why should I do that?' And I used to say this regularly: 'Look, the minute I find a Lutheran minister or priest who was on the scene when they were delivering 600 kilos of cocaine at some air base in Contra-land, I'll put him on the stand, but until then, you take what you can get.' The big papers stayed as far away from this issue as they could. It was like they didn't want to know."

There were two reporters, Blum said, who'd pursued the Contra drug story—Robert Parry and Brian Barger of the Associated Press—but they'd run into the same problems. Their stories were either trashed or ignored. There were also two reporters in Costa Rica—a *New York Times* stringer named Martha Honey and her husband, Tony Avirgan, an ABC cameraman, who had gone after the story as well, he said. Honey and Avirgan wound up being set up on phony drug charges in Costa Rica, spied on in the States by the FBI and former CIA agents, smeared, and ruined financially.

"I know Bob Parry is still here in Washington somewhere. He did the first stories and was one of the few who seemed to know what he was doing. You might want to talk to him," Blum suggested.

Parry sounded slightly amused when I called him in Virginia. "Why in the world would you want to go back into this?" he asked. I told him of my discoveries about Meneses and Blandón, and the latter's cocaine sales in Los Angeles. Had he or anyone else ever been reported this before? I wondered.

"Not that I'm aware of," Parry said. "We never really got into where it was going once the cocaine arrived in the United States. Our stories dealt mainly with the Costa Rican end of things. This is definitely a new angle. You think you can show it was being sold in L.A.?"

"Yeah, I do. Well, one of the guys has even testified to it before a grand jury. But this is an area I've never done any reporting on before so I guess what I'm looking for is a little guidance," I told him. "Have you got any suggestions?"

There was a short silence on the other end of the phone. "How well do you get along with your editors?" Parry finally asked.

"Fine. Why do you ask?"

"Well, when Brian and I were doing these stories we got our brains beat out." Parry sighed. "People from the administration were calling our editors, telling them we were crazy, that our sources were no good, that we didn't know what we were writing about. The Justice Department was putting out false press releases saying there was nothing to this, that they'd investigated and could find no evidence. We were being attacked in the *Washington Times*. The rest of the Washington press corps sort of pooh-poohed the whole thing, and no one else would touch it. So we ended up being out there all by ourselves, and eventually our editors backed away completely, and I ended up quitting the AP. It was probably the most difficult time of my career."

He paused. "Maybe things have changed, I don't know."

I was nonplussed. Bob Parry wasn't some fringe reporter. He'd won a Polk Award for uncovering the CIA assasination manual given to the Contras, and was the first reporter to expose Oliver North's illegal activities. But what he'd just described sounded like something out of a bad dream. I told him I didn't think that would be a problem at the *Mercury*. I'd done some controversial stories before, but the editors had stood by them, and we'd won some significant awards. I felt good about the paper, I told him.

"One place you might try is the National Archives," Parry offered. "They're in the process of declassifying Lawrence Walsh's files, and I've found some pretty remarkable things over there. It's a long shot, but if I were you, I'd file a FOIA for the men you mentioned and see if anything turns up."

It *was* a long shot, but Parry's hunch paid off. My Freedom of Information Act request produced several important clues, among them a 1986 FBI report about Blandón that alluded to a police raid and reported that Blandón's attorney, Brad Brunon, had called the L.A. County Sheriff's Office afterward and claimed that the CIA had "winked" at Blandón's activities. I also obtained 1987 FBI interviews with a San Francisco Contra supporter, Dennis Ainsworth, in which he told of his discovery that Norwin Meneses and a Contra leader named Enrique Bermúdez were dealing arms and drugs.

I tracked down Ainsworth and had another disconcerting conversation. You've got to be crazy, he said. He'd tried to alert people to this ten years ago, and it had ruined his life. "Nobody in Washington wanted to look at this. Republican, Democrat, nobody. They wanted this story buried and anyone who looked any deeper into it got buried along with it," Ainsworth said. "You're bringing up a very old nightmare. You have no idea what you're touching on here, Gary. No idea at all."

"I think I've got a pretty good idea," I said.

"Believe me," he said patiently, "you don't understand. I almost got killed. I had friends in Central America who were killed. There was a Mexican reporter who was looking into one end of this, and he wound up dead. So don't pretend that you know."

"If the Contras were selling drugs in L.A., don't you think people should know that?"

Ainsworth laughed. "L.A.? Meneses was selling it all over the country! Listen, he ran one of the major distributions in the U.S. It wasn't just L.A. He was national. And he was totally protected."

"I think that's the kind of thing the public needs to know about," I told him. "And that's why I need your help. You know a lot more about this topic than I do."

He was unmoved. "Look, when I was trying to tell Congress, I was getting death threats. And you're asking, you know, if I'm Jewish, would I like to go back and spend another six months in Dachau? Leave this alone. Take my advice. You can go on and write a lot of other things and maybe win a Pulitzer Prize, but all you're going to be after this is over is a persona non grata. Please. Everyone's forgotten about this and moved on with their lives."

A few days later I got a call from Coral. My one chance to hook up with Blandón had just fallen through. "He isn't going to be testifying at Rafael's trial after all," she told me. "Rafael's attorney won his motion to have the DEA and FBI release the uncensored files, and the U.S. attorney decided to drop him as a witness rather than do that. Can you believe it? He was one of the witnesses they used to get the indictment against Rafael, and now they're refusing to put him on the stand."

I hung up the phone in a funk. Without him, I didn't have much to go on. But there was always his boss—this Meneses fellow. Getting to him was a tougher nut to crack, but worth a shot. Coral said she thought he was in jail in Nicaragua, and the *Chronicle* clip I'd found noted that he'd been arrested there in 1991. Maybe, I hoped, the Nicaraguans locked their drug lords up longer than we did. I was put in touch with a freelance reporter in Managua, Georg Hodel, an indefatigable Swiss journalist who spoke several languages and had covered Nicaragua during the war. He taught college journalism classes, knew his way around the Nicaraguan government, and had sources everywhere. Better yet, with his Swiss-German-Spanish accent, it was like talking to Peter Lorre. I persuaded Dawn to hire Georg as a stringer, and he set off to find Meneses.

Meanwhile, the San Diego attorney who had been out of town when I was looking for Blandón returned my call. Juanita Brooks had represented Blandón's friend and codefendant, a Mexican millionaire named Sergio Guerra. Another lawyer in her firm had defended Chepita Blandón. She knew quite a bit about the couple.

"You don't happen to know where he is these days, do you?"

"No, but I can tell you where he'll be in a couple of months. Here in San Diego. Entirely by coincidence, I have a case coming up where he's the chief prosecution witness against my client."

"You're kidding," I said. "What case is this?"

"It's a pretty big one. Have you ever heard of someone named Freeway Ricky Ross?"

Indeed I had. I'd run across him while researching the asset forfeiture series in 1993. "He's one of the biggest crack dealers in L.A.," I said.

"That's what they say," Brooks replied. "He and my client and a couple others were arrested in a DEA reverse sting last year and Blandón is the CI [confidential informant] in the case."

"How did Blandón get involved with crack dealers?"

"I don't have a lot of details, because the government has been very protective of him. They've refused to give us any discovery so far," Brooks said. "But from what I understand, Blandón used to be one of Ricky Ross's sources back in the 1980s, and I suppose he played off that friendship."

My mind was racing. Blandón, the Contra fund-raiser, had sold cocaine to the biggest crack dealer in South Central L.A.? That was too much.

"Are you sure about this?"

"I wouldn't want you to quote me on it," she said, "but, yes, I'm pretty sure. You can always call Alan Fenster, Ross's attorney, and ask him. I'm sure he knows."

Fenster was out, so I left a message on his voice mail, telling him I was working on a story about Oscar Danilo Blandón Reyes and wanted to interview him. When I got back from lunch, I found a message from Fenster waiting. It said: "Oscar who?"

My heart sank. I'd suspected it was a bum lead, but I'd been keeping my fingers crossed anyway. I should have known; that would have been too perfect. I called Fenster back to thank him for his time, and he asked what kind of a story I was working on. I told him—the Contras and cocaine.

"I'm curious," he said. "What made you think this Oscar person was involved in Ricky's case?"

I told him what Brooks had related, and he gasped.

"*He's* the informant? Are you serious? No wonder those bastards won't give me his name!" Fenster began swearing a blue streak.

"Forgive me," he said. "But if you only knew what kind of bullshit I've been going through to get that information from those sons of bitches, and then some reporter calls me up from San Jose and he knows all about him, it just makes me—"

"Your client didn't tell you his name?"

"He didn't know it! He only knew him as Danilo, and then he wasn't even sure that was his real name. You and Ricky need to talk. I'll have him call you." He hung up abruptly.

Ross called a few hours later. I asked him what he knew about Blandón. "A lot," he said. "He was almost like a godfather to me. He's the one who got me going."

"Was he your main source?"

"He was. Everybody I knew, I knew through him. So really, he could be considered as my only source. In a sense, he was."

"When was this?"

"Eighty-one or '82. Right when I was getting going."

Damn, I thought. That was right when Blandón said he started dealing drugs.

"Would you be willing to sit down and talk to me about this?" I asked.

"Hell, yeah. I'll tell you anything you want to know."

At the end of September 1995 I spent a week in San Diego, going through the files of the Ross case, interviewing defense attorneys and prosecutors, listening to undercover DEA tapes. I attended a discovery hearing and watched as Fenster and the other defense lawyers made another futile attempt to find out details about the government's informant, so they could begin preparing their defenses. Assistant U.S. Attorney O'Neale refused to provide a thing. They'd get what they were entitled to, he promised, ten days before trial.

"See what I mean?" Fenster asked me on his way out. "It's like the trial in *Alice in Wonderland*."

I spent hours with Ross at the Metropolitan Correctional Center. He knew nothing of Blandón's past, I discovered. He had no idea who the Contras were or whose side they were on. To him, Danilo was just a nice guy with a lot of cheap dope.

"What would you say if I were to tell you that he was working for the Contras, selling cocaine to help them buy weapons and supplies?" I asked.

Ross goggled. "And they put me in jail? I'd say that was some fucked-up shit there. They say I sold dope all over, but man, I *know* he done sold ten times more than me. Are you being straight with me?"

I told him I had documents to prove it. Ross just shook his head and looked away.

"He's been working for the government the whole damn time," he muttered.

1

"A pretty secret kind of thing"

In July 1979, as his enemies massed in the hills and suburbs of his doomed capital, the dictator huddled in his mountainside bunker with his aides and his American advisers and cursed his rotten luck.

For the forty-six years that Anastasio Somoza's family had ruled the Republic of Nicaragua, the Somozas had done nearly everything the U. S. government asked. Now, after all his hard work, the Americans wanted him to disappear. Somoza could barely believe it. He was glad he had his tape recorder going, so history could bear witness to his cruel betrayal.

"I have thrown many people out of their natural habitat because of the U.S., fighting for your cause… so let's talk like friends," Somoza told U.S. ambassador Lawrence Pezzullo. "I threw a goddamned Communist out of Guatemala," he reminded the ambassador, referring to the role the Somoza family had played in the CIA's overthrow of a liberal Guatemalan government in 1954. "I personally worked on that."

When the CIA needed a secret base to prepare for the Bay of Pigs invasion, Somoza couldn't have been a more gracious host. "The U.S. called me, and I agreed to have the bombers leave here and knock the hell out of the installations in Cuba," Somoza stormed, "like a Pearl Harbor deal." In 1965 he'd sent troops into the Dominican Republic to help the United States quell another leftist uprising. Hell, he'd even sent Nicaraguans off to fight in Vietnam.

And now, when Somoza needed help, when it was his soldiers who were locked in a life-and-death struggle with Communist aggressors, the Americans were selling him out—all because of some nonsense about human rights violations by his troops.

"It is embarrassing for you to be good friends with the Somozas," the dictator told Pezzullo sarcastically. Somoza then tried his trump card: If he went, the Nicaraguan National Guard, the *Guardia*, would surely be destroyed. The *Guardia*, as corrupt and deadly an organization as any in Central America, served as Somoza's military, his police, and his intelligence service.

Somoza knew the Americans would be loath to let their investment in it go to waste. They had created the *Guardia* in the 1930s and nurtured it carefully since, spending millions of dollars a year supplying weapons and schooling its officers in the complex arts of anticommunism.

"What are you going to do with the National Guard of Nicaragua?" Somoza asked Pezzullo. "I don't need to know, but after you have spent thirty years educating all of these officers, I don't think it is fair for them to be thrown to the wolves.... They have been fighting Communism just like you taught them at Fort Gulick and Fort Benning and Leavenworth—out of nine hundred officers we have, eight hundred or so belong to your schools."

Pezzullo assured Somoza that the United States was "willing to do what we can to preserve the Guard." Putting aside its international reputation for murder and torture, Pezzullo recognized that the *Guardia* was a bulwark against anti-American interests and, as long as it existed, could be used to keep Somoza's successors—whoever they might be—in line. "We are not abandoning the Guard," he insisted. "We would like to see a force emerge here that can stabilize the country." But for that to happen, Pezzullo said, Somoza and his top generals needed to step down and give the *Guardia* "a clean break" from its bloodstained past—before the Sandinistas marched in and it became too late to salvage anything. "To make the break now. It is a hell of a mess," Pezzullo said sympathetically. "Just sitting here talking to you about it is strange enough. We are talking about a break."

Somoza knew the game was over. "Let's not bullshit ourselves, Mr. Ambassador. I am talking to a professional. You have to do your dirty work, and I have to do mine."

In the predawn hours of July 17, 1979, Somoza and his closest associates—his top generals, his business partners, and their families—boarded two jets and flew to Homestead Air Force Base in Florida to begin a vagabond exile. The vaunted National Guard collapsed within hours.

Sandinista columns swarmed into the defenseless capital, jubilantly proclaiming an end to both the *Guardia*—which had hunted the rebels mercilessly for more than a decade—and Somoza. Those National Guard officers who could escape poured across the borders into El Salvador, Honduras, and Costa Rica, or hid inside the Colombian embassy in Managua. Those who couldn't, wound up in prison, and occasionally before firing squads.

Nine days after Somoza and his cronies were overthrown, a handful of congressmen gathered in a hearing room in the Rayburn House Office Building in Washington, D.C., to discuss some disturbing activities in Latin America. Though what had happened in Nicaragua was on everyone's mind in the nation's capital that week, these particular lawmakers had concerns that lay farther to the south: in Colombia, in Bolivia, and in Peru.

They were worried about cocaine. The exotic South American drug seemed to be winning admirers everywhere. References were turning up in movies, songs and newspaper stories, and surprisingly, many of them were positive. To Republican congressman Tennyson Guyer, an elderly former preacher and thirty-third-degree Mason from Findlay, Ohio, it seemed like the media was hell-bent on glamorizing cocaine.

Guyer, an ultraconservative fond of loud suits and white patent leather shoes, was the chairman of the Cocaine Task Force of the House Select Committee on Narcotics Abuse and Control, and he wasn't just going to stand by and watch.

"Recent developments concerning the state of cocaine have come to my attention, which call for decisive and immediate action!" Guyer thundered as he opened his cocaine hearings in July 1979. "The availability, abuse, and popularity of cocaine in the United States has reached pandemic proportions.... This is a drug which, for the most part, has been ignored, and its increased use in our society has caught us unprepared to cope effectively with this menace."

But if Guyer was feeling menaced by cocaine, not too many others were.

Many Americans who'd grown up during the drug-soaked 1960s reasoned that an occasional sniff of the fluffy white powder was no more menacing than a couple of martinis—and considerably more chic.

Cocaine didn't give you a hangover. It didn't scramble your brains. Many doctors believed you couldn't get hooked on it. It made you feel great. It kept the pounds off. And there was a definite cachet associated with using it. Just the price of admission to Club Cocaine was enough to keep out the riffraff. At $2,500 an ounce and up, it was a naughty pleasure reserved for a special few: the "so-called elites" and the "intellectual classes," as Guyer derisively termed them.

Even the paraphernalia associated with the drug—sterling silver cocaine spoons and tightly rolled $100 bills—carried an aura of decadence. In the public's mind, cocaine was associated with fame and fortune.

"The rediscovery of cocaine in the Seventies was unavoidable," a Los Angeles psychologist gushed to a convention of drug experts in 1980, "because its stimulating and pleasure-causing properties reinforce the American character, with its initiative, its energy, its restless activity and its boundless optimism."

While the street corners played host to lowbrow and much more dangerous drugs—angel dust, smack, meth—coke stayed up in the penthouses, nestled in exquisitely carved bowls and glittering little boxes. It came out at private parties, or in the wash rooms of trendy nightclubs. Unless some celebrity got caught with it by accident, street cops almost never saw the stuff.

"My first ten years as a narcotics agent, my contact with cocaine was very minimal," recalled Jerald Smith, who ran the San Francisco office of the California Bureau of Narcotics Enforcement during the 1980s. "As a matter of fact, the first few years, the only cocaine I ever saw was an ounce some guy would take around as a training aid to teach you what it looked like. Because it was something you saw so rarely. Our big thing[s] in those days were pills and heroin and marijuana."

But if Reverend Guyer thought the experts he'd summoned to Washington were going to help him change the public's mind about cocaine sniffing, he was badly mistaken. Witness after witness trooped up to the microphone to tell Congress that cocaine was not only a relatively safe drug but so rare that it could hardly be called a nuisance, much less the "menace" Guyer was advertising.

"Daily cocaine use is extremely uncommon, simply because of the high cost," testified Robert C. Petersen, assistant director of research for the National Institute on Drug Abuse. "Under present conditions of use, it has not posed a very serious health problem for most. Rarely does it cause a problem."

Lee I. Dogoloff, the White House's drug expert, concurred. "It is our assumption," he said, "that the current relatively low level of health problems associated with cocaine use reflects the relatively high price and relatively low availability of the substance."

To make the point, the head of the Drug Enforcement Administration, Peter Bensinger, told the committee he had brought $800,000 worth of cocaine to show them. He pulled out a little bag and dangled it before his rapt audience.

"That is simulated, I trust?" Guyer inquired.

"No, that is actual coca," Bensinger replied. A sample, he said, of seized contraband.

"I can't believe you are holding almost $1 million there!" Guyer sputtered. "We ought to have security in the hearing room!"

"We have some special agents in the room, I assure you," Bensinger said.

The experts were careful to note that if cocaine became cheaper, it would be more widely available and might pose a bigger problem than anyone realized, but no one seemed to think there was much chance of that happening. Most of the smugglers, Bensinger said, were just bringing amounts small enough to put in a suitcase or stash on their body. "We don't think people are bringing cocaine across the border, to a large extent, in a car from Mexico." He recommended that Congress, instead of trying to prevent the drug from coming in over the borders, concentrate its efforts on getting the Peruvians and Bolivians to stop growing coca plants.

Dr. Robert Byck, a drug expert from Yale University, sat in the audience listening patiently to the testimony all day. When it was Byck's turn to speak, Guyer warmly welcomed him up to the witness table, complimenting him on his "very, very impressive" academic and professional credentials.

Byck thanked Guyer and then politely ripped into the federal government for spreading misinformation about the drug. "What I would like to talk to you about for the most part is the importance of telling the truth," Byck, a professor of psychiatry and pharmacology at Yale Medical School, began. The truth was that cocaine wasn't the horrible health hazard Americans were being told it was. "Cocaine doesn't have the kind of health consequences that one sees with drugs such as alcohol and cigarettes. Right now, if we look at the hospital admission records and death records, cocaine doesn't look like a dangerous drug.... We have given a great deal of cocaine to many individuals and find it to be a most unremarkable drug. We are giving cocaine by nose to normal young men. When anyone visits our laboratory, they look at the TV screen and say, 'That guy took cocaine?' They don't jump around, they don't get excited; they sit calmly and experience a drug high and don't become dangerous."

"What about five years later?" Guyer cried. "Are the membranes and so on not affected at all?"

"The damage to people's membranes is quite rare with cocaine. It does occur, but it is a rare phenomenon," Byck answered. "Part of this is because people don't use very much cocaine. It is expensive. Tell me the last alcoholic you saw with cirrhosis of the liver when cirrhosis was caused by Dom Perignon. You almost never see it."

As most Americans were using it, Byck said, cocaine "is a very safe drug. You almost never see anesthetic death due to cocaine. There have been a series of 14,000 consecutive doses of cocaine given with no deaths. Deaths from cocaine are very, very rare. They do occur, and I think it is important to recognize that they occur. But actually, the drug, in terms of the risk of killing people, is comparatively safe. If you want a dangerous drug, take digitalis or digoxin.... It is a heart drug. And that is really deadly, one of the deadliest poisons known."

"But that is used to save lives," Guyer countered.

"Yes, it is used to save lives," Byck said. "Cocaine is also used medically. So you cannot take whether or not something can kill you as a measure of dangerousness."

What the government was doing with its scare campaigns about cocaine, Byck complained, was poisoning the well. It was ruining the government's credibility with the public, just when the government needed its credibility to be impeccable. "I think we make a mistake when we say that snorting cocaine every once in a while is a dangerous habit and is going to kill people, because it does not," Byck said flatly. "There are a great many people around who have been snorting cocaine and know that their friends haven't gotten into trouble. If you then tell those people that cocaine is very dangerous, they won't believe it. Then, when you get to the next step—when you are talking about something that *is* really dangerous—they are not going to believe you the second time." And that brought Byck to the real reason he was in Washington on a humid day in late July.

He was there to deliver a warning from the scientific community.

Something bad was coming, Byck knew, something so deadly awful that the only way to prevent a catastrophe was for the government to tell the truth, and pray to God that it was believed. "I think we have to be careful that the government is believed about cocaine, because there are dangers associated with the drug," Byck said vaguely. "These dangers are not particularly associated with the present use pattern."

Byck told the committee that he'd hesitated for a long time about coming forward with the information and was still reluctant to discuss the matter in a public hearing. "Usually when things like this are reported, the media advertises them, and this attention has been a problem with cocaine all along."

Chairman Guyer, who'd spent two decades as a public relations man for an Ohio tire company, told Byck to spit it out. "[The purpose of our panel] is to bring into the open what has been, up to now, a pretty secret kind of thing."

The information Byck had was known to only a handful of drug researchers around the world. And it was as frightening a spectacle as any they'd ever seen.

For about a year, a Peruvian police psychiatrist named Dr. Raul Jeri had been insisting that wealthy drug users in Lima were being driven insane by cocaine. A psychiatrist in Bolivia, Dr. Nils Noya, began making similar claims shortly thereafter. Their reports, written in Spanish and published in obscure medical journals, went largely unnoticed in the United States because, frankly, they sounded so weird.

The first problem was that all of recorded history was against them. Peru and Bolivia had been producing cocaine products for thousands of years, with few reports of the drug causing serious medical effects. At the same time, some of America's leading researchers were claiming that cocaine was nonaddictive and perhaps should be legalized.

Jeri, a professor of clinical neurology at the National University of San Marcos, claimed a cocaine "epidemic" had swept through Lima's fashionable neighborhoods in 1974 and spread like a grass fire to Peru's other major cities: Piura, Trujillo, Chiclayo, Chimbote, Huaraz, Ica, Arequipa, and Cuzco. Within two years, he said, the alleged epidemic had engulfed Ecuador and Bolivia.

No one had heard of anything like it before. It also didn't help that the psychiatrists' studies read like the script of *Reefer Madness*, painting scenes of jails and insane asylums filling up with legions of half-mad drug fiends.

"When seen, these patients were generally very thin, unkempt, pale and looking suspiciously from one side to the other," Jeri wrote. "These movements were associated... with visual hallucinations (shadows, light or human figures) which they observed in the temporal fields of vision."

Many of the patients bore scratches from trying to dig out the hallucinations they felt crawling under their skin, and they claimed they were being "followed by persons or shadows that seemed to want to catch, attack, or kill them... three patients died in this series, two by acute intoxication and one by suicide."

It wasn't a new drug that was causing this reaction, Jeri and Noya reported, but a new trick from an old dog. Instead of sniffing tiny crystals of cocaine up their nose, as Americans were doing, the Peruvians and Bolivians were smoking a paste known variously as *pasta basica de cocaina, basé,* or *basuco*. It was all the same thing—the gooey mess that leached out of solvent-soaked coca leaves. Coca paste was an intermediate substance created on the way to manufacturing the white powder known to most cocaine users. People had started drying the paste, crumbling it into cigarettes, and smoking it.

For the serious drug abuser, paste's advantages over powder were enormous.

You could smoke as much as you wanted. With powder, only a small amount could be stuffed up one's nose, and it took time for the drug to kick in, because first it had to be absorbed by the nasal membranes. Eventually the nose got numb.

Cocaine vapor, on the other hand, hit the vast surface area of the lungs immediately and delivered an instantaneous sledgehammer high. Users described the feeling as more intense than orgasm; some called it a "whole body orgasm." And there was no limit to the amount of vapor the lungs could process. Paste had the added advantage of being richer in actual cocaine than the powder commonly sold—40–85 percent as opposed to 12–20 percent—and was far cheaper. In terms of bang for the buck, it couldn't be beat.

"Many patients said they found no other drug as pleasurable as this one," Jeri wrote. "Paste was almost unknown six years ago. Now it is the main drug reported by patients who are admitted to psychiatric hospitals or drug treatment centers in Lima. There is no zone of this city where youngsters do not get together to smoke coca paste and where pushers do not sell the drug in their own homes or in the street. They even come to the school entrances to do their business."

But there was a price to pay for such a blissful rush. The feeling lasted only a few minutes, and nirvana could only be reattained by another hit—quickly—or a crushing depression would follow, the devil's own version of the cocaine blues. It was a roller-coaster ride, and invariably the user couldn't keep up the pace.

Jeri was deeply troubled by his research, comparing paste smokers to those suffering from a malignant disease. "It is hard to believe to what extremes of social degradation these men may fall, especially those who were brilliant students, efficient professionals, or successful businessmen," he wrote. "These individuals became so dependent on the drug that they had practically no other interest in life."

The Bolivian psychiatrist Nils Noya claimed that the drug caused "irreversible brain damage" and wrote that cocaine smokers literally could not stop once they started. Some users, he reported, smoked sixty to eighty cocaine-laced cigarettes in a single session. Cocaine-smoking parties would go on for days, ending only when the supplies dried up or the smokers passed out. "Immediately after smoking a cigarette, they have diarrhea," Noya said in a 1978 interview. "I mean immediately. But the worst part is they have to go on smoking until they finish the box [of paste]."

Jeri wrote that cocaine smoking was largely confined to Peru, Bolivia, Ecuador, and Colombia, but there were ominous signs that it was moving northward. "We do not know if coca paste has been introduced to America, but Panamanian authorities have reported heavy transportation of coca paste by American and Peruvian citizens," Jeri wrote in 1979, citing an unpublished Panamanian police report.

Byck, who among other things had collected and edited Sigmund Freud's cocaine papers, had been skeptical of the South American reports until he sent one of his students down to Peru on a summer project. In the spring of 1978 a first-year Yale med student named David Paly came to Byck with an idea the scientist found intriguing: Paly wanted to measure the blood plasma levels of Peru's coca-leaf-chewing Indians to see what it was that got the Indians high. Plenty had been written about the cultural aspects of the habit, Paly told Byck, but no one had ever done any real experiments to see what it was that the leaf put in the Indians' bloodstream, and how much of it got there.

Paly, who had in interest in Peru from earlier travels there, said he "dreamed up" the project in order to start work on his thesis. "It was a fairly rudimentary proposal, but Yale has a thesis requirement for an M.D.—it's the only medical school in the country that does—so you have to start a proposal early in your career."

Coincidentally, Byck had recently gotten a letter from a prominent Peruvian neurosurgeon, Dr. Fernando Cabieses, who proposed some cooperative research on cocaine. At the time, the Peruvian government was cracking down on coca chewing and Cabieses believed the Indians were being harassed unfairly. He was looking for some scientific evidence to back up his arguments that the Indians' social customs should be left alone. Both Byck and Cabieses liked Paly's idea, and the Peruvian agreed to provide the lab facilities, test subjects, transportation, and assistants.

Soon a delighted Paly was winging his way to South America to spend his summer among the Indians in the mountains of Peru. Cabieses squired the young Yalie around Lima and introduced him to his friends in the arts and sciences. One man Paly met through Cabieses was Dr. Raul Jeri, who latched onto him and began telling him of his research into cocaine smoking. Jeri, who was also a general in the Peruvian military police, insisted on showing Paly the wretched victims of this new drug habit he'd discovered. Mostly to humor his influential new acquaintance, Paly agreed to accompany Jeri to the psychiatric institute where Jeri worked as a consultant. Paly left the hospital more doubtful than before.

"I interviewed some of these quote unquote *pastaleros*, and to my mind, one of them was clearly schizophrenic," Paly said. "Another one appeared to be a poly-drug abuser. I mean this guy had done everything from Valium to Quaaludes. So I was very unimpressed when I went around with him that first time."

Reading Jeri's studies did nothing to enhance Paly's opinion, either. They "were mainly observational and not very scientific," he said. It wasn't until Paly began making friends in Lima that he started changing his mind about the insistent general's work.

"I began to hear...about their friends who were dropping out of medical school and dropping out of college and basically turning into raging cocaine addicts," Paly recalled. "They were good kids who had essentially abandoned their lives and turned into wildly addicted base smokers. They were stealing from their grandmothers and doing all the kinds of things that you would associate with a heroin addict...and there were thousands of them."

On motorcycle trips through Lima with his friends, Paly said, he'd "drive down these streets and the places would stink of cocaine. They would stink of it. You'd come around a corner and you could smell it for miles. It has a very characteristic, sweet odor. And these weren't slums either. These were middle-class neighborhoods that my friends had grown up in, and now their friends were hanging out in the middle of the street, gaunt, and totally strung out."

Alarmed, Paly called Byck at Yale and told him what he'd seen. "The substance of my conversation with Byck, if I remember correctly, was that if this shit ever hits the U.S., we're in deep trouble."

Said Byck, "I remember the phone call very vividly. He said something was going on down there, and I told him to get some bloods [samples] and bring them back with him." Paly drew blood samples from random smokers and had them analyzed at the Laboratories of Clinical Psychopharmacology at Yale that fall.

"Peter Jatlow, who was the lab director, said they had the highest plasma levels of cocaine that he'd ever seen in someone who wasn't dead," Paly recalled. "If the average experimental plasma level they were getting in the lab from ingesting—snorting—cocaine was 100 [nanograms per mil], these—these were in the thousands."

Byck quickly got some federal grant money and sent Paly back to Lima to do some controlled experiments on cocaine smokers. Jeri, with his police connections, obtained the necessary permits and approvals, procured a half-kilo of coca paste and some cocaine smokers, and allowed Paly to bring them all to a room at the Peruvian Museum of Health Sciences. Most of them were young men in their twenties. Paly put on some music, served food and refreshments, and then brought out a box of coca paste.

"All subjects, calm while sitting in the room before the experiment, became markedly anxious as the box containing the paste was brought into the room," Paly wrote. "This nervousness became pronounced as they were preparing their first cigarettes and was evidenced by shaky hands and extremely sweaty palms and foreheads. This nervousness was borne out by the high blood pressure and heart rates taken immediately before smoking. This anxiety reaction is common to most experienced cocaine smokers and will often be brought on by the mere thought of smoking."

Paly was both fascinated and repelled. "It was Pavlovian," he said. "It was just unbelievable. Some of these kids, in the lab, would smoke twenty grams of paste and then, after you had paid them for their time, they would run out on the street with the money and buy more."

While Paly was running his experiments in Peru, further evidence was emerging in the United States that Raul Jeri's laughable predictions of a North American "cocaine invasion" were right on the mark. In February 1979 a psychologist from UCLA, Ronald K. Siegel, had a letter printed in the prestigious *New England Journal of Medicine* warning of "a growing trend" toward cocaine smoking in the western United States. Siegel, who'd been researching cocaine use in the Los Angeles area since the early 1970s, was a well-known drug expert who had become something of a media darling, always ready with a good quote for reporters wanting the inside scoop on the latest drug craze in La-La Land.

Siegel had started a pioneering research project in 1975 by taking out newspaper ads seeking longtime cocaine users. L.A. being L.A., he got plenty of responses. He selected ninety-nine cocaine users, mostly young males, and proposed keeping in touch with them over the next four years so he could monitor the results of constant, long-term cocaine use.

His findings were great news for cokeheads. Not only did cocaine make you feel good, Siegel reported, but it had very few adverse psychological effects, and as a bonus, it helped you lose weight. "By the end of the study, approximately 38% of the subjects had shown increased elevation of the Euphoria Scale, indicating increased happiness and contentment with life," Siegel wrote. Only 5 percent of the subjects reported psychological problems, such as suspiciousness or paranoia, and Siegel dismissed those complaints as hypochondria or "perceptual" disturbances.

"Taken together, individuals reported experiencing some positive effects in all intoxications and negative effects in only 3% of the intoxications," he wrote. Even those negative effects "were usually of short duration and infrequent occurrence." All in all, Siegel concluded, the long-term negative effects of cocaine use "were consistently overshadowed by the long-term positive benefits."

There was, however, a curious footnote to Siegel's study, which the psychologist mentioned in passing. Over the course of his study, which ran from 1975 to 1978, six of the original ninety-nine cocaine users had become confirmed cocaine smokers, puffing something known on the streets as "freebase." Siegel was sufficiently intrigued to perform some cocaine-smoking experiments on monkeys, discovering that three out of three apes, given a choice between smoking lettuce or cocaine, clearly preferred coke.

So when Siegel read Jeri's reports about the cocaine smoking epidemic in South America, he realized the Peruvian was wrong about one thing: the habit wasn't confined to South America anymore. It had already planted its seeds in L.A. and was starting to pop up in other cities as well, building a devoted following among certain circles of rich drug users. Worse, Yankee ingenuity had already been at work, improving upon the deadly product, making it easier to use and more appealing to refined American tastes.

The substance Jeri's subjects were using, coca paste, came mostly from the jungle cocaine-processing labs that dotted Peru and Bolivia. Paste was an ugly gray glob laden with residues of the toxic solvents used to extract it from the coca leaves—kerosene, acid, and other chemicals.

Some analyses had even found brick dust and leaded gasoline in it. Paste was hardly ever sold in the United States.

What Americans got for their drug dollars was the finished product, the sparkling white crystals of cocaine hydrochloride powder. But cocaine powder was made to be snorted. It was extremely difficult to smoke because of its high boiling point. So what was it that Siegel's patients were using, this cocaine they called "freebase"?

Siegel learned that it was cocaine powder that had been reverse-engineered to become smokable again. He traced the discovery of the process to the San Francisco Bay Area in January 1974, around the time that coca paste smoking had started becoming popular in Peru. According to Siegel, California cocaine traffickers who were journeying to Peru and Colombia for their wares "heard of the people down there smoking *basé*." Though the Colombians were referring to coca paste, Siegel said, the Americans "mispronounced it, mistranslated the Spanish, and thought it was cocaine base. So they looked it up in the Merck Manual, saw cocaine base and said, 'Yeah, that's just the alkaloid of cocaine hydrochloride,' which is street cocaine."

By a relatively simple chemical process, Siegel said, the dealers took the powder and "removed the hydrochloride salt, thus freeing the cocaine base. Hence the expression 'freebasing.' That was something they could smoke, because it was volatile. And they were wowed by it when they smoked it." The traffickers "thought they were smoking *basé*. They were not. They were smoking something that nobody else on the planet had ever smoked before."

By 1977, kits to extract freebase from cocaine powder were available commercially; ads were appearing in the underground press and in drug magazines. But since cocaine powder was so expensive, freebasing was a habit practiced only by a few rich drug dealers or avant garde celebrities. "They had very inefficient processes in those days and thought you needed large bags of cocaine to reduce to the cocaine freebase. So during the early years, only dealers and very wealthy users engaged in this," Siegel said.

Dr. Sidney Cohen, another California scientist who recognized the dangers of cocaine smoking early on, wrote in 1980 that the only good thing about freebase was that it was "the most expensive of all mood changers when price is measured against euphoria time. Affluent hedonists are the only ones who can afford it."

In December 1978, after comparing notes with Jeri, Siegel fired off his letter to the *New England Journal of Medicine*, alerting the medical profession that there were problems afoot. "Users are now experimenting with smoking cocaine alkaloid or base," he wrote. "Free-base parties have become increasingly popular and the practice has spread from California to Nevada, Colorado, New York, South Carolina and Florida."

Siegel's letter appeared in the *Journal* in February 1979. Five months later, in July, he, along with Paly, Byck, Jeri, and other cocaine researchers, found themselves together in Lima for an international symposium on cocaine. It was the first chance North American and South American drug researchers had had to compare notes and discuss their latest work.

While the experts split on what to do about powder cocaine, those who'd been studying cocaine smoking were unanimous about their findings: there was a monster loose, a drug capable of totally enslaving its user.

At the Lima conference, the stories continued to pour in. Two Bolivian psychiatrists from La Paz, Gregorio Aramayo and Mario Sánchez, told of seeing patients coming in for treatment in bare feet and borrowed clothes. "One of the patients said, 'This damn drug, doctor, I have had to sell even my clothes in order to buy it.'" Eighty percent of their patients, they reported, had committed "impulsive acts such as thefts, swindling, clothes-selling and others in order to buy more drug."

The Lima conference had taken place only two weeks before Byck appeared in Washington, and the stories he'd heard were fresh in his mind as he sat before Guyer's committee and listened to America's drug experts pooh-pooh the dangers of cocaine.

Once, Byck testified, he was in their camp. No longer. "I have come to the absolute, clear conclusion that it should not be legalized under any circumstances," he said. Cocaine smoking "can represent the same threat that the speed epidemics of the 1960's represented in their time.... We are on the verge of a dangerous drug use phenomenon."

Byck also wasn't the only American scientist who attended the Lima conference and came back alarmed. "The impact of these experiences was impressive, and observers from the National Institute on Drug Abuse (NIDA), the White House, and the Department of State reported on the growing problem in South America when they returned to the U.S.," said a 1982 study. Two of those observers, from NIDA and the White House, backed up Byck's warnings at the hearing.

But there was still time to prevent a catastrophe, Byck told the committee. "We do not yet have an epidemic of freebase or coca paste smoking in the United States. The possibility is strong that this might occur," Byck testified. "I have reports from California, from Chicago, and from

New York about people who are smoking the substance, and I hear there are numbers of people now in San Francisco smoking the substance. Here is a chance for the federal government to engage in an educational campaign to prevent a drug abuse epidemic." The government needed to do three things "as rapidly as possible. Number one, find out about it. Number two, establish some kind of collaboration with the media; and number three, show what happens when this drug is used, so that we don't get an epidemic. We need our best minds to figure out how to do this without advertising the drug."

But the congressmen weren't interested in discussing educational campaigns or public service announcements. That wouldn't get any cocaine off the streets. What they wanted to know was this: What about the DEA's plan to ask the Peruvians and Bolivians to please quit growing coca plants?

Byck scoffed. "I don't think you can eliminate the growing of coca in Peru and countries which have had it for thousands of years."

"Not with [crop] substitutions?" Guyer asked.

"I don't think so."

"That is not going to work?" Guyer persisted.

"It *can't* work," Byck said, "if you consider these are crops grown on the slopes of mountains near jungle, and grown by people for their own use for 2,000 years. And talking about wiping it out? You have a better chance of wiping out tobacco in Virginia."

"We'll come back to this," Guyer promised, and the Cocaine Task Force hurried from the room for a break.

They never came back to Byck's warnings.

When the hearings resumed, the congressmen peppered the witnesses with such questions as whether they thought Hollywood cocaine use was contributing to the deterioration of quality TV shows (as one of them had heard recently on the *Mike Douglas Show*); if it was true that Coca-Cola once contained cocaine; and if the TV series *Quincy*, in which Jack Klugman played a coroner, was "accurate" or if it was "way out." Not another word was said about doing research or warning the public about the dangers of cocaine smoking. Byck left the hearing stunned. "Nobody paid any attention," he recalled. "They listened to it, and everyone said, 'So what?' I felt very strongly that the information that I had should have caused somebody to say, 'All right! We've got to start finding out about this stuff!' But they didn't."

Instead, Congress and the Carter administration did exactly the opposite of what Byck advised. It embarked on "the Andean strategy" advocated by the DEA to wipe out the coca plant, a tactic that even its supporters now concede was a failure. Nor did the federal government seem all that eager to allow scientists to do their own research into cocaine smoking, or to help them spread the alarm.

When Siegel, under U.S. government contract, finished a massive report on the history and literature of cocaine smoking, he couldn't get the government to publish it, allegedly due to concerns that readers would rush out and start smoking once they found out how to turn powder into freebase.

"They wanted me to do a scientific paper about cocaine smoking, but not to tell anyone how it was done," Siegel said disgustedly. "I tried to explain that people already knew how it was done. That's why there was a problem." Concerned that the information might never get out, he published it himself in a small medical journal two years later.

In 1982, Raul Jeri came to the United States to deliver his warnings in person.

He showed up at the California Conference on Cocaine, a well-attended affair held at a hotel in balmy Santa Monica, a few miles south of Los Angeles. Surrounded by palm trees and hibiscus, with the sounds of the ocean breaking in the background, the setting was perfect for a gabfest about such a sexy topic. Reporters flocked to the event, mobbing LSD guru Dr. Timothy Leary for a few witticisms about cocaine.

If any of them sat through Raul Jeri's presentation, it is likely they came away with the conviction that the thin, dark Peruvian was even stranger than Leary. Jeri showed his American colleagues a few slides, and in broken English tried to bang the drum about the dangers of cocaine smoking, which he claimed would result in "grave incurable cases of dementia." He trotted out his horror stories about the walking dead, the coke zombies that populated Peru. He showed more slides. "I would like to warn the U.S. against the plague which has reached its borders!" Jeri said dramatically, as the lights came back on. "The trivialization of cocaine use is a curse on humanity!"

The speech was "followed by an uneasy silence," a doctor in the audience remembered. How did Jeri treat such patients? someone asked.

Nothing worked really, Jeri said. They'd tried everything. Long periods of confinement, heavy doses of tranquilizers, lobotomies. It didn't matter. The relapse rate was between 50 and 80 percent, he said.

Um, lobotomies, did you say?

"Yes, surgical lobotomy—cyngulotomy, to be precise," Jeri said. He assured the audience that the brain surgery was done "only in desperate cases on incurable repeaters, often upon request by the family and with the patient's consent."

It was hard for Jeri's listeners to imagine how cocaine could become so addictive that a person would volunteer for brain surgery. "How barbaric," one muttered.

Byck said the Food and Drug Administration shut down attempts to do any serious research on addiction or treatment, refusing to approve grant requests or research proposals and withholding the government permits necessary to run experiments with controlled substances. "The FDA almost totally roadblocked our getting anything done. They insisted that they had total control over whether we could use a form of cocaine for experimental purposes, and without a so-called IND [an Investigation of New Drug permit] we couldn't go ahead with any cocaine experiments. And they wouldn't give us an IND."

Why not? "Once you get into the morass of government, you never understand exactly who is doing what to whom and why," Byck said.

Eight months before he appeared before Guyer's task force, Byck had requested official government permission to bring a coca paste sample into the United States for laboratory analysis. He filled out many forms, turned the sample over to a DEA agent in Lima, and never saw it again. "I now have a number of licenses I never had before, but no samples," Byck told Guyer's committee sarcastically. "The regulations which govern the legal importation of cocaine and coca research are much more effective than the regulations which seem to govern smoking or smuggling."

2

"We were the first"

The same day the world's cocaine experts were gathered in Lima to discuss the approaching drug epidemic—July 5, 1979—a man who would help spread it across Los Angeles was touching down at LAX. It had been a rough couple of weeks for Oscar Danilo Blandón Reyes, a pudgy twenty-seven-year-old refugee from the Nicaraguan civil war.

Not long before he'd had the world on a platter. He'd been rich, the second son of a wealthy landowner. His wife, Chepita, had been rich, a daughter of one of the country's most prominent political families. He had a brand-new M.B.A., a cushy government job, and a couple of businesses—an import-export company and a travel agency—on the side. One of his firms had a lucrative contract to supply American food to the Nicaraguan National Guard, the institution that ran the country.

Danilo and Chepita Blandón were solidly plugged into the power structure of General Anastasio Somoza's dictatorship, which was benevolent only in the ways that it rewarded its friends. The Somoza family owned nearly all of the country's biggest corporations—the national airline, the power company, the biggest hotel, the biggest department store, the cement factory, a newspaper...you name it, they owned it. It was hard to earn a living in Nicaragua if the Somozas took a dislike to you. But those families who stayed loyal and pleased the dictator partook of the riches that only a wall-to-wall monopoly can provide. The Blandóns had been blessed by Somoza's smile.

Then the Sandinistas had come to town and spoiled everything.

As Danilo Blandón stepped off the jet from Miami into the vast terminal at LAX, he found himself jobless, nearly broke, and homeless—human driftwood from a faraway, conquered land.

"[He came here] with one hand in the front and one in the back, you know what I mean?" his cousin Flor Reyes said.

All he and his wife had grown up accepting as their birthright—the elegant mansions, the servants, the vacation homes, the elite private schools—was gone, and he dreaded would soon be the property of some grasping commandante.

Though Somoza's army had beaten them down time and again, the Sandinistas rose up from the earth in the summer of 1978 to begin an offensive that would flabbergast both Somoza and his American handlers. By the spring of the following year, they had captured many of the smaller rural cities and were closing in on the capital. Somoza's supporters, who called themselves *Somocistas*, were beside themselves. Who would have ever believed that "Tachito" Somoza, the self-described Latin from Manhattan, could have gotten his ass whipped—and so quickly—by a bunch of bearded radicals? More importantly, how could the Americans have allowed such a thing to happen? The CIA contingent at the U.S. embassy had been assuring everyone that things were fine, that the rebels weren't a real threat. It might get a little tough for the old boy a couple years down the road, the CIA opined, but Somoza would hang on until then.

But what Somoza and, apparently, the CIA didn't realize was that the deal his family had struck with every U.S. administration since Franklin Roosevelt's—a blood pact to combat Communism together—would be dissolved by a Georgia peanut farmer, Jimmy Carter. Instead of covering up or downplaying the brutality of Somoza's National Guard as past administrations had done, some of Carter's people went on a human rights crusade, complaining publicly that the longtime dictator was just *too* dictatorial, and that his *Guardia* was wantonly killing people. In 1977 some in Congress had begun wondering why the U.S. government continued putting up with Somoza and his ill-behaved brood. Asked by the chairman of the House Appropriations Subcommittee what harm would befall U.S. interests if Congress were simply to cut off all aid to Nicaragua, Undersecretary of State Lucy Benson replied, "I cannot think of a single thing."

Somoza told his *Guardia* cohorts to ease up on the rough stuff, and miraculously, complaints dropped off sharply. Satisfied, the

Carter administration backed off. "President Somoza is known to have instructed the National Guard on several occasions to eliminate abuses which led to many charges of extra-legal killings and torture, particularly in a northern rural area of insurgent activity," State Department official Sally Shelton proudly told Congress in 1978. That "northern rural area" was the stomping grounds of an especially efficient *Guardia* general, Gustavo "El Tigre" Medina, who would later play an important role in Danilo Blandón's life. Medina was Somoza's top counterinsurgency adviser, a short, steely-looking man hated and feared by the Sandinistas. They consider him responsible for some of the revolution's worst defeats.

The State Department reported in 1978 that, as far as the human rights complaints coming out of Medina's theater were concerned, "it appears that many of the allegations of cruel, inhuman and degrading treatment during the course of National Guard operations against the FSLN [the Sandinistas] were well-founded, but others were more dubious." But when the Inter-American Commission on Human Rights, a branch of the Organization of American States (OAS), did its own inspection in late 1978, the Latin American team, observers from other countries, saw things in much more graphic terms than had the Americans.

They spoke to a mother who told of picking body parts out of the dust to reassemble her five-year-old daughter after the girl was hit by an air-to-ground missile. They talked with survivors of "Operation Mop-Up," during which the *Guardia* went in after a street battle and killed everyone they found in the neighborhoods where the Sandinistas had hidden, shooting "numerous people, in some cases children, in their own homes or in front of the same and in the presence of parents and siblings." They visited the jails, reporting that in "all the jails visited, the prisoners alleged that they rarely saw a doctor but that when they did see one he was giving instructions as to the voltage of electricity to be applied during the torture, or examining the tortured persons to see if they could resist any more shocks."

In the northern mountains, the team concluded that of 338 peasants arrested between 1975 and 1977 by the Guardia, 321 of them "were never seen again and are presumed dead." The missing peasants' farms were "appropriated by members of the National Guard," the report said.

When the State Department went to Congress for more money to support Somoza's troops, one congressman was perplexed. "What possible interest does the United States have in training the National Guard of Nicaragua?" the lawmaker asked. "How does that help the American citizen?"

The training programs "have provided us a useful instrument for exercising political as well as professional influence over the Guard," the diplomat replied.

"I know," the congressman deadpanned. "We have been doing that for the last twenty or thirty years."

Because the National Guard had such a tight lock on the country, it was considered invincible by many of Somoza's followers. And it might have been, had the Carter administration backed up Somoza when the Sandinistas were at his throat. But Carter's people never really figured out what they wanted to do in Nicaragua, except to distance themselves from Somoza's excesses.

When it became obvious that the Nicaraguan people would no longer live under Somoza's rule, the American plan for dealing with the crisis boiled down to this: Dump Somoza and salvage the *Guardia*. Apparently the administration never realized that, to the Sandinistas and most other Nicaraguans, the *Guardia* and Somoza were like evil twins joined at the brain. One could not survive without the other.

As Sandinista attacks mounted, Washington let Somoza twist. Gradually, it dawned on Somoza's followers that the Americans weren't riding to their rescue. By early June 1979 Managua's airport was jammed with people frantically trying to catch a flight out before the rebels arrived. "Hundreds of Nicaraguans struggle daily at Las Mercedes International Airport to get a seat on one of the four commercial flights," Panamanian radio reported on June 9. "The situation here is such that if a donkey with wings appeared, it would be beseiged by travelers," an airport official said. "Departure from the country by land or by sea is impossible because of the danger involved in driving on the country's roads."

Yet Danilo Blandón stayed put, though he had every reason to fear the vengeance of the Sandinistas, to whom the Blandón family represented all that was wrong with the dictatorship. Blandón's father, Julio, owned the land on which was built one of the worst slums in Managua—OPEN #3—a low-rent district that began life as emergency government housing after an earthquake leveled Managua in 1972. Conditions there were so bad that the neighborhood, now called Ciudad Sandino and numbering more than 70,000 residents, was a constant source of new recruits for the Sandinistas and a hotbed of anti-Somoza activity. "It was called Via Misery," said economist Orlando Murillo, an uncle of Blandón's wife. "People there lived like the niggers in Los Angeles. But it made [Danilo's] father a very rich man."

The Blandóns were social friends of the Somozas and shared common business interests; Julio Blandón and Somoza were two of the biggest landlords in Managua. Blandón could trace his family's relationship with the dictatorship back several generations. Blandón's mother was from the Reyes family, which had an illustrious history in the Somoza regime, and his grandfather was Colonel Rigoberto Reyes, former minister of war and National Guard commander under Somoza's father, Anastasio I.

Danilo's in-laws, the Murillos, were stalwarts of Somoza's Liberal party. The Murillos had provided leaders for the National Assembly for generations; Orlando Murillo's father had been the assembly's president, and Chepita Blandón's father had been Managua's mayor. Like the Blandóns, the Murillos owned large tracts of the capital, including the national telecommunications company headquarters, along with cattle ranches and plantations in the hinterlands.

In some ways, Danilo Blandón had more to fear from the Sandinistas than other *Somocistas*. He was part of Somoza's government, the director of wholesale markets, and ran a program designed to introduce a free-market economy to Nicaragua's farmers. Blandón's job was to award grants for demonstration projects to create central distribution points for the country's agricultural riches, places where farmers could come and sell their goods to food wholesalers.

The $27 million program, Blandón said, was jointly financed by the Nicaraguan and U.S. governments. It paid for his master's degree in business administration from the University of Colombia in Bogotá.

Blandón and his wife held fast during the first jittery weeks of June. Heavy fighting was breaking out in Managua, where they lived; National Guardsmen and Sandinista rebels were shooting each other in the streets. By June 11 things were so far gone for Somoza that the rebels had set up a headquarters in the eastern part of the city, and shells from National Guard howitzers whistled over downtown Managua daily to explode in the Sandinista-held neighborhoods. Circling airplanes would drop 500-pound bombs or flaming gasoline barrels into the area. On the edge of town, a National Guard tank had rolled up outside the *La Prensa* building and pumped round after round into the shuttered offices of the paper that had been Somoza's fiercest critic.

The CIA hastily revised its estimate of Somoza's staying power on June 12, giving his government only a short time to live. Somoza "fired" the *Guardia*'s general staff four days later—many had fought the Sandinistas for decades—and most of them ran to the Colombian embassy for asylum. The exodus was on.

Somoza went on the radio June 19 to denounce the U.S. government for its ingratitude for his long years of service. "I want the U.S. people to help me, just as I helped them during thirty years of struggle against communism," he announced. "We want the North Americans to return what we contributed during the Cold War."

That same day the CIA shortened Somoza's life expectancy once more. Now, the agency estimated, he had little more than a week. Danilo Blandón decided he'd hung around long enough. He had a three-year-old daughter, and Chepita was pregnant with their second child. It was time to go. Blandón fell in with a Red Cross convoy on its way to the airport and put his wife and daughter on a plane for Los Angeles, where Chepita had relatives. For some reason, he did not accompany them. Instead Blandón and his older brother, Julio Jr., boarded a flight for Miami, where Blandón entered the United States on a tourist visa he'd been issued several years earlier.

How he managed to do what many others could not—namely, get four seats on jetliners bound for the States—is not clear, and the Immigration and Naturalization Service has refused to release any records of the Blandóns' immigration, citing privacy reasons. Nor is it clear why he first went to Miami.

Years later, Blandón would claim that he couldn't get a ticket to L.A. for himself, and barely could afford the tickets he got. He claimed that he sold a Sony color television for $200 to pay for them, and landed in Miami with $100 to his name. However, his wife's uncle, Orlando Murillo, says he paid for the airline tickets and also gave the couple $5,000 before they left the country. If that was true, Blandón had other reasons for choosing to spend his first few weeks in Miami.

As he tells it, he stayed with a friend and "got a job washing cars" until he could save enough for a plane ticket to Los Angeles. He rejoined his family on the West Coast in early July, and by August he had landed a job as a salesman at a used car lot in East Los Angeles, a heavily Hispanic section of town. His employers were two huge Nicaraguan brothers named Torres.

Blandón has said he knew one of the brothers, Edgar, from his days in college in Monterrey, Mexico, where Edgar was studying economics. Edgar's brother, Jacinto, was a former U.S. Marine and had served in Vietnam. Together they ran Torres Used Cars.

"They had a used car lot with only ten cars," Blandón said. "They just give me a favor to be there and pay me something because they know that I didn't have any money, and then they gave me [a job] like a salesman in the neighborhood."

But the Torres brothers weren't just car salesmen. They were also major-league cocaine traffickers. Other dealers called them "the Trees" because of their sequoia-like girth; both brothers were estimated to be at least six-six. To the cops they became known as "the Twin Towers." The Torres brothers lived with two sisters who were big in their own way: they were cousins of Pablo Escobar, a Colombian cocaine kingpin who was one of the founders of the Medellín cocaine cartel.

Escobar and his Colombian pals Jorge Ochoa and Carlos Lehder were then firmly in control of the blossoming Miami cocaine market, having wrested it from the Cuban-Americans after a long-running cocaine war. The Cubans had been using the city as a base for small-scale cocaine smuggling since the late 1960s, but the Colombians had bigger ideas. They intended to distribute mass quantities of cocaine all across the United States in an organized and businesslike fashion.

For three years, from 1976 to 1979, they fought the Cubans for supremacy in Miami, and the two sides killed each other in droves. Afterward the Colombians turned the city into a cocaine distribution hub, and it became the official port of call for cocaine dealers of every stripe. Local banks began swelling with drug profits.

Miami was convenient; the Colombians could blend in with the large Hispanic population and move about the city unnoticed. Escobar's associate Carlos Lehder set up shop in the Bahamas, buying an island where the drug planes coming out of Colombia could land, refuel, and wait for the right moment to fly into the United States.

Lehder's transportation system worked well and gave the Medellín cartel its first real toehold in America. Then he began jetting to the West Coast to scope out a distribution system for Los Angeles and the western United States.

When Blandón was working for the Torres brothers, he says, they had not yet begun dealing cocaine. But it apparently didn't take them long to get the hang of it; by 1982 they would be two of the more significant drug dealers in Los Angeles.

Blandón insists he wasn't dealing drugs in 1979 either. That was a couple years down the road. At the moment, he had plenty to keep him busy. Chepita was getting bigger with their second child every day, and he was struggling to pay the bills. In August 1979 he started a new job with another car lot, Rocha Used Cars, and was also hustling rental cars at an L.A. hotel, according to his friend Frank Vigil. And in his spare time Blandón was also trying to start an army.

"I was the first," Blandón boasted. "Well—we—we formed a group in

L.A. to—a group of our people to go and fight against the Sandinistas that we called FDN, *Fuerza Democrática Nicaragüense* [Nicaraguan Democratic Force]. We were in charge. We were five people in charge of it in L.A. We were in charge to get some money at that time."

Blandón said his counterrevolutionary group came together soon after he arrived in Los Angeles. At first it was just a group of Nicaraguan exiles who got together occasionally to bitch about the Sandinistas and help each other find a toehold in their new country. They would "talk about developments in Nicaragua," Blandón later told the CIA. "Other members of this group also opposed Somoza and the Sandinista regime.... [They] simply came together to share common experiences and discuss their mutual desires to see the Sandinista government out of Nicaragua." They had "meetings every week, every 15 days, okay, since we got to L.A., in 1980–81. And we raised money for the Contras." When it began, he said, his group was not officially connected to anyone. It had no formal structure, no officers, no membership requirements.

"You Americans have no idea what it's like to lose everything and be thrown out of your own country," commented Jose Macario Estrada, an ex-judge who later became Blandón's lawyer and business partner. "When you are in exile, you become very close to other exiles."

At the end of 1979 Blandón applied for political asylum in the United States, claiming that he would be killed by the Communists if he returned to Nicaragua. And he listed his membership in an "anti-Communist organization" as proof that his life was worthless back home. If Blandón's recollection is correct, his little L.A. group was one of the first flickerings of an organized resistance movement against the Sandinistas in the United States. Acquaintances and former college classmates say Blandón sometimes brags that he was one of the earliest founders of the FDN, which became the biggest and most famous of the various Nicaraguan anti-Communist armies that would later be called the Contras.

The FDN didn't officially come into existence until mid-1981, so if Blandón was raising money for Contra fighters as early as he says—in 1979–80—he was doing it on behalf of the FDN's predecessor: the Legion of September 15, a violent band of ex-*Guardia* men then based in Guatemala. The legion, a terrorist organization started by former Somoza bodyguards soon after Somoza's fall, was to become the hard core of the FDN after the CIA merged it into two smaller resistance groups in August 1981.

Blandón's Contra fund-raising efforts bore little fruit at first. "At the beginning, we started doing some parties, you know, some—how do you call—some activities in the park, until 1980 and '81," he said. "We have to have some rallies or whatever." The fund-raisers were disappointing, though, bringing in only "a few thousands or something." An acquaintance reported that Blandón also hawked copies of Somoza's bitter memoirs, *Nicaragua Betrayed*, and helped put out an anti-Sandinista newsletter that was printed at a little shop owned by a sympathetic Nicaraguan.

About the same time that Blandón and his compatriots began their fund-raising efforts in L.A., Somoza's cousin, Luis Pallais Debayle, began making the rounds of the various exile groups in the United States and Central America to see if anyone was interested in helping Somoza fight his way back into power.

Pallais contacted his cousin in Paraguay, and the ex-dictator promised to kick in $1 million to start a resistance movement. It was a promise he never kept. On September 17, 1980, Argentine revolutionaries blasted a rocket-propelled grenade and a hail of M-16 fire into Somoza's Mercedes-Benz limo, killing Somoza and scattering pieces of him and his German automobile across a block of downtown Asunción.

Another visit Pallais made, with happier results, was to former National Guard colonel Enrique Bermúdez, to see if Bermúdez would be willing to lead a resistance force if one could be put together. Bermúdez was a logical choice to be the Contras' military commander. Of all the former officers of Somoza's National Guard, he probably had the best contacts with the U.S. military and intelligence communities. Convincing the Americans to back them was going to be critical if the Contras were ever to get off the ground. And Bermúdez was a leader who was very palatable to the Americans. He was a known quantity.

"He fit the profile," one U.S. official later told journalist Sam Dillon. "He was malleable, controllable, docile."

In 1965 Bermúdez had been the deputy commander of an infantry company Somoza sent to support a U.S.-led invasion of the Dominican Republic, an excursion to put down a leftist political movement. It was another one of those favors Somoza had done over the years to help his American friends stamp out any hint of communism in Latin America.

Bermúdez had been in the United States since 1975, first as a student attending courses on subversion and counterinsurgency at the Inter-American Defense College in Washington and later as the Nicaraguan government's liaison to the American military. The Americans thought so highly of him that he was one of six *Guardia* officers they recommended to head the National Guard during the final days of the Somoza regime, in a last-minute public relations ploy by the Carter administration to change the *Guardia*'s murderous image and take some of the wind out of the Sandinistas' sails before their final offensive.

The State Department considered Bermúdez a safe choice; he had spent most of the revolution in Washington and, the reasoning went, couldn't be held responsible for any of the *Guardia*'s human rights violations—the tortures, the disappearances, the aerial bombardments of civilian neighborhoods. Somoza picked someone else, however, and Bermúdez rode out the remainder of the civil war from the safety of Embassy Row in Washington. When the Somoza government collapsed, Bermúdez began a new career as a truck driver, delivering *Newsweek* magazines.

He would not toil long at such a menial task. Soon after the uplifting visit from Somoza's cousin, Bermúdez got a call from Major General Charles E. Boyd, a top U.S. Air Force official, who invited Bermúdez to the Pentagon to kick some ideas around. There, after sounding out Bermúdez on the idea of running a rebel force to harass the Sandinistas, Boyd told him he had a friend at the CIA who was interested in speaking with him. By mid-1980 Bermúdez had packed his family and his belongings and left Washington behind, moving to a rented house in Miami. According to one account, Bermúdez was then on the CIA's payroll.

He began traveling widely, gauging the sentiment of vanquished National Guardsmen hiding in the United States and Central America and reporting his findings to his CIA handlers. Those who wondered how Bermúdez could afford his travels when he was jobless were told he was living off the profits from the sale of his home in Washington.

According to Boyd, the CIA "put Bermúdez in touch" with the Legion of September 15 in Guatemala. Soon Bermúdez would move there and become the legion's commander.

It was a motley crew, if there ever was one. Made up mostly of ex-*Guardia* officers who escaped from Nicaragua at the end of the war, the legionaires had a safe house in Guatemala City and were training on a farm near the Honduran border called Detachment 101. Coincidentally, the farm was located in the same small town, Esquipulas, that had served as the headquarters for the CIA-backed group that overthrew the Guatemalan government in 1954.

Since there was no war for them to fight—yet—the legion kept in shape by hiring itself out to perform a variety of warlike deeds for others. One writer, former *Washington Times* reporter and Contra sympathizer Glenn Garvin, reported that the legion started out with bank robberies, after which they branched out into kidnapping and other crimes, which were performed by a section called "Special Operations."

Garvin wrote that Pompileo Gadea, whom he described "as one of the most enthusiastic Special Operations men," was arrested on drug charges in the United States in the mid-1980s, as was the legion's former civilian leader, Eduardo Roman. During their crime sprees in Guatemala and El Salvador, the legionaires would leave behind political leaflets that suggested that leftist guerrillas were committing the crimes.

In his book *With the Contras*, former *Washington Post* reporter Christopher Dickey described the Legion of September 15: "There were robberies and kidnappings, threats and extortion. There were murders. Market vendors at the bus terminal in Guatemala City's fourth zone were prey to operations described as 'recuperating funds.'... There were jobs for the Guatemalan police and for certain Salvadoran exiles." One "job" laid to the Legion was the March 1980 assassination of the Roman Catholic archbishop of San Salvador, Oscar Romero, who was shot through the heart as he held Mass. Romero had the bad luck to interest himself in the fate of some parishioners who had been "disappeared" by the infamous Salvadoran death squads. The archbishop had been warned several times to butt out, but he hadn't taken the hint.

Records seized from a right-wing Salvadoran politician suspected of orchestrating Romero's murder, Roberto D'Aubuisson, revealed that D'Aubuisson had gone to Guatemala three days after Romero's murder and made two "contributions to Nicaraguans," one for $40,000 and one for $80,000. Written underneath these amounts was the name and telephone number of Colonel Ricardo Lau, a former intelligence and security officer for the *Guardia* who was running the Legion of September 15 prior to Bermúdez's appointment as commander.

Lau, who was never charged in connection with Romero's murder, would go on to become Enrique Bermúdez's right-hand man in the Contra organization. Garvin also wrote that the legion "stole cars in the U.S. and smuggled them to Central America, where they brought premium prices." Coincidentally, that's what Danilo Blandón was doing for the Contras in Los Angeles. His little exile group was moving up in the world, and had switched from cocktail parties to car theft and loan fraud. They had also become an official part of the CIA's new Contra army, the *Fuerza Democrática Nicaragüense*—the FDN.

In 1981 CIA agent Enrique Bermúdez paid Blandón's little group in L.A. a visit. "Bermúdez came to a meeting of the group to give a pep talk and to ask that the group keep the idea of a free and democratic Nicaragua alive by publicizing the Contra cause in the United States," Blandón told CIA inspectors. The colonel asked the group "to adopt the colors and the flag of the FDN," and, after that, the CIA inspectors wrote, "Blandón and other member of the group called themselves FDN and used the FDN's colors, flag and letterhead."

They also got an assignment, Blandón testified. "It came, you know, that we had to provide some cars and we got involved in another thing to get some money." By then Blandón had been working in L.A. long enough to establish a credit history, so he applied for an auto loan.

"My thinking was to get back to Nicaragua, never to stay in the States, so I used my car salesman job to get a [loan] application, to make an application and to get a car without—just giving them the down payment—and sending it to the Contra revolution in Honduras," Blandón said. "We were the first people, the first group that sent a pickup truck to the Contra revolution in Honduras." (In the spring of 1981 the Legion of September 15 moved its operations from Guatemala to a new headquarters in Honduras, where it would remain for the rest of the war.)

Blandón said the payments on the cars they sent to the Contras were to be picked up by "the organization...and they didn't pay the monthly payments, so I lost my credit. But at that time I didn't care because they [the Contras] were my idea, my cause."

3

"The brotherhood of military minds"

Danilo Blandón says he never intended to become a cocaine trafficker when he arrived in L.A. in 1979. He became a drug dealer out of patriotism. When the bugle sounded and the call to serve came, Blandón was hustling used sheet metal at H&L Auto Exchange in Los Angeles—an honest guy making an honest two thousand bucks a month. Next thing you know, he was selling cocaine instead of Chevys.

As Blandón tells the story, his transformation occurred shortly after getting a call from a friend from Miami, an old college classmate named Donald Barrios. Barrios told Blandón that someone wanted to meet with him, a man who would be flying into L.A. very soon. The passenger's name was Norwin Meneses. Blandón was to meet him at the airport and listen to what Meneses had to say.

"He had to talk to me about something," according to Blandón, who didn't know Meneses personally but "knew the family name and was aware that Meneses had a reputation as a Nicaraguan Mafia type." The men were also related; "[Norwin's] last name is Meneses Cantarero and Cantarero was my mother, grandmother also."

Barrios didn't say why he wanted Blandón to meet with the gangster, but Blandón figured it had to do with the Contras, "because he [Barrios] was in the Contra—in the Contra revolution organization."

People who know Barrios describe him as a wealthy former insurance broker and financier from Managua who emigrated to the States long before the revolution and married an American woman. They say Barrios is a relative of former Nicaraguan president Violeta Barrios de Chamorro, widow of the crusading journalist Pedro Joaquin Chamorro, whose 1978 murder sparked the uprising that eventually toppled Somoza. Norwin Meneses, records show, was a partner of Violeta Chamorro in a finance company before the revolution.

After the Sandinista takeover, Donald Barrios reportedly became a financial angel to dispossessed Somocistas, helping them settle in Miami and find jobs. He also became business partners with some of them, including at least two members of the dictator's general staff and the owner of the largest pharmaceutical company in Nicaragua.

At the time he called Blandón in Los Angeles, Barrios was partners with Somoza's old guerrilla hunter, Gustavo "El Tigre" Medina, the counterinsurgency expert who'd ravaged the northern mountains rooting out Communist sympathizers. Medina was head of G-4—the officer in charge of supplies—for the National Guard at the end of the war, and he fled Managua with Somoza on the morning his regime ended. "I was in the plane right behind his," Medina said. Because of his activities during the war, Medina is among the minority of Nicaraguans who have not gone home.

Medina and Barrios started a restaurant and an investment company in Miami, records show. Other partners included former colonel Aurelio Somarriba, head of G-1 for the *Guardia*, Somoza's chief administrative officer; and Enrique "Cuco" Sánchez, a member of a wealthy Nicaraguan family that would play a key role in the founding of the Contras.

Blandón's hunch about Meneses and the Contras turned out to be correct. The meeting, he said, was "to start the movement, the Contra revolution."

After picking his passenger up at the airport, Blandón said, the wiry Meneses "started telling me that we had to do some money and to send [it] to Honduras." Later, at a restaurant, Meneses explained his idea more fully: "He told me to make some drug business in L.A. for raise money to the Contra, and we started that way."

Blandón was shocked by the suggestion at first, he said. "I didn't agree at that time, because I had to think."

Joining up with a man like Norwin Meneses would be agreeing to work for a killer—a career criminal. Meneses's nickname, "El Perico," is a Spanish pun, and a telling one. The word usually means "parakeet," and given Meneses's quick, dark eyes and small beakish face, it's easy to see why such a moniker would stick. But in Argentinian slang the word means "cocaine." And to cops in Central America from the 1970s to the 1990s, cocaine often meant Meneses.

The CIA, in a recently declassified 1986 cable, described Meneses as "the kingpin of narcotics traffickers in Nicaragua prior to the fall of Somoza." The agency would later describe him as the Cali cartel's representative in Nicaragua, but Norwin wasn't finicky. He'd sell cocaine for anyone.

In fact, he'd been selling cocaine since before there were any cartels. In the small world of international cocaine smuggling, Norwin Meneses was a pioneer.

Back when Medellín kingpin Carlos Lehder was still just a car thief sitting in a cell at the Danbury, Connecticut, federal prison, Meneses was making multikilo deals directly with Peruvian cocaine manufacturers. According to Nicaraguan police officials, Meneses's relationship with the drug lords of Colombia began during the marijuana era of the early 1970s, and the story they tell of his first big deal is illustrative of Meneses's modus operandi.

Roger Mayorga is a former Sandinista intelligence officer who also headed up investigations for the Nicaraguan National Police narcotics unit. Mayorga says the drug kingpin's association with the Colombians began after an airplane full of marijuana made an emergency landing at a ranch owned by one of the Somozas. The Managua police were called, and they arrested the Colombian pilots, seized the airplane, and confiscated its load of prime weed.

In Somoza's Nicaragua, the Managua police department was a branch of the National Guard. And the *Guardia* officer who commanded the Managua police for many years was Colonel Edmundo Meneses Cantarero—Norwin's brother. Colonel Meneses came to an understanding with the Colombians who owned the aircraft. Mayorga said the pilots and the airplane were allowed to leave, but the load of marijuana remained behind as "evidence." Somehow the evidence got turned over to brother Norwin, and a drug kingpin was born.

The role played by the Nicaraguan National Guard in creating Meneses's criminal empire can't be overstated. The *Guardia*, which one researcher called "one of the most totally corrupt military establishments in the world," permeated the Meneses family. In addition to Edmundo, another brother, Brigadier General Fermin Meneses, commanded the *Guardia* garrison in the city of Masaya, a commercial and cultural center not far from Managua. The family's long ties with the *Guardia* and its history of staunch anticommunism help explain Norwin's later activities on behalf of the Contras.

"The whole [Meneses] family was anti-Sandinista to the death," the Nicaraguan newsmagazine *El Semanario* reported in 1996. "It is a hate that seems almost genetic, ancestral."

The *Guardia* wasn't just an army; it had its hands in everything. If the CIA, the FBI, the DEA, the IRS, the army, the air force, the Marine Corps, the National Guard, the Coast Guard, Customs, Immigration, and the Postal Service were all rolled into one, it would begin to approach Somoza's National Guard in its power over the everyday lives of the average citizen. "Nicaragua is one of the few countries we are aware of in which all arms shipments that go into the country, whether they are sporting goods or of whatever kind, have to be received by the National Guard," State Department official Sally Shelton told Congress in 1978. "We have been shipping hunting equipment, for example. They are in effect purchased by the National Guard and then resold in retail outlets."

"Say that again?" one stunned congressman asked. "The National Guard is a wholesaler for hunting ammunition?"

"They are passed through the National Guard and sold in retail outlets," Shelton repeated. "It is more an accounting procedure than anything else."

According to the hearing transcript, "general laughter" ensued.

But the pervasive corruption of the *Guardia* was no laughing matter to Nicaraguans. "Gambling, alcoholism, drugs, prostitution and other vices are protected and exploited by the very persons who have the obligation to combat them," Nicaragua's Roman Catholic bishops complained in a 1978 pastoral letter to Somoza. "Widespread corruption continues unchecked and public scandals further undermine the confidence and morale of the people."

To many the *Guardia* was little different than the Mafia. And if Somoza was its godfather, the Meneses brothers were his capos. Somoza was closest to Edmundo, known as Mundo, who was one of his favorite generals. In the 1960s Mundo—who'd been trained in irregular warfare and anticommunism at the U.S. Army's School of the Americas in Panama—conducted a series of bloody operations against Sandinista rebels near the town of Pancasan in northern Nicaragua. Those campaigns killed several key Sandinistas and crippled the guerrilla movement for years. Later Somoza gave Mundo the *Guardia*'s choicest plum, control of the Managua police, a perch from which a man so inclined could dip his beak into every imaginable scam. For the unscrupulous, the profit potential was unlimited.

"You have to realize that you did a lot of things in your career in the *Guardia* and you progressed up through the ranks so you might have been a lot of things," explained former Somoza secretary Juan C. Wong. "Now, Police Chief, that's one of the best. That's a nice job. That was the last job he [Edmundo] had in his military career. Then he retired and went into the diplomatic corps."

Under Mundo's watchful eye, Managua became an open city for brother Norwin, who by the late 1970s owned discotheques—the Frisco Disco and the VIP Club, among others—drive-in whorehouses with waterbeds and porno tapes, and a thriving drug business.

The Frisco Disco was burned down in a fire so suspicious that it is still talked about in Managua. But after Norwin turned up with one of Somoza's top lawyers by his side, the insurance company quickly wrote the check.

"Norwin ran all the rackets for the *Guardia*," said Mayorga. "And remember, his brother was the chief of police. No one could do anything."

San Francisco cocaine trafficker Rafael Corñejo, who has worked for the Meneses family since the 1970s, told of prerevolution jaunts down to Managua where he would spend weekends partying with the Meneses brothers. "You'd walk down the street with Mundo, and everyone would salute you," Corñejo recalled with a smile. "We went riding around in the Jeeps, you know, guys with big guns everywhere around us. It was a trip."

Though never a member of the *Guardia*, Norwin did his part for the Somoza regime. In his teens and twenties, acquaintances said, he worked as an undercover informant for the Office of National Security (ONS), Somoza's plainclothes secret police, which rooted out subversives and political dissidents. Before going to Guatemala to start up the Legion of September 15, Colonel Ricardo Lau spent much of his career with the ONS and was allegedly one of its chief torturers.

Former Managua police chief Rene Vivas, an early member of the Sandinista movement, said Norwin Meneses infiltrated pro-Communist groups for the ONS, sometimes posing as a news photographer, other times as the secretly disaffected son of a powerful Somocista family. In a magazine interview in 1996, Meneses told of starting up an armed guerrilla group to support Fidel Castro's takeover of Cuba but insisted that he was never a Communist.

With Mundo and the National Guard as his protectors, Norwin appears to have literally gotten away with murder. In the spring of 1977

Norwin found himself under investigation by the chief inspector of the Nicaraguan Customs Department, a particularly tenacious sleuth named Oskar Reyes Zelaya. Inspector Reyes and the FBI believed Norwin was running a massive car theft ring, which was using the National Guard to "import" stolen American cars into Nicaragua and then selling them to various potentates of the Somoza government. Importing cars through the *Guardia* allowed the buyer to evade the hefty tariffs the Nicaraguan government had placed on imports.

According to press reports, Norwin first tried to get the annoying inspector off his tail by setting him up with an attractive woman in a Managua hotel room. The woman, Pamela Cestoni, then went to the police, claiming that Inspector Reyes had raped her. When the investigation revealed that Cestoni was a friend of Norwin's, Reyes was cleared, and "the sexual maneuver was used only to exacerbate the prosecution against Norwin," *La Prensa* reported.

On the evening of June 2, 1977, the chief inspector got a phone call at his home, allegedly from a man who wanted to give him a payoff in order to drop the Meneses investigation. Dressed in a bathrobe and flip-flops, Reyes hopped into his Jeep Cherokee and drove to an alley behind a nearby supermarket, where the man was waiting to meet him. Whoever it was in that alley shot Reyes three times in the stomach and throat. But he didn't complete the job. Bleeding profusely, the inspector was taken to the emergency room of the Orient Hospital in Managua. As he lay writhing on a cot, the dying Reyes spotted his friend Pablo Zamora Moller, the chief investigator for the Managua police department, standing nearby.

"Pablo, protect me!" Reyes cried. "This is Norwin! Norwin Meneses sent away to kill me!" Reyes died a short time later.

Norwin was arrested and jailed on suspicion of murder. But after a "rigorous and exhaustive" investigation ordered by brother Edmundo, Norwin was cleared of any involvement and released. Meneses claimed he was at a motel when the killing happened, and both Rafael Corñejo, one of his San Francisco-based cocaine traffickers, and his nephew Jaime Meneses, who also was dealing cocaine in the Bay Area, backed up the story, testifying that Norwin was with them.

(A month later Corñejo would be arrested in Panama for attempting to smuggle some of Meneses's cocaine back to the United States in a false-bottomed suitcase and hollowed-out shoe heels. Corñejo said he was beaten and tortured by Manuel Noriega's security police for the name of his source but never talked. Meneses reportedly paid Corñejo $1 million after his release from a Panamanian prison, in gratitude for his silence.)

The Nicaraguan papers later reported that a triggerman imported from Puerto Rico had done the actual hit on Reyes and that his identity was known to the Managua police, since the man's picture had appeared in the social pages of *La Prensa*. But the police reportedly refused to assist the FBI when the American agents came down to investigate what had happened to their Nicaraguan colleague. No one was ever prosecuted for Reyes's murder.

Years later, the pro-Sandinista newspaper *Barricada* claimed that Meneses was running the stolen car ring on behalf of Somoza's minister of finance, Gustavo Montiel, and Somoza's mistress, Dinorah Sampson, who happened to own an auto dealership.

One longtime Contra supporter said Norwin's arrest and the subsequent scandal that enveloped Edmundo so upset Somoza that it may have triggered his heart attack in July 1977, after which he went off to the United States to recuperate. Edmundo soon left the police department, was promoted to brigadier general, and retired from the National Guard. Somoza then sent him off to Guatemala to be Nicaragua's ambassador.

It would be Edmundo's last assignment for Tachito.

On September 16, 1978, Ambassador Meneses was machine-gunned in Espana Park in Guatemala City, catching three bullets in his back. Two days later, as he clung to life in the Guatemala City Medical Center, a revolutionary group, the People's Guerrilla Army (EGP), claimed credit for the attempted assassination.

The EGP's communique described Meneses as being far more than a diplomat. According to the guerrillas, he was overseeing anti-Communist counterinsurgency operations all over Central America. "Meneses Cantarero enjoyed special privileges amongst Guatemala's authorities and army commanders," the guerrillas declared. "Exploiting his ambassadorial position in Guatemala as a smokescreen, he actually discharged the duties of coordinator between the Guatemalan army and the Nicaraguan National Guard, and also between Somoza and Guatemala's reactionary government. He coordinated political repression for all of Central America and the operations undertaken by the governments of this area against popular revolutionary movements." The EGP claimed that the ambassador was gunned down to "show solidarity with the struggle of the Sandinist National Liberation Front."

"The Sandinistas never forgave my brother Edmundo for the guerrillas of Pancasan," Santiago Meneses told *El Semanario* in 1996.

Edmundo Meneses lingered for another fifteen days before succumbing to his wounds. At his funeral, Somoza hailed him as a martyr in the worldwide struggle against communism.

The nature of Edmundo Meneses's relationship with the U.S. government is not clear. The CIA has refused to disclose any information about him, on grounds of national security. The State Department, incredibly, has claimed it can find no records that even mention his name, a stunning admission given Meneses's stature in the Somoza government—its chief law enforcement officer and ambassador to Guatemala.

In light of Edmundo's murder, Norwin figured the Sandinistas probably had the same fate in mind for him, and he left Nicaragua in early June 1979. He caught a flight to El Salvador, went to Ecuador for a while, then to Costa Rica—where he had businesses and at least six ranches—before finally emigrating to the United States in early 1980 and applying for political asylum. Meneses had homes in Florida and Alabama, he said, but spent most of his time in San Francisco, where he had begun buying property in 1978.

San Francisco has had a relatively large Nicaraguan population since the days of the gold rush. Before the Panama Canal existed, Nicaragua was the preferred overland route to the Pacific Ocean, and when would-be gold miners from the East Coast came through in the mid-1800s, many Nicaraguans tagged along on the trip north. Starting in the 1940s and 1950s, wealthy Nicaraguans sent their children to San Francisco if they wanted them to have an American education, because of the city's many Catholic colleges and universities. Some never went home.

After the Sandinistas marched into Managua, the Bay Area—like Miami, Houston, and Los Angeles—saw a large influx of Nicaraguans who had supported Somoza. Not surprisingly, Contra support groups quickly popped up in those cities. Once in San Francisco, Meneses posed as a successful businessman, purchasing a used car lot, a couple of commercial buildings, a travel agency, and a restaurant. He zipped around town in a gray Jaguar sedan. His nephews bought bars and nightclubs. Norwin purchased two houses in Pacifica, a small town just down the coast from San Francisco, one for himself and the other for his brother Ernesto.

He spent much time in San Francisco's Mission District, working out of a travel agency office owned by nephew Jaime Meneses. The Mission is a heavily Hispanic section of town, with a history of hospitality to Central American revolutionaries of all stripes. According to Roberto Vargas, a San Franciscan who later became the Sandinistas' ambassador to China, the Mission was home to several of the Sandinistas' future commandantes, who practiced their sharpshooting skills at rod and gun clubs down the coast.

Meneses's ability to freely travel in and out of the United States, buying properties, starting businesses, and applying for political asylum—all under his own name—speaks volumes about his lack of concern about attracting the attention of American law enforcement officials. "I even drove my own cars, registered in my name!" he boasted.

His carefree attitude certainly wasn't due to his being unknown to U.S. authorities. Of all the Meneses brothers, Norwin had the most extensive government files. Records show that Norwin was as well known to American drug agents as he was to those in Central America. In fact, it's difficult to imagine how someone with his record was allowed to enter the United States at all.

Court records show that the DEA first picked up word that Norwin was a drug dealer in 1974. By December 1976 its office in Costa Rica had identified him as a cocaine "source of supply" based in Managua, and noted that his brother was Managua's police chief.

The FBI became aware in April 1978 that Norwin and his brother Ernesto "were smuggling 20 kilos of cocaine at a time into the United States" and identified Norwin's nephew, Jaime Meneses, as their San Francisco distributor. A month later, a confidential DEA informant reported that the shipments were coming in every two months. The DEA learned that Meneses was dealing cocaine in Miami as well, bringing it into the country aboard commercial airliners.

In August 1978 one of Meneses's mules was arrested at Tocumen Airport in Panama City with a kilo of cocaine. The mule fingered Meneses as having "financed the smuggling venture," and the DEA was informed. The following year, the New Orleans DEA determined that Meneses was responsible for smuggling cocaine into that city also. The DEA's "Operation Alligator," as the sweep was called, resulted in the indictment of "numerous persons for smuggling cocaine. It was determined that Norwin Meneses was a source of supply for this group."

In June 1980 someone called the San Francisco DEA office to report that a man arrested in Tampa, Florida, a few months earlier had been hauling cocaine for Meneses. The same caller said another Meneses nephew—Edmundo's son Jairo—"had gone to Costa Rica to obtain approximately seven pounds of cocaine."

By the fall of 1981, the time Blandón says Meneses recruited him to sell dope for the Contras, the DEA had Meneses under active investigation for cocaine trafficking and possible gun running. "The Drug Enforcement Administration has developed information over the past several years that the Meneses Family has been involved in the smuggling and distribution of cocaine in the San Francisco Bay Area," stated a November 1981 affidavit by DEA agent Sandra Smith.

Smith, who was one of the DEA's first female agents in San Francisco, recalled that her investigation of the Meneses family was "the only thing that I ever worked, in all the time I worked there, that I thought was really big.... In this business, if you have people coming in from Nicaragua bringing in cocaine and the rumor was they were taking guns back...that's sort of an interesting combination."

Starting in the late 1970s, Smith said, she began gathering string on the Meneses family, "putting together the comings and goings." She said Meneses was living in "a gorgeous house" in Burlingame, a ritzy suburb of San Francisco. Periodically, she and a Customs agent would stake out the house, sitting in the parking lot of a nearby elementary school and jotting down license numbers of cars seen pulling up Meneses's thickly treed drive. "We really didn't have anybody on the inside," she said. "That was part of the problem."

The local San Francisco police were also running across various and sundry Meneseses, often in the company of large quantities of cocaine. Omar Meneses, another nephew, was arrested for cocaine sales at a bar in the Mission owned by nephew Jaime in June 1980. A month later nephew Roger Meneses was arrested with twenty pounds of cocaine and more than $8,800. That same month, Omar got busted again with a quarter pound of cocaine.

By mid-1981 Smith had put together enough information from her investigation and from the DEA's files to sketch out a fairly detailed portrait of a family steeped in drug trafficking. The Nicaraguan, it appeared, had cocaine coming in from everywhere. "Meneses had an endless supply of dope, from what I could see."

In June 1981, Smith got a break in her on-again, off-again investigation.

Detective Joseph Lee of the Baldwin Park police in southern California got a tip that a cocaine dealer in West Covina, a Nicaraguan named Julio Bermúdez (no relation to Enrique Bermúdez), was making two trips a month to San Francisco, "where he contacts a large cocaine smuggling organization headed by Norwin Meneses." The informant told Lee that Bermúdez was bringing down between fourteen and twenty pounds of cocaine on each trip. Another informant reported that Bermúdez called San Francisco and "places his order by telephone" before each trip.

The police subpoenaed Bermúdez's telephone records for the previous three months, and sure enough, they found fifty-one long-distance calls from Bermúdez's phone to a number in Daly City, a working-class suburb south of San Francisco. The number belonged to Norwin's nephew, Jairo Meneses.

It was enough for the Baldwin Park cops, along with members of the L.A. County Sheriff's Department and the U.S. Customs Service, to put a tail on Bermúdez and stake out his house at 1128 Greendale Street.

On November 12, 1981, Bermúdez left the house with a small beige suitcase and drove off in a 1972 Buick. The cops followed, observing him stop to pick up another man, Jose Herrera, before heading to the L.A. airport. The duo bought two one-way tickets to San Francisco on PSA Flight 425 and got there at 3:40 P.M., when DEA agent Smith picked up the surveillance.

Smith watched as the two traffickers were met outside the terminal by an unidentified Latino man driving a gold 1979 Toyota, a car registered to Herrera, one of the traffickers. They drove to a small house in Daly City, and the three men went inside. After a bit Bermúdez came out, opened the trunk, and got out the beige suitcase, which he placed behind the driver's seat; then he drove off.

Bermúdez managed to shake his tail in the traffic. Thirty-five minutes later, though, the cops spotted the car in another part of Daly City, parked outside Jairo Meneses's house. Bermúdez came out about two hours later and drove back to the first Daly City house.

While not exactly incriminating, the sequence of events gave the police enough evidence to get a search warrant. When Bermúdez showed up at his house in West Covina two days later, the cops were waiting for him. Bursting in, they caught him with three pounds of cocaine and $17,000. They also seized a ledger book that bore an entry reading "11-11-81 $90,000 to Jairo." Bermúdez was arrested and jailed, and Smith applied for a search warrant for Jairo Meneses's house.

On November 16 the police hit Jairo's place and caught him with drugs and drug paraphernalia. They found a plastic bag containing Thai stick, a potent form of grass, an envelope containing $9,000, an O'Haus triple-beam scale—the kind favored by drug dealers—a 12-gauge shotgun, a .22-caliber pistol, and "miscellaneous pictures, address books, photographs and passports."

Convinced that the family was a major trafficking organization, Smith said she asked her supervisor if she could work the case full-time. The answer was not encouraging. "He said, 'Well, that sounds like a good idea. Who would run it?'" Smith recalled, laughing. "I think it was just that, being a female, my credibility was somewhat in question."

The investigation soon fell apart. Julio Bermúdez was released on bail and promptly skipped the country, never to be seen again. Without Bermúdez, the DEA decided against prosecuting Jairo Meneses, Norwin's nephew.

Smith said she never worked the Meneses family again. "They had me assigned to other things, like the Hell's Angels case, and I really didn't have enough time," she said. "This was a pretty big case to me, and I think had I been given free rein and some assistance and some time to do it, I think I could have really done something." But, she said, "I'm not so sure the DEA management took it seriously enough to allow me the time and the assistance I would have needed." She quit the DEA three years later.

Norwin Meneses said he was well aware that the DEA was after him in 1981, and came close to catching him during its investigation of Julio Bermúdez. He was in love with Bermúdez's sister, Patricia, at the time, and was often at the house in West Covina. The DEA, in fact, described Norwin as the owner of the three pounds of cocaine found with Bermúdez.

But the arrests of one of his distributors and his nephews didn't slow him down a bit. According to Blandón, the Meneses organization moved 900 kilos of cocaine—almost a ton—into the United States in 1981, about $54 million worth at wholesale prices.

Blandón accepted Meneses's pitch to become a cocaine salesman for the Contras, he said, after he and the drug kingpin took a trip down to Honduras for another "pep talk" from CIA agent Enrique Bermúdez. At a Contra camp near the Nicaraguan border, Bermúdez "told them of the trouble the FDN was having in raising funds and obtaining equipment," and he exhorted them to raise money for the counterrevolution. "He was in charge, okay, how to raise money in California."

Meneses confirmed Blandón's account of the meeting with the CIA agent, who was an old friend of the Meneses family. "I've known him since he was a lieutenant," Meneses said, adding that his brother Edmundo had been friends with Enrique Bermúdez even longer: "They'd known each other since childhood." Meneses, who was on an FDN fund-raising committee, said Bermúdez put Blandón in charge of raising money in southern California. Meneses raised funds in the Bay Area and also screened and recruited potential Contra soldiers from the Nicaraguans who'd emigrated to the United States.

Meneses became Bermúdez's intelligence and security adviser in

California, he claimed; anyone recruited to fight for the Contras in Honduras had to pass his muster first, so the organization would be safe from Sandinista infiltrators. "It was an understanding between old friends," Meneses said of the job Bermúdez gave him. "Nobody would join the Contra forces down there without my knowledge and approval."

Blandón confirmed that, telling the CIA that Meneses's role in the FDN operation in California was "primarily that of a personnel recruiter for the group."

Adolfo Calero, the CIA agent who was the head of the Contras' political directorate, denied that the two cocaine traffickers had any official positions with the FDN. But Calero confirmed that Meneses had come to Honduras to meet with Bermúdez and had brought him a crossbow as a gesture of his esteem.

Another top Contra, former FDN director Edgar Chamorro, acknowledged that Meneses was involved with both the FDN and Bermúdez. "It was very early, when the Contras did not have as many supporters as later," Chamorro said. "Very early the Contras were trying all kinds of things to raise funds. This man [Meneses] was connected with the Contras of Bermúdez, because of the military kind of brotherhood among the Somoza military—the brotherhood of military minds."

Blandón insisted that Bermúdez never mentioned drug sales during his fund-raising pitch, but from Blandón's description of Bermúdez's instructions, that didn't appear necessary. The Contra commander apparently had a pretty good idea of what they were getting into. "There's a saying that the ends justify the means and that's what Mr. Bermúdez told us in Honduras, okay?" Blandón said. "So we started raising money to the Contra revolution." Blandón doubted that Bermúdez knew specifically they would sell cocaine to raise the cash, but Contra commander Edén Pastora has said it would be naive to think that Bermúdez didn't know he was asking drug dealers for financial assistance. It was well known in prerevolutionary Nicaragua "that [Meneses] was involved in illicit or dirty business," Pastora said. "He had hotels and it was also said that he was involved in the sale of cocaine. In those days, cocaine sales was not very common."

Senator John Kerry of Massachusetts has accused Bermúdez of being a drug trafficker himself. "He was the target of a government-sponsored sting operation," Kerry told the Senate Foreign Relations Committee in a closed-door hearing in June 1986. "He has been involved in drug running and that sting operation saw him get tipped off. And the law enforcement officials know that the sting operation was pulled back in the interests of protecting the Contras."

No further details about that case have ever been made public, and Kerry's statements could not be corroborated.

At their meeting with Bermúdez, Blandón said, Bermúdez asked if he and Meneses "could assist in the procurement of weapons." In court testimony, Blandón called it "a mission" that took them to Costa Rica to "contact some people to get some connections from where to construct the Contra revolution.... We have to get in contact with someone that was going to—we were going to give some money to buy some weapons."

The trip had an inauspicious start, Blandón later told the CIA, describing his departure from Honduras with Meneses, from where they had planned to travel first to Guatemala, then to Bolivia on business, before returning to the United States.

"Both he and Meneses were escorted to Tegucigalpa airport by armed Contras," a summary of his CIA interview states. "Unbeknownst to Bermúdez and the Contras, Blandón says, he was carrying $100,000 in drug proceeds to be used in [a] Bolivian drug deal. In the process of departing the airport, Blandón was stopped and detained by Honduran officials. Blandón states that his Contra escorts, seeing that Blandón had been detained with money, assumed that Blandón had been given the funds by Bermúdez to purchase arms for the Contras. As a result, the Contras interceded on Blandón's behalf, effected the return of the money, and secured Blandón's release."

In doing so, Blandón said, "the Contra escorts told the Honduran airport authorities that Blandón and Meneses were Contras. Blandón states he was allowed to leave the next morning and that he then joined Meneses, who had not been detained and who had been allowed to travel to Guatemala."

They were unable to contact the arms dealers they were looking for, Blandón said, and he returned to California with Meneses to begin his career in the cocaine business.

Meneses didn't simply hand him the dope. He brought Blandón to San Francisco for a two-day seminar on the intricacies of drug dealing. "Mr. Meneses explained to me how I, you know, how to see...the quality, how they sell it by the ounce, by kilo," Blandón said. Meneses also showed him how to transport the drug undetected in pickup trucks by putting the cocaine in "the compartment of the door, the driver's side door." Meneses brought in a one-eyed Nicaraguan exile, Raul "El Tuerto" Vega, as a transportation consultant. Vega, who lived in L.A., was an old hand at driving dope cars for Meneses, and "Norwin wanted that I went with Raul Vega to show me how to drive, how to do it because he used to work more often."

Meneses was a fount of advice on how to avoid problems, Blandón explained. He told Blandón not to give out cocaine on credit; "Don't this, don't do a lot of things. But I didn't know to whom to sell it. But he told me go and visit a few people and I start." Meneses gave him two kilos of cocaine—worth about $60,000 each at the time—and the names of some customers in Los Angeles, and told him to hit the streets. The cocaine was provided at no cost, but with the understanding that Blandón would pay Meneses back out of the profits.

When Blandón began doing this is a matter of some conjecture. Blandón insists that he didn't actually sell his first ounce of cocaine until early in 1982. But others who knew him at the time say he was dealing drugs in L.A. much earlier. Still others insist Blandón, like Meneses, was already a trafficker back in Somoza's Nicaragua, before the Sandinista revolution.

The Torres brothers would later tell the FBI that Blandón picked up his two kilos from Meneses in 1980. "Shortly after Blandón moved to the Los Angeles area Blandón was introduced to Norwin Menesis [sic] in the San Francisco, California, area by Donald Barrios," Jacinto Torres told the FBI. "In approximately 1980, Danilo Blandón, Frank Vigal [sic] and Douglas Diaz travelled to the San Francisco area where they obtained two kilograms of cocaine from Menesis. Blandón, Vigal and Diaz returned to the Los Angeles area where they had thirty days to sell the cocaine."

Frank Vigil is a Contra supporter who had worked as a public relations director for Norwin Meneses in one of Norwin's nightclubs in Managua. Though he admits being in Los Angeles in 1980, he denies traveling with Blandón to meet with Meneses or selling cocaine himself, although he says he knew Blandón was doing it. Blandón has identified Diaz as a man who would drive Meneses's cocaine to L.A. occasionally, but he said Diaz was not with him during his training period at Norwin's house.

Blandón's wife's uncle, economist Orlando Murillo, also agrees that Blandón was selling drugs for Meneses before 1982. "I was in Costa Rica and Chepita called me and said, 'I have serious problems with Danilo,'" Murillo recalled. Chepita told him they'd started a small business, but that Danilo was dealing drugs and had gotten in debt to Meneses, who was now pressing her for the money. "I sent her another $5,000," Murillo said. He acknowledged that his money was probably used to pay off

Meneses, but said Chepita "is my niece and my only relative. And Danilo is a very dangerous man. So I help her when I can."

Murillo placed the call from his frantic niece in "1981, February or January."

Others say Blandón was a drug dealer even before he came to the United States, and had known Meneses for years, long before meeting up with him at LAX that day. Longtime Meneses employee Rafael Corñejo claimed that Blandón and Meneses "knew each other back in Nicaragua before the war. Danilo was sort of in the background of the group that hung around with Mundo. I'd see him at parties sometimes."

In an interview with journalist Georg Hodel, former Sandinista leader Moises Hassan—who is related to Blandón's mother-in-law, Vilma Peña Alvarez—said Blandón "was involved with drugs and contraband prior to the Sandinista takeover." Hassan had known Blandón since college, where Blandón was a student activist on behalf of Somoza's Liberal party.

The DEA, in a sworn statement filed in San Diego federal court, corroborated Hassan's statements. In a sealed search warrant affidavit filed in May 1992, DEA agent Chuck Jones wrote, "Blandón fled Nicaragua after the Samoza [sic] regime was deposed. Blandón had been a cocaine trafficker in Nicaragua prior to the fall of Samoza [sic] but had enjoyed protection through family political influence. Since about 1982, Blandón has been a cocaine trafficker in the United States."

At the time Jones made that statement, he was Blandón's case agent. Four years later, though, when defense attorneys accused federal prosecutors of hiding Jones's revealing affidavit from them, Agent Jones would suddenly remember that it wasn't Blandón he'd been referring to when he prepared the affidavit to search his storage locker. No, he claimed, he'd confused Blandón's background with Meneses's.

Regardless of when Blandón's career as a cocaine trafficker began, by the time he says he started selling drugs for the Contras, they were no longer just a ragtag group running around the jungles on their own. They were, by early 1982, the property of the Central Intelligence Agency.

4

"I never sent cash"

Between July 1979 and March 1981, Somoza's exiled supporters had made little headway in putting together any kind of organized opposition.

It wasn't for lack of trying. It was for lack of money.

The Legion of September 15—the hundred or so ex-*Guardia* men hiding out in Guatemala—survived through thievery and contract killings. Another group of exiles coalesced in Miami, calling themselves the National Democratic Union (UDN), which had a small armed branch in Honduras called the Revolutionary Armed Forces of Nicaragua (FARN). Both the legion and this second group—UDN-FARN—tapped into Miami's Cuban community, drawing financial support and volunteers from the rabidly anti-Communist Cubans, including men who had worked with the CIA on the Bay of Pigs operation in the 1960s.

The union of the Nicaraguan and Cuban exile communities in Miami was an obvious marriage. The Nicaraguans hated Daniel Ortega and the Sandinistas almost as much as the Cubans hated Fidel Castro. Castro had been giving the Sandinistas aid and comfort since the mid-1970s. After the war, Cuba provided key advisers to the Sandinistas on how best to beef up their own army and, most of all, their intelligence services.

As the Cubans had learned from twenty years of covert war with the United States and the CIA, the best defense against subversion was information. Who were your enemies? Who were the infiltrators? What were they planning?

The combination of the Cubans' advice and the Sandinistas' own experiences at the hands of Somoza's secret police led them to build an efficient and deadly secret police unit inside the Ministry of the Interior.

The Sandinistas made it difficult for any organized opposition to take root inside Nicaragua. As a result, the Contras were forced to rely on help from outsiders—exiles, many impoverished by their flight, and foreign governments. The first donation of military supplies appears to have come from the Miami group UDN-FARN in the fall of 1980. Its members scraped together enough money to buy a couple boxes of rifles from Miami sporting goods stores and a little radio equipment, which was boxed up and mailed to Honduras.

The crates were sent to the head of the Honduran national police, Gustavo Álvarez, an ardent anti-Communist who took up the Nicaraguans' cause. Álvarez saw that the guns from Miami got to the soldiers, who were still learning how to march and drill.

Meanwhile, Bermúdez and other ex-*Guardia* officers with the Legion of September 15 made the rounds of South America's military governments, seeking donations to the cause. They found much sympathy but little cash.

One of the places they visited was Argentina. At that time, Argentina's military dictatorship was one of the most brutal in the world, and its generals were regarded as pariahs even by other military regimes in Latin America. The generals there had a deal for them.

A radio station in Costa Rica was broadcasting unpleasant news about the Argentinian military government, accusing it—correctly, as it turned out—of murdering political opponents and nonpolitical citizens alike by the thousands, sometimes by dropping them out of helicopters or burying them alive. The radio station was getting on the generals' nerves. If the Nicaraguans were serious about fighting their way back into power, the Argentines said, a little demonstration of their sincerity might not hurt. Why didn't they try to put Radio Noticias del Continente out of the broadcasting business?

The legion agreed to take care of the radio station and infiltrated a sapper team into Costa Rica, hitting the station about two in the morning on December 13, 1980. But the raiders didn't find the target quite as easy as they expected. Earlier Argentine military attempts to close it down—air-dropping drums of homemade napalm onto the station's roof, for instance—had caused the broadcasters to beef up their security.

When the legion unit arrived, they found themselves attacking a pillbox. The raiding team was met by a hail of machine-gun fire and beat a hasty retreat, barely managing to toss a Molotov cocktail at a storage shed. Some were killed. On the way out the survivors were arrested by the Costa Rican police. All in all, it was a disaster.

But the Contras got a lucky break from the American political system that November. Jimmy Carter—whom the Contras despised for abandoning Somoza—was beaten in the November elections. A new team was coming to town, a different administration led by Ronald Reagan and George Bush, and it had a different outlook on what was happening in Central America.

When Reagan and Bush looked at Nicaragua, they didn't see a populist uprising against a hated and corrupt dictatorship, as did most of the world. They saw another Cuba taking root in their backyard, another clique of Communists who would spread their noxious seeds of dissent and discord throughout the region. And when they looked at the Contras, they didn't see the remnants of Somoza's brutal *Guardia*, or mercenaries doing hired killings and robberies. They saw plucky bands of freedom fighters.

Things couldn't have been clearer.

Within days of taking office, Reagan froze all aid to the Sandinista government. In March 1981 he authorized the CIA to begin exploring ways of undermining the Sandinistas and halting their shipments of arms to rebel groups in El Salvador, with whom the Sandinistas were ideologically aligned. CIA agents fanned out across the United States and Central America to begin taking stock of the scattered pockets of anti-Sandinista groups. They also began doling out money indirectly, to help keep the shoestring organizations afloat financially.

The Argentine military, which had been given the cold shoulder by the Carter administration, also noticed Washington's fresh new outlook. And they figured, quite correctly, that one sure way to get back into America's good graces was to help the Contras out. The next time the Contras came calling, in the spring of 1981, the Argentines were glad to see them, despite their bungled job on the radio station.

"We were practically official guests," former UDN-FARN commander William Baltodano Herrera told an interviewer in 1984. "The government took charge of everything. We were driven everywhere, invited out everywhere and we didn't have to pay for anything."

When it was time to go, the Argentines slipped Bermúdez's legion $30,000 and gave UDN-FARN $50,000, but Baltodano said the money "was just to cover absolute necessities. One can hardly build a movement with $50,000. We could pay for our trip with that money."

By mid-1981 Argentine military advisers were secretly slipping into Honduras and Miami to teach the exiles how to run a guerrilla war. Dozens of Nicaraguans were also taken to Argentina for training at special schools there. Because of the secrecy attached, the Nicaraguans weren't let outside the safe house where their training was taking place. "It was in Buenos Aires, in a residential district about half an hour from Ezeiza airport," former Legion of September 15 member Pedro Javier Nuñez Cabezas recalled in a 1985 interview. "The training was purely theoretical, there was no practical instruction. We were taught theories of espionage, counterespionage, interrogation techniques, beating techniques, how to lead troops and psychological warfare.... I didn't see anything of Buenos Aires." After the training, Nuñez said, the legion "divided us up into working groups and handed out various assignments. A couple of the groups travelled to Miami."

The U.S. ambassador to Honduras at the time, Jack Binns, told an interviewer that he tracked fifteen Argentine intelligence operatives in and out of Honduras in July 1981. The men had applied for visas to visit the United States and were identified as employees of Nicaraguan businessmen in Honduras. The embassy granted the visas, only to discover later that the men had used false Argentine passports to get them. No one in Washington seemed particularly interested in that fact, Binns said.

Outside Miami, Cuban Bay of Pigs veterans put up training camps for the Contras' new recruits and invited the press in to witness the Nicaraguans being drilled by former Green Berets. Other training camps were reported to have been set up in California and Texas, but little information about their locations and operations has emerged.

For the most part, however, the Contras were still disorganized, barely qualifying as an army. When the CIA got involved in early 1981, its first project became uniting the various groups under one umbrella. As things stood, the bands were too small to be taken seriously as a military threat, and dealing with them separately was too difficult for the CIA.

Enrique Bermúdez was persuaded to move his Legion of September 15 from Guatemala to Tegucigalpa, Honduras, where the CIA was sending in dozens of new agents and operatives. The agency pressured the Miami-based UDN-FARN group to link up with Bermúdez's men and form a new resistance group, to add yet another degree of separation from past image problems that might detract from the freedom fighter persona the Reagan administration was creating. "The gringos made no secret of the fact that if we wanted support from them, we'd first have to join forces," said former legion member Pedro Nuñez.

The problem was that the two Contra groups hated each other.

UDN-FARN's commander, Fernando "El Negro" Chamorro, was a rabble-rouser who had fought for the Sandinistas against Somoza and attained immortality by helping to shoot a couple rockets at Somoza's bunker from the roof of the nearby Intercontinental Hotel in 1974. He was also known to have a drinking problem and a questionable work ethic, and he hadn't managed well within the new Sandinista government. Eventually, he broke completely with the ruling Sandinistas and drifted down to Costa Rica to join his older brother, Edmundo Chamorro, another former Sandinista. Together the Chamorro brothers became the military leaders of UDN-FARN.

The Chamorros' Contra group, with its connections to the Miami Cubans, was actually further along in developing an organized, regional opposition force than Bermúdez's scruffy legionnaires. Though based in Costa Rica, UDN-FARN had established a small military camp in Honduras at the Cuban-owned Hacienda El Pescado, just outside the capital city of Tegucigalpa. "At that time, the UDN-FARN had the best connections with the Honduran capital and with the Honduran military and government," said former UDN-FARN commander Baltodano.

Baltodano's group wanted nothing to do with Bermúdez's brutish outfit, resisting the CIA's desire that it join forces with the legion. The Chamorros regarded many of the ex-*Guardia* men of the legion to be war criminals who could never win popular support back home. "The Legion was entirely composed of ex-National Guards. Naturally one couldn't make a big splash with that in Nicaragua," Baltodano said. There were also indications that Bermúdez was personally corrupt. In 1981 a group of legion officers voted to expel him from the organization for misuse of funds and lying. The mutiny was put down by Bermúdez's Argentine backers.

The CIA eventually got its way. After top CIA officials met with their allies in the Honduran military, the Hondurans withdrew their support of the Chamorros' group and backed Bermúdez's legion instead. If UDN-FARN wanted to stay in the Contra business, it would have to merge with Bermúdez's ex-*Guardia* men.

And if it didn't want to merge—well, it would merge anyway.

An odd kind of "unity" meeting was held in August 1981 in the upstairs rec room of the legion's rented safe house in Guatemala City.

With an Argentine military officer looking on, Bermúdez signed a one-paragraph document stating that the Legion of September 15 and UDN-FARN "agree to join efforts and constitute a single organization that will be called the Nicaraguan Democratic Forces (FDN) in order to fight against the Sandinistas."

The Chamorro brothers boycotted the meeting rather than sit in the same room with Bermúdez, which was fine with Bermúdez, who regarded the Chamorros as closet Communists.

The legion moved to Honduras, and the FDN was officially born. Quickly the UDN-FARN Contras were pushed into the background and assigned to subordinate roles. The top jobs were filled by Bermúdez and his murderous crew from the Legion of September 15. "By choosing to support Colonel Bermúdez and the FDN over other Contra factions, the United States threw in its lot with the single most detested group of Nicaraguans," former *New York Times* reporter Stephen Kinzer, who covered the Contras, wrote in 1991. "American planners never seemed to grasp the simple fact that Nicaraguans hated the National Guard and would never support an insurgency directed by ex-Guardsmen."

The CIA's role in the FDN's creation—hidden at the time—was spelled out by former FDN director Edgar Chamorro in an affidavit filed with the World Court in the Hague in 1985. Chamorro, a former advertising executive and distant relative of the UDN-FARN Chamorro brothers, said the CIA paid for the meeting, rented the building, and drafted the agreement. "The name of the organization, the members of the political junta and the members of the general staff were all chosen or approved by the CIA."

As luck would have it, the CIA selected another one of Norwin Meneses's friends to assist Bermúdez in running the FDN: Aristides Sánchez, a wealthy landowner whose brother Fernando had been Somoza's last ambassador to Guatemala after Edmundo Meneses was assassinated. Another Sánchez brother, Troilo, had been one of Norwin's friends and business partners in Managua. And yet another brother, Enrique, was partners in a Miami restaurant with Danilo Blandón's "friend from Miami," Donald Barrios, the man Blandón claims introduced him to Norwin Meneses.

Like Bermúdez, Aristides Sánchez went on the CIA's payroll and began reporting daily to his CIA overseers. Together, Bermúdez and Sánchez would become the heart and soul of the military side of the Contra organization. (The political side was left to CIA agent Adolfo Calero, the former manager of the Coca-Cola bottling plant in Managua, who also worked closely with Aristides Sánchez. Oliver North later called Sánchez "Calero's hatchet man.")

Though the FDN would change and merge with other groups over the years, the Bermúdez-Sánchez alliance stood unchanged, thanks largely to the backing of the CIA. "Sánchez became one of the Contras' top political and military strategists, plotting logistics, buying supplies and delivering weapons," wrote the *Miami Herald* in his 1993 obituary. Throughout the 1980s, Sánchez was consistently described in the press as the Contras' supply chief. Norwin Meneses explained that when he was buying and delivering weapons and supplies to the FDN, "I dealt directly with Bermúdez, and occasionally his assistant on minor things. I also worked with Aristides Sánchez. He was a very good friend of mine."

By November 1981 the Contra project was far enough along that the CIA moved to make its sponsorship of the FDN official. President Ronald Reagan was presented with a document known as National Security Decision Directive #17, which served as a blueprint for the U.S. government's plan to overthrow the Sandinista government. It called for the CIA to conduct a variety of covert operations—military and political—against the Sandinistas and asked for $19.95 million to do it with. The document made it clear that it was only a start. "More funds and manpower" would be needed later.

It was obvious to anyone that the CIA's $19 million wasn't going to go very far if a serious paramilitary operation was being planned. The paucity of the allocation, in fact, was used by former CIA deputy director Admiral Bobby Inman to ridicule a reporter's suggestion that the CIA was financing a Contra war machine. "I would suggest to you that $19 million or $29 million isn't going to buy you much of any kind these days, and certainly not against that kind of military force," Inman told a press briefing in 1982.

The covert operations, according to Reagan's directive, would be conducted "primarily through non-Americans." In particularly delicate situations, the agency would send in UCLAs—Unilaterally Controlled Latino Assets—to do the dirty work. That way, if any of them got caught, Langley could throw up its hands and insist it had no idea what was going on.

Reagan approved the intelligence finding, and in December 1981 he sent CIA director William Casey to present Congress with it, saying that the covert operations planned for Nicaragua were in the interest of U.S. national security. Under the law, a "finding" from the president and congressional notification was required if a major covert operation was being planned.

From that point on, the Contras were the CIA's responsibility. From late 1981 through most of 1984, the agency ran the show directly, doling out weapons and money, hiring subcontractors, ferrying supplies, planning strategy and tactics, and keeping tabs on its hirelings. As the Nicaraguans soon learned, their role was to fight and to obey orders. Someone else, usually an American CIA agent or an Argentine military trainer, would do the thinking for them. One order the Nicaraguans were repeatedly given was to vehemently deny any connection to the CIA.

Bermúdez played that role to the hilt, angrily brushing off any press suggestions that the U.S. government had a hand in running the FDN. "We would never accept the role of American mercenary," Bermúdez huffed.

Former FDN director Edgar Chamorro claimed that CIA advisers prepped them for their press conferences and told them to deny they had received any money from the U.S. government. "It was particularly important that we deny having met with any U.S. government officials," Chamorro recounted in his book *Packaging the Contras*.

Blandón said that when he began selling drugs for the FDN in Los Angeles, he was aware the U.S. government had somehow become involved with his organization but saw no direct evidence of it himself. "Maybe in the principal office in Honduras they were helping, but, no, because we were being helped by the Argentina people at that time," Blandón said.

To further insulate themselves from the Contras, CIA officials worked out a deal with the Argentine and Honduran generals. The Americans would supply the cash if the Argentines would supply the training and military advisers. The Hondurans would provide the clandestine bases from which the Contras would operate. As their part of the deal, both countries would get a lot better treatment—increased foreign aid and military support—from the U.S. government.

This tripartite agreement, however, did nothing to ease the financial woes of the Contra commanders. The $19 million in CIA money that Reagan had approved did not go to the Contras. In fact, they saw very little of it. Nearly all of that money was channeled through the Argentine military, both to preserve the CIA's "deniability" and to make sure the Argentines retained some semblance of control over the Nicaraguans. In essence, the CIA was paying the Argentine military to run its covert war. When the Contras needed cash, they had to go begging it from the haughty Argentines.

"They handled all the money. The Nicaraguans—from Bermúdez, needing several hundred dollars for the rent on the Tegucigalpa safe houses, to a foot soldier on leave in the capital, asking for a couple of bucks to see a movie—had to get it from the Argentines," journalist Glenn Garvin, a Contra sympathizer, wrote in 1992. "That was just one of the ways, some subtle and some anything but, that the Argentines let it be known that they were in charge."

While the Contras were forced to beg for scraps, the Argentines were being paid $2,500 and $3,000 a month, "some just for sitting around at a desk cutting up newspapers," said Argentine adviser Hector Frances. Frances described "multi-million dollar purchases carried out by the Argentinian advisors in Honduras...furniture, equipment, tools, and office equipment; million-dollar purchases from a pharmacy near the Hotel Honduras Maya...where in a few months, the owner made himself a multi-millionaire, and also multi-million dollar accounts rung up at the Hotel Honduras Maya, where the Argentinian advisors lived for almost six months, occupying nearly an entire wing of the hotel." That the Contras had to grovel for handouts from the high-living Argentines rankled mightily. And though the Americans had promised to start sending guns, ammo, and equipment, it would be nearly a year before those supplies began arriving.

It was against that backdrop that Meneses and Blandón had been called to Honduras to meet with Enrique Bermúdez, where they were told by the new FDN commander to raise money in California. It is understandable that they would have translated this to mean, by any means necessary. After all, crime had ensured the survival of Bermúdez's legion in Guatemala.

And what was a little cocaine trafficking when compared to kidnappings and contract killings?

Danilo Blandón's first illegal Contra fund-raising efforts met with the same lack of success as had his legal rallies and parties, he said; the two kilos Meneses had given him to sell weren't moving because he knew nothing about the cocaine business.

"Well, it took me about three months or four months to sell those two keys because I don't know what to do," Blandón said. "Meneses told me, 'You go to—with two customers.' That wasn't enough, you know? Because in those days, two keys was too heavy."

Jacinto Torres, Blandón's large Nicaraguan car dealer friend, told the FBI that Blandón was unable to unload all the cocaine Meneses had dumped on him. "Torres stated that Blandón and the others only sold a few ounces of the two kilos to someone in the San Diego area. They gave the rest of the unsold cocaine to Raul Vega" (the one-eyed driver for Meneses who had helped train Blandón in San Francisco), the 1992 FBI report said.

"Mr. Meneses was pushing me every—every week, you know, 'What's going on?'" So Blandón said he had to turn to friends and acquaintances in the automobile business to cultivate customers. "I started getting some people," he said, but his cocaine deals were still small potatoes, selling only "ounces, ounces and grams at that time.... It's only for the money that we had to send. We start sending trucks, pickups, to the Contra revolution. We started sending clothes, medicines at that time."

He told CIA inspectors that he bought a pickup truck and "filled it with medical supplies and radios and turned it over to others to drive to Central America. He says that the truck was, in fact, later used by the FDN in Honduras." Between 1981 and 1982, he said, he also provided several thousand dollars in drug profits to finance the FDN's wing in Los Angeles. The drug money "was used to support the operating expenses—plane tickets, rent, office supplies, etc." Meneses was doing the same, Blandón said, estimating his in-kind contributions at about $40,000.

Most of the money he made from cocaine sales, Blandón said, was turned over to Meneses. How it got from Meneses to the Contras "was Meneses' problem, not mine. I give the money to Meneses. I bought some cars or whatever, some pickups, but the money, we gave him the money.... I bought a lot of things, but I never sent cash."

Cash deliveries to the Contras, it turned out, were being handled by someone else—the unidentified Latin male whom DEA agent Sandra Smith had seen pick up two cocaine traffickers from L.A. at the San Francisco airport and drive to a modest row house in Daly City. And Agent Smith's gut feelings about the Meneses drug ring had been right on target. She'd discovered the first direct evidence of a Contra drug pipeline into California.

5

"God, Fatherland and Freedom"

In the fall of 1981, before his troubles began, Carlos Augusto Cabezas Ramirez was living, breathing proof that America could still be the land of opportunity for anyone willing to roll up his sleeves and work. The chubby thirty-five-year-old had always been willing to work his way to where he wanted to go. In Nicaragua, by the age of fourteen he was helping his mother support nine brothers and sisters. In 1970 he went to the United States, where he spent four years studying to become a commercial pilot, working nights as a janitor to support himself. He took his pilot's license back to Nicaragua and joined the National Guard, flying for Somoza's army and managing a crop-dusting company on the side.

Later Cabezas enrolled in the National University of Nicaragua, got an accounting degree, and was hired by the Bank of America. He became head of the Managua branch's foreign division, supervising seven employees in the sleek blue-and-white skyscraper that was the country's only high-rise office building. He got a law degree next, becoming a licensed attorney in 1978 and setting up a practice in Managua. But the next year, when the Sandinistas were on the outskirts of the capital, Cabezas was recalled to active duty as a fighter pilot. An ardent anti-Communist, he was happy to defend Somoza's government against the Sandinistas.

Near the end of the war, when the *Guardia* was desperately striking out at every perceived enemy, Cabezas took part in the terror bombings of the city of Masaya, something he still doesn't like to talk about.

On July 15, 1979, four days before the shooting stopped, Carlos Cabezas caught the last flight out of Managua. He came to San Francisco, where his wife, three young daughters, his mother, his brothers, and his sisters were already living. With a family to support, Cabezas needed a job—fast. He hired on as a sales agent for the Lincoln Insurance Company in San Francisco. He also took a second job as a night janitor at San Francisco's Hilton Hotel. In 1980, after only a year on the job, the Lincoln Insurance Company named him Sales Agent of the Year. He was given a plaque with an engraving of Abraham Lincoln on it, a prize he still proudly shows off to visitors at his tiny law office in Managua.

By 1981 his hard work was paying off. He sold his car, his wife Angela sold some jewelry, and, throwing in some savings, they scared up $10,000, enough for a down payment on a small row house in Daly City. In just two years he'd gone from being a homeless refugee to owning a piece of the American dream.

When time permitted, Cabezas did legal research for a couple of lawyers, mainly to keep his skills in tune. That work made him realize how much he missed the practice of law and the income that came with it. To be a lawyer in California, though, he would have to go back to law school and study for the grueling California bar exam. With a family to support, a $1,200-a-month mortgage, and two jobs, Cabezas couldn't think of any way to do it, until he thought of his ex-brother-in-law, Julio Zavala.

Two years older and recently divorced from Cabezas's sister Maritza, Zavala had plenty of money. Once Cabezas had been at Zavala's house when a friend of Julio's named Nestor Arana came by lugging a suitcase. It was full of cash, neatly wrapped and stacked. Zavala told the goggle-eyed Cabezas that part of his job involved taking money to Miami, and he was paying Arana to do it for him. Cabezas had asked if Zavala needed any help, but the inquiry was gently brushed aside.

The more Cabezas thought about it, the more it seemed that Julio Zavala was his ticket out of the dilemma he was in. If he could persuade Zavala to give him a loan, Cabezas figured he could quit his jobs long enough to go to law school and pass the bar. So in October 1981 he called Zavala and asked if he could come over and talk to him about an idea he had. Zavala said sure. And at that moment, Carlos Cabezas was screwed.

The reason Julio Zavala had so much money is because he was a cocaine dealer, and a fairly busy one at that. He wasn't anywhere near

Norwin Meneses's global perch, but few were. Zavala was solidly midlevel. He sold kilos and ounces to street-level dealers, who then sold grams to users. For several years he'd been buying directly from a Colombian in San Francisco and a Nicaraguan in Miami, picking up a kilo for around $54,000 and turning it over for up to $68,000, more if he ounced it out. Business had been good. The day Cabezas called him, however, Julio Zavala was a worried man. Bad things had been happening all around him, and he was starting to get nervous.

His problems stemmed from some loose talk last spring in the lock-up at the San Francisco County Jail.

Local DEA agents had busted several people in South San Francisco for possession of a half-kilo of cocaine. One of the women arrested was a Contra fund-raiser named Doris Salomon. She and a codefendant, Lilliana Blengino, were cooling their heels in the jail when Salomon ruefully mentioned that the cocaine they'd been busted over wasn't even hers. It had belonged to her boyfriend, Noel.

A month later, DEA agent Luis Lupin stopped by Blengino's house to see if she could be of some assistance to the authorities. Blengino didn't know much, she told Lupin, but Doris Salomon did say that she'd gotten the coke from her boyfriend, some guy named Noel. Lupin made a note of the name and filed it away.

When Salomon appeared in federal court five months later for a bail hearing, she made a passing reference to a boyfriend, a fellow named Julio Zavala. Agent Lupin, sitting in the courtroom, perked up. Could Julio Zavala be this "Noel" character that Blengino had told him about?

The agent hurried over to the jail and asked to see the visitors' log for the time Doris Salomon had been there. Bingo. Julio Zavala had come to see her three times in a span of eleven days. Unless she had more than one boyfriend while she was in jail, Zavala had to be Noel, Salomon's source of supply.

Checking with the San Francisco Police Department, Lupin discovered that Zavala, a Nicaraguan immigrant, was no angel. Just a month before Salomon was arrested, Zavala and another man had been nabbed trying to bust into a woman's apartment, allegedly to collect a drug debt from her husband. She called the police, and when the irate dealers were hustled out to the curb, the cops found five ounces of cocaine in the Cadillac that Zavala had parked outside. To be precise, it wasn't actually Zavala's Caddy—it had been stolen in Florida and presented to him as a gift from his Miami cocaine connection.

Lupin noticed that the other man arrested with Zavala that day, Edmundo Rocha, had been one of those pinched with Doris Salomon a month later. And there in Rocha's wallet the police had found a slip of paper with "Julio 349-2790" written on it. It was a small world. The DEA started an investigation.

That was the way Zavala's luck had been going all year.

He'd been busted twice, his girlfriend had been busted, his friend Mundo Rocha had been busted twice. The charges against Zavala had been dropped each time, but he didn't like the odds of it happening again. Zavala was moving a lot of cocaine. He had customers in Miami, Los Angeles, Chicago, and San Francisco. He was also making inroads into Oakland's black community, selling to a couple of African-American dealers there. Unfortunately, the growth of his business was making it increasingly difficult for him to disguise what he was doing.

When asked, Zavala said he worked as a buyer for some supermarkets in Costa Rica, which helped cover his frequent travels to Miami and Central America. But that story didn't explain why the telephone in his apartment in San Mateo never stopped ringing, or the steady stream of people who came and went at all hours. What he needed to do was fade into the background for a while and lower his profile. Let someone else take the heat.

So when Carlos Cabezas came around with his hand out, Zavala didn't give him the brush like the last time. This time, he listened.

Cabezas told him of his plans to become a lawyer in the United States, "because I knew that there was no way for me to go back to my country since the revolution had taken over the power." He told Zavala that "in order for me to go to law school, I have to become a full-time student and I couldn't, you know, catch up if I was working two jobs."

Zavala appeared sympathetic, and when Cabezas was through, he "said he was going to help me to finance some and support my family since I had to quit my job." He couldn't actually give him a loan, he said, but if it was time and money Cabezas was after, Zavala had a suggestion: Come work for me. He could make as much as he did at both of his present jobs put together, and then some. Plus, he could do it in his spare time. It was the perfect job for him.

"He said I was going to be delivering cocaine and collecting money so he can stay a little bit cool," Cabezas would later testify. "At that time Mr. Zavala was having problems himself with some legal problems. And he said, 'I was lucky that the charge was dismissed and I don't want to get myself in this transaction, so I want you to work for me. I trust you. And then, you know, the heat is going, it would be off me for awhile.'"

Zavala told Cabezas he'd pay him $500 for each kilo of cocaine he delivered, plus a percentage of the drug debts he collected. And there was an added bonus that Zavala knew Cabezas would like, given his former brother-in-law's feelings about the Sandinistas: some of the cocaine they sold would help to finance the Contras.

So Carlos Cabezas, who'd been a lawyer, an accountant, a pilot, an insurance salesman, a banker, a janitor, and a crop duster, became a cocaine dealer for a while.

At first he stayed around the San Francisco area, running errands, meeting Zavala's customers, delivering a few kilos here and there. The work was easy, Cabezas found, and the money was very good. One of his first errands had been to pick up a gold Toyota and drive it to the airport, where he was to meet a couple of Julio's friends from L.A. and bring them into town. Cabezas agreed to put them up at his house for the couple of days they would be around.

That was when Carlos Cabezas first drew the attention of the federal government.

As part of her investigation into the Meneses drug ring, DEA agent Sandra Smith was watching when Cabezas arrived at the airport to pick up the two L.A. dealers she'd been tailing. When Cabezas drove them back to his little row house in Daly City, 8 Bellevue Avenue was added to the government's list of potential wiretap locations. Within two months the FBI had joined the chase. Scattered among Zavala's customers, the bureau had at least four confidential informants who were giving them chapter and verse: when the cocaine loads were arriving, when the couriers were coming and going, how much cocaine Zavala and Cabezas were selling, how much money was leaving the country. The evidence that the two Nicaraguans were involved in a major cocaine trafficking network piled up fast.

A recently declassified CIA Inspector General's report shows that the Agency had been wise to Zavala since 1980. That year a CIA operative reported that Zavala was supplying drugs to a Nicaraguan official who was a drug addict. The operative would keep the Agency apprised of Zavala's activities for years. In addition, the CIA has admitted that a relative of one of the people involved in the drug ring was working for the CIA at the time.

To Zavala, blissfully unaware of the gathering storm, it seemed as if things were finally looking up. Hiring Cabezas had been a stroke of genius. The customers liked him. He was dependable, a hard worker, and would probably start bringing in some customers of his own soon. Zavala was so pleased with himself that he decided to take some time off and celebrate. His girlfriend, Doris Salomon, had jumped bail and was waiting for him down in Costa Rica, he told Cabezas. He was flying down to join her, and his plans were to get married and spend his honeymoon down in Central America. He told Cabezas he'd see him after the holidays, and off he went.

So, after just a month and a half in the business, Cabezas began running a major drug ring, doing Zavala's job as well as his own. He started dealing directly with Zavala's cocaine suppliers and keeping the books, his accounting background helping him to record the operation's income and expenses meticulously.

Cabezas said the cocaine he and Zavala were selling came from two separate sources. One was Alvaro Carvajal Minota, a Colombian who lived in San Francisco. Carvajal was part of a ring of international cocaine dealers located in Cali, Colombia, a group that would later become known as the Cali cartel. By the early 1990s the Cali dealers would operate the world's biggest cocaine sales network, eclipsing the rival Medellín cartel in terms of power and money. But in late 1981 few in U.S. law enforcement circles were even aware of the cartels. Cabezas began making trips to Cali in 1982 to negotiate deliveries for Zavala.

The other source, Cabezas said, was someone down in Costa Rica. That cocaine would arrive by courier via Miami and would sometimes be brought to Cabezas's house for safekeeping.

Because each source had different prices and delivery costs, Cabezas kept two sets of books—one for the Costa Ricans and another for the Colombians—so everyone got paid what they were owed, without any mix-ups. The cocaine from Costa Rica was of a far higher quality than the Colombians' powder. It was Peruvian. And it was this cocaine, he said, that belonged to the Contras.

He got proof of that in December 1981 when Zavala called him from Costa Rica and told him to catch a plane down. Zavala wanted him to meet some friends of his.

The friends turned out to be two exiled Nicaraguans who were working with Norwin Meneses: Horacio Pereira Lanuza, a drug dealer and gambler known as *La Burra* (a female donkey), and Troilo Sánchez Herdocia, a playboy brother of FDN leaders Aristides and Fernando Sánchez.

Fernando Sánchez had been Somoza's last ambassador to Guatemala, replacing the slain Edmundo Meneses. The U.S. State Department, in a 1988 publication, described Fernando as the Contras' "representative in Guatemala." Troilo Sánchez had been a partner of Meneses in one of Norwin's nightclubs in Managua, and was one of his drinking buddies. A pilot, Sánchez said he flew for the CIA in the early 1960s during preparations for the Bay of Pigs invasion, which was partly staged from Nicaragua. But by the late 1970s he was a hopeless drug addict, spending large sums of his family's fortune on heroin, cocaine, women, and gambling. The Sandinistas seized what was left, and Troilo Sánchez and his wife, Isanaqui, fled to Costa Rica, where they became partners with Meneses in a bean-processing factory there.

"We are like family," Meneses said of Sánchez's wife in a 1986 interview. "She came many times to visit my brother Mundo, who was a general and the police chief of Managua and was later assassinated in Guatemala for the Sandinistas."

Horacio Pereira had also been a business partner of Meneses before the revolution. Meneses said they owned cattle and cattle ranches together and had known each other since childhood. Both were from Esteli, where Pereira controlled some gambling clubs.

Cabezas told CIA investigators that his December 1981 meeting in Costa Rica "was the genesis of an effort to raise money for the Contras by selling drugs. Although the original reason for the meeting was purely social, Cabezas says Sánchez and Pereira raised the idea of selling cocaine as a means of raising funds for the Contras. Cabezas says Pereira and Sánchez discussed the idea with him because both knew of Cabezas' role in the Zavala organization. Although it was Sánchez's and Pereira's idea to raise funds for the Contras by engaging in drug trafficking, Cabezas says it was Zavala who came up with the idea that Cabezas serve as a go-between by collecting the money from street dealers and delivering it to Central America." Zavala and Sánchez have denied any involvement in drug trafficking for the Contras.

On January 23, 1982, Zavala sent Cabezas back to Costa Rica with two other men to pick up two kilos of cocaine from Pereira. But Pereira was suddenly uncomfortable with the arrangements. "I went down there with those two people to Costa Rica, but apparently Mr. Pereira changed his mind because he said he had some information that Mr. Zavala was drinking very heavily and he was scared that Mr. Zavala was going to misuse that money that supposedly he said that he was helping the Contra revolution in Nicaragua," Cabezas would later testify. Pereira told

Cabezas that "he was representing the UDN-FARN and FDN in Costa Rica and that they had chosen Zavala's organization to sell the cocaine they were getting in from Peru. He said the money was going to the Contras and that the CIA would control the delivery of the money."

Pereira's information about his ex-brother-in-law was correct, Cabezas conceded. Zavala *had* been drinking quite a bit, and he was starting to neglect his responsibilities, falling behind in his payments to the Colombians, who were getting annoyed. His dicey relationship with them would be the source of several arguments, Cabezas said. Sometimes, when the Colombians were really pressing for money, Zavala would take some of the Contras' cocaine and sell it to pay the Colombians, which played hell with Cabezas's accounting.

The wary Pereira suggested an alternative: He would deal directly with Cabezas. He would sell him the cocaine, and then Cabezas would become responsible for getting the Contras' money back to Costa Rica. But Cabezas was hesitant. "I explained to Mr. Pereira that I didn't have no clients and that if I have to sell the cocaine, I have to tell Mr. Zavala because I wasn't going to jump him," Cabezas later testified. "I wasn't going to do anything behind his back."

But Pereira insisted that Cabezas had to assume responsibility for the cash, "because the money belonged...to help the Contra revolution," Cabezas said. That was the only way, Pereira told him, that he would let go of the cocaine.

Cabezas called Zavala and explained the situation, and Zavala agreed to Pereira's terms. But Cabezas was no fool. Instead of his usual $500 per kilo payment, he wanted half of Zavala's profits, "because I am taking the responsibility of the money." Stuck, Zavala had no choice but to agree. In an interview with the CIA, Zavala confirmed that he was then cut off from Cabezas's dealings with Pereira and Sánchez.

Cabezas traveled with Pereira to San Pedro Sula in Honduras, where he met other members of Pereira's family. While there, he said, he stayed at the home of Pereira's brother-in-law, an exiled Nicaraguan attorney named Francisco Aviles Saenz, who had been educated in the United States. He spent two or three days in Honduras, waiting for "a Peruvian who would be bringing drugs for shipment to the United States." Before he left, Pereira gave Cabezas a bottle of whiskey, some souvenirs, and two hand-woven baskets from Peru, saying, "This one is for you and the other one is for Julio." Baffled that there was no cocaine, Cabezas took the gifts back to San Francisco.

When he showed the baskets to Zavala, Cabezas said, Zavala

exclaimed, "These are not gifts!" and began ripping them apart. As Cabezas watched, Zavala stripped the basket down to its internal framework and, from inside the frame, pulled out long, thin, waxy strings that resembled skinny candles. Taking a razor blade, he slit them open and poured out a small pile of cocaine powder. Cabezas said each "candle" held about three ounces of cocaine, and each basket contained about a kilo.

Cabezas would later testify that he personally brought back twelve kilos from Pereira during the first part of 1982, earning about $17,000. He would tell CIA inspectors that "Contra mules, typically airline flight attendants" were also bringing the baskets into the United States, one kilo at a time. When the baskets arrived in San Francisco, it was Cabezas's job to dismantle them and extract the cocaine. How many kilos Pereira sent into the States is anyone's guess, but Costa Rican authorities claimed that he was the biggest cocaine trafficker in their country during the early 1980s.

For the next year, Cabezas said, he and others made regular trips to Miami and Costa Rica carrying money for the Contras. He told CIA investigators that "on average...he carried $64,000 on each of his 20 trips to Central America, although he also claims that he and another person once delivered about $250,000 to Pereira and Sánchez." FBI records show Zavala made a money-hauling trip to Costa Rica in early 1982, and said the amount he was carrying was a quarter million dollars. Another man, a Nicaraguan dental student named Ernesto Linsig Caballero, admitted to having delivered $40,000 to Pereira's wife in Miami and then continuing on to Costa Rica to meet with Pereira and Troilo Sánchez, court records show. When no one in San Francisco was available to make the trips, former ambassador Sánchez would fly up from Guatemala and take money back. Sometimes Horacio Pereira would do it, Cabezas said.

An FBI teletype shows that by November 1982 the bureau—thanks to its wiretaps and inside informants—knew exactly what was going on inside Zavala's drug ring. According to the report, from the San Francisco FBI office to the FBI director in Washington, "Zavala's sources of supply of this cocaine are: Troilo Sánchez, Fernando Sánchez and Horacio Pereira. All three are operating out of Costa Rica." As for Cabezas, "Cabezas's sources of supply for cocaine have been established as Troilo Sánchez, Fernando Sánchez, Horacio Pereira of Costa Rica, Humberto and Fernando Ortiz of Colombia, Sebastian Pinel of Los Angeles and Alvaro Carvajal Minota of San Francisco." The FBI had taped conversations that discussed "Horacio going to Costa Rica to bring money";

"Miami Cuban arriving at Cabezas"; "Troilo arrival from Costa Rica on Sept. 13 or 14"; "Don Troilo in Costa Rica has $30,000"; and "Fernando arrival through Tijuana on Sept. 26."

"The use of couriers to bring cocaine from Costa Rica via Miami is a common method of operation by Zavala," FBI agent David Alba wrote in a lengthy affidavit requesting a wiretap.

Cabezas was also taking $50,000 a month to the Contras' Miami offices, located in a shopping center near the Miami airport. Often he would give the money directly to FDN leader Aristides Sánchez, the brother of his suppliers Troilo and Fernando. Aristides Sánchez died in 1993; he was still working on behalf of the Contras at the time of his death, according to a laudatory obituary in the *Miami Herald.*

Cabezas told the CIA that "he never specifically told Aristides Sánchez that the money came from drug proceeds but only that it was from Troilo. Cabezas said he assumed Aristides Sánchez must have known what Troilo was involved in." Other Contras certainly did. Former Contra official Leonardo Zeledon Rodriguez told UPI in 1986 that "Troilo sold 200 pounds of cocaine and received $6.1 million for it."

The money Cabezas took to Central America was given to Pereira or an FDN logistics officer, Joaquin "Pelon" Vega, who lived in Danli, Honduras, Cabezas said. He assumed the money was used to buy food and clothing for the newly formed guerrilla army. (Vega could not be located by the author.)

On one of his trips to Costa Rica with Contra cash in April or May of 1982, Cabezas told CIA investigators, he was called to a meeting at a San José hotel, where Pereira and Troilo Sánchez introduced him to a curly-haired, solidly built man he'd never seen before. The man called himself Ivan Gómez and told Cabezas that he was with the CIA—the agency's "man in Costa Rica." Gómez said he was there, Cabezas said, "to ensure that the profits from the cocaine went to the Contras and not into someone's pocket." Cabezas saw the CIA agent only once more, in late summer, when he was met at the San José airport by Pereira and the CIA man, but Gómez never spoke during the second meeting.

Three former Costa Rican Contra officials with direct knowledge of the CIA's operations in that country in the early 1980s—Edén Pastora, Carol Prado, and Marcos Aguado—independently confirmed in interviews that they dealt with a man who called himself Ivan Gómez, and they all described him as a CIA agent assigned to help build up the Southern Front at the beginning of the war. All three described Gómez as a Venezuelan who was a relative of Venezuelan president Carlos Andrés

Pérez. A 1995 book about Contra activities in Costa Rica offered similar descriptions of Gómez's work there.

Pastora identified Gómez as the CIA agent in charge of logistics for the Contra group Pastora led in Costa Rica starting in mid-1982. Gómez had retired from the CIA following the war, married a Nicaraguan woman, and moved to Spain. Marcos Aguado, Pastora's chief pilot and later his son-in-law, said the woman Gómez married was one of his old girlfriends. "I didn't know that motherfucker was even after her," Aguado said with some amusement.

In an interview with a British television crew in late 1996, former CIA official Duane "Dewey" Clarridge said he'd never heard of Ivan Gómez. Clarridge was the CIA officer who headed the Contra project from 1981 to 1984 and was later indicted for lying to Congress about the Iran-Contra scandal. He was pardoned by President George Bush, a former CIA director.

The 1998 CIA Inspector General's report strongly suggests Dewey Clarridge was lying once again. "CIA records indicate that a CIA independent contractor used 'Ivan Gómez' as an alias in Costa Rica in the 1980s," the CIA report admitted. The report implied, however, that Cabezas might not have actually dealt with the CIA agent, since he was unable to pick his photograph out of a lineup of sixteen photos—hardly surprising considering that Cabezas met the agent only twice, fifteen years earlier. And while admitting that Gómez had curly black hair, as Cabezas said, the agency described Gómez as "much shorter" than Cabezas recalled.

"Gómez" told the CIA inspectors he'd never met Cabezas or the other traffickers.

Based on Cabezas's statements and the historical record from the early days of the Contra conflict, it appears that most of the cocaine profits Cabezas was delivering to Costa Rica in 1982 went to assist the Contras of the UDN-FARN faction, which at that time was under CIA supervision. A 1984 DEA report described UDN-FARN's deputy commander, Edmundo Chamorro, as "well known to 'The Company.'" During a Costa Rican police investigation of Horacio Pereira in 1984, the authorities would tape phone calls between Pereira and Edmundo Chamorro regarding cocaine shipments and transportation for the Contras.

For most of 1982, UDN-FARN served, however unwillingly, as the southern branch of the CIA's primary Contra force—the FDN—run by Meneses's friend Enrique Bermúdez and his Honduran-based former

Guardia men. But in September of that year, when former Sandinista commander Pastora announced he was taking up arms against his old Sandinista colleagues, UDN-FARN jumped ship, leaving the FDN and officially uniting with Pastora's group to form a brand-new Contra army in Costa Rica, known as ARDE.

At that point, it is likely that the cocaine profits from Meneses's San Francisco operation began being used to benefit ARDE. Even then, however, the CIA retained oversight responsibility. When the Chamorros switched from the FDN to the ARDE, they simply changed their line of command. Instead of reporting to Bermúdez, as they had been doing, they now reported to Pastora. But both Pastora and Bermúdez were still reporting to the CIA. Like Bermúdez, Pastora was put on the CIA's payroll, where he remained until mid-1984.

The merger between the Chamorro brothers and Pastora's group made sense politically because they had one trait in common, aside from their preference for fighting from Costa Rica: as former Sandinistas, they hated the ex-*Guardia* officers who made up the FDN. Pastora frequently outraged his CIA handlers by publicly complaining about his purported allies to the north, once picturesquely referring to them as "criminal mummies and gorillas." Bermúdez and the FDN considered Pastora a closet Communist and suspected him of being a Sandinista mole.

Carlos Cabezas said his Contra money flights to Costa Rica continued throughout 1982 but were interrupted near the end of that year, when Horacio Pereira was arrested in Florida. Cabezas said one of the FBI's informants, Donald Peralta, a man who had accompanied him to Costa Rica on several occasions to deliver cash, tipped off the FBI that Pereira was heading south with a wad of greenbacks.

FBI records show that on December 1, 1982, a confidential source told FBI agent David Alba that "Horacio Pereira and Augusto Monkel would be traveling from San Francisco via Miami to San José, Costa Rica, with between $80,000 and $100,000, which was the proceeds of cocaine sales in San Francisco." Alba called U.S. Customs, and the next day Pereira was arrested in Miami, boarding Air Florida Flight 473 to Costa Rica. The agents found $70,000 on him, which he had failed to declare.

FBI wiretap records show that Cabezas was in contact with Pereira's cousin, Rosita, soon afterward. "Horacio going to court tomorrow," the FBI's notes of that phone call say. "Carlos has some money to help Horacio. The money taken by Customs will be kept. Carlos asked why Troilo has not called. Horacio was interviewed but did not mention Carlos' name. Carlos wants Horacio to call tomorrow."

On Christmas Eve, after he was bailed out, Pereira called Cabezas and told him that he'd been set up and needed some money. Cabezas replied that "Jairo is giving him money," an apparent reference to Norwin Meneses's nephew, Jairo Meneses.

Then something inexplicable happened.

Pereira, whom the FBI knew to be a major international cocaine trafficker, was turned loose after paying a small fine for not declaring the $70,000. He returned to Costa Rica and immediately resumed drug trafficking, which the FBI learned while monitoring a phone call from Pereira to Cabezas on January 21, 1983. "Fine was completed. No probation, no prison," Pereira was recorded as telling Cabezas. "Horacio wants to get ready to send Carlos some material."

By then the feds were crawling all over the drug ring. All of the traffickers' phone calls were being taped and transcribed; eventually the FBI would monitor more than 13,000 conversations. Cabezas and Zavala were being shadowed everywhere. Their dealers and their dealers' customers had their phones tapped as well.

The wiretaps revealed that the Colombian side of Zavala's drug operation was using freighters registered to the Gran Colombiana shipping line to bring cocaine into the United States. Agents began following the Gran Colombiana ships as they plied the waters off the West Coast and watched as kilos of cocaine were unloaded by Cabezas's associates in San Francisco and Seattle. Right before Christmas, the FBI started taking the operation apart.

On December 22, 1982, they intercepted two men coming off the freighter *Ciudad de Nieva* in Los Angeles, carrying thirty-nine pounds of cocaine. Another Gran Colombiana ship, the *Ciudad de Cucuta,* pulled into Pier 96 in San Francisco shortly after the first of the year, and the FBI set up a stakeout. It was a vessel that, according to one report, "had been raided in previous drug seizures."

Nearly two weeks went by without anything happening. Then, just before 2 A.M. on January 17, 1983, during the heaviest fog of the winter, a silver-and-orange Chevy van and a Toyota Celica pulled up to a hole in a fence near a swampy marsh leading to Pier 96. Seven men got out and began wading through the swamp toward the docked freighter, disappearing into the darkness. Two hours later the Celica and the van returned, and the seven men materialized out of the gloom, carrying heavy duffel bags. Two of them wore divers' wet suits.

The stakeout agents moved in, and one of the suspects unleashed a short burst from an Uzi submachine gun, but no one was injured, and they quickly surrendered. The agents found that all the men were heavily armed—a wise precaution, considering the value of what they were carrying: an astonishing 430 pounds of cocaine. Five other men were also rounded up that night, most of them Colombians who had been seen in Los Angeles and Seattle during earlier freighter stakeouts.

It was the biggest cocaine bust in the history of the West Coast.

The next day the *San Francisco Chronicle* blasted the news of the drug raid across its front page. Headlined "Cocaine Seized from Frogmen at S.F. Pier," the story told of "a fog-shrouded scene right out of a B-movie" and featured a large front-page picture of a Customs agent in a windbreaker piling football-sized bricks of cocaine on a table.

It was the first case made by President Ronald Reagan's new federal Drug Task Force in San Francisco, and U.S. Attorney Joseph Russoniello, a right-wing Republican close to the Reagan administration, made sure the media understood what a momentous seizure the president's new drug warriors had made. Russoniello told reporters that the street value of the cocaine the frogmen were carrying was, after "routine dilution," a whopping $750 million—three quarters of a *billion* dollars. Even the agents working the case couldn't swallow that one. Russoniello's quote in the *Chronicle* was followed by one from the DEA saying the load was worth no more than $100 million on the street, and between $11 million and $12 million wholesale.

Two weeks later agents in Los Angeles raided the Gran Colombiana freighter *Ciudad de Santa Maria* and arrested fifteen people, again mostly Colombians, in the act of unloading 150 pounds of cocaine. A UPI story noted that "the arrests were made as the suspects tried to transfer the drug ashore by way of couriers and a scuba diver." That story said the cocaine was worth $22.8 million.

(Amazingly, cocaine continued arriving in the United States aboard Gran Colombiana freighters all the way through 1986. The very same ship docked at Pier 96 that night in January 1983—the *Ciudad de Cucuta*—was found in Houston the following year with $18 million worth of cocaine secreted behind a steel wall. The shipping line was partly owned by the Colombian and Ecuadoran governments.)

The hammer fell next on Carlos Cabezas and Julio Zavala.

At 7 A.M. on February 15, federal agents and local police simultaneously raided fourteen locations in the San Francisco area, including Cabezas's house and Zavala's apartment, scooping up everyone and everything they could find. The haul included the Colombian supplier Alvaro Carvajal Minota; Cabezas; his mother, Gladys; Zavala; the low-level dealers they had been selling to; and some of their customers. In a bookcase in a San Francisco apartment, records show, police found "five flyers for Nicaraguan Benefit."

Once again U.S. Attorney Russoniello hosted a media event, and the San Francisco papers ate it up. "Big Drug Ring Raid," the *Chronicle* blared on its front page next morning. Russoniello described Zavala's Colombian supplier, Carvajal Minota, as "the linchpin of the operation." Referring to the earlier arrests of the frogmen at Pier 96, Russoniello said, "Before, we got the mules. These are the higher-ups in the operation."

But while Russoniello and the federal agents who accompanied him were more than happy to give out detailed tidbits concerning the Colombians—such as the fact that Carvajal Minota sent boxloads of cash and jewelry each month to his mother in Cali—they had nothing at all to say about the cocaine and the cash the Nicaraguans were hauling to and from Costa Rica.

The involvement of Pereira and the Sánchez brothers was never disclosed, nor were they ever charged with anything. For some reason, the fact that the former Nicaraguan ambassador to Guatemala was bringing cocaine into the United States wasn't deemed newsworthy—or indictable. "Little information was given on the background of those arrested," the *Chronicle* reported. "Their listed occupations varied from handyman to housewife, PBX installer to produce salesman. One, said to have been an attorney in Nicaragua, was believed to have advised the ring on legal procedures to thwart the law."

The Meneses family's involvement with the drug ring was also suppressed. Defense lawyers had to get a court order to force the Justice Department to reveal that the 1981 searches targeting Jairo Meneses and Julio Bermúdez had even occurred. After the lawyers got those files, they accused the FBI of "serious misrepresentation" for concealing the identities of individuals "who are, clearly from the government's point of view, either distributing cocaine obtained from some of the principals in this case, or supplying it to them." The records, they argued, revealed that there was "a direct and ongoing connection between the Meneses organization and Carlos Cabezas."

The government replied that the searches had been of little importance.

When news of the arrests reached Central America, reporters there saw an angle that their American counterparts missed. "Somocistas traffic in drugs," is how the pro-Sandinista daily, *Barricada*, headlined the story that appeared on February 20, 1983. "Narcotics police of San Francisco, California, carried out a haul last Wednesday of 20 cocaine traffickers, among whom are several Nicaraguans who supported through this criminal activity the economic needs of Contra groups."

The paper quoted unnamed Nicaraguan diplomatic sources, asserting that "one could not establish how many of those captured are of Nicaraguan origin, but there were several, and they were tied to groups of former Somocista Guards in San Francisco, and that through the crime of trafficking in cocaine they are contributing economically to the Contras." It would take another three years before an American journalist would make the same connection.

Julio Zavala complained to the court that similar stories had appeared in the Spanish-language press in Costa Rica, making it impossible for him to return to Central America. Both Zavala and Cabezas were held in prison on $1,000,000 bail, which Cabezas was unable to raise. After getting a look at the evidence the FBI had compiled against him, Cabezas's attorney advised him to cut a deal with the government and testify against Zavala, which Cabezas did.

About a year later, shortly before his trial was to begin, Zavala's attorney, Judd Iverson, walked into U.S. District Court judge Robert Peckham's office and dropped a bombshell on his desk. Iverson handed Peckham two letters addressed to the court, written by Nicaraguan exiles in Costa Rica, regarding Julio Zavala's activities on behalf of the Contras. One was written by Horacio Pereira's brother-in-law, the exiled attorney Francisco Aviles Saenz, who identified himself as the international relations secretary for UDN-FARN. A published account said Aviles had also helped set up the Committee in Defense of Democracy in Nicaragua, a CIA front in San José, Costa Rica, with money from Venezuelan sources. The other letter was also written by Aviles, together with businessman Vicente Rappaccioli Marquis, on behalf of a group called the Conservative Party of Nicaraguans in Exile (PCNE). In the early 1980s he was part of UDN-FARN, according to a former UDN-FARN commander who'd been recruited by Rappaccioli.

The Contras' letters said Julio Zavala, who stood accused by the Justice Department of being a cocaine kingpin, was actually a Contra official who had been working for the resistance forces at the time of his arrest; Zavala was the assistant treasurer of the PCNE and a longtime member of UDN-FARN, which "fights for the restoration of the democratic system in the Republic of Nicaragua…under the slogan 'God, Fatherland and Freedom.'" The reason they were writing Peckham, the Contra leaders stated, was because the FBI had something that belonged to them, and they wanted it back.

When Zavala's apartment was searched the morning of his arrest, the police—in addition to finding an M-1 carbine, a practice grenade, a variety of passports, and a catalog of machine guns and silencers—found slightly more than $36,000 in Zavala's nightstand, which was confiscated as illegal drug proceeds. That was not an unreasonable assumption, given all the cocaine and drug paraphernalia the police found scattered about the place. But the Contras insisted that the money in the dealer's nightstand was theirs, and they had given it to Zavala so he could make some "purchases characteristic of this organization" while in San Francisco. "The retention of this money is prejudicing the progress of liberation, with natural consequences," Aviles warned Peckham.

According to the letter, Zavala had made several trips between California and Costa Rica on UDN-FARN's behalf, and during his last visit in January 1983 he was given $45,000 that UDN-FARN had "collected amongst our collaborators here in Costa Rica." To prove it, the Contra leaders provided copies of a letter appointing Zavala as the assistant treasurer of PCNE, and authorizing him "to collect within the United States money for the liberalization of Nicaragua from international communism"; a receipt showing the group had given him $45,000; his UDN-FARN credentials; and Aviles's sworn statement that he was willing to testify to Zavala's position if necessary.

Defense attorney Iverson told Judge Peckham that he wanted to go down to Costa Rica and take the Contras' depositions. If what they were saying was true, he argued, Zavala was going to defend himself on the grounds that "agents of the U.S. government were intricately involved in the alleged conspiracy and either sanctioned the use of cocaine trafficking to raise funds for Contra revolutionary activity and/or entrapped the Defendant into participating under the belief that such activity was sanctioned."

Peckham quickly scrawled his signature on an order sealing the Contras' letters and the other papers Iverson had submitted. Iverson had requested the secrecy order to keep the U.S. government from discovering the documents, which he felt might expose Aviles and Rappaccioli "and/or their families to harm or political pressure." In court a few weeks later, Iverson again raised the issue of the depositions, a request Peckham was still considering. Assistant U.S. Attorney Mark Zanides scoffed at the notion, saying that Iverson hadn't come close to showing a need to go "trudging off in the middle of the trial to Costa Rica without a firm basis for it."

Judge Peckham disagreed.

"It would be very important testimony to corroborate what they apparently claim is his defense. It has to do with the source of the money. My understanding is the Government will assert the money came from narcotics transactions?"

"It is very likely," Zanides answered.

"Well, he claims another source for another purpose," Peckham said. "And this evidence would corroborate that. It is very important evidence."

"I don't know, I have not seen any reason why the government isn't entitled to know the identity of the witnesses," Zanides complained. "I don't know what the source of this information is, or alleged information. I'm flying blind."

"There were letters from the people involved that were filed under seal with the court," Iverson reminded the prosecutor.

"I don't know who they are," Zanides protested. "These letters could come from anybody. I don't know if Mr. Iverson has ever spoken with them personally. I don't know how he can vouch... it is just a letter."

The prosecutor told Peckham that it wasn't "a situation where we are talking about a threat to the lives of the witnesses."

"They think so," Peckham replied.

"I think it is," Iverson said.

After holding two hearings in the secrecy of his chambers, Peckham had the lawyers come to his courtroom on July 16, 1984, to hear his decision. Prosecutor Zanides again complained that he was being kept in the dark about the identity of the Contra officials. "You are talking about some unknown people in a foreign country with allegedly revolutionary affiliation," he argued.

"The concern, I suppose, is that these people will be intimidated," the judge said, "not necessarily expressly. They are revolutionaries in Nicaragua. They want to overturn the Nicaraguan government, as I understand it. The Contras. They are based in Costa Rica and they have monies. Where those monies came from, nobody knows. There is speculation about that, but there is no evidence. They want to show that this money that was found in his possession came from the Contras."

"I appreciate all that. That's been apparent," Zanides said. "Let's assume for a moment that I don't believe these people, that I think they're lying. I mean, I have to be able to make inquiry of those persons or agencies whom I believe possess that information."

"Judge, these people probably have very close contacts with the CIA,"

Zavala's cocounsel, Marvin Cahn, argued. "We don't want the CIA saying to them, 'Don't testify.' I see no reason why an investigation can't be done after the deposition."

"Oh, that's ridiculous," Zanides said.

"I don't see anything ridiculous about it," Cahn retorted.

"Would you look to the CIA?" Peckham asked the prosecutor.

"I look anywhere I think there might be some information."

"That is troublesome," the judge said.

"Absolutely, I might look to the CIA."

"Is that troublesome?" Peckham inquired of the lawyers.

"Not to me," Zanides said. "I need to know. It may turn out that they may be telling the truth."

"It is very troublesome to us to have the CIA involved because I think our witnesses won't be there if that happens," Cahn said. "It seems our witnesses should be afforded the same degree of protection that the government's informants are afforded."

"That just doesn't add up," Zanides said.

"There is a far more dangerous situation in Costa Rica than an informant has in the United States!" Cahn said.

Peckham gently intervened. "They fear, you see, that there will be disclosures made," the judge explained to Zanides. "And again, I don't accept this because I have no evidence. So by my saying it, I don't want it understood that I am finding what I say to be fact. They are afraid. Just like you are afraid about the safety of informants, they are afraid that if the CIA is, in fact, financing these people that they will not want it disclosed and that they will take measures to make certain people don't get funding or be advised strongly not to cooperate. I don't know if you have control over that."

"So the fear," Zanides asked, "is that the CIA is going to bring some pressure on these people not to testify, is that it?"

"That's very much the fear," Cahn said. "And I think it is a realistic fear in this case."

"I don't see any evidence...I can't even respond to that," Zanides argued. "What is the evidence the CIA—"

"That is fairly well documented," Iverson interjected. "I don't think there is any question that they are down there and intimately involved with the group that is trying to overthrow the Sandinista government."

"All we are saying," Judge Peckham told Zanides, "is that nobody should discourage them from testifying in this proceeding by way of deposition. I don't know what is so horrendous about that."

Peckham granted the defense lawyer's motion to fly to Costa Rica during mid-August "for the purpose of taking depositions of Francisco Aviles Saenz and Vicente Rappaccioli Marquis." He instructed the government to pay $5,000 in travel expenses for the attorneys.

Six days later the Costa Rican CIA station fired off a cable to Langley to warn that a federal prosecutor and an FBI agent were planning a trip to San José "to question two anti-Sandinistas in connection with the prosecution of a cocaine trafficking case." The problem, the station told Langley, is that both Aviles and Rappaccioli were Contra officials and belonged to an organization that had "unwittingly received CIA support."

Both men were also CIA assets, the station said. Langley was advised to search its files for anything it had on them and their connection to the cocaine traffickers, and the cable ended by saying that the CIA station was "concerned that this kind of uncoordinated activity (i.e. the assistant U.S. attorney and FBI visit and depositions) could have serious implications for anti-Sandinista activities in Costa Rica and elsewhere."

CIA headquarters discovered that Aviles was indeed a Contra official and had attended an August 1982 conference in Miami, where he was elected to the board of directors of the PCNE, which was receiving CIA money.

Various branches of the CIA were alerted, and the agency sprang into action. The Justice Department and the federal prosecutor handling the Zavala case, CIA officials decided, needed to be "discreetly approached."

On August 3, 1984, CIA headquarters instructed the Costa Rican station to keep away from Aviles and Rappaccioli, "to avoid giving Zavala's defense attorneys a possible issue." Langley reassured the nervous Costa Rican station that "there was no reason to believe that Zavala's attorneys knew Rappaccioli had any association with CIA." The whole thing could just blow over "if planned legal action is successful," the cable said.

CIA lawyer Lee S. Strickland flew into San Francisco from Washington, and on August 7, 1984, he sat down with prosecutor Mark Zanides and had what Zanides recalled as an "opaque conversation" with him. The CIA, Strickland told him, "would be immensely grateful if these depositions did not go forward." But Strickland "provided little or no explanation regarding what the CIA's interests were in the case," Zanides said. Strickland appeared "very concerned about the public identification of the individuals who were to be deposed."

There was one problem, however. Neither the CIA nor the prosecutor knew what was in the letters the Contras sent to the judge. Before they could do anything, they needed to see those letters.

That afternoon Zanides filed a motion asking Peckham to unseal the Contras' letters so government lawyers could read them. "Keeping it under seal at this point would result only in preventing the counsel for the United States from preparing properly for the deposition," he wrote. "At present the government is undertaking an inquiry with respect to the identities of these persons and counsel for the government is attempting to ascertain precisely what the facts are."

At a hearing the next day, Zanides wanted to clarify the government's position. When he asked for the records to be unsealed, he told Peckham, he hadn't meant for the general public to be able to read them. All he was asking for was that the documents be shown to government lawyers under a protective order.

Judge Peckham bristled at the prosecutor's suggestion.

"I think it ought to be made public," he said. "Why should we not make it public? What is there left to keep—"

"Your Honor," Zanides interrupted, "before I could comment on that—"

But the judge abruptly cut off the prosecutor.

"I am going to make it public. If it is unsealed it is going to be public," he warned.

"Well, as Your Honor knows, I can't comment since I really haven't seen those materials," Zanides said.

"I am ordering it made public. It is unsealed," the judge said. "I don't have to put it that way. I will just order it unsealed."

"Very well," Zanides replied. "May I obtain a copy from your clerk this morning?"

"Certainly," the judge said, taking out his pen. "So I will sign this...there is no restriction on the public disclosure of this."

When Strickland and Zanides saw the letters the two CIA operatives had sent to Peckham, their faces must have fallen. They had put the Contras right in the middle of the biggest cocaine bust in California history. Zanides went running back to Judge Peckham with a request that he make the documents secret again, until the government could make a private "presentation to the court why the record re Costa Rica depositions should not be made public." Zavala's attorneys weren't invited.

Whatever the Justice Department told Peckham during the private meeting in his chambers, it worked. Peckham issued an order that afternoon sealing up the records he'd made public only that morning. Five days later Zanides filed a three-paragraph agreement that said simply that the "United States will not introduce the $36,020 in United States currency seized from the residence of Julio Zavala" and "agrees to return said currency to Julio Zavala." In exchange, the agreement stated, Zavala would not press the issue of the Costa Rican depositions.

"As the matter stands now," a CIA cable stated, "CIA equities are fully protected." The cable bemoaned the fact that both Aviles and Rappaccioli "planned to testify at their deposition as to the source of the money in question. We can only guess at what other testimony may have been forthcoming."

A U.S. embassy official in Costa Rica, after hearing that the depositions had been called off, quipped that they "had been canceled by The Funny Farm." His remark quickly got back to Langley, which instructed its Costa Rican agents to tell the diplomat "that CIA had no hand in cancellation of the trip."

"The government just folded up its tents and went home," remembered defense cocounsel Cahn, now retired. "In my whole career, I had that happen only twice." The other case, he said, also involved "the whole Iran-Contra affair and Oliver North and when I got down to the point where I was really going to make things public, showing the DEA and CIA involvement in drug smuggling operations, again, the government just folded."

Years later, when questioned about the case by the author, former U.S. attorney Russoniello said the only reason he agreed to return the drug dealer's cash was because it would have cost the government too much money to go to Costa Rica and take two depositions. There never was any evidence to suggest that the Contras were involved with the drug ring, he insisted. But recently declassified CIA cables contradict Russoniello's explanation. The money was returned because the CIA did not want its involvement with drug dealers publicly exposed, the cables reveal. And the CIA took full credit for Russoniello's decision to give the cocaine dealer his money back, saying he was "most deferential to our interests."

Even after the depositions were canceled, the agency continued to fret that its dirty secrets would somehow leak out. CIA officials were instructed to "monitor the prosecution closely so that any further disclosures or allegations by defendant or his confidants can be deflected." CIA lawyer Strickland argued in a memo that the Costa Rican station "must be made aware of the potential for disaster. While the allegations may be entirely false, there are sufficient factual details which would cause certain damage to our image and program in Central America." A memo from CIA general counsel Stanley Sporkin observed, "This matter raises obvious questions concerning the people we are supporting in Central America."

In a lengthy cable to the Costa Rican station on August 24, 1984, Strickland detailed his concerns. "While this particular aspect was successfully resolved, the possibility of potential damage to CIA interests was not lost on the U.S. Attorney or headquarters. By virtue of Rappaccioli's relationship as a former covert action asset and a member of board of directors of a Contra organization, Aviles' role as director of the Contra support group office in San José, and their formal claim of drug-tainted money, case could be made that CIA funds are being diverted by CIA assets into the drug trade," he wrote. "Indeed, close relationship between Zavala, a convicted drug dealer, and Rappaccioli and Aviles could prove most damaging especially if any relationship, no matter how indirect, were to continue. As long as Rappaccioli and Aviles continue to play any role in the anti-Sandinista movement, any public disclosure of the foregoing would have as a certain element the fact that they were 'linked to' or 'assets of' CIA."

Strickland told the Costa Rican station to look into whether the Contras were dealing drugs but warned "no action other than discreet inquiries should be undertaken without headquarters approval."

What the CIA found was censored from the report, but the agency clearly didn't cut its ties with the two Nicaraguans. Aviles, in 1985, was appointed to the general staff of UDN-FARN. A 1988 State Department biography of Vicente Rappaccioli identified him as the secretary of the Contras' political division. Incredibly, the 1998 CIA Inspector General's report that contained all the cables claimed Aviles and Rappaccioli really hadn't worked for the CIA after all. The repeated references to them as CIA assets in the 1984 cables were mistakes, the IG claimed.

In October 1984 the federal government returned $36,020 to Aviles and Zavala. And not a moment too soon: eight days after the check was issued, the U.S. Congress—outraged by the disclosure that the CIA and the Contras had dropped antiship mines in Nicaraguan harbors—cut off all CIA funding for the Contras.

Despite the CIA's efforts to keep Contra involvement in the so-called Frogman case from becoming public, some of the truth got out when Carlos Cabezas took the witness stand in late 1984 against his ex-brother-in-law. Under oath, and as a U.S. government witness, Cabezas admitted that some of the cocaine money was going to the Contras. He told the jury of his meetings with Horacio Pereira, and of Pereira's nervousness over the Contras' profits being misspent by the hard-drinking Zavala. Pages from the ledger books in which Cabezas kept track of the Contras' cocaine were introduced into evidence and made public, showing cocaine transactions with Contra official Fernando Sánchez.

Zavala was convicted of trafficking and sentenced to prison. Cabezas's testimony went unchallenged. It also went unreported. Though the San Francisco news media had fairly swooned when Cabezas and Zavala were arrested, not a single reporter stuck around to cover the trial. The evidence of Contra involvement in cocaine trafficking in San Francisco would lie undisturbed in a federal court file for another two years.

6

"They were doing their patriotic duty"

Unlike Carlos Cabezas, who walked into an existing cocaine sales operation and began dealing dope the next day, Danilo Blandón was forced to make his own way, finding his own buyers in a city he really didn't know. If he had been in San Francisco, it would have been a different story. Meneses's drug network there was well established and, according to Blandón, flourishing. After distributing 900 kilos—nearly one ton—in 1981, Blandón said, Meneses's business in San Francisco "got bigger and bigger, because all the family was working at that time with him, in the drug business."

By contrast, Meneses's network in Los Angeles was of more recent origin and had been dealt a serious blow in late 1981 with the arrest and subsequent flight of his West Covina dealer, Julio Bermúdez, who had been moving about twenty kilos a month before he was arrested.

While Blandón struggled to establish a customer base, he made himself useful to the Meneses organization in other ways. He became "like a secretary for Mr. Meneses, because he already saw that I could do a lot for him. He started telling me, 'Go out and collect some money to somebody else in L.A.' and I started doing it, and he started getting trust, trusting in me."

Blandón said he would not only pick up money from customers in L.A. but deliver it as well, taking cash from Meneses to pay his cocaine suppliers in Los Angeles, men

Blandón described as Colombians. He also began keeping the books for the L.A. drug operation, describing himself as Meneses's "administrator."

"I wasn't working with him in San Francisco. He was working alone," Blandón said. "I keeping the books from L.A."

"You were keeping his books in L.A.?" Blandón was asked.

"Yes."

"So he was up in San Francisco, and you're down here in L.A.?"

"Yes."

"So you were running his Los Angeles operation, isn't that correct?"

"Yes," Blandón said. "But remember, we were running just a—whatever we were running in L.A. goes—the profit is—was going to the Contra revolution. I don't know from San Francisco."

The relationship between Blandón and Meneses quickly transcended the cocaine business. Meneses opened up a restaurant on Hoover Street in East Los Angeles, which Blandón helped oversee, called the Chicalina. Blandón described the establishment somewhat curiously to a federal grand jury, calling it a "marketing" operation. "That was not my restaurant. That was Meneses's restaurant," he said, but he admitted that he'd told others he was one of the owners.

Another of Blandón's jobs involved looking after the welfare of Meneses's wife and children. Meneses had sent them from San Francisco to L.A. after he started yet another affair. In 1982, Blandón said, Meneses "was in love" with a woman in South San Francisco named Blanca Margarita Castaño, a Nicaraguan who would later become his fifth wife.

Blanca was a cousin of a top Sandinista official, Bayardo Arce Castaño, one of the Nicaraguan government's nine commandantes and one of the most hard-line radicals among them. Blanca's apartment near the Cow Palace, an old auditorium made famous by Jefferson Airplane, was used to store cocaine. "I went one time to pick it up right there," Blandón said.

A frequent houseguest of Meneses during this period was John Lacome, a San Franciscan who was friendly with Norwin's nephews, Jaime and Jairo. Lacome said he lived at Meneses's home for long periods during the early 1980s, and told of cocaine-fueled parties that went on for days. Meneses appeared totally unafraid of being arrested; "There was a woman he was selling to, and this woman would drive by his house, honk, and he'd come walking out to the street with two kilos in his hands, in broad daylight, and give them to her," Lacome said.

Meneses was fond of expensive leisure suits, wore a fairly obvious toupee, and took pains to surround himself with women, as did his nephews. A former girlfriend of Jaime Meneses, Gloria Lopez, said the nephews all drove flashy new cars, which they would trade in as soon as they tired of them. That was how she first noticed Jaime, she said. She was tending bar in the Mission District, and he would drive up in a different new car every couple weeks.

Lopez, who later had a child with Jaime Meneses, said Jaime started off driving trucks for his uncle Norwin right out of high school. Initially the loads were military uniforms; then he graduated to moving a more lucrative product—and started earning a substantially bigger paycheck.

"You give a kid like that out of high school all that money, and what do you think is going to happen?" Lopez asked. "I can't say that I blame Jaime for what he did. Then. I blame him for a lot of things that happened later though."

Jaime's father, Jaime Sr., was also pressed into service for the cause, hauling money to Central America for brother Norwin. "Jaime Sr., I respected him very much," Rafael Corñejo said. "He really wasn't too much involved with drugs. He had a brake factory in Nicaragua before the revolution, called FRICA. He was a very decent man. During, I can't remember which year, he was incarcerated in the U.S., 1984–85.... He'd been stopped at the border with $70,000 or something. He was taking the money down to Nicaragua. Once I told him, 'Look, Jaime, let me do that for you.' But he said, no, he could do just fine." Jaime Meneses Sr. was murdered in 1990 in the offices of his money-changing business—FRECERSA—in San José, Costa Rica.

Such were the hazards of being a Meneses. So it was not surprising that when Maritza Meneses and her children arrived in L.A. in 1982, someone would be assigned to watch over them and help them along. Norwin gave Danilo the job.

In August 1982 Blandón and Maritza Meneses set up a business together in Los Angeles, a company they named JDM Artwork Inc. The name was an acronym made up of the first initials of the incorporators' first names: Josefa Maria Pelligatti, a friend of the Meneseses; Danilo Blandón; and Maritza Meneses.

The company did silk screen printing, and Blandón said it was started by Meneses to provide an income for his relocated family. But there may have been other motives behind Meneses's investment in the silk-screening business. The company quickly became part of the Contras' support network in Los Angeles. ARDE commander Edén Pastora said he visited the firm during a trip he made to L.A. in 1982, and it printed up T-shirts with his likeness on them. Former Pastora aide Carol Prado claimed that a Los Angeles printing company connected to Blandón was used to launder money from drug sales for the Contras.

Another former associate of Blandón, a Puerto Rican man convicted of counterfeiting U.S. currency, believed that the company also dabbled in funny money, printing up fake twenty-dollar bills that provided operating cash for the FDN. The former associate produced Polaroid photographs that showed him at work in an office with FDN banners and slogans on the wall, and a picture of Blandón in the same office, smiling, his arms thrown over the shoulders of other laughing Hispanic men. A blue-and-white FDN flag was clearly visible on the wall.

The associate's claims of counterfeiting could not be independently corroborated, but according to CIA cables filed in federal court, the CIA had information by 1984 that Norwin Meneses was involved in counterfeiting—both American dollars and Costa Rican *colones*. In a 1986 interview, Meneses said he allowed FDN members to use his wife's Los Angeles T-shirt factory as a meeting place.

As the Contra support organizations in San Francisco and L.A. grew more active, Meneses's role with the FDN became much more public. Former FDN director Edgar Chamorro told the *San Francisco Examiner* in 1986 that he and FDN director Frank Arana flew to San Francisco in October 1982 to select local leaders for the FDN's support committee there. Meneses attended the organizational meeting, standing quietly in the back of the auto body shop where the meeting was held. Meneses "appeared like a fund-raiser, an organizer," Chamorro told the paper. The next day, Chamorro said, Meneses helped set up a similar meeting in Los Angeles, providing refreshments beforehand and throwing a party afterward.

"He was one of the main contacts in L.A.," Chamorro told *Examiner* reporter Seth Rosenfeld. "He was in charge of the organization of the L.A. meeting, the reception. He drove us to the place. He gave us the schedule for that day. He knew people, he was recommending names" (for leadership positions in the L.A. organization).

According to a recently declassified CIA cable, Meneses was known to other Nicaraguan expatriates as the man to see if one wanted to be a Contra.

The CIA reported that one Nicaraguan was looking around in south Florida in October 1982, "hoping to contact a friend named Norbin [sic] Meneses in Miami, who would direct him to counter-revolutionary training camps in South Florida and eventually to join Miskito combat units in Honduras." The censored cable said Meneses was not in Florida; he was living in California.

In a recent interview with the CIA, Meneses said that "between 1983 and 1984, his primary role with the California sympathizers was to help recruit personnel for the movement. Meneses says he was asked by Bermúdez to attempt to recruit Nicaraguans in exile and others who were supporters of the Contra movement." The drug lord told the agency's internal investigators that "he was not directed to recruit people with any specific skills, such as pilots or doctors, but was simply told to seek out anyone who wanted to join with the FDN. Meneses states that he was a member of an FDN fund-raising committee, but was not the committee's head." He did not raise much cash but was "involved in 1985 in attempting to obtain material support, medical and general supplies" for the Contras.

When asked in 1995 where he got the money to pay for these war materials, Meneses gave a slight smile. "There was money available for these purchases," he said.

Meneses associate Rafael Corñejo said he attended some of the parties Meneses hosted for the FDN at his homes in the San Francisco area.

"You can say what you want about that man, but his heart and soul was into the movement, and that was his priority more than anything else," said Corñejo, whose father had been a sergeant in Somoza's National Guard. "It's kind of hard to be kicked out of your own country and that's what his passion was. He was straight-up pro-Somocista."

Blandón complained that Meneses was so tightfisted with the cash he was raising for the Contras that he was making little or no money selling cocaine. "I didn't make any money, you know. It was only for the people in the mountains, you know, for the Contra Revolution," Blandón said. Meneses allowed him to keep enough "just to pay the rent and to pay the food for my daughter... just to pay my expenses." Among the Nicaraguan exile community, it was strongly suspected that Meneses was dealing cocaine for the Contras. And it was not unadmired. Somoza's former secretary, Juan C. Wong, one of the first Nicaraguan exiles to begin recruiting ex-*Guardia* men to join the Contras, said he visited Meneses in San Francisco in 1983. "It's true, it was widely spread around that he was involved with drugs," said Wong, a University of San Francisco grad who knew the Meneses family from before the revolution. "And I don't doubt that they wanted to raise money for the FDN. That's only natural. They were doing their patriotic duty."

Bradley Brunon, Blandón's lawyer, said Blandón was on[e]
former Somoza supporters dealing cocaine in L.A. in the earl[y]
met Blandón while defending a middle-class Nicaraguan exile accused of drug trafficking. "People were being arrested who had high government connections, or high military connections, in the Somoza regime, who didn't have any particular lifestyle consistent with being cocaine dealers, didn't have a background consistent with that, but they were highly politicized individuals," Brunon said. "And the only politics I was aware that they were involved with was this attempt to fund the Contra revolutionary insurgency."

Brunon said it was his understanding that "the Contras, and I don't even know if they were known as that then...had no above-the-line funding. Everything was sub rosa and one of the ways they were trying to raise money was importing cocaine. That was information that I didn't specifically receive from Blandón, but that I had surmised based on a series of events that were happening."

Blandón was fairly close-mouthed about his role with the Contras, according to Brunon. "I don't know the formal particulars of it other than there was this kind of atmosphere of CIA and clandestine activities and so forth that surrounded him when I met him," Brunon said of his longtime client. "He never was specific. I mean, I believed he was involved with the Contras. I don't think there's any doubt about that. Beyond that, I never got into the particulars with him, because I didn't have a need to know at that point."

An air of mystery also surrounded another associate of Blandón, an odd, cherubic, balding man in his mid-thirties Blandón picked up as a partner shortly after going to work for Meneses. The man would remain at Blandón's side for seven years, though mostly in the shadows. Considering his work history and the activities he was involved with at the time, his appearance in the Nicaraguan's cocaine trafficking entourage is both strange and worrisome. He would give Blandón's drug ring a whole new sideline—weapons and sophisticated electronics equipment—and a whole new smell, the unmistakable aroma of the U.S. intelligence community.

Brad Brunon met him in 1986, when he showed up unannounced at the lawyer's office and began asking very detailed questions about Blandón's background. "It was just like the hair on the back of your neck goes up. What does this guy want? What's he doing here? Is he investigating Blandón?" Brunon said. "I never knew what his true role was. I mean, he covertly insinuated that he was CIA. At least, if not a sworn member, whatever the hell they do to get to become employees—some sort of operative." Brunon "really didn't have much communication with the guy because he scared me."

His name was Ronald Jay Lister, a southern California native who began working as a cocaine dealer and money hauler for Blandón in late 1981 or early 1982, just as the CIA was taking over the funding and operations of the newly formed FDN. The CIA has publicly denied any relationship with the man.

Before launching his life of crime as Danilo Blandón's faithful sidekick, Ronald Lister had been a police officer of one sort or another for nearly fifteen years. He'd started out as a military policeman for the U.S. Army and U.S. Army Reserve, stationed in Orange County with the 414th Military Police company. His service records show he had a degree in political science and was trained in processing prisoners of war captured during the Vietnam conflict. He regularly received excellent fitness reports. While an army reservist, Lister hired on as an officer with the police department of Maywood, a small suburb of Los Angeles that once employed a handful of uniformed patrolmen. He was also a reserve deputy for the L.A. County Sheriff's Office at the same time.

Lister was called to active duty in the army for a few months in 1969, and later, when his enlistment ended, he volunteered for the U.S. Coast Guard, serving as a reserve port security officer at Terminal Island, in San Pedro, California. In late 1973 he found a home with the Laguna Beach Police Department, which patrols a posh Orange County suburb south of Los Angeles. There, among the rich and famous, he rose through the ranks to become a detective in the burglary division.

Lieutenant Danielle Adams said Lister was a veteran by the time she arrived in burglary; her recollection of him was that he was "always very successful, very tenacious and got the job done."

His former chief, Neil Purcell, who was on the hiring board that gave Lister his job, remembers him differently. "You hear lots of things about Ron Lister," Purcell said. "The man, in my opinion, is a lying, conniving, manipulative person who likes to play with people's minds. He's very evasive and loves living on the edge. He's the biggest bullshitter that has ever been placed on this earth."

Toward the end of Lister's twelve-year stint with the police department, he was traveling in some pretty fast company. "When he worked here, that silly son of a gun was in with—what do they call themselves?—the Royal Highnesses from Iran!" Purcell recalled with a hoot. "Sporting Rolex watches for himself and his wife. Getting wined and dined by these people until finally they [the Iranians] were asked to leave this country. Anything. He threw out names and organizations. He's a very bright guy. As far as intelligence, he's very, very smart." It was the one point upon which Adams and Purcell agreed.

"Don't ever underestimate him," Adams warned. "He's very, very bright and very tenacious."

Both Adams and Purcell said Lister became involved in private security work on the side toward the end of 1979. He quit the Laguna Beach police department in May 1980 to pursue that vocation full-time. "He was in the alarm business, is what he originally started off as," Adams recalled. "And he had some muckety-mucks from the Arab countries, so he says, in his alarm business and this was getting pretty elaborate, and that's when he left the police department. I know there was a lot of involvement and a lot of travel while he was still here."

A few weeks before he resigned, corporate records show, Lister incorporated a company called Pyramid International Security Consultants Inc., based in Newport Beach. What Pyramid was doing between 1980 and 1981 is not known, but Lister stated that this was around the time he first met Blandón, "through a Beverly Hills business connection." He said Blandón introduced him to Norwin Meneses, and that he "provided physical security for both men," who "always paid him in cash."

Soon after Lister paired up with Blandón and Meneses, his security company began doing business overseas. According to an attorney who worked for Lister at the time, Lister "began working in Central America as security. I'm not sure what kind. My impression was that he was working for a private company that provided security services in Central America. During the 1980s, particularly during the Reagan administration, there were...companies that would provide services to the U.S. government. My understanding is that Ron was working for one of these companies that provided security. He could have been doing anything."

Blandón's attorney, Brad Brunon, described Lister as "one of these guys who would boast about having bugging capabilities, would boast about having wiretap capabilities, you could get any information any time, one of those...I-can-uplink-to-the-satellite sort of guy."

Christopher W. Moore, a former reserve Laguna Beach police officer who met Lister in 1979, said Lister hired him as an office manager in 1982 while Moore was working his way through law school. "I think I was actually an officer in Pyramid International. Ron put my name down as treasurer or director or something because he needed to have some directors for the incorporation papers." Moore confirmed that Lister had extensive business dealings in Central America, specifically in El Salvador. Lister explained his travels there to Moore as involving gun running and "helping the Contras, supposedly on behalf of the [U.S.] government. I remember the longest conversations with him—'I'm protected. You're working for the government. Don't worry about anything. I'm protected, I'm protected.' I don't know if that was true or not, but I do know that we stopped worrying about domestic security jobs and started concentrating on foreign ones."

During the early 1980s, when Lister began doing business there, El Salvador was wracked by a vicious civil war and murderous political repression. A tenacious revolutionary guerrilla group, the FMLN, had been running circles around the country's corrupt and inefficient military. The rebels' fight was being assisted by the Sandinistas in Nicaragua, who have admitted supplying them with tons of Eastern Bloc arms and ammunition.

The Reagan administration was far more concerned about what was happening in El Salvador than they were about Nicaragua, which Reagan's advisers considered already "lost" to the Communists. One of Reagan's top foreign policy objectives in 1981 and 1982 was to keep what had happened in Nicaragua from spreading to El Salvador, and the administration pushed hard for increased military and economic support for the beleaguered Salvadoran government, particularly after a January 1982 rebel attack on the main military airport in El Salvador demolished dozens of aircraft.

"Indeed, what came to be known years later as the 'Reagan Doctrine' may have been born in El Salvador in 1982," former Reagan State Department official Robert Kagan wrote in 1996. Halting Sandinista arms shipments to El Salvador was the official reason CIA director William Casey gave to Congress when he informed lawmakers of Reagan's decision in late 1981 to turn the CIA loose in Nicaragua. The Contras were being trained to police the borders to make sure no Sandinista arms got out to the FMLN, Casey claimed.

Like many of the things the CIA said about the Contras, that explanation was a lie, a smoke screen to hide the agency's true agenda, which was to run a full-scale covert war against the Sandinistas. The Reagan administration found its Salvadoran aid program a tough sell in Congress because of the horrendous human rights abuses then occurring in the country. Frustrated by its inability to crush the FMLN guerrillas in the field despite an overwhelming firepower advantage, elements of the Salvadoran government were striking back at the rebels by murdering thousands of their supporters with death squads—right-wing, quasi-military posses that would snatch suspected rebel sympathizers off the streets and leave their mutilated bodies on the outskirts of town a few days later. At the height of this campaign, residents of the capital city of San Salvador would wake up to find forty new bodies every morning.

The Salvadoran government officially denied any connection with the death squads, but the denials rang hollow in Washington, even among Reagan's stalwarts. "Under the guise of anti-Communism, the death squads terrorized the entire country—murdering nuns, teachers, labor organizers, political opponents and thousands of other civilians," Lieutenant Colonel Oliver North wrote in his 1991 memoirs, *Under Fire*.

North wrote that it was clear most of the death squad activity was the responsibility of the ultraright ARENA party and its leader, former Salvadoran army major Roberto D'Aubuisson. D'Aubuisson was reportedly running one of the death squads linked to the assassination of San Salvador's Archbishop Oscar Romero—allegedly by hit men from the FDN's predecessor, the Legion of September 15.

The official whose men were committing some of the worst abuses was a $90,000-a-year CIA asset, Colonel Nicholas Carranza, head of the government's feared Treasury Police. According to one account, CIA director Casey met personally with Carranza in the summer of 1983 and told him to "knock it off," or the CIA would kick him off the payroll.

In phone conversations with Lister, Christopher Moore learned that his boss was "supposedly doing security consulting for the government of El Salvador." In June of 1982 Lister asked Moore to fly down and "babysit" a government contract for a few days while Lister returned to the United States to take care of some unspecified business.

Moore agreed, and was off on what he would call the strangest trip of his life.

Accompanying him on the eleven-day excursion, Moore said, was a man who introduced himself as the Salvadoran consul in Los Angeles. Since Moore spoke little Spanish, the man served as Moore's guide and interpreter. "They flew me down to this airbase that the French were building, and I had to take pictures of it," Moore said; it was his impression that Pyramid was bidding on a contract to provide security for the base. When he returned to El Salvador's capital, San Salvador, he settled into the downtown Ramada Inn. Then he and the Salvadoran consul attended a series of meetings with none other than Major Roberto D'Aubuisson. "That was probably the highlight of my life at that point," chuckled Moore, now an attorney in Los Angeles. "There I was, a reserve police officer who'd only been in the country for a couple days, and I was sitting in this office in downtown San Salvador across the desk from the man who ran the death squads. He had a gun lying on the top of his desk and had these filing cabinets pushed up against the windows of the office so nobody could shoot through them."

At another meeting, Moore and D'Aubuisson were joined by Ray Prendes, the newly elected head of the Salvadoran Assembly and a powerful figure in the ruling Christian Democratic party. Prendes was on friendly terms with D'Aubuisson, Moore said, and both appeared to have some role in the award of the security contract Lister was seeking.

Lister, in an interview with police, "said that Moore was a good kid who had gone down to El Salvador to take pictures of poorly planned and constructed security work at a port on the southwest tip of El Salvador."

Moore was unsure if Lister's company ever got the security contract for the airbase, but he thought not. He left Lister's employ in 1983, soon after his boss began dealing in heavy weapons. "Ron was an arms dealer and was buying these semiautomatics, the ones the bad guys use, called MAC-10s. He also had semiautomatic Uzis, and he had gotten involved in selling something called RAW, which was a rifle-fired hand grenade. He was into a lot of things."

Former Laguna Beach police chief Purcell said Lister "also came up with a type of thing, it was being tested out somewhere out by Mammoth [ski resort]... a special sensor you could put in the ground, all this kind of shit, where anything that flew into the area, dropped down into the area, this and that, he had the schematics of it, this elaborate... whether or not he ever did that, I don't know."

Gary Shapiro, an Orange County attorney who did corporate legal work for Lister, "heard rumors of illegal arms trafficking. I don't know how true they were. I know Lister called me a couple of times from El Salvador, trying to work on the U.S. side of things down there... but to tell you the truth, I really didn't want to know too much."

But the owner of the Ramada Inn in downtown San Salvador, where Moore and Lister stayed while in the city, said he knew exactly what Lister was doing: selling guns to the Contras. In May 1987 the Ramada's owner, Frederico Cruz, walked into the FBI's office in Mobile, Alabama, and said he wanted the FBI to hunt down Lister for stiffing him. "Lister was in San Salvador in 1981 or 1982 and stayed two or three months," Cruz told the FBI in a once secret report released by the National Archives. "Cruz claimed that Lister was selling weapons to the Contras. Lister allegedly left El Salvador owing Cruz a large amount of money. Cruz requested that the interviewing agents assist him in collecting this money. This request was declined."

In October 1982 Lister's company, Pyramid International, made a security proposal to Salvadoran defense minister General Jose Guillermo Garcia, a man linked by one human rights organization to death squad activities and the slaughter of hundreds of peasants at a village called El Mozote in December 1981.

Pyramid's proposal, which L.A. police found in a 1986 drug raid, was written in Spanish and had "Confidential" stamped all over the front of it. It was entitled "Technical Proposal for an Urgent Project to Implement an Integral Security System for the Defence Ministry and the Major General of the Armed Forces of the Republic of El Salvador." The thick report described Pyramid as a unique consulting firm "dedicated to the maintenance of freedom, independence and free enterprise." The company only served clients "with a similar political orientation."

That political orientation was spelled out in no uncertain terms: Pyramid International Security Consultants would "assist the new government in its goal to combat the tyrannical forces of the left side, promoted and assisted by the current governments of Nicaragua, Cuba and the Soviet Union."

Lister's company outlined a variety of services it would provide for the sum of $189,911: bodyguard and armed escort services for Salvadoran public officials, including the president and top political and military leaders; protecting sensitive installations from sabotage and terrorism; and installing sophisticated electronic technology, including radio sensors and explosives detectors, at key military and industrial installations. Lister later explained the document as "a proposal to the current government in El Salvador to implement programs to assist them in different types of security operations, counter-measures type operations, dealing with the types of problems they had.... We did a whole study down there."

But one of Lister's associates at the time, a San Diego arms manufacturer, said Pyramid's security proposal was actually just a cover for another operation, a covert one directed by the CIA. The company's real mission in El Salvador, he said, was to set up a weapons manufacturing facility to supply guns to the Contras in neighboring Honduras. In a series of interviews with investigative reporter Nick Schou of the *L.A. Weekly* in 1996 and 1997, arms maker Timothy LaFrance described Pyramid International as "a private vendor that the CIA used to do things [the agency] couldn't do." LaFrance, whose handiwork is so highly regarded that he has created custom-made weapons for *Rambo* films and episodes of *Miami Vice*, said he accompanied Lister to El Salvador at least twice, becoming involved as a weapons specialist and helping to set up facilities to make pistols for the Contras.

Among the series of nameless biographies attached to Pyramid's proposal to the Salvadoran government, one employee is identified a "specialist in the design and manufacture of unique weapons." Lister's former office manager, Chris Moore, confirmed that "one of his [Lister's] friends, and I can't recall the name, was an arms maker in San Diego. He had a custom gun shop down there."

LaFrance, who makes and modifies exotic automatic weapons for the military and law enforcement agencies in his San Diego manufacturing facility, was convinced Lister's consulting company had friends in high places. When he applied in Pyramid's name for a State Department permit to take high-powered weapons out of the United States, for example, LaFrance said, "It came back approved in two days. Usually it takes three months. We went down to Central America with two giant boxes full of machine guns and ammunition."

LaFrance told Schou that their cover story for the trip was that they were there "to provide security, armor-proofing for vehicles, limos and homes. My end was the weapons [and] how to make a three-car stop if you're shot at." But the real purpose, LaFrance said, was to "set up an operation in El Salvador that would allow us to get around U.S. laws and supply the Contras with guns. It's much easier to build the weapons down there and that's eventually what we did." Pyramid's security proposal discusses the company's unique ability "to design and manufacture special equipment—at the point—and in any part of the world, in the majority of cases saving their foreign clients important sums in currency."

According to LaFrance, the Pyramid team moved into a mass-transit center run by the military in downtown San Salvador. "That's where we made the weapons. You could have 50 guys working in a machine shop and nobody would know it," he said. After the finished guns were transported to a Salvadoran military airstrip in Morazon province, they were airlifted to Contra camps in Honduras. "We made almost all of our drops by helicopter, buzzing the treetops," LaFrance said.

While LaFrance's story is by its nature difficult to corroborate, some independent documentation suggests he was definitely the man to see in the early 1980s if one needed to build a weapons plant. In May 1983 LaFrance was solicited by the tiny Cabazon Indian tribe in southern

California to build an arms factory on their desolate, tumbleweed-strewn Riverside County reservation. "We need the know-how from an organization engaged in the manufacturing of armaments of various types, all consisting of technology not currently found on the marketplace," the Cabazons' letter to LaFrance Specialties stated. Another letter spelled out precisely what the Cabazons were looking to build: "A 9-mm machine pistol, an assault rifle with laser sighting, a long-distance sniper rifle, a portable rocket system, a night-vision scope, and a battlefield communications system 'that cannot be detected by current technology.'"

According to the *San Francisco Chronicle*, the Cabazons were working on "a series of international military and security projects that seem to be lifted from the pages of a spy novel." The tribal administrator was a man who claimed to have long experience working for the CIA, helping out on the agency's Chilean destabilization program in the 1970s. He had paired the tribe up with Wackenhut International Inc., a security firm the *Chronicle* described as being "led by former officials of the CIA, the FBI, National Security Agency, Defense Department and federal law enforcement."

Wackenhut was very active in El Salvador during the Contra war, providing employees to protect the U.S. embassy and other installations, and doing "things you wouldn't want your mother to know about," one Wackenhut employee told *Spy* magazine in 1992. Apparently the firm was using the Cabazon reservation's tax-exempt status and its freedom from federal oversight to gain a competitive advantage in soliciting federal weapons projects.

Freelance investigative reporter Danny Casolaro was looking into the Cabazon/Wackenhut projects as part of a larger conspiracy investigation at the time he was found dead in a West Virginia motel room in 1991, allegedly a suicide victim. He had told friends he was convinced that "spies, arms merchants and others were using the reservation as a low-profile site on which to develop weapons for Third World armies, including the Nicaraguan Contras." The *Chronicle* stated that Contra leader Edén Pastora had visited a firing range near the reservation for a weapons demonstration in 1981, a claim Pastora has both confirmed and denied on separate occasions.

In early 1994 the U.S. Justice Department announced that it was opening "a nationwide investigation" into Casolaro's suspicious death—a probe ordered by then–associate attorney general Webb Hubbell. Not long afterward Hubbell pleaded guilty to crimes he'd committed while

…wyer and resigned from the Justice Department. What … from the Casolaro investigation, or even whether it ever went …rward, has not been made public.

Hubbell's interest in the journalist's death may have been more than passing curiousity. Hubbell had his own connections to a company that was making weapons parts for the Contras.

Tim LaFrance's story about setting up an arms factory with Ronald Lister in El Salvador bears striking similarities to one told by Terry Reed, a former air force intelligence officer and FBI informant who became involved with the CIA's Contra project in the mid-1980s. Reed, a pilot and machine tool expert, said he was initially recruited to train would-be Contra pilots at a clandestine airstrip near Nella, Arkansas. Later, he claims, he was asked to help the CIA set up secret weapons parts facilities in Arkansas and, later, in Mexico.

In his memoirs, *Compromised,* Reed wrote that he scouted locations and provided the corporate shell for CIA agents working with the Contras to set up and run a sophisticated machine-tool shop in Mexico in 1985–86, in order to keep a supply of untraceable weapons parts flowing to the Contras during a time when Congress had cut off the rebels' CIA assistance. He claims CIA operatives were shipping cocaine through the machine-tool company he'd helped the agency set up in Guadalajara, Mexico. One of the companies Reed worked with in Arkansas was a small manufacturer of parking meters called Park On Meter Inc., located in the town of Russellville. Reed claimed that the company was secretly manufacturing parts for M-16 rifles as a subcontractor on a CIA weapons project to supply the Contras.

The *Washington Post* sent a reporter to Arkansas in 1994 to "investigate" Reed's story. While the resultant article was a snide and ham-handed attempt to portray Reed as a crackpot conspiracy theorist, it nonetheless confirmed many of the basic elements of his story. "Some of the key relationships described in the book did exist in some form," the *Post* grudgingly admitted. "The Iver Johnson arms company near Little Rock, which the book portrays as being at the center of the gun-manufacturing effort, did ship a load of weapons to Nicaragua through a Mexican distributor, according to former plant engineer J. A. Matejko. But Matejko, described in the book as part of the CIA plan, says the rifles were M-1s, not M-16s." Moreover, the *Post* found, the parking meter company Reed named "did make some gun parts for Iver Johnson, another relationship characterized in the book as part of the CIA weapons scheme." But, the *Post* scoffed, the parts were "firing pins, not M-16 bolts as the book contends."

Park On Meter's former secretary and corporate lawyer was Webb Hubbell, who also happens to be the brother-in-law of the company's owner. Hubbell admitted to a *Time* magazine reporter that POM was also making rocket launchers.

Another similarity between the weapons operations described by Reed and LaFrance is that they both involved admitted drug traffickers who appeared to be working for the U.S. government. A central figure in all of Reed's dealings with the CIA, he wrote, was a CIA and DEA contract agent named Adler Berriman Seal. A former airline pilot, Seal moved in 1982 from Baton Rouge to a tiny airfield in isolated Mena, Arkansas, Intermountain Regional Airport, and began running drugs and weapons.

In the early 1980s, Barry Seal was one of the biggest cocaine and marijuana importers in the southern United States, flying loads in directly for the Medellín cartel and air-dropping them with pinpoint precision across Louisiana, Arkansas, and other southern states.

"Seal detailed his cocaine-smuggling activities in '81, '82 and '83. What he testified to was that he was involved in 50 trips during those three years," IRS spokesman Henry Holms told the *Baton Rouge State Times* in 1986, explaining a $29 million lien that the IRS filed against Seal for back taxes. A letter that year from Louisiana's attorney general to U.S. Attorney General Ed Meese said Seal "smuggled between $3 billion and $5 billion worth of drugs into the U.S."

Seal's farm in Baton Rouge, according to a 1983 U.S. Customs report, was allegedly used as a drop site for cocaine and marijuana flown into the country aboard a DC-4 aircraft, N90201. That same plane subsequently turned up flying supplies for the Contras in 1985 through an air cargo company the FDN hired called Hondu Carib Cargo Inc. The operator of Hondu Carib, records show, was FDN leader Adolfo Calero's brother, Mario Calero.

Hondu Carib's owner was pilot Frank Moss, identified in a 1989 Senate report as having "been investigated, although never indicted, for narcotics offenses by ten different law enforcement agencies." The report said Moss flew FDN supply missions for both Hondu Carib and a Honduran air freight company called SETCO, which was owned by Honduras's biggest drug trafficker, Juan Matta Ballesteros.

Another DC-4 Moss controlled was chased by Customs pilots off the coast of Florida on a suspected drug flight. When the plane was searched upon landing, the Senate report stated, the agents found an address book containing "the telephone numbers of some Contra officials and the

Virginia telephone number of Robert Owen, Oliver North's courier." (In 1985, records show, Owen reported to Oliver North that a DC-6 owned by Mario Calero "which is being used for runs out of New Orleans is probably being used for drug runs into U.S.")

During the time he was dealing with Terry Reed, Seal was also working for the DEA as a top-level informant; in 1984 he participated in a joint CIA-DEA sting operation in an attempt to snare Sandinista government officials in drug smuggling. Congressional records show North was being regularly briefed by the CIA on Seal's sting operation, was supplied with some of the evidence it produced, and allegedly leaked the information to the press shortly before a critical vote on Contra aid was coming up in Congress. North maintains that his only involvement in the Seal sting against the Sandinistas was as an observer, but a statement he gave to the FBI in June 1986 suggests that his relationship with the trafficker was considerably more complex than that.

On February 17, 1986, Seal was murdered in New Orleans by Colombian hit men. Four months later, in June, North called the FBI and claimed that there was an "active measures program" being directed against him by the Sandinistas. People were following him, he fretted, directing death threats and smears against him. "North expressed further concern that he may be targeted for elimination by organized crime due to his alleged involvement in drug running," a Washington-based FBI agent wrote. North pointed to "the murder on Feb. 17, 1986 of a DEA agent, Steele [sic], on the date prior to Steele's testifying against the Sandinistas for drug involvement."

Seal's "personal records showed him to be a contract CIA operative both before and during his years of drug-running in Mena in the 1980s," historian Roger Morris, a former NSC staffer, wrote in a 1996 book, *Partners in Power*, about Bill and Hillary Clinton.

The same Senate subcommittee that looked into the Contras' connections with Hondu Carib in 1988 also poked around at Mena and concluded that "associates of Seal who operated aircraft service businesses at the Mena, Arkansas, airport were also the targets of grand jury probes into narcotics trafficking. Despite the availability of evidence sufficient for an indictment on money laundering charges, and over the strong protests of State and federal law enforcement officials, the cases were dropped. The apparent reason was that the prosecution might have revealed national security information."

Clinton's critics have charged that it was impossible for the governor of Arkansas to have been unaware of Seal's activities at Mena. Indeed,

Reed and former Arkansas state troopers L. D. Brown and Larry Patterson, both of whom have been critical of Clinton, insist he knew quite a bit about it—including the fact that cocaine was involved. Patterson, a member of Governor Clinton's security detail, testified that he and other troopers were aware "that there was large quantities of drugs being flown into the Mena airport, large quantities of money, large quantities of guns, that there was an ongoing operation training foreign people in that area. That it was a CIA operation."

A mechanic at Mena airport, John Bender, swore in a deposition that he saw Clinton there three times in 1985. Ex-trooper Brown said that when he confronted Clinton about the cocaine flights Seal was involved in, Governor Clinton replied, "That's Lasater's deal," referring to his close friend and campaign contributor, Little Rock bond broker Danny Ray Lasater. In 1986 Lasater was indicted by a federal grand jury in Little Rock on drug charges, and Clinton's brother Roger, a cocaine addict, was named as an unindicted coconspirator. Lasater pleaded guilty to drug trafficking; he received a thirty-month prison sentence but served only six months in prison. Clinton pardoned him in 1990.

Clinton's supporters have maintained that Lasater was no drug dealer, simply a high-flying businessman who got a little too caught up in the fast life. But that's not the way the FBI described it in a 1988 report citing the bureau's successful battles against major drug trafficking organizations. According to the FBI's description of its investigation, Lasater was part of a huge drug ring. "In December 1986, the Little Rock, Arkansas office of the FBI concluded a four-year Organized Crime Drug Enforcement Task Force investigation involving the cocaine trafficking activities of a prominent Little Rock businessman who operated several banking investment firms and brokerages in Arkansas and Florida," the FBI report stated. "The investigation revealed that this businessman was the main supplier of cocaine to the investment banking and bond community in the Little Rock area, which has the largest bond community in the United States outside of New York City. This task force investigation resulted in the conviction of this businessman and 24 codefendants to jail sentences ranging from four months to 10 years, as well as the seizure of cocaine, marijuana, an automobile, an airplane and $77,000."

Typically, investigations conducted by federal Organized Crime Drug Enforcement Task Force (OCDETF) units target top-level criminal organizations, not businessmen who take a few toots every now and then. Researchers familiar with the Lasater investigation say that the FBI's description of its Little Rock investigation goes far beyond anything that has ever been publicly released about the Lasater probe.

Roger Morris's book, in fact, describes an investigation that was shut down prematurely and ended only with Lasater's arrest, not that of twenty-four others. But Morris also suggested that there was much more to the case than met the eye: "Whatever the limits or extent of Lasater's cocaine trafficking or the nature of his other dealings, most believed that beyond him the larger corruption in Little Rock and elsewhere pointed unmistakably to organized crime, not to mention the vast crimes of Mena—none of which would be pursued."

Morris wrote that "in sworn testimony, a former staff member of the Arkansas State Police Intelligence Unit would describe 'a shredding party' in which she was ordered to purge the state's Mena files of nearly a thousand documents, including those referring specifically to Iran-Contra conspirator Oliver North and Seal associate Terry Reed." Reed claims that North, who was the National Security Council official overseeing the Contra project at the time, was his CIA contact for both the pilot-training program and the machine-tool company front.

A Clinton spokesman called the reports of Clinton's alleged knowledge of the Mena operations "the darkest backwater of the right wing conspiracy industry." North, who certainly knew about Barry Seal, has denied knowing anything about Terry Reed or what was going on at Mena. But something was certainly happening at that little airport, and it was far from routine. While denying that the CIA was involved in any illegal activities at Mena during the time Seal's drug-smuggling operation was based there, the CIA's Inspector General's Office confirmed in 1996 that the CIA ran a "joint training operation with another federal agency at Mena Intermountain Airport." The IG report, which has never been publicly released, reportedly claims the exercise lasted only two weeks, but conveniently omits the year this occurred. The CIA also used the Mena airport for "routine aviation related services" on CIA-owned planes, according to a declassified summary of the report.

Coincidentally, it was Seal's drug-hauling airplane, a Fairchild C-123K called *The Fat Lady*, that a Sandinista soldier blew out of the skies over Nicaragua in 1986 with a SAM-7 missile, breaking open the Iran-Contra scandal. The plane had been based at Mena before Seal sold it and it began flying weapons-hauling missions for Oliver North and the FDN.

Morris wrote that Seal also worked for the Pentagon's spy service, the Defense Intelligence Agency (DIA), "where coded records reportedly showed him on the payroll beginning in 1982." Tim LaFrance told L.A.

journalist Nick Schou that the DIA was also involved in Ronald Lister's weapons manufacturing plant in El Salvador, and that the meetings Lister and his associates had with death squad commander D'Aubuisson "happened because the DIA wanted them to happen." Records found in Ronald Lister's house in the 1986 raid disclosed connections between Lister and "a DIA subcontractor."

Another man involved in Lister's Salvadoran weapons operation, LaFrance said, was Richard E. Wilker, a former Laguna Beach resident whom LaFrance described as an ex-CIA agent. Wilker appears as the "technical director" on Pyramid International's proposal of the security project to the Salvadoran government. The biography section of the proposal boasts that the company had "technicians with the Central Intelligence Agency in physical security for 20 years."

"I met Lister through Wilker," LaFrance said. "Wilker had heard about my stuff from the Agency. He said he had a friend who wanted to talk about a deal. I called to check and Langley said he [Wilker] was still working for the Agency. So I started doing business with Lister and Wilker." Lister was not officially a CIA employee, according to LaFrance; "He wasn't getting a paycheck from them. He may have said he did but his connection was...with Wilker. Very few people ever work directly for the Agency."

Former CIA officer John Vandewerker, who once employed Wilker as a salesman, said he knew Lister and Wilker were involved in some business activity in El Salvador. "It was kind of touchy...as far as getting out of the country and all that kind of stuff." He did not elaborate. (Coincidentally, Vandewerker's name was found in the notebooks of investigative reporter Danny Casolaro after his death, in connection with the goings-on at the Cabazon reservation.)

Pyramid was eventually tossed out of El Salvador at the urging of the U.S. Army, which took over the weapons plant that he and Pyramid had started, LaFrance said.

Lister dismisses any suggestion that he was "knowingly" working for the CIA. In an interview with police in 1996, he claimed "that if he were affiliated with an organization like the CIA, he wouldn't talk about it." He confirmed, the detectives wrote, that he had been a "security consultant and had dealings and offices down in El Salvador. Lister said he had a 'Munitions Control Permit' at that time and was involved in legal arms sales." The detectives noted that "Lister did display some knowledge of the U.S. intelligence community during our interview."

Danilo Blandón met Lister very early through the FDN's organization in Los Angeles and began an association with him that would last until the late 1980s. Lister and a partner named Bill Downing, Blandón said, "went to the meeting that we have in the Contra revolution, the meeting that we have every week and they, they offer us, they show us, you know, they show us a demonstration for the weapons, okay? They show the machine guns and the weapons. They have the, the license to sell them."

Lister never sold guns to the Contras, according to Blandón. That was true, but not entirely accurate, Norwin Meneses said during a 1996 interview: "We, in fact, did make arrangements to sell arms to the Contras, but the FDN couldn't collect sufficient funds in order to finalize the deal." Meneses, Blandón, and Lister then "traveled to Honduras, Guatemala and, El Salvador to make arrangements with local governments" for the *donation* of arms, Meneses said.

"Lister and Blandón then continued their mission in South America without me.... I know Danilo says that the weapons he got came through Ronnie Lister, but that isn't true. If I told you where we got them, governments would fall," Meneses said mysteriously. "I'm not going to do it while I'm in this place." He motioned to the walls of the Nicaraguan prison where he was interviewed and made a pistol with his thumb and forefinger, which he pointed at his head.

Meneses's own involvement in Contra gun running was confirmed in 1996 by the *New York Times*, which quoted an unnamed Clinton administration official as saying that Meneses had "contacts with the Contras in Honduras in 1982 or 1983 and 1984, and that he was believed then to have had some involvement in arms smuggling as well as money laundering and drugs." The *Times* also quoted two other unnamed government officials as saying, "Intelligence reports showed that Mr. Meneses was thought to have sent some weapons for the Contras on at least one occasion. But the size and nature of the shipment are unclear."

"There is a mention of weapons with him but not an indication whether it was a standard or large pipeline," the *Times* quoted "one official" as saying. The *Times* article provided no further details on this stunning revelation.

The *Los Angeles Times*, in a 1996 profile that portrayed Lister as a loudmouth who told tall tales, confirmed Meneses's statements that Lister was involved in weapons transactions with him. Quoting an unidentified "former business associate" of Lister, the paper wrote that Lister "led a sales team on a futile mission to civil war-racked [sic] El Salvador in the summer of 1982 to market surplus American arms, military equipment and used school buses to the Salvadoran military.... The trip was financed, the associate said, with an investment of at least $20,000 from Norwin Meneses."

The trip was a failure, according to the *Times*, because Lister tried to arrange the deal through an unnamed leader of an unnamed political party. Afterward Lister tried to get involved in the cocaine business with Meneses, but the drug kingpin allegedly turned him down, supposedly because Meneses regarded Lister as "a loose cannon." The story did not explain how or where Lister would have picked up enough "surplus" American arms to approach the Salvadoran military about making a weapons deal.

When defense attorneys tried in 1996 to quiz Blandón about Lister's alleged relationship with the CIA, a federal prosecutor immediately objected, and the jury was ordered out of the courtroom. During a whispered conversation with the judge, the prosecutor said that while it was true that "Lister made a claim...that he was an employee of the CIA," the government believed it was false, made only to "impress [his] illegal business partners," and was an attempt "to deter prosecution."

Nevertheless the prosecutor asked the judge to halt that line of inquiry because it was "muddying the waters." The judge decided that since Blandón had denied that Lister worked for the government, there was no need for any more questions like that. An internal CIA investigation in 1997 declared that Lister had no relationship with the agency.

Chris Moore, who regarded Lister's claims of CIA connections with some skepticism, said Lister told him he had a "big CIA contact" at an Orange County company.

"I can't remember his name, but Ron was always was running off to meetings with him supposedly," Moore said. "Ron said the guy was the former Deputy Director of Operations or something, real high up there. All I know is that this supposed contact of his was working at the Fluor Corporation [an international construction management company based in Orange County] because I had to call Ron out there a couple times." Years later, evidence would surface suggesting that Lister's claims of having a "big CIA contact" at Fluor were not as wild-eyed as Moore thought. And there is no doubt that Lister, in addition to all his security and weapons wheeling and dealing, was heavily involved with the booming Meneses-Blandón cocaine operation in 1982. In an interview with police in 1996, Lister admitted dealing cocaine with Blandón from 1982 to 1989, and hauling between $50 million and $60 million in cocaine profits to Miami for him.

Lister when he first met Blandón, "knew nothing about narcotics and could not tell you coke from flour. I had never seen the shit." But after Lister returned from his Central American travels, his former San Diego attorney said, he appeared to be an expert in the cocaine business. "When he came back, he seemed to know a lot about what was going on in Colombia with drug trafficking. I thought it was interesting because in the mid-1980s, no one knew very much about these cartels. But he knew quite a bit. And he knew names and dates, places, et cetera.

"I can remember one incident in particular. In the papers at the time all of a sudden there were these stories about the Medellín cartel, and Ron just snorted and said, 'What the hell is with the news media? There are all these stories about the Medellín cartel and nothing about the Cali cartel.' Ron said the Cali cartel is where all the power is concentrated, that's where the power structure is, and no one is even bothering them. They're getting ready to expand their market to Europe. They're buying cargo ships and airplanes.' Well, I'd never heard of the Cali cartel at that point. Subsequent events certainly proved him right."

The attorney surmised that Lister could have gained "this information from the CIA, or through his work with them. He knew some pretty damned good details and professed to being through the area. Now, I have traveled extensively through Central America, and the only thing I can tell you is, his information about the area was true. I know he'd been there." Lister told CIA inspectors that he had been to Colombia with Blandón and observed Blandón negotiating drug deals with the Colombians.

As 1982 drew to a close, Blandón's cocaine trafficking business in Los Angeles exploded. Almost overnight, it appears, he went from receiving little one- or two-kilo packages that could be tucked inside a lunch box to getting multimillion-dollar loads that wouldn't fit on a wheelbarrow. "I'd go over to D's [Blandón's] house, take my Mercedes over there, put three U-Haul boxes which will cover about 100 keys, about 33 per box plus one you'd squeeze in, in the trunk, go over to south L.A.," Lister told police. "It was the slickest deal you've ever seen."

There were two interrelated reasons for this huge expansion of Blandón's cocaine trafficking. One is that Dr. Raul Jeri's much-ridiculed "epidemic" of cocaine smoking had finally arrived in Los Angeles. And the other was a street-smart ghetto teenager who would come to be known as Freeway Rick.

7

"Something happened to Ivan"

The man who would be king of the L.A. crack market saw his first rock of cocaine around Christmastime in 1979 and didn't believe it was a drug. Ricky Donnell Ross knew what drugs looked like. He was nineteen. He'd seen drugs before. But this sure didn't look like cocaine to him. It was a little whitish chunk of something that could have been bird shit, for all he knew. And you were supposed to put it in a pipe and smoke it? Right.

Ross had seen people on TV using cocaine before, and they never smoked any shit that looked like this. When they used it, they cut it up on a mirror with a razor blade and tooted it up with a hundred-dollar bill.

"It was glamorous. It was, you know, you was in the 'in' crowd if you was into cocaine, if you was using. You know, whatever. It was in," Ross said. "It was what the movie stars were doing."

Ross's skepticism seems hard to believe now, with crack dealers more plentiful than policemen in urban communities. But in 1979 it was understandable. At that point, hardly anyone had seen rock cocaine. The friend who gave Rick what he called "a fifty-dollar rock" knew about smokable cocaine only because he was traveling in the fast lane. He was on the San Jose State University football team. He went to a lot of high-class parties. He knew what was happening.

"He's like, 'Man, I'm onto something new,'" Ross would later tell the *Los Angeles Times* in 1994. According to the

Times, "Ross ventured out and showed off his acquisition to an old pimp, who fired it right up and ordered $100 more."

The problem was, Ross didn't have any more. He didn't know how to make it or where to get it. And it's doubtful he could have found more even if he had the money, which he didn't.

If he'd searched hard enough in the right neighborhoods, maybe in Malibu or Hollywood, Ricky Ross might have been able to come up with something close—freebase cocaine. Freebase was becoming popular in the upper echelons of the drug underground in the late 1970s. It was not crack, however. Making freebase was more complicated and dangerous, requiring exotic and highly flammable solvents. It was also different in content.

Freebase resulted from mixing cocaine powder with ether. When the ether evaporated, it took the adulterants and cutting agents with it, leaving behind smokable crystals of pure cocaine base. For the process to work, however, it required a very high-quality cocaine; the cocaine powder that most people snorted wouldn't do because it was so heavily cut. Adding ether to a mishmash of mannitol, lidocaine, or milk sugar caused some "cocaine" to evaporate entirely.

Freebasing was what comedian Richard Pryor had been doing when he set himself on fire on June 9, 1980, and ran screaming from his bedroom in Northridge, outside L.A.—a ball of blazing polyester leaping across neatly kept lawns. "His polyester shirt had melted onto his arms and chest and he suffered third-degree burns from the waist up," *Time* magazine reported. "The Los Angeles police say Pryor told them that the accident occurred while he was 'free-basing' cocaine."

Pryor would later say freebasing was only tangentially related to his fearful scorching. The fire happened because he accidentally ignited some 151-proof rum while in a daze from a seventy-two-hour freebasing binge. If he'd been smoking freebase, in fact, he might never have burned himself at all; Pryor said he started drinking the rum because he'd run out of cocaine.

The distinction didn't matter much to the news media. The fact that Pryor—a major celebrity—had an accident while in the clutches of some weird, exotic new drug habit made it big news. "When Cocaine Can Kill," *Newsweek* trumpeted. "A dangerous drug craze" is how *People Weekly* put it. The *Los Angeles Times* discovered to its alarm that in the mostly black NBA, freebase use was spreading among pro basketball players.

As one cocaine expert wrote in 1982, the coverage of Pryor's accident was "reminiscent of the pre–Harrison Act yellow journalism [and] told the story of how cocaine was becoming the modern version of the Black cocaine menace of the early 1900s." The Harrison Act of 1914, which outlawed recreational cocaine use in the United States, resulted from a wild—and bogus—newspaper campaign mounted by southern sheriffs who linked coke-crazed black studs to the rapes of white women.

For a variety of reasons, including the bad press from Pryor's misfortune, freebasing was largely a passing fad, never really taking hold except among a few rich, hard-core drug users. "The relatively high cost and difficulty of producing cocaine free-base made it less accessible to most cocaine users," drug researcher Steven Belenko wrote in 1993. "An estimated 10% of cocaine users in the late 1970s also used free-base cocaine. But the need for large quantities of relatively pure cocaine and volatile chemicals to produce free-base limited its appeal to the broader group of cocaine users."

Unlike Richard Pryor's neighborhood, the neighborhood where Ricky Ross lived rarely saw cocaine in any form. As hard as the drug was to find in white, middle-class communities, it was ten times as scarce in South Central L.A., where the Ross family had lived since the early 1960s. People in the projects didn't have that kind of money, and if every once in a while they did, they sure as hell didn't go out and spend it all on white powder that barely got you high.

According to a Rand Institute study of street prices paid by DEA agents and informants, an ounce of cocaine powder in L.A. was selling for $4,844 in 1979. Other sources place it at roughly $2,500 an ounce, suggesting that DEA agents weren't the savviest shoppers around. In any event, a tiny bit cost about half the average annual income of a South Central resident. Little wonder that marijuana and angel dust—a dangerous chemical known in the projects as "Sherm" or "water"—were the drugs of choice where Ricky Ross lived. They were far less expensive. That was why Thomas C. "Tootie" Reese, the alleged king of cocaine in black L.A. at the time, lamented that he never sold as much coke as the cops and the press claimed.

"When you mentioned drugs, whether it was heroin or coke, you heard Tootie's name," said former LAPD narcotic detective Steven Polak. "He was the kingpin, especially in the fifties and sixties. Everybody was working Tootie Reese. Tootie Reese was probably one of the first blacks who really did big dope." But the man himself had a different story for the *L.A. Times*, which interviewed him a few months after his arrest in December 1983 for selling two kilos of cocaine to undercover officers.

"I ain't never been big," Tootie told the *Times*. Some evidence gathered during the investigation of Reese backed up his assertion that his cocaine-dealing prowess had been greatly overrated. During a taped conversation with undercover agents, Reese told them that "most of his customers purchase only five ounces or 10 ounces and that he had only five kilo-size customers." That admission was made at a time when a much bigger dealer in South Central—Danilo Blandón—was moving dozens of kilos a month through just one customer. Reese was mostly a heroin and marijuana dealer. By the early 1980s, when cocaine started seeping into the inner cities in noticeable amounts, Reese was a dinosaur.

"These new kids, once the eighties hit and these gangs hooked up with this dope, he was nothing anymore," ex-detective Polak said. "He was just an old grandpa who'd lost his teeth and wasn't worth anything anymore." A 1989 *L.A. Times Magazine* piece wrote him off in similar terms: "The amounts of cocaine he allegedly dealt were infinitesimal contrasted with the tonnage now sold monthly by his successors in the black community."

Reese's first major successor would be Ricky Ross, though that was not readily apparent in late 1979. Looking at him then, one would not have imagined the slender, slightly pop-eyed teenager to be a successor to anything but a hard row to hoe. A sometime thief, sometime student, he was clinging to a tattered dream of becoming a professional tennis player. Though too small for football or basketball, Ross had quick reflexes. When he was in middle school, about eleven or twelve, two family friends, Dr. Mal Bouquet and Richard Williams, encouraged him to take up tennis.

Ross's own father, Sonny, an oil tank cleaner by trade, had left home while Ross was still a small child in Tyler, Texas, in 1963. The rest of Ross's life would be spent in a sometimes tragic quest to find someone to replace him. Bouquet and Williams became Ross's first father figures. "They picked me up, took me to tennis tournaments. They took care of my racquets and tennis shoes, stuff like that," Ross said. "They fed me. You know, we'd leave a tournament, we'd go to McDonald's, something like that."

Ross said the tournaments and tennis practices kept him out of the 74 Hoover Crips, his neighborhood gang. He was friends with many of them, he said, but was never a gang member himself. Federal prison records appear to back up that claim. "There exists no information to substantiate your membership in the Los Angeles based 'Crips' street gang," stated a 1993 letter to Ross from the Federal Correctional

Institution in Phoenix. "All information in your file has been deleted which reflected gang participation or membership."

"He does not have the culture of a gang member when you talk to him," said *L.A. Times* reporter Jesse Katz, who spent months interviewing Ross in 1994 for a major series on the L.A. crack market. "He doesn't have the attitude and the—I mean, he was a capitalist."

It wasn't because Ross had anything against gangs necessarily. Most of the 74 Hoovers were homies he'd grown up with, gone to school with. He would put them to use in the future. But for now, he just didn't have time for gang-banging. "Once I started playing tennis, we'd start practicing as soon as school was out, so we'd get off the tennis court probably around 6:00 or 7:00 when it was time to go in the house."

It was hard to get away with anything there. His mother, Annie, a heavyset woman with bottle-thick glasses, a janitor in downtown office buildings, was strict. She was always checking up on him and his older brother David, snooping in their rooms to make sure they weren't getting into trouble. When she was at work, her younger sister Luetha Wilson watched the boys.

By the time Ross enrolled in Dorsey High School, his tennis skills were well honed. "I made All-League my first year. My second year, I made All-City second team and my senior year, I made All-City first team," Ross said. But he didn't fare as well in tournaments. "I'd win a few rounds. I never got ranked."

Still, Ross played well enough to retain a spot on the Dorsey High tennis team. Playing tennis for a major university was his immediate goal in life. There were about five players on his high school team that the coaches were grooming for college scholarships, and he was proud to consider himself one of them.

Ross had a bit of a problem, though. By his senior year at Dorsey, he still couldn't read or write. "My teachers just passed me, gave me C's and let me go through," Ross shrugged. It hardly seemed to matter, he said, because you didn't need it to play tennis. And in truth, it hadn't mattered. It hadn't kept him off the courts. It hadn't kept him behind in school. It only mattered when he started practicing with the Long Beach State University tennis team.

Ross had played in a tournament in Griffith Park, "and I had beat the number three or four guy from Long Beach State and a [Long Beach] coach asked me what school I was going to, when I was graduating from high school. Basically, he asked me, you know, what was I doing and how is my tennis going and stuff like that." The coach invited him over to the university for practice, and Ross worked out with the Long Beach State team a couple of times. "Then he found out about my grades and that I couldn't read or write," Ross said. To Ross's shock, that was the end of the university's interest. "I thought it basically would be the same as it had been all the time," Ross complained. "That they would just keep passing me through."

Disillusioned, he dropped out of Dorsey soon afterward, saying that it seemed pointless if he couldn't get into college. "I didn't graduate. I made it to the 12th grade and I was a few credits from being able to graduate." Ross said he was "kinda like in no man's land, almost, I would say.... My life was like at a standstill." On July 7, 1978, he was arrested by the LAPD for burglary and disorderly conduct. The charges would be dismissed—Ross said it was a case of mistaken identity—but the incident was an indication of the path he was on.

Ricky's other passion in life was automobiles, so he channeled his efforts in that direction. Since childhood, his mother said, "Ricky was taking things apart and putting them back together." Every summer she took the boys back to her brother's house in Overton, Texas, where Ricky and David would work on the brother's farm. Ricky began tooling around on tractors at an early age and developed driving skills quickly.

"When Ricky was about four years old he tried to drive my brother's car," Annie Ross said. "By the time he was eleven or twelve, he was driving by himself. You know, out in the country, where nobody minded. When he got older, he'd bring these cars home, work on them all the time, fix them up, and sell them. He always kept himself real busy."

In 1979, as Ross prepared to leave tennis behind, he prevailed upon someone he'd met through the sport, Mr. Fisher, a young auto upholstery teacher at the Venice Skills Center, to give him a shot at a new career. Fisher, a sometime tennis partner, got Ross into an open slot at the skills center.

"It's like a trade school where people that don't have nothing going can go and get them a trade, and they pay them," Ross said. "They pay them something really for going, you know, like help you with your expenses and stuff like that for going to the school." It was a nice favor, and Ross began attending auto repair classes. Then tennis came calling again.

Pete Brown, a coach at L.A. Trade Tech Junior College, asked Ross if he'd like to come to the technical school, learn a trade, and play tennis for him. Jubilantly, Ross quit the skills center and went running to Trade

Tech. He had made a college team after all. "He was a very good player," recalled Brown. "I'd say he was probably my number-three guy on the team at the time." Ross recalled that he "played number one and number two at different times of the season. You know, like sometimes one guy would beat me and sometimes I would beat him. So we would go back and forth."

By then Ross had drifted away from his two childhood tennis mentors, Bouquet and Williams. Ross was embarrassed by his failure to get a scholarship, and he sensed that Williams wasn't eager to have him around anymore, since it was clear he wasn't going to make a major university team.

Ross began spending more time with Mr. Fisher, the upholstery teacher, and the two played tennis together frequently. Ross soon adopted Fisher as a father figure. "Me and him, we would go play, you know, what we called hitting. I would hit with him, because they like to hit with people that's better than them, and in return he would buy me tennis shoes, racquets, help me get—like if I couldn't get a racquet strung, I could call him and say that, you know, 'I need my racquet strung' and he would pay for it."

Fisher, Ross said, "was considered an uppity black guy. He was single. He stayed in the Baldwin Hills area, which is a nicer part of Los Angeles. He had a brand-new Cadillac, you know, nice jewelry, school teacher." Ross said he would "go by his house from time to time" after getting off school at Trade Tech, where the illiterate Ross, ironically, was studying bookbinding.

As the two became closer, Fisher let his guard down. In 1981, shortly before he left Trade Tech, Ross found out why Mr. Fisher was able to afford jewelry and brand-new Cadillacs on a trade school teacher's salary. "We had a conversation one day. I found out that he was dealing and also using narcotics. I'm not exactly sure how the conversation came up but we started talking about it and he started explaining to me what it was all about."

Ross said he was glad the topic arose. At this point in his life, he was looking for any way to make a buck, and it really didn't matter if it was legal or not. He'd crossed that threshold already. "Actually, when he explained it to me, I wanted to know more about it, so I started asking him more questions," Ross said. "He showed me some. It was about as big as a matchhead and he said, 'Well, this right here is worth $50 and you can sell this and it just keeps getting better and better,' is basically what he said."

Ross mulled it over. Selling cocaine certainly seemed a lot better and a lot less risky than stealing and stripping cars, which is what he'd been doing to put himself through Trade Tech. He discussed it with his running partner, Ollie Newell, known as "Big Loc" because some people thought he acted crazy. Newell, who'd just gotten out of jail and needed money, agreed that selling dope looked like a lot less work for a lot more money.

But Ross had one reservation: all the dope dealers he knew eventually got fucked up on their own product. Nothing was more pathetic than seeing a burned-out old dealer begging nickels and dimes from his former clients. That wasn't the way Ricky Ross envisioned his life ending.

"Ollie was kinda like the one that kinda like coerced me into getting into the business," Ross said. "You know, he's like, 'Come on, man, you can do it, you don't mess around with nothing, you don't smoke, you don't drink, you're clean, you can handle it.'"

Ross made up his mind. They went back to see Mr. Fisher and announced that they were ready to try it out. Ross said Fisher gave them "a fifty-dollar piece" and "we went to a neighborhood and tried to sell it."

It was not an encouraging start. "We got beat out of it," Ross said. "We gave it to somebody and they said they was going to pay us later and it didn't happen." Ross said he had to go slinking back to Fisher to tell him about the "sale," but he assured the teacher that "the guy was going to pay me the money, and he said, 'Okay, don't worry about it.'"

Chastened, Ross and Newell regrouped for another try. They scoped out the parking lot at Bret Harte Junior High, their alma mater, and stole a car from a faculty member. Selling the fancy wheels brought them $250, and a week or so after their first debacle, they went strutting back to Fisher's house with their hard-earned cash.

"We bought what's called an 8-track of cocaine from him. It's three grams of cocaine. At that time, it probably was about a gram of cocaine and about two grams of cut." Taking the 8-track for $250, they cut it again and sold it off in bits and pieces. "We could take it to our neighborhood where we stayed at and it would sell for [a total of] five, six hundred dollars.... I think the first time we might have made about $600 off it...an awful lot of money."

Instead of spending the profits, Ross said, they went back to Fisher's house and ordered more cocaine. "Sold it, made more money," Ross said. "I didn't really know the game. It was like we were just stumbling through, you know what I'm saying? Picking up as we go."

Ross said the amount of cash he was able to bring in scared him.

"I was selling, and Ollie was standing back, you know, and watching me, you know, make sure didn't nobody try to rob me or nothing like that," Ross said. "So I would make like three hundred dollars, I would take it home and put it up, because I didn't want to be standing out there with a whole lot of dope and a whole lot of money. Because the police raided the spot all the time, you know. They might be raided every 15 or 20 minutes. It was a PCP street. They was selling PCP there. But they wouldn't pay no attention to me unless I had a lot of money on me."

Ross said the cops mostly just smelled dealers' hands, looking for the telltale stench of PCP. "They would just smell my hands, pat me and let me go. But if I had a wad of money, it would draw attention, so we never wanted to get over two or three hundred dollars."

Acquaintances who were dealing PCP—"slanging Sherm" or "selling water," as it was called—made fun of him for selling coke because there was a much bigger market for angel dust. "All the guys selling PCP used to tell us, 'Ya'll can make more money, ya'll should sell PCP.' And I was like, 'No, that's all right, I don't want to mess with PCP. That's too hard.' And cocaine was more, like, fly-er, more like the uppity people, you know, wasn't nobody going crazy, you know? When they smoked the PCP they would go crazy and stuff and I would think, 'I ain't gonna be involved with that.' Cocaine is like, mellow, and it was cool. So I didn't mind doing it."

Still slightly unsure of the future of the cocaine business, Ross kept his hand in the auto business as well. He was still stealing cars and fencing them or stripping them down in his body shop and parting them out. On March 19, 1982, he was arrested by the LAPD for grand theft auto. The police found a Mercedes Benz in his garage with parts that didn't match. Ross dipped into his cash reserves and hired a Beverly Hills lawyer named Alan Fenster, a former prosecutor and film studio lawyer who had little trouble getting the auto theft charge tossed out of court.

"There was no evidence Ricky had any knowledge about that car," said Fenster, whose performance in that felony case would lead him to many years of lucrative employment with Ross. Fenster, who'd been defending drug dealers and drug users since the early 1970s, said it was "my recollection that when I met Rick, he was already dealing drugs. Ricky was introduced to me by another client I had, who was a dealer, and I recall that he told me Ross was someone who was into some serious dealing then."

Early 1982 was an exceptionally good time to be in the cocaine business. It was like getting in on the ground floor of Amway. "At first we was just going to do it until we made $5,000," Ross said. "We made that so fast we said, 'No, we'll quit when we make $20,000.' Then we was going to quit when we saved enough to buy a house...."

Though it would not become apparent for some time, the cocaine industry was then undergoing dramatic changes that would boost the fortunes of dealers everywhere. The drug was finally beginning to filter down from the penthouses into the real world, opening up a whole new audience for its seductive charms.

The most basic reason was supply and demand. In some cities, Miami in particular, supply was beginning to outstrip demand, thanks largely to the efforts of Carlos Lehder and his pals in Medellín, Colombia, who had revolutionized the import/export part of the business. By early 1982, the Medellín cartel had gotten its act together and—using special airplanes, radar avoidance techniques, and specially designed speedboats—began bringing in unheard-of amounts of cocaine, mostly through the Bahamas.

Ten days before Rick Ross's auto theft arrest in March 1982, Customs agents in Miami searched an airplane, owned by a tiny Colombian air cargo company, that had flown in from Medellín. By the time agents arrived, workers were busy unloading dozens of boxes labeled "jeans." But when an inspector stuck a screwdriver into one of them, he didn't hit denim. White powder came pouring out of the hole.

When the Customs men had finished weighing the cocaine, the scales topped out at 3,906 pounds, nearly four times the size of the previous U.S. cocaine seizure record. It was, authors Guy Gugliotta and Jeff Leen wrote in *Kings of Cocaine*, the DEA's "first look at the shadow of the beast."

As more loads like that got through, the wholesale price of cocaine in the U.S. began dropping. But it never dropped dramatically enough to make it popular in low-income neighborhoods. According to the 1994 Rand Institute study, between 1979 and 1982 ounce prices in L.A. fell from the stratospheric to the merely exorbitant: $4,844 vs. $4,011. Gram prices fell slightly during the same period, from $321 to $259. Kilo prices dropped more significantly, from around $75,000 to around $60,000. Major importers and top-level dealers began seeing big price breaks. But if the Rand study's figures are accurate, for the average Joe who bought by the gram, cocaine was still extremely expensive.

And that was okay with Ricky Ross and Ollie Newell. At those prices, they didn't need a lot of customers. By the end of 1981, they were finally starting to make some real money. The number of users in the neighborhoods wasn't growing that much, but they were stealing customers away from other dealers. "We just had a price," Ross said. "Nobody in the neighborhood could touch us."

The cocaine they were getting from Fisher was slightly cheaper than what others were paying, and when Ross asked him why, Fisher told him he "had a really good connection." Since Ross could charge less, it wasn't too hard to find customers willing to pay $125 a gram instead of the $150 or $200 they'd been paying. Any chance to save a buck—especially after being gouged all these years—made for very happy and loyal clients. "People would come from everywhere, man. They would come from Pomona, Pasadena, Riverside, Long Beach. It wasn't just like an L.A. thing."

Ross also exercised some of the same type of discipline that had kept him out on the tennis courts, swinging the racquet and running, hour after hour, day after day. "I mean, listen, when you got in the dope business, everybody wanted to get high. Nobody wanted to sell dope," Ross said disgustedly. "It was like...even Ollie! Ollie was, was, was straight and always wanted to get high, get high, get high. So...I finally got in it, I said, 'Well, man, you're using up all the profit!' This was in the early stages, and he said, 'Well, I ain't gonna do no more.' But everybody else wanted to get high. [It was] the whole motto, you know, in our neighborhood—because we never left our neighborhood; we was like confined to South Central L.A.—everybody was just getting high. Let's party, man."

Ross was not the party-hearty type, not when it came to business. He considered himself first and foremost to be a professional cocaine trafficker. It was his job to move dope, and he did it with his usual intensity. "You know how some people feel that God put them down here to be a preacher? I felt that he had put me down to be the cocaine man," Ross told the *L.A. Times* in 1994. And like a missionary for a new religion, Ross began creating cocaine dealers.

"Eventually, all the guys that was selling PCP started seeing everybody coming [to me] with their hundred dollars, and they were selling like ten dollars worth, five dollars worth, you know, sticks. They knew every time somebody came to me, it was a hundred dollars. So I didn't have to see that many people, maybe, fifteen people a day, you know, I make fifteen hundred dollars and they started seeing to that and knowing how much money I was making.

"So then they started saying, 'Well, I'm gonna sell some water and you know I'm going to buy two hundred dollars worth from Rick and start, you know, investing it in cocaine and start doing it myself. So the next thing I know, all these guys were coming to me saying, 'Man, I want to get an eight-track.'"

But Ross's source, Mr. Fisher, was getting antsy about all the cocaine Ross and Newell were ordering. An occasional gram here and there was fine, he told Ross, but he was a schoolteacher, not Super Fly. The only reason he did a little dealing out the side was to pay for his own supply. Rick and Ollie were making a business out of it, and if they wanted to do that it was their business, but he didn't want anything to do with it.

"I think he was getting tired of us calling him up all the time and having him get us some more," Ross said. "Mr. Fisher was working so he told me to go ahead and deal directly with Ivan and we met at Mr. Fisher's house and I got the stuff."

"Ivan," a handsome, smiling Latino, had been supplying Mr. Fisher with cocaine for about a year. Ross had seen him around Fisher's house before, but they'd never been introduced.

During their first meeting, Ivan brought along another Hispanic—Henry—but Ricky wasn't clear what part Henry played, other than that he was Ivan's brother-in-law. Maybe he was his partner. Or maybe he'd just come along for the ride.

In halting English, Ivan told them that he would be happy to be their supplier from now on. If they wanted any more product, they should call him directly, instead of bothering Mr. Fisher. He slipped Ross a folded paper with a phone number on it. On the way out, Ivan told Ross that he would get them a better price than Mr. Fisher had. "We moved up fast," Ross said. "We went from moving grams to moving ounces." And Ivan proved true to his word. "After I started dealing directly with Ivan, it got better. We could take…the same thing we was buying from Mr. Fisher for $200 and turn it into $900, because we found out Mr. Fisher had been taking some of the money. He might have been making like $50, $75 off each one [8-track]. So we started making more money."

With more cash flow, Ross was able to order larger amounts of cocaine from Ivan and get a better price, a volume purchase break. And then he could cut his street prices even further. "He kept incrementally expanding his quantity, and every time he could do that, he was bringing the price down just a little bit more, and then what he would gain from volume, he would put right back into the operation," *Times* reporter Katz said. "It was just classic economics. And he saw all this in a way I guess others didn't, or weren't as disciplined as him to act on."

Some of this discipline was not entirely of Ross's choosing. One reason he and Newell began reinvesting their profits so faithfully was because they didn't dare spend the money on anything else. "My momma was strict, right? Both our mothers, me and Ollie's mother, was strict, right? So we couldn't show the money! We had like…we had $1,000 and we didn't even buy new tennis shoes! Because my mother woulda knew: 'Where'd you get them shoes from?'

"So we, like, hid our money. We was hiding our money from our mothers!" Ross laughed, shaking his head at the idea of two badass cocaine dealers so afraid of their mommas they couldn't spend their loot. "So even if we buy clothes, we'd hide them in the garage and put them on after we'd leave so she wouldn't find out."

But the nature of his business made it difficult to hide forever. Eventually Annie Ross figured out what was going on.

"When she found out I was selling dope, she had a fit. Threw me out of the house," Ross said. "I never rented no apartment or nothing like that. I had some money but I didn't know how to rent an apartment. I was living in her garage. I fixed it up like a little house. She was like, 'Boy, something going on. I don't know what you're doing but you ain't doing something right. You got all these people coming around here. Tell them people to stop coming round my house,'" Ross said.

He "really didn't do business there," he said, but when a customer wanted something, someone had to come by and let him know. "And she was like, 'There's too many people coming over here, I know something is wrong.' One day she just said, 'Get your stuff and leave. Don't come back over here. And Ollie, don't you come back either.' Because you know Ollie is like her godson. So she threw us out. But I had a little bit of money then and I moved in with one of my cousins and started paying her to let me stay there.

"But that's basically how we got started."

After eight months with their new supplier, just as their business really began expanding, "something happened to Ivan," Ross said. He'd disappeared. Ross and Newell panicked. Their only supplier had dropped off the face of the earth. Where were they going to get their cocaine now? From afar, Danilo Blandón watched events unfold. It was time for him to make his move.

8

"A million hits is not enough"

Ivan's whereabouts were no mystery to Danilo Blandón. He'd been observing Ivan's dealings with Ricky Ross for quite some time, seeing their sales expand, watching the venture become more and more profitable. He had to admit it; he was jealous. Despite all the work he'd been doing for Norwin Meneses personally—keeping the books, working for the Contras, helping Norwin's wife run the restaurant and the T-shirt company—the drug kingpin was still nagging him to move more cocaine. Every couple of months Blandón would drive all the way to Meneses's house in Pacifica, a nine-hour trip, pick up another kilo or two, drive back to L.A., and then have to put up with Meneses flogging him to sell it.

Blandón had been hitting up other car salesmen he knew, helping other cocaine dealers through dry spells now and again, but he wasn't making any great strides. He estimated that he spent "about a year, year and a half, you know, with the same two, one or two keys."

But Ivan Arguellas, another Nicaraguan exile scuttling around L.A. with cocaine to sell, had found this kid in South Central, Ricky Ross, and they were really starting to move the powder. Blandón knew Ivan, who also used the name Claudio Villavicencio, because of their shared heritage and their new profession. He sold Ivan a little cocaine every once in a while. But Ivan had other sources of supply.

The Torres brothers—the two giants with the little car lot—also got into the cocaine business around this time, according to Blandón, who surmised that they were supplying Ricky Ross. "I supposed that maybe they start with Rick," Blandón said. "I know them so well, you know, they are Nicaraguan people.... When I saw them getting rich, getting money, so I saw that they start doing business with him."

If the Torres brothers were dealing with Ross, as Blandón claims, it is likely that they were doing so as Ivan's suppliers, because Ross said he never met the Torreses face-to-face until long after Ivan disappeared.

Blandón had no other sources. He was stuck with Norwin Meneses, who was squeezing him dry for the Contras, charging him $60,000 a kilo and taking nearly every penny he made. Norwin was holding him back, he believed. "I didn't have my own car," Blandón complained. "I have to rent cars, you know. I used to work with him [Meneses], you know, coming from San Francisco, going back, and I thought, 'Hey, what are you doing? You're not doing nothing, you know? You're not making no—no money.'"

That's why Ivan's deal with Ricky Ross looked so good to Blandón. This little kid was a mover, and he was getting bigger all the time. "I wished I could have known Ricky...because all the time I want to grow in the business," Blandón said. "He [Ivan] and his brother-in-law [Henry] was selling to Rick. So I wish I could [have known] him.... I knew how much they were selling."

Blandón got his wish. Ivan Arguellas caught a bullet in the spine that crippled him from the waist down. He was hospitalized for months and forced to quit the cocaine business while he recuperated. "He got shot by his wife," Blandón said. "He's paralyzed right now." A tough break for Ivan, but it was the break Danilo Blandón had been waiting for. Ivan's customers had fallen to his brother-in-law, Henry Corrales, a drug dealing amateur. "Henry was kind of a knucklehead," Ross recalled. "He was a nice guy who just wanted to party all the time. He didn't know what he was doing."

Blandón agreed. "When he [Ivan] got in the accident, it started Henry Corrales getting in [the business]," he said. "Henry was running the business because his brother-in-law was in the hospital. And when the guy that got paralyzed get in the hospital, he lost that [cocaine] contact. And Henry didn't have any contact more than me when he took over."

In all the time he'd been hanging around Ivan, Henry apparently hadn't made any connections of his own. In a business where a man is only as good as his sources, Henry Corrales was hurting. Ivan's people expected him to deliver. And where the hell was he going to come up with the cocaine for these black gangsters downtown?

When Blandón came by to offer his sympathies and lend a hand, Henry must have seen him as a savior. "When he doesn't have any sources, [he] asked to me and that's when we began the relationship with him," Blandón said. Corrales told him Ross was "the best customer" he and Ivan had, "a big customer that they were selling five or ten [kilos] a week.... For me, it was a big customer."

Henry was so grateful for Blandón's help that he agreed to share his profits on every kilo he sold, fifty-fifty. "We split the commission," Blandón said, but he couldn't remember how much that was. "I was selling to Henry Corrales and Henry Corrales was selling to him [Ricky]. Henry was coming to me to pick up the stuff."

Ross denied he was receiving that much cocaine from Henry when he started his relationship with him. He and Ollie were still dealing mostly ounces at that point, he said. It was in multi-ounce lots, to be sure—they'd buy four or eight ounces a day. But he said they did not graduate to buying kilos until later. Blandón said he knew how much Ross had been buying from Ivan because the quantity he sold him determined his price.

Ross said he did not know that Danilo Blandón had adopted him as a customer. Just as he hadn't known where Ivan got his coke from, he didn't know where Henry got his. It's not that he wasn't curious. It was just a question cocaine dealers didn't ask each other.

In the cocaine business, serious dealers had good reason to cut out their wholesaler and buy directly from the source. The closer they got, the cheaper and purer the cocaine became. The more hands it passed through, the more times the product got stepped on, or cut, and the lower the profits became.

All Ricky knew was that once he started dealing with Henry, his cocaine prices fell again. Maybe Ivan's disappearance wasn't going to be such a bad deal after all, Ross decided. "After we started dealing with Henry, it got even better."

Not long afterward, Ross started noticing a slight change in the cocaine market around South Central. Some of his customers were taking the cocaine powder he was selling them and turning it into weird little rocks—just like the one he'd seen back in 1979. A couple dealers had actually starting trying to sell rocks, he noticed, but the dopers Ricky knew regarded the product suspiciously.

"At first, nobody wanted rock," Ross said. Nobody wanted to mess with cocaine that didn't look like cocaine. Secondly, the price was too low. How could anything claiming to be cocaine cost only $25? It had to be a rip-off.

But Ricky vividly recalled his Christmastime experience with the pimp a couple years back, when the man had smoked a rock and come running back waving $100. If this stuff catches on, Ross considered, it might be worth looking into. Then one of his customers asked him if he had any rock to sell, and Ross got the message.

"See, the way rock came into play, it would be like, say somebody was going to work early in the morning and they wanted some cocaine. They wanted to get high and they'd say, 'Damn, I gotta cook this shit up and I'm late for work,' and they'd ask me, 'Can you cook it up for me?'" It was a question of convenience. Ross said sure, and promptly hired someone to make it for him.

"Know what I got in chemistry in school? A 'F'!" Ross laughed. "First started out, I was paying someone to cook it. But everybody always used to make it more complicated than it was. Like the cookers never wanted you to learn how to cook it. So everybody kind of kept it like hush-hush. 'Oh man, you *got* to let me do it. You goin' to *mess* it up.'"

In truth, rock cocaine is easy to make. Put cocaine powder in a pan, add some water and baking soda, and heat until it starts crackling. Done.

The recipe had been floating around a little while before it caught hold in South Central. In November 1979, Tennyson Guyer's Select Committee investigating cocaine provided the first public airing of the ingredients needed to turn powder into crack. "A saucer, a glass, a paper towel and Arm & Hammer baking soda are about all that is needed," testifed Dr. Franklin Sher of Walnut Creek, California, a Bay Area physician whose family owned the country's largest freebase paraphernalia company at the time.

In 1981 an author named T. Davidson published a pamphlet, *The Natural Process: Base-ic Instructions and Baking Soda Recipe,* out of Tustin, California, an Orange County town about thirty miles east of L.A., which contained step-by-step instructions on how to make crack. Davidson hailed the simple procedure as "safe, healthy and economical."

Ross said he watched his cooker for a while and thought, "'What the hell, I'm going to try it.' Because the first person that ever tried it was me. Ollie didn't try it first. I tried it first. Then I told Ollie, 'You can do that shit too.' So we started cooking it ourselves and we started selling what we called 'ready rock.'" He crumbled the rock up and delivered it in $20 hits—nuggets about the size of a ball bearing—first in tiny bits of aluminum foil, then later in tiny glass vials.

Ross smoked some himself and found the craving for more so powerful that he vowed to stay as far away from the shit as possible.

But, man, what a product.

He saw how his customers reacted. Once they tried it, they never wanted anything else. "I think what made us start smoking was curiosity and frustration. I know that it wasn't the Black brothers' or sisters' intention to smoke cocaine as a career. It's just so addicting. It's like one hit is one too many and a million hits is not enough," explained Big Shiphead, a Shotgun Crip since he was twelve years old. "In my opinion, it's the worst drug that ever hit the face of this earth."

What happened next was just what the scientists had been predicting since 1974. As *basé* had done in Lima and La Paz eight years earlier, rock caused a sensation in South Central. But it was an underground sensation initially.

A 1985 study by two University of Southern California social scientists provides some of the only existing documentation of crack's progression in South Central in the early 1980s, when Ross and others began selling it. It is like reading the origins of the Black Death.

"We...reviewed the LAPD South Bureau Narcotic Division activity reports from January of 1982 to the present [April 1985]," sociologists Malcolm Klein and Cheryl Maxson wrote. "From January to April of 1982 there are notes of cocaine increase with freebase as the most popular method. In May there is a random comment about 'rock hard' pre-freebased cocaine. With continuing increases in arrests, the first real mention of rocks came in September 1982 in the Southeast division. It showed up in 77th Division after another five months. Thereafter, monthly reports continued to report the presence of rock cocaine throughout the Bureau in increasing amounts."

And that was only what the LAPD was finding when they busted somebody stupid, according to Ross; "They mighta got some dude with a few rocks in his pocket, but the LAPD didn't know nothing about what was really goin' on. The LAPD didn't mess with us at all."

Former LAPD narcotics detective Steve Polak, who was riding the streets of South Central at that time, said Ross's viewpoint was essentially correct. Street cops like him, Polak insisted, saw what was happening. As the USC study showed, many of them were putting it in their reports. But none of them really knew what they were looking at, and the brass didn't seem that interested in finding out. "We didn't know what it was. I was there as a cop in uniform. I was stopping people on the streets and seeing these rocks. I'd see them throwing these rocks, these little things, and I'd go, 'What the fuck is this?' I didn't know what the fuck it was, you know?"

When Polak asked, he was told they were bleached peanuts. "I'd put the handcuffs on them and I'd say, 'You know this is dope. I carry bleached peanuts all the time in my pocket and throw them away when I see the cops, so, you know, come on, give me a break.' It's just a matter of sending it to the lab and seeing exactly what he had and, you know, it was coming back this coke stuff."

Polak started seeing other strange items as well. "We were stopping these people and they had these little bottles of Puerto Rican rum and little glass pipes and what we called a torch, a torn-off piece of a coat hanger with a cotton swab wrapped around it. What they were doing was dipping the swab in the rum because of its high alcohol content and then they'd put the rock on top of the glass pipe and then they'd flame [the swab] up. But then again, you learn, you know? There's nothing written on this shit."

Once word got out that the Five-O was wise and was starting to bust people with rocks on them, Polak said, "We'd drive by and see them put their hands in their mouths. And we'd come back an hour later and they'd either be overdosed or wired like a motherfucker, jumping all around like little tops. They'd put it in their mouths and they'd leave it in so long it would start to dissolve, like an aspirin. These guys were falling all over."

Smarter users found crack to be an ideal drug for the streets of South Central, where the cops tend to frisk young black men just for looking at them funny. Now you could actually carry dope with you in public, and the cops couldn't get there fast enough. "It's easy to get rid of in a pinch. Drop it on the ground and it's almost impossible to find," complained a Miami narcotics detective in 1986. "Step on it and the damned thing is history. All of a sudden your evidence ceases to exist."

The inner city of Miami started seeing crack about a year after the Los Angeles market started, but on a much smaller scale. Longtime Miami area drug researcher James Inciardi, a criminology professor, wrote in 1988 that "although crack in one form or another appeared in Miami as early as 1982, at first it was generally limited to the Caribbean and Haitian communities." The drug "advanced to the wider drug subcultures in 1984," Inciardi wrote. "By early 1985, crack had become widely available in every inner-city neighborhood in the greater Miami area."

According to several sources, 1985 was the year Jamaican posses took over the nascent crack market in inner-city Miami and began organizing and expanding it. Though the Miami market trailed the L.A. market by about a year or two, the similarities between them are striking in some respects. Both markets exploded following political upheavals in foreign countries—upheavals in which the CIA played an active role.

Just as the South Central crack market began flourishing when political exiles from Nicaragua arrived to raise money for themselves and their political causes, the Miami crack market didn't really take off until political exiles from Jamaica moved in. The intelligence division of the Drug Enforcement Administration, in a 1994 report on crack cocaine, offered a startling explanation for the evolution of the Jamaican posses from small-time dopers to "one of the most effective trafficking groups" in the United States, rivaled only by the Crips and Bloods of Los Angeles.

Since the 1970s Jamaica had been run by a socialist government headed by Michael Manley, a graduate of the London School of Economics, who immediately angered U.S. officials by recognizing the Cuban government of Fidel Castro and supporting socialist rebels that a CIA proxy army was battling in Angola. In 1977 two investigative reporters exposed a "destabilization program" against Manley's government reportedly being run by the CIA's Jamaican station chief, Norman Descoteaux. The campaign included covert shipments of arms to Manley's opponents, the use of selective violence, bombings, and assassinations, covert financial aid to the conservative Jamaica Labour party, the fomenting of extensive labor unrest, and bribery.

One of the CIA agents who would later play a key role in the Contra project, Luis Posada Carriles—a Cuban Bay of Pigs veteran with a history of engaging in arms-for-drugs deals—was sighted in Jamaica near the scene of at least one bombing, the reporters wrote.

During the course of a bitter election campaign in 1980 between Manley and a candidate from the CIA-backed Jamaican Labour party, rival political gangs killed "more than 700 people," according to the DEA. Manley lost the election. What happened next was in many ways a carbon copy of what had happened in Nicaragua and Los Angeles a year earlier, despite the fact that here the political changing of the guard was roughly the reverse of the Nicaraguan situation. "Following the election, many of these political gunmen left or were driven out of Jamaica and immigrated to the United States. They settled into the large Jamaican and Caribbean communities in Miami and New York City," the DEA intelligence report stated. "In the early 1980s, the U.S. posse leaders maintained a sense of allegiance to their political parties in Jamaica, sending weapons and drug profits back home." Eventually, the DEA said, the Jamaican traffickers in the United States "evolved from small-time marijuana sellers into nationwide cocaine and crack distributors."

The political leanings of Miami's and South Central's major cocaine suppliers were not known to lower-level dealers and hustlers, who probably wouldn't have cared anyway. Dope was dope. Politics was politics. And it wasn't until one got to the very top of the cocaine business that the two worlds intersected.

Ricky Ross had no political interests at all, and never would. His worldview was limited to South Central, and how much cocaine he could move into it. What his Nicaraguan suppliers were doing with their money was their business, he figured.

What he was concerned with in late 1982 was that the new crack market in South Central wasn't turning into the money-maker he'd been expecting. Dealers had gotten away with charging more for powder, he said, because it sold in more expensive doses. When you were talking to someone about $300 for a gram or $3,000 for an ounce, you could pack a little more profit in around the edges, and nobody would say anything. "We was making more money when it was powder," he groused. "[The market] went to powder and rock, and eventually just went straight to rock because *everybody* had stopped snorting. I had to get out on the street myself and sell $20 rocks, run at the cars."

The reason crack became so popular in South Central and elsewhere was that it only cost a few bucks to become a customer. Crack normally sold in $25 hits, but you could find tiny rocks for as little as $5. "One of the principles of modern marketing is to develop products for increasingly small market segments at prices each segment can afford. Crack pushers accomplished this by creating prepackaged units at more-or-less standard sizes and prices," drug experts David Allen and James Jekel wrote in 1991.

Yale cocaine expert Dr. Robert Byck agreed that crack was a triumph of modern marketing principles. But there were more reasons than packaging for why it took off so quickly, he said. "I think the crack phenomenon is not just a matter of smoking freebase. What happened with crack was a change in the selling, distribution, and price. It was sold in a very convenient form, which was accessible to a wide range of people. Smoking, unfortunately, in our society is not an abnormal behavior. Injecting something intravenously is. Snorting something into your nose is abnormal.

"So here was a way of taking a drug that was completely within the range of so-called normal behavior. And...gave you the same kick that you got from shooting it intravenously, but this was free of the risk of AIDS. It was socially acceptable and, on top of that, the drug was sold in a very convenient unit package. This was to drugs like McDonald's was to hamburgers. They knew how to sell it. And I think that what happened to crack was, they knew how to sell it."

Crack's second big advantage over powder was that it democratized cocaine not only for users but for dealers as well. It didn't take a large investment anymore to call yourself a player. You could buy half a gram of powder for $150, rock it up, and get ten to twelve doses of crack, each of which would give the buyer a bigger blast than ten times as much powder. And you doubled your money.

"Crack increases its own on-the-street sales force because many addicts find they must become pushers in order to make enough money to sustain their own habits," Allen and Jekel wrote. "And they can get cocaine powder at 'wholesale' prices this way and make their own crack."

For Ross, that was the biggest problem with crack. Now he had to worry about competition from customers as well as other dealers. Competition meant fewer customers, and that meant less volume, negating the very advantage of selling crack in the first place. At the same time, his costs were going up; crack cost more to make. When he sold powder, all he needed was a scale and a bag of lactose. Now he needed a place to cook the shit up, because he couldn't do it in his cousin's apartment. He had to rent an apartment and pay rent bills and power bills. And then he needed vials, and people to help put the crack in the vials. To get the necessary volume, they had to pay people to go out and sell it, because he and Ollie couldn't do it all by themselves now. Overall, it was a bigger headache, with lower profits.

Since standardization had eliminated Ross's strategy of cutting street prices and boosting volume, he had to figure out another way to raise his profits. Fortunately, Danilo Blandón was a stickler for quality, and Henry's cocaine was of a very high purity. By experimenting, he found that he could dilute the cocaine even further, *before* he mixed it with the baking soda, and his customers couldn't tell the difference. Because the dope was being cooked and smoked, purity and appearance didn't matter as much as it once had.

"We called it 'blowup' and what we would do is cut it with procaine," Ross said. "You could get more weight and it would look bigger." Ross settled on a three-to-one cut, which turned one ounce of powder into four ounces. "You could turn it into as many as you wanted but the more you cut it, the less it was acceptable...one batch we cooked up we couldn't sell it. Customers wouldn't take it no more."

Now he had four times as much crack to sell for roughly the same cost. But a couple months later, other dealers began using blowup too. That's when he decided to get out of street-corner crack sales and get into wholesaling, selling to other crack dealers.

There was a new thing happening in parts of South Central and the San Fernando Valley suburb of Pacoima: rock houses, which some dealers had set up as one-stop shopping centers for crack. You made your crack in the kitchen, sold it in the dining room, and the customer smoked it in the living room. When they were out, the cycle began again. Since crack-heads smoked hit after hit after hit until they ran out of money, it made more sense to get them in the house and keep them there, rather than go to a park or stand on the street drawing a crowd by making repeat sales all day long. Some of the more enterprising rock house operators had "strawberries" back in the bedroom if that's what you wanted, crack whores who would suck a dick for a suck on the pipe.

James Inciardi had been a drug researcher in Miami for years and considered himself to be a hardened and streetwise observer. But nothing, he wrote, prepared him for the nightmarish world of a crack house. "I observed what appeared to be the forcible gang-rape of an unconscious child. Emaciated, seemingly comatose, and likely no more than 14 years of age, she was lying spread-eagled on a filthy mattress while four men in succession had vaginal intercourse with her," Inciardi wrote. "After they had finished and left the room, another man came in and they engaged in oral sex." Inciardi discovered that she was a "house girl," who got food, clothing, a roof over her head, and all the crack she wanted if she put it out for the customers.

That was where he could still use his high-volume, low-price strategy, Ross decided. Those new rock houses and those baby brand-new dealers out there—those hustlers buying half-grams and "slanging" on the corners—they would be his customers. Ricky would sell his "ready rock" in batches, cheaper than they could make it themselves, prepackaged and ready to peddle. And the other dealers could have the street trade and the competition and cops that went along with it.

The move, which Ross places near the end of 1982, worked. It reduced his operation's costs and took him off the streets. It reduced his customers' costs as well. He moved once again into an arena with no competition, where he was free to set his own prices, cherry-pick the best customers, and undercut anyone who tried to move in on him.

"We was like... the first quantity dealers," Ross said. "Because there wasn't nobody really dealing quantity in L.A. at that time." Others agreed. "Ricky, as far as I'm concerned, I mean, there had to have been someone before him to hand him a rock, but he had to be one of the very first people, if not *the* first guy, to really sense the economic potential of street-level marketing," *L.A. Times* reporter Jesse Katz said in 1995. "In my story I called him the first crack millionaire to rise from the streets of South Central." Katz's 1994 profile, headlined "Deposed King of Crack," said of Ross, "He didn't make the drug and he didn't smuggle it across the border, but Ricky Donnell Ross did more than anyone else to democratize it, boosting volume, slashing prices and spreading disease on a scale never before conceived."

Ross told CIA inspectors that he was South Central's biggest cocaine dealer by the end of 1982. "I knew this because it was my business strategy to know my competitors and stay on good terms with them," Ross told the agents.

James Galipeau, a longtime probation officer in the South Central area, said Ross was indeed a pioneer. "The thing about Rick that set him apart from the other guys who started out selling when he did, guys like Honcho Day and Michael Harris, is that pretty soon, they ended up buying from him. And they were learning from him."

But it seemed that as soon as Ricky got one problem solved, another one would crop up. Now Henry was freaking out on him. Henry had never been all that reliable to begin with, Ross said, but he was getting worse all the time. He wasn't showing up when he said he would. Sometimes at night he didn't want to come down to the 'hood. And he was looking real nervous when he came. Rick didn't like it. Henry was still his only supplier. If he took a hike like Ivan did, Rick would have to find another quantity dealer with Henry's prices. Fat chance of that.

As it turned out, something *was* going on with Henry. He didn't have the stomach for the business. And the more cocaine he sold to Ricky Ross, the more fretful he became. By late 1982 or early 1983, Ross said, Henry had gone from selling him ounces to selling him kilograms. And Blandón said he was selling many, many kilos to Ross through Henry.

"How many kilos a week?" Blandón was asked.

"To Henry?"

"To Henry, to Ricky."

"To Henry could be 10 or 15," Blandón said.

"Ten to fifteen?"

"Yes."

"Would 50 a month be a fair estimate?"

"In 1983, it…through Henry, yes."

That means Ricky Ross—within a year of crack's first real appearance in South Central L.A.—was selling between 1,000,000 and 1,250,000 doses of crack every single month (using DEA estimates of 20–25 rocks of crack per gram of powder, 20,000 to 25,000 per kilogram).

During 1982 and 1983, Blandón said, he and Meneses brought "three or four" planeloads of cocaine from Miami to Los Angeles. According to the Torres brothers, each one of those loads from Miami ranged between 200 and 400 kilos. These "regular" flights continued until at least 1984, they said. (Whether all of that was sold to Ross, or was divided among other customers of Meneses and Blandón, is not clear.)

Blandón said Henry's cocaine deals with Ross began frightening the novice dealer. "He was selling him so often he was getting so paranoid, you know?" Blandón said. "Somebody from his organization was in jail.... He told me, 'I've got $200,000, $300,000, I'm going to leave.'"

Corrales, Blandón said, planned to retire to the relative safety of Honduras. "He feel that he got a lot of money and he told me, 'Let me introduce you to my guy because my brother-in-law is still in the hospital.'" Blandón explained that Ivan Arguellas was still considered "the owner of Ricky Ross" by Henry, but since Ivan was laid up, and Henry was leaving town, Henry wondered if Blandón would mind dealing with Ricky.

Henry was not turning over his best customer for free, though. Blandón would have to continue splitting commissions with him. "He wanted to leave to Honduras, be there and get some commission," Blandón said. "He wanted that I give some commission to him, you know? That was the proposal." Blandón agreed, and Henry took him down to South Central to meet the rising young crack magnate.

"He introduced me, right in front of the house of Mary," Blandón said, referring to Mary Monroe, a friend and employee of Ross. "It was in South L.A.... that was the house that later came to be the warehouse for money, and to deliver."

Ross recalled the meeting well. "We had a place, one of the ladies in our neighborhood, we used to hang out in her back yard and play pool, mess with her daughters. Danilo met us in the front yard. Henry came in the back and knocked on the door and said he wanted to talk to me. He said, 'Come on. Let's go for a ride.' So we got in the car and we were riding around and he said, 'I'm leaving and I'm going to turn you over to the man. He's gonna do a better business than what we been doing and you gonna have a better price. Everything is gonna be better for you."

The price he paid for his cocaine fell once again. "After we started talking directly with Danilo, I mean the price was just...everybody was saying it was the bottom. That's what they used to say. 'You've got the cheapest price in town.' Everybody else was paying like $3,000 for an ounce of cocaine and when me and Ollie started dealing directly with Danilo, I think we was getting it for like $1,800 an ounce."

After his trip to South Central, Blandón knew why Henry was nervous. It was "a rough area" of town, he said, and the place fairly bristled with firearms. For his first drug delivery, "We went to an apartment that was on the second floor and there was a door, an iron door. And there was a guy, you know, with a shotgun: 'Who are you?' We identify ourselves, then you have to pass another guy with another machine gun, or shotgun. And inside, near the dinner table in the living room, there were about five guys, and all the guys were there with a gun at the table."

When asked to date that encounter, Blandón was unclear. "1982," he said under oath. "Excuse me. Sorry. 1983. 1983, I think so really. 1983. Excuse me, I make a mistake. 1984, because I was living in Northridge. Yes, 1984." Ross said he was introduced to Blandón about six or seven months after he started dealing with Henry, which would put his first face-to-face meeting with Blandón some time in the fall of 1982 or early 1983.

Henry's retirement also seemed to improve the quality of the cocaine Ross was getting. When he took it to the dealers who were his customers, they raved about it. "They said that the stuff was not cut. It was pure." Ross had finally reached the source, the wellspring from which pure, uncut cocaine flowed in abundance. His street-dealing days were over. Now, he was the man to see.

And true to form, he began to innovate. If there was a neighborhood where the dealers were not pushing his supply, Ross said, he would find the hood's top dealer and pay him a friendly visit, bringing with him a couple kilos of Danilo's finest, which he would give the rival dealer free as a measure of his respect. Try it out and see what you think, he would tell them. And then Ross would tell them the price, and he would have another customer.

Other times, he would invite dealers to smoke parties, where all the crack they wanted would be available on the house. There was plenty more where that came from, they would be told. And the price…

Ross said his first deal with Blandón was for "around eight ounces." Blandón, however, said it was much more than that, at least a kilo, and that their business grew geometrically from there. "In those times, there were one, two, three, four, five, six, maybe seven a day," he said. "Every day."

At seven kilos a day, Ross was moving more than 200 kilos of cocaine every single month. That meant he was pumping out around 165,000 vials of crack a day—5 million rocks a month.

"I had as many as five cookhouses. Because that was our hardest thing, to cook. Once you cooked it, it was sold," Ross said. Compton crack dealer Leroy "Chico" Brown told of visiting one of Ross's "cookhouses," and his description matched the one Ross gave. A house in a cheap neighborhood would be purchased by a front man and gutted. The windows would be barred and steel doors installed. Large, restaurant-size gas ranges and big aluminum pots would be brought in at night and set up. And then the cookers went to work. They would work in shifts, arriving and departing as if they lived in the house. The only visitors would be the couriers, one to drop off the powder and the other to pick up the crack.

"They were stirring these big pots with those things you use in canoes," Brown said with wonder. "You know, oars."

"Working around the clock, taking the age-old axioms of good business to ominous extremes, [Ross] transformed a curbside operation at 87th and Figueroa into the Wal-Mart of cocaine," the *L.A. Times* wrote in 1994.

South Central L.A. had become a boomtown of sorts. What happened there was reminiscent of what occurred in the hills and hollows of Kentucky during the coal boom of the 1970s, when seemingly worthless land was suddenly worth millions. While most of the residents remained poor and poorly educated, a few struck it rich overnight. Satellite dishes started popping up near shacks. Big, expensive cars—Cadillacs, BMWs and Mercedes Benzes—began rolling through the streets.

In early 1983 stories began appearing in the *Los Angeles Sentinel*, the South Central area's black-oriented news weekly, about the crack houses that were springing up here and there. "I would say that things got worse when cocaine hit the streets in '83 because prior to that all the brothers that were slangin' were selling water, Sherman, angel dust, PCP, or whatever you wanted to call it," said Leibo, an East Side Crip. "About '82 or '83 is when rocks hit the streets hard."

Fed by an unending supply of cocaine from Danilo Blandón, Ricky Ross's crack trafficking organization prospered and grew unhindered by law enforcement in the ghettos of Los Angeles. The cocaine business was turning out to be exactly as he'd seen it in the movies.

"Right when I was starting to sell drugs *Scarface* came out," Ross said, referring to the 1983 remake starring Al Pacino as a cocaine kingpin. "A whole bunch of us went and saw it, like 10 or 15 of us. We took our girlfriends, and we see this guy who . . . don't have nothing and the next thing, he's on top of the world." Like his fictional hero, Ross said, "I became a drug-dealing legend."

Chico Brown, a Corner Pocket Crip who was also heavily influenced by *Scarface*, agreed. "You ask any of the people who they looked up to back when they was startin' out, and all of them will tell you it was Ricky Ross. He was like a legend in the neighborhoods. He got a lotta people started."

9

"He would have had me by the tail"

Barely a year had passed since the CIA had taken over the financing of the Contras, and already the covert war was no longer a secret. The week before the 1982 elections, *Newsweek* magazine published the first detailed account of the Reagan administration's support of the Contras: "America's Secret War: Target Nicaragua." The cover story portrayed the Contras—whose forces had built up to around 4,000 men by this point—as being in a position to overthrow the Sandinistas. There were full-color photographs of paratroopers dropping from the sky, which made it appear as if the invasion was already under way.

But that was a gross exaggeration of reality. The Contras, in truth, had just started receiving the American weapons and supplies that Reagan had promised them a year earlier. According to one account, the main source for *Newsweek*'s story was none other than CIA director William Casey, who wanted to ensure that the Contra project didn't get shelved. Now that it was public knowledge that the Reagan administration was helping the Contras, Casey's reasoning went, it would look like a sellout—another Bay of Pigs—if it stopped.

The reporting incensed some members of Congress, particularly those who had been told by CIA officials that the Contras were merely border guards, keeping the Sandinistas from sending arms into El Salvador. The Contras' first major act of war, in fact, had nothing to do with El Salvador. Under CIA direction, two bridges linking Honduras and Nicaragua were blown up in March 1982, an operation Contra commanders considered to be the opening shots of the war.

In response to the *Newsweek* report, Congressman Tom Harkin proposed a complete cutoff of funding for all paramilitary activities against the Nicaraguan government. The fact that the war was illegal, Harkin argued, was nothing compared to the U.S. government cozying up to "perhaps the most hated group of Nicaraguans that could exist outside the borders of Nicaragua, and I talk about the *Somocistas*." Harkin called them "vicious, cutthroat murderers" and urged Congress to "end our involvement with this group."

When the Reagan administration heard about Harkin's proposed amendment to the annual defense budget bill, Oliver North later wrote, it "hit the roof.... The President let it be known that if Congress approved the Harkin Amendment, which was unlikely anyway, he would promptly veto it." Instead, Congress passed the first Boland Amendment, named for the Missouri Democrat, Edward P. Boland, who authored it. Boland, a member of the House Intelligence Committee, knew full well that the CIA was funding the Contras, and he was not opposed to it. But Harkin's move—making a public issue out of a secret CIA project—had put Boland on the spot and riled up other liberals. Boland told Harkin that Congress had no business passing laws like the one he was proposing. That's why there was an Intelligence Committee, Boland lectured, "to keep the nation's secrets and exercise sensible and prudent oversight." The Intelligence Committee, a body generally protective of the CIA, had been one of the few committees told of the secret Contra project.

To quiet Harkin and other liberals, Boland agreed to an amendment that prohibited the use of taxpayer funds "for the purpose of overthrowing the government of Nicaragua or provoking a military exchange between Nicaragua and Honduras." The House passed it on Christmas Eve 1982 by a vote of 411–0.

No doubt the lawmakers were eager to get home for the holidays, but the reason the Boland Amendment received unanimous support was because it accomplished nothing. It was largely a fraud, designed to make it look as if Congress was cracking down on the Contra project without actually doing so.

Internal government memos show that the CIA, the White House, the Defense Department, and the Contras' congressional supporters knew that the Contras had no hope of defeating the Sandinistas. Since there was no way in hell the Contras were ever going to overthrow the Nicaraguan government, their supporters reasoned, they could continue spending CIA funds despite the Boland Amendment. If the Contras were given money for one purpose—arms interdiction—and decided to use it another way, well, that wasn't the CIA's fault, was it? The money hadn't been given "for the purpose" of an overthrow.

Indeed, by early 1983, CIA dollars were pouring into Honduras and Costa Rica in torrents. Best of all, the Contras no longer had to ask their Argentine advisers for permission to spend it. Most of the Argentines were called home in 1982 after their country's disastrous war with Great Britain over the Falkland Islands.

Enrique Bermúdez and the other top-ranking FDN officials started living like real generals. In Tegucigalpa, Honduras, Bermúdez moved into "an elegant two-story place, all dark wood and balconies, overlooking the Tegucigalpa basin from a lovely hillside lot in the exclusive neighborhood of Ciudad Nueva." Bermúdez and his staff spent their evenings dining on roasts, puffing cigars, quaffing tequila, or carousing in the excellent casinos downtown. "Bermúdez had developed a taste for the teenage girls his men were recruiting in Nicaragua," journalist Sam Dillon wrote in his 1991 book *Comandos*. "Bermúdez was inviting them from the base camps back to Ciudad Nueva, one at a time, to try out as his 'secretaries.'"

Dillon wrote that the CIA was sending "tens of thousands of dollars a month to Bermúdez's general staff to pay the 'family aid' salaries of his field commanders, and other prodigious sums to buy food for the thousands of FDN fighters." But much of that aid was being diverted and never reached the soldiers in the field. The Southern Front commanders in Costa Rica, Edén Pastora and "El Negro" Chamorro, constantly complained that Bermúdez and his CIA friends were stiffing them on the supplies, raking off the best weapons and the best food and sending them garbage—planeloads of diapers, feminine napkins, and extra-large underwear. It wasn't merely unfair, they argued, it was an insult to their manhood.

"Bermúdez's staff officers were pocketing the money," Dillon wrote. "They were also stealing half the CIA's food budget. Though they routinely shipped only half the necessary beans, rice and other foodstuffs to the base camps, they were billing the CIA for full rations."

Several accounts, including Dillon's, paint a picture of massive corruption inside the FDN, perpetuated by Bermúdez and his closest associates, death squad leader Ricardo Lau and millionaire land baron Aristides Sánchez. At one point, dozens of midlevel FDN field commanders petitioned to have Bermúdez fired for stealing money and squandering supplies. Some CIA field officers were pushing for his removal on the same grounds.

But Bermúdez had friends at CIA headquarters at Langley, and after he contacted them about the incipient mutiny, the complainers were the ones booted out of the FDN. The CIA brass felt they couldn't dump "the obedient asset who'd helped construct their entire project," Dillon wrote.

Still, congressional discomfort over the CIA's army was growing. In May the House Intelligence Committee issued a special report suggesting that the "operation is illegal" and that the administration knew plainly that the Contras were trying to overthrow the Nicaraguan government. On July 28, 1983, the House passed a resolution by a 228–195 vote to stop all aid to the Contras. "Opposition in the House to aiding the Nicaraguan rebels seemed almost insurmountable and it would be easier for House Democrats to block passage of a new aid authorization in 1984 than it had been to cut it off in 1983," former State Department official Robert Kagan, a Contra supporter, wrote.

Yet it was somewhere around this time, according to Danilo Blandón, that he stopped sending the profits from his L.A. cocaine sales to the Contras. At other times he has said it was late 1982. In either case, Blandón said that the reason he was given for halting the donations was that the Contras had plenty of money.

"In 1983, okay, the Contra gets a lot of money from the United States," he told a federal grand jury in 1994. "And they were—when Reagan get in the power, Mr. Reagan get in the power, we start receiving a lot of money. And the people that was in charge, it was the CIA, so they didn't want to raise any money because they have, they had the money that they wanted."

"From the government?" Assistant U.S. Attorney David Hall asked.

"Yes, for the Contra revolution."

"Okay."

"So we started—you know, the ambitious person, we started doing business by ourselves," Blandón said.

"To make money for yourselves?"

"Yes."

"There's a lot of money to be made?"

"Yes."

Blandón told CIA inspectors that FDN commander Enrique Bermúdez came to California sometime in 1983 and told him personally that it wasn't necessary for the Los Angeles group to raise any more money. "The FDN needed people, not money, because the CIA was providing money," he said Bermúdez told them. But Blandón's mentor, Norwin Meneses, said Blandón remained a loyal financial supporter of the Contras for the duration of the war. Asked when Blandón stopped giving the Contras monetary support, Meneses replied, "Never, as far as I know."

Blandón said he was working for Meneses at the time the Contra cocaine kickbacks ended. "I continued working for a period of time, about six months, and then I changed because Meneses was—it was the same thing. I wasn't making any money." Blandón was tired of being stuck in the middle of fights between Norwin and his estranged wife, Maritza. Meneses was still charging him too much for cocaine and was refusing to let him share in the spoils. "When I was with Meneses, you see, I didn't make no money at all," Blandón griped. "Meneses was charging me, you know, a big price, that I couldn't meet. I couldn't make enough money, you know, because all the time I owe him."

Blandón said he owed Meneses around $100,000 and couldn't seem to reduce the debt because "I didn't make any money. So I start looking for my own resource, or my own sources." He found them by going behind Meneses's back and dealing directly with Norwin's L.A. suppliers—a couple of Colombians he knew only as Luis and Tony, to whom he had been delivering cash for his miserly boss. "I used to deliver money to the Colombian connection from Meneses, and I got a friendship with them and they know how hard I was working at that time. It was easy for me to ask them for credit because they knew how, how hard I work at that time for them."

The Colombians were happy to help, Blandón said, and encouraged him to strike out on his own. "When I fight with Norwin, the Colombian people started, you know, pushing me along, trying to cross Norwin, and they go with me and talk to me that I can make it myself." Asking the Colombians for cocaine on credit was not difficult. They were used to working cocaine deals that way. They would give you the cocaine and a few days to sell it. Then you'd pay them what you owed. It was a clever way for the cartels to expand their customer base in the United States and keep their own exposure to a minimum.

The Colombians advanced Blandón fifteen kilos—worth about $885,000—and they were off to the races. He started out getting fifteen kilos a month and within a couple months had progressed to thirty kilos a month. He left Meneses and the Contras behind and concentrated on making money for himself, he said.

But several parts of Blandón's story don't add up. He testified that when he was supplying Henry Corrales in 1983, Ross was already selling up to seven kilos a day, and Blandón said he had other customers as well. If

Blandón's testimony about the size of his initial dealings with the Colombians is true, he wouldn't have had enough cocaine to supply Ross for a week, much less a month. Before his purported split from Meneses he had been selling far larger quantities of cocaine than that, he admitted.

"And do you remember if you were getting large amounts or small amounts from Mr. Meneses?" Blandón was asked in 1996.

"At the end, large."

"And what is a large amount?"

"About 40, 50, at this time," he testified.

During his federal grand jury appearance in 1994, Blandón was asked to estimate "how much total you would have gotten from Norwin" during the time he was receiving cocaine from him.

"How many I received from Norwin?"

"Yes."

"Well, it was—I received from him, okay, not for me, because it was—I was only the administrator at that time. I received, in L.A. about 200, 300," he said.

But if Blandón didn't make his first sale until the spring of 1982 and spent a year to eighteen months dealing only ounces and grams, as he testified, it would have been impossible for him to have sold 200 to 300 kilos for Meneses by late 1982 or early 1983, when he claims he broke from him.

In fact, evidence turned up by the FBI and DEA in later years showed that Blandón and Meneses were still working together as late as 1991. In August 1986 Blandón's and Meneses's NADDIS files—computerized intelligence profiles maintained by the federal government on suspected drug traffickers—showed both men as current associates. Moreover, if Blandón double-crossed Meneses in 1982–83 by stealing his sources and his L.A. customers, it is doubtful the men would have remained friends and business partners, yet they continued to operate hotels and other businesses together in Nicaragua.

What appears to have happened is that Blandón acquired additional sources of supply sometime in 1984 and became his own boss in L.A., while Meneses remained in charge of the San Francisco drug operation. And they continued working with each other and with the Contras for years, more or less as equals.

Others who were present at the time confirm that this, in fact, is exactly what occurred. "The principal group is controlled by Blandón and is the focal point for drug supply and money laundering for the others," an August 1986 DEA report stated. "The other group is run by Meneses and is located principally in the San Francisco area.... Per CI [confidential informant] cocaine is often transported to the Blandón association and then from Blandón to Meneses in San Francisco." That DEA report, based on debriefings of an informant inside Blandón's drug ring, showed Blandón and Meneses working together so closely in mid-1986 that they were sharing the same cocaine supplier and money launderer.

In a 1992 interview with the FBI, Blandón's associate Jacinto Torres told agents that Blandón continued receiving cocaine from Meneses for at least two years longer than Blandón admits. "As of approximately 1984, Blandón was involved in cocaine sales in the Glendale, California area. Blandón's supplier as of 1984 continued to be Norwin Meneses," Torres told the FBI. Torres said Blandón's cocaine business "dramatically increased" in 1984, and that Meneses was flying planeloads of dope in from Miami to keep up with the demand; "Norwin Meneses, Blandón's supplier as of 1983 and 1984, routinely flew quantities of 200 to 400 kilograms from Miami to the West Coast. Blandón eventually 'separated' from Meneses and obtained other sources of supply."

On a different occasion Blandón timed his break from Meneses and the Contra drug operation to when "we received the $19 million help." If that's true, it places his departure somewhere in 1984. The Contras got two injections of $19 million from the CIA. The first one came at the end of 1981, when Reagan first authorized the CIA's involvement, before Blandón says he began selling drugs.

The second $19 million, congressional records show, was approved at the end of 1983, combined with some leftover CIA funds from the year before, and was delivered to the FDN during the first six months of 1984. It was the last bit of financial assistance the CIA was authorized to provide the FDN before Congress officially took the CIA out of the Contra business. After that, the FDN began running out of money, and CIA director William Casey turned to Lieutenant Colonel Oliver North of the National Security Council staff and asked him to start setting up a funding and supply operation outside the CIA.

That Blandón continued dealing with Meneses through 1984 was unwittingly confirmed by the *Los Angeles Times* in a 1996 story that attempted to demonstrate that Blandón and Meneses had split in 1982. The *Times* claimed to have interviewed an unnamed "cocaine trafficking associate" of Blandón, who said he was present at Meneses's house in the Bay Area on a day when Meneses and Blandón were celebrating the consummation of a big drug deal. "Danilo and Norwin had done some business," the *Times* quoted the associate as saying. "The deal involved 40 or 50 kilos. The money was all divvied up. There was cash all over the place. Norwin had steaks on the grill. It was going to be a big party."

The phone rang, and Meneses's girlfriend, Blanca Margarita Castaño, answered it and then shrieked, "'Jairo's been arrested!' Well, everybody cleared out in a heartbeat. They grabbed the money and ran.... I don't think anyone turned off the steaks."

Records show Jairo Meneses was arrested on November 26, 1984, roughly two years after Blandón claims he quit dealing with Norwin. San Francisco cocaine dealer Rafael Corñejo, a longtime wholesaler for Meneses, also confirmed that Blandón and Meneses were still working together then. "I didn't see him a lot, but I know he was with Norwin in '84," Corñejo said. Blandón and Meneses had paid him a memorable visit in San Francisco that year, stopping by a commercial building Corñejo owned on Chenery Street. Norwin wanted to store something in his building, and Corñejo didn't ask what. "It didn't matter to me. You know, if Norwin wants to do something...I said, 'Anything you want.' I like Norwin, I respect Norwin."

During that visit, Corñejo said, "Blandón starts telling me he'd been doing lots of things with the black people down there [in L.A.]. And I said, 'Yeah, so?' And he wanted to see if I was interested in doing something up here. And I said, 'Why?' And he said I should get into the black thing. No one cares about them, he tells me. When they start killing themselves no one cares." Corñejo told Blandón "not to play me with that race thing. Business is business, but don't play me with that race thing. The difference between him and me was that I grew up in San Francisco and it didn't mean that much to us. But he grew up in Nicaragua, with these rich and powerful people, and that's the way he thought."

Blandón's own experience had taught him that no one cared about the cocaine that he was pouring into South Central in 1984. By then, he'd been dealing ever-increasing amounts to Ricky Ross for two years and had received no interference from the police whatsoever. The only media in L.A. that seemed alarmed by the spread of crack in black neighborhoods was the African-American press. The white newspapers didn't even know what crack was.

In December 1983, for instance, former L.A. Dodger legend Maury Wills was arrested for driving a stolen car. The *Los Angeles Herald-Examiner* noted that the "arresting officers also found a small vial on the automobile's front seat containing a white, rock-like substance believed to be cocaine. Police said a clear glass water pipe was found next to the vial." An LAPD officer "refused to speculate if the water pipe may have been used for free-basing, a technique in which cocaine is smoked to intensify the high." The story said Wills was "booked on the grand theft auto allegation pending further identification of the white substance by the LAPD's narcotics laboratory."

Starting in 1984, unlike what they'd been seeing one or two years earlier, street cops like Steve Polak were arresting low-level dealers in South Central with more cocaine than they had ever seen before. The patrolmen were reporting their finds to the LAPD's Major Violators Unit but were getting nowhere, said Polak, who was one of the LAPD's crack experts and lectured police departments around the country. "A lot of detectives, a lot of cops, were saying to them, 'Hey, these blacks, no longer are we just seeing gram dealers. These guys are doing ounces, they were doing keys.'" The Major Violators Unit, which dealt primarily with Colombians and South Americans, found such reports hard to swallow. "They were saying, basically, 'Ahh, South Central, how much could they be dealing?'" Polak laughed. "'The money's not there. We're not going to bring in millions of dollars in seizures or large quantities of coke down there.'" As a result, the crack dealers of South Central "virtually went untouched for a long time. They enjoyed quite a run there without anyone ever working them."

The same could not be said for the Meneses organization in San Francisco. Since 1981, it had been under constant investigation by the DEA, the FBI, and the California Bureau of Narcotics Enforcement (BNE). But aside from a couple of nickel-and-dime busts of Norwin's nephews, nothing much happened.

"Norwin was a target of ours, and his organization was one that we'd worked on," said Jerry Smith, former head of the BNE's San Francisco bureau. But Smith said Meneses's network was so tight-knit that it was impossible to get anyone inside. The Meneses organization, one federal prosecutor wrote in 1993, had been "the target of unsuccessful investigative attempts for many years."

Meneses, on the other hand, seemed to have much better luck at infiltration than the police.

"There were some things that happened and I'm really kind of reluctant to go into that particular thing," Smith said. "It had nothing to do with the CIA or the FBI. It had to do with one of my guys, who subsequently was fired...I think he was trying to broker some information to somebody for some money. And we got onto it very quickly and so he's no longer around, and I don't think anything ever came to fruition. But it was something that bothered us at the time."

Meneses, in an interview, boasted that he had a DEA agent on his payroll who was feeding him information about the government's many investigations, allowing him to stay one step ahead of the law.

Even if that's true, however, it does not fully explain the drug lord's complete imperviousness to prosecution. It's hard to imagine how one or two corrupt narcotics agents could have held off the entire U.S. law enforcement community, especially when the DEA and FBI had been aware of Norwin's criminal activities since the 1970s. It becomes even harder to fathom given the events that would unfold in late 1984.

"Oh, he [Meneses] was totally protected by the U.S. government," insisted Contra supporter Dennis Ainsworth, a former San Francisco–area economics professor. "He was protected by everyone under the sun."

That conclusion had been a difficult and painful one for Ainsworth to reach. A staunch conservative and Republican party stalwart, the tall, patrician Ainsworth had believed in the Contras, and threw himself wholeheartedly into their cause starting in late 1983, when he became involved in efforts to assist Nicaraguan refugees who had settled in San Francisco after fleeing the Sandinistas. The Nicaraguans, he said, most of whom had been Somoza supporters, had difficulty getting help from the liberal churches in San Francisco, which Ainsworth claimed were interested only in assisting refugees from right-wing Central American dictatorships. "All of a sudden, bang, we've got a problem in our backyard, and nobody wanted to help them," Ainsworth recalled. "And so, I met some of the Nicaraguans and we started helping. Getting clothing donations and stuff like that."

In February 1984, Ainsworth said, he saw an announcement in the *San Francisco Chronicle* about a seminar at the Sir Francis Drake Hotel concerning Central America and the Contras. He attended and met Julio Bonilla, a Nicaraguan who was the local coordinator of the FDN. The men chatted briefly and exchanged phone numbers. (According to one published source, Norwin Meneses helped finance that seminar at the Drake.) About three weeks later, Ainsworth said, Bonilla called him and invited him to an informal gathering at a house on Colon Avenue in San Francisco, to meet with some of the Nicaraguans who had helped put the seminar together. Ainsworth found a pleasant group of middle-class husbands and wives, many of them recent immigrants. One, he said, had been Anastasio Somoza's dentist. Their leader was a jovial pharmaceutical salesman, Don Sinicco, known to others in the trade as "Mr. Maalox" because he sold the popular antacid to local hospitals. Sinicco was not Nicaraguan; he was born in Italy and lived there until 1938, when Mussolini came to power. He later married a Nicaraguan, Nydia Gonzáles, the daughter of a powerful Nicaraguan general, Fernando Gonzáles. Through them, he became fascinated with Nicaraguan politics.

As the covert war in Nicaragua escalated, stories about the conflict began popping up in San Francisco's newspapers, and Sinicco read them avidly, but not happily. He believed the press was cheerleading for the Sandinistas, and he fired off dozens letters to the newspapers, chiding them for their "slant." Many were published. "I got a reputation," he said proudly.

In late 1983, Sinicco said, he got a call from a man named Adolfo Calero, the head of the political wing of the FDN. Sinicco said Calero called him because of his letter-writing campaign, which flattered him considerably. "He said, 'We need someone like you to help us get the word out. People will listen to you because you're an American.' So they contacted me, and I said that's fine." At Calero's suggestion, Sinicco formed a small organization called United Support Against Communism in the Americas (USACA), and he and his friends began holding regular meetings, casting about for ways to publicize the Contras' plight.

Sinicco said he'd never met Calero before, but his wife and Calero's wife were old friends. In Managua, Calero had been a well-known businessman, a Chamber of Commerce type who'd run the bottling plant for the local Coca-Cola distributorship. He was also a CIA asset, someone the U.S. government had hoped might replace Somoza as Nicaragua's president before the Sandinista takeover. According to former FDN director Edgar Chamorro, Calero "had been working for the CIA in Nicaragua for a long time. He served as, among other things, a conduit of funds from the United States Embassy to various student and labor organizations." In early 1983 the CIA had brought Calero out of Nicaragua and installed him as the political director of the FDN; his broad, acne-scarred visage soon became the most familiar face of the Contra rebels in the United States. Tall and imposing, Calero spoke English well, not surprisingly for a graduate of Notre Dame University in South Bend, Indiana. "Calero and Bermúdez were our main links with the CIA," Chamorro declared. "They met constantly with the CIA station chief."

In 1984 Calero began visiting San Francisco frequently, Ainsworth and Sinicco said, and would usually stay at their homes while in the city attending to FDN business. While finding Calero personable and smooth, Ainsworth was dismayed by the lack of political sophistication displayed by the FDN support group Sinicco had assembled at Calero's request. The Nicaraguans were eager and committed to the Contra cause, Ainsworth recalled, but there wasn't a soul among them who knew anything about working the American political system. "That little group that used to meet at his house...would have done nothing if I hadn't come over and said, 'Look, I'll set these things up.' All Sinicco and his friends were thinking of doing was writing a few letters to the editor. They had no connections whatsoever. And I happened to walk in and I was a well-connected guy."

Ainsworth gently suggested to the Nicaraguans that there were other ways of drawing attention to their cause. Why not sponsor a speaking tour for some Contra officials, such as Adolfo Calero? Bring him to town, show him around, get some press coverage. Sinicco, who was USACA's president, said he and his friends were "very impressed" with Ainsworth's ideas and his political connections and voted to make him a director of their new group. "As far as I knew, he was presumably very active in Republican politics. He knew senators, he knew representatives, both federal and in Sacramento. He knew the chairman of the party. He seemed to be influential and was active internationally in anti-Communist efforts," Sinicco said. Ainsworth, he said, began opening doors all across San Francisco. "He was the one who appeared to be able to get us these bookings at places like the Olympic Club, the Commonwealth Club. None of us belonged to those kind of places. But he either did or knew people that did. He was able to devote his full-time attention to the group. Most of the rest of us were working men. We had businesses to run, jobs to go to."

On June 4, 1984, Ainsworth arranged a private reception for Calero at the exclusive St. Francis Yacht Club in San Francisco with about sixty of the city's most influential business leaders and Republicans. "It was just a chance for everybody to meet and greet. It wasn't a fund-raiser. Calero was in the news, he was a newsmaker, and some people I knew had expressed an interest in meeting him," Ainsworth said. Calero gave a short speech, answered a few questions, and mingled. "The cocktail party went very smoothly," Ainsworth would later tell the FBI.

Afterward, Calero, Ainsworth, Sinicco, and about twenty others drove over to Caesar's Italian Restaurant, one of the many near Fisherman's Wharf. When the bill came, Ainsworth said, a small neatly dressed man he had not noticed before called the waiter over and picked up the tab for the entire party. Ainsworth leaned over and asked a Nicaraguan friend who Mr. Generosity was. "You don't want to know," was the response he said he got.

Sinicco said he initially assumed one of the Mendoza brothers—two strident Cuban anti-Communists who were members of USACA—had paid the bill. "When we called for the check, we were told it had been taken care of, and I thought it was one of the Cubans who'd paid for it. I thought Max [Mendoza]'s brother had paid for the dinner, and in fact I went up and thanked him afterwards and I'm sure he wonders to this day what I was thanking him for." Before the evening was over, Sinicco was set straight by another Nicaraguan: the big spender was named Norwin Meneses. He owned a restaurant and a travel agency in the Mission District. "I'd never heard of him," Sinicco said, "but we were glad for the financial assistance."

At the end of the dinner, Ainsworth stood and announced that in two days, Don Sinicco was going to be hosting a cocktail party for their esteemed guest, Adolfo Calero, and that everyone in the room was invited.

At the party two days later, Norwin Meneses came in with the crowd dressed in an expensive white linen sports coat with a cashmere overcoat draped over his arm. Sinicco said Meneses spoke to Calero briefly, and the two men retired to a back bedroom, apparently for a meeting. Ainsworth confirmed that. Calero has said he never met privately with Meneses.

Later, as the party was winding down, Sinicco got out his Instamatic camera and began snapping pictures of the historic occasion. He got a shot of some of the wives posing behind a handmade cloth map of Nicaragua. He snapped one of Max Mendoza, the Cuban, with a big grin on his mustachioed face. Sinicco found Calero in the kitchen, huddled by the refrigerator with Meneses, San Francisco FDN coordinator Julio Bonilla, and some other local FDN officials. He told the group to smile and lined up the shot, but just as he snapped the shutter, Meneses closed his eyes and turned away. "Let me get another real quick," Sinicco said. This time Meneses kept his eyes open, but he didn't smile. He looked at Sinicco and glared. Calero posed with a tight smile on his face.

Sinicco suddenly remembered Meneses from the restaurant two nights earlier, and he approached him and thanked him for his kindness. "I told him that now that he knew where we lived, he should come to our next [USACA] meeting and he said that he would, but that he really needed to leave now."

After that Meneses began attending USACA's meetings, Sinicco recalled, usually arriving with the Mendoza brothers, who ran a Cuban anti-Communist group in San Francisco. Ainsworth said he did not believe there was a connection between Meneses and the Cubans, other than a political one. However, a former FDN mercenary from Florida, Jack Terrell, said Meneses was plugged tightly into the Cuban exile community in Miami. "He assisted the Cuban Legion in their radio propaganda shows coming from Miami," Terrell said, adding that Meneses was an associate of several members of the 2506 Brigade, which was made up of Bay of Pigs veterans.

Sinicco showed the author attendance records, minutes of meetings, and other assorted paperwork he kept as USACA's president. One of the documents he provided was a handwritten note that he said were his talking points for one of USACA's earliest meetings. "Our first time venture as USACA has proven highly successful," Sinicco had written, and he listed "seven successes." The first was that "Adolfo was brought over."

Success No. 6: "We are receiving some attention from some Cuban people who appear eager to help."

Success No. 7: "Mr. Meneces' [sic] contribution." Meneses dropped a $160 contribution on the little group one night, Sinicco said, and picked up another dinner for $324.20.

According to Sinicco's files, another founding member of USACA was Father Thomas F. Dowling, a San Franciscan whom Sinicco said was "some kind of a priest." Though he sometimes passed himself off as a Roman Catholic priest, Dowling was an ordained member of a tiny splinter church called the North American Old Roman Catholic Church of the Utrecht Succession, a church whose legitimacy is a matter of some debate. While working with USACA and the Contras, Dowling appeared before Congress in 1985 sporting a clerical collar and identifying himself as a Catholic priest, to testify as a purported witness to Sandinista atrocities. His appearance had been arranged by the State Department's Office of Public Diplomacy for Latin America, later described by congressional investigators as an illegal CIA-run domestic propaganda mill.

"Senior CIA officials with backgrounds in covert operations, as well as military intelligence and psychological operations specialists from the Department of Defense, were deeply involved in establishing and participating in a domestic political and propaganda operation run through an obscure bureau in the Department of State," a 1992 House committee staff report concluded. "Almost all of these activities were hidden from public view and many of the individuals involved were never questioned or interviewed by the Iran/Contra committees."

Through that office, the CIA and the National Security Council engaged in "a domestic, covert operation designed to lobby the Congress, manipulate the media and influence domestic public opinion," the report said, echoing a 1987 investigation by the Comptroller General of the United States, which said the State Department had engaged in "prohibited, covert propaganda activities."

Dowling later admitted receiving about $73,000 in cash and travelers checks from Oliver North, CIA agent Adolfo Calero and other members of North's operation between 1986 and 1987 "to affect public opinion favorably toward the Reagan position inside, regarding Central America." Dowling testified that the money went to a non-profit organization he'd set up in San Francisco called the Latin America Strategic Studies Institute (LASSI). In addition to Dowling, LASSI employed a recently retired CIA officer with extensive Latin American experience, G. James Quesada, a Nicaraguan who lived in the San Francisco area. "I met [Quesada] when I spoke before the retired group of intelligence officers a few years back," Dowling testified in 1987.

Quesada confirmed that he worked with Dowling but said he did so as private citizen, not for the CIA. "I know nobody thinks a CIA agent ever retires, but I really did retire," he said in an interview, with a laugh. Quesada also met Norwin Meneses and Danilo Blandón at an FDN meeting, and instantly, he said, his antennae went up. "I found out what Meneses was pretty quickly, but he was not involved in our side of things, which was the political side," Quesada said. Meneses and Blandón had something to do with "the other side," meaning the military part of the Contra operation. "As I recall, Blandón was looking for medical students or was recruiting medical students to go down to Honduras. I stayed away from both of them."

In addition to his work with Oliver North and the San Francisco FDN, Father Dowling was also heavily involved with CAUSA, a conservative political organization that was part of the Rev. Sun-Myung Moon's Unification Church. During the time of the CIA funding cutoff, Moon's organization—which was linked in the 1970s to the Korean Central Intelligence Agency—stepped in and began funneling money and supplies to the Contras. Dowling was a member of CAUSA's national advisory board and a frequent speaker at CAUSA rallies and conferences. Among the documents USACA founder Sinicco showed the author was an August 1984 letter from CAUSA's president, retired air force general E. D. Woellner, thanking Sinicco's organization for attending the annual CAUSA convention and suggesting that the groups work more closely in the future.

Though the combination of fringe religions and the Contras may seem strange, partly declassified CIA records show that the agency had evidence as far back as 1982 that there were unwholesome connections between Meneses's drug ring, the FDN, and an unnamed religious organization in the United States. According to a 1998 CIA Inspector General's report, the CIA's Domestic Collection Division picked up word in October 1982 that "there are indications of links between (a U.S. religious organization) and two Nicaraguan counter-revolutionary groups." The heavily censored CIA cable said, "These links involve an exchange in [the United States] of narcotics for arms."

The CIA's domestic spies reported that "there was to be a meeting among the participants in Costa Rica regarding this exchange" and that two U.S. law enforcement agencies were aware of it. Though the agencies were not named in the censored CIA cable, the FBI had the Meneses organization under investigation at the time and had learned through wiretaps that Norwin's Costa Rican Contra associates—Horacio Pereira, Troilo Sánchez, and Fernando Sánchez—were shipping cocaine to San Francisco.

CIA headquarters ordered its domestic agents to get more information about the upcoming meeting in Costa Rica, and a few days later another cable arrived at Langley with additional details. "The attendees at the meeting would include representatives from the FDN and UDN, and several unidentified U.S. citizens," the CIA cable reported. It "identified Renato Peña as one of four persons—along with three unidentified U.S. citizens—who would represent the FDN at the Costa Rica meeting."

Renato Peña Cabrera was one of Norwin Meneses's San Francisco drug dealers and a friend of Dennis Ainsworth. Peña was dating Danilo Blandón's sister, Leysla, and was a top official in the San Francisco FDN. Peña told CIA investigators that he met Meneses in 1982 at an FDN meeting and served as an official representative of the FDN's political wing in northern California from 1982 until mid-1984. After that, he said, he "was appointed to be the military representative of the FDN in San Francisco, in part because of Norwin Meneses' close relationship with [Enrique] Bermúdez."

Jairo Meneses, who was in charge of Norwin's drug network in San Francisco, hooked Peña up with Norwin, and soon he was hauling cash and cocaine between Los Angeles and San Francisco. "Peña says he made from six to eight trips from San Francisco to Los Angeles between 1982 and 1984 for Meneses' drug trafficking organization," the CIA Inspector General reported. "Each time, he says, he carried anywhere from $600,000 to $1,000,000 to Los Angeles and returned to San Francisco with six to eight kilograms of cocaine. Peña says that a Colombian associate of Meneses told Peña in general terms that a portion of the proceeds from the sale of the cocaine Peña brought to San Francisco were going to the Contras."

Even with the inflated cocaine prices of the early 1980s, the amount of money Peña was taking to L.A. was far more than was needed to pay for six to eight kilos of cocaine. It seems likely that the excess—$300,000 to $500,000 per trip—was the Contras' cut of the drug proceeds.

When the information about Renato Peña's involvement in the upcoming Costa Rican meeting was relayed back to Langley, CIA headquarters immediately ordered the Domestic Collection Division to halt any further investigation, allegedly because "of the apparent participation of U.S. citizens." But the agency began having second thoughts about sitting on the information. On November 17, 1982, Langley worriedly cabled one of its stations in Latin America to tell its agents that while headquarters didn't think the reports about the Contras and drugs were true, "the information was surfaced by another [U.S. government] agency and may return to haunt us. Feel we must try to confirm or refute the information if possible." Langley wanted to know if Contra leaders had "scheduled any meeting in the next few weeks? If so, what information do you have regarding the attendees?"

The response was probably not what CIA headquarters wanted to hear. "Several Contra officials had recently gone to the United States for a series of meetings, including a meeting with Contra supporters in San Francisco," the Central American CIA station reported back. (It was during October 1982 that FDN leaders met with Meneses in L.A. and San Francisco in an effort to set up local Contra support groups in those cities.)

The CIA Inspector General's report is silent about what, if anything, the agency did next. Peña told CIA inspectors that the unnamed U.S. religious organization mentioned in the CIA cables "was an FDN political ally that provided only humanitarian aid to Nicaraguan refugees and logistical support for Contra-related rallies, such as printing services and portable stages."

When Renato Peña and Meneses's nephew Jairo were arrested on cocaine trafficking charges in November 1984, Ainsworth began suspecting that the FDN was also involved in drug trafficking. "Renato wasn't a drug dealer," Ainsworth said. "He was a Contra and he was duped. When Congress cut off aid in the fall of 1983, these guys had nowhere else to turn and they wanted to get their country back. And once you say I'll do anything to get my country back, then they were easy prey for Meneses, who said, 'Hey, you do this for me and I'll help you guys out.'"

According to a DEA agent's affidavit filed in the case, Jairo Meneses and Renato Peña had been selling cocaine in San Francisco since at least March 1984 and, on several occasions, sold coke directly to undercover DEA agents. The cocaine deals were set up through Jairo Meneses, and Peña made the deliveries and picked up the cash. The DEA agent said he'd bought five ounces of cocaine from Peña at a Folsom Street recording studio for the astoundingly low price of $1,100 an ounce—$39 a gram. According to the Rand Institute study of cocaine prices, an ounce of cocaine in San Francisco was then selling for $2,350, or $166 a gram. As the dealing went on, the price of the cocaine dropped even further, and its purity reached medical quality levels. One deal, which was for 392 grams, ended up costing the DEA a mere $35 a gram. The cocaine tested out at 97 percent pure.

When Peña and Jairo Meneses were arrested, agents found a kilo of cocaine in the trunk of Peña's car. At an apartment Jairo Meneses maintained in Oakland as a cocaine storehouse, the DEA found half a kilo in a safe. Because the evidence against him was so overwhelming—hand-to-hand sales to DEA agents and a kilo in his car—Peña pleaded guilty to one count of possession of cocaine with intent to sell in March 1985. He admitted that he was selling cocaine but insisted that "the drugs were not mine." He also agreed to help the government prosecute Jairo Meneses, and was given a two-year sentence in return.

Ainsworth said that Peña was devastated by the drug trafficking charges, and that the young Nicaraguan admitted to him later that year that he'd been doing it for the Contras. Peña suggested that "the FDN is involved in drug smuggling with the aid of Norwin Meneses, who also buys arms for Enrique Bermúdez, a leader of the FDN," Ainsworth told the FBI in 1987. Meneses, in an interview with the author, acknowledged that Peña was one of "my employees" at the time he was arrested. Peña later confirmed to CIA inspectors that Norwin Meneses "had Contra-related dealings with Enrique Bermúdez."

Alarmed by Peña's revelations, Ainsworth began looking into the relationship between the FDN and drugs. He made "inquiries in the local San Francisco Nicaraguan community and wondered among his acquaintances what Adolfo Calero and other people in the FDN movement were doing and the word that he received back is that they were probably engaged in cocaine smuggling," Ainsworth later told the FBI.

During one of Ainsworth's trips to Washington in 1985, he said, "I went to see some friends of mine and started asking some questions." One friend slipped Ainsworth a copy of a Drug Enforcement Administration intelligence report dated February 6, 1984. The DEA report, prepared by agent Sandalio González in San José, Costa Rica, told of the results of a debriefing of a confidential informant. Ainsworth's heart sank as he read it. The informant "related that Norwin Meneses Cantarero, Edmundo's younger brother, was presently residing in San José, Costa Rica, and is the apparent head of a criminal organization responsible for smuggling kilogram quantities of cocaine to the United States." The discovery left Ainsworth reeling: "I had gone through the Looking Glass. I had crossed over into the nether world that 99 percent of the population wouldn't even believe existed."

In September 1985 Ainsworth was contacted by a U.S. Customs Service official who was "investigating the Nicaraguan role in a large narcotics ring extending from Miami, Florida to Texas and California." The Customs agent wanted to ask Ainsworth about the FDN. "During the contact, [name deleted] complained to Ainsworth that national security interests kept him from making good narcotics cases and he acted frustrated at this chain of events," Ainsworth would later tell the FBI. "According to [name deleted] two U.S. Customs Service officers who felt threatened and intimidated by National Security interference in legitimate narcotics smuggling investigations had resigned and had assumed false identities." The FBI report went on to say that the Customs agent "told Ainsworth that Norwin Meneses would have been arrested in a major drug case in 1983 or 1984 except that he had been warned by a corrupt [information deleted] officer."

Other law enforcement sources told Ainsworth "they had a file on Meneses that was two feet thick. I thought this bastard should have been arrested. I assumed there would be an outstanding warrant on this guy. I was amazed. There wasn't a single outstanding warrant on Meneses. Not one. They had no interest in him whatsoever. Here you had a major cocaine trafficker who was deeply involved with the Contras, and apparently, everyone but me knew about it. After I broke with Calero, I found out Calero and Meneses were very good friends."

Calero has admitted meeting with Meneses on at least six occasions in San Francisco, but he has portrayed them as simple greetings during large public gatherings. He has repeatedly denied knowing Meneses was a drug trafficker, yet he admitted to a Costa Rican paper in 1986 that he knew Meneses was "involved in some illegal things, but I don't know anything."

USACA president Don Sinicco said he never suspected Norwin Meneses was involved in criminal activities, but he confirmed that Ainsworth began muttering about it. "What always bothered me about [Dennis] is that towards the end, I don't know what, he seemed to get disillusioned or disgusted with Calero. Dennis got disillusioned about something," Sinicco said.

Ainsworth's disillusionment caused him to quit working with the Contras and seek out the FBI. In early 1987, records show, during his first meeting with FBI agents, Ainsworth warned them that the FDN "has become more involved in selling arms and cocaine for personal gain than in a military effort to overthrow the current Nicaraguan Sandinista government." He told the agents about Norwin Meneses and Renato Peña, about Tom Dowling and Oliver North, and about North's illegal Contra support network in the U.S. and Central America. Much of the information Ainsworth gave the FBI and, later, Iran-Contra prosecutor Lawrence Walsh's staff about the inner workings of the FDN and the relationships between Contra leaders and U.S. government officials was corroborated during the congressional Iran-Contra investigations.

Ainsworth was also getting death threats, he told the FBI, but the agents seemed unimpressed. "He had no information to substantiate this alleged threat," they wrote. Ainsworth never heard from them again. "I mean, here I am as a citizen, I complained to the FBI and they tell me they have no interest in the case. Then I call Walsh's people up and they sent a couple FBI guys out to talk to me and they have no interest in it. I couldn't find anyone who was interested in this. And I made a legitimate effort. And people were like, 'Den, leave this alone. Just leave it alone,'" Ainsworth remembered. "I thought I was part of the establishment. And all of a sudden I was a leper." Frightened and heartsick, Ainsworth fled California for the East Coast, where he went into semiseclusion.

Meanwhile, the narcotics investigation that began with the arrests of Renato Peña and Jairo Meneses seemed to fall into a black hole. The case federal prosecutors had assembled against the drug kingpin's nephew was a slam-dunk. They'd found cocaine in Jairo's apartment; his codefendant had cut a deal and was prepared to testify for the government. If convicted of the charges against him—one count of conspiracy to distribute cocaine and six counts of possession with intent to distribute—Jairo Meneses would spend the next fifteen years in the federal pen. His decision to plead guilty and rat out Uncle Norwin could hardly be considered a surprise.

At his sentencing in 1985, Jairo admitted that he was a delivery man and "bookkeeper" for his uncle, whom he described as a "large dealer" who sold about 30 or 40 kilos a week. In exchange for his cooperation, he was sentenced to three years in jail. But that's as close as prosecutors got to Norwin.

In an interview with a Costa Rican paper in 1986, Meneses scoffed at his nephew's testimony. Jairo had made it up, Norwin declared, because he'd refused to bail the boy out when he'd gotten arrested. "If Jairo supposedly was my accountant, like he says, I would have been interested in taking him out of jail because he would have had me by the tail," Meneses told *La Nacion*. "Isn't that logical?" (Norwin didn't mention that Jairo's bail was paid by Danilo Blandón's sister, Leysla Balladares, who also bailed out Peña, her boyfriend.) "Besides," Norwin added, "I remained in San Francisco. I have never hidden. There's never been a warrant for my arrest. I have not changed passports. That I directed a drug trafficking organization is totally false."

Some of Meneses's assertions were indeed irrefutable. With the testimony of Jairo Meneses and Renato Peña, and the stacks of other evidence the police had compiled against him over the years, it would have been a relatively easy matter to have convicted the drug lord on any number of trafficking and conspiracy charges. Many dopers have gone to jail on much less evidence. At a minimum, the government could have deported him as an undesirable alien and banned him forever from the United States; he was, after all, living in the United States as a guest of the government—a political refugee.

But it didn't happen. Nothing happened. Norwin Meneses continued living as a free man, crisscrossing U.S. borders with impunity, dealing cocaine and sending supplies to the Contras. And his relationship with the U.S. government grew even closer.

10

"Teach a man a craft and he's liable to practice it"

The potential exposure of Norwin Meneses couldn't have come at a more inopportune time for the Contras, or the CIA.

During the winter of 1984–85, the Contra forces were at their lowest ebb, both on the battlefield and in the battle for U.S. public opinion. For twelve months the Contras had staggered from one public relations disaster to another. There had been a major uproar in Congress in the spring of 1984, when it was revealed that the CIA cowboys running the Contra project had seeded Nicaraguan harbors with hundreds of small mines, which proceeded to indiscriminately blow holes in merchant ships from all over the world, including those from friendly nations. Shortly after that, a bomb went off at ARDE commander Edén Pastora's jungle headquarters during a press conference, wounding Pastora, killing or injuring a score of ARDE officials and journalists, and throwing the Contra armies in Costa Rica into turmoil.

Later in the year, in the midst of Reagan's reelection campaign, an illustrated terrorism manual the CIA printed up for the boys in the field ended up in the newspapers, creating yet another public outcry and much congressional breast-beating.

The hardest blow came in October 1984. With the administration off balance and desperately hoping to avoid any more CIA-Contra controversies before the elections, the Democrat-controlled Congress succeeded in passing yet another Boland Amendment. Unlike the earlier ones, though, this had some teeth.

It prohibited the CIA, the Defense Department, or any other agency of the U.S. government from giving any money or aid to anyone for the support of the Contras. The money spigot had been officially turned off; the loopholes were sewn shut.

The CIA and Defense Department began withdrawing their trainers, advisers, administrators, tacticians, and logisticians from Central America, and by the end of the year the Contras were alone and in disarray. Thousands of rebel fighters began retreating from Nicaragua for the safety of Honduras. Money was scarce; weapons and ammo were in even shorter supply.

In early 1985, as the Contras spent their last batch of CIA money, another mini-scandal erupted. Allegations of Contra battlefield atrocities surfaced in reports from human rights groups, spotlighting murders, tortures, assassinations, and "the deliberate use of terror" by some Contra field commanders, putting the lie to Reagan's characterization of them as "freedom fighters," showing instead their connection to Somoza's hated National Guard.

Even the FDN's normally optimistic handlers in Washington began to despair. Reagan's national security adviser, Robert McFarland, told FDN leader Adolfo Calero in January 1985 that maybe it was time to start thinking about "cutting both our losses and theirs." The administration's prestige was riding on the Contras; Reagan had gone so far during a speech as to compare them to the founding fathers of the American Revolution. The FDN's only ray of hope was to withdraw from battle and lie low until the spring, when Congress agreed to let the administration come back and make one more pitch for money.

Had Norwin Meneses popped up then with a federal cocaine trafficking indictment around his neck—after all the meetings he'd had with FDN directors Adolfo Calero, Enrique Bermúdez, Edgar Chamorro, and Frank Arana—the resultant scandal would likely have wiped out what little support the Contras had left in Washington. It would have also again tarred the CIA, which was reeling from the exposure over the harbor minings and assassination manuals. Even if nothing could have been proven conclusively about the CIA's involvement in the Contra drug ring, the agency was supposed to be the nation's primary intelligence-gathering arm—and its responsibilities specifically included monitoring the international narcotics trade. A plea of ignorance about dope dealing by its own paramilitary forces would have looked as bad as proof of complicity.

And that was assuming Meneses kept his mouth shut. If he started naming names, dates, and places, the scandal could well have spread into the CIA itself, as it would eleven years later. Former assistant U.S. attorney Eric Swenson, who was familiar with the investigations into Meneses, said the drug lord's activities with the Contras were well known to the Justice Department because he had personally reported it. And Justice wasn't the only agency that knew about it.

"The CIA knows about this guy," Swenson said in an interview. "I'm sure they do. I'm *sure* they do. The CIA knows a lot of crooks. I mean, the CIA knows." As it turned out, Swenson was right. A 1998 CIA Inspector General's report confirmed that, as early as 1984, the agency had information tying Meneses to a drug and arms network in Costa Rica, in partnership with top Contra official Sebastian "Guachan" González.

Against that backdrop, and given the cozy relationship that existed between the CIA and San Francisco's U.S. attorney, Joseph Russoniello, it is hardly surprising that Norwin Meneses was not charged with drug trafficking in the spring of 1985. Even though one of his top lieutenants had pleaded guilty to cocaine charges and publicly implicated him as a major trafficker, allowing Meneses take the witness stand was out of the question. The drug lord simply knew too much. Not only was he in a position to expose the FDN's long involvement with drug merchants, but he could have led the police and the press to Danilo Blandón's booming enterprise in South Central Los Angeles.

And what a fine picture that would have presented.

Blandón was dumping a small mountain of cocaine into L.A.'s black neighborhoods every week, as well as providing South Central's crack dealers with assault rifles, submachine guns, and sophisticated telecommunications and eavesdropping gear.

Blandón was having the time of his life. As far as he and Ricky Ross were concerned, 1984 had been a terrific year. And 1985 was only going to be better. For one thing, Blandón was now an official guest of the U.S. government. The State Department, after two earlier rejections, had suddenly changed its mind in 1984 and decided to approve his application for political asylum. Now he could stay in America indefinitely and no longer had to worry about being summarily tossed out of the country. Had that fact been made public, all the propagandists and spin doctors in Washington would have been hard pressed to explain why the "Just Say No" administration had allowed South Central's biggest cocaine trafficker to call the United States his home.

Though the administration could have claimed ignorance, there were easily obtainable records proving that the DEA was fully aware of what Blandón was doing. Further, it is State Department policy to check with the DEA before approving applications for political asylum.

Records showed the drug agency had opened a NADDIS file on Blandón on May 24, 1983, after getting a tip from a confidential informant that he was a member of a cocaine trafficking organization. His attorney, Bradley Brunon, said in court in 1992 that the DEA's voluminous knowledge of Blandón's dope dealing stretched back even further than that. "I have some 300 DEA-6 reports regarding Mr. Blandón, and the reports relate to activities between approximately 1981 and May 1992," Brunon told a San Diego federal judge.

In early 1984, while Blandón's asylum application was under review at the State Department, the DEA learned from an informant that Blandón was "the head" of his own cocaine distribution organization based in Los Angeles, information that, as history shows, was accurate.

The same odd sequence of events happened with Blandón's wife, Chepita. First the DEA learned she was a drug dealer, then the State Department gave her political asylum. In early 1985 she was reported to the DEA as a "member of a cocaine distribution organization," and on March 15, 1985, the agency dutifully opened a NADDIS file on her. Later that same year she was granted political asylum.

Immigration experts agree that, normally, even the slightest hint of drug involvement by an alien results in deportation. "I've had clients deported because anonymous sources, people who were never even identified to us, allegedly told the DEA they were involved in drugs," said one California immigration lawyer. "One of my clients, he was a college professor from Thailand, was denied entry because he'd been arrested for smoking marijuana when he was a *teenager*, for Christ's sake. When it comes to drugs, it's an almost automatic no." In an interview, a State Department official confirmed there was a blanket zero-tolerance policy for immigrant narcotics suspects.

Why those same standards didn't apply to Blandón and his wife is not known, because the State Department and the Immigration and Naturalization Service refused to release any information from the Blandóns' asylum and immigration files, saying it would be an invasion of their privacy. The DEA also refused to answer any questions about what it did with the information it was compiling about the couple's criminal activities. But from the looks of things, the answer is evident: nothing.

During 1984 and 1985, Ross and Blandón have admitted, their cocaine trafficking empire was at its zenith. Ross was selling dope so fast he didn't have time to turn it into crack anymore. He would just take Blandón's kilos, put a hit on them, and pass them along to smaller crack manufacturers, who more and more frequently were members of various Crips "sets" from across Los Angeles.

"It continued growing, growing, growing, until sometime he buy [from] me 100 a week," Blandón said. Ross was driving him nuts with his constant telephone orders for more kilos. "I was getting crazy because you have to move—I was the, the man that made the delivery every day, so he was calling me every day, two or three times. Sometimes we deliver at 2 o'clock, sometimes we deliver at 4 o'clock, and anytime—one o'clock, two o'clock, one A.M."

Blandón finally worked out an arrangement with his Colombian suppliers to give Ross large amounts of cocaine for little or no money up front—sell now, pay later. "I spoke with the Colombian and I told him, 'Hey, let's go and give some credit to this guy because he pays. He's a good payer.' I give 20, the first 25 keys on credit and tell him, 'Hey, don't bother me until you got the money.'" That initial advance by itself was worth about $1 million, wholesale.

There was a reason Blandón wanted Ross out of his hair for a while. The Blandón family had moved from Northridge, a suburb near downtown L.A., to neighboring San Bernardino County, settling into a sprawling Spanish-style home in the city of Rialto, some thirty miles outside Los Angeles. He'd withdrawn $175,000 in cash from his bank account in Panama and given it to Orlando Murillo, the former Somoza banker, who bought the house under his name to keep Danilo's name off the property rolls. From his hot tub on the terraced hillside behind his new house, Blandón could gaze out at the bucolic, rolling hills and towering pines of a country-club golf course.

In one sense, Blandón had a right to be proud of his accomplishments. He was the epitome of Reagan-era success, along with brigand financiers Ivan Boesky and Michael Milken. In only three years he'd gone from working in a car wash to running a multimillion-dollar-a-week operation, employing, directly and indirectly, hundreds of people, many of them inner-city residents who would have otherwise had little or no income. Thanks to Blandón, they were making thousands or tens of thousands of dollars a week.

He was the chief supplier to the largest minority-owned business in an area so forbidding that the government was offering to pay companies just for moving there. Blandón's "company" moved in and began producing high-paying jobs without ever once asking for a handout. Unlike many legitimate industries that merely pay lip service to the concept, the cocaine industry is a fervent believer in the get-government-off-our-backs philosophy of commerce.

The fact that Blandón's activities happened to be illegal—as were Boesky's and Milken's, for that matter—was a technicality. After all, it wasn't his idea to start selling drugs; he'd done it to help the Contras. He was furthering official U.S. foreign policy in a very unofficial way.

As his longtime attorney Brad Brunon said, with a slight laugh: "You teach a man a craft and he's liable to practice it."

Blandón had practiced his craft well, and he was now enjoying the fruits of his labors. He hired a live-in maid and nanny for Chepita and his daughters, opened a restaurant—the Nicamex—and bought a car lot in nearby Fontana with an old college buddy, Sergio Guerra, a Mexican millionaire whose family owned major automobile franchises in Guadalajara. Guerra had the distinction of owning the last parking lot on the California side of the Mexican border in San Ysidro, which is like having a license to print money. The government valued its worth at around $29 million in the early 1990s.

Blandón's businesses were merely fronts through which to launder his drug money and provide a respectable explanation for his wealth and lifestyle. The used car lot—a favorite ploy among Nicaraguan traffickers—was especially handy. It was a cash-heavy business; lots of different vehicles were moving in and out all the time and their trunks were perfect places to store cocaine overnight, providing a plausible denial in case of accidental discovery. Cars that were sold for $2,000 were declared as being sold for $4,000. The car lot paid taxes on $4,000—at a rate cheaper than any money launderer would charge—and suddenly, $2,000 in drug profits had a legitimate pedigree.

Now that Danilo was a suburbanite with businesses to run, Ricky Ross certainly couldn't expect him to hop in his Mercedes and come running down to South Central every time Ross began getting low on blow. Blandón started asking Ross to drive out to Rialto to meet him, or he would bring the cocaine only halfway into town, leaving it in a load car at a shopping center parking lot.

Ross didn't mind the trips to Rialto, at first. Danilo and Chepita were fun to be around, he said, and he grew close to the couple and their daughters. "It would be just like any other wife if one of the employees come by the house," Ross said. "She'd cook dinner for us. 'Here, this is your room where you'll sleep at tonight. Here's your towels.' Know what I'm saying? So, she was playing along with the whole thing." Ross said she also knew the kind of business her husband was in. Once, he said, he found kilos of cocaine stored in their freezer, nestled in among the steaks and ice cubes.

At other times Blandón would take Ross and Ollie Newell out to dinner, question them closely about their business dealings, and then offer advice on how to improve their operations and safeguard themselves against both the police and other dealers. One of the best pointers he ever got from Blandón, Ross said, was "not to flash. Don't buy a lot of jewelry. Don't dress too fancy. That was the way he was. Always had on a nice suit and tie. Drove a nice car, but not too nice, know what I'm saying? No way you would look at him and say he was a dope dealer. Told us to buy some businesses, invest our money, so you can explain that you got a job. He taught us a lot."

The Torres brothers, in an interview with police in 1996, confirmed that "Blandón became very close to Ricky Ross.... Ross looked up to Blandón as a 'father figure.'"

But Ross noticed a change in his mentor's demeanor after he joined the country-club set in Rialto. "Danilo started getting relaxed. He didn't want to leave the house. 'I'm at home, man, I dreenking.' Fuck that shit, man," Ross said.

Blandón was getting drunk frequently and snorting a lot of cocaine. "He would use so much his nose got red and he kept trying to get me to use it. 'Here, just take a little.' I didn't want no part of that shit," Ross said. "And I ain't never had a drink in my life."

Blandón's habits would leave him soft and bloated. The other Nicaraguan dealers began calling him *Chanchin*, "the fat pig." Ironically, that disparaging nickname turned up as an alias in Blandón's DEA files.

It all made Ross a little nervous. The way he saw it, people who got lazy got sloppy, and sloppy people made stupid mistakes. This was a business where you couldn't afford even one mistake. It had taken Ross two years to perfect his delivery and distribution system—using nondescript decoy cars and load cars, walkie-talkies, stash houses, cash houses, and safe houses—and everything was running smoothly. He'd never had any troubles with the cops. Nearly every big crack dealer in town was getting cocaine from him, and he'd done it without resorting to attention-getting violence.

The dollar was a powerful persuader, he discovered. There was no limit to the average cocaine dealer's greed. You could buy your way into anything, or out of any disagreement. But deep inside, Ross was gnawed by the fear that his cocaine empire could vanish as suddenly as his tennis career had, leaving him in jail, dead, or back out on the streets, running at cars again.

When he looked closely at his operation, he saw a glaring weakness: his exclusive relationship with Danilo Blandón. It didn't make sense to have his entire life resting in the hands of one person, Ross concluded. At first he'd had no choice. He was tied to Blandón by circumstance. "If Danilo had disappeared, we wouldn't have been getting no ounces, no nothing, you know what I'm saying? When we got started, if we wouldn't have had him, we wouldn't have been able to have found it nowhere else," Ross said. "Even if you had the money, you just couldn't get it."

But now that he was riding on top, Ross had no shortage of offers from other cocaine importers, major traffickers who dreamed of finding a customer the size of Freeway Rick.

Blandón once told an associate that the beauty of dealing with "the black people" was that they sold cocaine so rapidly there were no costs or security risks to be incurred by warehousing the dope and parceling it out over a week or two. They would take as much as you could sell them and it was gone in a day, he crowed; "The black people, you know, buy everything."

Ross said the other "players" who came around usually couldn't match Blandón's prices. Couldn't even come close, most of the time. "When everybody else in town was spending forty-five [thousand] for a key, we was getting them for thirty-eight. And we knew, with him, he like never ran out."

Blandón confirmed that the prices he charged Ross were lower than anything he charged his other customers; Ross sold so much, he said, he could "get good prices from my suppliers."

Still, price and supply were just part of the reason Ross had confined his cocaine purchases to Blandón. With someone else, who knew what kind of troubles you were buying into? A new supplier could turn out to be a head case, or a fly-by-night. A low price could simply be a snitch's offer.

Danilo, on the other hand, was his friend, his protector. Rick trusted him implicitly, and for good reason. Danilo had guided him, advised him, kept him out of trouble. And he genuinely seemed to like Ross. "All I knew was like, back in L.A., he would always tell me when they was going to raid my houses. The police always thought I had somebody working for the police," Ross said. "And he was always giving me tips like, 'Man, don't go back over to that house no more,' or 'Don't go to this house over here.'" The cops invariably raided the locations within a couple days.

Ross, realizing that he owed much of his phenomenal success to Danilo, felt almost superstitious about tampering with a winning formula. "I can't say I never would have found out about it, but before I met him, the chances of me being a big dope dealer were slim to none." But when Blandón wouldn't get his ass up off the couch, Ross decided to look seriously for other sources, people who would be there when Danilo didn't feel like making money. He also used the opportunity to teach his teacher a little lesson about complacency.

One of the offers Ross had gotten came from the towering Torres brothers, known to Ross and his crew as "the Greens." He'd met them through Blandón and assumed from their size that they were his bodyguards. They also delivered cocaine and picked up money for Blandón occasionally. One day—as most of Blandón's assistants eventually did—they slipped Ross their phone number, in case he ever needed something extra.

If Danilo trusted the Greens enough to work for him, Ross figured, that was a pretty good recommendation, and one particularly busy day he called the brothers up and said he was willing to talk some business. Their prices were about the same as Blandón's, he said, but Ross didn't intend to pay either supplier's price for very long. Once the Torres brothers started selling to him, Ross used them to whipsaw Blandón on his prices, pointing out that his "other suppliers" were offering him a much lower price than his good friend Danilo. And he'd play the same game with the Torreses.

Blandón acknowledged that Ross began getting cocaine from "another two suppliers...they were my friends.... He got the coke from me, from Torres, from—see, not only from me. I got a piece of the apple." And he confirmed that Ross started driving his kilo prices down even further. But the new relationship had a bit of a rocky start. Jacinto Torres quickly got into trouble with the police.

He and his wife Margarita had quarreled, and he'd moved out, renting a room at his friend Robert Joseph Andreas's new four-bedroom house in Burbank. On April 6, 1984, shortly before 9:00 P.M., a team of Burbank narcotics detectives acting on an anonymous tip came crashing in through the kitchen door. They found a number of Nicaraguan women sitting around the kitchen table.

Jacinto Torres was stretched out on the bed in his room. In his dresser the police found a half-ounce of cocaine, a .38-caliber pistol, $3,700 in cash, and "large men's clothing." He and Andreas were thrown into the back of a prowl car and whisked off to jail. In Spanish, Torres and Andreas cursed their predicament, unaware that the cruiser was equipped with a secret taping system that was recording their every word.

"Stupid," Torres spat. "My money, my ledger, my clients, all the names. They are going to find a house I have got rented and if they get there, the whores, I don't want to think about it. Great God."

He turned to Andreas and said, "Rick is the one who fingered us."

"No, I have known him for a long time."

"They came looking for him," Torres replied. "Don't say nothing."

"It's nothing," Andreas assured him. "It's just half an ounce, almost nothing. They can't do nothing. I don't know if they found the house. I don't believe they did."

Court records show the police later searched a house in Northridge they thought belonged to Torres, an address that shows up on Blandón's NADDIS report as being one of his residences. But no drugs were found.

During the preliminary hearing, one of the arresting officers was asked about the search he'd conducted of Jacinto Torres's Mercedes Benz, and a very odd conversation ensued.

"Did you find any contraband in the Mercedes?" Torres's attorney, Joseph Vodnoy, asked Burbank police officer James Bonar.

"No contraband," Bonar answered. "Just some property of the United States Customs. No contraband."

"Wait a minute…" the judge said.

"I move to strike that answer!" Vodnoy shouted.

"Just a minute," the judge said. "What is it now you want to strike?"

"I asked him did he find any contraband? The answer was no. Then he went on to say something about United States Customs," Vodnoy complained.

"Property belonging to U.S. Customs?" the judge asked Bonar.

"It was not contraband. No no," Bonar replied.

"It will go out," the judge decided.

What U.S. Customs property the police found in Torres's car is not known, as all the police files from that case were destroyed. The charges against Torres were quickly disposed of. Four months later he pleaded guilty to a lesser charge of cocaine possession; he was fined $500 and given no jail time.

That outcome didn't please Jacinto Torres's probation officer, who refered to him as "that big guy who always comes in here in short pants." He told Torres's attorney, "You know your client's guilty. All we want is for him to serve some time…. This guy was a troublemaker as far back as 1970."

But even though Torres would violate his probation several times, no action would ever be taken against him. He went right back to cocaine trafficking.

Ross eventually turned Blandón and the Torres brothers against each other, a situation that would have dire consequences for Blandón in later years. The longtime friends became bitter rivals, fighting each other for Ross's business. One night, Ross said, he realized just how heated the rivalry had become.

While Ross was twitting a drunken Blandón about how low the brothers' cocaine prices had fallen, Blandón looked at him blearily, announced that "Chepita was fucking one of them," and said he wasn't going to take such an insult sitting down. He had a little plan he wanted to discuss with Ross to even things up.

"Danilo wanted to kill him," Ross said.

Blandón suggested that Ross set up a cocaine buy with the adulterous brother and "'tell that motherfucker to bring it at such-and-such a place, and I'm going to have some guys there waiting and you keep the dope. I'm going to take care of that fucking guy.'"

Ross said he laughed off the idea, figuring it was the liquor talking.

But the Torres brothers confirmed the story and took it one step further. In an interview with police, they "explained that Danilo Blandón's wife told him she had an affair with one of the [brothers] in a fit of anger. Blandón became enraged and hired a former military officer of the Nicaraguan army to kill him." The brothers said Blandón "apparently realized his wife had lied to him about the affair and called off the hit man."

Blandón said he never knew just how much cocaine the Torreses were selling to Ross, but he estimated that their volume rose to a level comparable to his own. He saw them "getting rich," he said. "If I sell a week to him, a hundred, maybe they go buy 50 or something like that. If I didn't sell him 100, they will sell him like, like 100 to him, you know? It was all the competition."

The brothers admitted to the police that they were selling "large amounts of cocaine to Ross on some occasions."

If Ricky Ross was going through 150 kilos of cocaine every week—and Ross says the figure is a reasonable average—it means he was selling enough to put a staggering 3,000,000 doses of crack on L.A.'s streets every seven days. It also means Blandón and the Torres brothers were sometimes sharing about $5.7 million a week in cash from the prolific young dealer. "Sometimes, we'd spend $4 million or $5 million a week with that guy, in our hell days," Ross said, speaking of Blandón.

Blandón said Ross was using an apartment in South Central as a countinghouse, where the money from the drug sales was brought, sorted, and wrapped. He would pick up his payments there. "When he [Danilo] came over we'd be counting the money and he said, 'Man, I'm gonna have to get you a money machine.' Because you know, our problem had got to be counting the money. You know, I started telling him, 'Man, my fingers hurt!' We got to the point where it was like, 'Man, we don't want to count no more money.'"

Blandón agreed that Ross was being deluged with cash. "Those times, they were using two or three machines, counting machines, and they were counting day and night."

To hide it all, Ross followed Blandón's advice and started investing in real estate, buying houses, apartment buildings, an auto parts store, and a hotel near the Harbor Freeway called the Freeway Motor Inn. In addition to giving Ricky Ross his nickname, "Freeway Rick," the motel served as a secure meeting place for dealers and couriers.

There was so much cash and so much crack flying around South Central that even the mainstream media had started to notice. On November 25, 1984, one day before the DEA arrested Jairo Meneses and Renato Peña Cabrera in San Francisco, the first story about crack to appear in the national press was published by the *Los Angeles Times*. It was written by Andy Furillo, a freckle-faced police beat reporter who'd been hired away from the smaller *Los Angeles Herald-Examiner* .

When he talked to some of the officers at the South Central stations, Furillo said, several of them mentioned this flood of cocaine they were seeing in the ghettos. He hit the streets, knocked on some doors, and confirmed what the officers told him—and then some. There was, he discovered, a gigantic, wide-open cocaine market flourishing in the poorest section of Los Angeles—and no one except the neighborhood newspapers had written a single word about it. It was a hell of a story, he thought.

Headlined "South Central Cocaine Sales Explode into $25 Rocks," Furillo's scoop began: "Police say hundreds, perhaps thousands, of young men, most of them gang members, are getting rich off the cocaine trafficking that has swept through L.A.'s black community in the past 18 months." Furillo described the rock house phenomenon and the multitude of street-corner dealers. He quoted police as saying that there were several hundred rock houses in South Central at that time. And his story accurately predicted that crack was a threat that could "destroy South Central Los Angeles for years to come."

Naturally, the *Times* buried the story inside the paper. But it was enough to prompt an embarrassed LAPD to launch raids on several dozen rock houses shortly afterward, with tragic results. On December 13, a diversionary explosion the cops set off during a raid on a West Sixtieth Street rock house killed a woman who happened to be walking by at the wrong time.

The crack phenomenon, Furillo said, fascinated him, and he pressed to do more stories on it, but his editors at the *Times* showed little interest in having him pursue the topic. Furillo eventually quit the paper in disgust and returned to the *Herald-Examiner*, where he continued producing gritty, ground-breaking stories on crack's impact on L.A.'s inner-city residents.

Furillo's piece in the *Times* also caught the eye of the *Washington Post*'s L.A. bureau chief, Jay Matthews, who did a follow-up in December 1984. That story described rock cocaine as "a marketing breakthrough that furnishes this middle-class drug to the city's poorest neighborhoods" and said rock houses—described as "steel-door dispensaries"—were "growing like a new fast-food chain." But as rapidly as the drug was spreading, the *Post* reported, it was still only an L.A. fad, and the story quoted unnamed "narcotics experts" as saying that "the hard little pellets of cocaine powder, selling for as little as $25, have not been found in significant numbers outside Los Angeles."

Bobby Sheppard, intelligence unit supervisor for the U.S. Drug Enforcement Administration in L.A., told the newpaper that he "saw no sign of rock cocaine spreading to the rest of the country, 'but I've got to believe that if it isn't there yet, it probably will be in the future.'" The story ended somewhat strangely by comparing crack to the clove cigarette fad of middle-class white teenagers.

It would be another year before other East Coast papers would begin reporting on crack; this timing coincided with the drug's belated arrival in New York City. "Crack first came to the attention of the New York Field Office Division of the Drug Enforcement Administration in the fall of 1985. The New York Joint Drug Enforcement Task Force made the first significant seizure of crack on October 25, 1985," said Robert Stutman, the head of the DEA's New York office, in 1986 congressional testimony. "A form of cocaine similar to crack but known as 'rock' has been available in Los Angeles for the last five years." According to then NYPD commissioner Benjamin Ward, "In January of 1985, of all cocaine arrests made by the Narcotics Division, there were fewer than fifteen arrests for crack."

Furillo's story also prompted the first scientific look at the early L.A. crack market, done by USC sociologists Malcolm Klein and Cheryl

Maxson in early 1985. Their preliminary findings, published in a small social research journal, noted that "throughout the Black residential areas of Los Angeles County, there has been a recent, dramatic increase in cocaine dealing…in large part from the proliferation of cocaine 'rocks' and fortified 'rock houses' which, with certain refinements, constitute a new technology and organization for cocaine distribution. An increasing trend in the distribution system is the use of street gang members in various dealing roles."

The study said that "estimates on the number of [rock houses] in South Los Angeles, a Black area where the phenomenon is concentrated, range from one to two hundred at a time to as many as a thousand."

Some rock houses were even being franchised, they found, and said "gang involvement is a connected part of a very rapid process by which this system has been institutionalized." The distribution system "yields ready access to inexpensive cocaine in a very large Black community in Los Angeles."

One thing they were unable to explain was why crack was found only in L.A.'s black neighborhoods. The drug, the sociologists wrote, "at least currently seems to be ethnically specific. Cocaine is found widely in the Black community in Los Angeles, but is almost totally absent from the Hispanic areas."

The explanation for that seems obvious once the Danilo Blandón–Rick Ross partnership is factored into the equation. "There was no market until we created it," Ross said matter-of-factly. "We started in our neighborhood and we stayed in our neighborhood. We almost never went outside it. If people wanted dope, they came to us."

The USC sociologists' predictions for the future were frightening and, as history has shown, dead-on accurate. "The distribution system seems custom-made for other Black gang centers (Philadelphia, New York, Washington, Chicago, etc.)," they wrote. "There is absolutely nothing inherent in this distribution technology, nor in the Los Angeles context of its development, that would prevent its exportation to many other urban areas. Indeed, exportability seems very high…. All this makes for an intelligent, well-organized system that is maximally effective—in short, it works efficiently, is very impressive and could easily explode across the nation."

And that is essentially what happened.

While the *Washington Post* story made no mention of the L.A. street gangs, Andy Furillo's story tagged them as the prime beneficiaries of the new crack trade. He presciently predicted that crack would dramatically alter the power structure on the city's streets, by providing the gangs with the one thing they had previously lacked: money. "Tom Garrison, director of field operations for the Community Youth Gang Services Project, said the utilization of the gang structure by drug dealers represents 'a whole new challenge for us,'" Furillo wrote. "'They've always had the numbers and the firepower, but now they've got the economic power too.'"

Klein and Maxson later came to believe that the police were exaggerating the role of gang involvement in the crack trade, but two later studies by the California Department of Justice refuted that idea and said the gangs were an even bigger force behind its spread from L.A. than previously thought. "We think that law enforcement perceptions of gang involvement in the drug trade are sharper than the Klein and Maxson statistical study suggest," UC-Berkeley sociologist Jerome Skolnick wrote in 1988. "In fact, it appears difficult to overstate the penetration of Blood and Crip members into other states."

The U.S. General Accounting Office (GAO), in a 1989 report, echoed Skolnick's conclusions: "In the early 1980s the gangs began selling crack cocaine. Within a matter of years, the lucrative crack market changed the black gangs from traditional neighborhood street gangs to extremely violent criminal groups operating from coast to coast. The lure of profits coupled with increased pressure from local police have prompted the Los Angeles gangs to extend their territories far beyond their neighborhoods. Within the past three to four years, members of the Crips and the Bloods have been identified selling or distributing crack in Washington, Oregon, Kansas, Oklahoma, Colorado, Missouri, North Carolina, Arizona, Virginia, Maryland and elsewhere."

The GAO report noted that a Washington, D.C., crack ring in 1989 was distributing 440 pounds of cocaine there every week, which "illustrates the nationwide impact of the Los Angeles street gangs. Much of the cocaine distributed by the gang was allegedly purchased from the Crips and the Bloods, who had purchased their cocaine from the Colombians."

The report included a map of the United States showing ominous black arrows emanating from L.A. and streaking northward and eastward across the country. The map was pockmarked with black dots—all the cities where crack had been found. Miami for some reason wasn't among them, although by 1985 the Jamaican posses from Liberty City had reportedly started their trek westward. They also began bringing crack to some African-American neighborhoods, but their primary markets were in areas populated by Caribbean immigrants. One drug researcher, Nick

Kozel of the National Institute on Drug Abuse (NIDA), went to Miami specifically looking for crack after reading Furillo's article and, according to one account, "came up empty-handed."

Ross said that while he did not sell exclusively to Crips gang members, they initially formed a large part of his customer base simply because he and Ollie were from a Crip neighborhood. But that only mattered in the beginning, he said. By 1984 and 1985, they were so far removed from that level of dealing that gang colors or the 'hoods their buyers hailed from were trivialities.

Freeway Rick was the dealers' dealer. What his customers did with their cocaine, who they sold it to, and what they fought about afterward made no difference to him. One customer was just as good as another, as long as they paid. All that other stuff just got in the way of making money. "By the time the market exploded in 1984, Ross already was dealing directly with the Colombian cartels, who supplied him with 50 to 100 kilos a day," the *Los Angeles Times* stated in 1994. "With that, Ross was able to operate dozens of rock houses, catering to thousands of addicts across Los Angeles. He had another three 'ounce houses,' servicing 100 to 200 mid-level dealers. Finally, he had his own private list of V.I.P. customers, maybe 30 to 50 big-time dealers, who dropped tens of thousands of dollars at a time."

As the South Central crack market became saturated, Ross's gang customers started traveling to other cities in California to make their fortunes, setting up new crack markets and using their connections with Ross to supply them. It was the start of an unprecedented cross-country migration by the Crips, and later the Bloods, which would spread crack from South Central to other black neighborhoods across the United States.

And it was the start of Ross's expansion from a large regional drug trafficking network to what the *L.A. Times* would later call "a coast-to-coast conglomerate that sold more than 500,000 nuggets of the drug every day." One L.A. narcotics detective would describe it as "a cartel."

South Central—ground zero of the crack explosion—would never be the same again.

Like night follows day, crack brought a host of attendant plagues: a flood of automatic weapons, rock houses, motorized police battering rams, drive-by shootings, and pitched gun battles. At the same time, the Reagan administration began snipping away at the fragile social support services that had made life in the inner cities livable, if not luxurious.

A commission examining the causes of the 1992 riots in South

Central named crack as one of the contributing factors. The drug was the beginning of the end for many struggling inner-city neighborhoods in the 1980s. They changed from places where generations had raised families in relative safety to free-fire zones where children could be mown down as easily as if they were walking the streets of Beirut.

"With rocks hitting the streets hard, and the money that was generated... about '84 or '85, guns hit the streets hard. Around '86, '87, it was on. You name it, you could get it," Leibo, an East Side Crip, told authors Yusuf Jah and Sister Shah'Keyah. "You didn't hear that much about 9-millimeters, M-16's, M-14's and AKs unless you were hooked up and was high on the echelon, but after 1986 they were available to anybody."

Here again, Danilo Blandón was a trendsetter.

Blandón began selling high-powered weapons to Ross and his friends in 1984, courtesy of his spooky associate, Ronald J. Lister, the ex-cop. "We started handling more and more money and then the first gun that I ever had, Danilo gave it to me for free," Ross said. "He just came by the house and said, 'I've got a present for you.' It was a .22 pistol. I think it was a 15-shot, with a silencer on it.... He started selling us guns after that. Everybody that worked with me—*everybody*—bought a gun from him."

Blandón had access to every imaginable firearm, he said. "I mean, he sold what is called a Streetsweeper, the Thompsons, he sold those. I think he sold those for like $3,000 apiece. It's a fully automatic that you see like in the movies, you know, in the old gangster movies," Ross said. "He sold Uzi's, he sold pistols, brand new pistols, .38, .357, any kind of pistol that you wanted...any kind of gun that you wanted, he got it for you."

Ross, who bought a silver-plated Uzi submachine gun, said his partner, Ollie Newell, became one of Blandón's biggest arms customers and soon had enough firepower to equip a platoon. One of his prize possessions was a tripod-mounted .50-caliber machine gun, which can down small planes.

"Like, I started buying houses, right? Well, Ollie started buying guns. He'd buy anything Danilo would walk through the door with. We had our own little arsenal. One time, he tells me Danilo was gonna get him a grenade launcher. I said, 'Man, what the fuck do we need with a grenade launcher?'"

He and his fellow dealers, Ross said, bought more than a hundred guns from Blandón. He sold so many to other dealers and friends that, by 1987, the L.A. police would list "weapons sales" as among Ross's various enterprises. Blandón denies selling Ross that many weapons, but he did admit selling him a .22 pistol, an Uzi machine pistol, and an Armalite AR-

15 assault rifle, the civilian version of the military's M-16. The AR-15 was a weapon the Contras bought by the thousands. Blandón owned one himself.

Blandón described his weapons sales as nothing more than a convenience for Ross and insisted he was no arms dealer: "I don't sell guns, okay? I sold that gun because he ordered [them from] me—because I knew the people who sell the guns." He said he never used weapons in his business and tried to pass that practice along to Ross.

So how was it that Danilo Blandón, a drug dealer, knew arms merchants?

"Because I was in the Contra revolution," he replied.

The guns sold to the crack dealers, Blandón explained, came from Ron Lister and his associate William Lee Downing, through their "security business" in high-class Laguna Beach. Lister admitted to the CIA that he began acquiring weapons for Blandón between 1982 and 1983, "some of which Blandón claimed were going to 'my friends down South.'" Lister said he sold Blandón one or two guns a week: "Assorted handguns, semi-automatic Uzi machine pistols, KG99 Tec Nine machine pistols, and possibly semi-automatic AK47's." He also admitted "purchasing a small number of commercially available, off-the-shelf night vision devices for Blandón. Lister says he does not know what Blandón did with the devices."

Blandón told CIA inspectors that Lister had access to such a wide variety of weapons that, in 1983 or 1984, he arranged for him to give a sales presentation to the leadership of the Contras. "Blandón recalls that, in addition to the usual attendees, several top Contra leaders were also in attendance, including Edén Pastora, Adolfo Chamorro and Mariano Montealgre. Blandón also says Ivan Torres was present," the CIA report stated. Mariano Montealgre, a CIA-trained Contra pilot, was implicated in a scheme to haul drugs for the Contras but never charged. Ivan Torres was a drug-dealing subordinate of Blandón, identified in DEA records as having "political connections to the FDN."

"Blandón said the attendees showed no interest in Lister's offer and Blandón received the impression that the military arms of the Contras was already being supplied by CIA or another U.S. government agency," the CIA reported.

During a 1996 court case, Blandón was asked if he went to Lister's security company and bought weapons "off the rack."

"No, he brought them to me."

"Brought them to you?"

"Uh huh."

"Where?"

"To my house."

"What did you do—call him up and order some?"

"No sir. He'd shown me that, and he told me that. And I offered them like a salesman, you know? He [Ross] ordered and I sold it."

"So you were doing another one of your brokerage things?"

"Yes."

"Sir, this business that you were in is not like selling paper to offices, is it?"

"Excuse me," Blandón huffed. "In those times you can buy a gun from the gun shop and you can sell it to anybody, okay?"

"But you sold Uzis!"

"Those guns," Blandón said calmly, "they weren't stolen."

The "security business" that provided Blandón the weapons was Mundy Security Group Inc., which Lister incorporated in Laguna Beach in mid-1983. Lister, an attorney named Maurice Green, another attorney named Gary Shapiro, and his reserve police officer buddy, Christopher W. Moore, were named as directors and officers. A business card found in a drug raid three years later identified Blandón as a vice president of that company.

Moore said the goings-on at Mundy Security Group's offices were enough to scare anyone. Director Maurice Green, he said, was a self-proclaimed legal genius with a severe drug and alcohol problem. He had a special wall constructed behind his desk that was hollow, Moore said, so he could kick through the paneling and run out of the building in case he needed to beat a hasty retreat. "I walked by his office one day and he was sitting at his desk looking down the barrel of a gun," Moore recalled. "I went into Ron's office and said, 'Hey Ron, you know Maurice is sitting in there playing with a gun?' He just laughed about it." Once, director Gary Shapiro said, the office was besieged by a mob of angry doctors who "were screaming and yelling about how Maurice had screwed up with their money." Lister was so wary of Green that he secretly videotaped him, Shapiro said.

Green was prosecuted and disbarred in 1987 for forging prescriptions to obtain narcotics. In 1992 he was sentenced to two years in prison for grand theft and practicing law without a license.

Aside from a few burglar alarm installations, Moore said, the only other business that he knew Mundy Security Group was involved in was an attempt to market a laser sighting device for AR-15 assault rifles.

Lister's partner, Bill Downing, was designing that gizmo, which used a tiny laser beam to put a small red dot on the target—perfect for killing people at night.

According to a 1996 report from the U.S. Customs Service, Mundy Security Group was licensed with the U.S. State Department in 1983 to export U.S. Munitions List items to other countries. "This firm received three DSP-73s [temporary export licenses] to export laser components and spare parts to 'various countries,'" the Customs report stated. "Unfortunately, the data base here at the Department of State does not contain abundant information on registrations/licenses that old, so I am unable to provide...more specifics on the types of equipment and countries exported to."

Blandón also did a brisk business selling electronics equipment to other cocaine dealers, he said. He sold walkie-talkies to Ross and his crew, who used them to keep in touch during cocaine and money pickups. He sold pagers, police scanners, voice scramblers, cellular phones, and anti-eavesdropping equipment to the dopers. "I could sell to all the people that was in the coke business," he said. Again, Ronald Lister procured that equipment for him. Blandón said Ross "used to live in an apartment beside the freeway, you see, in San Pedro, San Pedro Freeway in L.A. It was an apartment by Florence, if I remember, by the freeway. So I get him [Ross] a scanner, telephone security, you know, when you put the thing in the telephone and you can get on another phone and talk to him and nobody will listen."

Ross said his crew carried the police scanners in their cars while out on drug deliveries, eavesdropping on the conversations between the patrol cars in the neighborhood. They also used one in the counting house when there were large sums of money on hand. During one 1987 raid, some of their equipment fell into the hands of the L.A. County Sheriff's Office, and the cops were suitably impressed. "They've got electronic police-detection systems, sophisticated weapons—better equipment than we have," Sergeant Robert Sobel complained to a reporter.

Sobel and his team had raided Ross's "Big Palace of Wheels"—a well-stocked but curiously customer-free auto parts store that was one of his many front corporations—and they also hit an apartment belonging to one of Ross's dealers. At the store, Sobel said, "We found hand-held, programmable 800 megahertz radios which are better than our radios, which they use in their counter-surveillance thing, when they communicated with one another when they transported cocaine."

The apartment coughed up "several sophisticated firearms, including an Israeli .357 automatic pistol with a laser-type sighting device, which facilitates its use during darkness," according to the affidavit of one of Sobel's partners. The search also found Teflon-coated bullets, commonly known as "cop killers" because they can easily pierce an officer's bulletproof vest.

In an L.A. Police Department summary of searches at locations associated with Ross, Deputy Chief Glenn Levant wrote that "numerous 9-mm Uzies [sic] were seized, along with an AK-47 assault rifle, a fully automatic Mac-11 machine gun, a fully automatic machine gun complete with silencer, and state-of-the-art handguns, rifles and shotguns."

Eventually Ronald Lister's skills in procuring such high-tech marvels brought him to the attention of the FBI. On April 3, 1985, two FBI agents, Richard Smith and David Cook, came knocking on the door of Lister's well-tended home in Mission Viejo. They had a grand jury subpeona to deliver and a statement to take. They "hammered on who I might know in East block countries. See's a spy situation," Lister wrote after they left.

He confirmed to police in 1996 that he had been the subject of a "grand jury investigation on my relationship with Soviet agents. Crazy, huh?" Lister "went on to say that he had sold an FBI 'scrambler system' to somebody overseas and the FBI had investigated only to find out that the equipment was declassified and available on the open market."

But FBI agent Smith, now retired, remembered things a little differently. He told the police that "he had received information that Lister was attempting to sell classified electronic equipment to Soviet KGB agents. They conducted an investigation, which included a sting operation in which FBI agents posed as KGB agents. [He] said Lister was attempting activities which were completely illegal and clearly in violation of United States national security."

Lister's former chief, Neil Purcell, confirmed that the FBI had Lister under investigation but recalled that the gear involved high-tech camera equipment. "They came down to see me. They were absolutely convinced he was selling this stuff to the Russians and tried to get background on the guy and after I listened to them, I said, 'Pardon me for laughing, but he's taking you guys for a ride, believe me.' And they said, 'We've got photographs!' and [they] showed me photographs of him meeting in San Francisco and New York with the Russians and at the Embassy in Washington—on and on."

Purcell said the FBI discovered that Lister was "bullshitting the Russians, charging them four and five times what he paid for it. The kind of thing that's really laughable about this is the Russians think they've really got something and they could have gone to the camera store themselves and bought it."

Former agent Smith claimed that Lister was never prosecuted because he turned out to be "full of hot air" and was "determined to be incapable of producing the equipment which he was attempting to sell to the KGB. Lister's lack of 'present capability' to commit the crime made prosecution impractical." But Smith acknowledged that "the Assistant U.S. Attorney who handled the case felt, however, that Lister's activities were serious enough to warrant a grand jury hearing."

Lister admitted to L.A. police that he had been called before the grand jury and questioned about his activities. When the police asked him about the nature of the equipment involved, he said, "I can't get into that stuff with you guys." Lister was never indicted and told police he was unclear as to the outcome of the grand jury investigation. "That's all classified, incidentally," Lister told them. When the detectives asked him why the information would be classified, Lister said, "I can't answer that for you."

If the L.A. detectives were as skeptical of Lister's cloak-and-dagger work as ex-FBI agent Smith and former chief Purcell seemed to be, they must have gotten quite a jolt when they called the FBI to ask for a copy of their old files on the Lister investigation. "Special Agent Tim Bezick…stated that the FBI reports and the transcripts of Lister's grand jury testimony were protected by the National Security Act," Detective Axel Anderson wrote on November 20, 1996. "At Bezick's suggestion I called Joel Levin, chief of the Criminal Division of the San Francisco office of the United States Attorney. Mr. Levin researched the issue and confirmed the necessity of a court order."

They got similar reactions when they checked on Lister's background with the Maywood Police Department and the Laguna Beach Police Department, his old employers. "The personnel jacket for Ronald J. Lister has been sealed by the City of Maywood," they reported in November 1996. In Laguna Beach they learned that "the actual personnel files related to Ronald Lister no longer existed…all the information and documents in the Lister file had been purged, with the exception of the original employment application."

The FBI never turned over the documents, and the L.A. detectives were unable to determine why the files of a decade-old investigation of a dope dealing arms merchant with an allegedly overactive imagination would still be a matter of national security.

A significant clue, however, can be found in some documents seized during a 1986 narcotics raid on Lister's house. One of the many curious items the police carted away that day was a ten-page, handwritten document that details weapons and equipment deals by Lister. Lister admitted to the police that he had written the document in preparation for his 1985 grand jury appearance. The notes chronicled a series of meetings with a customer named "Ivan" at the Fairmont Hotel in San Jose, California. Ivan was uninterested in Lister's scramblers, the notes said, but asked Lister to procure some "Varo night vision equipment." The notes also told of Lister visiting the Russian embassy in Washington, D.C.

After jotting down a description of the April 1985 visit from FBI agents Smith and Cook, Lister wrote down a list of seven names. "Lister said he gave the above names to the FBI agents Rich Smith and Dave Cook," the police detectives wrote in their 1996 report. "He said the names 'came up in his business' for some reason and he wanted to have the names in writing when he went before the grand jury.... Lister said the people listed were only 'business people.'" The last two names on the list were Roberto D'Aubuisson, the right-wing Salvadoran death squad leader whom the CIA later acknowledged to be a drug and weapons trafficker, and Ray Prendes, the former head of the Salvadoran Christian Democratic party, which received substantial CIA financial assistance during the 1980s.

The detectives didn't ask why Lister would be having business dealings with CIA-linked Salvadoran politicians, or what the nature of that business was.

But the most intriguing name on Lister's list was at the very top of it: Bill Nelson. "Lister said that Bill Nelson was an A.S.I.S. member, which he said stands for the American Society of Industrial Security. Lister said that Nelson was the security director for the Fleur [sic] Corporation," the detectives' report said.

William Earl Nelson was far more than that, but Lister didn't elaborate, and the detectives didn't push him. Had they done so, they might have gotten a better idea about why the FBI's files on Lister would still be classified eleven years later.

Before becoming Fluor Corporation's vice president for security and administration, Bill Nelson had been the CIA's deputy director of operations—the head spook—the man in charge of all CIA covert operations around the world from 1973 to 1976. A Fluor spokeswoman initially denied to journalist Nick Schou that Nelson had been affiliated with

Fluor until Schou confronted her with documentary evidence of his employment there. Only then did she admit it, saying Nelson had worked at Fluor from 1977 to 1985.

A former CIA officer, John Vandewerker, confirmed to Schou that Nelson and Lister knew each other. Apparently, when Lister was running out to Fluor's headquarters in 1982 and 1983, it was Bill Nelson with whom he was meeting—"Ron's big CIA contact," as Lister's former office director, Chris Moore, described him.

They didn't get much bigger than Nelson, a protegé of former CIA director William Colby. A native of New York, Nelson had been a CIA officer since 1948, serving under a variety of military and State Department covers, mostly in the Far East. Japanese newspapers exposed him as CIA after they learned he was asking travelers to the Soviet Union to literally dig up dirt around Russian missile bases.

As head of covert operations, Nelson oversaw the CIA's controversial destabilization program in Chile, which resulted in the overthrow and murder of Chile's elected president, socialist Salvador Allende. Later, Nelson commanded 'Operation Feature,' a covert plan to place a "friendly" group in power in Angola after the former African colony was granted independence from Portugal in 1975. He was named as a defendant in a civil suit filed by the widow of an American mercenary the CIA recruited to fight in Angola in 1976. The widow claimed the CIA misled her husband about the hopelessness of his mission and then engaged in a smear campaign to distance itself from him when he turned up dead. The suit was eventually dismissed.

Nelson's Operation Feature bore many similarities to the Contra project, particularly in terms of how the CIA's proxy army received its weapons. That could explain why Lister—who has admitted dealing arms in Latin America—was meeting with Nelson. In both operations, arms and equipment for the CIA's secret armies were laundered through the armies of neighboring countries friendly to the United States in order to disguise their origins and preserve deniability for the CIA. In the Angolan conflict, the countries of Zaire and South Africa were used. Guatemala, Honduras, and El Salvador fronted arms shipments for the Contras. In both cases the CIA turned to the People's Republic of China to supply additional weaponry and missiles to its chosen fighters.

Evidence of Lister's involvement in sophisticated international arms transactions was found in the notes Lister made, naming Nelson and the Salvadoran politicians. Lister had drawn a flow chart containing boxes labeled "Swiss Bank," "U.S. State Department," "H.K.," "X Country," and "Factory USA." Strange acronyms and abbreviations were jotted alongside each box.

When the L.A. County Sheriff's Office sent Lister's flow chart to the U.S. Customs Service for analysis in 1996, Customs said it appeared to diagram a scheme to illegally divert American-made weapons to a third party, using fraudulent end-user certifications (EUCs) from another country to conceal the true identity of the weapons' recipients. EUCs are sworn declarations in which the government buying the weapons certifies that it really did order them. It is supposed to provide the U.S. government with some assurance that American-made weapons aren't ending up in the hands of terrorists or Communist guerrillas. When Oliver North began supplying arms for the Contras after the CIA funding cutoff, he frequently used phony EUCs from the Guatemalan and Honduran governments to divert weapons to the Contras, records show.

"The Contras can't buy weapons on the international arms market. Only countries can buy weapons, and certain countries can't buy weapons if they're embargoed or if they're embroiled in a political confrontation," explained former CIA official Alan Fiers, who ran the Contra program for several years. "So what happens is an arms broker will get an intermediary country to issue false end-user certificates. There is generally some consideration involved and the end-user certificate is issued, but the arms are either not shipped to the country that issued the certificate or are trans-shipped through that country on to a disguised end user, in this case, the Contras."

That was precisely what the flow chart seized from Lister's house illustrated, according to the U.S. Customs Service arms expert who analyzed the document. "Were this transaction taking place today," Senior Special Agent James P. McShane wrote, "I would assume that there was to be a [weapons] diversion to either Iran or the People's Republic of China, neither of which can get licenses for exported munitions."

Just what the CIA's former boss of covert operations, who by most accounts was an upright individual, could possibly have had to discuss with an admitted cocaine trafficker, drug addict, and gun runner like Ronald Lister is hard to fathom, and the exact nature of their relationship is likely never to be known. In April 1995, wracked with pneumonia, Nelson died of respiratory failure in an Orange County convalescent hospital at the age of seventy-four. But it is conceivable that their connection had something to do with the Contras and weapons. At the same time that he was reportedly meeting with Nelson, Lister was also advising the Contras on security matters and peddling arms.

"Lister did tell us that he was a Contra sympathizer in the 1980s," police detectives wrote in 1996. "He seemed reluctant to discuss this subject in depth but he did say that he was just one among many 'private people' who supported the Contras during those years." But Lister took pains to specifically disassociate himself from the one agency he'd bragged of working with. "It wasn't like I was doing it for the CIA or anyone else," he insisted.

11

"They were looking in the other direction"

Norwin Meneses was in a suspicious mood. He sat stiffly on a wooden bench and parried with two journalists who had come to question him about his relationship with the Contras some fifteen years earlier.

It was January 1996. Meneses had been locked up in the primitive Tipitapa prison outside Managua for five years, but he had none of the flourescent-tube pallor that men in American prisons have after such long periods of confinement. The drug lord was tanned, comfortably dressed; he had adapted well to his surroundings.

Or, perhaps more accurately, the old *Guardia* prison—where FDN founder Ricardo Lau once held court as warden and chief torturer—had adapted itself to him. Meneses strolled freely through the grounds, and the guards looked respectfully at their shoes and murmured "*Señor*" when Meneses and his entourage passed by. His cell door was closed only when he wanted it that way.

His sandals slapping loudly through the high-ceilinged halls, he had led the reporters to a breezy and secluded corridor that looked out on the prison's bright courtyard. A young dark-skinned inmate who seemed to take directions from Meneses stood by a tree outside, observing intently.

Just getting this far had been a chore for Meneses's visitors, a process as protocol-driven as arranging an audience with a potentate. They had been run through a screening process of Meneses's own devising, one that had nothing to do with the Nicaraguan penal system or its security concerns. The prison warden admitted that he had no say. He simply signed the passes and opened the gates when Meneses told him to.

First, Norwin's wives, Maritza and Blanca Margarita, had to approve. Then their attorneys needed to be personally satisfied. Then Norwin's attorneys—all three of them—had to sign off. And he wanted letters from them proving it.

The DEA and the CIA also got involved. "I'll be right up front with you," said DEA public affairs chief James McGivney, after reviewing Meneses's intelligence files in Washington, D.C. "I've already talked to the CIA people, because obviously there's some implications in some of the things I've seen that he may have been or at least he represented himself to be, and frankly, the CIA says, 'Hey, you know, that's fine. If he wants to talk to the reporter, he can tell them whatever he wants.' Their thinking on it was: 'We've been through this before' and they didn't think they had anything to hide on it."

Nor did the DEA, McGivney assured the reporter, though no one had suggested otherwise about either agency. The DEA was even willing to set up the interview, McGivney said. "I think I could probably represent to you that we might be able to facilitate any meeting you have with Meneses, in arranging it," he said carefully. "I can represent that I can go out and try to facilitate [an interview with] Meneses. And what he ends up saying, who knows? I'm willing to let the chips fall where they may. That's the kind of confidence I've got that…that the DEA back in the 1980s had no problems in those areas."

But the DEA's help came with a price, "a quid pro quo," as McGivney put it. In exchange, the DEA wanted the reporters to leave something out of their story: Danilo Blandón's relationship with the DEA. The reporters arranged the interview themselves.

Even after they jumped through all of his hoops, though, Meneses gave nothing away for free. Every suggestion of criminal conduct was protested as a calamitous slur by a foolish detective or Communist. But when he was confronted by hard evidence—such as a photograph or his own words—he would shrug, smile, and admit it.

As the minutes stretched into hours, Meneses became relaxed and expansive but never let his guard down. Every so often, he would tell an obvious lie, just to see if his audience was paying attention. He denied having any connection to the Contras, a falsehood he immediately retracted when confronted with a photograph of himself standing with FDN commander Adolfo Calero. Or he would casually drop a bombshell—like mentioning Ronald Lister's name unbidden—to see how it resonated, doing his own soundings to test which paths the journalists had taken before arriving in his presence.

He laughed heartily only once during the afternoon, when he was reading an interview U.S. authorities had done with his old associates, Jacinto and Edgar Torres, who later became informants for a variety of police agencies. In May of 1992 the FBI, the DEA, the IRS, and the LAPD sat the Trees down in the U.S. attorney's office in Los Angeles and grilled them about Meneses and Danilo Blandón. Meneses was asked to read the Torres's statement and point out areas where he disagreed. He rested a forefinger on his lips, and his eyes darted across the four-page FBI report. He nodded occasionally, pursed his lips angrily once, and then let out what could best be described as a guffaw.

Holding the document open to the second page, he pointed to the second paragraph: "Torres estimated that between 1980 and 1991 Blandón moved over 5,000 kilograms of cocaine."

"It would be more accurate if you multiplied that by ten," Blandón's longtime supplier smiled.

Fifty thousand kilos? Fifty-five tons of cocaine?

"Easily," he said. And not without a little pride.

Meneses's figures are impossible to verify, but as he was Blandón's supplier for many years, no one is in a better position to know. The amount is not inconsistent with law enforcement estimates of Blandón's ten-year-long operation. The Torres brothers later raised their estimates of Blandón's cocaine sales dramatically. According to a 1996 L.A. County Sheriff's Office report, the brothers told police "they heard that Blandón sold 10,000 kilos of cocaine, mostly in South Central Los Angeles and the San Francisco Bay area" during a two-year span in the mid-1980s. At Ricky Ross's conversion rate, that's enough cocaine to make 30 million doses of crack. "Danilo Blandón was the biggest dealer in the Los Angeles area for about two years," the Torres brothers concluded.

U.S. government officials were even more generous in their appraisals. "Mr. Blandón was considered to be probably the largest Nicaraguan cocaine dealer in the United States, is that correct?" Assistant U.S. Attorney L. J. O'Neale asked Blandón's DEA case agent, Charles Jones, during a 1995 federal grand jury hearing in San Diego.

"I believe so, sir," Jones testified.

Both men had reason to know. O'Neale had been monitoring the activities of Blandón and his associates since the 1980s. Jones had been watching him since at least the early 1990s, and would describe Blandón in a sworn statement in 1992 as a "multi-ton dealer."

Becoming the biggest dealer in the biggest cocaine market in the United States in less than four years is no small testament to Blandón's sales and marketing skills. But what makes his rise to the top even more remarkable is the fact that his friend, mentor, and cocaine supplier, Norwin Meneses, was working for the DEA toward the end of Blandón's ascendancy.

If the *New York Times* can be believed, it was a very strange bargain indeed that the antidrug agency struck with Meneses in the mid-1980s. "After narcotics agents for the Drug Enforcement Administration and the State of California were unable to build a strong case against Mr. Meneses in 1985, law enforcement officials said they approached the trafficker about becoming an informer. He agreed," reporter Tim Golden wrote in 1996.

Why a dope dealer of Meneses's cunning and stature would so readily agree to become a rat—especially when the DEA had no case against him—is a critical bit of information missing from Golden's story. Court records in Nicaragua show that U.S. prosecutors had a solid case against Meneses in 1985—one that they would later persuade a grand jury to file charges on. The star witness was his own nephew, Jairo Meneses, who admitted dealing cocaine and keeping his uncle's drug ledgers for years. Another was a woman who'd bought a kilo of cocaine from him directly. The DEA had other witnesses as well, people who could testify about his drug dealings in New Orleans and Miami.

No charges were filed in 1985 because Meneses became "a cooperator" and moved overseas, said Eric Swenson, the former assistant U.S. attorney who handled the case. The trafficking charges were held back by the U.S. government as insurance, Swenson said, to guarantee the drug lord's continued assistance. In other words, Meneses was pressed into service by the DEA. From then on, presumably, the DEA began monitoring his activities, and to some extent directing them.

Just what kind of work Meneses was doing for the U.S. government during those years is hard to know, because the DEA has so far withheld from the public nearly all of its voluminous files on him, citing concerns for the drug lord's privacy. But one detective familiar with Meneses says the trafficker was working for the CIA in Costa Rica. "They used Meneses in Costa Rica basically for money laundering operations," said Roger Mayorga, former director of criminal investigations for the Nicaraguan national police. "He was really in the background."

Whatever it was that Meneses was doing, quitting the drug business and helping L.A. authorities snuff out Blandón's roaring cocaine enterprise in South Central obviously wasn't part of the deal. To Meneses's friends, it appeared as if nothing had changed.

Rafael Corñejo, one of his Bay Area distributors, said it never occurred to him that his boss could have been working as a DEA informant then because he continued to supervise a flourishing cocaine trade in the Bay Area and L.A. "Those were very big years in terms of...well, the contraband," Corñejo said hesitantly. "That's why I have a hard time believing Norwin was working with the feds."

Soon after his nephew's arrest, Meneses sold his used car lot in San Francisco, his gray Jaguar, and his Mission District office building and moved to his beachfront ranch in Costa Rica.

"I went to Costa Rica to see him right after he moved and I spent about six months on his ranch down there," said John Lacome, a Bay Area friend of Meneses and his nephews. "He would take us into town, take us to the clubs, get us some girls. I got a great picture of him while I was there. He's standing next to one of his cows and he's wearing this black baseball hat with a picture of a clock on it that says, 'It's Party Time!'"

Meneses was no stranger to Costa Rica, a picturesque and normally placid little democracy on Nicaragua's southern border. Like Somoza, Blandón, and other wealthy Nicaraguans, Meneses had had a home there since before the Sandinista takeover. Meneses owned not one house but several, and large ranches in northern Costa Rica, near the war zone. The *L.A. Times*, citing an unnamed source, reported that "beginning in November 1982 Meneses was spending much of his time in Costa Rica and commuting back to San Francisco."

He also had important friends in Costa Rica.

"Norwin receives political protection from Jose Marti Figueres, the son of former Costa Rican President Jose 'Pepe' Figueres," an informant told DEA agents in 1984. Jose Marti Figueres, the older brother of Costa Rica's current president, was accused in 1995 of swindling the Costa Rican State Lottery of six million dollars. He was also implicated in the 1970s with fugitive financier Robert Vesco in a scheme to profit from the nationalization of Costa Rica's gasoline distributors.

Political or otherwise, Meneses clearly seemed to have some kind of protection while living in Costa Rica. Records show that by 1984 his activities there were well known to the CIA, the DEA, and the Costa Rican OIJ, an agency similar to the FBI. Yet, in all the years he lived there, he was never arrested or expelled. "There were some stories in the Costa

Rican papers about me, planted by the Communists, which said I was involved in drug trafficking, but nothing ever came of it," Meneses said dismissively.

The DEA was first informed of Meneses's Costa Rican drug operations in February 1984, when a confidential informant was debriefed at the U.S. embassy in San José and reported that Meneses was in charge of a major cocaine trafficking ring. Six months later the DEA learned that a small cocaine shipment destined for Meneses had been seized at the international airport in San José by the Costa Rican police.

Costa Rican authorities knew him as "one of the most important traffickers of drugs, as much in the Nicaragua of Somoza, as at the moment in Costa Rica." That 1985 report from an OIJ investigation stated, "He was one of the first economic supports of the FDN in Costa Rica. There are rumors that he works as an informant for the DEA." The report noted that Meneses had "various businesses" in Costa Rica, including a factory for canning and processing beans. His partner in the canning factory was FDN leader Aristides Sánchez's brother Troilo Sánchez, the former Nicaraguan playboy named by the FBI in 1982 as a supplier to Meneses's Contra drug ring in San Francisco.

Sánchez, who told CIA inspectors that Meneses was dealing cocaine for the Contras, said Meneses was the moneyman behind the factory, and he and his wife were only paper owners of the company, which exports beans to the States under the name "Autumn Flower." Meneses confirmed that business relationship.

"We had the idea in Nicaragua before the revolution, and so when we were in exile we went to Norwin and he agreed to put up the money," Sánchez said. "We had nothing of our own. The Sandinistas had taken everything." Asked in an interview in 1997 if he knew Meneses was dealing drugs when he sought his financial aid, Sánchez shrugged. "Maybe I did. Maybe not."

Meneses also had another business in San José, one that made it easy for his DEA handlers to find him. It was right across the street from the U.S. embassy—a chicken restaurant called El Pollo Loco ("the Crazy Chicken"). Meneses said his partner in that venture was Frank Vigil, the former Nicaraguan public relations man who, along with Danilo Blandón, was allegedly part of a group of exiles dealing cocaine for Meneses in Los Angeles in the early 1980s. Vigil acknowledged his part ownership of the restaurant but denied being a drug dealer.

The DEA also learned that "Norwin owns a private aircraft which he uses to transport cocaine, and that in late October 1983 this aircraft was used to bring an unknown quantity of cocaine to Guanacaste province in Costa Rica." Isolated Guanacaste Province, in northern Costa Rica, was the center of the Contra drug trafficking universe during the war. According to a special Costa Rican legislative commission, during 1984 and 1985 the area served as the headquarters for "an organization made up of Panamanians, Colombians, Costa Ricans and citizens of other nationalities who dedicated themselves to international cocaine trafficking, using Costa Rica as a bridge for the refueling of planes that came from Colombia." That drug ring, which was being run with the help of Panamanian dictator Manuel Noriega, worked closely with the Contras, the legislative commission found. "Specifically, use was made of the same landing strips and the collaboration of the same Costa Rican authorities that had aided the Contras," the commission's report stated, adding that Contra pilots provided "the gasoline that was used for refueling the planes of the organization."

Evidence produced during the DEA investigation of Manuel Noriega revealed that his drug trafficking ring loaded up planes with cocaine in Colombia; the planes refueled at Contra airstrips in northern Costa Rica before continuing to the United States and dumping their loads in Louisiana and Texas. Former Costa Rican government pilot Werner Lotz Octavio confirmed to a U.S. Senate subcommittee in 1988 that Noriega's pilots would fly up weapons for the Contras along with the drugs, leaving the guns behind in Costa Rica, before hitting two routes north: one through Mexico for the West Coast market, and the other through the Bahamas for the East Coast's coke buyers.

"The people who were flying in the weapons used and made contacts with certain people in Costa Rica to be able to use their airfields as a jump point to carry drugs for them, for refueling stops," Lotz testified. "There was a charge, you know, the allowing of the aircrafts to land, to drop the weapons, and to proceed with the drugs. Or to better explain, the landing fees, to put it this way, were paid with weapons."

"How was it possible for these drug planes to go in and out of the airstrips without being detected and without creating problems in Costa Rica?" a Senate investigator asked Lotz.

"Very simple, sir. Costa Rica has got a very poor radar."

"So there was no radar to detect them? Wasn't there danger that they would be arrested on the ground?"

"None, because it was previously arranged. All the landings were arranged. They were supported by the revolutionaries themselves," answered Lotz, who admitted to flying weapons and drugs for several years.

"Were there many police or Rural Guard people in that region?" the investigator pressed.

"To be very clear with you, sir, our Guard down there is barefooted, and you're talking 50 men to cover 400 kilometers maybe," Lotz explained. (The head of the Costa Rican Rural Guard in Guanacaste Province, Colonel Edwin Viales Rodriguez, was convicted in 1988 of providing security for those drug and weapons flights. He allegedly told a friend that he was doing it for the CIA and was paid between $20,000 and $30,000 a flight.)

While the barefoot Costa Rican Rural Guard may not have been able to keep up with such a well-oiled drug operation, the CIA and DEA couldn't use the same excuse. The number of American agents stationed in Costa Rica exploded during the Contra war years, and U.S. reconaissance aircraft and spy satellites made routine overflights, photographing miles of northern Costa Rica for the Contra war effort and monitoring Sandinista troop movements and the rural airfields the Contras used for their supply flights.

Yet in spite of all this cutting-edge technology, plus firsthand human intelligence from Norwin Meneses, the Americans proved surprisingly inept at catching drug dealers. "Despite obvious and widespread trafficking through the war zones of northern Costa Rica, the Subcommittee was unable to find a single case against a drug trafficker operating in those zones which was made on the basis of a tip or report by an official of a U.S. intelligence agency," a U.S. Senate subcommittee reported in 1988. "This is despite an executive order requiring intelligence agencies to report trafficking to law enforcement officials and despite direct testimony that trafficking on the Southern Front was reported to CIA officials."

Costa Rican law enforcement officials said in interviews that the contingent of DEA agents working from the U.S. embassy in San José showed little interest in helping them probe reports of Contra drug trafficking. Jorge Chavarria, a former prosecutor who investigated several such cases in the 1980s for the Costa Rican OIJ, said he was convinced the DEA "knew about the Contras and drugs. All these flights and pilots that were flying in and out with drugs could not have been ignored by the DEA. They were looking in the other direction."

There is some evidence to substantiate that accusation. During a

1987 Senate subcommittee hearing, Senator John Kerry of Massachusetts told DEA director Jack Lawn that "the head of the DEA office in Costa Rica was interviewed by this committee and he told us that the infrastructure that was used to supply the Contras was used to smuggle drugs. This is *your* DEA officer in Costa Rica. Are you familiar with that report?"

"No, sir, I am not," Lawn said. The DEA's position, said Lawn and aide David Westrate, was that there was "no credible evidence" to support such allegations. The DEA officer in Costa Rica who was questioned by Kerry's committee, Robert J. Nieves, was in a perfect position to know, however. According to Norwin Meneses, Nieves was his control agent, and would be throughout the remainder of the 1980s.

The timing of drug kingpin Meneses's appearance in Costa Rica as a DEA informant is interesting for a couple of reasons. First, it coincided with the congressional cutoff of CIA funds to the Contras in late 1984, and with a renewed emphasis by the Reagan administration on beefing up the Contra forces in Costa Rica, despite the lack of CIA money.

"Within the administration, there was no doubt that the resistance would continue to be supported," Oliver North wrote in his memoirs. "The only question was how." One idea North had in mid-1984 was to use drug money, congressional records show. After learning that the CIA and DEA were involved in a sting that would snag $1.5 million from Medellín cartel traffickers, North asked top DEA officials if they wouldn't mind turning the cash over to the Contras. DEA officials told Congress that they spurned North's suggestion.

By then, the Contras had set up an elaborate network of offshore bank accounts to conceal the source of the funds that would sustain them during the cutoff in congressional funding. North, who helped the Contras set up the accounts on the advice of CIA director William Casey, wrote that Casey didn't want the Contras' "unofficial" funds coming into U.S. banks because of fears that Treasury agents, on the lookout for drug money, would be alerted by the large sums of cash that would be arriving.

It was a time when the Contras and top U.S. officials—North, National Security Adviser Bud McFarland, Assistant Secretary of State Elliott Abrams—were scrambling to find funds for the Contras, putting the arm on the Saudis, the racist government of South Africa, the Israelis, and the sultan of Brunei to come up with cash, with the full knowledge that such solicitations were illegal.

Meneses's appearance in Costa Rica also coincides with a time when his drug network there had been suddenly rendered leaderless, accidentally disrupted by a Costa Rican police investigation.

In May 1984 the OIJ raided the San José home of Meneses's business partners Troilo and Isanaqui Sánchez, whom they suspected of moving thousands of dollars worth of cocaine every month. According to newspaper reports, Sánchez's wife ran to the bedroom and tossed a package out the window containing nearly a pound of cocaine.

One former Costa Rican Contra official, Leonardo Zeledon Rodriguez, told UPI in 1986 that Sánchez "was caught in Costa Rica with pillows full of cocaine. Troilo is a brother-in-law of Adolfo Calero." Both Sánchez and his wife were arrested on trafficking charges, but the charges against his wife were dismissed. Troilo was acquitted after convincing the jury that he was an addict and the cocaine was for his own use. Nonetheless, the raid provided the Costa Rican authorities with the break they needed to land an even bigger fish in the Meneses organization.

While searching Sánchez's house, the agents were interrupted by a banging on the front door. Opening it, they came face-to-face with a very surprised Horacio Pereira Lanuza—"La Burra"—the Meneses lieutenant who had been supplying cocaine to Carlos Cabezas and Julio Zavala in San Francisco and funneling the profits to the UDN-FARN Contra army of Fernando "El Negro" Chamorro.

In August or September 1984, a recently declassified CIA cable shows, Meneses had approached "Negro" Chamorro and asked the Contra leader "to help move drugs to the U.S." Neither Chamorro's nor the CIA's response to Meneses's overture was disclosed.

Though Horacio Pereira's drug trafficking activities had been known to both the FBI and the U.S. Customs Service since 1982, those agencies apparently never bothered to inform the Costa Ricans that they had a major dealer in their midst. According to the Costa Rican paper *La Nacion*, the OIJ agents had no idea who Pereira was the day he put in his unexpected guest appearance at Troilo Sánchez's house. Once they made his acquaintance, however, they were loath to let it end. In November 1984 they placed wiretaps on his phones and those of two associates. They quickly learned that Pereira "was one of the biggest narcotraffickers to have operated from this country," *La Nacion* reported—the man behind nearly every major drug trafficking case in Costa Rica since 1981, with "connections in Honduras, Colombia, San Andrés and the United States."

As the OIJ agents listened in on Pereira's phone calls, they were stunned to find themselves eavesdropping on Costa Rican Contra commanders, who were discussing cocaine shipments, drug labs, weapons deliveries, and international politics with the cocaine dealer. Among those captured on the wiretaps were UDN-FARN subcommander Edmundo Chamorro; Ernest Hidalgo Abuanza, UDN-FARN's logistics chief and the personal assistant to UDN-FARN commander "El Negro" Chamorro; Guillermo Bolt, a CIA-trained Contra pilot who flew for Edén Pastora's ARDE Contra group; and Sebastian "Guachan" González, the man in charge of the Panamanian logistics for ARDE and UDN-FARN. During one conversation, a caller mentioned that González was building a cocaine processing lab in Panama, and hinted that he was kicking back $20 million a month to Panamanian authorities for the privilege of doing business there.

The Pereira wiretaps were an intelligence bonanza for the Costa Rican police. "Guachan" González was a wanted man at the time of his calls, having recently fled Costa Rica after he and UDN-FARN's logistics chief were caught with 600 grams of cocaine in a house in Guanacaste Province. González was overheard calling Pereira from his hideout in Panama, where he was living under the protection of Manuel Noriega, then head of the Panamanian military.

A charismatic and intelligent smuggler, González had worked for the CIA since 1983 as the Panamanian quartermaster for all the Costa Rican Contra armies, arranging supplies and deliveries from Noriega's armed forces. He was "a personal friend of Manuel Noriega since high school years. His job was to manage the arms flights from Panama to the ARDE forces in Costa Rica," ARDE commander Edén Pastora said.

According to a 1998 CIA report, Norwin Meneses "was known to be involved in the drug trafficking activities of Sebastian González." A 1984 cable from the Costa Rican CIA station to CIA headquarters in Langley said Meneses and "another trafficker, Tuto Munkel, were involved in drug trafficking with Sebastian González Mendieta in Costa Rica.... It was reported that Meneses owned a restaurant in which González might have had a financial interest." According to the cable, "Meneses, González and Munkel were well-known as the 'Nicaraguan Mafia,' dealing in drugs, weapons smuggling and laundering of counterfeit money." (The "Tuto Munkel" mentioned in the CIA cable may be Augusto Mönkel, a Contra supporter who was detained in Miami with Horacio Pereira for currency violations during the FBI's investigation of the Frogman case in 1982.)

In a 1990 interview with journalist Douglas Vaughan, Gonzales said Horacio Pereira had offered him money to help finance a new Contra movement he started when he broke with Pastora in 1983: the M-3. "Horacio Pereira earlier had loaned money to Edén Pastora and he offered to help M-3 but we rejected this because Norwin Meneses and Troilo

Sánchez were involved in drugs," González said. "They were close to [FDN founder] Aristides Sánchez."

Largely on the strength of the wiretaps, Horacio Pereira was convicted of drug trafficking in 1986 and sentenced to twelve years in jail, one of the harshest sentences a Costa Rican court had ever handed down for a drug crime. The verdict was significant enough to attract the attention of the *CBS Evening News*, which aired a brief report in June 1986 on Pereira's trial and the undercover tapes. "The wire-tapped phone calls show the drug dealers have ties to the highest level of Contra leadership in Costa Rica," CBS correspondent Mike O'Connor reported. "Costa Rican narcotics officers say much more dope has been flowing through their country to the United States since the Contras began operating from here and they don't believe it's a coincidence."

Pereira never served a day of his sentence. He was released on bail and immediately disappeared. Meneses said his friend was "chopped into tiny bits" in Guatemala a few years later, when he became embroiled in a dispute over a drug debt.

The Costa Rican government's indictments of Pereira, "Guachan" González, and Troilo Sánchez might have been expected to put a crimp in cocaine trafficking in that small nation. After all, Costa Rica's biggest dealer, Pereira, was out of business, González was on the run, and their supplier, Norwin Meneses, was now working as an undercover informant for the DEA.

But that wasn't the case. "It was precisely in that period when the transshipment of weapons and drugs in our country grew," a Costa Rican legislative commission reported. Again, this growth can traced to a drug ring involving the Contras and the CIA.

CIA records and the declassified testimony of former CIA officials who oversaw the Contra program in Costa Rica confirm that the intelligence agency began receiving reports of drug trafficking by Edén Pastora's ARDE faction in late 1984. In a secret congressional hearing in April 1987, former CIA Costa Rican station chief Joseph Fernández testified that "there were certainly substantiated cases—and we can name names if you wish—of people in [Pastora's] coterie, of supporters and his lieutenants that did have connections with drug traffickers and, in fact, he himself received funds from a person who was known to be affiliated with drug traffickers."

Pastora admits all that, but says it was due entirely to the CIA. In an interview, the former Contra commander claimed he was the target of an elaborate CIA scheme to force him out of the war, a plot that involved the use of drug dealers working for the intelligence agency. This occurred, he said, after he refused CIA orders to unite his forces with the former National Guardsmen in the CIA's northern Contra army, the FDN, which was being run by Norwin Meneses's friends.

The problem for the agency, Pastora said, was that many of his fighters refused U.S. government entreaties to desert him for the new Costa Rican Contra army the CIA was putting together, and they decided to fight on without the agency's assistance. The CIA had to get Pastora out of the way because it needed his veteran commanders and his men to run its new army.

While it is tempting to dismiss Pastora's theory as the paranoid grumblings of an embittered and abandoned asset, a considerable amount of documentary evidence suggests he may be right. In the spring of 1984, the CIA cut off Pastora's funding and began a concerted effort to both discredit him politically and isolate him from the rest of the Costa Rican Contra forces. He had pissed off his CIA handlers once too often. "His actions, and particularly his public comments, frequently provided the Sandinistas with propaganda benefits, particularly his statements about alleged National Guard control of the FDN and FDN atrocities," complained a secret 1986 cable to CIA director William Casey entitled "Disruptive Actions of Edén Pastora."

To get rid of him, Pastora claimed, Nicaraguan CIA assets approached him with offers of financial assistance, which he desperately needed after his CIA funding was cut off in May 1984. Pastora said he accepted their money and their supplies, not knowing that the men were drug traffickers.

When it came time to dispose of him, Pastora said, the CIA leaked the information that he was getting help from drug dealers, both to drain his support in the United States and to make him the fall guy for the cocaine trafficking being done by the CIA's "approved" Contra armies—the FDN and UDN-FARN—which was about to be exposed by the American press.

Former CIA station chief Fernández disputed Pastora's claims. "We attempted to diminish his influence by showing other political leaders that he was an irresponsible person and so forth, but never did we ever use narcotics or even the rumor of narcotics trafficking or anything like that as a means of bringing about this diminishment," Fernández testified. It is interesting, though, that the men who came to Pastora with offers of drug money and drug-tainted supplies all had ties to the CIA or to DEA informant Norwin Meneses, sometimes both. Two of them have since publicly admitted the CIA was aware of their drug dealing on behalf of Pastora's army and had, in fact, okayed it.

Pastora's first offer of assistance came from Octaviano César, the former social director of Meneses's VIP nightclub in Managua, who maintained a financial relationship with the CIA for many years. According to the memoirs of former Contra political leader Arturo Cruz, César was receiving CIA political funds and "using his special communications equipment to keep the Americans informed of activities between the Sandinistas and the Cubans."

In March 1984 César and two other Contra officials close to the CIA—ARDE logistics chief Adolfo "Popo" Chamorro and ARDE air force commander Marcos Aguado—met with a major Colombian drug trafficker named George Morales at his offices in Fort Lauderdale and asked him to contribute to Pastora's army. "During our conversation they told me they were CIA agents. Two of them said they were, Octaviano César and Marcos Aguado," Morales said in 1986 congressional testimony. "I knew that they belonged to the Central Intelligence Agency and [I] also knew this through several pilots, who at the time worked for me and who had also been directly involved in operations with the Contras flying airplanes." Like Octaviano César, Marcos Aguado was another old friend of Norwin Meneses. He was also a close associate of the CIA's man in northern Costa Rica, John Hull, who served as the agency's unofficial liaision to the Contras.

Morales, the Colombian trafficker, had supplied a few shipments of guns to the rebels in 1983, and he was surprised that the Contras still wanted his help in early 1984, since he had just been indicted by a federal grand jury on conspiracy and cocaine trafficking charges. But Morales said César and Aguado made it clear that if he assisted them again, they could make his legal problems disappear. César "told me he had plenty of friends, being him, the CIA, can advise the superiors about my financial support and airplane and training and therefore they will finally, eventually, will take care of my problem, which they did," Morales testified. During the entire time he was working with the two Contras on drug deals, no action was taken on his pending cocaine indictment. It was one postponement after another, Morales said. When he started talking to U.S. Senate investigators about his Contra dealings two years later, however, the case moved quickly to trial and conviction.

Morales later passed a DEA-administered lie detector test about his drug dealings with the Contras. In addition, two of the pilots who flew the Contra drug missions for him confirmed Morales's story—under oath as U.S. government witnesses.

Morales and the pilots, Fabio Ernesto Carrasco and Gary Wayne Betzner, said planeloads of weapons were flown to a ranch in northern Costa Rica owned by CIA operative John Hull, whose cover was that of an aw-shucks midwestern farmer managing some plantations for rich gringos. In reality, Hull's ranch was a training area and hiding place for Contra soldiers; it was where the Legion of September 15 gathered before its bumbling raid on the Argentine radio station in 1980.

After they dropped off arms, Morales and the pilots said, large green duffel bags full of cocaine belonging to the Contras were loaded aboard and flown back into the United States, usually to the public airport at Opa Locka, Florida. "Every one of the flights I make to Costa Rica, the cocaine was the Contras', not mine," Morales testified. "I have my suppliers in Colombia. I don't need to go to Costa Rica."

While Hull has vehemently denied accusations that drug trafficking was occurring at his ranch, a once-secret FBI report shows that the CIA official who was overseeing the Contras from Washington during that time, Alan Fiers Jr., was convinced that Hull's ranch was being used for Contra drug flights. "There is no doubt in Fiers's mind that Pastora's men trans-shipped drugs out of the airstrip on Hull's ranch," investigators for Iran-Contra prosecutor Lawrence Walsh reported in 1991. "Fiers realized this around 1986 when he heard all the evidence from Senator John Kerry's hearings and from the newspapers. Fiers is adamant that he has no knowledge of CIA complicity with drug activity in Central America."

Hull, when told of Fiers's statement, was astonished. "Hell, here I thought that all this time the people spreading rumors like that were the Sandinistas and the Communists. Now I find out it's my own government."

One of the Morales pilots who flew in and out of Hull's ranch, "Tito" Carrasco, testified that one of Pastora's commanders assured him he had nothing to worry about because the CIA was protecting the flights from Costa Rica all the way into Florida. "Octaviano and Popo tell George [Morales], 'Listen, these people supposed to work for the CIA, those people are supposed to have, you know, everything under control, so the people tell George, 'Do it at Opa Locka. Nothing will happen if the plane arrives at Opa Locka,'" Carrasco testified.

"And you flew into Opa Locka?" he was asked.

"Yes."

"Did anyone stop you?"

"Nobody," Carrasco said.

Carrasco's opinion was that the entire operation was being protected from police interference all the way from Panama, where his drug flights originated. "Every week I flew to Panama, between Panama and Costa Rica, with different passports and different names and they never asked me why," Carrasco testified. "So if that is not protection, I don't know what is protection."

The Contra officials gave Carrasco and Morales "good passports" from Nicaragua during a party at Morales's house in Miami. The passports were complete with entry and exit stamps from a variety of countries, Carrasco said; they lacked only a name and a photograph.

Carrasco's copilot, Gary "Hippie" Betzner, also testified that their flights were protected by the CIA. "And did these CIA people permit you to fly airplanes into foreign countries carrying weapons?" a defense lawyer asked him during a federal trial in Oklahoma.

"Why, sure," Betzner said.

"And bring drugs back?"

"Yes."

"And did these CIA people know what you were doing with the drugs?"

"Certainly," Betzner insisted. (Like Carrasco, when Betzner gave that testimony, he was on the stand as witness for the Justice Department, not as a defendant.)

Asked if he was surprised that his boss Morales was helping the Contras, Betzner, who'd pleaded guilty to federal drug charges, said, "No, actually, I wasn't surprised by it because I knew that George was anti-Communist, as are most Colombians. So the Cartel and people like that are definitely anti-Communist to the—I don't suppose their world would function too well in a Communist world. It's strictly a capitalist movement, this drug business."

When money from the drug sales was collected, Carrasco said, he would deliver it to CIA operatives Chamorro and César, "sometimes in the United States, sometimes in Costa Rica." He said he delivered bags of money "sometimes two, three times a day.... I paid a lot of money, maybe millions."

In 1996 interviews with the *Washington Post*, César and Chamorro both said the CIA was fully aware of their involvement with the Colombian drug trafficker and had approved of it beforehand. César informed a CIA officer stationed at Ilopango air base in El Salvador. Chamorro went higher than that—to Langley. "I called our contact at the

CIA, of course I did," Chamorro told the *Post*. "The truth is we were still getting some CIA money under the table. They said [Morales] was fine." While the *Post* thoughtfully omitted the name of the CIA official who okayed the arrangement, in an interview Chamorro identified him as the head of the CIA's Central American Task Force, Alan Fiers.

In congressional testimony, former Costa Rican CIA station chief Joe Fernández said Fiers once ordered him to use two suspected drug traffickers in a still-secret CIA operation involving the Contras. "For political considerations, there were two individuals who were associated with Pastora who had allegations against them for drug involvement and [the chief of the Central American Task Force] wanted [censored]," the declassified hearing transcript states. "I objected to it in cable traffic, in person, and it was deemed necessary [censored], at least since these were only allegations and not proof, and so I was overruled and we proceeded to do it and we did it."

"But in your mind it went beyond allegation, didn't it?" Senator Daniel Inouye of Hawaii asked.

"Yes, sir," Fernández replied. "[Censored] there were indications that our suspicions might be more well founded than..."

The rest of Fernández's exchange with Inouye was censored for national security reasons.

After his first meeting with the Contras, Morales testified, he agreed to give the men an aged C-47 cargo plane that he had stored in Haiti, and $10,000 with which to fly the lumbering transport to Ilopango. Pastora's planes had been hangared there since 1983 under an arrangement worked out between CIA pilot Aguado and the Salvadoran Air Force. The C-47 was the first of many aircraft the Colombian trafficker would give to the Contras. According to a Senate subcommittee investigation, the airplane was officially transferred from Morales to Marcos Aguado for $1 on October 1, 1984, and saw considerable service on the Southern Front.

In 1987 investigative reporter Jonathan Kwitny obtained the refueling receipts for the C-47 and reported that the plane "was repeatedly piloted into and out of Ilopango Air Force Base in El Salvador by Marcos Aguado." Another one of the C-47's pilots, Kwitny found, was Gerardo Duran, a Costa Rican drug pilot who also served as chief pilot instructor for the Southern Front Contras. Duran was convicted of narcotics trafficking in Costa Rica in 1987 and jailed.

"Morales contends that his C-47 would continue on from Ilopango to Colombia, where it was reloaded with drugs before flying back to Florida," Kwitny reported. "This assertion is entirely plausible, and is even somewhat corroborated by Justice Department charges that Morales was importing cocaine at the time for the largest Colombian cartel."

Morales told Congress that his old C-47 remained part of the Contras' air force for years, which both Aguado and congressional investigators confirmed. "Chamorro gave the Subcommittee a list of flights made by that C-47 to ferry arms from Ilopango to Costa Rica," a Senate subcommittee report stated. "Between Oct. 18, 1984 and February 12, 1986, some 156,000 pounds of material were moved from Ilopango to air fields in Costa Rica."

When he quit the war in May 1986, Aguado said he sold the airplane for $30,000. The buyer? Norwin Meneses. In 1997, Aguado said, the C-47 was still being used by Meneses in Venezuela.

Soon after Morales began supplying him with money, Pastora said, Danilo Blandón popped up waving cash. Pastora knew Blandón from before the Sandinista revolution, when Blandón headed a pro-Somoza student group in college. "We knew of him as a man who always had money," Pastora said. "In fact, he was regarded in Nicaragua as a millionaire. He was a member of the Blandón family, a family that had always been well-to-do."

Pastora said he met with Blandón during a trip to Los Angeles in late 1984. Marcos Aguado confirmed that and said he accompanied Pastora to the meeting. Both men agreed that Blandón provided cash—according to Pastora, $6,000; according to Aguado, $20,000—two pickup trucks, and the keys to Blandón's vacation home in San José, Costa Rica, where Pastora lived rent-free for several years. Blandón told the CIA he could have charged Pastora $1,000 a month for rent if he'd wanted.

"The only time Danilo came down to Costa Rica was for the parties," shrugged Meneses's partner, Troilo Sánchez.

It was around this time, according to former CIA official Fiers, that the CIA learned Pastora was getting drug money. "We knew that everybody around Pastora was involved in cocaine," he testified in 1987. "We knew it from November of 1984 forward. We reported it."

Pastora assumed Blandón was a successful car dealer, not a dope peddler, and he said he thought nothing of the donations at the time. "It seemed to me totally natural that a friend of mine who was in very comfortable financial straits, as are the Blandón family in Nicaragua, it just seemed very natural to me that a person like that would give to me two pickup trucks."

Another Blandón associate who came to Pastora's aid after the CIA cutoff was a Nicaraguan pediatrician named Dr. Felix Saborio who,

Pastora said, volunteered to become his representative to the anti-Communist Cuban community in southern Florida, his liaison with the U.S. news media, and an ARDE fund-raiser. Saborio was frequently quoted in the *Miami Herald* and other papers as Pastora's spokesman during 1984 and 1985. "Felix Saborio was a close friend of Blandón from childhood," said Pastora's former aide, Carol Prado. "I also knew them from childhood. They were very rich people. I went to a party in Miami at Felix's house with Edén and that's where I saw Blandón."

Saborio was also acquainted with Blandón's spooky associate Ronald Lister. Lister told the CIA that he had "travelled to Hialeah, Florida sometime in 1982 or 1983 and met with a Contra member named 'Dr. Sabario' in an effort to sell 'military supplies' to the Contras." The CIA report stated that "the military supplies were commercially available equipment such as non-reflective paint for equipment and surveillance detection gear of the type that can be purchased at electronic shops and 'spy' stores."

In 1992, court records show, Saborio posted part of Chepita Blandón's bond after she was arrested on drug trafficking charges in San Diego. The doctor did not return phone calls inquiring about his relationship with the trafficker or his wife. No evidence has surfaced implicating Saborio in drug dealing.

"Blandón and Saborio...both vanished from my ranks when it became clear that I was not willing to march to the tune of the CIA," Pastora said. Blandón's interest in helping ARDE always mystified him, "because I knew he had been with the FDN from the very first. I thought he gave me a little bit of money just so he could tell people that he had helped Commandante Zero."

Pastora's involvement with the Colombian trafficker Morales remained a secret until late 1985, when two Associated Press reporters looking into allegations of Contra drug dealing discovered some of the donations. The source of their information was a leaked CIA analysis of the narcotics trade that alleged that "one of ARDE's top commanders, loyal to ARDE leader Edén Pastora, used cocaine profits this year to buy a $250,000 arms shipment and a helicopter." The AP story also mentioned that "Guachan" Gonzales's M-3 group and the FDN were suspected of being involved in drugs as well, but offered no details.

Robert Parry, one of the AP reporters who wrote the groundbreaking story, said his editors sat on the piece for weeks and edited it heavily, only to spike it at the last minute. When it was accidentally transmitted over the AP's Spanish-language wire, his editors rewrote the story once again, and all references to the alleged involvement of CIA operatives were deleted before it was released to the American public. Parry later discovered that the AP's Washington Bureau chief was having regular meetings with Lieutenant Colonel Oliver North, who was running the Contra program at the time.

Though emasculated by its editors and ignored by most of the American media, the AP story kicked up a heated controversy in Washington and prompted Senator John Kerry's staff to begin an investigation. As the evidence of Contra drug trafficking piled up and suspicions mounted, CIA and State Department spokesmen immediately pointed to Pastora as the only drug-dealing Contra they knew, citing him as an example of how ridiculous were accusations that the CIA would condone drug dealing. Pastora's CIA funding was cut off, they said, at the first whiff of impropriety.

To this day, Edén Pastora remains the only Contra commander the U.S. government has ever officially admitted was involved with drug money. A few months after the AP story appeared, Pastora quit the Contra war and became a fisherman. The CIA-linked ARDE commanders who got him involved with the Colombian trafficker Morales—Octaviano César and "Popo" Chamorro—quickly joined forces with the CIA's new Contra army.

Pastora's claim of a CIA plot becomes even more believable when one considers who the agency selected to replace him as the Southern Front's military commander: none other than Fernando "El Negro" Chamorro, the drunken leader of UDN-FARN, which had been getting cocaine money from the Meneses organization since the early 1980s. Former Costa Rican station chief Fernández confirmed to Congress in 1987 that the CIA decided "to diminish Pastora's influence" and "raise up the stature of the Negro Chamorro people...what we needed to do was put [Pastora] aside and at the same time enhance the organization that we were supporting."

Why the CIA was so eager to promote such a drug-tainted organization as UDN-FARN is one of the enduring mysteries of the Contra war. Independent Counsel Lawrence Walsh, in his memoirs of the Iran-Contra scandal, wrote that Chamorro was picked because he "had been acceptable to Contra leader Adolfo Calero and responsive to the CIA." The agency's choice demonstrates just how contrived the official shock was over Pastora's involvement with drug dealers. Chamorro's Contras had far more links to drug traffickers than Pastora's organization ever did, and those ties could be traced all the way back to the beginnings of the

Contra war. The leadership of UDN-FARN had been directly implicated in the Frogman case in 1983, a fact the CIA had strived mightly to conceal from the American public. Moreover, "El Negro" was just as erratic and unstable a military commander as Edén Pastora had been—perhaps more so—and far less effective in recruiting volunteer fighters. Most of Chamorro's band were Cuban mercenaries and terrorists he and the CIA had scoured from the Miami underworld.

But even when reports of UDN-FARN drug dealing reached the highest levels in Washington, the U.S. government's financial and material support for the organization never wavered. The money and the CIA assistance kept right on coming.

"The concern about Chamorro is that he drinks a fair amount and may surround himself with people who are in the war not only to fight but to make money," Lieutenant Colonel Oliver North's Costa Rican emissary, Robert Owen, nervously wrote North in April 1985. Owen, one of the CIA's top informants in Costa Rica, listed eight of Chamorro's associates as having "past indiscretions." The list included UDN-FARN's air force chief, Jose "Chepon" Robelo, whom Owen described as having "potential involvement with drug running," and Meneses's partner, Sebastian "Guachan" González, whom Owen said was "now involved in drug running out of Panama." That Meneses and González were dealing cocaine together had been known to the CIA since late 1984, records show.

One of the men closely involved in the Contra operation around that time, retired air force general Richard Secord, told writer Leslie Cockburn in 1987 that he heard the same allegations about the UDN-FARN commanders, and that "most of them were true. I didn't pick them. The Agency picked them."

As a fighting force, UDN-FARN was an unmitigated disaster, probably the most inept Contra group there was. Never numbering more than a couple hundred fighters, UDN-FARN caused more grief for the U.S. government than it ever caused the Sandinistas. Chamorro's boys were creating "such a difficult situation" that CIA station chief Joe Fernández, who'd been instrumental in throwing the CIA's support behind UDN-FARN, was catching flak from both the Costa Rican government and the U.S. ambassador to "get those people under control. 'They just do this and that' and I mean it was just one headache after another," Fernández testified. (If he elaborated on the "this and that," it was deleted from the heavily censored transcript of his testimony.)

According to Fernández, Chamorro and his men couldn't be driven into battle with a cattle prod. "They certainly had to get their act together and their guts in place and say, 'No more [Costa Rican] sanctuary, let's go in and fight the Sandinistas,'" Fernández told Congress in April 1987. "They were extremely—and that is not an overstatement—they were extremely reluctant to do so. Negro Chamorro to this day that I know of has yet to get inside Nicaragua."

CIA informant Rob Owen confirmed that. "The Costa Ricans wanted the people—they were up near the Costa Rican/Nicaraguan border, they were in several camps—they wanted them moved out. They wanted them moved at least 40 kilometers inside Nicaragua," Owen testified. "There was a hesitancy on the part of Negro Chamorro and his people.... Their hesitancy was based on going deep inside Nicaragua. They would not have Costa Rica to be able to run back into should something happen."

Blandón's drug-dealing friends, the Torres brothers, told L.A. County Sheriff's Office investigators that "during the height of the Contra war, they would continually run into supposed Contra commandantes in swank casinos throughout Costa Rica. These 'commandantes' would laugh and say they were just spending the CIA's payroll money of about $7,000 a month," a 1996 report stated. (Why two L.A. cocaine traffickers were cavorting through Costa Rica at the height of the Contra war was not a question the Torreses were asked.)

CIA officer Fernández testified that "the last time I remember Negro Chamorro being inside Nicaragua was in 1983 when he crossed the border [censored] and attacked, if you can imagine, a guard post, a guard house 30 meters or 30 yards inside Nicaragua. And then when he started to get his—when the Sandinistas counterattacked he ran to a telephone on the [censored] side and dialed me in Washington D.C., at Langley headquarters, asking for mortars! So help me God! And I asked him, 'Where in the hell are you calling from?' and he said, 'From the guard post at [censored].' He said, 'We are under attack, you need to send me arms!' and I said, 'You've got to be out of your mind.'

"This is no joke," Fernández assured the laughing congressmen. "He called our outside line." The lawmakers were apparently so amused by Fernández's stories that none of them thought to ask why the CIA continued to train and finance such a clownish crew.

But El Negro and company weren't the CIA's headache for long.

Shortly after UDN-FARN became the agency's anointed force in Costa Rica, the CIA was forced to give up its active role in the Contra project, and it left the mess it had created for someone else to clean up.

When the Boland Amendment went into effect in October 1984, day-to-day control of the Contra project passed to the Reagan White House and Lieutenant Colonel Oliver North at the National Security Council. "As the summer of 1984 came to an end, I felt like I was straddling a canyon," North wrote. "On one side was the resistance, always expanding, always needing more. On the other side was the CIA, which was steadily withdrawing its support."

If the CIA's blindness to Contra drug trafficking was bad, it was nothing compared to what happened after North and his network of spooks and mercenaries took the wheel. Perhaps for the first time in history, the U.S. goverment became business partners with cocaine traffickers. And Norwin Meneses's cocaine began arriving in the United States aboard military transport planes.

12

"This guy talks to God"

When they found Dr. Hugo Spadafora in September 1985, they found everything but his head. The rest of him had been tied up in a U.S. mail sack and dumped under a bridge on the border of Costa Rica and Panama.

His body bore evidence of unimaginable tortures. The thigh muscles had been neatly sliced so he could not close his legs, and then something had been jammed up his rectum, tearing it apart. His testicles were swollen horribly, the result of prolonged garroting, his ribs were broken, and then, while he was still alive, his head had been sawed off with a butcher's knife.

The horrors of Hugo Spadafora's death brought thousands of people into the streets of Panama City, where they formed a miles-long human chain of outrage and lament. The dashing young doctor had been a hero to many Panamanians—an unusual mix of revolutionary warrior and middle-class professional.

When he was murdered, Spadafora had been fighting for the Contras in Costa Rica, at the side of his old friend Edén Pastora. They had fought together in the 1970s against the Somoza dictatorship, with Spadafora leading an international brigade of jungle fighters—the Brigada Internacional Simón Bolívar—in support of Pastora's southern forces. After the Sandinistas became too oppressive for Pastora's liking, he joined the CIA and took over command of a Contra army in Costa Rica. Hugo Spadafora gave up his medical practice in

Panama and, with his wife Winy, moved to Costa Rica to take up arms with Pastora once again—this time against their old Marxist comrades.

The Reagan administration's Contra PR machine couldn't have dreamed up a better freedom fighter than Hugo Spadafora. The DEA called him "reportedly the best known guerrilla fighter in Central America." He was so popular in Panama that the country's civilian president, Nicolas Barletta, announced an immediate investigation into his shocking murder. It was to be one of Barletta's last official acts. A few weeks later he was forced to resign by Manuel Noriega, the commander of the country's military, and the promised investigation never occurred. Telephone intercepts by the U.S. National Security Agency (NSA) showed fairly convincingly that Noriega had ordered Spadafora's beheading. Later, others close to Noriega would say so publicly.

The *New York Times*, in a June 1986 story that first exposed Noriega as a drug dealer and money launderer, cited Spadafora's murder as an example of why U.S. government officials were growing tired of the tyrant. "Officials in the Reagan Administration and past Administrations said in interviews that they had overlooked General Noriega's illegal activities because of his cooperation with American intelligence," the story said. "They said, for example, that General Noriega had been a valuable asset to Washington in countering insurgencies in Central America and was now cooperating with the Central Intelligence Agency in providing sensitive information from Nicaragua."

But the *Times* story left unaddressed a rather obvious question: why would a cunning political strategist like Noriega take the risky step of having the popular Spadafora, Panama's former vice minister of public health, kidnapped by government security men in full view of dozens of witnesses, and decapitated?

The answer, which may be the reason the *Times* sidestepped the issue, involved drugs and the CIA. When Noriega's goons hauled Spadafora off a bus at the Panamanian border, he was on his way to Panama City, where he intended to publicly release evidence of Noriega's cocaine-smuggling activities—activities that also involved the Contras in Costa Rica. Before leaving for Panama, Spadafora had excitedly told friends that he now had the proof he needed to document the dictator's participation in cocaine trafficking, and he was convinced that the revelations would sink the tyrant.

In the months before his murder, the doctor had befriended a drug and arms smuggler who once ran Noriega's drug operation, Floyd Carlton Caceres. Carlton, who also served as Noriega's personal pilot, began confiding in Spadafora, sharing intimate details of Noriega's drug trade. "Dr. Spadafora was a very honest man," Carlton said. "He was an idealist and he tried to get the best for anyone needing justice."

If anyone needed justice right then, it was Floyd Carlton. The smuggler was lying low, trying to avoid a hit man Colombian dealers had sent after him. Carlton had lost $1.8 million in cash the Colombians had entrusted to him to fly from Los Angeles to their banks in Panama City. Since he was too busy to do it himself, he'd delegated the task to an underling, who later turned up in Miami, sans cash.

"I had to pay that money," Carlton said, which he agreed to do by flying a drug load north for free. But again, he'd sent someone else to fly the mission, one of his partners, Teofilo Watson. Watson had never returned, disappearing with 530 kilos of cocaine. Now the Colombians were really angry.

"They thought I had agreed or made a plan with Mr. Watson to steal the drug," Carlton said. Carlton suspected that Costa Rican Contra leader Sebastian "Guachan" González and his strange M-3 Contra group had done Watson in, leading him into an ambush at an airstrip owned by the local CIA man, John Hull. "They killed him and then took the airplane and the drugs to Mr. Hull's ranch," Carlton testified. The plane was cut up and thrown into a river that ran through Hull's property, and the cocaine was spirited to the United States, where it may have been traded for weapons.

The Colombians sent a hired killer named Alberto Aldimar out to find Carlton and the cocaine. Aldimar started by kidnapping Carlton's friends and employees and slapping them around. One of his relatives, Carlton said, "was brutally beaten." Then the power shovels arrived and began digging up Carlton's ranch. "They spent weeks there looking for some type of metal and found nothing," he said. Next the Colombians kidnapped the daughter of the Contras' CIA liaison, John Hull, on whose ranch the theft supposedly had taken place. Hull ransomed the girl back unharmed and blamed it on the Communists.

After that, Carlton bolted Central America altogether and took refuge in Miami, the U.S. headquarters of his cocaine transportation network. That's where Spadafora found him, in hiding. "He was trying to unmask Noriega and he was successful in obtaining truth that could imperil Noriega," Carlton later testified.

That in large part was due to Carlton, who would later astonish DEA officials with his photographic recall of Noriega's drug deals. Carlton eventually became the U.S. government's star witness against the

Panamanian dictator at his trial on drug charges. The pilot gave Spadafora the names of other pilots involved and the dates of specific drug flights through Costa Rica. He also implicated Noriega's high school buddy, "Guachan" González, who was then hiding out in Panama from a Costa Rican cocaine indictment.

When he was finished, Carlton said, Spadafora announced, "I am going to have a bomb explode in Panama. I am going to set it off with all this information which I have." Hurrying back to Costa Rica, Spadafora began sharing his discoveries with law enforcement and intelligence officials, which may have been his worst mistake.

According to Carlton and Noriega's political adviser José Blandón, one place Spadafora went with his allegations was the U.S. Drug Enforcement Administration offices at the American embassy in San José, Costa Rica. Shortly before his death Spadafora had three meetings with the DEA's country attaché, Robert Nieves, the last one occurring just two days before Spadafora's death.

If Nieves needed a way to confirm the doctor's explosive claims, he had just the man for the job—his deep-cover informant Norwin Meneses. In addition to Meneses's connections within the Contras, the trafficker was a close friend and trafficking partner of the Contra official Spadafora was trying to unmask, "Guachan" González.

Somehow Meneses's lieutenants got wind of what Spadafora was planning, and they began devising a counterattack. During their investigation of Meneses aide Horacio Pereira, the Costa Rican police taped Gonzales and Pereira discussing Spadafora's probe and plotting ways to silence him. The Costa Rican newspaper *La Nacion* obtained copies of the tapes and printed partial transcripts. One ploy González and Pereira batted around was paying a witness in Guanacaste Province between $200,000 and $300,000 to falsely accuse Spadafora of drug trafficking and exonerate González of his pending Costa Rican drug charges.

"Now he's surrounded because if he comes over here, he's finished," González confidently told Pereira in a phone call from Panama.

"Yes," Pereira replied. "If he shows up over there, you'll get him."

The district attorney in the Panamanian province where Spadafora was murdered ordered González arrested in 1990 for allegedly offering to pay someone to kill the doctor, but no charges were filed, and González was quickly released. He has strenuously denied any involvement in Spadafora's death, but Spadafora's family remains convinced González played a major role.

Though Noriega apparently felt the information Spadafora possessed was important enough to kill him over, DEA official Robert Nieves had a very different reaction. He told *La Nacion* that his discussions with Spadafora were "not important" and said he did nothing with the information the doctor had risked his life to bring him. Since Noriega's drug dealing was the official reason the United States invaded Panama four years later, Nieves's professed inaction is astounding. But it would not be out of character for the DEA at that time.

Floyd Carlton testified that he got the same cold shoulder from the DEA office in Panama City when he tried telling them about Noriega's drug dealing in January 1986. "I did actually make contact with intelligence agents in the United States Embassy in Panama," Carlton related. "And I asked, 'Have you not heard my name?' And they said, 'Yes, we have.' And so I said, 'On different occasions I have sent people to speak to you so that you interview me. But you have always told them that you have nothing to talk to me about. And the fact is that I believe that I can go before the American judicial system and speak of a lot of things that are happening in this country, and I can even prove them.'

"So they asked, 'Such as what?' So, I said, 'Money laundering, drugs, weapons, corruption, assassinations.' When I mentioned the name of General Noriega, they immediately became upset." Carlton said the DEA agents "did not try to contact me again. And the only thing that I asked for was protection for myself and my family. And at that time I had no problems with the American justice system."

Judging from the DEA's response to a Freedom of Information Act request, Nieves took a similarly incurious stance when his informant turned up with his head missing. Apparently, none of the DEA's Costa Rican agents ever looked into the doctor's gruesome death. All the agency had on Spadafora, it claimed, was a couple of paragraphs culled from Panamanian newspaper stories written a year after the murder.

The CIA's reaction was even more bizarre. Its Costa Rican station chief, Joe Fernández, helped Noriega plant false media reports about who really killed Hugo Spadafora.

José Blandón, then Noriega's consul general in New York, told Congress that he and Noriega discussed Spadafora's murder a few weeks after the body was found, during a long flight home from New York aboard the dictator's private Lear Jet. Noriega, who'd been in France when Spadafora was killed, wanted an update on how the public was reacting to the killing, the diplomat said. "Especially, he was interested in the developments regarding a witness whose name is Hoffman, a witness of German origin who appeared on Panamanian television saying that he knew who had killed Spadafora and publicly said that Spadafora had been killed by the FMLN [leftist guerrillas] of El Salvador," Blandón testified.

The German, Manfred Hoffman, "was a witness who was created by Noriega, and he was obtained through the CIA operating in Costa Rica," Blandón testified. "He is a specialist in electronics and he worked for the CIA in some cases." Blandón, describing the episode as "an absurd farce," said he told Noriega "nobody believed that story."

No one was ever held accountable for Hugo Spadafora's hideous death. A show trial of some minor military officers resulted in acquittals all around, and the case was closed.

Unfortunately for Spadafora's wife and family, the good doctor had the bad luck of being murdered at a politically inconvenient time. It was in no one's interests right then—Noriega's or the U.S. government's—to delve too deeply into the crime for fear of what would be exposed: the apparent complicity of two CIA assets—Noriega and González—in the murder of someone trying to expose government drug trafficking.

At that point the Reagan administration was nuzzling up to Noriega as it had never done before, frantically searching for ways around the 1984 congressional ban on CIA support to the Contras. For months, a steady stream of high-ranking visitors from Washington had been paying courtesy calls to the despot, reminding him of how much Uncle Sam liked and needed him.

In June 1985, aboard a luxurious yacht anchored in the Pacific port of Balboa, North and Noriega struck a very important bargain, said José Blandón, who attended the meeting. "Colonel North was interested in gaining Panama's support for the Contras and he particularly requested training assistance in bases located in Panama," Blandón told Congress in 1988. "General Noriega promised to provide training in specific locations to members of the Contras, training to be provided at bases located in Panama." He was also willing to allow Contra leaders free access to the country, and made it clear to North that he was willing to do much, much more.

According to government documents filed during North's trial, Noriega offered to have the entire Sandinista leadership assassinated in exchange for "a promise from the U.S. government to help clean up Noriega's image." North raised the proposal at a top level meeting in Washington and made it clear that "Noriega had the capabilities that he had proffered." North was instructed to tell Noriega that the administration wasn't keen on murdering Nicaraguan government officials, but that Panamanian assistance with sabotage would be another story.

A month after Spadafora's body was found under the bridge, North went back to Panama for another visit, this time to assure the dictator that the U.S. government would be boosting Noriega's foreign aid payments. Within a year an additional $200 million in U.S. taxpayer funds and bank loans was sent his way.

Meanwhile, a former staffer on the National Security Council, Dr. Norman A. Bailey, was frantically trying to alert various high-ranking government officials to the fact that Noriega was in bed with drug traffickers and other criminals. Bailey, the NSC's former director of planning, had discovered that Panamanian banks were taking in billions of dollars in $50 and $100 bills, money that Bailey concluded could only have come from criminal activities.

Bailey set off on a quixotic quest to persuade the Reagan administration to distance itself from Noriega, pressing his reports into the hands of Reagan's top advisers, including national security adviser Admiral John Poindexter. "I took the initiative myself after the murder of Dr. Spadafora," Bailey testified. "As far as I know, the only thing that actually took place was that Admiral Poindexter added Panama to a trip he was making to Central America in December of 1985."

But Poindexter's meeting with Noriega was hardly what Norman Bailey had envisioned. According to Jose Blandón, who was in attendance, Poindexter did bring up the Spadafora murder, but only to give Noriega some friendly advice on how to handle it; Poindexter "spoke of the need to have a group of officers be sent abroad, outside of Panama, while the situation changed and the attitudes changed regarding Spadafora's assassination."

At that point, Poindexter had to be aware of the NSA intercepts showing Noriega's role in ordering the killing, and under those circumstances, his meeting takes on a decidedly different hue: the president's national security adviser was advising a suspected murderer on how best to handle the bad PR resulting from his crime.

Noriega met CIA director William Casey after that, again to discuss his help for the Contras. According to a Senate subcommittee report, Casey decided not to raise the allegations of Noriega's cocaine trafficking with him "on the ground that Noriega was providing valuable support for our policies in Central America."

While all of this official ring-kissing was going on, Oliver North and the CIA were quietly knitting parts of Noriega's drug transportation system into the Contras' lines of supply—and hiring drug smugglers to make Contra supply flights for them.

At the time of his visits with Noriega, North was firmly in control of the Contra project, having been handed the ball personally by CIA director Casey. Far from being the dopey, gap-toothed zealot portrayed by the Reagan administration and the press, North was one of the most powerful men in Washington. "The spring of 1985, he was the top gun," testified Alan Fiers, the CIA's Central American Task Force chief and North's liaison at Langley. "He was the top player in the NSC as well. And there was no doubt that he was—he was driving the process, driving the policy."

Former Iran-Contra special prosecutor Lawrence Walsh, who indicted and convicted North on a variety of felonies, suspects the Marine officer was a cutout for the CIA, a human lightning rod to keep the agency from becoming directly involved in illegal activities. "The CIA had continued as the agency overseeing U.S. undercover activities in support of the Contras after the Boland amendments were enacted," Walsh wrote in his memoirs. "The CIA's strategy determined what North would do."

In a city where information is power, North had access to the nation's deepest secrets, subjects so highly classified even top CIA officials didn't know about them. "He told me in 1985 that there was [sic] two squadrons of Stealth bombers operational in Arizona and I just thought he was crazy," Fiers testified. "It was the, one of the greatest secrets the government had and then all of a sudden we, in fact, ended up with two squadrons of Stealth bombers operational. And there were many, many other instances when he told me things, and I thought they were totally fanciful and, in fact, turned out to be absolute truth."

One of the many surprises North had for Fiers was the fact that he had received specialized training usually reserved for CIA officers. During one late-night conversation about the Contra supply operation in Costa Rica, Fiers testified, North blurted out that he had "put together a whole cascade of cover companies, 'just like they taught us at the CIA clandestine training site.' And I thought that was pretty interesting because I went there and I didn't learn how to put together a whole cascade of companies. And I also didn't know that Ollie North had gone down to the training site."

Savvy bureaucrats in Washington knew North was not someone to be taken lightly. Fiers called him "a power figure in the government…a force to be reckoned with." When he asked for something, people jumped. When he gave orders, they were followed. "Ollie North had the ability to work down in my chain of command and to cause [it] to override me if and when I didn't do something," Fiers testified. "And, I would like to

"El Rey de la Droga" (The King of Drugs), Norwin Meneses Cantarero, during an interview with the author and Georg Hodel at Tipitapa Prison outside Managua in 1996. PHOTO BY GARY WEBB

FDN supporter Don Sinicco snapped this picture in his kitchen in San Francisco during a cocktail party he was hosting for CIA agent Adolfo Calero, center. Drug lord Norwin Meneses is on the far right. The other men are local Contra supporters. At the time this photo was taken, June 1984, Meneses was engaged in a cocaine smuggling conspiracy, according to federal prosecutors. PHOTO COURTESY OF DON SINICCO

Danilo Blandón, circa 1995.

ABC Park and Fly, near the Miami International Airport. Blandón established his car rental company in this building during his brief "retirement" from the cocaine business in 1987. The day this picture was taken Anastasio Somoza's former counterinsurgency expert, Maj. Gen. Gustavo "El Tigre" Medina, was working behind the counter.
PHOTO BY GARY WEBB

Enrique Miranda Jaime, shortly after the FBI kidnapped him in Miami and sent him back to Nicaragua to face escape charges in late 1996. Miranda, a former double agent for the CIA and the Sandinistas, was Meneses's top aide after the war and would later help send his boss to prison. PHOTO BY GARY WEBB

Former Contra cocaine courier Carlos Cabezas, at his law office in Managua. PHOTO BY GARY WEBB

The Oval Office, August 5, 1987. A gathering of Nicaraguan resistance leaders to mark yet another CIA-inspired merger of the Contra armies from the FDN to the United Nicaraguan Opposition (UNO). Second from left is Aristides Sanchez. Adolfo Calero is on the far right.
COURTESY OF THE RONALD REAGAN LIBRARY

The Oval Office, April 4, 1985. From left: CIA agent Adolfo Calero, political boss of the FDN; Lt. Col. Oliver North and President Ronald Reagan, after the CIA handed off the day-to-day management of the Contra project to North and the National Security Council. COURTESY OF THE RONALD REAGAN LIBRARY

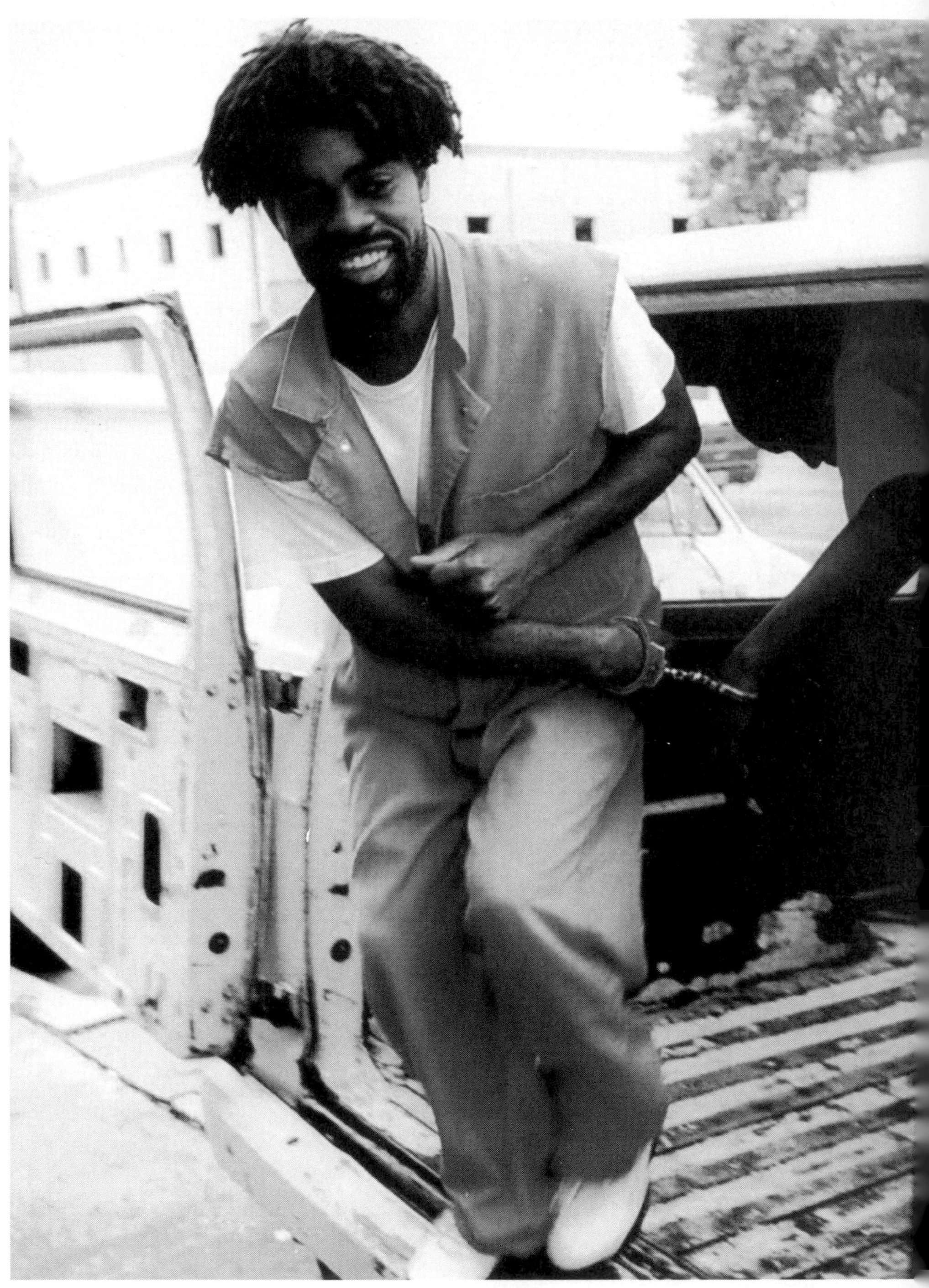

L.A. crack kingpin "Freeway" Ricky Ross was all smiles as he was released from a Texas prison in 1994 after serving a short stint for cocaine trafficking. Though he had vowed to go straight, a few months later he would be lured back into the drug business by his old friend and cocaine supplier, Danilo Blandón. ROBERT GAUTHIER/LOS ANGELES TIMES

Ricky Ross was captured March 2, 1995 in National City after his truck careened into a hedgerow.
PHOTO BY GARY WEBB

Part of the $160,000 seized by the DEA from crack dealer Leroy "Chico" Brown during the 1995 sting that snared "Freeway" Ricky Ross.
DEA PHOTO

Ricky Donnell Ross, shortly before he was sentenced to life in prison without the possibility of parole in October 1996. ROBERT GAUTHIER/LOS ANGELES TIMES

add, subsequently I saw that happen in other ways, other places and other agencies."

Fiers's boss at the CIA, Clair E. George, echoed that. "I suffer from the bureaucrat's disease, that when people call me and say, 'I am calling from the White House for the National Security Council on behalf of the national security advisor,' I am inclined to snap to."

CIA Costa Rican station chief Joe Fernández was more blunt. "To a GS-15, this guy talks to God, right?" Fernández said of North during a secret congressional hearing in 1987. "Obviously, I knew where he worked in the Executive Office Building. He has got tremendous access.... I mean, North is not some ordinary American citizen that is suddenly in this position. This is a man who had dealings with, obviously, the Director of the CIA.... You know, he deals with my division chief."

North was even telling U.S. ambassadors what to do.

In July 1985, before taking his new job as ambassador to Costa Rica, Lewis Tambs said North sat him down and gave him his marching orders. "Colonel North asked me to go down and open up the Southern Front," Tambs told the Iran-Contra committees. "We would encourage the freedom fighters to fight. And the war was in Nicaragua. The war was not in Costa Rica, and so that is what I understood my instructions were."

But with the CIA's billions officially banned from the scene, North had a big problem if he was going to get the Contras out of their Costa Rican border sanctuaries and into Nicaragua to do some actual fighting.

He had no way to supply them; the CIA had been doing all that.

It takes tons of material to sustain an army in the field, particularly one that is going to be warring deep inside enemy territory, separated by days from its supply depots. The CIA had plenty of experience handling such complicated logistical problems, but North didn't. It was a problem he took up with his friends at Langley, who, according to CIA official Fiers, "spent major time, major effort" trying to come up with a solution.

"Air resupply of the Contras was the key," Fiers testified. "We had a 15,000-man army of guerrillas operating in Nicaragua and had to supply them. All of the supply went by air. They carried in what—their boots and their clothes, and then their new ammunition and such had to be dropped in by air. So the success or failure turned on air resupply operations."

One of the vehicles North selected to handle that chore was a new unit set up inside the U.S. State Department called the Nicaraguan Humanitarian Assistance Office (NHAO). The office was officially created in mid-1985 to oversee the delivery of $27 million in "humanitarian" aid

Congress agreed to give the Contras, under considerable pressure from the White House.

North and the CIA first tried to get the operation placed inside the National Security Council, where it would be free from public scrutiny and North could control it directly, but that move failed. Instead, Fiers said, North simply "hijacked" it from the State Department. In November 1985 he pressured the NHAO to hire one of his aides as a consultant, a tall, blond former L.A. prep school counselor named Robert W. Owen. A Stanford University grad and onetime advertising executive, Owen idolized North. Since 1984 he had been, in his own words, North's "trusted courier" in Central America, zigzagging through the war zones for Ollie, listening to the concerns of Contra officials, setting up arms deals, and solving problems.

Owen's work had drawn rave reviews from his CIA contacts. "That man has all of the attributes that we want in our officers," Costa Rican station chief Fernández told Congress during a 1987 hearing. "I met with him on a number of occasions...introduced him to one of my officers who regularly met with him when he was in town." Fernández said his superiors were "so impressed with Mr. Owen that he was being considered as a possible applicant for the clandestine service."

Owen, in 1989 court testimony, admitted that "there was a possibility that I might have gone with the CIA on contract."

But because Owen was a private citizen, Fernández said, he couldn't legally send him out on intelligence-gathering missions. He could listen when Owen reported back but couldn't, in CIA jargon, "task" him. But that all changed once Owen began working for the NHAO, which probably explains North's insistence that Owen be hired. "When he did that, then we did have a much more operational relationship," Fernández confirmed. "Because then he was a government employee, I did ask him to find out things."

NHAO director Robert Duemling and his aides couldn't figure out why they needed to have Rob Owen around, and initially they rebuffed North's suggestions. "I certainly didn't see the necessity for a middleman," Duemling testified in a once-secret deposition to the Iran-Contra committees. But North kept pushing. Duemling said North had Contra leaders write letters demanding Owen's hiring, and he lobbied Duemling's superior at the State Department, Assistant Secretary of State Elliott Abrams, a fervent Contra supporter. After one stormy meeting with North and Abrams, Duemling said, "Elliott Abrams turned to me and said, 'Well, Bob, I suppose you probably ought to hire Owen.' Well, in bureaucratic terms the jig was up, since I was the only person who was speaking out against this."

Owen was given a $50,000 contract as a "facilitator," a job that mystified Duemling's aide, Chris Arcos. Arcos testified that no one was "sure what, in fact, Rob Owen could do or bring or offer to the office that we couldn't do. He didn't have much Spanish, he didn't have an expertise in medical or anything like that."

The minutes of that November 1985 meeting show that for some reason, Abrams and North were extremely concerned about the fallout if someone discovered Owen's involvement with the NHAO, and they began working on a cover story to explain his presence there in case it leaked. "Abrams and North agreed that Owen will be expendable if he becomes a political or diplomatic liability," the minutes state. If that happened, Congress would be told that he was "an experiment that hadn't worked out."

It was an experiment right out of Dr. Frankenstein's lab.

Rob Owen's mission was to serve as the CIA's unofficial liaison to the drug traffickers and other undesirables who were helping the Contras in Costa Rica, people who were too dirty for the CIA to deal with directly. Like North, he was another "cutout." "He probably had the most extensive network of contacts among the resistance leaders," CIA station chief Fernández testified in 1987, "including people with whom we did not want to have contact with and who, however, were involved with the Nicaraguan resistance."

The untouchables Fernández was referring to were the Cuban anti-Communists in Costa Rica—the rough mix of mercenaries, bombers, assassins, and drug dealers recruited in Miami by UDN-FARN commander Fernando "El Negro" Chamorro and CIA agent Ernesto Cruche. The agency, Fernández testified, was "very leery of these people. However, Rob Owen had an entrée to them."

And now, thanks to his NHAO job, he had an official entrée—as an operational CIA asset. Owen's specific assignment, in fact, put him directly over the drug traffickers Fernández and the CIA didn't want to be seen with.

He was assigned to "monitor" an NHAO contract with a Costa Rican shrimp company called Frigorificos de Puntarenas, S.A. This consisted of a small fleet of fishing boats based in the humid Pacific Coast village of Puntarenas, and an import company in Miami called Ocean Hunter, which brought Frigorificos' catch into the United States. In reality, however, it was "a firm owned and operated by Cuban-American drug traffickers," according to a 1988 Senate subcommittee report.

That conclusion was based partly on the congressional testimony of former Medellín cartel accountant Ramon Milian Rodriguez, a suave Cuban-American who was the cartel's money-laundering wizard until his arrest in Miami in 1983, when he and $5 million in cash were taken off a Lear Jet bound for Panama. Frigorificos, he testified, was one of an interlocking chain of companies he'd created to launder the torrents of cash that were pouring into the cartel's coffers from its worldwide cocaine sales. Drug money would go into one company and come out of another through a series of intercompany transactions, clean and ready to be banked or invested. In 1982, Frigorificos was taken over by a group of major Miami-based drug traffickers, who began using it to help the Contras.

"Were payments or arrangements made by which the Contras could receive money through Frigorificos?" Senator John Kerry asked Milian during a Senate subcommittee hearing in 1987.

"Yes sir," the accountant answered.

"You arranged that?"

"I, through my intermediaries, made it possible."

"Was any of the money that you provided Frigorificos traceable to drugs or to drug-related transactions?" Kerry asked.

"No, sir."

"Why was that?"

"Because," said Milian, "we were experts at what we do."

Milian, a graduate of Santa Clara University in Silicon Valley, told Kerry's committee that he used the firm to launder a $10 million donation from the Medellín cartel to the Contras, a donation he said was arranged by and paid to a former CIA agent, Cuban Felix Rodriguez. Kerry's committee didn't believe that tale, especially after Milian flunked a lie detector test on the question.

But during the drug trafficking trial of Manuel Noriega several years later, one of the government's star witnesses, former Medellín cartel transportation boss Carlos Lehder, confirmed under oath that the cartel *had* given the Contras $10 million, just as Milian had testified. Lehder said he arranged for the donation himself.

Contra leader Adolfo Calero has always denied the Contras received such a sum, but Calero is hardly a credible source when it comes to Contra fund-raising. He denied for many years that the Contras ever got money from the CIA, or assistance from Oliver North.

The FBI first picked up word of Frigorificos' involvement with drugs in September 1984, while the CIA was still running the Contra program. An investigation of a 1983 bombing of a Miami bank had led police and FBI agents into the murky underworld of Miami's Cuban anti-Communist groups, who were suspected of blowing up the bank.

Miami police questioned the president of the Cuban Legion, Jose Coutin, who told them what he knew of the bombing and then unloaded some unexpected information about the Contras and drugs, naming a host of Cuban CIA operatives and Bay of Pigs veterans he said were working for the Contras in Costa Rica. One drug dealer Coutin named was Francisco Chanes, whom Coutin said "was giving financial support to anti-Castro groups and the Nicaraguan Contra guerrillas. The monies come from narcotic transactions." He identified Chanes as one of the owners of Ocean Hunter, the sister company of Frigorificos. The Miami cops quickly turned the information over to the FBI, records show.

Coutin's statements were corroborated years later by former drug pilot Fabio Ernesto Carrasco, who admitted flying cocaine and weapons loads for the Contras in 1984 and 1985. As a U.S. government witness, Carrasco testified that Frigorificos was being used by the Contras during the war as a front to bring cocaine into the United States to finance the war effort.

"To make sure I understand, is this company Frigorificos de Puntarenas in any way involved in drug trafficking?" defense attorney Richard "Racehorse" Haynes asked Carrasco during a 1990 drug trial in Tulsa, Oklahoma.

"That's correct."

"In what way was it involved?"

"As I have said, they would load cocaine inside the containers which were being shipped loaded with vegetables and fruit to the United States," Carrasco said.

"Did this company have a role in your drug operations dealing with the Contras and the weapons that you believed to be involved with the CIA?"

"It did in my opinion," the pilot testified.

So how could a company started by the Medellín cartel and used as a front to run drugs into America ever wind up with a contract from the U.S. State Department's Nicaraguan Humanitarian Assistance Office?

Through Rob Owen and the CIA, court records show.

"The people that were involved in Ocean Hunter in Costa Rica were ones that had been helpful to the cause," Owen testified in a 1988 civil deposition. He identified those helpful souls as Frank Chanes, the Miami Cuban who was reported to the FBI as a drug trafficker in 1984, and Moises Nuñez, another Bay of Pigs veteran who was suspected by Interpol of being a drug trafficker as well as an intelligence operative.

Another man involved with Frigorificos was the exiled Nicaraguan lawyer Francisco Aviles Saenz, the CIA asset who claimed the $36,000 police had seized during the investigation of the Frogman case in San Francisco in 1983 belonged to the Contras. On several occasions Aviles, the brother-in-law of Meneses's lieutenant Horacio Pereira, notarized affidavits submitted by the shrimp company to obtain payment from the State Department, records show.

Owen claimed the shrimp company was used mainly for its international bank accounts, serving as one of several Central American "brokers" for the humanitarian aid money going to the Contras on the Southern Front. In all, more than $260,000 in U.S. taxpayer funds flowed through Frigorificos's bank accounts during 1986.

"We needed an account in Miami that the [State Department] money could be deposited to. [There were] constant financial transactions between Miami and Costa Rica, between Frank Chanes and Moises Nuñez. They had been helpful and supportive of the cause. They were willing to do it," Owen testified. "I felt that they were honest and that the money would go where it was supposed to go."

Where it ended up is anybody's guess. Some of the money paid Frigorificos, bank records show, was wired out in never-explained transfers to banks in Israel and South Korea. When the U.S. General Accounting Office audited the NHAO's "broker" accounts, it was unable to trace most of the money. Of $4.4 million that went into the accounts, less than $1 million could be accounted for, and much of that was in payoffs to Honduran military officials. The rest was traced to offshore banks and then disappeared.

Owen insisted that the traffickers at Frigorificos had been cleared by the CIA and presumably the FBI. "U.S. intelligence sources were involved in Costa Rica to provide a check and a balance on this. They would be knowledgeable, they knew the lay of the ground. I thought it important and appropriate to talk with them," Owen testified. "To the best of my knowledge, I talked to U.S. intelligence officials regarding Moises Nuñez. I believe I would have asked about Frank Chanes as well."

In addition, Owen said, "their names were given to NHAO and it was my understanding that any account that NHAO provided funds to was checked through the FBI. The FBI was informed who was being used as a banker. Now, whether they did any check on it or not, I'm not sure. I guess I assume that they did."

The director of the NHAO testified that the FBI never answered his letters of inquiry.

"So, is it fair to say, then, that you were the one that suggested these gentlemen be utilized?" Owen was asked during a deposition.

"It is fair to say…in consultation with U.S. intelligence officials," Owen replied. Owen refused to identify them further, other than to say that it was "someone who works for the CIA."

One reason the CIA gave Frigorificos a clean bill of health may have been because its Costa Rican manager, Moises Nuñez, was a CIA agent. John Hull, the CIA's Costa Rican liaison with the Contras, confirmed in an interview that Nuñez was working with the agency as an intelligence source, and a 1988 UPI story said Nuñez was "identified as an Agency officer by two senior Costa Rican government officials, a U.S. intelligence source, and American law enforcement authorities."

In addition to distributing State Department money to the Costa Rican Contras, Nuñez was also permitting Frigorificos to be used by North and CIA station chief Fernández as a cover for a secret maritime operation they were running against the Sandinistas, records show.

In February 1986, one of the Cubans working with North in Costa Rica, a longtime CIA contract agent named Felipe Vidal, devised a plan for a "small, professionally managed rebel naval force" that would serve as a supply line for the Contras, an intelligence-gathering operation, and a transportation unit "to infiltrate into the [Nicaraguan] mainland rebel cadres for specific missions."

Vidal recommended using a Costa Rican shrimp company as "a front" and getting two shrimp boats to act as motherships and to gather intelligence. "These boats could be acquired from U.S. government auctions," Vidal wrote, noting that "existing connections with a high-ranking official in the DEA would facilitate the purchase of said boats. The cost of these boats, with cooperation from the DEA, could come to as low as $10,000 per boat."

Vidal's "existing connections" with a top DEA official are fascinating, considering the Cuban's shady background. Published reports indicate that Vidal was arrested at least seven times in Miami for drug and weapons violations. Even CIA station chief Fernández admitted to Congress that Vidal, whom he referred to as one of "our people," had "a problem with drugs." Nonetheless, Vidal's plan was approved. The following month, Owen informed North that "the first hard intelligence mission inside by boat has taken place and the people are now out." He said five small boats were being constructed and "a safe house [in Costa Rica] has been rented on a river, which flows into the ocean."

"Moises Nuñez, a Cuban who has a shrimping business in Punteranous [sic] is fronting the operation," Owen wrote North. "He is willing to have an American come work for him under cover to advise the operation.... If we can get two shrimp boats, Nuñez is willing to front a shrimping operation on the Atlantic coast. These boats can be used as motherships. I brought this up awhile ago and you agreed and gave me the name of a DEA person who might help with the boats."

In other words, in early 1986 the DEA was being asked to provide cheap oceangoing vessels to a company started by the Medellín cartel, run by drug traffickers, for espionage missions planned and fronted by suspected drug traffickers.

The identity of Vidal's high-ranking DEA contact was not divulged, nor is it known whether the agency ever provided the boats, but records show the maritime operation was going strong in April 1986 and would soon be running "several trips a week," according to a memo Owen sent to North. Curiously, the Iran-Contra investigations barely looked at this clandestine operation, which was a clear violation of the Boland Amendment since, according to Owen, it directly involved CIA station chief Joe Fernández.

Despite his background, Moises Nuñez also maintained a chummy relationship with antidrug agencies, both American and Costa Rican. "Nuñez got to be known by our authorities as a collaborator of the DEA and of other police bodies," said a 1989 Costa Rican prosecutor's report, adding that the Cuban carried credentials from the Costa Rican Ministry of Public Safety's Department of Narcotics, provided funds and vehicles for an antidrug unit, and went out on raids with them, though his effectiveness was somewhat questionable. The report said he blew a four-month investigation of a Colombian drug ring by making a "premature" arrest.

Most of this strange activity was occurring with the knowledge and apparent approval of CIA station chief Fernández and other CIA agents in Costa Rica, records indicate. Fernández admitted to the Iran-Contra committees that he knew Nuñez and knew he was meeting with Owen to discuss Contra operations. Fernández was asked if he knew that Nuñez claimed to have met North, but his answer was classified for reasons of national security.

Former CIA official Fiers confirmed that the CIA played a critical role in the "humanitarian" aid operation involving Frigorificos; without the agency, Fiers said, the NHAO was simply "a shell entity.... We were to be the eyes and ears of the NHAO office. The only way that they could monitor alignments, verify shipments and receipts was by having CIA capabilities in the region perform that function for them. And so that's what we did." But since at least three other drug-dealing companies ended up working for the NHAO during its brief lifespan, either the CIA's oversight was woefully incompetent or it was seeking a special kind of contractor.

One such company was DIACSA, the Miami aircraft company that Floyd Carlton had used for years as the U.S. headquarters for his Panamanian drug-smuggling venture with Noriega. It was in DIACSA's offices, Carlton admitted, that he and his partners plotted their drug flights and arranged the laundering of their cocaine profits. DEA records confirm that.

Just like Frigorificos, DIACSA was run by a Cuban drug dealer who had been part of the CIA's Bay of Pigs operation, Alfredo Caballero. Carlton testified that Cabellero was "involved with drug trafficking and to a certain extent he helped the Contras. But to be more specific he was helpful to Mr. Pastora's organization [ARDE]."

According to a Senate subcommittee report, the Contras were dealing with DIACSA even before it was hired by the State Department. "During 1984 and 1985, the principal Contra organization, the FDN, chose DIACSA for 'intra-account transfers.' The laundering of the money through DIACSA concealed the fact that some funds of the Contras were deposits arranged by Lieutenant Colonel Oliver North," the report stated.

The State Department's selection of DIACSA as a "humanitarian" aid contractor is perhaps even more egregious than its choice of Frigorificos. At the time DIACSA got its government contract, the company had been penetrated by an undercover DEA agent, Danny Moritz, who was churning out eyewitness reports of Caballero's drug dealing and money-laundering rackets. Moreover, both Caballero and Carlton were under indictment in the United States for conspiring to import 900 pounds of cocaine and laundering $2.6 million in drug profits. Both were convicted, and both became U.S. government informants.

How the CIA missed those clues has never been explained. It is highly likely the agency knew exactly what DIACSA was, since its owner was said to be working for the CIA. "Alfredo Caballero was CIA and still is," insisted Carol Prado, Edén Pastora's top aide in ARDE. "I say that because I knew him very well. A lot of times I went to DIACSA in Miami." Caballero also worked for the DEA.

During Noriega's trial in 1991, Floyd Carlton testified that his smuggling operation was flying weapons to the Contras at the same time he was flying dope to the United States and he said some of the arms flights were organized by Caballero. When Noriega's lawyers asked Carlton about Oliver North's knowledge of those flights, federal prosecutors vehemently objected, and U.S. judge William Hoeveler became angry. "Just stay away from it," the judge snapped, refusing to allow any more questions on the topic.

Another Miami company the NHAO hired to ferry supplies was Vortex Aviation, which was being operated by a Detroit drug dealer named Michael Palmer. Palmer, a former airline pilot, had worked since 1977 for "the largest marijuana business cartel in the history of the country," according to a federal prosecutor in Detroit. Yet in 1985 Palmer became a freedom fighter and volunteered for the Contra war effort, transporting humanitarian aid for the State Department.

In a recently declassified interview with FBI agents in 1991, CIA official Fiers admitted that the CIA had information that Palmer was dealing drugs during that time. "Fiers heard that some of Palmer's people got caught taking a plane of drugs into the U.S. and this is what caused a lot of problems for Palmer," the FBI reported. "CIA thought the northern Contras were clean but Palmer was an exception."

One DC-4 Palmer was using to deliver Contra aid was shot up in February 1986 as it attempted an airdrop over Nicaragua, and it made an emergency landing on San Andrés Island off the coast of Nicaragua, a notorious haven for cocaine traffickers. Four days later Owen wrote to North, saying, "No doubt you know that the DC-4 Foley got was used at one time to run drugs and part of the crew had criminal records. Nice group the Boys chose." Pat Foley was the owner of a Delaware-based company, Summit Aviation, a longtime CIA and U.S. military contractor, often for clandestine air operations. Foley was reportedly overseeing Palmer's operations at Vortex.

Francis McNeil, at the time one of the State Department's top narcotics intelligence officers, confirmed to Congress that the DC-4's appearance at San Andrés caused red flags to go up in Washington. "A stop at San Andrés Island for a Contra resupply plane is a bit suspicious since San Andrés is known to be a transshipment point for drugs," McNeil testified.

The pilot of that unlucky DC-4, former CIA contract pilot Ronald Lippert, said in an interview that neither his trip nor his crew were involved with drugs, though the plane had been involved with drug flights "long before I acquired it." He said the landing at San Andrés was for repairs only. But he acknowledged that his plane was probably used for drug flights while Vortex was hauling humanitarian aid for the Contras. Those flights were piloted by Vortex's own crews, Lippert said. He knew one of the flights wound up in Colombia, because he got a call from the FAA in Miami "asking what my plane was doing, taking off from a dirt strip on the northeast coast of Colombia during its two-day mysterious absence on the Nicaraguan Contra flight."

Lippert, a Canadian who flew for the CIA in the early 1960s until his imprisonment by Cuban intelligence agents in 1963 for espionage, said that "the most I was able to find out from a friend in the intelligence community was the name 'Operation Stolen Mercedes' and that aside from Costa Rica, its itinerary may have included a stop in Panama and Mexico after it left Colombia."

On another Contra flight, Lippert's plane came back with an unexplained twelve and a half hours of excess flying time on it; Palmer told him the pilots had to make an emergency detour to Costa Rica. In his testimony to the Iran-Contra committees, Rob Owen confirmed that the airplane was involved in an unexplained "embarassing situation" in Costa Rica. "That's when I decided some real strange shit was happening," Lippert said. "It came back all messed up with bullet holes in the tail and the engine burned out and, after that, I told them that was it. Unless I'm flying the plane, it was no dice. So Palmer says, 'Fine, I'll buy the damned thing from you.'"

Palmer, whom Lippert believes was working for Oliver North and the CIA, arranged to buy Lippert's DC-4 through some associates of his: a Cuban lawyer from Miami named José Insua and an aircraft company executive, Richard Kelley, both of whom intimated to Lippert that they were working with the CIA. After the sale, Lippert said, the DC-4 was used to airdrop explosives off the coast of Cuba. Then, a month after he signed the installment sale papers, it was seized in Mexico with 2,500 pounds of marijuana on board.

A story in the Mexican newpaper *La Opinion* quoted the attorney general of Mexico as saying that the plane was being used by a "powerful gang of drug-smugglers ...known to have been operating for a long time using large aircraft to transport arms southbound and bring back marijuana through here."

Lippert never got the plane back, nor was he ever paid for it. The company that issued the letters of credit that "guaranteed" the purchase of his plane was later shut down by the state of Florida, which announced that its owners were drug traffickers and fugitive stock swindlers. "Can't we close a bank or even a supposed bank anymore without finding some sort of tie to the Contras?" bank examiner Barry Gladden wondered to a *Miami Herald* reporter in 1987. "What's the world coming to?"

One of the DC-4's buyers, José Insua, was later exposed as a drug trafficker and DEA informant himself, and was used by the agency in an unsuccessful attempt to snare the former chairman of the Florida Democratic party in a bribery sting. During the trial, the government admitted that Insua was "involved in the brokering of aircraft for narcotics smugglers on approximately 12 occasions."

As Lippert aptly observed in 1997, "José Insua is a drug dealer and he's hanging around a company [Vortex] with a State Department contract. Michael Zapedis is a drug dealer and he issues two letters of credit for planes that are used by the CIA. Mike Palmer is a drug dealer and he's running an airline for the CIA. You tell me what's going on."

Owen confirmed to Congress that the CIA had been behind the NHAO's hiring of Palmer's company, which was paid more than $317,000. In 1994, the *Washington Post* reported that Palmer was indicted in Louisiana for allegedly hauling 300,000 pounds of marijuana into the United States in 1982. "Palmer boasted to prosecutors that his drug running was sanctioned by the government and the prosecutor, Howard Parker, said he dropped the indictment to avoid a sideshow," the story said.

The NHAO also hired a Honduran air freight company, SETCO, which happened to be owned by the Honduran drug kingpin Juan Matta Ballesteros, a fact that the U.S. Customs Service had known since 1983. SETCO was another cargo carrier the Contras had been using since the early days of the war. In fact, that appears to have been the reason behind *all* of the State Department contracts that were awarded to cocaine smugglers: they were the same people the CIA had hired to do that work when the agency was running the show.

In a 1987 deposition taken by Iran-Contra investigators, the NHAO's director, Robert Duemling, said he was given very specific instructions along those lines when he took the job. "One of the policy guidelines was do not disrupt the existing arrangements of the resistance movement unless there is a terribly good reason," Duemling testified.

"Who told you that, by the way, going back to the beginning of this?"

"Ollie North," Duemling said. He said North instructed him not to "dislodge or replace their existing arrangements, which seemed to be working perfectly well."

They certainly were, in one sense. According to Danilo Blandón's lawyer, Brad Brunon, the Contra's cocaine was arriving in the United States literally by the planeload. "The transportation channel got established and got filled up with cocaine rather quickly," Brunon said in an interview. "As I understood it, these large transports were coming back from delivering food and guns and humanitarian aid and things like that and they were just loading them up with cocaine and bringing them back. I think 1,000-kilo shipments were not unheard of. That scale. Because all of a sudden they seemed to have unlimited sources of supply."

According to former Meneses aide Enrique Miranda, Meneses's drug-laden planes were flying out of a military air base in El Salvador called Ilopango. Like the CIA before him, North had selected that base as the hub for his Contra air force; his operatives worked there "practically unfettered," according to the report of Iran-Contra prosecutor Lawrence Walsh.

And it was at Ilopango where the whole sordid mess first started to unravel.

13

"The wrong kind of friends"

It didn't take DEA agent Celerino Castillo III very long to discover that something very strange was going on at Ilopango Air Force Base in El Salvador. Two days into his new job at the DEA's regional office in Guatemala City in October 1985, Castillo said the agent-in-charge, Robert Stia, took him aside and told him that the U.S. government was running a covert operation at the air base. Castillo should be careful not to interfere with it.

It struck the former Texas policeman as odd advice. Why would a DEA field agent need to be warned about interfering with a legitimate government operation? Castillo was there to fight drug dealers. Whatever they were doing at the military airfield outside San Salvador couldn't possibly concern him. At any rate, it wasn't as if he was going to be spending a lot of time in El Salvador. Though he was the country's only DEA agent, Castillo lived and worked in neighboring Guatemala and had duties there also.

Besides, El Salvador in late 1985 had all the makings of a very sorry posting. The war-torn country produced no drugs, and as far as anyone knew there were no major drug rings operating there. It was of such little concern to the American government that the DEA never opened an office in the country. If El Salvador was anything, it was a resting place for cocaine mules on their way north.

Flipping through the reports of his predecessors, Castillo could see that the DEA's role in the country had been limited to intelligence gathering, collecting information about drug shipments passing through and filing them away, making few seizures. "We were playing traffic cop, taking down the license numbers of speeders but never writing any tickets," Castillo would later observe.

Castillo put his boss's warning about Ilopango down to bureaucratic caution and got on with his job, which was to train and recruit Guatemalan and Salvadoran policemen to become soldiers in America's worldwide war on drugs. Since the DEA couldn't legally make any arrests in Central America, his assignment was to put together local antinarcotics squads the DEA could trust enough to work with, and develop informants who could provide real-time intelligence.

But no matter where he went, it seemed, Ilopango kept coming up.

Castillo was out one day with a DEA informant in Guatemala, a Cuban named Socrates Sofi-Perez, who proudly informed Castillo that he was a Bay of Pigs veteran and a Contra supporter. After learning that his new control agent had been decorated for fighting Communists in Vietnam, Sofi-Perez confided that he was helping the Contras fight Marxism in Nicaragua and laid out a scheme that was remarkably similar to the operation Frigorificos was then conducting in Costa Rica: a shrimp company he owned was being used as a front to launder money for the Contras. The Contras were also dealing in cocaine, he told Castillo, using a small air force based at Ilopango that was ferrying war materials for the cause. He justified the trafficking by blaming the U.S. Congress for ill-advisedly cutting off Contra aid.

Castillo wasn't sure if his informant was trying to impress him, pull his leg, or waste his time. The idea of a U.S. government–sponsored operation dabbling in drugs struck the six-year DEA veteran as absurd. But there was one way to find out. The next time he was in El Salvador, Castillo said, he bounced the Cuban's story off one of the few informants the DEA had there, Ramiro Guerra, who owned a coffee shop in San Salvador. Guerra was working for the DEA as the result of a pending cocaine trafficking indictment in San Francisco, where he had lived for many years. While hiding out in El Salvador, Guerra picked up pocket money by acting as an informant for the very agency that wanted him in jail back in the United States. He had also insinuated himself into Roberto D'Aubuisson's right-wing ARENA party, and had risen to a high level inside the party structure.

To Castillo's surprise, Guerra told him that the information about drugs at Ilopango was probably true. He'd heard the same rumors himself. And he confirmed that there was indeed a small air force based there that was illegally flying supplies to the Contras, but it really wasn't very secretive. While headquartered on the restricted military side of the Ilopango airport, the Contra air supply operation was being run quite openly, and a lot of his friends in the Salvadoran Air Force knew about it, Guerra told Castillo.

"The woman selling tortillas at the gate of Ilopango could tell you what was going on," the assistant regional security officer for the U.S. embassy in San Salvador told Iran-Contra investigators in 1991. "Anyone who ever flew into or over Ilopango air base could see something like that was going on. When looking down at Ilopango from the air, one could see one side of the airfield having a ragtag operation of inferior planes, dilapidated buildings and the like. On the other side of the airport were nice facilities, lift trucks unloading supplies from more sophisticated and bigger aircraft, and gringos running around."

The modern facilities "all belonged to the American operation," the officer said, adding that he didn't know "if it was a CIA operation or what, but he knew there was Contra resupply activity at Ilopango."

While CIA officials denied they were running the show, they admitted they were keeping a very close eye on it. "We had a capability and indeed a responsibility for reporting what had been happening at Ilopango," said Alan Fiers Jr., the former CIA official who headed the Contra program from 1984 to 1988.

Guerra told Castillo that a Cuban named Max Gómez was doing the actual day-to-day management of the operation for the U.S. government. "Gómez" was the name then being used by CIA agent Felix Rodriguez, a Bay of Pigs veteran who'd had a remarkable career with the agency as a paramilitary specialist. Among other operations, he'd been in on the capture and execution of Che Guevara. In early 1985 Rodriguez appeared in El Salvador as an adviser to the Salvadoran Air Force, working on a helicopter-based counterinsurgency operation against the FMLN guerrillas.

While Rodriguez has always claimed—sometimes under oath—that he was retired from the CIA and in El Salvador merely as a volunteer and private citizen, former CIA officer Fiers suggested otherwise. He testified that Rodriguez was sent there in early 1985 as part of a CIA reorganization that began after Fiers took over the Central American Task Force. "As a result of the change in management of the task force...we undertook a complete review of our efforts in San Salvador...and made adjustments in that undertaking that left certain operations, certain activities that we had—left a void," Fiers testified in 1992. "Felix Rodriguez was put into—sent to El Salvador to work in the areas where we had left a void and was going to take over those responsibilities, or at least in part take over those responsibilities."

Rodriguez's journey from "retirement" to Ilopango began with a very strange step. Shortly before he left for Washington, D.C., to get final approval for his mission to El Salvador, he received a call from a friendly private eye in Miami who wanted him to meet "a client who could compromise the Nicaraguan Sandinista government for drug-money laundering," Rodriguez wrote in his memoirs.

The client turned out to be former Medellín cartel accountant Ramon Milian Rodriguez—the man who had set up the Costa Rican shrimp company Oliver North would later use to funnel money to the Contras. Rodriguez said Milian was trying to broker information to obtain help in the money laundering case pending against him. Not only did he tell Rodriguez of Manuel Noriega's drug activities, but he claimed he could provide proof of Sandinista drug dealing. Rodriguez said he passed the info along to the CIA and FBI and heard nothing back.

Milian tells a very different story. He met with Rodriguez to offer $10 million to the Contras in exchange for the U.S. government dropping the money laundering charges against him, he says; Rodriguez accepted the offer, and money was delivered to him on five separate occasions. Milian later failed a lie detector test when asked about making payments to Rodriguez, but the examiner reached no conclusions about his claim that he'd given money to the Contras. In congressional testimony, Noriega's former political adviser described Felix Rodriguez as "a very close friend of Milian." Both were Cubans who had been active in Miami's anti-Castro movement.

Most accounts date the Contras' use of Ilopango to September 1985, when North wrote to Rodriguez, asking him to use his influence with Salvadoran Air Force commander Juan Rafael Bustillo to secure hangar space for Contra supply flights. Rodriguez claimed he "greased the skids" with Bustillo and eventually became the overseer of North's Contra resupply operation at the air base.

In actuality, the Contras had been using Ilopango with General Bustillo's blessings since 1983, when Norwin Meneses's friend, CIA pilot Marcos Aguado, made arrangements to base Edén Pastora's ARDE air force there.

Since he could not devote all of his time to North's secret air force, Rodriguez wrote, "I found someone to manage the Salvadoran-based resupply operation on a day-to-day basis. [At Ilopango] they knew that person as Ramon Medina. I knew him by his real name: Luis Posada Carriles."

With men like Luis Posada and Marcos Aguado running things at Ilopango, it's little wonder DEA agent Castillo was hearing rumors about Contra drug trafficking. Luis Posada was a veteran CIA agent with a history of involvement with drug traffickers, mobsters, and terrorists. He was recruited by the CIA in the 1960s after years of working with anti-Castro Cubans in Miami and was implicated in a number of terrorist incidents conducted by various Cuban extremist groups. In 1967, CIA records show, Posada was investigated by the Justice Department for supplying explosives, silencers, and hand grenades to Miami mobsters "Lefty" Rosenthal and Norman "Roughhouse" Rothman. Rothman was a close associate of South Florida's Mafia chieftain, Santos Trafficante. A memo in Posada's CIA file said, "Posada may have been moonlighting for Rosenthal," but in late 1968 he was transferred by the agency for "unreported association with gangster elements, thefts from CIA, plus other items."

Posada was sent to Venezuela and began working as an official of the Venezuelan intelligence service. In 1973 the DEA received a report that Posada "was in contact with two Cubans in Miami who were reportedly smuggling narcotics into the United States for Luis Posada." According to the informant, Posada was to be "the main contact" in a major cocaine smuggling operation involving members of the Venezuelan government. The DEA placed Posada under surveillance and he "was observed by agents in Miami to meet with numerous identified upper echelon traffickers in Miami during March 1973."

Records show the CIA was fully aware of its agent's reported involvement with drug traffickers. It received word in February 1973 that "Posada may be involved in smuggling cocaine from Colombia through Venezuela to Miami, also counterfeit U.S. money in Venezuela." But the agency decided "not to directly confront Posada with allegation so as not to compromise ongoing investigation."

According to the notes of a congressional investigator who reviewed Posada's voluminous CIA files in the late 1970s, cables in the file "indicate concern that Posada [was a] serious potential liability. Anxious to terminate association promptly if allegations prove true. By April 1973, it seems sure that Posada involved in narcotics, drug trafficking—seen with known big time drug trafficker." But after questioning the Cuban about his contacts, the agency found him "guilty only of having the wrong kind of friends" and continued his employment.

His choice of friends continued to plague Posada, however. In January 1974 he asked the CIA to provide a Venezuelan passport for a Dominican military official, which the agency refused to do on the grounds that it "cannot permit controlled agents to become directly involved with illicit drug trafficking." A few months later the DEA received a report that Posada was trading weapons for cocaine with a man the DEA believed "is involved in political assassinations."

According to records at the National Archives, the CIA formally terminated Posada in February 1976. Eight months later he was arrested in Venezuela and accused of participating in the midair bombing of a Cuban DC-8 airliner, which killed seventy-eight people. Though never convicted of the crime, he spent nearly ten years in Venezuelan prisons before escaping in the summer of 1985 and going underground. He resurfaced at Ilopango in early 1986 as Felix Rodriguez's right-hand man, telling investigators that "Rodriguez and other Cuban friends" helped him "get out of Venezuela and relocate in El Salvador. Upon arriving in El Salvador, Posada stayed with Rodriguez for two or three days. Rodriguez then helped Posada get a house in San Salvador, where Posada lived for the next year or so."

Though allegations of Contra drug trafficking were swirling around Ilopango, DEA agent Castillo was having difficulty getting firsthand evidence of it. For one thing, the air base was in a very protected position, high atop a plateau, surrounded by imposing cliffs. The area where the trafficking was supposedly going on was off limits to the public, tightly guarded by the Salvadoran military. If he was ever going to find out the truth, Castillo figured, he needed to get onto that side of the base.

He went to Salvadoran Air Force commander Bustillo, lord and master of Ilopango, for permission, but got the cold shoulder. "An agent from the DEA's branch office in Guatemala City came to San Salvador seeking access to Ilopango," the *New Republic* reported in 1990, adding that Bustillo "stalled" the requests. "There was never a good reason why [the DEA] couldn't get on Ilopango," the magazine quoted an unnamed U.S. official as saying. "They just kept putting off meetings, stuff like that."

So Castillo improvised. He recruited a Salvadoran named Murga, who wrote the flight plans for the private planes on the civilian portion of the base. Murga had excellent contacts on the military side and could come and go at will. He became Castillo's eyes and ears inside Ilopango.

Murga knew all about the Contras' drug running, Castillo said, because he was filling out their flight plans and inspecting their aircraft; the pilots were so brazen that they told him they were flying dope to the United States and money to Panama. Sometimes they left with the kilos in plain view, or arrived with boxloads of money, Castillo said.

In a once-secret 1992 interview with the FBI, ex-CIA agent Posada recounted that "the resupply project was always looking for people to carry cash from the United States into El Salvador for Posada to dispense. They were always worried about the restriction on only taking $10,000 out of the United States at one time. Any time any of the resupply people went up to the United States for any reason, whether it was a personal visit or whatever, they would be asked to bring money back." Posada was told "the money came from Washington," but never got a better explanation than that.

The drugs often arrived in private planes flown by Contra pilots from Costa Rica, Murga told Castillo; on other occasions they came in military aircraft from Panama.

When Castillo typed the names of the Contra pilots Murga had given him into the DEA's computers, nearly all of them came back as documented narcotics traffickers. Among the busiest of the pilots was Francisco Guirola Beeche, the scion of one of El Salvador's most influential families. How Chico Guirola wound up at Ilopango flying for the Contras is an illuminating tale; he should have been sitting in a federal prison cell in the United States.

On the morning of February 6, 1985, a white T-39 Sabreliner jet took off from John Wayne Airport in Orange County, California, with Guirola and three other men—Cuban-Americans—aboard. It stopped briefly at the Kleberg County Airport in Kingsville, Texas, to refuel, and was met by a posse of U.S. Customs Service agents wielding search warrants. The agents had been tracking the men since the month before, when they were spotted in the same plane leaving Orange County for Florida. In mid-flight, they had suspiciously diverted to Panama, where they landed with $1.2 million in cash.

Guirola and his crew were all listed in Customs databases as suspected drug traffickers, and their airplane was on a watch list as a suspected smuggling craft—for good reason, it turned out. In the Sabreliner's cargo hold were fourteen suitcases, which Guirola claimed as his. He pulled out a Costa Rican diplomatic passport and advised the agents not to search the suitcases, or it would "cause trouble."

He was right. They were bulging with cash, a total of $5.9 million in small bills, the largest cash seizure in Texas history. When the agents announced they were arresting the men for trying to smuggle the cash out of the country, Guirola claimed diplomatic immunity because his mother was the Costa Rican vice-consul in New Mexico.

In court records, federal agents charged that the cash was drug money destined for El Salvador. They cited DEA records that said Guirola had been "reportedly involved in cocaine and arms smuggling in El Salvador and Guatemala" and noted that he was a top aide to Salvadoran death squad leader Roberto D'Aubuisson.

The latter claim was confirmed by the *Los Angeles Times*, which reported that Guirola had accompanied D'Aubuisson to a "very sensitive" meeting with former CIA deputy director Vernon Walters in May 1984. According to the story, Walters had been dispatched in a frantic attempt to talk D'Aubuisson out of assassinating Thomas Pickering, the U.S. ambassador to El Salvador.

Guirola, who attended college in California with one of Anastasio Somoza's nephews, had allowed D'Aubuisson to use his house as a campaign headquarters when he ran for Salvadoran president in 1984. Guirola's passport, which was signed by D'Aubuisson, identified him as a "special adviser" to the Salvadoran Assembly. He was also carrying credentials from the Salvadoran attorney general's office.

Since Guirola was using an Orange County airport as his departure point, it is possible that the millions he was hauling out of the country came from Los Angeles–area drug sales. But the source of the funds was never made public. "The investigation came to a sudden, abrupt halt with a lot of questions unanswered," U.S. Customs agent Ernest Allison complained.

That was because the Justice Department had made a quick deal with Guirola: If he let the U.S. government keep the money, he'd be let off with probation. Guirola and one of his companions pleaded guilty to a minor currency violation charge and walked. Charges against another passenger and the pilot were dropped, and the plane was given back.

"I have a hard time swallowing it," federal judge Hayden Head Jr. told Guirola after the Justice Department announced its plea bargain with the smuggler. "The punishment doesn't fit the crime.... I don't know what you were up to, but this conduct cannot be tolerated."

Less than a year later, DEA agent Castillo and his informants were watching Guirola zoom in and out of Ilopango, hauling drugs in, carrying cash to the Bahamas, and flashing credentials from the Salvadoran Air Force and the Salvadoran president's office. "When I ran Guirola's name in the computer, it popped up in 11 DEA files, detailing his South America–to–United States cocaine, arms and money laundering," Castillo wrote in his memoirs.

In response to a Freedom of Information Act request filed in 1997, the Customs Service claimed it could not locate any records relating to the Guirola case.

Castillo said that in January 1986 he began firing off a string of reports to DEA headquarters in Washington about the suspicious activities of the Contra pilots, listing their names, destinations, tail numbers, and criminal records. He got no replies, and no offers of assistance. It was, he wrote later, as if his reports were "falling into some faceless, bureaucratic black hole." But in mid-April he got his first ray of hope, a cable from the DEA office in Costa Rica. In it, Castillo was advised to check out Hangars Four and Five at Ilopango; a reliable informant had reported that cocaine was being flown from Costa Rica to the air base.

Finally, Castillo exulted, here was proof that he was on the right track. Someone else was getting the same intelligence that he was. The cable had been sent by DEA agent Robert Nieves, Norwin Meneses's control agent in Costa Rica, and if anyone was in a position to know about Contra drug flights into Ilopango, it was Meneses. According to his former top aide, Meneses was overseeing the cocaine shipments through that base. But Nieves's reasons for sending Castillo that memo may have been the opposite of what Castillo at first assumed.

Enrique Miranda Jaime, who became Meneses's emissary to the cartels of Colombia in the late 1980s, testified in a 1992 trial in Nicaragua that "Norwin was selling drugs and funneled the benefits to the Contras with help of high-ranking military officials of the Salvadoran Army, especially with the help of the head of the Salvadoran Air Force and a Nicaraguan pilot named Marcos Aguado."

Aguado, the chief pilot for the ARDE Contra forces in Costa Rica, was identified in 1987 congressional testimony as a CIA agent. Soon after North set up his resupply operation at the air base, Aguado moved to Ilopango permanently, working as an aide to a high-ranking Salvadoran air force commander. The pilot, who had been instrumental in arranging the Contras' 1984 arms-and-drugs deals with Colombian trafficker George Morales, was no longer welcome in Costa Rica, having been formally accused of cocaine trafficking. "Aguado became a colonel in the Salvadoran Air Force, sharing all the privileges of a high-ranking military officer in El Salvador and was accepted by subordinate ranks as Deputy Commander of the Salvadoran Air Force," Miranda testified. "The flights he directed went as far as Colombia, where they were loaded with cocaine and then redirected to the United States, to a U.S. Air Force base located in the state of Texas."

In recent interviews, Miranda and former Nicaraguan antidrug czar Roger Mayorga, who arrested Miranda, said the U.S. air base was near Fort Worth, but neither knew the name of it. The only air force base near

Fort Worth at the time of the alleged drug flights from Ilopango was the now-closed Carswell Air Force Base, the home of a Strategic Air Command bomber squadron. In response to a Freedom of Information Act request filed in 1997, the U.S. Air Force said all flight records that may have shown arrivals and departures of Salvadoran military aircraft during the mid-1980s were destroyed years ago.

Miranda, a former Sandinista intelligence officer who became a double agent for the CIA during the Contra war and has worked as a DEA informant in recent years, said the cocaine brought from Colombia by Medellín cartel pilots arrived in Costa Rica in square twenty-five-kilo packages. It was unloaded at various airstrips there, including one located on CIA operative John Hull's farm in northern Costa Rica, where it was placed aboard Contra planes and flown into Ilopango.

Once it had arrived at the Salvadoran base, Miranda said, Aguado and Meneses supervised the loading of the cocaine onto U.S.-bound aircraft owned by the Salvadoran Air Force and, on occasion, a Miami-based CIA contractor, Southern Air Transport. SAT has denied any association with drug trafficking. The cocaine operations were handled inside Hangars Four and Five. "On some occasions Norwin himself…even went aboard to travel to the U.S.," Miranda said.

For reasons that he refused to disclose, Meneses claimed that during the 1985–86 period DEA agent Nieves was allowing him to fly in and out of the United States unsupervised, preclearing his border crossings with the U.S. Customs Service—a real boon, since Meneses was listed in government computers as a Class One cocaine trafficker. "When I tried to come in without [Nieves] knowing, I would set off all the computers [at the U.S. airport] and then I'd have to go to the little room," Meneses laughed. "He called me once at the airport when I got stopped and told me that I should have known better than to try and get in without telling him."

Nieves refused to answer any questions about Meneses or Contra drug dealing in Costa Rica. "I have very little to say to you. In fact, I'm insulted you called," he said.

Records recently declassified by the National Archives offer some independent evidence to substantiate Miranda's statements about trafficking at Ilopango. According to a 1991 interview with investigators for Iran-Contra special prosecutor Lawrence Walsh, former CIA official Alan Fiers Jr., who was in charge of the Contra program at the time, said that "the only thing [he] heard about Ilopango and drugs were allegations that

Hangar Number Four had drugs moved in and out." Fiers also said that he was convinced some Costa Rican Contras had used CIA operative John Hull's ranch in Costa Rica to transship cocaine. Hull denied that.

What, if anything, the CIA did about the Ilopango allegations, or where they came from, is not known; many portions of Fiers's 1991 interrogation are still classified. The topic was completely avoided in the 1998 CIA Inspector General's report of Contra drug trafficking allegations.

Interestingly, the hangar that Fiers pinpointed, Hangar Four, was being used by the National Security Council's Contra resupply operation, which was run by Oliver North and his Cuban friends. The hangar Fiers didn't mention, Hangar Five, was the CIA's. "The North-Secord group and the CIA had had adjoining hangars at Ilopango, with a common parking lot," former Iran-Contra prosecutor Lawrence Walsh wrote.

Miranda testified that he met CIA pilot Aguado for dinner at Meneses's mansion in Managua in 1991, where Aguado regaled them with tales of flying for the Colombian cartels. Aguado told him that he once took a Salvadoran Air Force bomber and leveled a warehouse full of Medellín cartel cocaine on behalf of the rival Cali cartel. Another time, he made plans to bomb the prison where Medellín cartel chief Pablo Escobar was briefly imprisoned. Aguado also boasted of flying weapons from the Salvadoran military to the Colombian cartels, a story Miranda said he doubted until a Salvadoran Air Force colonel and his associates were arrested in 1992 for selling bombs and high explosives to Colombian drug dealers.

Miranda said Meneses told him that U.S. military hardware stockpiled at Ilopango was loaded onto Salvadoran transport planes and flown south, where the guns were traded for cocaine and flown back to Ilopango. As wild as that scheme sounds, records show Enrique Miranda is not the first drug trafficker to have reported such a fantastic operation. During the 1980s the U.S. Justice Department received at least two other reports from reliable Colombian informants detailing arms-for-drugs swaps involving the Medellín cartel, the Contras, and elements of the U.S. government. Secret Justice Department records declassified in 1996 by the National Archives show that the U.S. attorney's office in Tampa, Florida, debriefed a Colombian trafficker named Allen Raul Rudd in 1988 after Rudd had agreed to become an undercover government informant.

In a February 1988 memo marked "Sensitive," Assistant U.S. Attorney Walter E. Furr told his boss that Rudd "is a very articulate individual and there has been no indication to date that he has not been totally candid. In a real sense his life is on the line for the cooperation he has given so far." Furr probably thought it necessary to add his testament to Rudd's credibility in light of what he was about to report next: the Medellín cartel reportedly had made a deal with Vice President George Bush to supply American weapons to the Contras in exchange for free passage for their cocaine deliveries to the U.S.

Rudd told the officials that in the spring of 1987 he'd met in Medellín, Colombia, with cartel boss Pablo Escobar to arrange a drug deal. In the course of their conversation at Escobar's palatial home, Rudd said, the cocaine lord began ranting about Bush and his South Florida Drug Task Force, which was making the cartel's deliveries to the Miami area more difficult.

"Escobar then stated that Bush is a traitor who used to deal with us, but now he is tough," Rudd told the federal officials. Escobar described "an agreement or relationship between Bush and the American government and members of the Medellín cartel which resulted in planes similar to C-130s (but smaller) flying guns to the cartel in Colombia. According to Rudd, Escobar stated that the cartel then off-loaded the guns, put cocaine aboard the planes and the cocaine was taken to United States military base(s). The guns were delivered and sold to the Contras in Nicaragua by the Cartel."

Escobar, Rudd said, explained that "it was a swap of cocaine for guns…Rudd has stated that while Escobar did not say the CIA was involved in the exchange of guns for cocaine, that was the tenor of the conversation. Rudd has stated that Escobar and the rest of the cartel members are very supportive of the Contras and dislike the Sandinistas as they dislike the guerrillas which operate within Colombia."

Rudd claimed that Escobar had photographic proof to back up his story. Not only were there "photographs of the planes containing the guns being unloaded in Columbia," but he claimed to have a picture of Bush posing with Medellín cartel leader Jorge Ochoa, in front of suitcases full of money. "After Escobar talked about the photograph, Rudd said that if the photograph was not genuine (and was merely two individual photographs spliced together somehow) it would be easily discredited," Furr wrote. "In response, Escobar stated that the photograph was genuine, it would stand up to any test...Escobar stated that the photo would be made public at the 'appropriate time.' Rudd indicated that the photo is being held back as blackmail if the cartel ever needs to bring pressure on Bush."

By 1993 Escobar was dead, killed in a shoot-out with Colombian police, and Jorge Ochoa was in jail. The photos, if they ever existed, were never heard of again.

Rudd's story is very similar to one told by a Miami FBI informant, Wanda Palacios, who reported in 1986 that she had witnessed Southern Air Transport planes being loaded with cocaine and unloading guns in Barranquilla, Colombia, in 1983 and October 1985. Palacios, the wife of a Colombian trafficker, said she'd accompanied Pablo Escobar in a limousine to the landing site and had spoken about it as well to Jorge Ochoa, who bragged that he was working with the CIA to get cocaine into south Florida.

Palacios was interviewed in 1986 by the staff of Senator John Kerry of Massachusetts, which was looking into allegations of Contra drug smuggling. Kerry's staff found her and her story credible and took an eleven-page statement from her. The senator and an aide took it to the Justice Department in September 1986, and met with William Weld, one of Attorney General Edwin Meese's top assistants.

"Weld read about a half a page and chuckled," Kerry aide Jonathan Winer wrote in a memorandum after the meeting. "I asked him why. He said this isn't the first time today I've seen allegations about CIA agent involvement in drugs...he stated several times in reading Wanda's statement that while he couldn't vouch for every line in it...there was nothing in it which didn't appear true to him, or inconsistent with what he already knew."

But when her allegations leaked out to the press, Palacios was publicly dismissed as a crank by top Justice Department officials, who said polygraph tests she'd been given were "inconclusive." Southern Air Transport called her "a lunatic" and sued or threatened suit against news organizations that aired her allegations.

Her story was buttressed mightily by subsequent events, however.

When the Sandinistas blew a Southern Air Transport C-123K out of the sky over Nicaragua in early October 1986, the dead pilot's flight logs revealed that he had flown several Southern Air Transport flights to Barranquilla, Colombia. The flights had occurred during October 1985, exactly as Palacios had claimed, and she was able to identify the pilot's picture in a lineup. Southern Air said in a statement that the planes were carrying drilling equipment, not drugs.

The wrecked C-123K in which those flight logs were found had a history of involvement with cocaine, the Medellín cartel, and the CIA. It was the same airplane Louisiana drug dealer Barry Seal used in a joint CIA-DEA sting operation in 1984 against the Sandinistas. In that case the CIA had taken Seal's plane—which he'd recently obtained through a complicated airplane swap with the cartel—to Rickenbacker Air Force Base in

Ohio and outfitted it with hidden cameras. Then Seal, who was working as a DEA informant, flew the aircraft to an airfield in Nicaragua and snapped pictures of men loading bags of cocaine into his plane.

One of Seal's grainy, almost indistinguishable photos was later shown on national television by President Ronald Reagan the night before a crucial vote in Congress on Contra aid. "This picture, secretly taken at a military airfield outside Managua, shows Federico Vaughn, a top aide to one of the nine commandantes who rule Nicaragua, loading an aircraft with illegal narcotics, bound for the United States," Reagan announced. "No, there seems to be no crime to which the Sandinistas will not stoop—this is an outlaw regime."

After the president's remarks were uncritically spread across the country by the national media, both the DEA and the Justice Department admitted there was no evidence, other than Barry Seal's claims, to support Reagan's accusations. (The Seal photos were also used in televised political ads that year attacking liberal California senator Alan Cranston, a staunch opponent of Contra aid.)

A 1988 congressional investigation raised troubling questions about whether or not the Seal sting was even a real sting. It produced evidence suggesting that the whole episode had been stage-managed by Oliver North and the CIA as a domestic disinformation operation. Among other things, the House Judiciary Committee investigation revealed that the alleged Sandinista official named by Reagan, Federico Vaughn, may have actually been working for the U.S. government. Committee chairman William Hughes of New Jersey told reporters that "subcommittee staff recently called Vaughn's number in Managua, Nicaragua, and spoke to a 'domestic employee' who said the house belonged to a U.S. Embassy employee," and that his investigators were told the house had been "continuously rented" by the United States since 1981.

Recently declassified CIA cables lend additional support to the idea that Vaughn was in fact a U.S. double agent. In March 1985 the CIA reported that Vaughn "was said to be an associate of Nicaraguan narcotics trafficker Norwing [sic] Meneses Cantarero." Meneses at that time was working with the DEA in Costa Rica, assisting the Contras. And Oliver North's daily diaries for that period contained several references to "Freddy Vaughn," including a July 6, 1984, entry that said, "Freddy coming in late July."

Far from being a "top aide" to a Sandinista commandante, Vaughn was a deputy director of Heroes and Martyrs Trading Corporation, the official import-export agency of the Sandinista government, a firm that had been heavily infiltrated by CIA operatives. Records show that one of the Costa Rican–based drug traffickers working for North and the CIA, Bay of Pigs veteran Dagoberto Nuñez, obtained a contract with H&M Corp. in order to cover an intelligence-gathering operation aimed at Nicaraguan president Daniel Ortega, his brother Humberto, and Interior Minister Tomas Borge. According to a 1986 memo from CIA operative Rob Owen to North, Nuñez was preparing to sign an agreement with H&M for shrimping rights off the Pacific Coast of Nicaragua. "Nuñez is doing this so he can help us. He will cooperate and do anything we ask," Owen told North. "He believes this will provide an opportunity to use his boats for cover operations, or to implicate the Ortegas and Borge in taking money on the side for their own pocket. He is right on both counts."

Four DEA officials testified before Hughes's committee that they'd received pressure from North and the CIA to leak the news of Vaughn's involvement with drugs to the press. They also said North wanted to take $1.5 million in drug profits Seal had collected from the Medellín cartel and give it to the Contras. When the DEA refused to do either, the DEA officials testified, the story was leaked by the White House to the right-wing *Washington Times*, which was supporting the Contras both financially and editorially.

The leak accomplished two things. It publicly linked the Sandinistas to drug trafficking right before a crucial Contra aid vote. And by prematurely exposing the sting, it blew the DEA's investigation of the Medellín cartel, which DEA agents said had been their most promising chance ever to break up the Colombian drug conglomerate. The drug lords went free, and Vaughn disappeared.

"The [Seal] sting operation has North's fingerprints all over it," columnist Jefferson Morley wrote in the *L.A. Times* in 1986.

After Seal flew his CIA/DEA missions, he never used the C-123K cargo plane again, parking it at the tiny Mena, Arkansas, airport for a year, then selling it back to the same company he'd gotten it from originally. In early 1986 it wound up with CIA contractor Southern Air Transport, where it was used for Contra supply runs and based at Ilopango until its last, fatal flight.

Unfortunately, Rudd's and Palacios's allegations of a guns-for-drugs deal between the Reagan administration and the Medellín cartel were never seriously investigated. The memo of Rudd's debriefing was sent to Iran-Contra prosecutor Lawrence Walsh by the Department of Justice a month later, with a note from Associate Attorney General Stephen S. Trott, which said that "no action is being taken by the Department pending a determination by your office as to whether you intend to assert jurisdiction." Walsh's office apparently just filed the memo away; National Archives researchers found it while working their way through the Iran-Contra prosecutor's closed investigative files.

One of the lawyers who worked for Walsh told the CIA in 1997 that investigating Contra drug dealing comprised "only about one percent" of the Walsh probe's interest. "For the most part," the CIA reported, "any drug trafficking activity would have been 'stumbled on' in the course of the investigation of other issues, especially money laundering."

In an interview, Walsh said he tried to stay away from the Contra drug trafficking issue as much as possible because it was outside his jurisdiction and because he knew Senator John Kerry's Senate subcommittee was investigating the topic. But it appears that Walsh's office never passed the Rudd memo along to Kerry's investigators.

And despite the confirmation by Costa Rican DEA chief Nieves of Celerino Castillo's reports of Contra drug shipping at Ilopango, that issue was never seriously investigated either. In fact, Castillo says, he was advised repeatedly by State Department personnel in El Salvador—including Ambassador Edwin Corr—to forget about the whole thing. "Corr said, 'It's a White House operation, [you] should stay out of it,'" Castillo said.

Corr, who called Castillo "an excellent and very dedicated DEA agent," said he was told by Castillo's superiors in Washington that "a lot of [Castillo's] information was just totally inaccurate." But he has confirmed telling Castillo to back off the Ilopango investigation. "I certainly would not say that he did not go away with that impression," Corr said elliptically, in a 1993 interview. He said he doubted using the words "White House" in his conversation, however. But Corr's message to Castillo was the same one the CIA's station chief in El Salvador, Marsh Niner, got from his bosses when he began demanding information about what Felix Rodriguez and Oliver North were doing at Ilopango.

In a heated February 1986 memo entitled "End the Silence," Niner informed his bosses that a small airplane making "an ill-fated supply run to Ilopango via Mexico" crash-landed on a Salvadoran highway. According to a *New York Times* story that month, "local peasants said several bundles were thrown out of the plane before it landed."

Felix Rodriguez "apparently has been coordinating all of this with Ollie North (one supposes on an open phone)," Niner cabled. "What is going on back there?"

His memo sent CIA headquarters into a tizzy.

CIA official Alan Fiers testified that his boss, Clair George, "said to me in no uncertain terms: 'You tell Marsh to stay away from it. And if he doesn't stay away from it, I'll take him—I'll yank him out of there. You get down there and tell him that.'"

Fiers flew to Ilopango and informed Niner that "this is a State Department, White House operation and we're to stay out of it." While at the airfield, Fiers said, he saw to his horror that a huge cargo plane clearly marked "Southern Air Transport" was sitting in the middle of the runway apron, in full view. Fiers halted the flight, and the inquisitive station chief was soon transferred out of El Salvador, retiring from the CIA soon afterward.

Castillo now suspects that Nieves's cable alerting him to Contra drug trafficking at the two hangars was less a request for him to investigate it than a way to cover the DEA office in Costa Rica in case his investigation got anywhere. Since Castillo had been sending his Contra drug reports to Washington for months, it is likely they were being shared with Nieves, the top DEA official in the country where the drug flights were allegedly originating.

If, as Meneses aide Miranda claims, the Ilopango operation was part of Meneses's drug pipeline into the United States, Castillo's probe might have raised some very sticky questions about how well the DEA was monitoring its top-level informant.

Meneses confirmed in an interview that he was working closely with Nieves and the DEA in 1985 and 1986. Among other things, he said, he helped the DEA gather intelligence on the February 1985 torture-murder of DEA agent Enrique "Kiki" Camarena in Mexico. Meneses claims he provided information that assisted U.S. authorities in their capture of a Mexican drug lord suspected of involvement in the DEA agent's murder, Rafael Caro Quintero, who was nabbed at a mansion outside San José, Costa Rica, in April 1985. Meneses's claim could not be corroborated.

Coincidentally, though, the issue of the Contras and drugs arose during some of the trials stemming from the Camarena murder. Federal informants, including the pilot of Mexican drug lord Miguel Felix-Gallardo, insisted that the CIA had been collaborating with Mexican drug traffickers, who agreed to provide money, arms, and Mexican training facilities for the Contras in exchange for CIA protection.

In a lengthy 1990 *Washington Post* story about alleged CIA connections to the Camarena murder, a senior DEA official confirmed that there were a "series of large arms seizures in Mexico around that time, including cases of AK-47 assault rifles." The DEA official told the *Post* that at first "we thought it was for the traffickers. Naive us."

According to one theory, Camarena was interrogated and killed because he'd discovered the CIA's involvement with the Mexican drug lords and the Contras. A 1988 court motion filed by defense lawyers who reviewed secret DEA files stated that there was "compelling evidence that the freedom fight of the Contras was fueled by illicit drug revenues with the tacit approval of branches of the U.S. government." The *L.A. Times* reported that "some of the evidence comes from a mysterious new transcript of the interrogation of Camarena which was produced by the government three weeks into the trial.... The government had refused to disclose in open court how the transcript was obtained."

Defense attorney Gregory Nicolaysen told the *Post*, "The CIA obviously was cultivating a very powerful and efficient arms transport network through the cartel, and they didn't want DEA screwing it up." The CIA disputed that.

Denied access to the military side of Ilopango, DEA agent Castillo settled on another tactic: he would hit an off-base location linked to the Ilopango operation. He and his informants zeroed in on a likely suspect: a New York weapons dealer and U.S. military contractor named Walter "Wally" Grasheim. The tall, bearded arms broker was the Salvadoran sales representative for the Litton Corp. and other American weapons makers, and had a booming business selling night vision goggles, Steyer sniper rifles, and assorted other gear to the Salvadoran military. He was also advising and training Salvadoran army units in long-range reconnaisance operations on behalf of the U.S. government. One of Castillo's informants at Ilopango told him Grasheim was intimately involved with the Contra drug operation there, and Castillo claims that DEA computers turned up several references to Grasheim as a suspected drug trafficker.

On September 1, 1986, Salvadoran police working with Castillo raided Grasheim's elegant hillside home in San Salvador. A pound of marijuana was reportedly found, but that was nothing compared to what else was in the place. "Some of the rooms in the house had munitions and explosives piled to the ceiling, including automatic weapons, M-16's, hand grenades and C-4 (plastic explosives)," Castillo later told the FBI. "The raid at Grasheim's house uncovered Embassy license plates, radios and ID's in Grasheim's name. Castillo...showed Grasheim's U.S. Embassy ID to the interviewer."

Grasheim, who says the weapons were legally his, strenuously denied he had anything to do with either the Contras or drugs and believes Castillo was duped by his informants, whom he says were secretly working for the CIA. "The Agency put Castillo onto me as a way of getting him away from whatever it was they were doing at Ilopango," Grasheim insisted in an interview. "The person who claimed I was a drug trafficker was on the payroll of the CIA. I've never been involved with drugs in my life." The marijuana found at his house, Grasheim said, probably belonged to a U.S. Army colonel who was a frequent visitor.

Though no criminal charges resulted, Castillo's raid sent shock waves all the way to Washington because it threatened to expose the CIA and NSC operations at Ilopango, which were officially not occurring. Castillo's investigation was quickly shut down.

"Word of this incident began circulating in the White House and other government agencies and some senior officials became very, very worried that Ollie [North] really had stopped that investigation and this would be the next big scandal in the evolving Iran-Contra affair," the *New York Times* reported in January 1987. "The officials' concern increased in light of the recent disclosure that Colonel North had told the Federal Bureau of Investigation last October to stop investigating Southern Air Transport."

Because of the potential for scandal, the *Times* reported, "intelligence agencies were asked this month to investigate the matter." They discovered that by the fall of 1986 "the Drug Enforcement Administration office in Guatemala had compiled convincing evidence that the Contra military supply operation was smuggling cocaine and marijuana." The *Times* noted that "although the drug investigation was not officially closed it was no longer actively pursued. 'It was not one of the big smuggling rings anyway,' a drug enforcement official said."

In an ironic turn of events, Castillo soon found himself under investigation by the DEA. He spent the next five years fending off accusations that he had gotten too close to his Central American informants, accepted improper gifts, inappropriately handled firearms, and a number of other technical, administrative failures. Castillo's boss complained to his superiors that the charges against Castillo were unfair, and ultimately the DEA gave Castillo a disability retirement. In his 1994 memoirs, he blamed the fallout on his investigation of Ilopango.

The DEA declined to respond to questions about Castillo, and in response to a Freedom of Information Act request, it claimed it had no reports from Castillo about drug trafficking at the Salvadoran air base. If that's true, it means they've been destroyed: a DEA spokesman specifically mentioned them during a 1994 interview with the Associated Press.

The quashing of Castillo's investigation ended any official U.S. government interest in trafficking at Ilopango. But the issue refused to stay buried. At the same time the Contra drug pipeline in El Salvador was being hastily covered back up, police officers thousands of miles away in Los Angeles were starting to prying the covers off the other end of it.

As one of them would sadly remark ten years later, they had no idea what a Pandora's box they were opening.

“It’s bigger than I can handle”

Victor Gill had no job and no business license, but for some reason he found it necessary to buy eight money-counting machines in the space of a month in early 1986. To U.S. Customs agent Fred Ghio and IRS agent Karl Knudsen, Gill might as well have been wearing a neon sign that said, “Arrest Me!”

The two agents were on the prowl for money launderers. A good way to find them, they reasoned, was to check with companies that made cash-counting machines. One such firm was the Glory Business Machine Co. in Bell, California, a rundown suburb of Los Angeles that in better days had been Hollywood gangster Mickey Cohen’s stomping grounds. After seeing how often Gill was visiting Glory, they decided he could stand some scrutiny.

Ghio and Knudsen dropped by the Bell Police Department to see if anyone there knew their quarry. As luck would have it, the city of Bell’s only narcotics detective, Jerry Guzzetta, was on duty, and he knew Gill well. He’d arrested him on cocaine charges a few years earlier and was more than happy to help the two federal agents bust him again. “You can’t investigate money laundering without getting into dope. There’s just no way,” Guzzetta said.

Jerry Guzzetta went after dopers with a vengeance, and his one-man investigations had produced some impressive results. In November 1985 he’d been the subject of a glowing piece in the *Los Angeles Times* for his work in taking down a large Colombian trafficking ring. Some of his fellow officers regarded him as a loose cannon and a publicity hound, always trying to make a name for himself. But his friends said Guzzetta's zeal was largely misunderstood.

"He hated dope dealers. He hated them with a vehement passion, because a dope dealer had killed his brother, and that's one of the things that spurred him to go after these people so aggressively," Officer Tom McReynolds said.

"In a sense, a drug dealer killed my entire family," Guzzetta said. "After the guy shot my brother in the head, my father died of a heart attack. And then my mother died a couple years later. And he got off with two years for involuntary manslaughter."

Knudsen and Ghio liked Guzzetta's enthusiasm, and they invited him to join their surveillance of Gill. The trio soon discovered that Gill was buying the money machines for Colombian traffickers who didn't want their names turning up on purchase orders. He was arrested and eventually pleaded guilty to conspiracy charges.

It was the start of a mutually beneficial relationship for Guzzetta and the two federal agents, who specialized in money-laundering cases. For a small-town police department like Guzzetta's, busting a money launderer was an answered prayer, because the police got to keep a percentage of the spoils.

After California voters passed Proposition 103, which slashed local property taxes, many local police departments became hooked on drug money, using asset forfeiture laws to replace their lost tax revenues. Cash seized from traffickers and money launderers began being used to pay officers' salaries, for overtime, new patrol cars, uniforms, guns, and even helicopters.

The cash-strapped Bell PD was delighted to loan Guzzetta out to work with the federal agents. They would find the suspects, Guzzetta would help with surveillance and the search warrants, and afterward the city of Bell and the federal government would divvy up the booty—a win-win situation all the way around.

The trio "did some very good work together at first," Ghio said. "[We] took a lot of dope off the streets and seized a lot of cash." He said Guzzetta "became somewhat a local hero. He got a lot of recognition from his fellow officers, the public, and the Bell City Council, mainly due to the funds they got through asset sharing, which was generated from the seized cash."

Later that summer IRS agent Knudsen received notifications from vo L.A. banks about a pair of customers who were making large cash deposits on a regular basis, officially known as "suspicious transactions." Banks routinely report them to the IRS. "They did a bank account check and found out [the customers] had no visible means of support but had over $1 million in the bank," Guzzetta said. The federal agents approached Guzzetta and asked him if he wouldn't mind helping out "because one of the banks was in the city of Bell and I had a good rapport with [the bank officers]."

Guzzetta began tailing the two depositors, which was easy because they stood out in a crowd. They were the Trees—Jacinto and Edgar Torres, Danilo Blandón's gigantic associates. The Torres brothers were running all over L.A., picking up packages, dropping off packages, making strange nighttime trips into South Central Los Angeles.

Jacinto, Guzzetta discovered, was on probation for cocaine possession. That, combined with the bank accounts, the surveillance, and the lack of employment, provided all the ammunition he needed to get a search warrant for the addresses the Torres brothers had been visiting. On August 11, 1986, Guzzetta and his federal friends raided them—and they hit the jackpot.

"We found $400,000 in the closet of one of the houses," Guzzetta said. "That was their spare change." But the Torreses were too smart to mix their money with their cocaine. Like their friend Blandón, they kept the two far apart, hidden in nondescript rental houses around the city. The raid produced not an ounce of dope.

Guzzetta said the brothers disclaimed ownership of the $400,000 and handed it over to the feds, which satisfied Ghio and Knudsen. "They'd seized some money, cleared some paper, and made their bosses happy. They weren't interested in prosecuting them federally because all they really had them on was a currency violation. Even if they were convicted they'd have pulled three years and been out in a year and a half," Guzzetta said.

But Guzzetta wasn't willing to just turn the brothers loose. If he couldn't put them away, he'd put them to work—for the police.

As imposing as they were, the Torreses had an Achilles heel that Guzzetta and the federal agents skillfully exploited: their live-in girlfriends, who were close relatives of Medellín cartel boss Pablo Escobar. (In a 1996 interview, Norwin Meneses confirmed the relationship between the women and Escobar.)

Guzzetta said the Torreses were informed that no charges would be filed against them, but their girlfriends would be prosecuted on conspiracy and tax evasion charges, imprisoned, and then deported as undesirable aliens who would never be allowed to set foot in the United States again.

To the rest of the world, it would seem like the brothers had sacrificed their women to save themselves, offending traditional Latin machismo. Even worse, it would appear as if they'd ratted out two of the cocaine lord's relatives. "You give up Pablo Escobar's family, and you're dead," Guzzetta chuckled. "So we turned them."

To keep the brothers on a short leash, it was arranged with the Los Angeles County District Attorney's Office for the Torreses to plead guilty to drug charges under false names. They were given suspended sentences, put on probation, and turned over to Guzzetta, who was assigned as their sole law enforcement contact to minimize their chances of exposure.

"They were scared to death," Guzzetta said. "They believed very strongly, and I agreed with them, that if anyone found out they were informants—including their girlfriends—they'd be killed in a minute."

During a debriefing on August 22, 1986, the Torreses told Guzzetta that they were convinced their girlfriends had already hired a couple of assassins. They told the detective they would check in with him every twenty-four hours to let him know they were still alive. "The informants advise that if...they are found dead in some other location, that it was their girlfriends who had contracted their killing," Guzzetta's report stated. "The informants relate that if, in fact, they are found dead, that the method which would probably be used upon them is a lethal injection of drugs, which will show up as a drug overdose."

Guzzetta and the federal agents began debriefing the brothers, and slowly, like an ocean liner emerging from a fog bank, the size of the operation they were part of began to take shape.

It was mind-boggling.

They revealed a drug ring that was dumping hundreds of kilos of cocaine every week into the black neighborhoods of Los Angeles, generating truckloads of cash. "The CI [confidential informant] has admitted laundering approximately $100 million since Jan. 1986," Customs agent Ghio wrote a few days after the debriefings began. "They currently have approximately 1,000 kilos of cocaine currently stored in the Los Angeles area as well as between $250,000,000 and $500,000,000 secreted in various locations locally that they have been unable to get out of the U.S."

Guzzetta said he initially doubted the brothers' story. Crooks trying to wiggle out of a jam often made extragavant claims, but this took the cake. No one he had questioned claimed to have a half a *billion* dollars stashed somewhere. "These guys were right off the street. They had absolutely no credibility as far as I was concerned," Guzzetta recalled.

To prove what they were saying, the Torres brothers invited Guzzetta and his friends to follow them while they made their rounds, dropping off dope and picking up cash from their customers in South Central Los Angeles. "The reliability of the CI has been substantiated," Ghio reported to his bosses a few days later. "Under the control of Det. Guzzetta, Bell, P.D., the CI has picked up and delivered 40 kilos of cocaine and collected and delivered $720,000." Within two weeks, Guzzetta wrote, he had "observed the movement of monies totaling $750,000, $230,000, $130,000, $150,000 respectively, which have been moved by informants and picked up from the Black market area."

Guzzetta began compiling his debriefing notes into a series of reports he titled "Project Sahara," because he figured the Torreses could help dry up the cocaine supply in South Central. Portions of his Project Sahara reports were located by police investigators ten years later, in 1996. "Basically, there is one major market which informant 36210 and 36211 are dealing with, which for the sake of argument in this report will be designated the Black market, because it is solely controlled by two male Negroes by the name of Rick and Ollie," Guzzetta wrote in his first report.

Guzzetta listened gape-mouthed as the brothers rattled off names, dates, delivery sites, and routes of transportation. The two black dealers in South Central, they reported, "are generating a conservative figure of approximately $10 million dollars a month."

The Torreses told him that the blacks were getting their cocaine from three Colombians and "a fourth peripheral source." Two of the Colombians, they knew only by nickname; the "peripheral source" they knew quite well: Danilo Blandón.

"Informants relate that Danilo Blandón is extremely dangerous because of his access to information," Guzzetta wrote, "and further, is extremely dangerous because of his potential to override the informants' market, thus cutting off the informants from the supply source of cocaine and currency, thus cutting off the informants' source of information."

Guzzetta said the brothers told him that Blandón had "a lot of inside information as to law enforcement activity, as to people that are working him," and they warned him to "be extremely careful about releasing any information to other law enforcement agencies…because they were afraid that Blandón had somebody inside the police department or whatever that was feeding him information."

Ricky Ross confirmed that Blandón had an uncanny ability to accurately predict upcoming police raids but said he was never able to explain Blandón's clairvoyance.

The Torres brothers told Guzzetta that "Blandón is working with an ex-Laguna Beach police officer by the name of Ronnie, who lives in an expensive house in Mission Viejo and drives a new Mercedes automobile.... Ronnie transported 100 kilos of cocaine to the Black market and has transported millions of dollars to Miami for Danilo Blandón." Once Blandón's cash arrived in Florida, the brothers reported, a relative of Blandón's, Orlando Murillo, would launder it. They described Murillo as "a bank chairman under Somoza prior to his being thrown out of power."

Roberto Orlando Murillo, the uncle of Blandón's wife, was an influential Nicaraguan economist who'd been appointed by President Somoza in 1978 to the Central Bank of Nicaragua, which is similar in function to the U.S. Federal Reserve Bank. The debonair investment banker was also the official representative of two Swiss banks located in Panama and Managua, and had managed a number of the Somoza family's businesses before the revolution.

It was when the Trees started talking about Murillo and the Contras—and the airfields in New Orleans and Brownsville, Texas, where Contra cocaine was allegedly being flown in under armed guard—that Guzzetta knew he was way out of his league.

Even if only half of what the Torreses were saying was true, the detective realized, he was up against an organization that could roll over a small-town cop like he was a bug. "I took it to the chief of police. I told the chief, 'It's bigger than I can handle. These guys are talking about millions of dollars in cocaine, they're talking about a Nicaraguan [leader] named Calero being involved in this, Colombian families that strike fear into the hearts of mortal men. I can't handle this by myself.'"

His chief, Frank Fording, asked him if he would mind teaming up with one of the L.A. County Sheriff's Major Violators squads, the "Majors," as the elite units were known.

Guzzetta didn't mind at all. In fact, he was thrilled by the prospect. "The Majors were hot shit," Guzzetta said. "They had all the resources, they had the funding, they had the manpower, they had the surveillance equipment, the night vision stuff, the helicopters, the overtime. They had everything."

They were semilegendary in L.A. law enforcement circles as the best the 8,000-man sheriff's department had to offer. Any cop with the slightest amount of ambition lusted for an assignment to the Majors. They got the biggest cases, seized the largest amounts of cash and cocaine, got the fattest overtime checks, and worked virtually unsupervised.

As L.A. defense attorney Jay Lichtman put it: "This was really the cream of the crop, the elite, the top officers of the Sheriff's Department." They were considered some of the best drug detectives in the nation.

They also won notoriety for their boozy off-duty carousing. A drunken crew member had once pulled out a pistol at a restaurant to hurry along a lazy waiter. On another occasion Deputy Daniel Garner, regarded as the best drug detective in the department, relieved himself on the pants leg of an aspiring narcotics officer Garner deemed unworthy of joining the Majors.

The squads—Majors I, II, and III—worked out of trailers at the Whittier and Lennox stations, each team of seven or eight detectives commanded by a sergeant. Guzzetta was put together with Majors II, headed by Sergeant Edward Huffman, whose brother was a friend of Guzzetta's. "Huffman was great," Guzzetta said. "A real straight arrow."

Guzzetta gathered up his "Project Sahara" reports and delivered them to the Majors, where they landed on the desk of Detective Thomas Gordon, a tall, soft-spoken officer who had spent sixteen years with the Los Angeles County Sheriff's Department.

By 1986, Tom Gordon had become a hard man to impress. Since 1982 he and his cohorts on the Majors had been tangling with the biggest criminals L.A. had to offer: the Mexican mafia, the gangbangers, Medellín cartel cells, international money launderers. But "Project Sahara" had a bit of everything, and it had an element the Majors had never before faced—a CIA-linked guerrilla army that was allegedly dealing in dope. There was no telling where this investigation could take them. Former lieutenant Mike Fossey, the unit supervisor and intelligence officer for the Majors II squad, called it one of the biggest cases he'd ever handled.

One of its main attractions was that it would provide the law enforcement community with a wealth of information on the inner workings of the L.A. crack market. Though the crack epidemic had been raging in South Central for three years by then, drug agents still had very little understanding of its dynamics.

They knew the street gangs that dominated the trade rarely left their own neighborhoods, which meant that somehow, someone was bringing in massive amounts of cocaine and delivering it to them. But no one—from the DEA on down—had been able to figure out where it was coming from, who was importing it, or who was reselling it to the gangs.

Many narcotics detectives assumed that the normal rules of the drug trade—where one or two major drug rings control a "turf"—didn't apply to crack, because the marketplace appeared so disorganized and fragmented. There were crack dealers everywhere, on every corner. The problem seemed uncontrollable.

"We haven't encountered any major network. We're conducting these little skirmishes. It's very frustrating," one narcotics detective complained to the *Los Angeles Times* in early August 1986. Robert Stutman, the head of the DEA office in New York in the mid-1980s, wrote that "the marketing of crack was thought to be a cottage industry, a low-level blip in the drug trade like the selling of single marijuana cigarettes."

But that was only because the cops had never gotten much beyond the streets. In June 1986, DEA intelligence revealed that "what looked like independent street corner pushers were actually the bottom rung of carefully managed organizations," Stutman wrote in his 1992 memoirs. "It came as a revelation."

Analyzing the information provided by the Torres brothers, the Majors reached the same frightening conclusion. The L.A. crack market, they realized, was far more disciplined and well organized than anyone had ever dreamed.

And worse, through these two mystery dealers named Rick and Ollie, it appeared that the gangs had established a direct pipeline to the Colombian cartels, which meant they had access to as much cocaine as they could sell. Since the circle was so small, it was little wonder that its bosses had escaped detection for so many years.

It had been one long cop-free party, but it was coming to an end. The Majors now had the names and addresses of everyone at the top of the distribution chain, from the Colombian importers to the Nicaraguan middlemen to the black wholesalers who controlled the South Central marketplace. If everything went right, Gordon and his men could take down the biggest crack operation ever uncovered—one whose tentacles reached all the way to South America—and cut off the L.A. ghettos' main source of supply.

"This was going to be my last hurrah," said Gordon, who was scheduled to be rotated out of the Majors in a few months. "Like anyone, I've got an ego, and I wanted to go out with a bang."

15

"This thing is a tidal wave"

That summer, three years after crack exploded in South Central L.A., the national news media finally figured out what was happening.

Within weeks of each other in May 1986, NBC News, *People* magazine, and the Associated Press trumpeted the news that a deadly new drug plague was stalking the countryside. According to Tom Brokaw, crack was "flooding America." The AP, in a special weekend feature, said "crack is becoming the nation's drug of choice," spreading "like wildfire." The *New York Times* drew a picture of "a wave of crack addicts" engulfing the city, spreading "prostitution and other crimes."

Then came the cataclysmic event that is needed to convert any problem into a National Disaster: celebrity deaths. Two well-known black athletes dropped dead from cocaine abuse.

What Richard Pryor did for freebase, college basketball star Len Bias and pro football player Don Rogers did for crack. With their deaths in June 1986, crack went from being a long-ignored problem in a few black neighborhoods to "a threat to our national security," as one U.S. senator described it. Before the year was out, *Time* and *Newsweek* would run five cover stories apiece on crack and the drug war; *Newsweek* would anoint it as the biggest story since Vietnam and Watergate. *Time* said it was the "Issue of the Year." By November NBC News alone had run more than 400 stories on the topic.

As with most drug stories, the mainstream reporting tended to be half-baked, or just plain wrong. The coverage "followed a typical pattern in which exaggerated claims were supported by carefully selected cases and fueled with evocative words such as 'epidemic,' with its implications of plague, disease, crisis and uncontrollable spread," drug researchers Andrew Golub and Donna Hartman wrote in a study of the media's role in the 1986 crack scare.

The Crack Attack began with a faulty premise, based largely on the news media's myopia. Because there had been few previous reports about crack, many editors assumed that it hadn't existed until then, or they surely would have heard about it. And now crack was seemingly everywhere: in Houston, Detroit, Newark, New York, Atlanta, Kansas City, San Francisco, Los Angeles. Thus, the nation's editors and news directors concluded, crack had spread from coast to coast *overnight*. While we slept, we had become the victims of a dastardly sneak attack—a kind of chemical Pearl Harbor.

That crack had been ravaging South Central L.A. since 1983 was not mentioned. None of the stories reported how vast the L.A. crack market had become by the summer of 1986, or how enterprising Crips and Bloods were fanning out across the country, introducing it into other black neighborhoods in the West and Midwest, precisely as the two USC sociologists Malcolm Klein and Cheryl Maxson had predicted. The spread of crack by the L.A. gangs would not become generally known for another two years.

Nor did the press notice that a similar migration had been occurring on the East Coast for about eighteen months, as the Jamaican posses and Dominican gangs from Miami began expanding their markets westward. A typical observation was contained in the *Washington Post* of June 13, 1986, which reported that crack was "virtually unheard of nine months ago on the East Coast." In the *Post's* newsroom, perhaps.

The only explanation a frightened and bewildered public was given for this "sudden" deluge of crack was a modern-day theory of spontaneous combustion, which holds that people can simply burst into flames. "Crack hit our society with a suddenness unprecedented in the history of illicit drug use," Senator Sam Nunn of Georgia stated. "Literally an overnight phenomenon, crack caught many police agencies by surprise."

"Eight months ago I had never heard of crack," said Senator Lawton Chiles of Florida, who would write the harshest anticrack laws on the books. "This thing is a tidal wave that has hit everywhere.... We are talking about a phenomenon that basically has hit this country in the last year, nine months, eight months, six months."

Representative Hamilton Fish of New York declared that "nine months ago, addiction to crack was virtually unheard of and today it's an epidemic, a plague, that is sweeping the country."

If one believed the papers and the politicians, the crack "epidemic" simply happened, and no one knew how or why. During two well-publicized congressional hearings that superheated summer, the government's top drug experts and law enforcement officers lined up to proclaim their official shock and surprise.

Top scientists at the National Institute on Drug Abuse (NIDA) testified that the agency had never even heard of crack until 1985, which is why it still had no information about it a year later. "We have not had enough time elapse since then for us to get epidemiological data about crack use per se," NIDA official Charles Schuster explained. The DEA's director of operations, David Westrate, said his agency could only guess at how prevalent the problem was, since "crack has emerged as a major drug problem in less than a year. As a result, data on usage, emergency room mentions and arrests have not been focused on crack as an individual category of drug abuse apart from cocaine."

Westrate confirmed that "there is no comprehensive analysis of the crack problem, either from a health or enforcement viewpoint.... DEA's own enforcement information on crack is also incomplete."

Representative Benjamin Gilman of New York could scarcely believe what he was hearing. "Well, of course you are telling us that crack is just beginning to spread across the country like wildfire in the past year. We have no current data, is that correct?" Gilman asked the government experts.

"I think it would be fair to say that we do not have any accurate estimate at this time," replied Dr. Jerome Jaffe of NIDA.

"Am I correct, then," Gilman continued, "that at this point we really don't have any definitive knowledge of how extensive the use of crack is in our country? With all of our expertise? Is that right?"

"That's correct," admitted Edgar Adams, NIDA's head of epidemiology and statistical analysis.

"Is that right, Dr. Jaffe?"

"That's fair."

Gilman looked at the DEA's representative. "Mr. Westrate?"

"Yes, I would say especially with statistically valid information."

But the government's experts weren't quite as ill-informed as they claimed. There was a method to their ignorance.

Pretending that crack was something that had appeared out of nowhere was, politically, much safer than admitting the truth—that the federal government had been warned about it very specifically many years earlier and hadn't lifted a finger to stop it, effectively surrendering the inner cities to an oncoming plague. If that information became too widely known, the public might start asking prickly questions, such as: Why weren't we told?

And how could a question like that be answered? Because we didn't believe it? Because we didn't care? Because we thought it might encourage people to try it? Or was it because the drug problem looked as if it would be confined to lower-income neighborhoods, ghettos, as it had been in South America, Jamaica, and the Bahamas?

Sitting in the audience at one of the congressional hearings that summer of 1986, listening to all the official excuses, was a man who knew the sorry truth better than anyone: Dr. Robert Byck, Yale University's top cocaine expert. It had been seven years since he had appeared before Congress to sound the alarm about the approaching drug plague, only to have his warnings ignored. He had no intention of letting the government get away with the charade he was witnessing.

"In 1979, I testified before the House Committee on Narcotics Abuse and Control and I said that we were about to have the worst epidemic of drug use this country had ever seen, something like the speed epidemic of the 1960s, except on a national scale, and that it was going to be the use of free-base cocaine," Byck said, hunching over his microphone. "I begged people, and I begged people at NIDA, for goodness sake, this is a chance to stop, if not to stop it, at least to take a chance on an educational campaign to avert a drug abuse epidemic.... This advice went unheeded. We are not significantly more knowledgeable about cocaine smoking. No educational campaign was mounted. Today we are in the midst of the predicted epidemic."

DEA official Westrate hastened to assure Congress that the drug agency was on full alert now: "DEA *last week* began an extensive, in-depth intelligence survey through all of the domestic field offices to try to discern the use and availability of crack, its purity and its price." Westrate mentioned that the administration's top drug experts were meeting with President Reagan that very morning to discuss crack.

Byck renewed his plea for research money so scientists could get the answers they needed about crack use and find some way to slow its spread. "I hope my testimony today will have a greater effect than my warnings in 1979," Byck said bitterly.

It didn't.

"Every problem that comes before us, everybody says that money is the answer," scoffed the committee chairman, Senator William Roth of Delaware. "I think you have to use it pretty intelligently and we don't have it in large supply."

Instead of authorizing money for crack research and educational campaigns, the congressmen voted for tougher laws against crack dealing. If crack was more dangerous than regular cocaine, they said, its sellers needed to be dealt with much more severely. And that kind of medicine didn't cost the federal government a cent—up front.

At least, that was the rationale behind one of the laws Congress created that summer, the so-called 100-to-1 weight ratio, which would fill America's prisons with tens of thousands of black street-corner crack peddlers and users over the next decade without making a dent in the crack problem. Under the 100-to-1 ratio—a law Congress passed without any hearings—crack dealers were singled out for particularly harsh punishment. The scales of justice became so lopsided that a powder dealer had to sell $50,000 worth of cocaine to get the same five-year mandatory sentence as someone who'd sold $750 worth of crack. (As if crack could be made without powder cocaine.)

It was, Byck said years later, absolutely senseless. "That all comes from one of the congressmen, the one from Florida, Lawton Chiles," he recalled. "Chiles was asking me a question in which he stated something up front: 'Dr. Byck, isn't it true [crack's] 50 times more addicting?' or something like that. And I said, yes, and that 50 is the number that got doubled by people who wanted to get tough on cocaine and some expert's opinion on addictiveness got translated into weight.... The numbers are a fabrication of whoever wrote the law, but not reality."

As drug expert Steven Belenko of the New York City Criminal Justice Agency later observed, "One interesting aspect of the anti-crack crusade is that it occurred in the presence of a real vacuum of knowledge about the drug."

Meanwhile, drug experts who were reading and hearing about this "tidal wave" of crack began wondering which planet the media was reporting from. When the scientists looked around, they didn't see any epidemic, except for a few hot spots here and there—specific neighborhoods in Los Angeles, Miami, New York, Houston. It was certainly not the grand nationwide epidemic the press was portraying. A Chicago drug expert went so far as to call the whole issue "a hoax."

"Researchers were finding crack to be, not a national epidemic, but a phenomenon isolated to the inner cities of less than a dozen urban areas," drug expert James Inciardi observed in 1987. Even in New York, Inciardi wrote, "the fact of the matter was that if you lived outside of Washington Heights, crack was just plain unavailable."

Belenko wrote that "during the period of strongest concern over crack, 1986 to 1990, crack was actually the least-used drug among all illicit drugs." In Miami, at the supposed height of the crack epidemic there, cops running a sting operation in Liberty City had to call it quits because few cocaine customers wanted crack; they were looking for powder. (It was a different story in South Central L.A., of course. There, crack clearly was the drug of choice.)

But those who deviated from the official line of nationwide crack pandemonium were ignored or chastised. After NIDA officials called a press conference to announce the good news that cocaine use appeared to be leveling off, Senator Lawton Chiles sternly reprimanded the head of NIDA, Charles Schuster. "What kind of message are we sending out there, on the one hand, when we are saying that it is an epidemic, you have your *Newsweek* story, you have *Time* magazine, the *New York Times*, you have everybody in the world saying we have an epidemic, and then along comes NIDA which says that the figures are level, not to worry, and uses numbers that go back to 1982?" Chiles huffed. "Was it really necessary to call a press conference?"

After finishing its review of local field offices, the DEA initially sided with the scientists. "Crack is currently the subject of considerable media attention. The result has been a distortion of the public perception of the extent of crack use as compared to the use of other drugs," the DEA noted in an August 1986 press release. "Crack presently appears to be a secondary rather than primary problem in most areas."

The DEA's findings went virtually unreported; that kind of news was not what the politicians or the media wanted to hear. But when DEA officials changed their tune and began denouncing crack as the scourge of scourges, those comments got plenty of ink and air time.

One truly remarkable thing about the crack scare was the degree to which the national press—particularly the *New York Times*—walked in lockstep with the federal government on the issue, fanning the flames of hysteria and unquestioningly parroting the official line, a media phenomenon usually seen only in times of armed conflict.

While First Lady Nancy Reagan was off on a world antidrug tour in the spring of 1986, the *Times* began almost daily reporting on the "growing public outcry over the spread of crack." Throughout July and August, the *Times* featured leaks from "White House sources" who confided that the president himself was taking this crack issue very seriously. Television news was a steady barrage of hair-raising stories. (Years later, Nancy Reagan would pine for what she called "the steady drumbeat" of antidrug stories produced by the government/media partnership.)

Robert Stutman, chief of the New York DEA office, would later admit that the crack panic of 1986 had been largely his creation. He didn't think the Justice Department was taking the issue seriously enough so "to speed up the process of convincing Washington, I needed to make it a national issue and quickly. I began a lobbying effort and I used the media. Reporters were only too willing to cooperate, because as far as the New York media was concerned, crack was the hottest combat-reporting story to come along since the end of the Vietnam War." By the end of August, Stutman noted, the "groundwork that had been carefully laid through press accounts and my own public appearances" had produced incredible results: *Newsweek* was calling crack "a national scandal" and the New York papers were blaming every crime on crackheads. "Crack was a national menace," Stutman wryly observed in his memoirs, "and 1986 was the Year of Crack."

The PR campaign worked so well that the *New York Times* was reporting a "frenzy in Washington over drugs." The "frenzy" created a bonanza for the media. CBS News' *48 Hours on Crack Street*, which aired in the fall of 1986, is still one of the highest-rated TV documentaries in history. A *New York Times*–CBS News poll done in early September showed that 13 percent of the American public considered drugs America's number-one problem; five months earlier, only 2 percent had felt that way, a remarkable shift in public attitude in a very short time.

For politicians facing critical midterm elections a few months down the road, the crack panic had been heaven-sent. Lashing out at crack and crack dealers was a painless way to get a lot of free publicity, a perfect issue for any politician—almost too perfect. "Crack could not have appeared at a more opportune political moment. After years of dull debates on budget balancing, a 'hot' issue had arrived just in time for a crucial election," professors Craig Reinarman and Harry Levine wrote in the journal *Contemporary Drug Problems*.

In their analysis of media coverage during the crack panic, drug researchers Golub and Hartman found that most of the information appearing in the *New York Times*, *Newsweek*, and *Time* came from two types of sources: cops and politicians. Drug researchers or academics were quoted much less frequently. The *New York Times*, in particular, showed a remarkable aversion to experts: fewer than one in ten *Times* stories about crack carried an expert opinion. "It is interesting to note that the top two sources—law enforcement and public officials—are among those who stand to gain the most from a drug panic," Golub and Hartman observed.

The crack hysteria continued unabated through the elections until something else arose to divert the public's attention. "It was not until the revelations about Lieutenant Colonel Oliver L. North and the Iran-Contra connection toward the close of 1986 that crack media coverage experienced significant declines," drug researcher Inciardi wrote.

Law enforcement seemed to lose interest as quickly as the public, although the crack problem remained as fierce as ever. In October 1986, about a week after the Iran-Contra scandal began, the *L.A. Times* carried a story inside the paper about the LAPD "quietly disbanding" its thirty-two-member anticrack task force in South Central Los Angeles. Chief Darrell Gates told the *Times* that the task force was needed "in other parts of the city" but assured the residents of inner-city L.A. that they were not being abandoned because "conventional law enforcement efforts will continue."

As the Reverend Charles Mims, a South Central minister, observed, "It seems illogical to move this task force from what most everybody grants is the most active rock cocaine area on earth."

Just how quickly the crack problem was forgotten by the Reagan administration was demonstrated when DEA director Jack Lawn—following up on Reagan's pledge to crack down on crack—asked for $44 million to hire an additional 200 agents to focus solely on crack. The Justice Department's budget committee rejected his request. "They didn't treat it like a major issue," a surprised Lawn told *U.S. News and World Report*. The magazine identified the Justice Department official responsible for that decision as Associate Attorney General Stephen S. Trott.

By then, however, Steve Trott had bigger worries than inner-city crackheads: he had Iran-Contra to deal with. Not only was Congress screaming about North and beginning to scrutinize the Justice Department's involvement in the scandal, but Trott was monitoring a pesky Senate investigation into allegations of Contra drug trafficking. Trott viewed this probe with considerable agitation. Oliver North and the FBI were also keenly interested in its progress, North's notebooks reveal.

The administration's concern was understandable. By the spring of 1986, the Contras were almost out of money. While North and his agents were able to replace some of the Contras' lost CIA funding with donations from Saudi Arabia and Taiwan, the amounts were only a fraction of what it took to keep the Contras trained, armed, fed, and fighting. Reagan administration and CIA officials estimated that their monthly food bill alone was between $1 million and $2 million. Some estimated the annual cost of the Contra war to be $100 million to $200 million.

In March 1986 the White House began lobbying Congress to turn the money spigots back on and put the CIA back in charge, and to overtly provide what it truly cost to fight the Sandinistas: $100 million a year. The early indications were that Congress was willing to consider the matter seriously.

But then Senator John Kerry of Massachusetts and his staff started making noises about the Contras being involved with cocaine. They had been interviewing mercenaries, former Contras, and Cuban-American sympathizers, making trips to Costa Rica and Miami, talking to foreign officials and federal prosecutors. They started pushing for an official investigation of Contra connections to drug traffickers. With the public's crack hysteria at a fever pitch, a more deadly or untimely accusation could not have been made against the Contras, and the Reagan administration knew it.

"The obvious intent of Senator Kerry is to try to orchestrate a series of sensational accusations against the Contras in order to obtain massive press coverage at about the time of the next Contra aid vote," Trott was informed in a May 1986 memo from the Justice Department's congressional liaison. "It will be Senator Kerry's intention to try and twist facts and circumstances in order to unjustifiably defame the Justice Department, the Federal Bureau of Investigation and the Drug Enforcement Administration. Indeed, we have been informed that Senator Kerry will take every opportunity to make the implication or express claim that there is a conspiracy within the Administration to cover up illegal activities of the Contras and their supporters." The fact that Kerry, a former federal prosecutor, had been an outspoken opponent of Contra aid made Reagan administration officials even more distrustful.

By June 1986 Kerry's staff had compiled enough information for the senator to approach his colleagues on the Senate Foreign Relations Committee and seek authorization for an official investigation. According to a transcript of that secret meeting, Kerry warned the assembled senators that some of what he was about to tell them "strains credulity at moments in time and it strained my credulity. When I first heard this stuff, I said 'I do not believe this, you know? It cannot be true.'"

But after talking to many current and former Contras, Kerry said, there was ample evidence to suggest that the Contra leaders were corrupt, dealing in drugs and weapons, using their supply lines to run both, and that some U.S. government officials were protecting them. "We can produce specific law enforcement officials who will tell you that they have been called off drug trafficking investigations because CIA is involved or because it would threaten national security or because the State Department did not want it to happen," Kerry told the committee. "Our sources have suggested in direct testimony that agencies of the United States government may be failing to stop or punish those engaging in these criminal activities because those individuals are otherwise engaged in helping United States foreign policy."

Kerry warned: "When the State Department begins to say that we should not be pursuing the drug trafficking because it would threaten our national security, this committee ought to understand why we are making a decision that it is okay to have drugs coming into this country."

Kerry's chief investigator, Washington, D.C., attorney Jack Blum, detailed some of the charges Kerry's staff had looked into and told the senators that "the narcotics are coming into the United States not by the pound, not by the bag, but by the ton, by the cargo planeload."

And, Kerry added, the leadership of the FDN knew about it and was involved in it. "It is clear that there is a network of drug trafficking through the Contras, and it goes right up to Calero, Mario Calero, Adolfo Calero, Enrique Bermúdez. And we have people who will so testify and who have," he said.

But the idea of diving into such a stinking swamp made some of the other senators squeamish. Senator Joe Biden of Delaware warned that "we should understand that this thing may take us places we would have rather not gone. But we should be aware of it and I think there is no choice but to go there." Senator Nancy Kassebaum of Kansas said she didn't think the committee had the authority to get into the issue. Instead of holding hearings or subpoenaing records, she suggested an alternative approach: "It seems to me that we should be able somehow to really work with the CIA, the DEA. There are channels, it seems to me, that have that ability."

Kerry almost laughed. "Well, let me say that I would be amazed if the CIA were to be very cooperative in this," he said. "We had a meeting with the CIA, Justice Department.... CIA jumped out of their seats at some of the stuff that they heard we were thinking about looking at. I mean, they just literally jumped out of their seats. They were amazed that we were going to look at this stuff."

At the request of Foreign Relations Committee chairman Senator Richard Lugar of Indiana, Kerry gave the committee a list of areas that needed investigation. Among them: "The murder of Dr. Hugo Spottiforo [sic] by contras engaged in drug smuggling in Costa Rica"; "An ongoing drug smuggling operation connecting Colombia, Costa Rica, Nicaragua and the United States, in which Contras and American supporters, with the apparent knowledge of Contra leadership, handled the transport of cocaine produced in Colombia, shipped to Costa Rica, process[ed] in the region, transported to airstrips controlled by American supporters of the Contras and Contras, and distributed in the U.S."; and "Allegations [that] have also surfaced regarding other drug smuggling operations involving shrimp boats operating out of Texas, Louisiana and Florida."

The Foreign Relations Committee voted to approve Kerry's request for a behind-the-scenes investigation, but grudgingly, and the Republican staff members on the committee kept the Reagan administration fully informed of what the investigators were unearthing. Those timely tips allowed the Justice Department to head off attempts to obtain certain records, or interview certain witnesses.

When Kerry's investigators sought to interview Contra drug dealer Carlos Cabezas about the San Francisco Frogman case, the Justice Department announced that he couldn't possibly be questioned, since he was going to be a federal witness in an upcoming drug trial. Cabezas said that was "bullshit. I was never a witness in that case. They just didn't want anyone talking to me."

Justice Department official Mark Richard later admitted in a deposition that the department "was seemingly just stonewalling.... DEA was saying they won't do it. They didn't want to respond. They didn't want to provide any information." But some information trickled out anyway. And it got awfully close to exposing the Norwin Meneses–Danilo Blandón drug operation.

In the spring of 1986, *San Francisco Examiner* reporter Seth Rosenfeld broke the story of the Frogman case, exposing the Justice Department's bizarre handling of the $36,000 found in Julio Zavala's nightstand in 1983. It also reported Zavala's claim, from a prison cell in Arizona, that he had personally delivered about $500,000 in drug profits to the Contras in Costa Rica. Rosenfeld also unearthed Carlos Cabezas's long-buried testimony about selling Horacio Pereira's cocaine to raise money for the Contra revolution.

Coming on the heels of several Associated Press reports by Robert Parry and Brian Barger about Contra cocaine trafficking in Costa Rica, Rosenfeld's story provided the first hard evidence of a Contra drug ring operating in the United States. The Associated Press picked up the story, and several other newspapers printed it, but cautiously, burying it deep inside the paper and surrounded by plenty of official denials. Nonetheless, the Reagan administration reacted with fury.

San Francisco U.S. attorney Joseph Russoniello mailed a four-page letter to the *Examiner*'s editor, calling Rosenfeld's work "one of the most blatant attempts at contrived news-making we have witnessed in recent years," and suggesting that it was a political stunt to harm the Contras' chances of getting aid from Congress. Though Rosenfeld never made the charge, Russoniello indignantly wrote that "there is absolutely no evidence of CIA involvement." Incredibly, he made the same claim regarding the Contras. "There is no evidence to warrant the insinuation the defendants were connected to the Contras except…their own statements offered after the fact of arrest and in a futile attempt to explain away their own conduct."

Russoniello did not disclose that Carlos Cabezas—as a witness for Russoniello's office—had testified about selling dope for the Contras under oath in 1984. Nor did he mention that two high-ranking UDN-FARN officials had written letters to the court attesting to Zavala's official position in the Contra organization. He also forgot about the 1982 FBI teletypes that named Contra officials Fernando and Troilo Sánchez as the drug ring's suppliers.

In a White Paper subsequently circulated to Congress by the U.S. State Department, Zavala and Cabezas were portrayed as liars and opportunists, and Rosenfeld's story was dismissed as malarkey.

One-upping Russoniello, the State Department claimed that Cabezas and Zavala had never said anything about the Contras until "long after their conviction…. [They] did not raise these issues as a defense in their trial or at sentencing but waited two years before making these allegations, which, as indicated, could not be confirmed." Congress was assured that "DEA has examined allegations of linkages between members of the UNO/FARN and suspected traffickers. It has found no information indicating that members of this group have been involved in narcotics trafficking."

But it couldn't have been looking very hard. In April 1986, a UPI story featured an interview with former Contra official Leonardo Zeledon Rodriguez, who said he was beaten, paralyzed, and left for dead because he had denounced Contra involvement in drug dealing. Zeledon specifically identified Norwin Meneses's partner, Troilo Sánchez, as being involved and said Sánchez had been arrested for cocaine trafficking in Costa Rica.

Then, a month before the State Department White Paper was sent to Congress, Rosenfeld had another major front-page story in the *Examiner*, exposing Norwin Meneses's cocaine trafficking network and his involvement with the FDN in San Francisco and Los Angeles. Rosenfeld reported on Meneses's meetings with CIA agents Enrique Bermúdez and Adolfo Calero and other Contra leaders. He reported that the FDN's spokesman in San Francisco had been convicted of cocaine charges. He disclosed Meneses's donations at FDN fund-raisers.

The Meneses story was considerably more damaging to the Contras than the Frogman story because it directly involved the CIA's primary army, the FDN, with a major international cocaine and arms trafficker. Yet it drew no response from the administration, no angry denunciations from federal prosecutors. The State Department's White Paper—which belittled every other allegation of Contra drug trafficking that had surfaced in the past year—studiously avoided any mention of Meneses and his well-connected gang. And it wasn't just the government that was keeping mum.

Though the *Examiner*'s exposé appeared just two days before the House of Representatives was scheduled to take up the highly controversial issue of Reagan's $100 million Contra aid package, not a single major newspaper in the country touched the Meneses story. It drew nothing but silence, almost as if it had never appeared.

After Kerry Committee lawyer Jack Blum saw the *Examiner*'s stories, he asked the Justice Department to turn over its files on Meneses and the long-closed Frogman case. He ran into a buzzsaw, he said. "We had a terrible, terrible time getting information about Meneses from the fellow who was the U.S. attorney out there at the time, Russoniello, who was as rabid a right-wing true believer as ever came down the road and who was bound and determined to prevent anyone from learning anything about that case," said Blum. "He and the Justice Department flipped out to prevent us from getting access to people, records, finding anything out about it. It was one of the most frustrating exercises I can ever recall." Blum said Kerry and Russoniello got into "a screaming match" over the telephone.

On October 15, 1986, the controversy over the Frogman files reached Oliver North's ears. "46 boxes of transcripts of SF Frogman case," North wrote in his diary. "Justice never provided."

"It's a burn"

It was time to put the Torres brothers to the test. Providing intelligence and letting the cops follow them around was one thing. But if the investigation was going to progress beyond that level, the Majors had to be sure the two Nicaraguans could take the next, critical step: they had to give someone up.

The brothers chose one of the Colombians they'd named as a source for the black dealers, Jaime Ramos. One day in early September 1986, they told Bell narcotics detective Jerry Guzzetta that Ramos and another man were going to be making a pickup from two dealers that day at an abandoned apartment house in South Central. Around 1:00 P.M., the Majors set up surveillance on the building.

Within an hour, a red Chevy carrying two Latinos and a black Mustang with two black men inside rumbled up the driveway. They chatted briefly and drove off, leading the detectives on an aimless six-hour ride around Los Angeles.

About 8:00 P.M., near the intersection of 159th and Vermont Streets, the cars pulled over, and one of the black men got out and tossed a blue nylon gym bag into the Chevy. The Chevy sped off to a restaurant in Glendale, where the bag was transferred to a white car and driven to a house on Kenwood Avenue.

After a short wait, the Majors burst in, yelling and waving their guns. Jaime Ramos and the blue gym bag were found in the bedroom, the latter stuffed with $120,005 in small bills and $101,000 in cashier's checks. In a closet, they found a suitcase and six more nylon gym bags—with 114 kilos of cocaine inside. At another house a brown suitcase contained 17 kilos. Ramos, who was carrying ID from the Colombian military, and three other Colombians, were arrested.

Two million dollars worth of dope and a quarter million in cash. Not bad for an afternoon's work. It looked as if the Torres brothers were for real. While Detective Tom Gordon and the Majors plotted their next moves, Jerry Guzzetta asked the Torres brothers to show him around South Central. He wanted to know more about this mysterious black dealer they called "Rick," and needed to determine how well the Torreses really knew him.

They drove Guzzetta by a vacant two-story apartment complex off South Avalon Boulevard and told Guzzetta that a cocaine lab was located there. The building was occupied only when the dealers were at work, measuring, testing, and packaging the product. The rest of the time it was vacant, so there would be no suspicious traffic in and out of the dilapidated structure.

Near an entrance ramp to the Harbor Freeway, they pointed out a multistory apartment building, which they said served as one of Rick's distribution centers. Even during the middle of the week there was a lot of activity—young men lounging along the curb, hanging in the doorways—but the Torreses told Guzzetta to come by the place on a Friday or Saturday night if he really wanted to see some action. "There are numerous drug dealers that come to the location to party and there are numerous new vehicles, like Mercedes and Cadillacs, which would be parked on the street at the time of the parties," Guzzetta's report stated.

Swinging by 75th and Figueroa, the brothers pointed out a newly constructed motel, the Freeway Motor Inn. Rick had bought the land for a million dollars, they told Guzzetta, and had the motel built to his specifications. Rick's mother, Annie, worked the front desk.

Suddenly, everything clicked.

Rick. The Freeway Motor Inn. This was too good to be true, Guzzetta marvelled. The Torres brothers had led him to the legendary Freeway Rick, the elusive crack lord whose existence had only become known to the Majors within the past few months.

While rumors of a super crack dealer had been floating around South Central since late 1985, it wasn't until April 1986 that the police received informant information suggesting that there might be truth behind the rumors. The Majors I squad asked Detective John Edner to see what he could find out, and Edner confirmed that "Freeway Rick" had a name—Ricky Donnell Ross. While Edner couldn't track him down, he did find Freeway Rick's girlfriend, Marilyn Stubblefield, and got her address.

On May 15, 1986, the Majors introduced themselves. According to Stubblefield's brother, Steve, they kicked the door in, ransacked the apartment, arrested Marilyn, and beat Steve with a flashlight, telling him to pass a message along to Freeway Rick that he had some real bad hombres looking for him.

During the search of the Stubblefields' house, which turned up a bit of cocaine, some marijuana, and some empty kilo wrappers, Ross's cousin, George Mauldin, stopped by, and the Majors gave him the same warm welcome they'd given Steve Stubblefield. "Mauldin showed up while we were in the process of searching the house. We had most of the subjects detained in the living room. Mauldin showed up and got into a shoving match with [Detective Robert] Tolmaire after he was told not to interfere with what we were doing," Majors I supervisor Sergeant Robert Sobel recalled. "I believe Tolmaire hit him with a flashlight."

In late August Majors I struck again, rousting two of Ross's cousins, Anthony and Eric Mauldin, on suspicion of possessing stolen firearms. They didn't arrest them. They "tuned them up" and told them to tell Rick to watch his ass. For the first time in his young life, Rick Ross started worrying about the cops.

Years later, Ross surmised that the Torres brothers gave him up because he'd quit buying cocaine from them in 1986, reverting back to an exclusive relationship with Danilo Blandón. "Danilo's price was so low, that the Torres brothers simply could not continue to compete," Ross told police investigators in 1996. In addition, Ross and Blandón had become very close friends. "We got more personal with Danilo. We started to get more like friends than just selling dope. You know, first it was just like businesses, you know, like we'd meet him in the street. Eventually we started goin' over to his house and hanging out with him and stuff like that."

While the Majors I crew worked Ross's organization from the bottom up, Majors II was working it from the top down, trying to zero in on Ross's suppliers. The Ramos bust had been impressive in terms of cocaine and cash seized, but ultimately it had been a dead end. Despite the Torres's claims that the Colombian was one of Ross's big suppliers, no evidence was found linking him to Ross. In later interviews with police, Ross and his partner, Ollie Newell, both specifically denied that any of their suppliers had been arrested in September 1986, and both said they had not lost any money that month as the result of an arrest.

The Ramos case was eventually plea-bargained down to nothing, "and they let a guy who we found with 230 pounds of coke plead to a five-kilo bust and deported him," Gordon said. Later events led him to believe that Ramos had been a CIA operative, but according to court records, his light punishment may have been due to the fact that the Majors had no search warrant when they busted into his house.

Gordon went back to square one.

He started working his way down the list of other men the Torres brothers had identified as supplying Ross. It was not promising. He had only first names—Diego and Stefano—for the other two Colombians. All he knew about Diego was that he was a flashy dresser and a womanizer. Stefano, reportedly a college student, appeared to be working with some Italians who owned a fish processing plant in Riverside. Neither path seemed to point to South Central L.A., and the Torres brothers seemed vague on details about those two.

The information was much harder on the fourth man, Danilo Blandón, and his ex-cop sidekick, Ronnie Lister. These were the guys who, according to Guzzetta, the Torreses were really afraid of. If they were able to frighten a pair of heavily armed behemoths like the Torreses, they must be something.

Blandón's attorney, Bradley Brunon, said he didn't find out for years who'd led the sheriffs to his client. Then, while researching another case, he ran across a stray reference in some police records he was reviewing, and concluded that it had been the Torres brothers. "I would think the motivation for them at that time was to simply put him [Blandón] out of business and take his customers," Brunon said. "It's like watching snakes. It's interesting but it's revolting at the same time." Blandón shared that opinion. He said the Torres brothers led the police to him because "they were jealous" of his success.

On the afternoon of September 17, 1986, Gordon ran the names the Torres brothers had provided through two computer databases, NIN and NADDIS, which collect information from narcotics investigations around the world. They can instantly provide an officer with a criminal history of the suspect, his known associates, aliases, addresses, and the case file numbers of all DEA investigations in which the suspected trafficker's name has turned up.

Running a NIN and NADDIS check is a routine way to begin a narcotics investigation; it lets the investigator know if anyone else is working on the same suspects. If a doper has a NIN or NADDIS file, the protocol dictates that whoever entered the trafficker into the database "owns" that doper from then on. (Narcotics cops frequently complain abou who enter everyone they run across into the databases, just to clai ership in case the person one day turns out to be a major traffic NADDIS also alerts the "owner" if someone else accesses the compu file. "The idea is so that we don't end up shooting each other," Gordon explained.

The computer screen brought up Blandón's file first. He was listed as a Class One trafficker, the biggest. He had some addresses in Glendale, which showed up in connection with the Torres brothers. A couple file references from 1983 and 1984 described him as the head of a cocaine distribution organization in Los Angeles. He had only two known associates: Roger Sandino and Norwin Meneses.

Gordon decided to check them out with the computer.

Sandino's criminal history included a 1981 conviction in Hialeah, Florida, for attempting to sell 50,000 Quaalude tablets, while in the country illegally from Nicaragua.

The next name Gordon typed into the NADDIS computer was that of Norwin Meneses. When his file came up, it seemed as if it would never end. On and on it went, screen after screen.

This guy, Gordon observed, was in a league of his own. Another Nicaraguan, he had been in the NADDIS database since 1976—a decade. A Class One trafficker. Twelve aliases. Houses all over the Bay Area. A mansion in Managua. Mentioned in thirty-two DEA investigations, some as far back as 1974. A couple of classified files from 1976. Bringing in cocaine from Colombia, Costa Rica, and Ecuador, sending it to New Orleans, Miami, San Francisco, Los Angeles. Among a host of current associates were a cross-match: Roger Sandino and Danilo Blandón.

The report also revealed that someone else had been in Meneses's NADDIS file recently. The date of the last update was only nineteen days earlier. When Gordon started checking the status of the DEA investigations in Meneses's file, he learned that a number of them were still open. Yet despite all the official interest, Meneses had never been charged with a single thing. He was clean.

Gordon called up Ronald Lister's file next. It was short and sweet. He was an ex-policeman who was under active DEA investigation. The case was so active, Gordon noticed, that Lister's NADDIS file was less than a month old.

Another live wire.

But all the details of that case were classified, the NADDIS report stated. Gordon jotted the name of Lister's "owner" on the bottom of the ebb

DEA agent Sandalio "Sandy" González, U.S. Embassy, San ...osta Rica—the same agent who "owned" Blandón.

...omething didn't add up. Lister lived in Orange County. Blandón ...d in San Bernardino County. Why would a Costa Rican DEA agent ...ave them under investigation—unless they'd been down in Costa Rica recently? Then Gordon noticed that Meneses had been under investigation in Costa Rica also.

When Jerry Guzzetta brought the case in the door, he'd been insisting that he'd uncovered an international crack ring. It was sure beginning to look that way.

Gordon picked up the phone and called DEA agent González to find out what was going on. The reaction he got was memorable. González "goes through the ceiling," Gordon recalled. "He starts screaming that all the phone lines go through Nicaragua and [says] 'You can't call me on an open line and talk about this!' He said he'd fly to Panama and call me from there."

Now the detective was really baffled. So what if the phone lines went through Nicaragua? They probably went through a lot of other places on their way down there and back. What's the big deal?

Gordon didn't hear from González for five days, and when the DEA agent finally called back, Gordon was out. González asked the cop who answered the phone to take a message for him, which Gordon found on his desk: "Tom, got a call from Sandy González of Costa Rica DEA. He said [local DEA agent] will let you read the info. Sandy can not talk on the phone because all the lines are through Nicaragua. Sandy asks that you don't mention anything in your s/w [search warrant affidavit]. It's a burn."

There's those Nicaraguan phone lines again, Gordon saw. And what's this crap about "a burn?" That was cop slang meaning that his investigation had been exposed and the bad guys knew he was investigating them. González was telling Gordon not to put any details of his investigation into the sworn statement he had to file with his application for a search warrant because the search would come up dry and he would tip his hand for nothing.

Gordon didn't get that one at all. How the hell could his investigation of Blandón and Lister have been burned? It hadn't even started yet. The case was still sitting on top of his desk. Nobody had done anything except run a couple of computer checks, and no one besides Jerry Guzzetta—and now the DEA—even knew the Majors were working on it.

Besides, how would a DEA agent a couple thousand miles away know that a newborn investigation by the L.A. County Sheriff's O… been burned?

When Gordon called the DEA office in L.A., as González sugge… his uneasiness grew. No, he was told, the Costa Rican DEA office was n… investigating Lister and Blandón. But an agent in Riverside, in San Bernardino County, was.

Gordon found that Riverside DEA agent Thomas A. Schrettner was only too happy to help him. "They've got a gold informant right in the middle of the operation that they'd been using for three years or so," Gordon said. "They did their own case on these guys a year prior and during a raid one guy gets shot so they were hot on it. But they got word not to do it from some higher-up. No dealings, no surveillance, no nothing. So they gave us this guy [Blandón]." The DEA refused to release any information on this or any other aspect of its Blandón investigation.

In retrospect, Gordon said, that should have set off some alarms. The DEA was notorious among local lawmen for coming in and stealing the best cases, mainly for the publicity value. It almost never handed off a big case to a smaller department. Yet here was a case involving major international cocaine traffickers, crack in the ghettos, multikilo shipments, and hundreds of millions of dollars—the kind of case the DEA exists for—and the agency didn't want to investigate it?

At the time, though, Gordon thought Schrettner's offer was a clever way to get around a bureaucratic roadblock and still bring a dope dealer to justice. And when Schrettner sent Gordon a copy of his latest report on the investigation, the detective quickly forgot his concerns about the unusual behavior of the federal agents. The case was everything Gordon imagined it would be. It was worldwide.

In late August 1986 Schrettner had debriefed a Nicaraguan informant who'd known Blandón since meeting him in Miami in 1983. The informant admitted hauling cocaine and millions of dollars across the country for Blandón during 1984 and 1985, but said he felt bad about doing it and was planning to turn Danilo in eventually. As a matter of fact, he said, he'd already tried to turn him in once. Before starting a drug-hauling trip to the West Coast, the informant said, he "informed the FBI in Miami of the shipment and route but no action was taken."

Schrettner's informant described the drug ring as consisting of "loosely associated Nicaraguans located principally in the Southern California area. Said groups together purchase/distribute approximately 400 kilos of cocaine per month.... Cocaine is often transported to the Blandón organization and then from Blandón to Meneses in San

.” For Gordon, that information held special meaning. It pro- n independent verification of the accuracy of the information that zetta had gotten from the Torres brothers and the data he'd pulled NADDIS.

According to Schrettner's informant, Norwin Meneses was involved. Roger Sandino was involved. So were Jacinto Torres, Ronald Lister, and Anastasio Somoza's former bank chairman, Orlando Murillo, who was allegedly laundering Blandón's cash in Miami and serving as a front man in property deals.

The informant told the DEA that Blandón's millions were being driven to Florida in motor homes and taken to the Fontainebleu Apartment Complex between Miami and Sweetwater, “which had been purchased for Blandón by Orlando Murillo.” The *Miami Herald* wrote about the Fontainebleu area in 1983, noting that it was home to thousands of Nicaraguan exiles who'd fled the Sandinistas. It was, the *Herald* reported, “jokingly dubbed ‘OPEN #3,’ after a poor Managua neighborhood.” (The original “OPEN #3” was emergency housing erected by the Somoza government for survivors of the 1972 earthquake that leveled Managua. Ironically, it was built on land owned by Danilo Blandón's family, which collected rent from the tenants.)

Murillo was identified as working at the Government Security Bank in Coral Gables, and acting as “the principal money-launderer” for Blandón and Meneses. While Murillo denied those accusations, Blandón admitted under oath that Murillo had handled cash transfers to Panama for him, and put his name on deeds to properties that Blandón owned but he said Murillo didn't know he was handling drug money. However, in an interview with the author Murillo said he'd known Blandón was a drug dealer since early 1981.

According to the DEA informant, the Nicaraguan drug ring was made up of “two separate organizations. The principal group is controlled by Blandón and is the focal point for drug supply and money-laundering for the others. Blandón utilizes the nickname ‘Chanchin’ [fat pig] and works closely with his wife Chepita in his trafficking. The other group is run by Meneses and is located principally in the San Francisco Bay Area.”

The informant filled seven pages with names, dates, cash deliveries, stash house locations, drug storehouses, and business fronts. History has proven that nearly all of the information was accurate. Among those named as members of Blandón's operation were Claudio Villavicencio, aka Ivan Arguellas, Rick Ross's first major supplier; Jacinto Torres; and Ronald Lister, accurately described as an ex-Laguna Beach cop. Another one of Blandón's employees, a cocaine distributor named Ivan T listed as having "political connections with the FDN."

Schrettner confirmed in an interview with police investigato 1996 that "his informant had told him that the Blandón organization sending the proceeds from drug sales to the Contras in Nicaragua."

As Gordon continued his probe, he found out that the DEA wasn't the only federal agency with its eyes on Danilo Blandón. A Riverside FBI agent, Douglas Aukland, had been working the Blandón organization for about a month and had developed his own source inside the drug ring. Aukland's informant was also reporting that "some of the proceeds from the sales of cocaine were being sent to the Contras in Nicaragua," Aukland told investigators in 1996.

When Gordon contacted him for assistance, Aukland said he "strongly suggested" to Gordon that the Majors halt their investigation because he believed "the information he was receiving would culminate in a much bigger case." But after his bizarre experiences with the DEA, Gordon was leery of accepting such advice from federal agents. He told Aukland that the drug ring was bringing in too much cocaine for him to sit around and wait for the perfect case. He now had three independent sources telling the same story. The Majors had enough evidence to obtain a search warrant and bust the whole operation, Gordon told the FBI agent, and that was what they were going to do.

Once it became clear that Gordon was not going to back off, Aukland said, he agreed to help the Majors with their probe. "Agent Aukland thought very highly of LASD Deputy Tom Gordon," police investigators reported later. "He said it was obvious Gordon was very knowledgable and had extensive narcotics experience."

Gordon also had enough bureaucratic experience to know he was heading into some very dangerous political territory. The DEA, the FBI, and Guzzetta were all saying that money from this drug ring was helping the Contras, and anyone who read the papers knew what the Contras were and just how strongly the U.S. government felt about them, particularly then. Congress had just approved Reagan's $100 million aid package, and Reagan was getting ready to sign the bill.

If Gordon was going to end up investigating his own government or its proxy army for drug trafficking, he realized, he'd better get someone to sign off on it. He approached Lieutenant Mike Fossey, the acting captain of the bureau, and laid out the whole scenario. "The allegations were that the Contras were selling cocaine throughout the United States and in Southern California in particular," Fossey recalled in a 1996 interview ce investigators. Fossey recalled being told "that the CIA was d with them, screened them, and protected their operation." He dered Gordon's claims to be "a major accusation," and told the ective to keep after it.

Gordon's immediate supervisor, Sergeant Ed Huffman, decided to brief the commander of the Sheriff's Narcotics Bureau, Captain Robert Wilber, just to make sure the top brass had no qualms about pursuing such a sensitive case. Wilber confirmed that Huffman and his men "believed the suspects were possibly Contras. During this conversation they also said they were reluctant to work with the FBI on the case because the FBI might 'burn' them."

Wilber wasn't sure if Huffman's suspicions were "a political thing," or if the veteran sergeant just felt uncomfortable working with the feds. During this period, Wilber told investigators in 1996, his "guys were not working with the federal agents very well and...he pushed his deputies to work with them on this case."

"It was a tough nut to crack," he said, "but I was constantly emphasizing that they had to work with the Feds." Huffman reluctantly agreed to bring the Justice Department's agents aboard. But had the L.A. officers known what was going on right then with the DEA office in Costa Rica, and the agents who were monitoring Meneses, Blandón, and Lister, it's doubtful they would have let the Feds anywhere near their investigation.

…re going to blow your fucking head off”

Joseph Kelso, an undercover informant for the U.S. Customs Service, slipped quietly into Costa Rica in April 1986 on the trail of an elusive drug dealer. Before his visit was over, he would be chased, beaten, shot at, clubbed, caged, threatened with death, and deported. Kelso's horrific misadventures would earn him a minor place in history, a footnote to one of America's worst scandals—the Iran-Contra affair. His case would be cited by the congressional Iran-Contra committees as one example of how Lieutenant Colonel Oliver North of the National Security Council impeded law enforcement investigations to protect his illegal Contra supply operation from public exposure.

But the four paragraphs about Joe Kelso—buried deep inside the official Iran-Contra report—tell only a fraction of his story. How the former fireman from Golden Valley, Minnesota, happened to attract the stony gaze of Oliver North and his preppy CIA informant, Robert Owen, was never explained by the congressional committee. That omission bothered several Democratic members of the Iran-Contra panel—Congressmen Peter Rodino of New Jersey, Dante Fascell of Florida, Jack Brooks of Texas, and Louis Stokes of Ohio—who decided to write their own report on the matter of Joe Kelso. “The significance of the Kelso section…of the Committee report is not entirely clear from the facts as stated,” the congressmen complained in a little-read appendix to the final report. “In order to understand why

…d North were so concerned about Kelso, one must understand …at Kelso was doing and learning in Costa Rica."

What Kelso was doing, records show, was investigating allegations …t the same Costa Rican DEA agents watching over Norwin Meneses and Danilo Blandón were trafficking in drugs and funny money. What he was learning was just how hazardous investigating such matters could be.

Kelso, a would-be spy and inveterate thrill seeker, had been working as a CIA informant since the early 1980s, after he befriended a German-born arms dealer in Denver named Heinrich Rupp. Kelso said he was approached by a CIA agent who called himself Bill Chandler and asked to gather information about Rupp's activities. Rupp was selling arms to the Argentines during their short war with Great Britain over the Falkland Islands, and the CIA wanted to know what they were buying. At the CIA's suggestion, Kelso began working for Rupp, posing as a weapons broker seeking arms for Iraqi president Saddam Hussein. The agency figured it would draw some interesting people out of the woodwork, Kelso said, but the mission ended in a minor disaster. The tough-talking twenty-six-year-old was arrested by the U.S. Customs Service and charged with attempting to buy Harpoon missiles—big radar-guided cruise missiles designed to blow up ships—for the Iraqi government. Unbeknownst to Kelso, the men he had been negotiating missile deals with were undercover Customs investigators.

Kelso's arrest presented the CIA with a problem; the agency's charter prohibits it from spying on people inside the United States. To keep the operation under wraps, Kelso was advised by his CIA handlers to keep his mouth shut and plead guilty to the weapons charges, and they promised that his legal problems would go away.

Federal court records lend support to Kelso's story. Despite the severity of his crime—attempting to acquire cruise missiles for an unfriendly foreign government—Kelso was put on probation and promptly vanished. Supplied with a new identity and a matching passport, Kelso went back to work for the federal government, this time as an informant for the very agency that had just arrested him: the U.S. Customs Service. His control officer, Special Agent Larry LaDodge, registered him as an informant under the name of Richard Williams and sent him to Europe to hunt down a fugitive methamphetamine dealer who was wanted in the United States on "numerous, numerous charges," Kelso said.

Kelso followed the dealer's trail around Holland and England, and then LaDodge picked up word that the doper had a ranch in Costa Rica. In mid-1986, Kelso went to find it. He also had another mission to perform while there: "a standing directive" from the CIA to gather intellig about Robert Vesco, the millionaire swindler and fugitive who lived Havana and had been flitting through Costa Rica and Nicaragua durin the time of the Contra war, always managing to stay one step ahead of the law. Kelso found the methamphetamine dealer's ranch, but not its owner; he "had a house on the Mexican border, so he could hop back and forth between the U.S. border and the Mexican border to continue to conduct his narcotics business."

But Kelso continued his search for Vesco; he found the financier's private jet, he says, parked in a hangar in San José. When he checked to see who was paying the storage bills, he learned that it was the owners of a shrimp company called Frigorificos de Puntarenas—the cocaine-dealing CIA front that was helping Oliver North funnel U.S. government money to the Contras.

"A decision was being made up here in the United States whether we were going to put a satellite pinger on it or not," Kelso later testified, "and they chose not to, even though we had such direct access."

While on his Vesco hunt, Kelso started frequenting a bar in San José across from the headquarters of a right-wing political group known as Costa Rica Libre. To hear Kelso tell it, the watering hole was like something out of *Casablanca.* It was "where most of the upper echelon of Costa Rica Libre hang out," he testified in a videotaped deposition taken in 1988. "Now the oddity that we found was that the ETA [a left-wing guerrilla group] would hang out there and drink with them. M-19 [a Colombian terrorist group] was there. The German Mafia people were there. And it was just—they were drinking together, and having a good time like they were old buddies."

From the carousing crooks and mercenaries Kelso picked up word that "the [U.S.] Embassy was dirty and the Embassy, you know, had leaks…in the visa and passport section. Some 'Ticos'—or Costa Ricans—that were hired there had been manufacturing passports for a long time and selling visas." Kelso said he forwarded a report to the FBI, "and they turned around and shut the embassy down for 45 days…while they did a security check." Then Kelso began hearing rumors that DEA agent Robert Nieves, the country attaché and Norwin Meneses's control agent, had been taking cocaine from seizures made by the Costa Rican narcotics police. Kelso said the allegations were largely conjecture, but he confided them to Department of Defense officials stationed in Costa Rica. "They just shrugged their shoulders and said, 'Geez, he found out' and, you know, left it at that."

Kelso claimed that Agent LaDodge authorized him to pursue the allegations further. He snooped around Nieves and the other DEA agents working at the embassy for a couple months, enlisting the aid of a Canadian who worked as a U.S. Customs informant, Brian Caldwell. By the end of that summer of 1986, Kelso testified, he had "hard-core, documentable, bring-it-into-court information." Six witnesses—current and former Costa Rican and American government officials—were willing to testify that the DEA agents were skimming cocaine from drug seizures, making counterfeit money, sanitizing intelligence reports to Washington, and protecting cocaine processing labs in northern Costa Rica, including at least two on Contra bases, Kelso testified.

"What did they say to you was their direct knowledge of Mr. Nieves and his activities?" Kelso was asked during his deposition, which was taken by the Washington-based Christic Institute as part of a civil racketeering lawsuit it filed in 1986 against a variety of current and former government officials involved with the Contras.

"Well, they were all reverting back to direct involvement with narcotics smuggling and—if you want to use the word—protection in that situation. And that's the bottom line. I mean, it was all relative to that, with exact situations, exact information, documentation." The witnesses also told Kelso that the Contras were "involved in coke. And these were the people that also reiterated that these are 'bad' Contras. These particular Contras were, in fact, involved in narcotics, and were, in fact, involved in smuggling. Period."

One of Kelso's "witnesses" was Warren W. Treece, the deputy director of the Narcotics Department of the Costa Rican Ministry of Public Affairs. Treece, according to a 1989 Costa Rican prosecutor's report, had had a strange experience with one of Nieves's men, Sandy González—the DEA agent who'd yelled at L.A. detective Tom Gordon about the phone lines running through Nicaragua. "Information of the existence of a cocaine laboratory in the Nicoya peninsula and another one in Talamanca were transmitted by Treece to an official of the DEA with the surname of González, in Costa Rica, but they were not investigated on account of the leak of information from this agent," Costa Rican prosecutor Jorge Chavarria wrote. "As Treece and Kelso affirmed, that person was protecting those laboratories."

González and Nieves were never charged with a crime either in Costa Rica or the United States, and the allegations were never proven. In response to a Freedom of Information Act request, the DEA claimed it could find no records about Kelso or his investigation—rather unbelievably, considering that some DEA records concerning Kelso were made available to Iran-Contra investigators in 1987. The DEA would not allow González to be interviewed, and Nieves refused to answer any questions.

Costa Rican attorney Gloria Navas, a former prosecutor and judge who advises the Costa Rican Legislative Assembly on drug issues, strongly believes that the DEA agents stationed in Costa Rica during the Contra war were not what they appeared. "In my opinion, both Nieves and Sandy González were connected with the CIA. There is no doubt," insisted Navas. "You aren't going to find hard evidence because these were covert operations. But I did my own investigations and you can't come to any other conclusion." The DEA refused to release any records or answer any questions about the agents' backgrounds or their possible work for other government agencies.

"Sometimes the lines really got blurred when you were working for Oliver North," agreed former Iran-Contra Committee attorney Pam Naughton, who investigated the Justice Department's role in the scandal. "He was using DEA agents in Europe as CIA. I mean, they were doing activities that were way beyond the scope of the DEA. Those were clearly, clearly covert activities."

One of those double-duty DEA agents was James Kible, a Madrid-based agent who visited jailed Medellín cartel boss Jorge Ochoa in Spain in 1984 and attempted to persude him to publicly implicate the Sandinistas in drug trafficking. According to a 1987 story in *The Nation*, Kible "was one of a select group of DEA operatives who conducted secret missions for Oliver North and the National Security Council. On October 24, 1986, Kible and another DEA agent, Victor Oliveira, were apprehended by Spanish customs officials while boarding a plane for Switzerland at Madrid's Barajos Airport. In their possession was a briefcase filled with $5 million in cash. According to Spanish government officials quoted in *El Pais* of May 9, 1987, the money was destined for a bank account in Zurich controlled by North's contra-aid team. Some of the funds were intended as ransom to free American hostages in Lebanon."

At the time DEA agents Nieves and González were stationed in Costa Rica, the CIA station chief was Joe Fernández, a close friend and confidant of North who was later forced to resign from the CIA for his illegal involvement with the Contras. Fernández was indicted by Iran-Contra prosecutor Lawrence Walsh, but the charges were dropped on November 22, 1989, when the U.S. Attorney General, Richard Thornburgh, refused to declassify records needed in the trial, the first time in history that had ever happened.

Kelso said his witnesses claimed the CIA was involved in the operation of a drug lab at a Contra base near Quepos, Costa Rica. "So, it was my problem, or my duty, to go and respond back to the CIA that this allegation is—is that we got two CIA agents at Quepos at this laboratory participating in drug manufacturing, okay?" Kelso said. He said it was later determined that the men may have been part of North's resupply operation "and not, in fact, CIA personnel."

Kelso claimed to have obtained maps pinpointing the locations of thirty-two cocaine labs in Costa Rica and some personal papers of the DEA agents, including their radio code names—Jaguar 1, 2, and 3. A Customs agent familiar with the case said Kelso stole Agent Nieves's briefcase from his car. In an interview with the author Kelso denied this, but laughed while doing so.

At the end of July 1986, Kelso felt he had enough information about the DEA's activities to report his findings to his control agent, Larry LaDodge, and to the U.S. military's Southern Command headquarters in Panama "to the CIA officer there. It was hand-carried, on a microcassette." The allegations of counterfeiting were sent to the Secret Service.

William Rosenblatt, then head of enforcement for U.S. Customs, confirmed in a deposition that "Mr. LaDodge had received communications from one of these two gentlemen by telephone that they had uncovered a counterfeit operation in Costa Rica, and there was other information that the informants wanted to provide…but they did not feel comfortable doing it over the phone." That "other" information, Rosenblatt said in once-secret testimony to Congress, concerned "narcotics allegations relative to the Drug Enforcement Administration." Rosenblatt said the allegations were taken seriously in Washington: the Customs Service "coordinated with the Secret Service as well as our Customs attaché in Panama, who is responsible also for the country of Costa Rica. Arrangements were made for one of the New Orleans agents to travel through Miami down to Costa Rica to meet up with the informants and the Secret Service, so that we could provide firsthand information to the Secret Service about this alleged counterfeit money operation."

The New Orleans agent, Douglas Lee Knochenberger, met with Kelso and Caldwell in early August "ostensibly to debrief them and also to pay them the money that Mr. LaDodge felt was owed to them," Rosenblatt testified. "He did not check in with the Embassy. He immediately met with the informant, paid the informant and to some extent debriefed the informant."

According to the Iran-Contra committee minority report, Kelso and Caldwell "told Customs that the DEA agents in Costa Rica knew the location of drug laboratories and had been paid to conceal the location of narcotics." Kelso said he gave Knochenberger maps showing the locations of the drug labs, cassette tapes of interviews, and other documents. But Knochenberger—whom Kelso called a "newbie" and Rosenblatt termed "relatively inexperienced"—became nervous, insisting that he had to report the information to DEA attaché Nieves at the embassy.

Kelso couldn't believe his ears. "If we had this rumor and either qualified it or disqualified it, going and telling this person that you're doing research on him, qualifying it or disqualifying it, would be stupid," Kelso testified, "because if he is doing it, he would normally head over the hill or protect himself well enough that no one could touch him." Kelso said Knochenberger "had explicit orders not to say anything to Nieves…to keep his mouth shut, go in there, tell him he found nothing, that it was a waste of time, get back on the airplane immediately with all the documentation and get the hell out of town."

The agent's response, Kelso said, was: "'Wow, that's not State Department policy. I can't do that. I'm going to get in trouble.'" Knochenberger made a beeline for the U.S. embassy and spilled everything to the very DEA agents Kelso and Caldwell had just fingered.

"Both the Customs representative from our Panama office, as well as the Customs agent from LaDodge's office sat down with the DEA personnel [deleted] and related, summarized, however you want to, discussed what the informant had said, to include the allegations of corruption by DEA officials [deleted]," Rosenblatt confirmed.

Iran-Contra lawyer Pam Naughton, who was questioning Rosenblatt, was incredulous. "Did they do that on your instructions, or was that their own idea to tell the DEA about the allegations of corruption in their midst?" she asked.

"That was their idea," Rosenblatt insisted. "They didn't do that on my instructions. I didn't even know about this until after they came back." He agreed that "one may believe it is not prudent to tell the very same office what the allegations were…and relate those allegations to them," but pointed out that it was "part of the agreements that we have that we fill in DEA about narcotics information."

The next day, while Kelso and Brian Caldwell were lounging in their rooms at the Irazu Hotel in San José, the DEA called the Costa Rican national narcotics police and asked them to arrest the two foreigners on the grounds that they were impersonating narcotics agents. One of

Nieves's subordinates, Kelso said, "came stomping in there and demanding to see Caldwell and the stuff...and he saw a couple rolled up maps and he started yelling, you know, 'Are those some of those goddamned maps,' you know, 'floating around here?' And, 'We want those,' and started taking them." The DEA agent, accompanied by two Costa Rican national police agents, "started confiscating everything in the room, tried to do notebooks, things like that, my briefcase."

Kelso and Caldwell were hustled off to a construction warehouse owned by the Costa Rican electric company, where they were shoved around and interrogated about whom they were working for. When Kelso told of finding Robert Vesco's airplane, he said, the DEA agent became "extremely nervous...then he says, 'Get in the fucking car,' so we go in there and we go down to the OIJ [the Costa Rican national police] main office, right up to the director's office there."

Soon, Kelso said, DEA agent Nieves "comes in and he starts screaming, 'I'm going to blow your fucking ass away!' and 'You son-of-a-bitch!' and on and on and on...he's short-tempered anyway. I said, 'All you are is a motherfucking Puerto Rican.' And that—that's the key word that makes him trip off, okay? And I mean, he gets psychotic and just goes bananas."

According to Kelso, Nieves told him, "'You're a dead son-of-a-bitch.' You know? And he must have repeated, you know, 'We're going to blow your fucking head off!' about 50 times. You know? I mean, he was furious, absolutely out of control." Kelso's story was confirmed by Costa Rican police officials who were questioned during the Costa Rican government's investigation of the incident.

According to the Costa Rican paper *La Nacion*, which asked Nieves about Kelso in 1986, "Nieves did not disguise his anger about the fact that the U.S. Customs was investigating a matter that is a priority task for the DEA."

Kelso was taken to the U.S. embassy, where he said the DEA agents began copying the documents in his briefcase until "a person that I never saw before came in, sat down at one of the desks, very nice suit, well dressed, which later I learned, that's Rob Owen." What Kelso didn't know was that Rob Owen was the eyes and ears of both the CIA and Oliver North on the Southern Front. Kelso testified that after Owen got a look at the documents seized from the hotel room, he ordered the DEA agents to stop making copies, whisked Kelso out of the embassy, and dropped him back at his hotel.

Owen, in a deposition, admitted being in Costa Rica during August

1986, right around the time Kelso was abducted, but he denied meeting him.

Shaken, Kelso ran to Costa Rican narcotics investigator Warren Treece's house and hid out. The next day, he said, Nieves called him there and ordered him back to the embassy. Kelso refused, and Nieves told him he would be at Treece's house in five minutes.

"I said, 'Fuck you, try to find me,' and I slammed the phone down."

And then he ran for his life.

Treece and Alexander Z. McNulty, the chief of security for Costa Rican president Oscar Arias, took Kelso "up in the jungle" and dropped him off, and then returned to San José to pick up weapons and one of the presidential security cars.

Kelso said he had been instructed by his handlers to rendezvous at CIA operative John Hull's ranch if he got into trouble, because Hull had an airstrip where he could make a speedy getaway. In the dead of night, Treece and McNulty drove Kelso north to Hull's well-guarded compound and dropped him off with a dentist friend of Hull's, where he spent the night. The dentist drove Kelso onto Hull's ranch the next day.

Rob Owen later recounted the meeting in a deposition: "This guy [Kelso] came in and said, 'Look, I have been told that you are the one guy I should contact. There is a real problem here. I think the DEA people are trying to kill me. I am convinced that they were involved in narcotics trafficking and looking the other way. And I don't know who else to turn to.'"

Hull, in an interview, confirmed that. He wrote a report on Kelso's visit the next day, noting that Kelso claimed "[name deleted] of the U.S.A.-D.E.A. has maps of coke lab locations in Costa Rica but is protecting them. One large lab located in southern Nicoya. And another in Talamanca region."

While Kelso talked, Hull carefully examined the stranger's passport, which bore the name Richard Williams and "showed immigration stamps for several European and Mideast countries."

Though Kelso clearly seemed in fear for his life, Hull—who'd been accused repeatedly of facilitating Contra drug trafficking—was wary, thinking Kelso might have been sent by the Sandinistas to set him up on drug charges. "Not being known for wisdom or prudence, but having just heard that the USA-DEA team had checked in their white hats for black ones…I decided to call the local Rural Guard and the local DIS Dept. internal security," Hull wrote in his August 9, 1986, report of Kelso's visit. He put Kelso in his guest house, under guard, until he could figure out what to do with him.

About three in the morning, Kelso said, he was jolted out of bed by automatic rifle fire. Peering into the darkness, he saw a yard full of Costa Rican Rural Guards armed with AK-47 assault rifles and heard "this guy yelling something in Spanish." Kelso, wearing only his undershorts, was pulled out of the guest house and, at gunpoint, marched across the yard toward Hull's house.

Suddenly, Kelso felt his head explode. One of his captors bashed him from behind with the butt of his assault rifle, "and I reach up there and fucking draw blood, and I turned around and, you know, this guy's serious, you know?"

Kelso was pushed forward again, "and then halfway up, he hits me again and knocks me right down to the ground."

Hull watched the impromptu parade from his porch with growing concern. "It was a very, very obvious attempt to get him to resist so they could shoot him," he recalled. "This colonel came running up and pointing his finger at me, saying, 'The [U.S.] Embassy says he's extremely dangerous. It's better I kill him than he kill me.'"

According to the Costa Rican prosecutor's report, the embassy official who issued those dire warnings was DEA agent Nieves. Hull's report stated that the embassy told the Rural Guard colonel that Kelso "should be shot if he resisted arrest."

The Contras on Hull's ranch surrounded the Costa Rican intelligence agents who were beating Kelso, Hull said, and pulled out 12-gauge riot guns, which they leveled at the Costa Ricans. "All their guns were down and all the Contra guys were ready to pull the trigger," Kelso said. The Contras reminded Hull of "Alabama guard dogs that had been told to bite a black and couldn't decide which one."

Hull ran down and broke up the standoff, permitting the Rural Guard to take Kelso away. The woozy Customs informant was tossed into the back of an Isuzu Trooper and taken to a Rural Guard facility in San José, where, he said, he was thrown "into this little dog—well, it's, you know, a cell, but it's like a dog cage."

U.S. Ambassador Lewis Tambs asked the Costa Rican government to deport Kelso for using a false passport to enter the country, he said. After several hours in the cage, Kelso was put aboard the next plane out of the country.

Hull typed out a detailed letter on Kelso's visit and gave it to CIA informant Rob Owen, telling him to deliver it to Oliver North once he got back to Washington. Owen testified that "I went in to talk to North and gave him a copy of the letter and said, 'I am concerned because I don't know whether Hull is being set up, whether there is a problem with the DEA, or what is going on.'"

In his letter, Hull wrote North: "Since you are in Wash[ington] you might check these things out. If the DEA people are in the drug business it should be stopped."

Hull eventually came to believe Kelso was telling the truth about his investigation: "He was giving me locations of cocaine labs in Costa Rica and who they belonged to and then a week later one of them was busted and it was right where he said it was."

By the time Kelso arrived back in Denver, bells were ringing all over Washington. Customs enforcement chief Rosenblatt received a blistering cable from Ambassador Tambs, chewing him out for "having informants in Costa Rica without the Embassy knowing about it.... I apologized profusely that it happened and I assured him that these informants had not gone down there with our approval, and if they had, we would have definitely let the Embassy or the Ambassador know about it and all I was doing there for about 15 minutes was apologizing profusely, assuring them it wouldn't happen again."

Back in Denver, Kelso met with his lawyer, former federal prosecutor Rod Snow, and told him he feared for his safety. He asked Snow to hold onto the evidence he'd gathered in Costa Rica—tapes of interviews he'd done with U.S. intelligence agents and Costa Rican officials. Snow listened to them and called U.S. Attorney Bruce Black, urging him to do the same. But before he turned the tapes over, Snow wanted Black to promise that the tapes would not wind up in Washington because Kelso was afraid they would fall into the "wrong hands."

Black agreed, but the tapes ended up there anyway.

After listening to Kelso's tapes, Black called the special agent in charge of the Denver office of U.S. Customs, Gary Hilberry, and had him listen. Hilberry immediately phoned Washington, telling Rosenblatt that "based on the contents that he was very concerned, that one could almost make a case from these conversations, that there was some connection between Kelso and some member of the intelligence community," Rosenblatt testified. "I have known Gary Hilberry a very long time. He is now our special agent in charge of New York. He is not an alarmist...therefore, I called Colonel North."

Asked why he would call the National Security Council about a Customs agent's investigation of the DEA, Rosenblatt bluntly admitted that he was covering the Reagan administration's ass.

"My objective was to save any potential embarrassment to the government," he testified. "My main purpose was to find out whether Kelso/Williams was working with the intelligence community because of the tapes that Gary Hilberry had, and the potential for embarrassment."

Rosenblatt "went through the whole story with [North] from beginning to end. The Costa Rica business." He told North that Kelso had tapes to back up his charges "and was threatening to go to the media about his connection to the intelligence community." It was a threat to be reckoned with. As Rob Owen discovered after talking to Kelso's control agent, Larry LaDodge, Kelso really was who he claimed to be. "He validated the claim that Kelso was an asset," Owen testified. LaDodge told him that "Kelso said he was working for the CIA. He passed the polygraph. LaDodge started using him as an asset."

Customs official Rosenblatt testified that North knew all about the Kelso affair and didn't seem eager to talk about it over the phone. "He indicated he was extremely busy, but he was going to have Rob Owen call me.... It was clear to me that he wanted me to deal with Rob Owen on this matter." When Owen came around, Rosenblatt testified, he assumed the young man was on North's staff at the National Security Council. He told Owen about the tapes—which he numbered at "around six or seven"—and agreed to let Owen listen to them "and see if he recognized any voices...we were looking to use the NSC as a vehicle to determine whether or not the accusations made by Kelso/Williams were accurate."

Owen confirmed that he picked up the tapes from Customs in Washington and listened to some of them. The tapes he heard were of Customs agents debriefing Kelso's chief informant, Warren Treece, Owen said. "There was some thought that, at least according to Mr. Treece, that the Drug Enforcement Administration officials may have been on the take," he remembered. "There had been accusations made about Drug Enforcement Agency officials being involved in receiving funds to look the other way regarding narcotics trafficking in Costa Rica."

Rosenblatt said he washed his hands of the matter after he turned the tapes over to Owen, and he never heard another word about it. "I assumed that by not hearing from Owen or Colonel North, they were not coming up with anything positive," he said.

The congressmen on the Iran-Contra panel were stunned by Rosenblatt's actions. "He gave his only copy of tape recordings made by an undercover source to a total stranger," the congressmen complained. "Owen did not tell Rosenblatt he worked for North or the CIA. He told him he worked for a private organization. Not surprisingly, Owen never returned the tape recordings. Instead, he made two trips to Costa Rica to meet with the DEA agents."

Owen said his last trip to Costa Rica to meet the DEA agents occurred in October 1986. Within a day or two of the Iran-Contra scandal breaking, Owen threw the Kelso tapes away. "They were thrown out, along with a bunch of other stuff, when I moved," he testified. They were never seen again.

When the Iran-Contra committees heard about the Kelso investigation, they asked the DEA to provide them with the records of the case. "It was like pulling teeth out of Justice to get any cooperation, and we finally had to threaten everything imaginable to get to these documents," Iran-Contra committee attorney Naughton said. "Finally they caved in. And we had to go over to Justice to look at them in their secure area, on the sixth floor or wherever it is, and it reminded me of *Get Smart*—remember all those doors you had to go through? That's how it was. We finally get to the situation room and they had turned down the heat to about 30 degrees so that we wouldn't stay long. So they said, 'Here are the documents'—and they're all in Spanish."

Naughton said that, to her knowledge, the DEA never investigated the drug trafficking allegations against the Costa Rican agents. DEA director Jack Lawn told Congress in 1987 he'd never heard of the case. The U.S. Customs Service also quit looking. Customs agent Hilberry said the DEA allegations were "turned over to the DEA."

Two Costa Rican intelligence officers were eventually charged with illegally arresting Kelso, but the only American agent to go to jail as a result of the investigation was Joe Kelso. In January 1987 he was charged with violating his probation on his 1983 weapons charge—by being in Costa Rica—even though the Customs Service had been sending him all over the world for four years.

During Kelso's probation hearing both Snow and U.S. Attorney Bruce Black vouched for his credibility. "Some of what he said has totally checked out to the best of my ability to corroborate it, but some is inherently unverifiable," Black told U.S. District Judge Sherman Finesilver. He confirmed that "Kelso worked around the world under another name for several U.S. Customs Service operations."

Argued Snow: "By his belief, and quite frankly mine, he is working for the government. I believe and the U.S. Attorney believes there is a fairly high percentage of truth to what he is saying."

But Judge Finesilver wasn't interested. He ordered Kelso to prison for two years for violating his probation, "and didn't discuss the matter further," a newspaper report stated.

Kelso served his time quietly at Pleasanton federal prison camp in California and later became involved in a short-lived attempt to help an Italian financier buy MGM studios in Hollywood.

The target of Kelso's investigation, DEA agent Robert Nieves, went on to have a long and illustrious career at the DEA, rising to great heights. He became head of cocaine investigations in Washington, then chief of major investigations, and at the time of his retirement in late 1995, he was serving as chief of the DEA's International Division. After his retirement, Nieves went to work for a body armor manufacturing company in Virginia—Guardian Technologies. That company is owned by Oliver North, and the CIA's former chief of station in Costa Rica, Joe Fernández.

18

“We bust our ass and the government’s involved”

On the morning of October 23, 1986, Sergeant Tom Gordon did precisely what Costa Rican DEA agent Sandy González had told him not to do: he drove down to L.A. County Municipal Court, went before a judge, and applied for a warrant to search the Nicaraguans’ drug operation. His twenty-one-page sworn statement described a “large scale cocaine distributing organization” made up of “well over 100 persons storing, transporting and distributing cocaine for Danilo Blandón.”

Gordon linked up Blandón with Freeway Rick’s first major drug supplier, Ivan Arguellas, exposing the Contra drug pipeline into South Central. Blandón, he wrote, “has up to 20 kilos of cocaine per week delivered to Arguellas who, in turn, sells mainly to blacks living in the south central Los Angeles area.” Another South Central distribution point was a bar at Central Avenue and Adams Street, which Blandón uses “to distribute as much as 10 kilos of cocaine per week,” the affidavit said.

And the detective didn’t pull any punches when it came to the Contras. “Danilo Blandón is from Nicaragua, a Central American country which has been at civil war for several years,” Gordon wrote. “One side of this civil war is the ‘Contra army.’ Inf[ormant] #2 stated to your affiant that Blandón is a ‘Contra’ sympathizer and a founder of the ‘Fronte [sic] Democratica Nicaragua’ [FDN] an organization that assists the Contra movement with arms and money. The money and arms generated by this organization comes through the sale of cocaine."

Gordon listed more than a dozen locations across southern California where Blandón and his cohorts were storing drugs and cash. He traced the money trail from Los Angeles across the country, writing that the "monies gained from the sales of cocaine are transported to Florida and laundered thru Orlando Murillo who is a high ranking officer of a chain of banks in Florida named Government Securities Corporation. From this bank the monies are filtered to the Contra rebels to buy arms in the war in Nicaragua."

Gordon's sworn statement would prove to be a remarkably accurate portrait of the drug ring. A decade later Blandón would admit under oath that he was one of the founders of the FDN, and that nearly all of the people and locations Gordon named in his warrant were part of his drug operation. Blandón would also admit sending money to Orlando Murillo, who did, in fact, work for Government Securities Corporation, a chain of securities brokerages in southern Florida that went belly-up in 1987 amid federal allegations of fraud. The one accusation Blandón denied was that his father—Julio Blandón, the ex-slumlord—stored cocaine in his San Gabriel apartment.

Gordon's affidavit was pure political dynamite. At the time, the Contras were the hottest story in the country. Less than three weeks earlier, drug smuggler Barry Seal's old C-123K cargo plane had been shot out of the sky over Nicaragua, carrying a full load of weapons. Since then, new revelations about illegal U.S. goverment involvement in the Contra war had been appearing in the media almost daily. The White House, the State Department, and the CIA had immediately denied that the cargo plane—which was part of Oliver North's resupply operation—had any connections to the government, but those lies began unraveling the moment Sandinista patrols got back from the site of the smoldering wreck.

"The Sandinistas announced that the flight crew had not been flying with what we call in the business 'clean pockets,'" said Alan Fiers, the CIA officer then in charge of the Contra program. "They had all sorts of pocket litter that identified and connected them back to Ilopango. They had the cards of some of the NHAO—one particular NHAO employee, flight logs, essentially enough information so that the Sandinistas could put together, and did in fact, a lot of information relative to the connections of that flight."

If that wasn't enough, the Sandinistas also had one slightly batte cargo kicker named Eugene Hasenfus, the only crew member carrying parachute. Hasenfus, who'd worked for the CIA's Air America airline during the agency's secret war in Laos, told the press that he was again working for the CIA—at a time when the agency was allegedly not involved with the Contras. Hasenfus identified his CIA handlers as Ramon Medina, the alias of the Cuban terrorist and suspected drug trafficker Luis Posada Carriles, and Max Gómez, an alias of former CIA agent Felix Rodriguez. Hasenfus also exposed the secret Contra air base at Ilopango.

Aside from the legal problems Hasenfus presented for the administration, he was an even bigger political headache—living proof that the CIA and the White House had been lying about U.S. involvement with the Contras. The burgeoning scandal threatened to derail the administration's hard-fought efforts to win congressional approval for $100 million the CIA needed to restart the Contra war.

When the cargo plane went down, the new aid bill was in the final stages of passage through Congress. Reagan administration officials scrambled to keep a lid on the incident, sending out false press advisories, booking administration spokesmen on political talk shows to spread the official line, and sending CIA officials to Capitol Hill to give false testimony to bewildered congressional committees. The disinformation campaign, combined with a strange reluctance by the congressional intelligence committees to delve too deeply into the matter, worked long enough to get the $100 million aid bill through Congress.

But now, with the legislation sitting on Reagan's desk awaiting his signature, a respected Los Angeles narcotics detective was formally accusing the Contras in court of raising money by selling cocaine to black Americans. It is not difficult to imagine what would have happened to the Contra project had that information gotten out. Unlike the earlier allegations of Contra drug dealing that had appeared sporadically in the press over the past ten months, Gordon's charges would not be easy for the law-and-order Reagan administration to dismiss as the fantasies of a Sandinista sympathizer or a convicted drug dealer. This time, the accusations were coming from the police—under oath—in black and white.

Gordon's affidavit was persuasive enough for Municipal Court Judge Glenette Blackwell. She gave the detective his search warrant.

The next day, October 24, Gordon conducted a lengthy preraid briefing at the sheriff's training center, handing out raid plans, briefing klets, raid assignments, and radio frequencies, and locating command centers.

As drug raids went, this was going to be a big one. "On Monday, October 27, 1986, a 30 day investigation will culminate by executing a search warrant that will be served at fourteen locations in Los Angeles, Orange and San Bernardino Counties," the briefing book stated. It would involve more than forty-five agents from the Majors, the DEA, the IRS, the ATF, the San Bernardino County sheriff, and Bell police. Gordon split the officers into seven groups, each responsible for searching two locations.

Gordon's briefing left no doubts about who and what the police were up against: "The investigation centers around a male Nicaraguan named Danilo Blandón. The Blandón organization is believed to be moving hundreds of kilos of cocaine a month in the Southern California area and the money is laundered through a variety of business fronts and then sent to Florida where the money goes toward the purchase of arms to aid the 'Contra' rebels fighting the civil war in Nicaragua."

Gordon also mentioned that the drug ring involved a crooked ex-cop from Laguna Beach, Ronald Lister, who was known to have access to large quantities of heavy weapons. He was to be considered extremely dangerous.

Several of the officers in attendance distinctly recalled being warned that the federal government was unhappy that the Majors were going ahead with the raids. Deputy William Wolfbrandt said Gordon reported that he had "been contacted by someone from the government who told him not to do the warrant.... I thought it was pretty bitchin' just going out and doing it anyhow."

Lieutenant Mike Fossey, the Majors' intelligence officer, said it "was before the warrant [was served] that we were forewarned that there may be a CIA link"; information had "filtered down" that the "CIA and the Contras were dealing in arms and cocaine for Nicaragua."

According to Deputy Virgil Bartlett, the general belief among the police that day was that "the U.S. government backed the operation.... The government was bringing drugs into the country and shipping weapons back out." Bartlett said he was informed that Ronald Lister "had done jobs for the federal government, and we weren't so sure he hadn't done hits for them." (No evidence has surfaced linking Lister to murder.)

Jerry Guzzetta, who was assigned to search Blandón's mountain cabin near Big Bear ski resort, glanced around the briefing room to see which federal agents were there. To his surprise, they were not the ones he'd been working with during the investigation. Guzzetta thought it "st that federal agents from the Riverside DEA and FBI offices initi worked with the L.A. Sheriff's Narcotics investigators on the Blando case, but Los Angeles DEA and FBI agents were present at the briefing and later during the warrant execution."

Around 7:00 A.M. on Monday, October 27, the raid teams gathered at their designated staging areas, taking their last few gulps of coffee and strapping on their bulletproof raid vests. As they methodically went through their final preparations, coincidentally, another kind of ritual was unfolding back in Washington.

That day Ronald Reagan would triumphantly sign his name to the bill authorizing the CIA to spend $100 million on the Contras. It was now official. After a two-year absence, the CIA was back in the Contra business.

As Danilo Blandón's neighbors stepped onto their porches to retrieve that morning's edition of the *L.A. Times*—the front page was headlined "Contras Seek Quick Results on Two Fronts"—four big cars roared up to Blandón's elegant home and disgorged eleven heavily armed men wearing flak jackets. They quickly surrounded the house and banged on the front door, hollering that they had a warrant. "We'd certainly never seen the likes of it," one elderly neighbor said. "It was the talk of the neighborhood for quite some time, I can tell you. And they seemed like such a nice family. They had a maid, and the two little girls were so cute."

Chepita Blandón, wearing a pink housecoat, sleepily opened the door, and Deputy Dan Garner of Majors II thrust Gordon's warrant in her face. The raid team shouldered her aside and fanned out through the two-story house, emptying drawers and closets. Blandón, wearing a pair of green shorts and a brown shirt, stood silently by his ten-year-old daughter and watched the agents rummage around. The maid, Rosa Garcia, cuddled the Blandóns' twenty-one-month-old daughter.

Jerry Guzzetta brought in a drug-sniffing dog, and the hound alerted in the master bedroom and the rec room. A search of the bedroom turned up an envelope with a gram of cocaine in it, a maroon briefcase with three-tenths of a gram of cocaine inside, an AR-15 assault rifle with five full magazines of ammunition, a Mossberg 12-gauge shotgun with three boxes of shells, $163, and some assorted papers.

Out in the detached recreation room, which had a full bar and pool table overlooking the golf course, Deputy Wolfbrandt found an envelope behind the bar with a folded $10 bill inside; the bill held one and a half s of cocaine. He also found "pay-owe" sheets—records of drug trans-ons.

It wasn't much, but a couple grams of coke and some pay-owes were all the detectives needed to justify an arrest for possession for sale of a controlled substance. They slapped handcuffs on both Blandón and his wife, read them their rights, and marched them out to the waiting cars for a trip to the San Bernardino County Sheriff's station—and jail.

"As the suspects were being taken from the location to be booked," the police report said, "suspect #1 [Danilo Blandón] spontaneously stated, 'The cocaine is mine. The cocaine is mine. It's mine.'"

Now the cops had a confession to go with the coke. The drug kingpin was as good as convicted.

Across town, however, the other raid teams were not doing as well. Location after location was coming up dry. Some of the houses looked as if they had been scrubbed clean. One officer reported finding an empty safe with a garden hose running into it. Another said an occupant told him he'd been expecting him for an hour.

The word started circulating among the raiders. Something was fucked. "We're just going through the motions," one of the officers griped.

Down the coast in Orange County, Detective Bobby Juarez and his team were banging on Ronald Lister's door in Mission Viejo. Receiving no reply, they kicked it open. The house was uninhabited, but it wasn't empty. The detectives came out carrying bags of records, card files, video monitors, and photographs, which they tossed in a patrol car. A neighbor wandered over and told them that the Listers didn't live there anymore. They'd moved recently to an even bigger house a couple miles away. "Male and female Latins were now living at the Lagarto address," the neighbor reported. Some of the seized paperwork showed the neighbor was right: there were letters, video rental receipts, and bank records for someone named Aparicio Moreno and his wife, Aura.

The discovery of those documents corroborated another accusation that the DEA informant inside Blandón's ring had made: that Aparicio Moreno, a Colombian, was involved in the Contra drug operation. The informant described Moreno as a cocaine supplier and money launderer to both Norwin Meneses's San Francisco–based branch and Blandón's network in L.A., and said Moreno, his wife, and his family had hauled millions in drug profits to Miami for the two Nicaraguans, hidden in an innocuous-looking motor home.

Blandón would later admit that Moreno had supplied him with "so many" thousands of kilos of cocaine in 1984 and 1985 that he cou put an exact number on them. He said he was introduced to Moreno Norwin Meneses and worked with the Colombian until 1987. It is likel that Meneses turned Blandón over to Moreno when Meneses moved to Costa Rica to work as a DEA informant. Ronald Lister would tell police in 1996 that Moreno was "affiliated with [the] FDN," and Blandón strongly suggested the same thing during his interviews with the CIA Inspector General's Office.

Blandón claimed that Moreno arranged "at least one 1-ton delivery that was delivered by air via Oklahoma," a summary of his CIA interview states. Blandón said "he and his associates thought the plane might be connected with the CIA because someone had placed a small FDN sticker somewhere on the airplane. This was just a rumor though."

It was a rumor that the CIA Inspector General apparently never bothered investigating, as there is no further mention of Aparicio Moreno in the entire declassified report. But considering what else is known about the mysterious Colombian, the omission is not surprising. Moreno had an affinity for dealing dope to people with CIA connections.

Records show DEA agent Celerino Castillo III ran across Aparicio Moreno's trail in Guatemala in 1988 while investigating allegations of drug trafficking by a Guatemalan CIA agent, Julio Roberto Alpirez. A high-ranking officer in the Guatemalan military and a fixture on the CIA's payroll there, Colonel Alpirez was accused by the president's Foreign Intelligence Oversight Board in 1996 of covering up the murder of an American innkeeper in Guatemala, Michael Devine.

Castillo said he discovered that Aparicio Moreno was both supplying Colonel Alpirez with cocaine and selling drugs for Alpirez that had been seized by the Guatemalan military. Castillo believes Devine was killed by Guatemalan soldiers after he had discovered that the military was moving cocaine, a theory that has never been proven.

DEA files obtained under the Freedom of Information Act confirmed that Castillo reported Moreno's activities in Guatemala to the DEA, but the agency censored all of the information in his reports. From the records, it appears Moreno was also working as a DEA informant, in addition to his other activities.

After securing Moreno's residence, Juarez and his crew raced over to Lister's new house and performed a "soft knock." Since they didn't have a warrant for that address, they needed Lister's permission to search it. A rumpled man in a bathrobe opened the door and stood there calmly while Juarez explained the facts of life to him. "If you don't give me permission me in, I'm going to stand out here with these guys until a judge signs nd then we're going to come later on today," Lister said Juarez told him. So that's your choice. What's it gonna be?" Lister said he was living in "a nice community" and didn't like the idea of heavily armed officers hanging around in public view, so he invited them in.

According to Juarez, he told Lister they were executing a search warrant for drugs and asked him to sign a consent form. Lister's response brought the deputy up short.

"I *know* why you're here," Lister told him, "but why are you here? Mr. Weekly knows what I'm doing and you're not supposed to be here." Lister "told me that he had dealings in South America and worked with the CIA and added that his friends in Washington weren't going to like what was going on," Juarez's report of the search stated. "I told Mr. Lester [sic] that we were not interested in his business in South America. Mr. Lester replied that he would call Mr. Weekly of the CIA and report me."

Juarez decided to call Lister's bluff. "I don't know who Mr. Weekly is," the detective told Lister. "Let me talk to him. If I find out I'm not supposed to be here, I'll leave."

Juarez silently urged Lister to make the call so "I could get a phone record trace and find out who it was he was calling." Lister walked over to the phone and started dialing a number. "He looked at me, smiled, and then put it back down again," Juarez said. "He figured out what I was doing."

"Never mind," Lister told the deputy. "I'll talk to him later."

Lister claimed later he was planning to call his attorney and decided not to antagonize Juarez by doing so. He denied telling anyone he was working with the CIA, but other members of the raid team had very different recollections.

Sergeant Art Fransen said Lister erupted in a "tirade" and began shouting, "You guys don't know what you are doing. Oh, you don't know who you're dealing with. I deal with the CIA. I got power!"

Deputy Richard Love said Lister warned them, "You don't know what you're doing. There's a bigger picture here. I'm working for the CIA. I know the director of the CIA in Los Angeles. The government is allowing drug sales to go on in the United States." Love said Lister also "seemed to have some intimate details about a plane loaded with guns that crashed in Nicaragua and about the pilot. Lister alluded to the fact that he had been on one of those planes before and had actually been down there on a gun run."

Sergeant Fransen, an ex-Marine, poked around in a file cabinet in

Lister's garage and said he found "stuff that a civilian shouldn't ... be privy to...paperwork, pamphlets and manuals relating to tech... stuff concerning armaments."

Lister would later say that the cops may have gotten the wrong idea about him because he "was involved in legal arms sales. The deputies saw various weapons, scopes, pictures, literature or paperwork on arms and items that were tagged 'Not for Sale in U.S.'" In Lister's account, members of the raid team "became fascinated with what they found," and Sergeant Fransen walked by him later and muttered, "Man, you've gotta be CIA."

No drugs were found, and Lister was not arrested. The raiders packed up the paperwork and hauled it back down to the sheriff's station, where it was logged into the Master Narcotics Evidence Control ledger as "miscellaneous CIA info." Another report noted that there was "a lot of Contra rebel correspondence found."

As the raid teams straggled back to the sheriff's headquarters throughout the morning and early afternoon, the deputies compared notes and concluded that they'd been had. Someone had burned their warrant—and their suspicions immediately fell on the federal agents.

"After the search warrants had been served, the word among the investigators was that the operation had been compromised," said former Lieutenant Mike Fossey. "It appeared to have been snitched off by somebody in another agency, which is probably not a local agency, but probably an agency back towards the east, a big agency, a government agency."

Guzzetta was convinced federal agents had burned the investigation, pointing out that previous raids they'd conducted on the basis of the Torres brothers' information had always produced large amounts of cocaine and money. The only difference between those raids and Blandón's, he said, was the involvement of the FBI and DEA.

Deputy Love said it "was mutually agreed upon between narcotics investigators that the suspects had been tipped off."

In a case chronology prepared in late 1986, Majors II supervisor Sergeant Ed Huffman noted that "items seized (such as scales, weights, cocaine cutting agents) indicate cocaine activity. The small amount of cocaine (approx. 3 grams) seized is in contrast to the investigation indicators (informant's information, surveillance observations, background information). Did a burn occur? Possible, but can't say where or by who."

The Torres brothers would claim that the investigation was uncovered by Lister, who'd spotted police surveillance teams outside of Blandón's car lot and near his old house in Mission Viejo. Lister told the and the CIA the same story and said he informed Blandón about o weeks before the raids. "Lister states that Blandón simply smiled, did not comment," a 1998 CIA report states.

However, Assistant U.S. Attorney L. J. O'Neale, who investigated Lister and Blandón for several years, said the sheriff's probe was compromised by an FBI agent who did "a clumsy investigation and contacted somebody who knew Blandón and this person told Blandón about the inquiry." In an interview with the CIA, Blandón said he "suspected there would be searches after FBI agents interviewed one of his employees."

O'Neale said Blandón had specifically denied Lister tipped him off; Lister never told him anything about spotting police surveillance until "after the search warrant was served."

The deputies' suspicions of federal interference grew even stronger once they began examining the stacks of papers they'd hauled out of the houses. These people weren't just dope dealers, they realized. They were dope dealers who were dealing with the Contras and, apparently, the U.S. government. Deputy Bartlett recalled seeing photos of Lister in a Contra military compound "standing with a general, and in the background were tents, munitions and automatic weapons." He also saw "U.S. Army training manuals and videotapes concerning deployment, supply, ordnance and bomb disposal," telephone records showing calls to Nicaragua, letters bearing Nicaraguan postmarks, and "possibly one document…which had an FBI letterhead."

"Some of the paperwork contained what he recognized from his military career as Department of Defense codes," according to Deputy John Hurtado. Other papers, Hurtado told police investigators, "contained some type of reference to the Central Intelligence Agency. Hurtado believed some of the papers had 'CIA' handwritten or typed on them. He also recalled a note pad was written in what he described as some type of Department of Defense code." When Hurtado questioned raid leader Tom Gordon, Gordon told him "they had gotten involved in something over their heads."

Deputy Dan Garner saw handwritten lists of weapons—specifically AR-15 assault rifles—and papers that involved "transporting weapons from one location to another." He also recalled "that there were manuals on various weapons, military training films, and photographs of military bases…the manuals and films seemed to have been standard U.S. government military issue." Garner said that they involved "higher-tech equipment such as ground-to-air missiles," and that it was "unusual to have recovered these items in a search warrant."

Deputy Juarez described some of the paperwork as containing "r ences about Mr. Weekly and his contacts in Teheran relating to hostages." He saw "training manuals and training films for state of the ar weapons—Stinger missiles, tanks, and other armored vehicles."

Observed Lieutenant Fossey: "If it was just arms they were talking about on that paperwork, it's still interesting that we had a drug investigation going here."

The documents partly solved one of the day's mysteries—the identity of Lister's purported CIA contact, Mr. Weekly. Weekly's name was found in a sheaf of handwritten papers dealing with weapons and equipment sales. The documents included a list of armaments: antiaircraft weapons, fire bombs, 1,000 AR-15 semiautomatic rifles, air-to-sea torpedos, and napalm bombs.

The next page bore a list of names and phone numbers. Near the name "Aparicio," Lister had written: "FDN coordinator." Another list of names included Bill Nelson, the CIA's former deputy director of operations; Salvadoran politicians Roberto D'Aubuisson and Ray Prendes; and someone named Scott Weekly.

In another document, Lister had written, "I had regular meeting with DIA subcontractor Scott Weekly. Scott had worked in El Salvador for us. Meeting concern my relationship with Contra grp. in Cent. Am." (The DIA—Defense Intelligence Agency—is the Pentagon's version of the CIA, responsible for collecting military-related foreign intelligence. It was heavily involved in the Contra war and in the civil war in El Salvador.)

Lister wrote that he had consulted Weekly about buying a scrambler system, and Weekly "said he could get one for me to sell if I had a customer. Want $10,000 for it, as he had to share cost with someone in DIA. He had used this system himself and thought it was very good."

The detectives were confused. DIA? Hadn't Lister said Weekly was with the CIA? What the hell was the DIA? When the detectives read the confidential security proposal that Lister's Pyramid International security company made to the government of El Salvador in 1982, they knew they were in unfamiliar territory. They'd never run into drug dealers who did business with heads of state.

Detective Juarez, who also translated the bulky document from Spanish to English for the flabbergasted detectives, said he became concerned that the records "would not remain in evidence for very long because of their sensitive subject matter." He made a copy of the Pyramid International proposal and took it home with him. That decision, Juarez suspects, probably cost his brother-in-law, Manuel Gómez, a 32-year-old doran jeweler, his life. Juarez told the author that in 1993 he gave mez a copy of Lister's security proposal. His brother-in-law sympa-nized with the leftist rebels in El Salvador and was active in the Salvadoran solidarity movement in Los Angeles. Gómez was going to get the documents to an underground radio station in El Salvador in hopes of publicizing this example of the U.S. government's unsavory involvement in Salvadoran internal affairs.

"Two weeks after the document made its way to the underground radio station in February 1993, Manuel Gómez was found murdered in his car," Juarez told police investigators. He said Gómez "had apparently been tortured and strangled with a wire. His body was found wrapped in a blanket." When the police checked out Juarez's claims, they found that Manuel Gómez had indeed been strangled in 1993, his body dumped in the trunk of a car in South Central L.A. They also found a note in the homicide case files reporting that Deputy Juarez had called the police five days after the murder to tell them that his brother-in-law "had government documents in his possession that may have provided a motive for the murder." But the homicide investigators decided politics had little to do with the killing. After picking up rumors that Gómez was dealing drugs in South Central, they wrote the death off as drug-related and didn't pursue it much further. The killer was never apprehended.

Juarez sat down at a computer terminal and entered Ronald Lister's name into the NIN (Narcotics Information Network) database to make sure that any other narcotics agents who encountered him knew what they were dealing with. He reported that Lister had been searched in connection with a narcotics investigation, "and locations were cleaned out. Documents recovered indicate that Suspect Lister is involved in buying and selling police and government radio equipment and heavy duty weapons. Suspect possibly FBI informant and private detective."

Other deputies also began furtively copying some of Lister's papers. Deputy Garner grabbed a handful of records, including Lister's handwritten notes, as did Lieutenant Fossey. Fossey and Garner took the copies home with them "to safeguard them from loss or theft," Fossey explained. It would prove to be a wise precaution.

A few hours after the raids, Blandón's lawyer, Bradley Brunon, called the sheriff's station to ask where his clients were and how he could bail them out. He said Tom Gordon answered the phone and tore him a new asshole.

"He was a vile, vicious son of a bitch," Brunon recalled. He said G screamed, "I'm not telling you anything! You're worse than they are!"

"'Fuck,' I said, 'I just called up to find out where you're going arraign the guy.'

"'Fuck you! I don't have to tell you!' I mean just, boom, off the wall."

So Brunon called Gordon's supervisor, Sergeant Ed Huffman. Huffman took notes of the odd conversation, which he later passed along to the FBI. Huffman had suspected all along that there was something creepy about the Blandón case, and the phone call from Brunon clinched it. "Thought you knew CIA kinda winks at that activity," Brunon told the astonished detective. "Now that U.S. Congress had voted funds for Nicaraguan Contra movement, U.S. government now appears to be turning against organizations like this."

In an interview, Brunon confirmed that as "not far from what I said."

According to former narcotics bureau captain Robert Wilber, Sergeant Huffman came to see him afterward and sourly remarked, "We bust our ass and the government's involved." The deputies "were upset about the incident," Wilber said, but he didn't take it too seriously because he thought they were using it as an excuse not to work with federal agents again.

If the Majors needed any more excuses, they got another one quickly enough. According to Deputy Bartlett, "Two federal agents came into the office looking angry. With the agents were a 'zone' lieutenant and the Narcotics Bureau admin lieutenant, both of whom also appeared angry.... The agents put some of the evidence into boxes and then walked out of the office." Sergeant Huffman's daily diaries and other records recently found in the Sheriff's Office's archives confirm that agents from the DEA, FBI, and IRS arrived at the narcotics bureau on October 30 and for two days pored through the seized files, making copies of everything.

Later that night, a cable from the CIA's Los Angeles office marked "Immediate Director" buzzed out of the teletype machine at CIA headquarters in Langley, Virginia. Entitled "Three Persons Claiming CIA Affiliation," the once-secret cable stated, "Three individuals claiming CIA affiliation have been arrested by Los Angeles County Sheriff's Department on narcotics related charges. Details received via FBI are sketchy. However, request preliminary traces to determine if any of the three listed below have CIA connections." The first person named was Ronald Lister, who "claims that for many years he has assisted in supplying small arms and helicopters to CIA contacts in Latin and Central

...ca." The cable also named Danilo Blandón, identified as an accom-... of Lister. Curiously, it also asked for a trace on Norwin Meneses, who ...s identified as another accomplice of Lister's. Why the Los Angeles CIA was asking about Meneses in connection with the Blandón raid is unclear, since he was neither arrested, named in the search warrant affidavit, nor even living in the United States.

"Please respond immediate indicating what portions of response may be passed to local law enforcement authorities," the cable concluded. Langley cabled back the next day; there were no headquarters traces on Blandón and Lister, but Meneses was "apparently well known as the Nicaraguan Mafia, dealing in drugs, weapons, and smuggling and laundering of counterfeit money." What happened next is still a matter of dispute.

After the raids, Sergeant Gordon and Deputy Juarez said they took a couple of days off. When they returned to work, Gordon said, he was told by deputy Dan Garner that the CIA had come into the offices and taken the records the Majors had seized during the raid. Gordon didn't believe it and went to the evidence room to check.

The papers were no longer there.

According to Garner, Gordon walked back into the squad room and announced, "The evidence is gone." Juarez said he ran over to the evidence lockup and confirmed what Gordon was saying. Nothing was left. Both Juarez and Gordon claimed they never saw the documents again.

In addition to the seized documents, said Blandón's attorney, Brad Brunon, the official police records of the raid seemed to disappear also. Despite his best efforts, he was unable to come up with more than an informal note about the preraid briefing, and that only by accident a couple years after the raid. "For a long time, they (the Sheriff's Office) never acknowledged the existence of this warrant. I mean the whole thing was quite mysterious. Boom, they did 15 locations. Nothing turned up. Nobody got busted. There was a little tiny bit of cocaine found in one location. Nobody got filed on. They gave all the stuff back. The whole thing just was very strange," Brunon said. "I'd never had a case where all the reports disappeared. I mean, early on, the only theory I had was the CIA involvement."

An investigation by the L.A. County Sheriff's Office in late 1996 strongly disputed the idea that "mysterious federal agents swooped down…and stole away with any documents relating to this case. Investigators have determined that this allegation was apparently spread through second-hand rumor and innuendo among some members of the

"He was a vile, vicious son of a bitch," Brunon recalled. He said Gordon screamed, "I'm not telling you anything! You're worse than they are!"

"'Fuck,' I said, 'I just called up to find out where you're going to arraign the guy.'

"'Fuck you! I don't have to tell you!' I mean just, boom, off the wall."

So Brunon called Gordon's supervisor, Sergeant Ed Huffman. Huffman took notes of the odd conversation, which he later passed along to the FBI. Huffman had suspected all along that there was something creepy about the Blandón case, and the phone call from Brunon clinched it. "Thought you knew CIA kinda winks at that activity," Brunon told the astonished detective. "Now that U.S. Congress had voted funds for Nicaraguan Contra movement, U.S. government now appears to be turning against organizations like this."

In an interview, Brunon confirmed that as "not far from what I said."

According to former narcotics bureau captain Robert Wilber, Sergeant Huffman came to see him afterward and sourly remarked, "We bust our ass and the government's involved." The deputies "were upset about the incident," Wilber said, but he didn't take it too seriously because he thought they were using it as an excuse not to work with federal agents again.

If the Majors needed any more excuses, they got another one quickly enough. According to Deputy Bartlett, "Two federal agents came into the office looking angry. With the agents were a 'zone' lieutenant and the Narcotics Bureau admin lieutenant, both of whom also appeared angry.... The agents put some of the evidence into boxes and then walked out of the office." Sergeant Huffman's daily diaries and other records recently found in the Sheriff's Office's archives confirm that agents from the DEA, FBI, and IRS arrived at the narcotics bureau on October 30 and for two days pored through the seized files, making copies of everything.

Later that night, a cable from the CIA's Los Angeles office marked "Immediate Director" buzzed out of the teletype machine at CIA headquarters in Langley, Virginia. Entitled "Three Persons Claiming CIA Affiliation," the once-secret cable stated, "Three individuals claiming CIA affiliation have been arrested by Los Angeles County Sheriff's Department on narcotics related charges. Details received via FBI are sketchy. However, request preliminary traces to determine if any of the three listed below have CIA connections." The first person named was Ronald Lister, who "claims that for many years he has assisted in supplying small arms and helicopters to CIA contacts in Latin and Central

America." The cable also named Danilo Blandón, identified as an accomplice of Lister. Curiously, it also asked for a trace on Norwin Meneses, who was identified as another accomplice of Lister's. Why the Los Angeles CIA was asking about Meneses in connection with the Blandón raid is unclear, since he was neither arrested, named in the search warrant affidavit, nor even living in the United States.

"Please respond immediate indicating what portions of response may be passed to local law enforcement authorities," the cable concluded. Langley cabled back the next day; there were no headquarters traces on Blandón and Lister, but Meneses was "apparently well known as the Nicaraguan Mafia, dealing in drugs, weapons, and smuggling and laundering of counterfeit money." What happened next is still a matter of dispute.

After the raids, Sergeant Gordon and Deputy Juarez said they took a couple of days off. When they returned to work, Gordon said, he was told by deputy Dan Garner that the CIA had come into the offices and taken the records the Majors had seized during the raid. Gordon didn't believe it and went to the evidence room to check.

The papers were no longer there.

According to Garner, Gordon walked back into the squad room and announced, "The evidence is gone." Juarez said he ran over to the evidence lockup and confirmed what Gordon was saying. Nothing was left. Both Juarez and Gordon claimed they never saw the documents again.

In addition to the seized documents, said Blandón's attorney, Brad Brunon, the official police records of the raid seemed to disappear also. Despite his best efforts, he was unable to come up with more than an informal note about the preraid briefing, and that only by accident a couple years after the raid. "For a long time, they (the Sheriff's Office) never acknowledged the existence of this warrant. I mean the whole thing was quite mysterious. Boom, they did 15 locations. Nothing turned up. Nobody got busted. There was a little tiny bit of cocaine found in one location. Nobody got filed on. They gave all the stuff back. The whole thing just was very strange," Brunon said. "I'd never had a case where all the reports disappeared. I mean, early on, the only theory I had was the CIA involvement."

An investigation by the L.A. County Sheriff's Office in late 1996 strongly disputed the idea that "mysterious federal agents swooped down…and stole away with any documents relating to this case. Investigators have determined that this allegation was apparently spread through second-hand rumor and innuendo among some members of the narcotics team personnel." The department said that for each item seized, "there is a consistent paper trail."

The paper trail, however, raises more suspicions than it quiets. If the Sheriff's Office files are accurate, nearly all of the seized evidence was given back to Blandón and Lister within days of the raid, and apparently no copies were retained by the department, even for intelligence purposes. The Sheriff's 1996 investigation failed to find a single document in the files that had been seized during the raids. The only surviving documents are the few the deputies managed to take home with them.

All of the property that wasn't claimed—including the cocaine and the weapons manuals—was allegedly destroyed within six months. That destruction occurred while the investigation was still listed as open and active.

As Jerry Guzzetta had done earlier, the L.A. County Sheriff's Office soon concluded that the Blandón case was just too big for it to handle alone. Sergeant Huffman "did not believe it was the proper responsibility of the L.A. Sheriff's Department to investigate the activities of the CIA," he said; he and his superiors "felt it would be more appropriately handled by federal agencies from that point because there was evidence that there was a continuing narcotics trafficking organization which involved a very large geographical area." When the U.S. Department of Justice stepped in and offered to adopt the investigation, the Majors had no objections. Sergeant Gordon, in fact, was no longer around, having been promoted and transferred out of the Majors.

According to Sergeant Huffman's notes, one of the first things the federal agents did was to put Gordon's bombshell search warrant affidavit under court seal, which kept it from becoming public. The affidavit also disappeared from the Sheriff's Office case files and was never found again. (In 1996 Sheriff Sherman Block sheepishly admitted that his investigators were unable to locate a copy of the affidavit in the department's files and had to use the author's copy, which had been posted by the *San Jose Mercury News* on its Web site. And again, the only reason that copy existed was because an officer took a copy of the affidavit home shortly after the raid.)

Huffman was then informed that no charges would be filed against Blandón, "to protect the ongoing investigation and informants." Despite being caught red-handed with cocaine—and admitting it was his—the drug kingpin was set free. Federal prosecutors interviewed called that a stunning decision, given Blandón's stature as one of L.A.'s biggest traffickers and the fact that he was in the U.S. seeking political asylum at the time. The mere fact of the arrest should have been enough to deport him, his wife, and every other Nicaraguan implicated. "If he was a major trafficker and we got him with even a little bit, he'd have been prosecuted," said former federal strike force attorney Brian Leighton, who worked in central California during those years. "You could also charge him with conspiracy, because in conspiracy cases you don't need any dope. I've done plenty of no-dope conspiracy cases. Just because he has [only] a half a gram doesn't mean you let him go."

But Blandón was not merely turned loose. On December 10, 1986, he has said, he was formally notified that the case against him had been dropped and that there would be no charges filed. That day, records show, he drove into Los Angeles and hired a lawyer to file an application for permanent residency with the Immigration and Naturalization Service, which would make it much more difficult to deport him in the future.

Blandón's choice of attorneys was interesting; he hired a man who was then under federal indictment for immigration fraud, and a cocaine addict to boot. Just a week before Blandón retained him, attorney John M. Garrisi had been charged with illegally smuggling Iranian scientists into the United States. Garrisi's lawyer, Roy Koletsky, said Garrisi had "a pipeline" into the Iranian community and had been bringing Iranians into the States since "around the time the Shah was deposed. He had a number of Iranians working in his office. They spoke Farsi at the office."

At Garrisi's disbarment hearing, it was alleged that he had been crisscrossing the globe in his quest to get Iranians into the United States, creating phony immigration records with an apparently genuine stamp from the Iranian Ministry of Justice and referring clients to an expert document forger. He was also accused of cheating clients of money. Garrisi "repeatedly stated he believed he had a duty (emphasizing repeatedly the word 'duty') to bring 'these people' (most of his visa clients are Iranian) into the United States," a California Bar Association report stated. "He strongly inferred that he would pursue that duty even against their expressed wishes."

Koletsky had no idea what "duty" Garrisi was talking about, he said, and Garrisi did not respond to interview requests. After one mistrial, he was convicted in 1987 of making false statements and sent to federal prison for a year.

Blandón's application for permanent residency, which disclosed his membership in an unnamed "anti-communist organization," reported that he had been arrested for "possession of drugs and weapons" in October

1986 but added, "They didn't find nothing." Under "Outcome of Case," Blandón wrote: "No complaint filed. They exonerated me 12-10-86."

But other records show that the case continued to be investigated by the FBI, which was zeroing in on Ronald Lister. Lister was being probed in connection with "Operation Front Door," the code name for the FBI's investigation of the Reagan administration's arms sales to Iran. According to a December 8, 1986, teletype from the Los Angeles FBI office to the FBI director in Washington, a retired Secret Service agent reported that he'd had an unusual conversation with the real estate broker who'd handled the sale of Lister's new house in Mission Viejo. According to the teletype, "Lister paid for the house by providing two sackfuls of cash.... Lister told [deleted] that his occupation was 'setting up security systems for foreign governments,' 'selling arms to the Contras,' and that he worked for an Iranian." The teletype noted that "Lister is the subject of an ongoing joint narcotics investigation" and that a search of his house located several documents "which tended to indicate that Lister was involved in selling or providing arms."

The Los Angeles FBI office reported that it would continue investigating and "will provide information pertaining to aforementioned narcotics matter and subsequent discussions with Lister's attorney who had indicated Lister may have some involvement with the CIA. (Previous lead sent to FBIHQ regarding this affiliation.)"

On December 11, 1986, one day after Blandón says he was "exonerated," the director of the FBI sent a long teletype to the CIA's deputy director for operations and the director of the DIA. The teletype said the FBI was doing an "investigation focused on a cocaine distribution operation principally comprised of Nicaraguan nationals. Significant quantities of cocaine are reportedly distributed throughout the West Coast." Furthermore, "Information provided to FBI Los Angeles indicates that subject Ronald Jay Lister has made statements concerning his 'CIA contact,' identified by Lister as 'Mr. Weekly.' Investigation has also identified documents indicating that Lister has been in contact with 'Scott Weekly' of the DIA."

The FBI director asked both the CIA and the DIA if "any of the captioned subjects are currently of operational interest to your agency." In addition to Lister and Weekly, the FBI requested information on Blandón, Meneses, the Colombian Aparicio Moreno, economist Orlando Murillo, and someone nicknamed "Oklahoma Dick," who was reportedly operating an air freight company near Tulsa, Oklahoma.

The CIA replied that it had information only on Meneses and Murillo. The DIA's reply, if any, has never been made public.

The next day, FBI agent Douglas Aukland questioned Lister's former real estate agent, who confirmed that Lister had told him in July 1986 that he was "self-employed in selling security systems to Third World countries" and "mentioned that his business was 'CIA-approved.'" When the broker had asked where Lister was getting the cash for the house, "Lister replied that he was involved in fund-raising for Contras or Sandinistas. Specific one unrecalled by [deleted] but believed to be Contras. Lister said that specific activity was 'CIA-approved.'" The broker denied, however, that Lister told him he was an arms dealer or working for Iranians, and that was good enough for the sleuths at the Los Angeles FBI office. Following this single inconsequential interview, the case was closed.

Even though notes seized from Lister's house specifically mentioned Iran and contained a schematic detailing the use of phony government documents to ship restricted U.S. arms overseas—precisely the same method used by Oliver North—Los Angeles FBI officials claimed to see "no connection between Ronald Jay Lister and captioned matter.... Los Angeles will not interview Ronald Jay Lister."

But that didn't keep Riverside FBI agent Doug Aukland from digging a little further. He decided to do some checking on "Mr. Weekly," Ronald Lister's alleged CIA contact.

"Scott Weekly is an arms dealer in San Diego," the agent told Sergeant Huffman in mid-January 1987. "Can't confirm Weekly is or isn't CIA connected." But that was only because Aukland wasn't asking the right people: his own bosses in Washington. By then, records show, senior officials at the U.S. Department of Justice had Weekly under investigation and were intimately familiar with him because they had been reading transcripts of his telephone conversations. Those transcripts suggested that Scott Weekly was connected not only to the CIA but to the National Security Council and the U.S. State Department as well.

19

"He reports to people reporting to Bush"

It really didn't take an FBI agent to figure out who or what Scott Weekly was. A librarian could have done it. Weekly had been something of an inadvertent celebrity back in 1983. A story in the *Los Angeles Times*, in fact, gave him the nickname that would stick with him for years: Doctor Death.

"Scott's kind of a tough little guy," said Ronald Lister's longtime attorney, Lynn Ball. "He got busted out of the Naval Academy and entered the service as an enlisted man. Went on to become a SEAL. Then after he got out, he had some friends in Virginia. Essentially, Scott was involved in the same kind of bullshit that Ron was—providing security."

A federal public defender told a judge in 1987 that Weekly was "some sort of a combination between John Wayne and Rambo and Oliver North, perhaps, and James Bond.... He does have an involvement, a lengthy involvement, in some rather mysterious activities."

Weekly, a classmate of North's at Annapolis, would later say he was kicked out of the Naval Academy in 1968 "because of the buildup of a large number of demerits." He joined the SEALs—the navy's most elite band of fighters—and became a demolition and weapons expert, thus earning his macabre sobriquet. He was awarded two Bronze Stars in Vietnam, where, according to his lawyer, he was involved in "extensive combat duty and numerous intelligence operations." He later married the daughter of an admiral.

Weekly said he "technically" left the military in 1970 and described his employment afterward as a consultant and adviser. Just what kind of advice he provided became clear in 1983.

That year, he and several other Americans were arrested in Nakhon Phanom, a small Thai village near the border of Laos, while on a covert mission to gather intelligence on American soldiers missing from the Vietnam war. The head of the Defense Intelligence Agency had wanted to find out, once and for all, if rumors of American POWs being held in Laotian prison camps were true. (It was from this incident that the Sylvester Stallone movie *Rambo* took its inspiration.)

Leading the expedition was former Army Green Beret lieutenant colonel James "Bo" Gritz, a decorated Vietnam war hero and former commander of the U.S. Special Forces in the Panama Canal Zone. Though he ostensibly retired from the military in 1979, Gritz said that for several years afterward he worked with an army intelligence unit known as the Intelligence Support Activity (ISA), trying to locate American POWs in Southeast Asia. According to author Steven Emerson, the ISA, known in military intelligence circles as "the Activity," provided Gritz with "tens of thousands of dollars' worth of cameras, polygraph equipment (to check the veracity of Indochinese sources), radio communications systems and plane tickets to Bangkok. Gritz was also given satellite photos and other intelligence data." The operation was code-named "Grand Eagle." Dr. Death was Gritz's right-hand man.

In congressional testimony, Gritz said "Grand Eagle" was officially shelved after a bureaucratic dispute between "the Activity" and the DIA. Deputy DIA director Admiral Allan Paulson confirmed to Congress that a "Department of Defense organization…proposed an operation using Mr. Gritz in a collection capacity," but Paulson said the operation was turned down "at the first level of the approval process."

The official rejection didn't end the mission, however. With the ISA's equipment and money at their disposal, Gritz and Weekly proceeded under the ironic code name "Operation Lazarus." Weekly's contributions, according to a 1983 *Soldier of Fortune* magazine story, included "having silencers altered to fit the 9-mm submachine guns to be used by Gritz and the team."

The first mission, in November 1982, resulted in a firefight with Laotian forces, and one member of Gritz's team was killed. As he prepared to make another stab at infiltrating Laos in early 1983, word of his mission was leaked to *Soldier of Fortune* magazine and picked up by the *Los Angeles Times* and the *Boston Globe*. Exposed, Gritz and his squad were arrested by Thai police at the edge of the Mekong River and charged with possession of an illegal radio transmitter. Gritz, Weekly, and two others—an antiterrorism expert and the daughter of a missing U.S. pilot—were jailed and held for trial.

In a letter to the *L.A. Times*, Gritz said that "CIA-DIA knew" of the mission and provided him with a variety of high-tech gear. Both agencies disavowed any knowledge of Gritz's missions but the denials were difficult to believe. "U.S. sources in Bangkok said the radio was the latest in U.S.-made spy gear with a powerful transmitter that was to have been used to send messages from Laos straight to Washington," United Press International reported. "The disclosure of the radio's type and purpose bolstered the credibility of Gritz's statements that his first mission into Laos last November and his apparently just-completed second mission was carried out with the blessing of U.S. intelligence officials."

UPI's perceptiveness was short-lived. Those telling paragraphs were cut from the UPI story that moved later that afternoon, and from then on most press reports uncritically accepted the government's denials. Gritz and Weekly were dismissed as beer-can commandos off on their own private mission.

A year later, however, syndicated columnist Jack Anderson reported that Gritz's team had been sent into Southeast Asia "with at least initial support from the CIA and the Pentagon." Anderson based that conclusion on confidential court records filed in a federal fraud case in Honolulu, Hawaii, involving a polo-playing investment banker named Ronald Ray Rewald, who was accused of stealing millions from his bankrupt company's clients. Rewald claimed his investment company had been a conduit for the CIA to secretly funnel money to covert operations around the world, and that the agency had suddenly yanked its accounts, causing the firm to collapse.

The CIA admitted to Congress that Rewald's company "had some ties to the CIA" and that several CIA officials had investment accounts there. Anderson put it more bluntly: "Rewald's investment firm was hip-deep in active or retired CIA employees."

In an affidavit, Rewald said the CIA "had originally committed its support" to Gritz's mission and that Rewald "did supply a few thousand dollars to support the mission at the CIA's behest." According to Anderson, the "bombshell of Rewald's exhibits is a confidential letter to Gritz on official DIA stationery" instructing Gritz to "pull together evidence to convince political skeptics of the POW existence."

(As an aside, Rewald also told Anderson that he was approached in

1982 by "a senior CIA official and asked if he would help in a CIA drug-smuggling operation. When Rewald told the CIA official that he had no one in his firm with experience in drug operations, the CIA man contradicted him and named [a Rewald] employee who had been a longtime CIA contract agent active in Southeast Asia." The CIA disputed Anderson's column, but the columnist never backed down. Rewald was convicted of fraud and sentenced to an astonishing eighty years in federal prison.)

When a police investigator asked Scott Weekly in 1996 about his relationship with the CIA, Weekly replied that it really didn't matter what answer he gave. There was no way the police could ever confirm it. "He also agreed that if he was in the CIA, he wouldn't tell me anyway," the officer wrote. In 1998, the CIA Inspector General reported it could find no evidence that Weekly "had any relationship with the CIA."

Another officer tried to check out Weekly's military background by calling the Office of Veterans Affairs in Los Angeles. According to his report, an odd thing happened: "Scott Weekly's name was found in the database. The person on the telephone calmly read Weekly's name to me and suddenly exclaimed, 'Whoa!' He quickly informed me that due to provisions of the Privacy Act, only the fact that he was a veteran could be confirmed. No information about length of service, branch, or MOS [Military Occupational Specialty] could be released without a subpoena or the consent of Weekly."

Notwithstanding Lister's claim to the Majors that "Mr. Weekly knows what I'm doing," it is difficult to say with certainty if Weekly knew of Lister's cocaine dealings with Danilo Blandón. Weekly denies it. But there is no doubt that between 1982 and 1986, Scott Weekly was helping out on the flip side of Blandón's criminal enterprise: the sale of exotic weapons and communications gear, some of which was being sold to Freeway Rick and his fellow crack dealers in South Central Los Angeles. A U.S. Customs agent, John Kellogg, testified in 1988 that he believed Weekly was an arms merchant who "was involved in international munitions deals."

"And how did you come to that belief?" Kellogg was asked by a federal judge.

"Though his various contacts with me and his foreign travels," Kellogg replied. "He would come back after several months' absence and come into my office and say, 'I believe you need to know about this,' and then detail very specific information concerning munitions dealers that were under investigation by the Customs Service and others."

Weekly confirmed that he had "considerable contact with arms merchants" but denied he was one himself. He admitted that he would periodically advise Lister on ways "he could make some money and not get in trouble" in weapons transactions. He told police that it seemed "Lister was going out of his way to make sure he wouldn't get in trouble with his dealings in this area.... [Lister] may be a bonehead but, in fact, he was fairly careful about that."

Lister confirmed that he "often met with Scott Weekly because Weekly was very knowledgeable in the area of commercially available military related systems." He said Weekly was "a dependable source of information as to which systems were declassified and, hence, legal to sell."

In the final weeks of 1986, less than a month after Lister identified "Mr. Weekly" to the sheriff's raid team as his CIA contact, evidence surfaced suggesting that Lister's description wasn't far off the mark.

At the time Lister made that claim, Scott Weekly was participating in at least two covert operations involving the National Security Council and a special unit inside the U.S. State Department that was working closely with Oliver North and the CIA.

Both Weekly and Gritz have testified that in early 1986 they were asked to conduct training exercises for another of the CIA's secret armies: the anti-Communist Afghan resistance movement—the Mujahedeen. Before undertaking that mission, they said, they sought and obtained the approval of two State Department officials in Washington: William R. Bode, a special assistant to the undersecretary of state for security assistance, and Bode's aide, army colonel Nestor Pino Marina.

Eugene Wheaton, a former air force security expert who knows both men personally, believes Bode and Pino were CIA agents working under State Department cover on the Contra project with Oliver North. "That office...was CIA through and through," says Wheaton, whose name shows up repeatedly in Bode's daily agendas and Oliver North's notebooks during 1985-86. There is some independent evidence to support Wheaton's conclusions. In an interview with Iran-Contra investigators, former CIA Central American Task Force chief Alan Fiers Jr. admitted that he and North in late 1985 discussed an unnamed "paramilitary covert action program" involving Pino and Bode and a company called Falcon Wings Inc. What that program involved is not known; the rest of Fiers's interview was censored on national security grounds.

Undersecretary of State William Schneider told the FBI in 1988 that Bode and Pino were responsible for Central America and their jobs involved "keeping in touch with DOD [Department of Defense] and other government agencies to determine if U.S. assistance programs to the area were working." One of those programs appears to have been the secret Contra maritime operations North and CIA station chief Joseph Fernández were running in Costa Rica, using Kevlar speedboats and offshore shrimp trawlers as motherships. As discussed in an earlier chapter, those murky missions were being spearheaded by two CIA-linked drug traffickers working with the Southern Front Contras—Bay of Pigs veterans Felipe Vidal and Dagoberto Nuñez. In an interview with Iran-Contra prosecutor Lawrence Walsh's office, Pino confirmed that he and Bode met with North to discuss the purchase of the speedboats. During that meeting, Pino said, North unexpectedly announced that he could wind up behind bars. "North did refer to going to jail," Pino confirmed, but he said his "impression was that the phrase was common usage in the military before an inspection."

Colonel Pino, another Bay of Pigs veteran, has a history of involvement with the CIA and covert operations. In 1982 he became the U.S. Army's "action officer" on the civil war in El Salvador. Pino was a close friend of former CIA agent Felix Rodriguez, who was overseeing North's Contra resupply operation at Ilopango air base in El Salvador at the time. Rodriguez, in fact, says he first met Ollie North through Bode and Pino. Like Rodriguez, Pino was close to Salvadoran Air Force general Rafael Bustillo, who ran the Ilopango base. Pino referred to Bustillo as "family," and the Salvadoran general sometimes stayed at Pino's house in Virginia while visiting Washington.

As for Bode, he was described by his boss, Undersecretary Schneider, as "a deployable asset…who was used on non-routine projects." Bode's desk calendars, obtained from the National Archives, show frequent meetings in 1985 and 1986 with North and CIA operative Robert Owen, North's liaison to the Contras and the Cuban mercenaries working on the Southern Front.

Gritz testified that he approached Bode and Pino to discuss the Afghan training program he and Weekly were asked to conduct because "I've worked for intelligence agencies and I wanted to make sure that we weren't doing something that was illegal…Mr. Bode was enthusiastic, as a matter of fact, I would call him excited. He said that not only did he approve of the proposal but that he would provide other Afghan groups, since there was a division of about six or seven subgroups, that he would provide other people for us to train also. Later, in further meetings, I did provide him with a detailed training proposal. Initially I gave him an outline for a training proposal of seventy-six days." Gritz said Bode shortened the training schedule to thirty days "and eliminated some of the classes that he felt were too sensitive for the Mujahedeen at the time. It included various secure communications [courses] that we had planned to give."

In a 1987 interview, Bode confirmed that he had met with Gritz about the training program and "gave him the names of one or two people to talk to," but he denied he authorized the operation. "Just the fact that we met and had talks didn't authorize anything," Bode insisted. "The Afghan program is a covert program, okay? All CIA, or perhaps a little bit of Defense Department. The State Department does not get involved in those things." (As anyone who has studied the CIA can attest, the State Department has provided cover for more CIA officers over the years than any other section of government save the military.)

One of the names Bode gave them, Gritz and Weekly testified, belonged to a CIA officer in Canada: "Rasheed," an expert in the Afghan conflict. Gritz said Rasheed "was doing a classified study...Bode told me the study was also to be provided to him and to the CIA. He called Rasheed on the phone and directed Rasheed to open that study, which was about seven volumes, and give us all of the details there so we could operate a comprehensive training program." Weekly also confirmed meeting Rasheed, who was "to advise us on certain key elements, with the permission of the Agency and with direction by Bode, to assist us in circumventing wasted time and making things a bit more efficient." Bode's desk calendars for that period contain several references to a man identified only as Rasheed.

In federal court, Weekly and Gritz testified that the money to pay for the Afghan training exercises came from Stanford Technology, one of the companies fronting for Oliver North's "Enterprise," the quasi-governmental arms dealership at the heart of the Iran-Contra scandal. Stanford Technology was used by North and his agents to launder the profits of the Iranian missile sales. During the Iran-Contra deposition of Stanford Technology's owner, Albert Hakim, he admitted that approximately $900,000 from his various front companies was paid out "for miscellaneous projects at the request of Lt. Col. North."

In late 1986 Gritz and Weekly's training program—conducted in the Nevada desert on land owned by the federal government—was accidentally exposed by a law student in Oklahoma City who was married to a policeman. "She was sitting in her apartment one night when Weekly and this cop show up with 200 pounds of C-4 plastic explosives," recalled former federal prosecutor Stephen Korotash, who handled the case. "They were looking to store it somewhere. She happened to mention it to her father and Dad called the ATF [Bureau of Alcohol, Tobacco and Firearms]." The

ATF learned that Weekly had loaded the C-4 aboard two commercial passenger flights to Las Vegas and then left the country. An ATF report on the Weekly investigation, found in the CIA's files during an internal probe in 1997, "indicated that Weekly claimed he had done this for CIA."

ATF agents initially suspected that Weekly might be a terrorist until they got a look at his long-distance telephone records for September and October of 1986. Among other things, they found calls to Colonel Pino at the State Department; to William Logan, southwest regional director of the U.S. Customs Service; to the National Security Council; and to defense contractor United Technologies.

The agents broke the news to federal prosecutor Korotash, who was not pleased. The storm over the Iran-Contra scandal was then reaching a crescendo and the last thing Korotash wanted was to be dragged into that maelstrom. "My first thought was: 'Oh, great. Here I am picking my nose in Oklahoma and now I've stumbled into a Contra deal.' That's what I thought this was and I can remember thinking, 'How in the hell did I get ahold of a case like this?'"

No stranger to the workings of government, Korotash bounced the Weekly investigation up the bureaucratic ladder, and it kept right on bouncing, all the way to the top of the Criminal Division of the U.S. Justice Department in Washington. Records show that on December 2, 1986, Assistant U.S. Attorney General William F. Weld was briefed on the case. According to Weld's notes of the briefing, Weekly was somehow connected to the U.S. State Department and had made long-distance phone calls to a Lieutenant Colonel Tom Harvey, who was on the staff of the National Security Council. (Gritz has said Harvey was supervising the POW hunt he and Weekly were on at the time and provided them with White House and NSC credentials. Harvey has denied that.)

Korotash's supervisor, Oklahoma City U.S. attorney William Price, asked Weld, if he should "proceed with such cases?" Weld told him to go ahead, and then asked one of his aides, Deputy Assistant Attorney General Mark M. Richard, to look into the case.

Richard already had some background in this area. Earlier that year he'd been given an award by the CIA for "Protection of National Security during Criminal Prosecutions." A CIA spokesman said Richard was honored for "his outstanding work in the case against Ronald Rewald," the Honolulu investment banker who claims his investment firm funneled CIA money to covert operations, including Weekly and Gritz's earliest POW missions. Thanks to Richard's efforts, Rewald's ties to the CIA were not permitted to surface publicly at his criminal trial.

Richard called U.S. Attorney Bill Price on December 11, 1986, and was briefed on the investigation. Several months later, Richard was grilled about that briefing in a deposition taken by Iran-Contra committee lawyer Pamela Naughton. According to a transcript of the deposition, Naughton confronted Richard with two sheets of lined paper filled with handwritten notes.

"Tell me what that is," Naughton said. "Is that your handwriting, first of all?"

"I'd plead guilty to that," Richard cracked. "This is the gist of the conversation I had with Mr. Price and his briefing of me regarding an individual who had been arrested and his possible involvement in some CIA/Contra-related activities."

"Now, about a third of the way down—individual's name was Weekly? Is that—am I reading that correctly?" Naughton asked. "W-E-E-K-L-Y?"

"Yes."

"About a third of the way down it says—if I'm reading correctly—'Weekly posts on tape that he's tied into CIA and Hasenfus. Said he reports to people reporting to Bush.' What does that mean?"

"I don't know what the 'post' means, but apparently there was a tape recording," Richard answered. "This is a matter which had just arisen in the U.S. Attorney's office. I was getting briefed…it's an individual who had been arrested and is asserting, or there is a suggestion of, a relationship to the CIA and Hasenfus and the exportation of explosives to the countries." (At the time of Richard's conversation with Bill Price, Weekly was actually about two weeks away from being arrested; he was still in Burma with Bo Gritz on their latest POW hunt. Price was apparently briefing Richard on the tapes of intercontinental telephone conversations Weekly was having with his police officer friend in Oklahoma City. Who made the tapes and how the Justice Department obtained them isn't clear.)

"And he's alleging or indicating to someone that he's connected with the CIA and that he is reporting to people who report to Bush?" Naughton asked.

"That's what he's asserting," Richard agreed.

"What is the current status, if you know?"

"I cannot—as far as I recall, it was referred to the—"

"Referred to the Independent Counsel?" Naughton asked.

"To the IC," Richard confirmed. "And I just don't know the status."

Because the case had been turned over to Lawrence Walsh, the Iran-

Contra committees didn't pursue the Weekly matter further, Naughton said. Unfortunately, neither did Walsh. According to the declassified files of Walsh's investigation, the information about Weekly was never given more than a cursory glance, possibly because Walsh had nothing but the sketchiest details about the Weekly case. The tapes on which Weekly discusses the CIA, Hasenfus, and George Bush do not appear to have been turned over, nor were Weekly's phone records made available to Walsh's office. It was unlikely his office would have done much work on the case anyway, Walsh said, since his mandate "was to go from Oliver North upwards. We really didn't have the manpower or the time to go after all of North's side activities or his associates."

Richard's notes show that Price also reported Weekly was working for Tim LaFrance, the San Diego weapons maker who says he helped Ronald Lister and the CIA set up the Contra arms plant in El Salvador. LaFrance, who knows Weekly, denied he was working for him at the time. Price also mentioned that a man named Albert Schnaper was "also related to Weekly. Schnaper on probation in San Diego dope/arms."

Despite those intriguing leads, the next day the FBI officially shut down its Iran-Contra investigation of Lister and Weekly in Los Angeles, which had begun with the police raids on Danilo Blandón's operation. Whether or not that decision was related to the Justice Department's top-level inquiries into Weekly's connections to the intelligence community could not be determined, since the FBI refuses to release any of its records involving the Blandón investigation. But it begs the question of how the FBI could have reasonably concluded that there was "no connection" between Lister, Weekly, and the unfolding Iran-Contra scandal when two separate criminal investigations simultaneously turned up evidence linking Lister and Weekly to the CIA and the Contras.

While no evidence has surfaced suggesting that State Department officials Bode and Pino knew of Blandón's criminal enterprises, records show that they were not neophytes on the subject of the Contras and cocaine. At the same time they were dealing with Scott Weekly, the two men were trying desperately to get another CIA-linked cocaine trafficker out of prison because of his past assistance to the Contras.

The federal prisoner, José Bueso Rosa, had been indicted in 1984 for his part in a bizarre scheme to assassinate the president of Honduras, Roberto Suazo Cordova, and stage a coup d'état, using the proceeds of a giant cocaine sale to finance it. President Suazo had drawn Bueso Rosa's wrath by dumping Honduran Army chief General Gustavo Álvarez, a fanatical anti-Communist who was one of the fathers and chief supporters of the Contras. Bueso Rosa, a Honduran general, had been one of Álvarez's top aides, and the cocaine coup was intended to restore Álvarez and his men to power.

Unfortunately for the plotters, the two American military officers they hired to murder Suazo went to the FBI. In late October 1984, a collection of Cubans and Honduran arms merchants was arrested at a remote inland airstrip in Florida with 764 pounds of cocaine, valued at between $10 million and $40 million wholesale. "The announcements at the time of the arrests made by the Departments of State and Justice quite properly categorized this case as a triumph for the Administration's policy against terrorism and against narcotics," former State Department official Francis J. McNeil would later testify. But not everyone in the Reagan administration was happy about it. Bueso Rosa was one of the CIA's main collaborators in Honduras on the Contra project, working closely with the agency in setting up Contra bases, supply lines, aircraft repairs, and a host of other, still classified, activities.

In the summer of 1986 the Honduran's attorney flew to Washington and met with Colonel Pino, who began a vigorous lobbying campaign at State and Justice to turn Bueso Rosa loose, even though he had been indicted for racketeering, conspiracy, and attempted murder-for-hire. "The colonel assert[ed] an American intelligence interest in Bueso Rosa, in getting Bueso Rosa off," McNeil testified. As Pino explained to Iran-Contra investigators, "General Bueso Rosa...had information which he could use against us, as he had been privy to a large amount of specific information."

To get Washington's attention, Bueso Rosa's lawyers subpoenaed Oliver North, CIA officer Duane "Dewey" Clarridge, former U.S. ambassador to Honduras John D. Negroponte, and former U.S. Army general Paul Gorman to testify at the Honduran's racketeering trial as defense witnesses. In several computer messages to NSC chief John Poindexter in September 1986, North fretted that the case could become a major headache for the Administration. "The problem with the Bueso case is that Bueso was the man whom Negroponte, Gorman, Clarridge and I worked out arrangements [censored]," North wrote. "Only Gorman, Clarridge and I were fully aware of all that Bueso was doing on our behalf."

North's computer messages about Bueso Rosa are revealing for another reason: they illustrate just how skewed the Reagan administration's sense of justice had become regarding its "War on Drugs." At the same time Reagan and Bush were whipping the American public into a frenzy over street-corner crack dealers, North and other top administration officials were livid that Bueso Rosa had even been charged with a crime. "Justice is justifiably upset that none of this info was made available to them prior to indictment or before/during trial," North griped. "Clarridge was totally unaware that CIA had responded to a Justice query on the case with the terse comment that they 'had no interest in the case.' Elliott [Abrams] was also somewhat chagrined to learn that some at State had been urging rigorous prosecution and sentencing." Bueso Rosa was advised to "keep his mouth shut and everything would be worked out," North wrote.

The general later agreed to drop the subpoenas and pleaded guilty with the understanding that he would be sentenced to a minimum security facility at Eglin Air Force base in Florida, North wrote, "for a short period (days or weeks) and then walk free." Justice Department official Mark Richard, who met with North to discuss the case, said he was told that Bueso Rosa "was going to go in from one entrance and out the other entrance, you know, out the rear." An all-star collection of U.S. government officials, including Colonel Nestor Pino, Bill Bode, and the former head of the DIA, appeared as character witnesses or sent glowing letters to Bueso Rosa's judge, urging him to go easy on the admitted racketeer. But since Bueso Rosa's coconspirators had been hit with sentences of up to thirty years, it was impossible to let the ringleader off scot-free. He was given a five-year sentence and assigned to a federal prison in Tallahassee, a much harsher environment than the "country club" camp at Eglin he'd been promised.

In North's view, that only made things worse. "Our major concern—Gorman, North, Clarridge—is that when Bueso Rosa finds out what is really happening to him, he will break his longstanding silence about the Nic[araguan] Resistance and other sensitive operations," North wrote to Poindexter. "Gorman, North, Clarridge, Revell [an FBI official], [Steven] Trott and [Elliott] Abrams will cabal quietly in the morning to look at options: pardon, clemency, deportation, reduced sentence. Objective is to keep Bueso from feeling like he was lied to in legal process and start spilling the beans. Will advise."

The next day, North told Poindexter there had been "a good meeting this morning with all concerned." The Justice Department had graciously agreed to transfer Bueso Rosa to Eglin, work out a deal to reduce his sentence, and buttonhole the federal judge to "explain...our equities in this matter. Revell/Trott both believe this will result in approval of the petition for probationary release and deportation to Honduras. Discretely briefing Bueso and his attorney on this whole process should alleviate concerns…that Bueso will start singing songs that nobody wants to hear," North advised. "Bottom line: all now seems headed in the right direction." But Colonel Pino and the Defense Intelligence Agency got a little too happy. A few days before Bueso Rosa was to report to prison, State Department official McNeil got a call from an upset Justice Department official, informing him that the DIA had scheduled a luncheon honoring the would-be assassin in the Pentagon's Executive Dining Room. McNeil, outraged by the news, called a meeting between State, the Justice Department, the DIA, and the CIA to get the invitation squelched. The ceremony was eventually canceled, but McNeil said he was warned by a superior that he was "looking for trouble" if he kept sticking his nose into the Bueso Rosa affair. "It was very nasty business," McNeil, a former U.S. ambassador to Costa Rica, would later testify. He told Congress he suspected something sinister was behind the frantic machinations of North and company to get the Honduran out of the United States.

"I must tell you this is circumstantial, but it seems to me that the circumstantial evidence is such that one has to wonder if there is not a narcotics angle," McNeil testified. "What was so embarrassing that at least eight senior officers of the U.S. government would think it necessary to get this man off?" In a deposition, Justice Department official Steve Trott claimed he didn't know why he went through such contortions for Bueso Rosa, other than that North had told him about the possible release of "sensitive" information.

And what information was that? "I never got into the substance of what it was," Trott claimed. Whatever it was, Bueso Rosa held his tongue, and after doing three years at Eglin he was shipped back to Honduras. In a 1995 interview with the *Baltimore Sun*, he gave a chilling insight into the kinds of secrets he possessed: he disclosed that the CIA had equipped and trained the Honduran army's official death squad, the 316 Battalion, which was blamed for the torture, disappearance, and murders of hundreds of Hondurans in the 1980s.

According to court records, similar promises of leniency were made to Scott Weekly to keep him quiet about his involvement with Bode, Pino, and the "Enterprise." As in Bueso Rosa's case, the efforts looks particularly unseemly, given the fact that, at the time they were undertaken, Weekly was under federal investigation in connection with Danilo

Blandón's cocaine ring—something that was known at the highest levels of the CIA, the Justice Department, and the DIA.

On December 21, 1986, just two days after Independent Counsel Lawrence Walsh was appointed to investigate the burgeoning Iran-Contra scandal, Weekly got a call at his home in San Diego and was asked to meet with federal agents at a room in the downtown Holiday Inn, overlooking the harbor. Weekly had just returned from his latest POW hunt with Bo Gritz, allegedly on behalf of the NSC, but he discovered that the agents—accompanied by Oklahoma City federal prosecutor Steve Korotash—didn't want to discuss that. They wanted to know about the C-4 he'd placed on the airliners before he departed for the Far East.

When Weekly explained that the C-4 had been safely detonated in the Nevada desert, he said the prosecutor offered him a deal: if he kept quiet and pleaded guilty to illegally transporting the C-4 to Las Vegas, he would be released on unsupervised probation, and the case would be closed. "One of the points specifically that we agreed on was that this investigation would start and stop with me, and that it would not affect other or involve other personnel," Weekly later testified. Prosecutor Korotash denied making any such promises.

The next morning Weekly and Korotash flew to Oklahoma City, where the prosecutor "began hurriedly telling me all the answers I was to give to the officials...and emphatically told [me] if things got out of hand he would answer for me or direct my answers." Weekly said Korotash advised him to "lie low and keep mum."

Weekly went before a federal judge that afternoon and, without ever having spoken to a defense lawyer, tersely pleaded guilty to interstate transportation of explosives. Under Korotash's gentle questioning, he admitted to shipping plastic explosives on two commercial airliners to Las Vegas but was never asked why. Korotash helpfully pointed out that the passengers were never in danger and asked that Weekly be released from custody without having to post bail. Federal judge Ralph G. Thompson said it was "not routine that people be released on bail in cases of this kind," but he acquiesced. The hearing was over in a matter of minutes and Weekly was soon on his way home with the whole episode safely behind him. Or so he thought.

Then Bo Gritz began shooting his mouth off about the CIA and drugs.

Following his last POW foray, the superpatriot had come home radicalized. He and Weekly had trekked into the mountains of northern Burma to visit an opium warlord named Khun Sa, who commanded a tribal army estimated at 40,000 men. Gritz has said their primary mission from Colonel Harvey at the NSC was to check out a tip Vice President George Bush had received, suggesting that the warlord knew something about missing American servicemen in Laos. (As with Gritz's earlier missions, the U.S. government denies any involvement. However, no one has explained why Gritz and Weekly were meeting and speaking with an NSC official.)

After a three-day hike into the jungles, Gritz said, they found Khun Sa and discovered he knew nothing about American POWs. What he did know about, Gritz claimed, was a CIA-run heroin trafficking network that had been operating in the region for more than a decade, helping to finance a secret CIA army of anti-Communist guerillas in Laos. Gritz said Khun Sa, who controlled much of the raw opium trade in the Golden Triangle, opened up his ledger books and provided him with the names of the CIA officials allegedly involved and dates of their meetings with him.

Gritz and Weekly returned to the United States in mid-December 1986 with videotapes of their talks with the opium king, and Gritz said he immediately turned them over to Colonel Harvey of the NSC. Gritz said Harvey told him to "erase and forget" what he'd learned from the opium trafficker because the information would "hurt the government." Instead, Gritz put on his medals and his fatigues and went public, charging that U.S. government officials had been dealing heroin and that the Reagan administration was trying to cover that fact up. He pointed to Scott Weekly's recent arrest and conviction on the explosives charges as "proof" of a high-level conspiracy to silence and discredit them because of their awkward discoveries.

While the national press largely ignored the flamboyant veteran's strange tale, it received some wire service and radio coverage, particularly in Oklahoma City. Weekly's prosecutor, Steve Korotash, was driving to the supermarket one Saturday morning when he heard Gritz come over his car radio "claiming that I was retaliating against Scott Weekly because of some information Gritz had gotten from Khun Sa," Korotash said. "I didn't know who the fuck Khun Sa was. I didn't have a clue." Korotash said he laughed off Gritz's charges as "idiotic."

But others didn't find Gritz quite so amusing. A month later, federal agents raided his house in Sandy Valley, Nevada, hauling away boxes of paperwork. Simultaneously, Weekly began receiving pressure from prosecutors to implicate Gritz in the illegal transportation of the C-4 to Nevada, he said. Weekly refused to cooperate, arguing that he'd made a deal not to finger anyone. "Weekly was protecting the hell out of Bo Gritz," former U.S. attorney Price confirmed in an interview. "I mean, that's what really pissed us off."

When Weekly's sentencing on the explosives case rolled around in April 1987, Korotash filed a confidential memorandum with the court, saying Weekly had refused to take a polygraph test and failed to cooperate with the government. A letter from the U.S. Customs Service commending Weekly for his help in other investigations was withdrawn at the last minute. Judge Wayne Alley told Weekly that it appeared he was "simply trying to protect the names of others.... That's your privilege but it comes at a cost." Alley sentenced Weekly to five years in federal prison, requiring him to serve a year before he could be eligible for parole, and fined him $2,000. "I got my brains fucked out," Weekly would later complain.

A month later, in May 1987, Gritz was indicted by a federal grand jury in Nevada for misusing a passport during his travels to Southeast Asia. Gritz admitted that he had used a phony passport but claimed the government had given it to him. Pointing out that Oliver North had committed the same "crime" during his overseas travels and had never been indicted for it, Gritz told UPI that the charges were "intended to silence his accusations that the CIA and Defense Department are involved in opium trafficking." Gritz and his attorney vowed to turn his trial into an exposé of government drug dealing, but things never got that far. The charges were dismissed by a federal judge before trial.

After spending 14 months in prison, Scott Weekly was ordered released after a hearing revealed that he had indeed been working for the U.S. government at the time of his offenses, and had also been working as a U.S. Customs informant for many years. He was placed on probation, with the unusual caveat that he report any future contact "with any officer or employee of the Department of State, the Department of Defense, the Central Intelligence Agency or any other intelligence agency of the United States."

While the Justice Department pounced on Gritz and Weekly for what seem to be trivial violations of federal law, it showed no such zeal when it came to pursuing Danilo Blandón and the South Central L.A. drug gang. That investigation, though it involved massive amounts of cocaine and millions of dollars in ill-gotten gains, couldn't seem to generate any interest in the halls of Justice.

20

"The Assistant U.S. Attorney was found dead"

When all was said and done, the October 1986 L.A. County Sheriff's raids were a mere irritant to the Nicaraguans. Blandón had lost a thimbleful of dope. None of his people were arrested, and he and Chepita were out of jail in a matter of hours. "He laughed about it," Ross said. "I thought it was some pretty bad shit, but he told me there was nothing to worry about. Nobody'd found nothing. Nothing was gonna change." Blandón and Ross continued buying and selling millions of dollars worth of cocaine every week, even as the FBI watched. Records show Blandón was under periodic surveillance through the first half of 1987.

Former L.A. County deputy DA Susan Bryant-Deason, now a Superior Court judge, told police in 1996 that she met several times in the weeks following the raids with Sergeant Ed Huffman of Majors II and federal agents in an effort to keep the Blandón investigation alive. Bryant-Deason, the supervising attorney on the Blandón case, had been "cross-designated" as a special assistant U.S. attorney, which allowed her to prosecute certain federal cases as well as state crimes. She said the agents "were frustrated and wanted to do something but had insufficient evidence."

Why three grams of cocaine and a confession were insufficient to charge Blandón with a crime has never been explained, particularly since the L.A. police were hauling street dealers into court by the hundreds for possession of lesser amounts. The evidence the agents *did* have was, to say the least, fascinating.

According to a 1996 interview conducted during an internal sheriff's department investigation, Bryant-Deason stated that "during one meeting with Sergeant Huffman she was shown a stack of documents which were photocopies of bank records. She believed that these records were obtained through federal subpoenas rather than having been seized during the service of the warrant. She did not remember whose bank statements were shown to her, but only that they were connected to the investigation. She remembered these bank statements showed deposits of as much as $2,000,000 at a time into the account *from the U.S. Treasury*. [emphasis added]. She does not know the significance of the deposits."

It doesn't take a genius to figure it out. If her memory is correct, someone or something connected to Blandón's drug operation was receiving large sums of cash from the federal government. Huffman said he had no memory of showing Bryant-Deason such records, and, if they existed then, have never publicly surfaced.

Afterward, Bryant-Deason said, she went to her supervisor, Robert Schirn, and told him that "the matter should go to the U.S. Attorney's Office, where resources existed to follow up. Mr. Schirn agreed [and] briefed up the ladder." Bryant-Deason was later called to a short meeting with L.A. District Attorney Ira Reiner and Deputy DA Gil Garcetti. She made the same pitch to them: the Blandón investigation was a case the feds should chase. Anyway, she told them, it had already "been forwarded to the authorities who seemed best equipped for this type of investigation."

Sergeant Huffman agreed with the decision. "We went as far as we could as Deputy Sheriffs. We handed this thing off to federal agencies to further investigate it. We did our job," he insisted. "Even though we knew Contras were involved we went after them and we went into other counties to get them.... We went after them because they were drug traffickers."

Bryant-Deason said the assistant U.S. attorney assigned to the case was Darrell MacIntyre, a fifty-two-year-old prosecutor who had been working in the Los Angeles U.S. Attorney's Office for eighteen years and was described as "one of the most senior attorneys on the Los Angeles staff of U.S. Attorney Robert Bonner." Since 1983 he had been assigned to the U.S. attorney's major narcotics violators section.

MacIntyre would have been a logical choice to adopt the Blandón investigation because he had previous experience with Norwin Meneses's organization: he had prosecuted the L.A. end of the Frogman case in

1984. Some of the Gran Colombiana line freighters that had dropped off cocaine at Hunter's Point in San Francisco for the Colombian frogmen had continued on to L.A., where they were raided by the FBI. MacIntyre had handled the cases resulting from those raids.

When Bryant-Deason first talked to MacIntyre about the Blandón case, she said he informed her that "he was going to Washington D.C. very soon and that he would review the case and paperwork." But MacIntyre, who had been prosecuting drug cases since the mid-1970s, apparently decided the case was out of his league. He called Bryant-Deason afterward and told her "that he had referred the matter and documents to a special prosecutor in Washington." Unfortunately, he told her, the prosecutor had "no interest in the case."

"Sometime after this," Bryant-Deason told police, "the Assistant U.S. Attorney was found dead, possibly the result of a suicide." One Saturday afternoon, two days after Christmas in 1986, Darrell MacIntyre's body was found slumped in the front seat of an unlocked car in the deserted parking lot of a Pacific Palisades office building. According to police, he apparently put a revolver to his head and blew his brains out.

U.S. Attorney Robert Bonner told the Associated Press the next day that he "hoped the FBI and police would conduct a thorough investigation, but said he knew of no connection between any criminal cases and MacIntyre's death." But by then the police had already put their notebooks away—almost before any investigation had begun. Though no suicide note was found, an LAPD lieutenant told UPI less than twenty-four hours after the body was discovered that "everything indicates it was a suicide" and there would be "no further police investigation unless there was new evidence in the case."

Whether the police knew that MacIntyre had been working on a case involving drug-running Contras with CIA connections is unknown. No evidence has surfaced indicating a link between his death and the Blandón case, but it appears no attempt was made to find such a link.

On December 29, the U.S. Attorney's Office announced that MacIntyre had died of a self-inflicted gunshot wound. His boss, James Walsh, lamented his passing, saying that "he was the toughest prosecutor I've ever come across. He was a fair guy, a decent guy—straight as a string." No further stories appeared, and no reason was put forward for why the hardnosed DA would have killed himself. One of MacIntyre's friends at the U.S. Attorney's Office at the time, prosecutor Curtis Rappe, said he'd had lunch with MacIntyre a couple days before his death, and MacIntyre had seemed fine, telling him that "he'd see me on

Monday." Rappe, now a judge, disclosed that MacIntyre had been having marital problems and was not adjusting to an antidepressant he was taking, but the suicide still came as a surprise to him "because Darrell was one of these macho types you would never believe would do something like that."

MacIntyre's suicide was the second allegedly self-inflicted death in the L.A. area in two weeks involving people with knowledge of Contra drug running. Just two weeks earlier in nearby Panorama City, a mercenary soldier who had witnessed Contra cocaine dealing and gun running in Costa Rica also was found dead.

Steven Carr, 27, had been recruited in 1985 by the Bay of Pigs veterans in Brigade 2506 to train Contras on CIA operative John Hull's ranch in northern Costa Rica. Carr ended up in jail there on charges of violating Costa Rica's neutrality laws. During his incarceration at a prison outside San José, he began talking to journalists and investigators from Senator John Kerry's subcommittee about what he'd seen during his short time as a Contra: drugs and illegal weapons.

Carr was the first person to expose the secret Contra air base at Ilopango and the illegal arms flights to Hull's ranch. He, like Joe Kelso, also knew of the mysterious counterfeiting ring that was operating in Costa Rica and had reported it to the U.S. embassy. He exposed the roles of Oliver North and CIA informant Robert Owen in directing the Contra supply operation. He also swore that he had been at the Miami home of Cuban Frank Chanes, one of the owners of the drug-dealing Costa Rican shrimp company North was using as a money-laundering front, to pick up weapons, and had seen three kilos of cocaine in the same room.

Carr's information turned out to be highly accurate. And he worried that he would be killed because of it. "One of these days they're going to find my body," he told a reporter from the *Fort Myers (Florida) News-Press*, shortly after his release from a Costa Rican prison in May 1986. "They'll probably call it a cocaine overdose." Carr, an admitted cocaine abuser, returned to L.A., where his parents lived. In the predawn hours of December 13, 1986, he came stumbling out of his apartment in his bathrobe and collapsed on the driveway, where he began going into convulsions. He died before help could arrive. Police immediately announced that the death was due to an accidental overdose of cocaine, but the autopsy was inconclusive. More than a month later, Carr's death was ruled an accident by the coroner after a police toxicology report said he had a large amount of cocaine in his system.

Carr died just as he had predicted, and in the same way Danilo

Blandón's associates, the Torres brothers, had predicted they would die if anyone found out they were snitching on Blandón.

"I'll tell you the one true thing about Steven Carr: he was a snitch," said LAPD homicide detective Mel Arnold, who investigated Carr's demise. "Out of all those who were involved in that stuff down in Costa Rica he was the only one who talked."

While the FBI has refused to release any of its files on the long-closed Blandón case, it is evident from the few records that have leaked out that at least one lawman—Riverside FBI agent Douglas Aukland—still hoped to bust the Contra ring. Two weeks after MacIntyre's death, Aukland met with Sergeant Ed Huffman and DEA agent Tom Schrettner in the office of Bryant-Deason. According to Huffman's notes of the January 14, 1987, meeting, Aukland announced that he would "present the case of Danilo Blandón to the Organized Crime Drug Enforcement Task Force (aka Presidential Drug Task Force) next week. At that time it is anticipated that the case will be adopted by the U.S. Attorney's office in OCDETF for investigation and prosecution. More informants have been developed and some are inside the group."

Aukland also reported at the January meeting that the FBI had sent the CIA a teletype asking about the Blandón crew, and that "the reply from CIA was only regarding Norwin Meneses. Their reply was 'he is a known cocaine trafficker.'" The FBI agent identified former Somoza banker Orlando Murillo as "still a suspected money launderer for Blandón in Miami."

Then the conversation turned to the Contras. "[There are] three main front men for the FDN (Contras) in the U.S. They are constantly in the newspaper. Eden Pastor [sic], Adolfo Calero. ? Chamorro. Last week, Eden Pastor was at Guerra Auto Sales." (In an interview with the author, former ARDE commander Pastora was unable to recall why he would have been at Blandón's car lot in early 1987, but he guessed that he might have been soliciting money to get back into the war in Costa Rica.) Aukland reported that Ivan Torres, who allegedly had "political connections" to the FDN, was "the dope mover for Blandón. Ivan makes daily trips to L.A. with an unknown male Latin."

Sergeant Huffman would later say he felt that "there might be a suspicious connection between the CIA, the Contras and the Blandón organization. This was due to Lister's statements, revelations in the press concerning the connection between the CIA and the Contras and the information provided by informants that Blandón was a Contra sympathizer and might be funneling drug proceeds to the rebels in Nicaragua."

Aukland called Huffman near the end of January with an update. He had good news—the "unknown male Latin" seen leaving Blandón's car lot on those daily trips to L.A. had been identified. It was Norwin Meneses, back on one of his periodic visits to the States from his safe haven in Costa Rica. "For eight consecutive days previous, Ivan made daily trips to L.A. with Norwin Meneses. They drove a Toyota Tercel and would leave from Guerra Auto Sales," Aukland reported. The reasons for Meneses's presence can only be surmised; he may have been assisting a staffing change since, as we will see, it was during this period that Blandón began liquidating his assets and extracting himself from the L.A. crack market, turning his cocaine accounts over to two of Meneses's associates.

Aukland's presentation to the federal Organized Crime Task Force had apparently gone well. "An Assistant U.S. Attorney had adopted the case for investigation," he told Huffman on January 23. What happened to the case after that has never been publicly revealed, but it is now obvious that it shared the fate of the first assistant U.S. Attorney assigned to it. It died.

Aukland continued poking around until mid-1987, he said, and then shipped his files off to the Miami FBI when he realized that Blandón had moved. He told police in 1996 that he "believed he sent copies of his Blandón investigation to Washington D.C. during the 'Iran-Contra' hearings in the late 1980s." Where he sent them wasn't asked, and Aukland refused to be interviewed by the author. The recently declassified files of Iran-Contra independent counsel Lawrence Walsh show no evidence that the Blandón case was ever referred to Walsh by anyone from the FBI or the Justice Department.

It was all over. At the height of the American public's outrage over the Iran-Contra scandal, a criminal investigation involving Contra cocaine sales in Los Angeles was dropped by the Justice Department, and a lid of secrecy was clamped on the case, one which would not come off for another ten years. In 1996, when the author began looking into the 1986 raids, sheriff's department officials would initially deny that they had ever occurred.

If the Blandón investigation produced anything useful for the L.A. police, it was the knowledge that Freeway Rick Ross was the Man in South Central. In order to make a dent in the crack trade there, they were going to have to shut him down. "Back then Ricky Ross was a major dealer and he was affecting South Central L.A. He was supplying most of the dope in that region," said Sergeant Robert Sobel, the supervisor of the Majors I squad. "We were hearing from informants about murders and dealing cocaine directly with the Colombians and all kinds of bad things happening in L.A."

Deputy LAPD chief Glenn A. Levant felt that it was "abundantly clear that Ross was a vital link between major drug suppliers and lower level distributors and dealers."

On January 12, 1987, the sheriff's department and the LAPD formally joined forces, creating the Freeway Rick Task Force. It was one of the few times in the history of L.A. law enforcement that a single man had been the target of a multi-jurisdictional police squad. Prevented from waging war on Blandón, the police lowered their sights and trained them on his best customer.

"Ricky Ross is a Seven Four Hoover Crip whose success amongst Black gang members is well known," the task force's organizational report stated. "He has developed a large organization which handles weapons sales, multi-kilo cocaine shipments, and business enterprises as a result of surplus cash. Investments are known to involve real estate, commercial and residential."

Though Ross had made a concerted effort to keep a low profile—tooling around town in a Ford station wagon with fake wood paneling, for example—by 1986–87 he'd become too successful for his own good. One day, he and Ollie Newell sat down and counted up the money they had stashed in their apartment. It took most of the afternoon, but by the time they were finished, Ross said, they were looking at $2.8 million "sitting on the floor, wrapped up in rubber bands." And that was the haul from just one house. They had cash squirreled away in apartments all over Los Angeles. "All of his locations had these big, huge solid steel floor safes," said Sergeant Sobel. "We had to call a locksmith to get him to drill the things. It took a long time to get in."

Ross could no longer hide his fortune, and after a while, he no longer cared to. When he was coming up, he said, "I was like this mysterious guy that everybody heard about but nobody knew." Now he began acting like another man he'd seen and admired in the movies—the Godfather—doling out favors, buying friendship, buying respect. (One L.A. television station would later run a special report entitled *Ricky Ross, Gang Godfather*.)

"He's become quite a heavyweight," LAPD captain Sandy Wasson told UPI. "He's sort of a local hero in the same way the drug cartel leaders are. He employs people. He spends a lot of money in the area and he owns a lot of property either through himself or through his family."

One of Ross's lieutenants, Cornell Ward, later tried to explain it to ABC News by saying: "He was a *good* bad guy."

"And the whole community saw him that way?" correspondent Forrest Sawyer asked.

"Exactly."

"God, that's hard to believe," Sawyer sputtered.

"It's easy," Ward assured him. "All you have to do is just go through the neighborhood and see." So Sawyer did, interviewing people who described Ross as a "well-liked person in the area." They told of the crack king buying new hoops and backboards for the neighborhood parks, field lights, uniforms for local teams. He bought turntables and sound equipment for struggling rap artists, and supplied the eggs for the neighborhood Easter egg hunt. He paid for new pews and an air conditioner for his mother's South Central church and sponsored a semipro football team. Any panhandler on the street would walk away with a wad of bills if he was lucky enough to bump into Freeway Rick.

"Everybody likes him, man, because he helps, he helps a lot of people," one South Central resident told the ABC News crew. "And the brother ain't really done nothing. It's just that he sold dope."

James Galipeau, a veteran probation officer in South Central, told the *L.A. Times* that Ross "was more like a Robin Hood–type guy. You never heard of him getting high or drinking or beating women or dealing dope to kids. The guy really had a reputation for helping people out and giving money back to the community." That popular opinion, along with his wealth and success, made Ross an ideal target for the L.A. law's first concerted attack on the crack suppliers of South Central. According to task force records, the police believed that cutting Ricky Ross down to size would not only be a propaganda victory for law enforcement but would "send a message to up and coming gang members that success is not guaranteed at any level."

"To successfully conclude an investigation aimed at Ricky Ross and his associates will be the genesis of future efforts directed at mid-level drug suppliers," the task force's initial report stated. "Success will send notice to others, and there are, that they are vulnerable and law enforcement can and will escalate the enforcement effort."

The cops estimated they would need sixty days "to infiltrate and conclude enforcement efforts to bring Ross's empire to a semi- or total conclusion." The sheriff's department assigned five narcotics detectives, and the LAPD contributed four, all of whom were "selected for their respec tive talents including knowledge of gangs and narcotics expertise."

Because Majors I had been sniffing around Ross since mid-1986, its supervisor, Sergeant Robert Sobel, was put in charge of the Freeway Rick Task Force. Sobel, a short, hard-charging narcotics detective, was nicknamed "El Diablo" by his men because of his fierce demeanor and penchant for working his detectives hard.

"He kind of fancied himself as a tough guy. Some guys, when they get a nickname, they say, 'Don't call me that.' But he kind of liked that one," said one of his former subordinates. "He'd stay out two or three days in the field. If he told you to be there at seven in the morning, he'd be there at six."

In keeping with Sobel's personal motto—"March or Die"—all nine task force detectives were put on full cash overtime, so they could keep up twenty-four-hour surveillances and soften the blow by earning extra spending money. "A great many man hours are anticipated by the detectives," a January 1987 LAPD report said. "The overall investigation will require extended hours of work involving standard investigative techniques and surveillance of the primary suspect and associates."

For task force detective Steve Polak, who had been working the streets of South Central since the dawn of the crack era, nailing Ricky Ross became his personal mission in life. He made no bones about his feelings toward the young dealer: He hated him.

"What he did, he poisoned tens of thousands of people. He overdosed them. He killed them. There are a lot of crack babies out there now because of him," said Polak, who holds Ross personally responsible for starting the L.A. crack plague.

"Yeah, I could say he caused it.... There's no telling how many tens of thousands of people he touched. And not just in California, but like I said, it spread throughout the entire United States what he did with his organization. So he's responsible. He's responsible for a major cancer that still hasn't stopped spreading, even here in Los Angeles."

With nine detectives assigned to look after him, Freeway Rick started feeling the heat very soon. "When the task force was finally formed, we just dedicated seven days a week on him," Polak said proudly. "And we just dogged him until he couldn't take it anymore." That was putting it mildly. On January 21, 1987, Polak and his men hit the Freeway Motor Inn like a tornado. "The entire motel (all rooms) were searched," a task force report stated. "In room #5 currency and paperwork were seized in Ricky Ross's ame, 31 grams of rock cocaine, $6,819 and a sophisticated 800 Mhz hand-held repeater radio was discovered. Investigation disclosed Ricky Ross had purchased six of these radios for approximately $10,000 in cash."

They raided Ross's mother's house on West Eighty-seventh Place the same day, finding "a stolen 9mm Uzi and two point blank bullet proof vests." The search on Annie Ross's house sent Rick into a tirade. He called during the raid and had it out with Polak. "Going after my mom, that was the kind of shit they was doing. Polak even went to court to get her day-care license taken away. Can you believe it?" Ross grumped. A week later, as Annie Ross and a minister friend arrived at the airport to catch a plane to Texas, the task force pulled them into a trailer, searched their luggage and their car, fired questions at them, and held them long enough so that they missed their flight. Then they let them go.

As the weeks went on, it got worse. Three task force detectives searched Ollie Newell's apartment and gave Newell a vicious beating, punching and kicking him and "smothering him with a plastic bag," court records state. Newell's friend, Robert Robertson, also got a beating and had $30,000 taken from him. "They would go raid my rental properties and break the furniture, kick holes in the walls and knock the windows out," Ross complained. "And then these renters would be mad at me, you know, and stop paying their rent."

Ross's attorney, Alan Fenster, started filing formal complaints with the department on behalf of Ross and his friends, accusing the officers of beatings, thefts, property destruction, and false arrests. Sobel and his men fired back with a search warrant for Fenster's financial records, accusing him of being a money launderer and cocaine fiend. Fenster's complaints were perfunctorily investigated by the sheriff's internal affairs branch and closed with no findings of wrongdoing. His complaints to the Justice Department's civil rights division were similarly dismissed.

By the end of January the task force had served fifteen search warrants, arrested five people connected with Ross's organization, and seized nearly eight pounds of cocaine worth an estimated $1.3 million on the street, $63,122 in cash, and twenty guns. They also seized enough paperwork and telephone records to give them an inkling of just how vast Ross's cocaine distribution system was. "The investigation has expanded to include other co-conspirators and demonstrated that Ricky Ross is resourceful, has elaborate communications and is well organized," a task force weekly activity report stated.

Sobel called Ross's enterprise "a cartel…it's a major cocaine dealing organization that stretches from California to Texas and Cincinnati,

Ohio. We hit one place that was a lab, a full-on laboratory to make r
cocaine, just 30-gallon garbage cans full of cocaine. We seized like 2
pounds of finished product there."

Despite Danilo Blandón's reassurance to Ross that nothing would change, the Nicaraguan had already made up his mind to get out of Los Angeles. The raids on his home and other locations had blown his cover, and now his best customer was under siege. In the aftermath of the raids, Blandón's wife Chepita had begun to show signs of a nervous breakdown. "When I went to Miami to visit my family, the doctor told me. My wife was sick from the nerves.... The doctor called me and told me I have to change from L.A. 'If you want to have a wife...change from that place, [or] your wife will be in a psychiatric hospital.'"

There were business considerations as well. Blandón's attorney, Bradley Brunon, said Blandón's used car business had been extremely successful and had enjoyed "widespread patronage from the Latin community." But the raids "engendered widespread publicity in that small community and Mr. Blandón was practically out of business." After getting word in December 1986 that no criminal charges would result, he quietly began closing up shop, selling his used car lot, his restaurants, putting his house up for sale, collecting his debts, and sending Chepita and the girls ahead to Miami to stay with her uncle, Orlando Murillo, while he tied up loose ends. By the time he was ready to go, he was packing $1.6 million in cash and a whole new attitude.

"I was prepared to change my life," he testified. But that didn't mean letting a perfectly good cocaine ring go to waste. There was still quite a bit of money left for his countrymen to wring out of the streets of South Central. "I handed it to the Nicaraguans," Blandón said, referring to his drug enterprise. "I introduced my customers to them and they continued doing the business."

"Using your old contacts?"

"Yes, and my supplier and my buyers."

In other words, despite the fact that the LAPD, L.A. Sheriff's Department, FBI, DEA, CIA, DIA, and IRS were now fully aware of their cocaine ring, the Nicaraguans kept right on dealing. The only thing that changed was the man on top—and even that was not much of a difference. Blandón's successors were two of Norwin Meneses's cocaine-dealing colleagues, Roger Sandino Martínez, known as "Chocoyo," and Jose "Chinito" González.

"Roger Sandino was one of these guys from the old days, the old ntra connection," Blandón's lawyer, Bradley Brunon, said. "He was an riginal Gangster Contra." He was also a veteran drug trafficker who seemed to enjoy the same kind of protection as Blandón. DEA records show that Sandino was arrested in October 1980 in Hialeah, Florida, in possession of 50,000 Quaalude tablets. He pleaded guilty to conspiracy and was sentenced to thirty months in federal prison. Despite his conviction and the fact that he was in the U.S. illegally at the time of his arrest, Sandino was never deported, and he continued dealing drugs. In 1984 he set up an import-export business in Miami with the help of a Coral Gables attorney who was in business with several of Blandón's FDN associates, including former National Guard major general Gustavo "El Tigre" Medina and businessman Donald Barrios.

Sandino was busted again in April 1986, this time as part of the biggest cocaine case on the Atlantic Coast. DEA agents in Norfolk, Virginia, charged him and fourteen other people—including the son-in-law of Bolivian cocaine kingpin Roberto Suarez-Gómez—with conspiracy to import 700 pounds of cocaine worth an estimated $158 million. The dope wasn't theirs, however. It belonged to the DEA, which brought it into the United States from Bolivia to use as bait in a reverse sting, a scheme in which the police pose as cocaine sellers in order to seize money from drug buyers. In this case, they seized $1.3 million from Sandino and his associates.

The DEA has censored many of its records dealing with Roger Sandino, citing privacy reasons, so his role in the Bolivian drug operation isn't known. What is clear is that he was never brought to trial. Though arrested, Sandino somehow managed to wriggle out of custody, and the DEA issued a fugitive warrant for his capture. (When L.A. detective Tom Gordon ran Sandino's name through NADDIS several months later, however, there was no mention in his file of the Virginia indictment or the fugitive warrant.)

The trial of his codefendants became a public relations problem for the drug agency when defense lawyers discovered that DEA agents had actually left Bolivia with 752 pounds of cocaine—not 700 pounds. DEA official David Westrate explained that the missing fifty-two pounds was given to Panamanian president Manuel Noriega's drug police. Defense lawyers charged that it was a DEA payoff to Noriega for turning in one of Sandino's Panamanian associates, but Westrate claimed it was to be used by Noriega's men in a sting of their own, which for some reason never came off. The revelation was an embarrassment for the DEA; Noriega had just been indicted on drug trafficking charges in Florida, and the dictator's long, cordial relationship with the DEA was being scrutinized r Congress.

Months after fleeing Virginia, Sandino showed up in Los Angeles, just in time to take over the South Central drug ring from the departing Danilo Blandón. After Blandón moved, Ross said, he would call him in Miami and place his orders, and Roger Sandino's partner, Jose González, would handle the pickups and deliveries. Blandón confirmed that he continued working with the Nicaraguan operation in L.A., solving problems, settling disputes, and collecting commissions from the drug sales. "They used to be calling me all the time if they have some problem," Blandón said. "I was the middleman, you see, like—I was making something. I was making something...then I had to call Rick to tell him, 'Hey, what's going on?'"

By then, Ross said, the cocaine business was losing some of its allure. His friend and mentor was three thousand miles away. He owned about $5 million worth of real estate and still had more money than he could spend. And for the first time, Ross said, he began having second thoughts about just how mellow his product really was. His current girlfriend, Mary Louise Bronner, the mother of two of his five children, was now a crack addict, thanks to him. The chickens were starting to come home.

"At first, I had never saw anybody addicted to cocaine. It took a while before—before it started to affect anybody that we dealt with. I mean nobody—at first, it was like everybody that was using cocaine drove big cars and, you know, stayed in the Baldwin Hills area and then it started to change and we started to see the effects that it was having." Ross said the first twinges of conscience came when Jocelyn Clements, a longtime friend and one of his earliest customers, turned into a raging crackhead. "I found out that she was taking all her welfare money and her food stamps and stuff and spending it on cocaine," he said.

But there were other reasons for his restiveness. By early 1987 the L.A. crack market had become saturated, so much so that many gang members were hitting the road to find greener pastures and emptier street corners. Crips and Bloods were bumping into each other in cities across the United States. "Everywhere you go, you know what I'm saying, anywhere you go, you're gonna see some people from L.A.," one Crip dealer told California Department of Justice researchers in 1988. "If they got, you know, a dope house out there or a dope street out there...you'll run into somebody on that street from L.A."

Said another: "Out of town where nobody else ain't at...that's where the money's being made because there's too much competition in Los ngeles. It's got too many dope dealers in Los Angeles competing against each other. So they take it out of town. The profits are better. Here you can sell an ounce for $600. Over there you can sell it for $1,500." Cocaine prices in L.A. had been dropping through the floor because so much of it was coming in. Kilos that had once cost Ross $50,000 were now going for $12,000, which the *L.A. Times* blamed partly on Ross, since he was buying in such volume.

By 1986–87, Ross said, a good chunk of his business consisted of exporting the drug to higher-priced areas, where he was able to undercut the local yokels by thousands of dollars a key. He'd made connections in Bakersfield, Fresno, St. Louis, Texas, and Alabama. Police in St. Louis said cocaine prices there went into a free fall once the Crips and Bloods arrived. "Gang members have flooded the market here with excellent cocaine at good prices. The local dealers have to succumb to these people," one detective complained to the *St. Louis Post-Dispatch*.

The L.A. market was also getting tougher. Ross was no longer the only crack dealer in South Central with Colombian connections. He had begun facing competition from Brian "Waterhead Bo" Bennett, a fast-rising young dealer who'd hooked up with a Colombian named Antonio Villabona in 1985 and started moving large amounts of cocaine. But Bennett was sloppy and obvious, carrying brown paper bags stuffed with cash around in public. Within a year the police were onto him and he was arrested in 1988. L.A. law enforcement officials held a press conference to announce that, for the first time, they had proof that the black gangs had made direct connections with the Colombian cartels.

"What they didn't realize," observed *L.A. Times* reporter Jesse Katz, "was that Ricky had hit that level about six years earlier."

Danilo's decision to move back east made Ross think. If Danilo felt it was time to hang it up, maybe it was. He was usually right about things like that. Ross started scaling back his drug sales, gradually turning over the business to his partner, Ollie Newell, and their lieutenants, Mike Smith and Cornell Ward. He began making plans for an early retirement.

"I had slowed down on my drug activity tremendously," Ross said. "I might have been selling once a week to maybe one or two people. They would call me and say that they needed something, and I would call Mr. Blandón and get it and give it to them. So it was hard for the police to catch me doing something because I was barely doing anything. You know, they thought I was still going full bore, but I wasn't."

The Freeway Rick Task Force wasn't slowing down a bit, though. Every week another batch of search warrants would be served, another pile of cash would be seized, and another one of Ross's friends or relat would get roughed up or hauled off to jail. "We had some very good info mants that were very close to Ricky Ross and he knew it. Ricky Ross was getting upset," Sobel said.

In their rush to put Ross out of business, though, the detectives' tactics became increasingly questionable. According to federal court records, the task force ransacked an apartment owned by one of Ross's girlfriends in February 1987, picked up a doll belonging to his daughter, and then "as a threat to Ricky Ross, they plunged a knife into the doll's head, pinning it to a wall, along with a note: 'This is you, Ricky.'"

Sergeant Sobel said that "as time went on it became common knowledge among the entire Task Force that [LAPD detective] Polak was carrying around a kilo of dope in the tire well of his vehicle. Polak would be bragging about a present for Ricky Ross when they ran into him. There were constant jokes made about the dope they had ready [to plant on] Ricky Ross when they found him."

One evening in mid-April 1987, Ross, Newell, and Cornell Ward closed up Rick's auto parts store on Western Avenue, the Big Palace of Wheels, and piled into the crack king's brand-new Ford station wagon, intending to cruise around for a while. "I looked in the rearview mirror and I saw some cars coming up behind me with no lights on and first I thought it was somebody maybe trying to rob us or something. We didn't know. So I started speeding in the car and then a red light caught me and a car pulled up right up on the side of me and the guy let his window down."

Newell recognized the driver. It was task force detective Sergeant Robert Tolmaire, a black officer who was regarded by Ross's crew as the most dangerous and violent detective on the whole squad. "He stuck this gun out the window, pointing it at the car," Ross said. Newell turned to Ross and asked what he intended to do. Ross said he didn't know.

"Well," Newell replied calmly, "you know they're going to kill you. They already said they're going to kill you."

Ross stomped on the gas and roared through the traffic light, with the detectives in hot pursuit. He raced down a side street and decided to make a run for it. The station wagon swerved violently into a driveway and Ross leaped out, sprinting through a yard and hopping a fence.

"Behind me, I could hear them shooting," Ross said. The shots missed him, and he managed to hitch a ride on a passing bus and escape.

Newell and Ward weren't so lucky. They said they were handcuffed and tossed into the back of a police car, and the deputies took turns beat-on them with metal flashlights and leather saps. Ward was also hacked with a shotgun.

Then, according to court records, LAPD detective Steve Polak drove up, opened the trunk of his car, and "retrieved a kilo of cocaine in a black gym bag. Polak then displayed the bag to the others present, claiming that Ross had dropped the bag as he ran." Since shots had been fired that had to be explained, the deputies also agreed to accuse Ross of shooting at them.

Ross was charged with a variety of crimes—four counts of conspiracy, three counts of transporting controlled substances, one count of assault with a deadly weapon upon a police officer—and was declared a fugitive from justice. Assuming that every cop in L.A. would be gunning for him as a result of the assault charge, Ross went into hiding, lying low for three weeks as the task force scoured the city, tearing through his friends' houses on an all-out manhunt. On May 5, 1987, he decided things had gone far enough.

"I felt that it went past just…duty," Ross explained in court testimony. "My whole thing, I felt, became personal. It wasn't like just Joe the drug dealer. It had become more of a personal kind of vendetta with them and me. I didn't have no vendetta with them because if they arrested me, that was their job, but it seemed like they had a vendetta with me."

Ross drove down to the sheriff's office and turned himself in. He was locked up in the L.A. County Jail on a $1 million bond. The LAPD issued a press release, announcing the demise of Ross's "multi-million dollar mid-level rock cocaine organization…estimated [to have] netted over $12 million during the first four months of 1987." The body count was impressive indeed: sixty-one search warrants; thirty-nine arrests, including that of the ringleader; and $13.3 million in cocaine seized, along with $240,000 in cash and sixty-two firearms, including "revolvers, semi-automatic pistols, shotguns, Uzi's, Mac-10's, a fully automatic Mac-11 machine gun" as well as "five bulletproof vests."

The investigation had also "developed comprehensive intelligence information regarding street gang involvement in rock cocaine trafficking throughout the Western United States," Deputy LAPD chief Levant wrote, and he called the Freeway Rick Task Force "a model for other jurisdictions to follow to attack mid-level cocaine trafficking in California."

But the celebrations were destined to be short. Apparently unable to resist the temptation, several members of the Freeway Rick Task Force dropped by the jail to inspect their prize. They started goading Ross about Alan Fenster, telling him that his coke-snorting lawyer had abandoned him and was leaving him to hang. His only hope, they told him, was to confess and go to work for them because if he didn't, he was going to be in jail for a very, very long time. Fenster was never going to get him out of this jam.

They'd set him up, the detectives crowed, and they'd set him up good. He was going down for the count because they had their stories worked out, and the case was tight as a virgin. "The discussion was tape recorded," U.S. Justice Department records state. "They discussed their frame-up of Ross and unsuccessfully tried to turn Ross against his Colombian cocaine source. Ultimately, Ross filed a motion to dismiss based on the encounter and the existence of the tape recording was revealed at the hearing. The judge insisted that the tape be produced."

Before it was turned over, amateurish attempts were made to doctor it. A forensic expert concluded that eleven erasures had been made in an effort to obliterate the detectives' accusations against Fenster and their discussions of a beating administered to Ross's brother, David.

After hearing the tape, the judge threw the charges out of court.

Freeway Rick was free once again.

In one month, he'd dodged bullets twice—both lead and legal—and he didn't intend to give the task force a third shot at him. Someone else could be the crack king from now on.

"I could go anywhere in the world and sell dope"

Ricky Ross moved as far away from Los Angeles as he could get, taking Mary Bronner and their children to Cincinnati, Ohio. It was where Bronner grew up; Ross had accompanied her home once as she attempted to kick her crack habit, and he had taken to the tidy conservative midwestern city on the banks of the Ohio River. The neighborhoods were green and quiet, lined with big leafy trees. The homes were spacious, set on seemingly endless yards, not stacked on top of each other like the dusty matchboxes in Los Angeles.

"It was real cool," Ross said. He would use his time in Cincinnati "to back away from the game, just mellow out. I thought I'd get away from it, you know." Though most of his assets were tied up in L.A. real estate, he'd taken $300,000 in cash with him. In a city where a palatial home could be had for a third of that, it was plenty of money. His businesses and rental properties in L.A. were still producing revenue. "Financially," Ross said, "I was set."

He moved to a townhouse on the east side of Hamilton County, in a comfortable Republican suburb of rolling hills and minivans. "We was trying to get away from drug life—her using and me dealing," Ross explained. "Basically, I just wanted to be a small-time person, you know, with a nice house, with a nice car. I wanted kids. I wanted my kids to play tennis. I wanted my kids to win Wimbledon. I wanted them to go to college."

But Ross had never been able to sit back and take things easy. He had to be in motion, working some kind of deal, so he indulged himself in his other great obsession: real estate. He liked to refer to himself half-jokingly as a property junkie. "I was buying property, old houses, rebuilding them...I had become pretty knowledgeable on how to rebuild houses." It was undramatic but satisfying work, and gradually L.A. began to seem farther than 2,400 miles away. Ricky Ross was twenty-seven years old, and as the weeks stretched into months he began to feel at ease. Years later he would look back on that period wistfully. "I look at myself now and say, 'Man, you had it made.'"

He would get occasional calls from Danilo in Miami, and they'd catch up. "We stayed on a relationship. You know, we talked and he was still dealing with Ollie. He didn't quit. When I quit, Ollie didn't stop." But Ross said the Nicaraguan didn't like dealing with Newell, whom he referred to as "Big Charlie."

"Basically, he would tell me: 'Why'd you quit? I need you. You know Big Charlie don't take care of the business like you do.... He was saying, basically, that Charlie didn't pay him like he was supposed to and, you know, he was slow, stuff like that. He said that I took care of my business the way I was supposed to, and I did what I told him I was going to do."

Blandón denied he was personally selling drugs at that time but admitted that he was overseeing the drug sales of his successors. "I knew everything," he said. Because of the way the cocaine business worked, he'd had to vouch for Roger Sandino and Jose González, and that meant mediating the disputes and solving the problems that arose between Ross's crew, the Nicaraguans, and their Colombian suppliers.

Blandón agreed that Ross's replacements "weren't taking care of the business" and said there were frequent feuds with Meneses's men. "They were calling me all the time: 'Hey, the order didn't come with the money. The order didn't come with the merchandise.' So that's the relationship I had."

But most of his time and attention, Blandón said, was devoted to what he called his "legitimate businesses." After he got to Miami, Blandón invested his L.A. drug profits in a string of companies, sometimes in partnership with an exiled Nicaraguan judge, José Macario Estrada, a family friend who was also Blandón's immigration lawyer. Like Blandón, Macario was deeply involved with the FDN and its Miami support network, working with the Contras to arrange travel papers and work permits for rebel soldiers and their families. He also helped to create a number of nonprofit foundations in Miami that supported the Contra cause.

"I was with the FDN here in Miami, working in Miami since 1980," Macario confirmed in an interview with the author. Before the revolution, acquaintances said, he'd worked at the U.S. embassy in Managua, helping out in the cultural attaché's office. "We always joked that he was working for the CIA," said one. Macario denied it, but it's easy to see why others might have gotten that impression. He had CIA agents for friends. In fact, they'd saved his life in 1979.

"A squad of Sandinista revolutionaries came to pass me by the arms, you know? Came to, what do you call it, eliminate me in a summary proceedings." The next day he decided to seek asylum in the embassy of Colombia, which, as it turned out, was located in the home of Macario's friend, attorney Carlos Icaza. A son-in-law of General Edmundo Meneses, Icaza was the personal attorney of Adolfo Calero, who had been a CIA agent before the 1979 revolution and would become the Contras' political leader. Icaza shielded Macario from the Sandinistas for a time, and Macario escaped the country seven months after the revolution on the last day of February 1980. "I have the anniversary of my escape once every four years," he joked.

Macario's protector, Carlos Icaza, was publicly accused by the Sandinistas of being a CIA agent in 1983, and a warrant was issued for his arrest. He was charged with being a central conspirator in a foiled CIA plot to poison Nicaragua's foreign minister with a bottle of thalium-laced Benedictine liqueur. Icaza fled Nicaragua and went to work for the FDN in Honduras, as did his wife. Later he became an attorney for Norwin Meneses (among other things, he arranged the sale of a Salvador Dali painting Norwin owned) and served as corporate lawyer for Norwin's suspected money launderer, economist Orlando Murillo.

In late 1986 José Macario was appointed to a blue-ribbon commission by the FDN to look into newspaper allegations that the Contras were squandering U.S. humanitarian aid money. Another member of that FDN panel was accountant Rene González of the Peat Marwick & Mitchell office in Caracas, Venezuela.

After exonerating the FDN, both men became business partners with Danilo Blandón in a company called Mex-US Import and Export Inc. Other directors of that company included Blandón's Mexican college friend and convicted money launderer Sergio Guerra and a Panamanian banker, José Fernando Soto, the longtime representative of the Swiss Bank Corp. in Panama and an old friend of Chepita's uncle, Orlando Murillo. Blandón also bought his wife a business: Pupi's Children's Boutique, which Chepita ran from a shopping mall in

Sweetwater. And he bought into a Nicaraguan restaurant in Miami called La Parrilla.

La Parrilla had been started by Anastasio Somoza's former counterinsurgency expert, Major General Gustavo Medina, and Miami businessman Donald Barrios, the FDN supporter who'd sent Blandón to fetch Norwin Meneses from LAX six or seven years earlier in 1980 or 1981. Ricky Ross's former cocaine supplier, Henry Corrales, also owned a piece of the action, court records show. The elegant restaurant became a hangout for Contra leaders and was the site of pro-Contra demonstrations and seminars. The *Miami Herald* lightheartedly described the cuisine as "Contra cooking from ex-Somoza General Gustavo Medina." Another story noted that "despite the proximity of Fontainebleau Park, the apartment complex that so reminds Nicaraguans of the Open Tres apartments in their native Managua, La Parrilla customers are primarily Cuban."

"The Cubans, our compatriots in exile, also are very fond of Nicaraguan food," General Medina explained.

Blandón's restaurant was also a big hit with the food critics. "The steak melts in your mouth," twittered one *Miami Herald* reviewer. "Service is akin to the poshest French restaurant." In 1987 the *Herald* named it "the best Nicaraguan restaurant in Dade [County]" and awarded it four stars, the paper's highest rating.

But the cocaine lord's main investment was in Alpha II Rent-a-Car, which began with an office outside the Miami International Airport and spread to twenty-four other locations in southern Florida. Blandón's rent-a-car business was so successful, court records show, he became an authorized outlet for Chrysler Corporation and General Motors vehicles.

Ross said he visited Blandón in Miami several times in mid-1987 and was treated like visiting royalty; Blandón provided him with free rental cars and complimentary hotel rooms. Meanwhile, Ross turned Blandón's daughters onto rap music, bringing them the latest CDs and amazing them with stories about the rappers he'd known and bankrolled from his neighborhood. "Danilo took me around and introduced me to his friends, like he was showing me off. I was probably the only black guy any of them had ever met," he said. Several times, Ross said, Blandón dropped hints that he'd like to do some business with him.

"He kept saying he could get me some stuff for really cheap and we could make a lot of money with it in Cincinnati." Ross knew Danilo was right. He'd checked around town and had been amazed at how much folks in Ohio were paying for their dope. "I got down there and started meeting people and they were telling me, 'Aw, man, it's this and it's that.'

Then my friend from Miami came by and said, 'Hey, man, come on, I'll give it for you for ten.' So he was talking about giving it to me for $10,000 and in Cincinnati, keys was selling for $50,000!" Ross laughed. "Ounces were like $2,400. It was like when I first started."

When Blandón called him from Detroit one day in the fall of 1987 and asked him to come up for a meeting, Ross said he knew what his old friend had in mind. And, just as surely, he knew that he would get in his car and make the four-hour trip north. It wasn't just because Danilo was asking, though Ross said his relationship with the Nicaraguan was such that he would have done almost anything for him. The real reason, Ross knew, was that he missed cocaine trafficking. He was good at it; it was in every fiber of his being.

"The business," as Danilo called it, had been custom-made for him. It was his calling. God, Ross firmly believed, had put him on earth to be the Cocaine Man. When he wasn't dealing, he was just like anybody else, maybe worse—an illiterate high-school dropout. A zero. But give him a pager and some dope, and he was a virtuoso. There weren't too many people in this world who could dance through a minefield of cops and snitches juggling multimillion-dollar drug deals and emerge unscratched.

"It got to the point where I enjoyed selling drugs so much that I could be in bed with my woman and, if the right person paged me, I'd get up," Ross told the *Los Angeles Times*. So when Danilo offered him fifteen kilos and a good price, Ross said, "I told him to bring them to me. I'll take them." He was back in play.

Making Cincinnati his own was effortless. By then, Ross was an old hand at creating new crack markets. "I knew the recipe. It's just like it was in L.A. If you want to get in with the blacks, you find out who the shot-caller [is]. And you talk to him and you get him on your side. If he gives you permission, you can go to his neighborhood and talk to his guys. So that's what I did in Lincoln Heights," Ross later told a Cincinnati reporter.

From there, he branched out to Over-the-Rhine, another poor inner-city neighborhood, and then took his show to the suburbs: Avondale, Mt. Airy, Bond Hill, St. Bernard, Lockland, and Walnut Hills, using the same marketing gimmicks he'd perfected in L.A.—free cocaine, smoke parties, volume discounts. Once those operations were up and running, Ross called back to L.A. and invited his friends to come out and staff them.

Suddenly, Cincinnati had two problems it never had before: Crips and crack.

"In 1987, we had lots of crack in the east and west but not in Cincinnati until Ricky Ross came here. There's no doubt in my mind crack in Cincinnati can be traced to Ross," said Sharonville, Ohio, police specialist Robert Enoch. Added Cincinnati's former U.S. attorney, D. Michael Crites: "One day we woke up and we had Crips in southwestern Ohio."

But Ross didn't limit himself to the Queen City. He began "going out of town," and the story was the same wherever he went. With Blandón's cocaine prices, he could blow the locals out of the water. So he did. "There was evidence that indicated not only was the organization distributing in the Cincinnati area, but as far away as Cleveland, Columbus, Indianapolis and Texas," Crites said. Cincinnati DEA agents said they traced Ross's cocaine to Hamilton, Middletown, and Toledo, Ohio, as well as St. Louis and Atlanta.

"That was a guy who could sell Popsicles to an Eskimo," said San Fernando Police lieutenant Ernest Halcon, a veteran undercover detective. "You want to say he's a low-life, no-good piece of crap. But you got to respect some of these guys for their ambition and cunning. You got to give the devil his due."

"I could go anywhere in the world and sell dope," Ross said. "I just need one person in a city."

Mike Horton, a police officer assigned to a DEA task force in Ohio, said Ross became known as the "10-million-dollar man" in Cincinnati because of the money he was supposedly making.

Ross said he made nowhere near that much. In ten months, he said, he sold 300 or 400 kilos of Blandón's cocaine in the Midwest, netting around $2 million in profits. He flew to Miami once a month to drop off cash. "Either we met there, or we met in New York. I think we might have met in Atlanta one time too," he said. He said he met with Blandón and a Colombian named Tony in New York City several times to place orders for cocaine.

Blandón confirmed that, and said he and Roger Sandino visited Ross in Cincinnati. Ross also wired money to Florida in Chepita's name, Blandón said, but claimed it was paid to Sandino "because Roge[r] Sandino was my partner in the business."

At other times, Ross said, his friends in L.A. would just stick the d[...] on a bus and let Greyhound do the driving. And that was how Cinc[...] authorities finally discovered who was bringing all that crack into th[...]

In September 1988 an eastbound Greyhound eased into a [...] New Mexico, and a state policeman walked by the silver behe[...]

a drug-sniffing dog. The canine got near the luggage compartment and went crazy. Inside, the officer found a suitcase carrying nine kilos of cocaine, worth around $100,000. The luggage tag said the bag was bound for Cincinnati. A call was placed to the Cincinnati DEA, asking for advice. Let it come through, the DEA said. We'll stake out the bus station and see who shows up.

A few days later one of Ross's employees, a young L.A. Crip named Alphonso Jeffries, ambled into the bus depot and claimed the suitcase, springing the DEA's trap.

Ross got the news and quickly assessed the damage. Nine kilos was enough to put Alphonso Jeffries away for a couple decades or more. The pressure would be on him to roll over and give up someone else, and if the dominos started falling, they would form a straight line to Freeway Rick. Ross contacted Jeffries and told him all his legal bills would be paid and he'd have the best lawyers in town, as long as he kept his mouth shut. Jeffries told him he would.

Then, as if he didn't have enough problems, Ross discovered that one his underlings was screwing his girlfriend. That clinched it; he was getting fucked every which way in Cincinnati. It was time to go home.

"I'd been gone a little over a year, so I felt that everything had died down and people had forgot about me," he said. "I sold what I had and I quit."

When he got back to L.A. in the fall of 1988, he wanted nothing to do with cocaine. He was too worried about Alphonso Jeffries, whose steadfast silence on Rick's behalf had been rewarded with a twenty-year prison sentence. That was straight federal time. No parole. For all Ross knew, Jeffries had already rolled over on him. Ross went into the home improvement business, buying specialized equipment to spray acoustic ceilings, painting, and waiting to see if the other shoe would drop.

"I guess about a month after I got back in L.A. he [Blandón] started calling me again and asking me what was the matter, why I'd stopped, and that Charlie and him wasn't doing what they were supposed to be doing." Ross said he told Blandón to forget it. He wasn't getting anywhere near dope. "I had enough money... I was working and I was just [illegible]le to resist him."

Blandón called two or three times a month, Ross said, until the word got [illegible]at Ross was under investigation. A grand jury in Smith County, Texas, [illegible]d an indictment charging Ross with cocaine conspiracy. He had [illegible] cousins, the Mauldins, in Texas in May 1988 and discussed a [illegible]l with them on a monitored line. A fugitive warrant was issued.

"About three months after I was in L.A., they did a program on CBS that was talking about me, that I was under investigation in Cincinnati and also in Texas," he said. "After the CBS program showed, [Danilo] stopped calling me."

A lot of people stopped calling after that. Ricky Ross was starting to smell like dead meat. As Ross had feared, Alphonso Jeffries had broken. He told the police about Ross's trips to New York City and California to pick up cocaine in the fall of 1988. They'd brought twenty kilos back from New York the first time, he said, and ten kilos the second. DEA agents found travel records and motel receipts that confirmed Jeffries's statements, and they found Ross's fingerprints on several incriminating documents.

In June 1989, Ross and thirteen other people were indicted on federal charges of cocaine conspiracy in Cincinnati, and another fugitive warrant was issued. Now he had the state of Texas *and* the U.S. government after him. Ross melted into South Central and kept his head down, staying busy with his construction work. Months went by, and he heard nothing. One afternoon in late November, he was pouring concrete at an apartment building when an unmarked police car came screeching up.

"One of the guys says, 'That was the narcs.' And so when he said it was the narcs, I ran, and when I ran they started shooting at me. I think they shot about twelve times at me." Bullets zipping by, Ross scampered down East Coldon Avenue, found an unlocked house, and barricaded himself inside, retreating to a bedroom closet. In the darkness, Ross pulled out a cell phone and frantically tried to call his lawyer, Alan Fenster, while the police yelled at him to come out. A two-man SWAT team arrived with a dog and approached the house cautiously.

"They told me to come out," Ross said, "and the next thing I knew they kicked the door in. They came in with a dog. The dog came to the closet and he alerted that I was in the closet."

The police pulled open the door, and Ross found himself staring into the glare of several flashlights. He was told to come out with his hands in front of him and to get down on his knees, which he did. He was handcuffed, and "then all of a sudden the dog just about went crazy. He started biting—he started biting me all up in between my legs, on my butt cheeks and he—he did it so long that I couldn't take th pain no more, so I kicked him."

All the pent-up rage and frustration that the Los Angeles police saved up for Freeway Rick erupted in the next instant.

"They started hitting me in the head with flashlights, and one of them broke his flashlight on the top of my head right here. And after he did that he went in the kitchen and got a big frying pan—I think it was a 15-pound frying pan, he said in court—and he clubbed me over the head with that. And then he was kicking me all over my back and in my stomach. I had boot marks all over me, all over my body." Ross was taken to a hospital and charged with assault on a police officer. The police claimed Ross had attacked them with a frying pan, so, naturally, they'd had to subdue him.

Bruised, sore, and swollen, the former crack king of L.A. was unceremoniously dumped into a cell at the Los Angeles County Metropolitan Correctional Center to await extradition to Cincinnati. In all his life, things had never seemed more hopeless. Politically, the timing of his capture couldn't have been worse. In the past year, the police and the media had finally discovered the connection between the L.A. gangs and the spread of crack and automatic weapons to cities and towns across America. Newspapers, magazines, and TV shows were filled with stories about L.A. gangbangers showing up in small-town USA, packing Uzis and terrorizing the locals.

"Los Angeles drug gangs are spreading cocaine and violence in cities nationwide and may become a new form of organized crime unless they are stopped soon," worried a July 1988 Associated Press story that appeared in many newspapers around the country. "Authorities say members of two prominent rival drug gangs from Los Angeles, the Crips and the Bloods, have infiltrated cities from Alaska to Washington, D.C."

During the 1988 presidential campaign Washington had gone on an antidrug crusade, in many ways more extreme than the one in 1986, because now there were some facts to back up the fear. Congressional hearings had unearthed the links between crack profits and the proliferation of assault rifles in the inner cities. Government studies had been done, showing that L.A. had indisputably become the main source of the nation's crack contagion, a giant chancre oozing death and violence. "Los Angeles has become the transshipment area for this problem," testified assistant L.A. County sheriff Jerry Harper. "We are being contacted regularly by officers from Oregon, Washington, Arizona, Texas, Kansas, Missouri, Ohio, Louisiana, Florida, Hawaii and all with regard to gang members, Crips and Bloods, and so forth, who have emanated from Los Angeles and are transporting their drugs to other states across the nation."

Los Angeles U.S. attorney Robert Bonner told Congress that "these [illegible]ging modern-day gangsters have set up raw cocaine distribution outlets in cities across the country. I can assure you and members of this committee that if these gangs are allowed to become entrenched in the drug distribution business on a nationwide basis, which is the direction they are headed, in the coming few years we will find ourselves with an organized crime problem that will put the Mafia to shame."

Alarmed by such reports, Congress passed a whole new set of anti-crack laws that, among other things, made even first-time offenders like Ross eligible for a mandatory ten-year sentence, no parole.

Ross knew there was a good chance they would nail him to the wall in Cincinnati, a city that had sent Larry Flynt to jail just for selling dirty magazines. If anyone ranked lower than a pornographer, it was someone like Ricky Ross. He epitomized everything that decent, upright midwesterners had come to hate and fear about the 1980s—a black crack kingpin bringing all his Crip friends in from the Left Coast to pollute their city with drugs and gangs. They knew how to deal with people like him.

And if, by some miracle, he managed to beat the federal rap, he had the folks in Texas waiting to get their hooks into him, with their hundred-year prison sentences and well-known love of black drug dealers. Try as he might, he could see no way out. He wasn't dealing with the goons from the Freeway Rick Task Force this time. These federal agents weren't going to do anything stupid. Barring some divine intervention, he was finished.

Ross passed several gloomy months awaiting extradition in the L.A. prison, growing more disconsolate with each passing day. His friends gradually quit coming to see him. His properties began going into foreclosure. Everything he'd worked for was crumbling away.

Then the people from the U.S. Department of Justice came calling, and by the time they left, he could barely stop smiling. God, it seemed, had not forsaken the Cocaine Man after all.

22

"They can't touch us"

When Ross was led from his cell at the MCC to meet the representatives of the Justice Department, his thoughts had been with Danilo Blandón. The feds, Ross assumed, wanted his source. It was what the task force had been after when they came to see him the last time he'd been locked up. That was the way things worked. You got busted, and they came to you with The Choice: be a rat or be a jailbird.

He'd managed to duck the situation the last time, but he wouldn't have that luxury again. The feds had him by the balls. Now, it appeared, he would be forced to confront the question he'd always dreaded: Could he rat out Danilo? "He was Danilo, you know? He was, he was like my God, my number one person," Ross said. "Hadn't many people been there for me, you know, when I was coming up. So Danilo was somebody that I felt had always been in my corner and he always showed like he cared about me."

But to Ross's surprise and relief, the federal people had no interest in the Nicaraguan. "They didn't ask me nothing about who I was getting it from," Ross said. All the Justice Department wanted to hear about were his experiences with the detectives on the Freeway Rick Task Force. They'd been reading those complaints he and his friends had filed against the officers. Were they true? And would he be willing to testify to it?

Ross was dumbfounded. He'd been willing to testify two years ago, but nobody had wanted to hear about it then.

Besides, the Justice Department's Civil Rights Division had already looked into his complaints and dismissed them for lack of evidence, or so he'd been told. Yet now they wanted to know if he would be a U.S. government witness against the police. A drug dealer helping to put narcs in jail? If that didn't beat all.

Ross had one question: What was in it for him? It could change the way certain people felt about him, he was told. If he cooperated and testified truthfully and honestly, it would help when he appeared before the judge in Ohio for sentencing. Plus, the government might decide not to seize his properties or his remaining cash under the asset forfeiture laws. And there was the added attraction of getting back at the cops who had harassed him and his family.

To the Justice Department, Ricky Ross was no longer a dope peddler. He had become "a percipient witness in a case involving allegations of serious misconduct" by members of the Majors and the Freeway Rick Task Force. An FBI sting called "Operation Big Spender" was behind Ross's newfound credibility with the federal government. "This may be a terrible thing to say," said L.A. County sheriff Sherman Block, "but as we got into this thing, it became obvious that the stories being told by the crooks were more credible than the stories told by our officers."

In the fall of 1989, after Block received anonymous complaints that the Majors were ripping off drug dealers, the FBI sent an undercover agent into the Majors' territory posing as a courier for a money launderer. The Majors were tipped off that he was carrying a load of cash, which could be found in his room at the Warner Center Marriott in Woodland Hills. The FBI had reserved three adjoining rooms at the hotel. The "courier" was in the middle. On one side were agents manning video and audio gear; on the other, a SWAT team.

It was like dangling a pork chop in front of a dog. Seizing cash had become the Majors' specialty by the end of the 1980s. They were no longer real narcotics detectives anymore. Thanks to expanded asset forfeiture laws, the Majors had become sin-tax collectors for Sheriff Block and L.A. County.

In 1988 alone, the sheriff's office hauled in an astonishing $33.9 million in cash, and another $33 million the following year—along with 66 houses, 110 vehicles, 4 airplanes, and 2 businesses. Of the $33 million seized in 1988, the Majors had brought in $13.6 million of it all by themselves, along with 4,470 pounds of cocaine.

The lion's share of that booty had been produced by the Majors II crew, which was now under the command of Sergeant Robert Sobel—"El

Diablo." After the Freeway Rick Task Force disbanded in late 1987, Sobel was hand-picked to lead Majors II, and he had driven his squad to Olympian heights. "My men are all trained to tear flesh when they scent blood!" Sobel had bragged in an interdepartmental newsletter.

The Majors zeroed in on the FBI's "courier" so fast they had a surveillance team in place before the FBI agents arrived at the hotel. The detectives quickly learned that the "courier" had reserved the rooms on either side of him and got suspicious, wondering if they were being led into some trap. Worried that the deputies would bust into the other rooms and expose the sting, an FBI agent cautiously approached Sobel's crew and told them they'd done their jobs too well. They had stumbled on a federal undercover operation and were about to expose it (which was technically the truth). Would they be so kind as to leave the area?

Two weeks later, the FBI tried again, this time renting a room at the Valley Hilton Hotel in Sherman Oaks. Again the Majors snapped at the bait. A hidden video camera was rolling as two plainclothes officers burst into the courier's room and found $480,000 in a garment bag. "'Ohhhhh ho ho!" one deputy exclaimed as she pulled the bag from under the bed and opened it. "Is this your bag?"

The deputies skimmed $48,000 of the marked cash, stuffed it into a gym bag, and left. Sobel and other deputies then entered the room and questioned the undercover FBI agent, Indalecio Guzman, about the money. After the agent claimed no knowledge of where the cash came from, one deputy persuaded him to sign a form disclaiming ownership of the remaining money. "[You] can say room service left it," Sobel joked.

In a series of lightning raids that night, the authorities found some of the marked cash in the homes and cars of the deputies. Sheriff Block immediately suspended nine members of the squad.

Within forty-eight hours, distraught and appearing heavily medicated, "El Diablo" Sobel approached the feds and volunteered to testify against his crew. He admitted that much of what Ross and his partners had accused them of was true: the task force had routinely beaten suspects, a practice known as giving someone a "tune-up"; planted dope, called "flaking" a suspect; lied in court; falsified search warrant affidavits; and stolen drug money—hundreds of thousands of dollars—by turning in only a portion of what they had seized.

With their ill-gotten gains, the Majors had gone on spending sprees, buying vacation homes on the Colorado River, big-screen TVs, jewelry, fancy cars, boats, helicopter lessons, and Hawaiian vacations. The FBI discovered that LAPD detective Polak had liposuction performed on his buttocks, and his wife had paid cash for a breast enlargement operation. The agents were told of Dom Perignon–drenched parties; officers were dabbling in stocks and bonds and starting side businesses. Remarkably, considering their line of work, the detectives had left a paper trail of their excesses a mile long.

On February 22, 1990, a federal grand jury indicted ten deputies on twenty-seven counts of theft, income tax evasion, and conspiracy. And prosecutors promised they were just getting started. There were more indictments to come.

One of the first to be charged was Deputy Daniel Garner, a hard-nosed detective who had been one of the spiritual leaders of Majors II. Garner decided that if he was going down, he was going down fighting. He hired one of L.A.'s most high-profile criminal lawyers, Harland W. Braun, who had defended Lee Marvin in his famous "palimony" suit and would later successfully represent one of the officers in the Rodney King beating case.

"Dan Garner came in my office and told me that there was nothing the feds were going to be able to do to them because he had proof that they were dealing in drugs and laundering drug money," Braun recalled in an interview. "He said, 'They can't touch us.' And he gave me these papers he said they had seized in a drug raid several years earlier." They were some of the documents the Majors had taken from Ronald Lister's house in 1986, which Garner had secreted away as "insurance." Though Braun privately doubted the records would have the impact Garner expected, he agreed they could be a useful bargaining chip down the road. Certainly, the Majors had little else to pin their hopes on. While the FBI had an incriminating videotape, marked cash, and tape recordings Sobel had secretly made of the deputies plotting their defense at a bar, all the detectives had were some lame stories about hitting jackpots in Las Vegas and loans from relatives.

Garner and his codefendants went on trial in October 1990, and the federal prosecutors led off their case by playing the devastating videotape for the jurors, who became noticeably upset at the sight of police officers helping themselves to bundles of suspected drug money and then joking about it. Braun decided it was time to spring the Lister papers on the government. While he was cross-examining one of the FBI agents who had participated in the Big Spender sting, he casually asked if the agent knew anything about seized drug money being laundered by the federal government and then diverted to the Contras by the CIA. Federal prosecutors leaped to their feet to object, and Braun let the question hang for a bit before moving on to another topic.

After court, Braun walked out onto the steps of the federal building in downtown Los Angeles and held his usual post-trial spin session with the reporters covering the case. One scribe asked about the strange question he'd put to the FBI agent about the Contras and the CIA. Braun calmly replied that he was laying the groundwork for his client's defense: outrageous government conduct. Deputy Garner, Braun pointed out, was a court-certified expert in money-laundering issues, and Garner would explain how some of the cash they were accused of stealing from drug dealers had been laundered by the CIA and used to buy arms for the Contras and other covert operations.

Braun's startling claims were mentioned in the seventeenth paragraph of the *L.A. Times*'s trial story the next day, but the Justice Department reacted as if he'd written them in the sky while riding a broom. Assistant U.S. Attorney Thomas Hagemann ran to Judge Edward Rafeedie and demanded a gag order against all of the defense attorneys in the case, complaining that they had "publicized matters that are likely to seriously impair the right of the defendants, the government and the public to a fair trial." He singled out Braun in particular, reporting his accusations that "the government laundered drug profits which were diverted by the CIA to the Nicaraguan Contras and Iran."

Braun responded with an inflammatory motion opposing the gag order, in which he exposed the long-hidden details of the Majors' 1986 raid on Ronald Lister's house. Lister, who wasn't identified by name, was referred to as "a money launderer who [Majors II] knew was associated with a major drug and money laundering ring connected to the Contras in Nicaragua."

Braun told of Lister's claim of CIA connections and the strange items the deputies had hauled from his house: "Films of military operations in Central America, technical manuals, information on assorted military hardware and communications and numerous documents indicating that drug money was being used to purchase military equipment for Central America. The officers also discovered blown-up pictures of the suspect in Central America with the Contras showing military equipment and military bases. The suspect also was discovered to have maintained a 'way-station' for Nicaraguan transients in Laguna Niguel, California. Officers also pieced together the fact that this suspect was also working with the Blandón family which was importing narcotics from Central America into the United States."

Braun's motion linked "the Blandón family" to the crash of Eugene Hasenfus's C-123K cargo plane in Nicaragua in October 1986, the same crash Scott Weekly claimed on tape that he'd been "tied into." It also told of the Lister files disappearing as "federal agents swooped down on the sheriff's headquarters and removed all the recovered property. Mysteriously all records of the search, seizure and property also 'disappeared' from the Sheriff's Department."

Garner, Braun wrote, had secretly made copies of "10 pages of the documents seized from the CIA operative," which he said "give the name of CIA operatives in Iran, specifically mention the Contras, list various weaponry that was being purchased and even diagram the route of drug money out of the United States, back into the United States purchasing weaponry for the Contras as well as naming the State Department as one of the agencies involved."

Braun said he'd asked the Justice Department to provide a letter "stating explicitly that no drug money was used by the United States government or any United States government agency to purchase weapons for the Contras or weapons to be traded for hostages from Iran" but it had refused to do so, which Braun interpreted as "a tacit admission" that Garner's claims were true. "The court will note that nowhere in the declaration by the United States attorney does he state that this allegation is false. From this counsel concludes that in fact the government concedes the truth of the statement and only attempts to again suppress it so the public will not know about these illegal activities," Braun wrote. "The government obviously fears the exposure of its drug financed Central American operations."

The seven deputies on trial, Braun noted, weren't the ones complaining about unfair publicity, even though they had been pilloried in the media by federal prosecutors since the day they were indicted. "The only party that complains about the publicity is the very party that was arguably using drug money to buy weapons for the Contras," Braun wrote.

The next day the Justice Department fired back with a motion of its own. Once again sidestepping the issue of whether Garner's allegations were true or false, prosecutors asked Judge Rafeedie to issue a court order "excluding any questions, testimony, or other evidence relating to any alleged CIA plot to launder drug money to finance Nicaraguan operations or operations in Iran." Those claims, prosecutor Hagemann wrote, were "wholly irrelevant" to the case, and "would be nothing more than a smokescreen to divert the jury's attentions from the issues." Since the raid had occurred in 1986, Hagemann argued, it was "well outside the time frame of any allegations in the indictment...there is thus no connection of any kind between this scheme involving the CIA and this case.

This evidence would do nothing more than confuse the jury and be a waste of time."

Judge Rafeedie called the lawyers into his courtroom the next morning and lashed out at Braun, calling him sneaky and unprofessional. The motion he'd filed, Rafeedie stormed, was a "bad faith" effort to get the information out to the public. "Even if everything that you have said in this document is true, it has nothing to do with whether or not your client filed a false income tax return or whether or not he was stealing money and making purchases with the money that was stolen," Rafeedie raged. "That is, what the CIA or the government did has nothing to do with that, so far as I can see. I cannot conceive of any theory under which that evidence would be admissible in the case and therefore, putting this information out in the guise of an opposition to a restraining order simply to ensure that it gets into the public print and perhaps might contaminate this case or create undue prejudice—frankly, I am disappointed in you, Mr. Braun. I do not believe that a lawyer of your ability and skill would ever even consider that this evidence would be admissible."

(Rafeedie would later display the same sensitivity to suggested CIA links during one of the trials involving the 1985 murder of DEA agent Enrique "Kiki" Camarena. When defense lawyers tried to introduce evidence alleging CIA and Contra involvement with Mexican drug lords, Rafeedie ruled the information was irrelevant to the murder and refused to allow the jury to hear it.)

Stunned by Rafeedie's vehemence, Braun tried to reply, but the judge told him to sit down and shut up. "This opposition which you filed is the most clear and convincing evidence that an order—a restraining order—in this case is necessary," Rafeedie told him. "This document manifests a continuing intention to use the media to make statements in the public...which violate the American Bar Association model rules of professional conduct and I have, after receiving this, decided that it is appropriate to issue an order in this case, and I intend to do that."

Braun once again asked to be heard, but Rafeedie told him it didn't matter what he had to say; he was issuing the gag order immediately. The order, he was informed, prevented him from saying anything "that a reasonable person would expect to be disseminated by means of public communication." Any violation would be "viewed as contempt of this court and punished accordingly." It was, Rafeedie noted, only the second time in his twenty-one years on the bench that he'd had to gag an attorney.

Finally Braun was permitted to speak. He asked Rafeedie to give him some time and some leeway to gather additional evidence to substantiate Garner's claims.

"We are not trying to determine the Iran-Contra affair," Rafeedie snapped. "Suppose I accept as true everything you have said...I don't see the relevance."

Braun complained that Rafeedie's gag order would make it impossible for him to find witnesses to corroborate Garner's contentions, but Rafeedie was unmoved, and he refused to allow Braun to pursue the subject. Garner, during his testimony, did manage to tell the jury that he discovered "the CIA was doing, conducting illegal activities in which the guys in the CIA were getting rich," but the jurors were told to disregard the comments.

Six of the seven deputies were convicted of corruption charges and sent to prison. Garner received one of the harshest sentences—fifty-four months. In 1996 he was released from prison. He emerged defiant. "I didn't pump 500 tons of cocaine into the ghetto," Garner said. "I stole American money and spent it in America. The United States government can't say that."

Before the Big Spender investigation was over, most of the officers who had worked on the Majors' investigation of Blandón and the Freeway Rick Task Force would be charged with crimes or forced out of law enforcement.

Bell PD detective Jerry Guzzetta—the narcotics officer who originally began the investigation into the Blandón operation—was accused of stealing cocaine, but never charged. In 1988 IRS agent Carl Knudsen, who'd had a falling-out with Guzzetta over his handling of the Torres brothers, blamed Guzzetta for the disappearance of six kilos of cocaine the police department had stored in a public storage locker. The L.A. County Sheriff's Office was called in to investigate but could find no evidence that Guzzetta had anything to do with the theft. (Indeed, it was discovered that the Bell police had given one of the keys to the locker to a convicted drug dealer working as a police informant.) Though two prosecutors examined the case and declined to press charges, Guzzetta said the investigation ruined his career. He filed a lawsuit against the city, which was later settled out of court, and retired on a partial disability.

He remains convinced that he and the Majors were targeted for destruction because of their investigation of Blandón. "Every policeman who ever got close to Blandón was either told to back off, investigated by their department, forced to retire or indicted," Guzzetta complained to police investigators in 1996. He "felt that he had been victimized by a conspiracy which damaged and ruined many police officers who had attempted to bring Blandón and his organization to justice."

Former deputy Virgil Bartlett, who assisted on the Blandón raids, disagreed. "Nobody humbugged Operation Big Spender. Nobody set us up. We screwed ourselves. Nobody prosecuted me for anything I didn't do."

The last Big Spender indictment to come down was against Sergeant Thomas Gordon, the chief investigator of the Blandón case, who was accused of spending stolen drug money to fix up his house in San Dimas. He was charged with money laundering and tax evasion and, representing himself, fought the government to a draw on money-laundering charges. He was convicted on the tax charges.

Defense lawyer Harland Braun had no way of knowing it, of course, but his efforts to drag Ronald Lister into the 1990 Big Spender case came perilously close to exposing the Contra drug connection—which may explain the Justice Department's frenzied efforts to gag Braun and keep the lid on the 1986 raids on Lister and Blandón.

By the time of the deputies' trial, Ronald Lister was working for the DEA as an informant, and had been briefing federal prosecutors about his work on behalf of the Contras and the CIA during the 1980s. The DEA considered him to be such a valuable source of information that it had interceded with local police to keep him out of prison.

Lister's transformation from a drug trafficker to a drug warrior began in August 1988, when he met a prostitute at a party and confided that he could get her some cocaine if she wanted it. The hooker, a police informant, ran to tell the cops, and the Costa Mesa Police Department sent out an undercover agent, who ended up buying two kilos of cocaine from the ex-detective. But after just two days in jail, Lister was released on his own recognizance and put back on the streets, apparently having convinced the Costa Mesa detectives that he would be more valuable to them as an undercover informant.

In late 1989, to the chagrin of Costa Mesa authorities, Lister was arrested by DEA agents in San Diego and charged with conspiracy to distribute thirteen kilos of cocaine. But instead of taking him off the streets, the DEA simply took him over.

Assistant U.S. Attorney Amalia Meza, in a 1997 interview with CIA inspectors, said San Diego DEA agent Chuck Jones suggested using Lister as an informant in an investigation he was conducting of Danilo Blandón, so she asked Lister's attorney, Lynn Ball, if Lister would be interested. The reaction from Lister's lawyer was memorable. "Ball indicated that Lister was going to have to check with 'the Agency' first to see if he could provide information regarding the Blandón organization," prosecutor Meza recalled. "Ball later indicated that Lister had been given 'clearance' to cooperate." Lister then began a series of extensive debriefings and grand jury appearances. "Lister alluded to the CIA during debriefings, but no one from the investigative team pursued that subject," Meza reported. "The focus of the U.S. Attorney's investigation was on cocaine smuggling." She claimed she "never questioned Lister about, *nor allowed him to discuss*, any involvement of CIA or any other U.S. government agency during these debriefings" [emphasis added].

Meza's reluctance to delve into Lister's alleged connections was not due to a lack of curiosity. More than likely, she didn't want to know. If Lister had confessed to a relationship between himself, the CIA, and drug trafficking, Meza would have been forced to reveal it during discovery if any criminal cases had resulted from Lister's undercover work.

Five times, according to court motions filed by Lister and his attorney, Lister appeared before a San Diego federal grand jury to discuss "his activities in Central America concerning certain key figures from Nicaragua alleged to have been involved in the Iran-Contra scandal" and his role in a "big Central American operation" that lasted from 1982 to 1986. Lister claimed he "provided the government with a written chronological debriefing from 1982 to 1986 and beyond, and I did it in detail, location, activity. I gave them physical evidence, phone bills, travel tickets, everything possible back from those days—which most people don't keep, but I do keep good records—to assist them in this investigation. They were excited about it."

In interviews with CIA inspectors, Lister said he was also working on an investigation with the FBI that involved Blandón and Meneses. "An FBI special agent was convinced that Lister, Blandón, and Meneses were connected with the CIA," the Inspector General's report stated. "Lister claims that an FBI special agent wanted to prove a connection between the U.S. government, the Contras and drug smuggling."

On December 20, 1990, ten days after the verdicts in the first Big Spender case were handed down, Ronald Lister was released from federal custody and sent out into the world as an undercover DEA informant "to assist the government in an investigation." He went to work as a salesman for a San Diego company called Markon Inc., an international barter brokerage owned by the man Lister had once claimed was his CIA contact during the 1980s—Scott Weekly, aka "Dr. Death." Whether the

DEA was using Weekly's company as cover or if Lister was also spying on Weekly is not clear.

Whatever the reason, DEA records show that Lister began engaging in some very unorthodox activities for a federal informant—moving mountains of cash for drug traffickers, just as he'd done while working with Blandón in South Central. Barely six months after he began working for the DEA, Lister strolled into Anthony's Fish Grotto, a waterfront San Diego restaurant, to have lunch with several Colombian drug traffickers and their associates. Unbeknownst to Lister, two of the men at the table were undercover DEA agents, posing as money launderers.

According to their reports, one of the Colombians demanded to know what Lister had done with some $500,000 he'd been given to launder. "At this time, Lister commenced to explain how he had originally received instructions from Colombia to wire transfer the money to a European bank, only later to be told to transfer it to another account," the DEA report stated. "Lister went on to say that he could not wire transfer the money from the account again since it was originally laundered with the assistance of the CIA. At this time, Lister explained how he and the CIA used to transport multi-hundred kilo loads of cocaine from Cali, Colombia and Costa Rica to the U.S." The DEA agent wrote that Lister had a paper in his hand that "appeared to be a copy of an outgoing wire transfer. On it, the agent noticed the following: 'Swiss Bank of New York, World Trade Center, #101-WA' (the rest of the numbers not obtained.)"

Lister was asked by one of the undercover agents "if he knew what would happen to him if he refused or failed to pay back the money. Lister replied that he had nothing to fear since he worked for the CIA. At this time the agent asked Lister if he was also employed with the FBI or the DEA, to which he replied, 'No.'" Lister's explanation apparently didn't mollify the Colombians. The group's leader, Osvaldo Montalvo, was overheard telling his associates "that Lister was a dead man."

A few days later, according to a federal prosecutor familiar with the case, "one of our undercover agents was being contacted by the Colombians and they said, 'By the way, we want to kill this guy Lister, and if we can't kill him we're going to kidnap his mother and put her on the phone and torture her so he pays us back the $600,000 he stole from us.' We ran Lister through the indices and he showed up as an informant, so we brought him in, actually brought him into San Diego PD and said, 'We have reason to believe there is a threat against your life, a serious threat. We are taking it seriously, we are offering to protect you if you want it.'"

Lister, he said, laughed off the offer to place him in the Witness Protection Program and said he wasn't afraid of any "fucking Colombians." The prosecutor made Lister sign a waiver of liability absolving the Justice Department of any responsibility in case he turned up dead.

Lister went back to one of the Colombians and told him that he knew what they were up to. He was so unconcerned, he said, that he had declined federal protection, which he proved by whipping out the liability waiver he'd signed. He told the Colombian that he "did not need any protection since he and his associate, Scott Weekly, could take care of themselves. Lister further commented that Weekly was a U.S. Seal and well equipped to take care of anything."

To show the Colombian he was serious, Lister also pulled out some surveillance photos of the undercover DEA agents who'd been at lunch with him. "The photographs appeared to have been taken from a top floor," a DEA report stated. "Lister claimed that the photographs were taken by his surveillance people."

In mid-June 1991, the prosecutor said, federal agents intercepted the hit team the Colombians had sent to kill Lister. "They were stopped at the Temecula immigration check point with a picture of Lister and a map to his mother's house and they were in the country illegally and we deported them," he said. "We saved his worthless life."

Embarrassed by the fact that another DEA team had discovered their prize informant was laundering money for Colombian drug dealers, Lister's DEA handlers threw him in jail for violating the terms of his plea agreement. In a motion filed to cancel their deal and send Lister to prison, the case agents claimed Lister was involved in money laundering through Weekly's company, Markon Corp., which they said "was set up to launder money from narcotics and weapons sales...defendant intended to sell weapons as well." Weekly insisted Markon was a legitimate trading company. In any event, no charges were ever filed against Markon or Weekly.

During a secret court hearing about the DEA's request to put him in jail, Lister testified that he was double-crossed by the federal government because of what he'd revealed about the Contras. He claimed the prosecutor handling the case took it out on him when her investigation was quashed by higher-ups.

"For reasons known to this court, the subject matter of the investigation was removed from the control of the U.S. Attorney's office in San Diego, California, by the Special Projects Department of the U.S. Justice Department in Washington, D.C.," Lister wrote in a 1992 motion. The prosecutor, Lister wrote, was "extremely upset.... She accused defendant of leading her down the primrose path knowing the subject matter would be suppressed."

Meza confirmed in an interview that her grand jury investigation was terminated, but she denied that the CIA or any other government agency influenced that decision.

In 1992, six years after the Majors had first tried to arrest him, Ronald Lister was finally sent to prison, sentenced to ninety-seven months for drug trafficking. He was inexplicably released in 1996, soon after the author contacted him for an interview.

For Ricky Ross, Operation Big Spender brought only glad tidings. He became one of the federal government's star witnesses in the second round of corruption trials in 1991, and his appearance on the witness stand was, in some ways, an historic occasion. It was the first time that the man who had helped touch off L.A.'s crack explosion appeared in public to tell his story.

The federal prosecutor handling the case called Ross "probably the most significant drug dealer" ever to testify for the government. Freeway Rick, along with a host of lesser dealers appearing as government witnesses, opened up the inner world of big-time crack dealing to a wide-eyed public.

Ross bluntly told the jurors that by the end of the 1980s he'd sold thousands and thousands of kilos of cocaine in South Central L.A., becoming a multimillionaire by the time he was twenty-two. He told of the properties he owned, the big speedboat he had docked at Marina Del Rey, his fleet of cars, his ski trips to Aspen, and his fourteenth-row seats at the Lakers games. Another major L.A. crack dealer who testified for the government, Alander Smith, corroborated Ross's story.

"Smith waxed at length on the economic empire—including a thriving tire shop, apartment investments and motel construction—of Ricky Ross, a convicted trafficker who has been described as the godfather of the rock cocaine trade in South Central Los Angeles in the mid-1980s," the *San Diego Union-Tribune* reported.

But Smith, who was serving a life sentence without the possibility of parole, made his federal handlers cringe when he launched into an impromptu lecture on the Drug War. Peering intently at the jury from behind steel-rimmed glasses and firmly gripping the microphone at the witness stand, Smith accused government officials of bringing drugs into the United States. "Yes, I mean President Bush," Smith told the jurors pointedly. "When he was with the CIA and now.... The government is the only people that have the access to the equipment, but the minorities are the ones who do the time for it."

Such comments, combined with the sentence reductions and other favors Ross and his cohorts had been given by the government to secure their cooperation against the deputies, didn't sit well with the jurors, who had difficulty accepting the testimony of drug dealers over the denials of the accused officers. Under cross-examination, Ross admitted that the Justice Department had agreed to cut his sentence in half and had permitted him to keep his remaining properties and his money, which he valued at around $2 million.

Outraged, the jurors acquitted most of the indicted officers and cited Ross's deal as one of their reasons. "They really gave away the farm on that one," one juror told the *Los Angeles Times*.

The LAPD detective who was the architect of the Freeway Rick Task Force, Ross's nemesis Steve Polak, was one of those acquitted. He was later reindicted on civil rights and income tax charges and pleaded guilty to violating Ollie Newell's civil rights by beating him up. Embittered, Polak retired from the police force, complaining that he'd been sold out by his own department and persecuted by government lawyers who'd "crawled into bed with drug dealers to go after cops."

Ironically, Danilo Blandón's longtime attorney, Bradley Brunon, defended one of the deputies Ross testified against. (It was during his pretrial preparations for the Big Spender case, Brunon said, that he first discovered that the Torres brothers had led the police to Blandón in 1986.)

Though the trial was a flop for the Justice Department, Ross had lived up to his end of the bargain, and federal prosecutors dutifully went to court in early 1992 and asked Ross's judge to cut the crack lord a break, citing his "substantial cooperation" and the fact that he had "complied fully with the terms of the plea agreement."

His sentence was trimmed from ten years to fifty-one months, which made him eligible for release in a little over a year. Ross was sent to the federal prison in Phoenix, Arizona, to serve the rest of his time.

23

"He had the backing of a superpower"

Though he had successfully navigated the treacherous waters of the cocaine industry for nearly a decade, Blandón learned that he was unprepared for the sharks of legitimate commerce.

His twenty-four-location rent-a-car business, Alpha II, suffered when a deal to rent thousands of cars to hordes of German sightseers in the 1988–89 season vaporized at the last minute. "I make a contract—3,000 cars to be rented to the German people," Blandón explained. "But I didn't have enough cars. So I get a credit from Chrysler for 250 cars, and I get a credit from General Motors of 300 cars." But when Chrysler discovered he was making deals with GM, he said, his $1.5 million line of credit was yanked. He was forced to go out and beg cars from other rental companies. "I lost $300,000 in three months." In early October 1988 his lender filed a notice to foreclose on the rental agency's office near the Miami airport, and by early January 1989 his company was bleeding money. "I had to get cash," Blandón said. Fortunately he knew just where to get it.

Alpha II Rent-a-Car had apparently been the Doper's Choice for wheels in sunny Miami, and Danilo had gotten to know some very heavy hitters. "I did a lot of favors to the Colombians in Miami with my rent-a-car [business]. They used to go—they don't have a credit card, so I rent it with a deposit, $500 deposit, and they rented the car. So I, I got a lot of connections in, in those three years that I was running my business.... They were my friends because of my business."

He felt particularly close to Colombian Humberto Cardona, because Cardona was supplying Danilo's Nicaraguan associates in South Central. "This guy used to go every week to my place, this Mr. Cardona. He used to go every week. He had a lot of business." Cardona, whom Blandón called "El Fruco," was one of Colombia's better known cocaine kings. When the Colombian government agreed to extradite him and five other traffickers to the United States in late 1985, it was international news, hailed as a sign of increasing cooperation between the Colombian and U.S. governments. (There was one trafficker the Colombians were refusing to extradite, UPI noted: Juan Matta Ballesteros, the Honduran billionaire whose airline, SETCO, was flying supplies for the Contras. Instead of turning Matta over to U.S. courts, the Colombians deported him to Honduras, which did not extradite its citizens, and he continued dealing drugs.)

Humberto Cardona's extradition to the United States appears to have been equally painless. A mere three years later, according to Blandón, he was jetting around the world, and supplying the South Central crack market through Meneses's men, Roger Sandino and Jose González Morales.

Blandón poured out his tale of financial woe to the chunky Colombian, and El Fruco had a novel idea: Why not get back into the cocaine business? It was hotter than ever. Why, he'd just sold Blandón's friends in L.A. a ton of cocaine—literally. Two thousand kilos. "So if you want to go back, I can get some merchandise in L.A. and you don't have to worry about the money that you have been losing down here," Blandón said Cardona told him. "So I started thinking. And I got back."

Blandón put his rental car agency into bankruptcy and moved his family back to California, settling in San Diego in a house owned by his old college buddy Sergio Guerra, the smooth Mexican millionaire. Guerra had become a well-known figure in San Diego business circles, owning profitable parking lots and car dealerships. He was on the board of the San Diego YMCA and had generously donated property in downtown San Diego to the Chamber of Commerce, to build a tourist information center. He was also smuggling cocaine and gold into the United States, court records say.

Perched high on a hillside overlooking San Diego's busy harbor, Blandón began the task of reassembling his cocaine network. He immediately reunited with the Meneses family. "In '89, back in business, I started doing business with Jose González in San Francisco. He was the contact with the Meneses family because I know all the Meneses family—their names, OK? But I never, at that time, I never come to deal with them because Norwin didn't let me be in touch with them. So I was in touch with Jose González, spoke with the people, with Omar [Meneses], with Guillermo [Meneses]—they introduced me to Guillermo by phone the first time—and all the people: [Rafael] Corñejo, Roger [Meneses], Omar, and Jairo Morales [Meneses]."

When Norwin was away in Central America, Blandón said, nephew Jairo Morales ran the family cocaine business in San Francisco, and Norwin was away a lot. About two weeks after former CIA director George Bush had been sworn in as president, the U.S. Attorney's Office in San Francisco brought a secret indictment against Meneses, finally charging him with a few of the crimes he'd committed back in the mid-1980s. The two-count indictment accused him of conspiracy to import cocaine between 1984 and 1985 and possession of one kilo in 1985—during the period when he was having meetings with CIA agent Adolfo Calero, hosting FDN breakfasts, squiring FDN officials around L.A., and holding FDN functions at the T-shirt factory Blandón was managing.

Norwin was declared a fugitive, and a federal magistrate signed an arrest warrant. Then, curiously, both the warrant and the indictment were locked away in the vaults at the San Francisco federal courthouse, where they still were in 1998—sealed from public view.

Neither Meneses's indictment nor the warrant was reported to NADDIS or NCIC, the computer databases police use to keep track of criminals. If Norwin had been stopped for a traffic ticket or detained at an airport, there was no way for an officer to know he was a wanted man. Meneses called the indictment "a phony," suggesting it was filed to protect the U.S. government in case its relationship with him was ever revealed. He hadn't been coddled or protected, it could now be argued; he'd been indicted.

Eric Swenson, the federal prosecutor who filed the case against Meneses, said the indictment was used as leverage to bring Meneses back in line. Swenson, now retired, said Meneses had been cooperating with the DEA overseas since he'd left the United States in 1985, so there was no need to file the indictment back when the crimes had occurred. But in late 1989 two things changed. The case against Meneses was so old that it was fast approaching the statute of limitations. If an indictment wasn't returned soon, it never could be. Secondly, Swenson said, "it materialized that there was some information that he was back in the [cocaine] business and it was like, 'All right, we'll indict his ass and if he gets arrested and comes back into the country, we'll see if he wants to cooperate then.'"

Whatever the motivation behind its belated filing, later events would show that its effect appears to have been to drive the cocaine kingpin back into the embrace of the DEA. Soon after he was indicted, he returned to Nicaragua on a clandestine DEA mission of extreme political sensitivity.

Toward the end of the 1980s Meneses began dividing his time equally between his beachfront sanctuary in Costa Rica and Nicaragua. Costa Rica wasn't feeling quite as safe as it once had. The Costa Rican police were after him again. Then his brother Jaime, who owned a currency exchange and money-laundering front, was assassinated in June 1989, gunned down in his San José office by three men in what police said was apparent robbery. Norwin claimed the killing was politically inspired and done by former Sandinista soldiers.

Nicaragua, on the other hand, had become much more hospitable. The Contra war was over, and Norwin's friends were back in power. The fighting had all but stopped in March 1988 with the truce of Sapoa, a military victory for the Sandinistas that left many Contras feeling betrayed. Contra officer Tirzo Moreno wrote an open letter to his comrades in July 1988 declaring that "our leaders never had the faintest intentions of winning this war.... For seven years we were used." Meneses's friend, Contra leader Aristides Sánchez, was among the most embittered, calling it the worst mistake the Contras ever made.

But the Sandinistas' battlefield victory was Pyrrhic. In 1990 a public weary of a decade of war and strife and tension with the United States voted the Sandinistas out of office. With U.S. backing, Norwin's former business partner, Violeta Chamorro, was elected president, and she immediately began returning to Anastasio Somoza's friends and relatives the companies and properties that the Sandinistas had confiscated.

Meneses and his family moved back into their mansion on the outskirts of Managua, and he began reclaiming the holdings—valued at $12 million—that had once belonged to him and his assassinated brother, Edmundo.

Norwin also began reconstructing his drug trafficking network in Nicaragua, a riskier business. Even though the Sandinistas were no longer running the government, they still controlled the country's military and national police. If they caught him dealing cocaine, he'd be at the mercy of his old enemies.

To cover his bets, Norwin recruited a turncoat Sandinista intelligence officer, Enrique Miranda Jaime, to help him reestablish his smuggling pipeline through Nicaragua. It was a move that would prove to be his undoing.

A slippery character who was a lifelong Sandinista, Enrique Miranda had been a paid CIA informant between 1984 and 1985, spying on his comrades and peeking into shipping crates to keep the agency up to date on the latest Sandinista weapons purchases. He says he was one of two CIA operatives working inside the Sandinista Ministry of the Interior's super-secret dirty-tricks unit, the Bureau of Special Operations.

In addition to having extensive political connections, Miranda was an experienced smuggler in his own right. During the early years of the Contra war, Miranda said, he was responsible for arranging clandestine shipments of Sandinista arms from Panama to revolutionary groups throughout Central America, and he had helped the Sandinistas design a string of secret arms caches in and around Managua—fortified concrete bunkers hidden in hillsides and in dense patches of jungle. As a result, he not only knew most of the smuggling routes through the isthmus but had places to hide cocaine that few people even knew existed.

In interviews with Nicaraguan police in 1991, Meneses corroborated many details of Miranda's past. He said Miranda, who is married to a cousin of Norwin's wife, Blanca, had been a friend of his for a decade, and he confirmed that Miranda "was the person who was sending guns to the FMLN in El Salvador." He also confirmed that Miranda "sold himself to the CIA" and provided the agency with intelligence on Sandinista leaders. The CIA refused to confirm or deny that.

In 1989 Meneses hired the former double agent to serve as his emissary to the Colombians, primarily the cartel of Bogota. Posing as Norwin's nephew, Miranda said he arranged the drug shipments, plotted the routes, and handled the cash deliveries, while Meneses negotiated prices, put up the money to finance the purchases, and arranged for the cocaine's transportation from Nicaragua to the United States.

Most of the cocaine they were shipping, Miranda said, was being sold in Los Angeles through Meneses's brother Luis Enrique, who was later convicted in Nicaragua of drug trafficking. In San Francisco, Miranda said, Norwin was dealing through his nephews, Guillermo and Jairo. The drugs were being smuggled into California through two different routes. Meneses "had on his payroll a series of American pilots and had taken charge of a control tower in the state of Texas," Miranda testified. Norwin's cargo planes, based in Costa Rica, had established flight plans to haul commercial goods to Texas. Before they left, Miranda said, a space would be cleared in the cargo hold big enough to conceal 300 kilos of cocaine. "When overflying their route to the U.S.A., they would be allowed to drop in for a quick landing at the airstrip at Rosita," he testified, referring to a 2,600-meter runway in the isolated jungles of northern Nicaragua, near the mining town of Rosita.

At the abandoned airfield, according to Miranda, Meneses had hundreds of kilos of cocaine hidden in underground bunkers. The kilos would be loaded aboard the cargo planes and hidden amidst the commercial cargo, and the planes would continue on into Texas. "This operation would last approximately 15 or 20 minutes," Miranda said. "The advantage is that here in Nicaragua there is no radar system with the capacity to reach this airstrip."

The other method was equally inventive. Meneses would purchase automobiles in the United States through a dealership, import them, fill their frames and hollow spaces with cocaine-filled PVC pipes, and weld them shut inside. Then the cars were loaded aboard an auto transporter—also packed with tubes of cocaine—and driven across the border in Texas or California. "For the amounts that were coming in, you almost needed flatbed trucks," recalled Meneses lieutenant Rafael Corñejo.

Blandón said his first job once he got back into the California drug market was serving as a broker for Norwin's nephew, Jairo, in San Francisco. He collected cocaine from hotel rooms all over the Bay Area and sold it to customers in Alabama, New Orleans, Los Angeles, San Jose, and San Francisco. At least two of Blandón's biggest customers, Mike Smith in L.A. and Reggie Rash in Alabama, were black dealers who'd worked for Ricky Ross before Ross went to prison.

Then Blandón had another well-timed series of lucky breaks. Jairo was arrested and sent to jail; Jose González moved back to Nicaragua; and the only experienced distributor left was Danilo Blandón. He took on the job of doling out cocaine to the other members of the Meneses ring and some of their Bay Area customers. Between 1990 and 1991, Blandón estimated, he provided somewhere around 425 kilos of cocaine to the Meneses family in San Francisco, about $8.5 million worth at wholesale prices.

Blandón also began putting his L.A. connections back together. Though he was reasonably sure the Torres brothers had ratted him out to the cops four years earlier—and they knew he'd hired a hit man to kill them after he became convinced that one of them was sleeping with his wife—the old friends let bygones be bygones and started buying and selling drugs from each other again.

Rafael Corñejo recalled visiting the Torres brothers in North Hollywood with Blandón in 1990, where Jacinto offered to sell him a chrome-plated .45. "There was a fight on TV and Danilo and I went over there to watch it. I was staying at a hotel...that's when I first met the Torres brothers. And he [Blandón] was working with them and to my belief he was involved with narcotics with them at that time. He offered some to me but I didn't take the offer. He told me he was back trying to open up the gates again that he had lost."

Blandón said Corñejo was very "picky" about cocaine quality and deemed the kilos Blandón offered substandard. Though Corñejo said he never liked Blandón personally—"he always had an agenda"—he valued his experience and his connections and began dealing with him on an almost daily basis. "Sometimes, you know, you gotta dance with the devil," Corñejo shrugged. "Danilo knew some very important people in Nicaragua, important people in society, and I was talking about taking my money and moving down there, you know, taking my assets and starting a business. And he told me he would use his connections with the World Bank to help me out." Whether Blandón actually had any connections to the World Bank is unknown, but undercover DEA tapes show that he was openly boasting of having received massive loans around that time from the Canadian government and, according to one DEA summary, the U.S. government.

Those discussions were secretly taped between 1990 and 1991 by DEA informant John Arman, a skinny, nasal-voiced drug dealer who'd been indicted in Nebraska in the early 1980s for cocaine trafficking and fled to Mexico. The Mexicans booted him out eventually, turning him over to FBI agents at the border, and Arman agreed to become an informant for the DEA office in San Diego.

He was one of the first people Blandón contacted when he reentered the southern California cocaine market, apparently due to a long-standing friendship with Arman's ex-wife. In March 1990, a week after the Sandinistas were voted out of office, Arman called San Diego DEA agent Charles Jones and told him that "Blandón is preparing to move back to Nicaragua from Miami, due to the favorable political climate at present. Blandón also reportedly had a large amount of cash in Los Angeles, California, that he was preparing to transport to Nicaragua." Arman reported that Blandón "owned property in Nicaragua that he rented to the government for $100,000 for five years," and was so tight with the new regime, he'd told Arman, he'd take him to the upcoming inauguration of Nicaragua's new president, Violeta Chamorro.

"Yeah, I know all the people from the government," Blandón boasted in one taped conversation with Arman. "They *like* you, see? Shit, they like you, all the fucking government—they know."

In July 1990, Blandón flew back to Miami to deal with his failing rental car company and returned to L.A. a few days later. Arman met him up at the airport, where an expansive Blandón announced that he'd just received a $40 million loan to build houses in Nicaragua.

On the drive to San Diego, Blandón killed time by filling Arman in on his latest cocaine deals. His supplier, Humberto Cardona, was now in France and was looking to cross 2,000 kilos he'd stored in Guadalajara, Mexico. A Canadian associate was bringing in a load from Mexico through Houston. Some of his Japanese customers had the bad luck of buying a boatload of cocaine in Colombia, and then having the trawler tracked and seized off the coast of Hawaii.

Arman dropped Blandón off at the Nicaraguan's hilltop home in Bonita, a few miles from the Mexican border, and they made plans to meet for dinner later that evening. Shortly before 7:30 P.M. on July 21, 1990, Arman arrived at the Old Bonita Store, a quaint lobster restaurant near Blandón's house, wired for sound. He was accompanied by undercover DEA agent Judy Gustafson, who was posing as a money launderer interested in doing business with Blandón and his friend Sergio Guerra, the parking lot magnate. Blandón rolled up fifteen minutes later behind the wheel of a silver Mercedes 450 SL, Guerra at his side.

The four made chitchat for a while—Guerra asked the DEA agent if she'd ever snorted methamphetamine—and then Blandón motioned Arman outside so they could discuss something privately. If Arman was looking to sell, Blandón said, he had customers looking for about 200 kilos. If he could get more, they'd buy that too.

"These people have been working with me 10 years," Blandón informed him. "I've sold them about 2,000 or 4,000, I don't know. I don't remember how many."

"It ain't that Japanese guy you were talking about, is it?" Arman asked.

"The Japanese? You know him?"

"No, you told me."

"No," Blandón insisted. "No, it's not him. These…these are the black people."

"Black?!"

"Yeah," Blandón replied. "They control L.A. The people that control L.A."

"I don't like niggers," Arman fretted.

"Well . . ."

"They pay cash though?"

"Yeah," Blandón said. "They pay cash."

"Can they come up with enough money to buy 50 at one time?"

"Yes."

"Oooh," Arman shivered. "That scares me, you know that?"

"No, no. Don't worry. I don't do with anybody else, just with black people," Blandón reassured him. "The thing is, with these people, you are making [money] every day or every week. They're all there. You don't have to be worried about nothing. You don't have to pay warehouses, because the warehouse would be only one day, you see?"

Arman told Blandón he'd see what he could do, and they returned to the table, where Arman pressed the Nicaraguan for details on his new housing project.

"What were you doing...what was the deal, you're doing some building, planning on doing some building, some houses down in...?"

"Nicaragua."

"Nicaragua?"

"I get a loan from the Canadian government, $40 million, for 5,000 houses," Blandón said.

"Like mass housing, neighborhood..."

"For the poor people, the poor people. You know, the government of Canada, they sometimes have, it's better for them, for construction, to give us 5,000 houses, a government loan for three years, you pay 3 1/2 % per year..."

"Then they get a United States company to...?"

"Well," Blandón said, "we will be supervising, see? Then they will build the house in Canada, how you say, prefabricated..."

Blandón also mentioned that he was due to receive a $1 million settlement from the U.S. government for some unspecified claim.

Arman steered the conversation to Roger Sandino, the Meneses associate wanted by the DEA in connection with the giant Bolivian drug bust in Virginia in 1986. Laughing, Blandón told the group how Sandino had a planeload of cocaine flown into Nicaragua, but the plane belly-flopped on a dirt field near a small town. The crash was swarmed by local peasants, who carted away much of the dope. "The people, the *campesinos*, they found it and they were selling it at the market—10 dollars, 20 dollars a fucking key!" Blandón chuckled. He said that when a horrified Sandino discovered the situation, he flew down from Miami and frantically tried to buy his remaining cocaine back from the peasants.

Nicaraguan aviation records show the airplane, loaded with 1,000 pounds of coke, crash-landed near San Rafael del Sur on June 4, 1990. The pilot, who was arrested, was a captain in the Colombian Air Force.

For the next two years the San Diego DEA would keep a close eye on Blandón, recording his telephone calls, tracking his movements, videotaping his meetings with informants and his negotiations to buy cocaine. They would hear him confess to many crimes and brag "about having customers in New York, San Francisco, Los Angeles, New Orleans and other locations." But even after hearing Blandón admit that he was back in South Central L.A., dumping cocaine into the ghettos again, the DEA made no move to arrest him.

"Blandón stated that one of the groups that he supplied cocaine to were black gang members in Los Angeles that didn't care about the quality of cocaine because they were going to convert it to crack anyway," a 1991 DEA report stated laconically. On the tape of that conversation, Blandón and Arman can be heard commiserating over the decline in standards in the cocaine business. A kilo of "beautiful" white flake meant nothing to these crack dealers, Blandón lamented. "They don't care. They, they, they, they cook everything."

The investigation of Blandón crept along at a snail's pace until July 1991, when Texas DEA agents finally nailed longtime fugitive Roger Sandino, who was tooling along outside Plano, Texas, with fifty-four kilos of cocaine in his car. The feds took him to Dallas for a detention hearing, shipped him to Oklahoma City, and indicted him, and within two weeks the San Diego DEA had him working the phones, making tape-recorded calls to Blandón in an effort to set him up for a reverse sting.

But Blandón's intelligence network was as good as ever. During one conversation, Sandino suggested that they do a deal with a certain couple in Miami. Blandón's voice suddenly hardened. "They are going to put you in jail, dumb fuck, but quickly," he said.

"Are they, are they working for the police?"

"Yes," Blandón said evenly. "They are the ones who fucked Jairo."

Sandino's suggestion apparently prompted Blandón to do a little checking up on his old friend. A few days later, Blandón called and asked Sandino to explain the circumstances behind his recent legal troubles in Oklahoma City. Sandino hurriedly made up a story about getting busted after an auto accident of no consequence. He insisted that everything was fine and encouraged Blandón to come to San Diego to complete a cocaine transaction they had discussed. Blandón assured him he would be there, but never arrived. He also quit returning Sandino's calls. Four days later, on August 16, 1991, the DEA admitted defeat. Blandón had once again beaten the narcs at their own game. "The investigation," a DEA report stated, "had been compromised."

"At first I thought it was just a keen sense of paranoia, but now I believe that he [Blandón] was tipped off," said a federal prosecutor who worked on the case. He declined to say whom he suspected.

When DEA agent Jones drove out the next morning to collect Sandino from the Chula Vista hotel where they had him holed up, he found an empty room. Just as he had done in Virginia five years earlier, Sandino had given the DEA the slip. He fled to Nicaragua "as a result of the pressure of cooperating," a DEA report stated.

The DEA refused to explain why it left unattended a federal fugitive who had just been captured after five years on the lam, or what attempts it had made, if any, to recapture him.

"He had a big wedding here a couple years ago out at the Montelimar resort," said Roger Mayorga, the Nicaraguan government's former antidrug czar, in 1997. "If the DEA wanted Roger Sandino he is very easy to find. They never asked us to arrest him, I can tell you that."

Just ten days after Sandino's disappearance, the federal government was presented with another golden opportunity to arrest Blandón. Once again, though, it declined. While on a trip to Tijuana on August 26, 1991, Blandón and Sergio Guerra stopped at the checkpoint on the international border in Guerra's silver Mercedes, and U.S. Customs inspector Phillip Lemon asked Guerra if he had more than $10,000 on him. The Mexican said no.

"How much do you have?" Lemon asked.

"About $100," Guerra answered.

Eyeing the $35,000 car and the expensive clothing the men were wearing, Lemon told them to pull over to the side for a vehicle inspection.

The Mercedes was a giant piggy bank. In the glove compartment, Customs agent Douglas Montone discovered $2,700 in cash rolled up with a rubber band. The trunk produced $110,550 in bank money orders and $1,300 in cash in a black bag. Guerra had $490 in his wallet and a second search of the trunk revealed an additional $2,000 in money orders. The money orders were blank and had been purchased within the past week.

Asked why he was driving around with a small fortune in his trunk, Guerra babbled that "he does not have a safe and he uses his two Mercedes Benzes in lieu of a safe deposit box to store his valuables." In truth, the money wasn't Guerra's. It was Blandón's. "The money orders were on their way to Mexico as a partial payment for cocaine," said Assistant U.S. Attorney L. J. O'Neale, who handled the case. Blandón had sent three of his assistants out to snap up 339 money orders, O'Neale said, because he'd "overloaded the delivery systems" of his cocaine suppliers with cash. After dumping $900,000 on them a few days earlier, O'Neale said, Blandón had been instructed to "hold off on the cash."

While a cursory check of the Customs database would have revealed that Blandón was a known cocaine trafficker and Guerra had no criminal record, it was Guerra who was arrested and indicted by a federal grand jury on two felony counts. He also had his Mercedes seized. Blandón was briefly questioned and released.

By Christmas, he would be three for three. In late December 1991 a special LAPD strike force arrested him and two other men on charges of money laundering and conspiracy after they caught him with $14,000 and a small amount of cocaine in his pocket. Blandón had been seen leaving the apartment of his old friend Raul "El Tuerto" Vega, the one-eyed Meneses flunky who'd helped break Blandón in when he started dealing coke for the Contras. In Vega's apartment, police found $350,000 in cash, a miraculous amount for a man who claimed to be a warehouse worker.

Then the LAPD got a call from the U.S. Attorney's Office in San Diego, asking that all the charges be dropped. Federal agents were working on an investigation, the police were told, which would be ruined if Blandón was put in jail. When the trafficker appeared for his arraignment, he was released without bail and the charges were subsequently dismissed. Once again, he'd walked away from an almost certain conviction. The federal prosecutor who made that decision said he intervened to protect the DEA's investigation of Blandón from a premature termination. "It wasn't done as a favor to Blandón," he insisted.

LAPD sergeant Ron Hodges heard a similar story while working his own case against Blandón in 1991. Hodges, a narcotics detective who was also looking into the Torres brothers, was attempting to arrange a hand-to-hand sale with Blandón, when he discovered that DEA agents were following the Nicaraguan around. The DEA asked Hodges to cooperate with their investigation, so he shelved his case and relegated himself to helping the DEA tail Blandón around L.A., surveilling his meetings with the

Torres brothers. "I actually had a better case against him if it would have come about," Hodges said. "I think they just let him run."

In stark contrast to their U.S. counterparts, Nicaraguan lawmen were onto Norwin Meneses from the moment they learned the drug lord was back in Managua.

René Vivas, the chief of the Nicaraguan National Police, and Commander Roger Mayorga, the head of its criminal investigations section, were well acquainted with Norwin and his family and the work they'd done for Somoza and the Contras. Mayorga, a short, stocky man with hard eyes, had been chief of state security in Meneses's hometown of Esteli. Vivas, one of the earliest members of the Sandinista underground, had known Norwin since his days as a teenage informant for Somoza's secret police, through his attempts to infiltrate anti-Somoza groups. They were itching for a reason to arrest him. And they got one sooner than they expected.

In November 1990 a white Volkswagon microbus was putt-putting through Chiapas, Mexico, on its way to Los Angeles when Mexican police pulled it over. Inside were forty-two kilos of cocaine and a beautiful Nicaraguan airline stewardess, Ivis Hernández, who had been one of the Sandinistas' fiercest urban guerrillas during the revolution, known as "La Negra."

"She was something else," sighed Roberto Vargas, an ex-Marine who fought with the Sandinistas and later became their ambassador to China. "La Negra was part of a special squad during the revolution that attacked National Guard buildings. They were the worst missions—suicidal almost—but oh my God, could she fight. I think every man who met her fell in love with her."

Certainly Enrique Miranda had. At the time of her arrest, she and Miranda were lovers. And it was his microbus she was driving. Roger Mayorga said the Mexican police told him about the arrest, which they said resulted from a DEA tip. Mayorga might want to look into it, they suggested, because he could have a drug ring operating in Managua. When Mayorga learned who owned the van and who was driving it, he was intrigued. He knew Ivis Hernández, and she'd never struck him as a cocaine trafficker. Enrique Miranda was a different story. Mayorga knew the kinds of things he'd done during the war.

Mayorga dropped by Ivis's house and asked her mother, who knew nothing of the arrest, if he could talk to Ivis. Her daughter was in Mexico, she said, receiving some medical treatment at the suggestion of her boyfriend, Enrique Miranda. "So I went to see him and I challenged him and I told him he was responsible for her arrest," Mayorga said. "He was very nervous and he denied everything, but I could tell. At that point, we decided to focus our investigation on him."

Miranda unwittingly led the police to Frank Vigil, the former advertising man who'd allegedly dealt cocaine with Blandón in L.A. in the early 1980s and was Meneses's partner in the Costa Rican chicken restaurant. Mayorga learned that Vigil had just formed a new company in Managua in partnership with a major Colombian drug trafficker, Hector Román Carvajal.

Mayorga saw from the incorporation papers that the company, called PZP S.A. (for *Processadora Zona Pacifica*), had been put together by a prominent Somoza lawyer, Adolpho Garcia Esquivel, a Nicaraguan assemblyman who also served as one of Norwin Meneses's lawyers. Among PZP's owners, the records showed, was Luis Henry Pallais, the son of Somoza's closest political adviser, and Nicaraguan assemblyman Frank Duarte, another longtime Somoza supporter who headed the Assembly's antinarcotics committee. The company, according to its records, planned to operate fishing boats to export seafood to Taiwan.

Miranda was also seen making trips to a motel in the hills overlooking Managua, the Auto Hotel Nejapa—one of a strange breed of small Nicaraguan hostelries that allow patrons to drive their cars into shielded carports and enter their rooms unseen from the outside. Such hideaways are usually used for trysts with hookers and mistresses. The Hotel Nejapa, police learned, had once belonged to General Edmundo Meneses. The Chamorro government had recently returned it to the Meneses family, and it was now being run by Norwin Meneses, business records showed. The incorporator of the new hotel business was—surprise—Somoza lawyer Garcia Esquivel, the incorporator of PZP.

Mayorga surmised that Miranda was working for Meneses and Frank Vigil, and he suspected they were plotting to use the fishing company as a front for a cocaine smuggling venture. In the summer of 1991, he said, his men began following Meneses and his wife, Blanca Margarita. One September evening Mrs. Meneses drove to a restaurant near her house, the Lobster Inn, and got a table. A few moments later, DEA agent Federico G. Villarreal arrived. Hot on his heels was Norwin Meneses.

To the shock of the Nicaraguan police, Villarreal was having dinner with Meneses and his wife. (Their shock would have been greater had they known that Meneses, at the time, was technically a fugitive from justice.) When his men excitedly returned from the stakeout with their news, Mayorga was dumbfounded. He regarded Villarreal, the agent in charge of the DEA office in Costa Rica, as a colleague who had always treated him with respect. What was he doing meeting with Nicaragua's top cocaine trafficker in Mayorga's backyard? Behind Mayorga's back?

Running a clandestine operation in a foreign country without informing the local authorities, Mayorga knew, violated just about every DEA policy there was. Either Villarreal was a friend of Meneses, which also violated DEA policy, or the DEA and the drug kingpin were up to something that the Nicaraguan National Police weren't supposed to know about. Something here was very fishy.

Mayorga went to see his boss, Nicaraguan National Police commander Rene Vivas, who shared his concerns. Checking with sources in Costa Rica, they learned Meneses and Villarreal had been seen together in San José as well. There was definitely something going on between Meneses and the Americans, they concluded. A lid of secrecy was clamped on their investigation. No one else in government, and especially not the DEA, would be informed until after it was all over. Their agents were sworn to absolute secrecy and given as little advance notice as possible of upcoming operations.

The precautions paid off. On a Sunday morning in early November 1991, Mayorga's men executed a series of simultaneous raids on Meneses's drug ring. At the Quinta Wichita, a small ranch ten miles south of Managua, they caught Norwin's engineers in the act of welding cocaine-filled PVC pipes into the frame of an auto transport trailer. A couple of Mercedes sedans were in the process of having the same alterations performed. They found 130 kilos there. In a bedroom in Miranda's mother's house, they found hundreds more hidden under blankets with spare tires thrown on top. In an abandoned military bunker they found more kilos, packed into air conditioner and television boxes that bore the address of the Auto Hotel Nejapa.

In all, the Nicaraguan police seized 725 kilos of cocaine, worth roughly $15 million wholesale. They also found Uzi submachine guns, Makarov pistols, and California license plates. Meneses, his brother Luis, Enrique Miranda, Frank Vigil, and the engineers and craftsmen Norwin had hired to prepare the vehicles were arrested.

(The auto transport trailer Meneses's men were busy stuffing with cocaine had recently been purchased for $125,000 in El Salvador from none other than former CIA pilot Marcos Aguado. Aguado, who'd helped run the secret Contra air base at Ilopango during the war, was not charged in the connection with the case, and his involvement was never publicly revealed. In an interview, he denied knowing how Meneses would use the trailer, although Miranda said he was present when Aguado and Meneses discussed drug trafficking one evening at Norwin's mansion.)

The Meneses drug bust was major news in Central America. It was the largest cocaine seizure in Nicaragua's history, and it prompted an uproar in the highly partisan Nicaraguan press, as two prominent Nicaraguan politicians were seemingly implicated. They were never charged.

The story made several U.S. newspapers as well. Reporter Jonathan Marshall of the *San Francisco Chronicle*—who had just coauthored a book called *Cocaine Politics: Drugs, Armies and the CIA in Central America*—wrote a detailed piece about Meneses and his relationship with the FDN and its leaders. Marshall's story also questioned the seeming inability of U.S. authorities to capture the drug kingpin during the years he was living in America. The *Chronicle* buried the story deep inside the paper, and it was ignored by the rest of the American media, which was then consumed with the "scandal" over Bush's chief of staff, John Sununu, using military planes for personal trips.

Commander Vivas went to the Tipitapa prison outside Managua to personally take charge of Meneses's interrogation. He found the trafficker relaxed—almost smug. "He said he wasn't worried about me because he had the backing of a higher power, a superpower," Vivas recalled. "He said he was working for the United States to get Sandinista officials on drug charges, and that I was one of his targets. I told him not to fuck with me because I didn't believe him. I thought he was just trying to impress me. But he insisted it was true and said I would find out for myself."

According to two Nicaraguan prison officials, Meneses gave his wife Blanca a letter to deliver to the U.S. embassy immediately after his arrest, addressed to two American officials there, which asked them to intercede with the Chamorro government. The sources were unaware if the letter was answered.

The evening of the raids, Mayorga called the Costa Rican DEA office to inform Villarreal of the arrests, but since it was Sunday no one was in. He stuck an arrest report into the fax machine and zapped it to the U.S. embassy in San José.

"Then, big surprise, I get to my office at 9 A.M. Monday, and Villarreal is there waiting for me," Mayorga grinned. "He wants more information. I asked him what was his special interest in this case?" After getting some evasive answers, Mayorga said, he provided Villarreal with the basic facts and waited for the American to tell him about Meneses's relationship with the DEA. Nothing was said.

Villarreal came back later looking for more information. By then, Mayorga said, "we'd had a chance to analyze the phone book that we had found on Norwin when we arrested him, and inside were phone numbers for Ronald Lard, the DEA country attaché in Costa Rica. I challenged Villarreal to explain this, and he couldn't."

Then Mayorga told the DEA agent that his men had seen him dining with Meneses less than two weeks before the raid. Why, Mayorga asked, was the DEA secretly meeting in Managua with a drug trafficker who was in the process of bringing 725 kilos of cocaine into his country? And why hadn't the Nicaraguan police been informed? "At this, Villarreal shuts his mouth and says nothing," Mayorga recalled. "Then he asks me what I want. I tell him I want help in building our case against Norwin, and he volunteered to help us." Villarreal later provided Mayorga with copies of the secret San Francisco indictment, the fugitive warrant, and a letter detailing Meneses's long career as a trafficker, which became important pieces of evidence at his trial.

It had been Meneses, Mayorga learned, who'd tipped off the DEA to the trip Ivis Hernández was taking in the cocaine-laden microbus. The cocaine Hernández was taking north was not Norwin's, he said; it was Frank Vigil's. He theorized that Meneses ratted out the shipment to allay the DEA's concerns that he was dealing on the side. "Villarreal made it clear to me that they did not completely trust Meneses," Vivas said. "He made me understand that Meneses was playing both sides."

Armed with that information, Mayorga paid Enrique Miranda a visit. He reminded him of his earlier denials regarding his girlfriend, and Miranda morosely admitted "having abused his relationship with her," Mayorga said. "Then he asked me why the police had stopped her car in the first place. How did they find out?"

It was your boss, Mayorga told him. Norwin. He'd told the DEA. And now your girlfriend is in jail in Mexico, undergoing God-knows-what humiliations. How's that for loyalty? Miranda repaid it in kind. He started talking. "We used Norwin's cooperation with the DEA to get Miranda to cooperate with us," Mayorga said.

Combining the information provided by Miranda, Villarreal, and Meneses, the Nicaraguan police pieced together a picture of what Meneses and the DEA were working on. Meneses, they believed, had been sent to Nicaragua on a secret DEA mission to snare high-ranking Sandinista military officials in a drug sting. The first person Meneses had approached was Commandante Bayardo Arce Castaño, a cousin of Meneses's wife Blanca and one of the most influential of the nine

Sandinista leaders. According to Meneses, Arce agreed to participate i. cocaine deal, and he offered to provide the protection of the Sandinist military. Arce admitted that Meneses had come to see him but denied making any drug deals.

Meneses's lawyers, who tried unsuccessfully to force Arce to testify, dug up some evidence to support their client's claim. According to affidavits they gathered from eyewitnesses, the Colombian airplane carrying the 725 kilos of cocaine had been met at the Rosita airstrip by a Sandinista army truck, which was loaded with boxes from the airplane. Two Sandinista army officers supervised the unloading, the witnesses said.

Mayorga discovered that there was also a DEA agent working inside Meneses's drug ring, a Nicaraguan who'd driven a Ford Escort full of cocaine to Houston, where an accident was staged so the drugs could be seized.

An indication of just how closely the U.S. government was monitoring the Meneses/DEA operation was contained in a 1998 CIA inspector General's report. It shows that both the Department of Defense and the State Department were tracking the operation and, in fact, had notified the CIA about Norwin's arrest.

"Those reports included reference to a trip to Colombia by Meneses and Miranda in September 1991 and to the group's loss of a Ford Escort 'loaded with cocaine' in Houston in September 1991," the CIA report stated.

But when the Nicaraguan police arrested the DEA's sting man, Meneses, the operation was blown.

If it had worked, the resultant drug scandal would almost certainly have crippled the last vestiges of Sandinista power in the new Nicaraguan government: their control of the military and the police. President Violeta Chamorro was being subjected to intense pressure to purge her government of Sandinistas by conservatives in Washington, particularly Senator Jesse Helms of North Carolina, whose staff had been intimately involved in the creation and funding of the Contra movement. Helms was then stalling a $50 million foreign aid bill for Nicaragua over the continued presence of Sandinistas—particularly Rene Vivas—in the national police and military.

The 1991 Meneses operation, in all likelihood, was simply another version of the 1984 DEA/CIA sting involving trafficker Barry Seal, which the Reagan administration had used to accuse the Sandinistas of drug trafficking right before a crucial Contra aid vote. Had the Meneses sting

..n successful, the Sandinistas would have been loudly denounced as ..rug dealers by the Bush administration—which already had a history of invading Latin American countries run by unfriendly traffickers—and might have been forced out of the Chamorro government.

The DEA refused to discuss its relationship with Meneses or release any records concerning his work for the agency, but unnamed DEA officials confirmed to the *Washington Post* and the *New York Times* in 1996 that Meneses was working as a DEA informant in the late 1980s and early 1990s. "There is no doubt that Meneses was working with the DEA when he was selling drugs here and in the United States," said Vivas, who now practices law in Managua.

At Norwin's trial in August 1992, Miranda took the stand against his former boss and bared all, explaining Norwin's relationship with the DEA and the Contras, the drug flights from El Salvador to Texas, and the meetings with CIA pilot Aguado and CIA agent Enrique Bermúdez, the FDN's former military commander. "Norwin even arranged a party in his residence for Bermúdez, celebrating his possible appointment as Army Chief by the new government," Miranda testified. "I also took part in meetings where Norwin Meneses and Bermúdez discussed the possibility to use the Army to send drug loads to the U.S. and Europe...but these plans were truncated by Bermúdez's sudden death."

Bermúdez had been murdered in the parking lot of the Intercontinental Hotel in Managua in February 1991 by someone who shot him in the back of the head. The slaying was never solved.

Meneses denied everything. The cocaine wasn't his, he insisted. It belonged to drug-dealing Sandinistas—Rene Vivas, Roger Mayorga, and Bayardo Arce. He claimed the Sandinistas had set up him and his brother on phony drug charges as "revenge" for their years of assistance to the FDN. "I was an important part of the FDN since 1982. And they [the Sandinistas] proclaimed themselves as my mortal enemies in 1984," he testified. Meneses blamed the Sandinistas for planting false stories about him in American and Costa Rican newspapers and pointed to his spotless record as proof that he was no criminal.

"I have never been arrested in the United States and in any other part of the world. I've never been the subject of a court trial. I've never been subpoenaed as a witness," Meneses testified. "I have been mentioned by some other people in some other cases, but that's because of the long arm of *Sandinismo*."

The Nicaraguan judges were bothered by Meneses's lack of a criminal record, court transcripts show, and they challenged Roger Mayorga on his public declarations that Meneses was "the king of drugs" in Nicaragua, and his country's representative to the Cali cartel. "How do you explain the fact that Norwin Meneses, implicated since 1974 in the trafficking of drugs, and where an arrest warrant exists issued by a court in San Francisco in the United States, has not been detained in the United States, a country in which he has lived, entered and departed many times since 1974?" one judge asked Mayorga.

"Well, that question needs to be asked to the authorities of the United States because I'm limited to the information that was supplied to us by. . . the DEA," Mayorga said stiffly.

"Explain then, that after 22 years, you have not been asked on the part of the anti-narcotics police in the U.S. to arrest the Nicaraguan citizen Norwin Meneses for drugs, if he has resided for much time in the United States and Nicaragua? He was very easy to find in the United States because of his residency card, and in Nicaragua, because he's highly well-known."

"With respect to his residence in the United States, in the previous answer I explained ignorance as to why the authorities in the United States had not stopped him," Mayorga testily replied. "With respect to Nicaragua, be clear that this Meneses had a year and a half in Nicaragua . . . and in the year and a half he was captured for drug trafficking."

Meneses was convicted and sentenced to thirty years in jail. As a result of his cooperation, Miranda was given a seven-year sentence. A few days after the trial, Nicaraguan prison authorities reported that Meneses had paid a deranged inmate $10,000 to knife Miranda in revenge for his damning testimony. Meneses denied it, but Miranda was quickly transferred to a prison in another city.

After a lifetime of crime and the ruination of countless lives, Norwin Meneses was finally behind bars. Almost single-handedly, an underpaid, middle-aged Nicaraguan policeman had, in eighteen months, done something that the entire U.S. government—with its spy satellites, international wiretapping capabilities, and an army of drug agents—had been unable to do for twenty years. Three weeks after the verdicts came down, under pressure from the U.S. State Department and the White House, the Chamorro government fired Rene Vivas as Nicaraguan National Police commander.

Roger Mayorga, who by then had begun looking into Danilo Blandón's relationship with the Meneses drug ring and its money-laundering tendrils in Central America, was fired soon afterwards.

24

"They're gonna forget I was a drug dealer"

In the summer of 1992, as one drug potentate, Norwin Meneses, was settling into the dreary Tipitapa prison for perhaps the remainder of his life, another, Ricky Ross, was preparing to rejoin society. Freeway Rick had done his time carefully at Phoenix, learning the basics of reading and writing, obtaining his high school equivalency certificate. He became a vegetarian and a devotee of self-help guru Anthony J. Robbins, whose motivational tapes Ross listened to incessantly.

He had a plan for the rest of his life, and ever the promotional genius, he used his notoriety as one of L.A.'s biggest crack dealers to jump-start his plan. In the wake of the nightmarish riots in South Central that April, which had fleetingly focused the nation's press on the problems of inner-city neighborhoods, Ross had begun granting interviews to reporters searching for reasons for the area's self-destruction. In quick succession, Ross was interviewed by CBS News, the *Cincinnati Post*, *Esquire* magazine, ABC News, and NBC News. Freeway Rick was an instant hit with the press. He was accessible and self-effacing. He answered reporters' questions directly and made sense. He would open up his prison records to anyone who asked and was disarmingly honest about the crimes he'd committed.

"Soft-spoken, dressed in sweats and sporting shoulder-length dreadlocks, Ross hardly seems like a man who spent about four years in prison for drug trafficking," an *L.A. Times* reporter wrote in 1993.

Asked by *The Cincinnati Post* if he'd ever felt regret when he was dealing cocaine, Ross said the feeling was just the opposite: "I felt I'd accomplished something. I'm a money-maker. A capitalist."

He not only made great copy, but his story had a terrific hook.

The final real estate acquisition he'd made before his arrest in 1989 was a huge abandoned theater at the intersection of Adams and Crenshaw boulevards in the heart of South Central. In its heyday, the 40,000-square-foot Adams Street Theater had been a major venue for touring R&B and Motown artists. Ross dreamed of restoring the dilapidated hulk to its former grandeur, becoming an impresario, and leaving a permanent mark on South Central. "One of the times I had met Danilo in New York I had went to the Apollo Theater and I saw what they was doing there, and I said that this would be a perfect idea for Los Angeles to reach out to the kids in my community," Ross said.

When he got out of prison, Ross told the reporters, he was going to make up for the damage he'd done to his neighborhood. He'd learned his lesson, he said. He'd destroyed lives. As his penance, he was going to take his last remaining drug profits and put them to good use, turning the old theater into a youth center for the children of South Central.

It would have a gymnasium, classrooms, recording studios, computer training rooms, and a performance hall. It would be a place where kids "could go and entertain because, you know, rap is big in my neighborhood. Most of the big rappers came from my area, where I grew up at. So I said, 'Well, we could do something like the Apollo Theater, give them a place where they can go and perform.' And then also, it would give the ones that's not performing a place to go and see what was going on, and we could also reach out and start giving them messages about how to deal with life because if you don't have something to interest the kids then they won't pay you no attention."

Ross was released from federal prison in August 1993 and returned home to South Central, moving into his mother's house and throwing himself into the theater project, which he was calling the Freeway Academy. He began making the rounds of local community groups and politicians, trying to raise money for the renovations, which his pro bono architectural consultants estimated at $18.5 million.

His efforts got a major boost in November 1993, when his quest to fund the Freeway Academy broke into the national media. First, the *Los Angeles Times* published a flattering profile under the headline "Ex-Drug Dealer Out to Stage Turnaround."

"Standing on the bare stage of the cavernous Adams Street Theater, s arms spread wide as if receiving a benediction, Ricky Ross speaks fervently of the second chance in life he never thought he would get," the story began. "Once the head of one of Los Angeles' most notorious cocaine rings that did business nationwide, Ross has embarked on a venture that he is determined will be just as big: helping youths."

"Young people have no safety valve these days that allows them to express themselves, develop their talents," Ross advised the newspaper. "Look at what happened to me. I had a lot of talent, but I never even read a book until I got to jail. I don't want other kids to end up there before they've even gotten a chance to do something."

The pastor of a nearby church told the paper that he'd been impressed when Ross addressed his congregation about his plans. "It's a blessing he wants to turn over a new leaf," the minister said.

Spurred by the *L.A. Times* story, the ABC News magazine *Day One* aired its own story on Freeway Rick, a piece it had had in the can for several months. It appeared right after Monday Night Football. "Next we have the story of a young man who set out to poison his entire community," correspondent Forrest Sawyer began, calling Ross "one of America's most powerful drug dealers."

"He lives in South Central Los Angeles and he was the area's biggest cocaine dealer," Sawyer intoned. "I say 'was' because today Ross claims he has changed his ways. He says he wants to make up for all the harm he's done by building something good for his neighborhood. Some people believe he really means it. Others say it's just a scam. Either way, Freeway's story proves that when you've been a major player in America's crime crisis, going straight is never easy."

Sawyer interviewed narcotics detectives and prosecutors who were openly skeptical of Ross's scheme, saying they doubted he'd ever straighten up. Ross was just trying to buy respectability, they charged, conning the community he'd been destroying for years. Sawyer also interviewed L.A. politicians who were working with Ross to raise the funds, and a representative of the Haagen-Dazs company, who said the ice cream maker had already agreed to pitch in.

Ross admitted to Sawyer that he didn't have much cash and he agreed that he could easily return to drug dealing to raise it. "Probably quicker than I used to make it because I'm smarter now," he said. But he insisted he wasn't going down that road again.

"What do you want to be remembered as?" Sawyer asked him at the close of the piece.

"As the guy that built this great youth center in South Central Los

Angeles, in the middle of where all the riots broke out," Ross answered. "The guy that really made an impact in the community, that changed lives. That's what I want to be remembered as. That's what I *will* be remembered as. They're going to forget I was a drug dealer."

Though Ross could barely believe it himself, the Freeway Academy project began gathering steam. In early December 1993, a Los Angeles–based community group, 100 Black Men, held a dinner in Ross's honor, "and more than 200 people filled the Regency West to make sure he has the right backing to accomplish his task," the *Los Angeles Sentinel* reported.

"Magic Johnson had came. He said he was going to help. Ice Cube, Snoop Doggy Dogg, I mean, all the rappers from L.A. that I had knew from the past said that they was going to come out and help," Ross said. "I was like on just another type of high, you know? I was going to churches and doing speeches.... I was talking to the president of Polygram Records, Ed Eckstein, who was talking about giving me a record company."

But, as *Day One* had predicted, there was no escaping his past. Shortly after the show appeared, Ross said, Danilo Blandón called him out of the blue. He'd seen him on TV, he told Ross, and was glad to hear he was out of jail and doing so well.

It was the first time Ross had spoken to Blandón in four years—not surprisingly, since drug dealers tend to shy away from prisons—and Rick was happy to hear his friend's voice again. Danilo said he and Chepita would love to see him when he had the time. But there was another reason for his call, according to Ross: "He said he had a great business and he needed my help. He wanted me to talk to his wife and she could settle everything. He had a connection for me and that it would be great like it used to be. I told him that I was trying a movie, you know, I was working on a book and I was out of the business. I didn't know nobody."

Blandón confirmed calling Ross around this time but said it was just a social call.

Ross said Chepita followed up by calling him up at the youth center offices and insisting that he come have dinner with them. They were having a get-together at her mother's house in Glendale, she said, and the girls were dying to see him. Ross agreed to go, but just to be on the safe side, he took a friend with him, Norman Tillman, who was working with former football star Jim Brown on similar youth projects for South Central.

"So we go up to the house. She hugs me and tells me she was glad I was out. Danilo loves me. She loves me. Her daughters was there and a couple other people was there," Ross said. "I liked their daughters. They was like my little sisters."

But it was apparent that something was on Chepita's mind, Ross said. She asked him to come outside with her for a moment. "She started telling me that my friends had lost a lot of money of Danilo's—Tone-Tone and Mike." Tony McDonald and Mike Smith were two of Ross's successors in South Central, picking up his accounts and buying from Blandón while he was in jail. Chepita claimed they owned Danilo $18,000 and had refused to pay it back, and now the Colombians were pushing Danilo for the money, which he didn't have. "She wanted me to find somebody to sell some drugs to," Ross said. "I told her no. I didn't know nobody. I'd just gotten out of jail, you know, I'm trying to get my life together, trying to stay away from the drugs."

Chepita, Ross said, told him she understood. But Danilo called him later and wondered why Ross was refusing to help him out. It wasn't like he was asking Ross to get back into the drug business to make money, Blandón said. He was asking as a friend, as a personal favor, to get the Colombians off his back. It was Rick's friends who'd gotten him into this mess, he pointed out.

"I told him I wasn't in the position," Ross said. "Basically, I was telling him, 'You see what I'm doing, you know? You saw me on TV. You've been reading the newspapers.' I mean, he kept up with me all the way. He knew everything about me, and he knew about me testifying against the Sheriffs and everything. So I told him basically, 'You know what I'm going through right now, you know, and I'm trying to stay clean.'"

Ross felt bad about turning his back on Blandón, but he didn't have much time to dwell on it. There was a little matter in Texas that still needed attending to—his indictment for calling his cousins and talking about a cocaine deal on the phone. The Texas authorities were still waiting for him to pay his debt to society.

Ross pleaded guilty to the Texas charges and reentered prison in December 1993. He said he thought he would be doing thirty days or so, but the weeks stretched into months, and it wasn't until the end of August 1994 that he was finally released from the Smith County jail in Tyler. *L.A. Times* reporter Jesse Katz, who was working with a team of reporters on a massive project to document the ravages ten years of crack had wrought on L.A., was there to record the scene: "The notorious Los Angeles drug lord known as Freeway Rick, who once boasted that his coast-to-coast cocaine empire grossed more than $1 million a day, walked out of a Texas jail Wednesday and vowed to return home in search of redemption," Katz wrote. He described the thirty-four-year-old parolee as "once one of the nation's most prolific cocaine wholesalers," a dealer who "probably rose faster and higher than any other drug trafficker from the streets of South Central Los Angeles."

Ross, Katz wrote, "said he hoped to head back to his old neighborhood as soon as possible and devote his life to warning youngsters about the mistakes that kept him locked up for most of the last five years."

After a short probation, Ross returned to South Central in mid-October, a free man at last. His ten-month absence had taken a toll on the Freeway Academy. It was out of money, and the bills were piling up fast. To tide the project over while he was serving his time in Texas, he'd borrowed $30,000 from a Compton crack dealer, Leroy "Chico" Brown, who was helping Ross put a recording studio in the theater, but that money was just a memory. Ross had $57 to his name when he walked out of jail in Texas. His motel and his auto parts store were gone; his remaining cash was eaten up by attorney's fees. The rental houses he owned, most of which had been placed in other people's names, had been sold, foreclosed upon, or abandoned.

But $30,000 was $30,000, and Chico wanted his money back.

He wasn't the only one. Blandón called from Nicaragua the day after Ross got back into town. They needed to talk, he told Ross, but he didn't want to do it over international phone lines. He would be back in L.A. soon and wanted Rick to call him from a pay phone. "He was telling me that he needed help. Tone-Tone and them had beat him out of the money and he wanted me to help him out," Ross said. "I told him I'd just got out of jail.... I couldn't buy no drugs. I ain't got no money to buy no drugs." Blandón denied making that call.

For the first time in years, Freeway Rick was forced to get a job—a real job—working for someone else. He was hired on at Wolf River Development Corp., a company that bought repossessed houses in L.A.'s slums and fixed them up for resale. It was Ross's task to go in and clean them up.

"People would leave furniture and the carpet would be just ruined and all kinds of stuff like that. So I started off, I would go in and I would pull the carpet up. I would take all the furniture out. Sometimes they'd have trash in the garages and it would be just sky high. I would clean the garage out. I would cut the grass, trim the trees, you know, make it where it's not just a total dump." The job paid little, however, and Ross kept his eye peeled for other ways to make some money. On October 16, 1994, Ross called Blandón in Nicaragua. The man who owned Wolf River, Ross said, had a 1991 Mercedes 560 he'd wrecked and had rebuilt, but he didn't like the workmanship. Ross thought they should buy it and have Blandón resell it in Nicaragua at a premium. Blandón said he'd have to look into it.

And then the conversation turned to cocaine. Ross asked Blandón if he could "get a little something right now," which Blandón said he interpreted to mean a couple of kilos. Blandón said he had some merchandise in Guatemala that he was planning to move to Los Angeles soon but didn't have the expense money—driver's fees and plane tickets and the like—necessary to move it across the border into the United States. Ross would have to loan him the money to pay the expenses, Blandón said.

Ross asked what price he was planning to sell the cocaine for.

"Eleven," Blandón said, meaning $11,000 a kilo.

"Okay, that's good," Ross replied. "Let me know as soon as possible."

Blandón asked Ross to call him the next day, but he didn't, and the negotiations for the cocaine sale went nowhere. Ross said it was pointless because he didn't have the money to pay Blandón's expenses. In a series of later calls, Blandón kept asking Ross for a loan and reminding him about the $18,000 Tone-Tone owed him. According to Blandón's notes of the conversations, Ross kept insisting he was "broke himself" and "wasn't ready to start the bussinees [sic]." Most of the conversations concerned buying cars and trucks and reselling them.

But Blandón and his wife kept pressing, Ross said, calling him, calling his mother, paging him constantly. His probation officer, James Galipeau, said he was driving Ross to a high school one morning to deliver one of his motivational speeches to the students when Ross's pager went off. Ross looked at the number and began cursing, "This guy won't leave me alone," Ross griped, explaining that the caller was a former cocaine supplier who wanted to resume business. "I mean, the son-of-a-bitch called him while he was in the car with his probation officer!" Galipeau said.

Ross said he met with Blandón in November at Meneses's old restaurant on Hoover Street and was told that if his friend didn't repay the money, Blandón was going to "take care of Tony." Ross believed Blandón meant it; when Mike Smith had gotten behind on some payments to Danilo, Smith and his house had been shot up. Blandón confirmed that he spoke to Ross several times about the debt Tony McDonald owed, but he denied ever threatening to kill him.

In December 1994 the *L.A. Times* published its opus on the ten-year anniversary of the city's crack plague, and once again, Ricky Ross was in the news. Reporter Jesse Katz crafted a poignant 2,500-word feature that chronicled "the saga of Ricky Ross' rise and fall." It pinned the explosion of L.A.'s crack market to his teenage dealings in South Central.

"If there was an eye to the storm," it began, "if there was a criminal mastermind behind crack's decade-long reign, if there was one outlaw capitalist most responsible for flooding Los Angeles' streets with mass-marketed cocaine, his name was Freeway Rick."

According to the story Ross's cocaine operation had so much influence on the L.A. drug market that "by the end of the decade, he had helped cut wholesale rates from $60,000 a kilo to just $10,000." The *Times* headline called him the "Deposed King of Crack" and described Ross as "a master marketer [who] was key to the drug's spread in L.A."

The Freeway Academy got another plug, and Ross's embittered nemesis, the recently convicted LAPD sergeant Steve Polak, took a shot at him—a verbal one—calling Ross a con artist. "Let him pay for all the people his drugs have killed. Let him put money into the hospitals for all the addicted babies. Let me see him turn over a million or two to the IRS and get a job...then maybe I'll give him some credibility," Polak told Katz. "Ross will fall again some day," the ex-detective said ominously.

Katz's story prompted another flood of calls to the Freeway Academy, Ross said, including more from Danilo Blandón. One day in February 1995 he was driving around with Chico Brown, his erstwhile recording studio partner, "and I got a page from Danilo. I called Danilo back and I start talking to him and Chico decoded the conversation." Brown, a veteran crack dealer with the Patrick Johnson organization, wanted to know what was up. Was Ross doing dope on the side, when he owed him money?

No, Ross told him. He didn't have enough to buy a car. He was six months behind on the rent for the theater. Chico had to loan him the $800 he needed to file a bankruptcy petition, to keep the bank at bay. Yet this friend of his kept trying to hit him up for the money Tone-Tone lost, Ross explained, wanting him to do a deal to pay it back.

Brown's moon-face broke into a wide smile. He had a solution to everyone's problems, he told Ross. *He* would put up the money for the dope deal. He had some friends back in Baltimore who were looking to make an investment. All Ross needed to do was introduce Chico to his source. If the deal went down, he'd not only forget about the $30,000 Ross owed him, but he'd *give* Rick $70,000 for his troubles.

Rick wouldn't really be buying or selling anything, Brown rationalized. All he'd be doing is making an introduction. Brown and his people would take all the financial risk and handle all the dope. Ross wouldn't have to come anywhere near it. Easy as pie. Unless, of course, Ross had a better idea about how to raise the 30 K he owed him.

Ross thought it over. When Brown put it that way, it didn't actually sound so bad. After all, it wasn't like *he* was selling dope, something he'd promised everybody he'd never do again. He sure wasn't buying any. Chico was. Danilo's cocaine—Chico's money. Their deal. Not his. All he had to do was make a phone call. One little call, and he'd have Danilo off his back, Chico off his back, the bank off his back. In and out. One time.

What the fuck. He was with it, he told Chico. He'd set things up.

In late February 1995 Ross, Chico Brown, and Brown's friend from Baltimore, Curtis James, met Blandón in the parking lot of the Popeye's chicken restaurant in National City, just south of San Diego. Ross introduced the Nicaraguan to his friends and told him they would be the ones he'd be dealing with. And they were ready to deal. Right now.

Surprisingly, Blandón demurred, as if not yet ready to seal the deal. The cocaine hadn't crossed the border yet, he told them. He had 150 kilos coming in. Fifty was for someone else. They could have the 100 that was left.

"I asked for $200,000 [up front] and they told me they only had $160,000 but they could do it today," Blandón said. "Impossible, I told them, today. We have to take a week or two or three days while the merchandise is crossing, so you have to wait."

He also tossed off one more threat against Tony McDonald, telling Ross, "That Tony—I want to get him."

Ross had heard enough about Tone-Tone and the $18,000. "He ain't gonna fucking pay you!" he said angrily "He ain't gonna pay you! It ain't worth it. Let it go. Let it go."

"Okay," Blandón replied. "I'll let it go."

"We're going to make a lot of money," Ross reminded him. Blandón laughed.

They met a week later, again in the Popeye's parking lot. Blandón told Ross that the Colombians wanted to meet his friends, to make sure they were reliable. They knew Ross could be trusted. But they'd never dealt with his friends before.

Ross, driving Chico's new Nissan Pathfinder, pulled into a parking slot, with Curtis James and Brown in the backseat. Blandón and a Hispanic man who did not speak English walked up to the driver's window. Blandón served as the man's translator. How much money were they bringing to the table? the Colombian wanted to know.

From the backseat, Chico told Blandón he had $160,000 now but would have $200,000 by the first of March, if the Colombians wanted to wait that long. Blandón was testy about it, but Ross said that was his problem—they'd done bigger deals with less up front before. If they could deliver it in L.A., Chico said, he'd guarantee them $500,000. The Colombian suggested a $300,000 down payment would be more appropriate. After all, this was $1 million worth of cocaine they were going to be giving them on faith.

Brown told him they'd get the money. "My word is bond," he said. "Whatever I say is the truth. My objective is to get you paid off as soon as possible."

Blandón told him the cocaine was crossing the Mexican border that night, and they'd call when it arrived in San Diego. Blandón didn't call, and Ross's partners refused to come up with any more money for the down payment.

At 7:30 A.M., March 2, 1995, Ross called Blandón at home and told him they were in San Diego, ready to deal. Blandón said he and the Colombian were ducking into Tijuana to pick it up and would call when it was over the border. Around four hours later, Blandón called Ross and his friends at the cheap motel they were staying in, the E-Z 8, and told them to be at the Denny's Restaurant off I-805 in Chula Vista in twenty minutes.

Ross and his old friend Michael McLaurin—the San Jose State football player who first told Ross about cocaine back in 1979—drove to the restaurant in McLaurin's new purple Ford Ranger pickup. McLaurin, who was working at an L.A. hospital and had been hitting up the medical staff for donations to the Freeway Academy, said Ross had called him and told him he was buying a car in San Diego, but didn't have a way to get down there. McLaurin agreed to give him a lift, eager to take his new pickup truck on a long ride.

With Chico and Curtis James following in Chico's Pathfinder, they met Blandón and the Colombian behind the Denny's shortly after noon. Blandón tried one more time to get Ross to pony up more cash. The Colombians had been expecting $300,000, Blandón complained, and Ross shows up with only around $170,000? Ross assured him he'd have the rest of the money by tomorrow. Where was the cocaine?

Nearby, Blandón told him. In a "load car" parked in a shopping center lot, just like always. Chico Brown said he wanted to see it, and Blandón got huffy.

"I told him, 'Hey, we don't have no time,'" Blandón recalled. "'Why don't you tell us that before?'"

But Brown dug in his heels, telling Blandón that he wasn't buying any dope he'd never seen. Ross jumped in to smooth things over. It's not necessary, Ross assured Brown. He and Danilo always did business this way. If Danilo says the dope is there, it's there. Relax.

"We trust each other," Blandón assured him. Now, where was the money?

Brown went to his Pathfinder, reached inside, and pulled out a black-and-green shopping bag full of cash bundles, which he handed to the Colombian. The trafficker put the bag in Blandón's car and told Ross to follow them to the load car, where they would get the car keys.

They drove about a quarter-mile to the Bonita Plaza Mall and pulled into the parking lot outside the Montgomery Ward. The Colombian got out and handed a key chain to Curtis James, telling him the cocaine was in the white Chevy Blazer parked about twenty yards away. Ross and McLaurin strolled nonchalantly to the Blazer, and Ross stuck his head inside, where he saw four cardboard boxes containing twenty-five kilos each, nestled in the back.

It was all there, just as Danilo had promised. A deal was still a deal. Ross told McLaurin to take the Blazer back to L.A., and he'd follow him in the purple pickup. As he walked to the truck, he saw Blandón and the Colombian driving away.

Then all hell broke loose.

From everywhere, police cars came screaming up, sirens blaring. Cops in raid jackets were running through the parking lot, waving guns. McLaurin revved the engine of the Blazer and dropped it into gear.

"They burned rubber," DEA agent Charles Jones said. "Federal agents blocked the vehicle...they burned rubber forward, he blocked it. They put it in reverse, he burned rubber in reverse and the kill switch finally kicked in." The DEA had booby-trapped the Blazer so it couldn't be driven.

Ross scampered to the purple truck and jumped in, tearing out of the parking lot with an unmarked DEA car roaring along behind him. He was sick to his stomach, sweating. How could be have been so fucking stupid? How could he have not seen this coming? Now what? "I was hoping to find a wall that I could just crash myself into. I wanted to die."

Ross "went out of the shopping center, blew through stop signs, intersections at a high rate of speed," Jones said. "He tried to turn onto Sweetwater Road and a police officer blocked him and he swerved and crashed in the bushes and jumped out and ran away." It was not a long chase. In a matter of minutes he was captured behind a house on a nearby street, handcuffed, and stuffed into the back of a police car. He had been a free man only six months.

Back at the DEA regional headquarters in National City, the jubilant agents counted and stacked up the pile of money they'd seized. It turned out that Chico had shorted the Colombians by a couple hundred bucks: $169,445 was piled on the table, and the agents snapped pictures. Ross was pushed into a chair and asked if he wanted to make a statement.

Sure, Ross said. Why not? He saw the lay of the land. Danilo had set him up, had probably taped all of their calls. Everyone else was under arrest. The cops had the dope and Chico's money. Case closed. Ross told them everything.

Two weeks later a federal grand jury returned a two-count indictment against Brown, Curtis James, Ricky Ross, and Mike McLaurin, charging them with conspiracy to possess cocaine and possession with intent to sell. This would be Ross's third strike. He was looking at life without parole this time.

His friends and family were crushed and embarrassed.

"I cussed his Mom out, I cussed his brother out, and my Mom and I cried together," said Ross's friend and partner in the youth center, Norman Tillman. "He was talking so positive, telling me in earnest how he was going to make it as big legitimately as he did illegitimately. He was going to prove it to the world."

"Sting Snares Drug Lord Who Vowed To Go Straight," the *L.A. Times* headline blared. A chagrined Jesse Katz was flown in from his new job at the *Times*' Houston bureau to write off Ricky Ross for good. "I had no doubt that he was going to fall again," former LAPD detective Polak crowed to Katz. "I just didn't know it was going to be this soon."

Katz interviewed Ross's brother David, who complained that the arrest "seems like entrapment. They set him up and he evidently fell for it." David Ross noted that the informant was a drug dealing acquaintance "who just kept bugging him, calling and calling, but Ricky wasn't doing anything like that anymore."

Katz called Ross afterward and demanded to know why he'd done it. Ross told him he'd set up the deal to help get a friend out of debt, "and I was like, 'Come on. Think about yourself here first.'"

Katz said he felt personally betrayed by Ross, who was swearing to Katz that he was going straight at the very same time he was setting up a drug deal. "I caught a lot of shit from the editors over that. I'd had a hard enough time getting that original story into the paper," Katz said, six months after Ross's arrest. "It was supposed to be a separate part of the [crack] series, but they cut it in half and made it a sidebar because some people said it looked like we were glorifying the guy. So you can imagine what the reaction was at the *Times* when it came out that he'd been busted."

Asked why he thought the DEA would target someone who had just emerged from prison, broke and vowing to go straight, Katz had a ready answer: "To fuck with him. They could go after *you* right now. That's the scary message in all of this. If the government decides to fuck with you and you take the bait, you are automatically fucked."

Ross was locked up without bail in the Metropolitan Correctional Center in San Diego. He had really done it this time. His fate seemed as predictable as the calendar. LWOP. Life without parole. He would never see the outside world again.

PART TWO

25

"Things are moving all around us"

I was swept into Ross's decade-long relationship with Danilo Blandón in late September 1995, two months into my investigation and six months after Ross's arrest. Quite unexpectedly, Coral Baca's tip on the CIA, the Contras, and cocaine had led me to the Metropolitan Correctional Center in downtown San Diego, a bleak, windowless skyscraper where the former crack king was being held without bail until his trial.

Entering the tiny interview room, Ross exuded an air of self-assurance and confidence. He appeared unfazed by his predicament, but by the time the interview was over, he had dropped the pretense. Blandón's betrayal had clearly left him hurt and bewildered. "I can't believe he done me like this," Ross commented as I packed up my tape recorder and notebooks. "Why'd he do it? You figure that out yet?"

I told him what I'd culled from the court files about Blandón's arrest in May 1992—how he'd faced a mandatory life sentence and the prospect of having his wife behind bars as well, leaving their two young daughters orphaned. It was hard to blame someone for trying to squirm out of a jam like that, I said. Ross nodded. "So how much dope did they catch him with?" None, I said. But they had him on tape talking to informants about cocaine deals, bragging about how many thousands of kilos he'd sold. Ross's reaction brought me up short.

"That's it?" Ross asked incredulously. "They didn't find

no dope on him? Then what would he roll over for? Think about it. You ain't gonna pull a life sentence just for talking to somebody about selling dope. That's bullshit. Somebody ain't tell you something."

LAPD narcotics detective Ron Hodges, who had investigated Blandón in conjunction with the DEA in 1991–92, made a similar observation when I interviewed him a few weeks later. "What's hard to understand [is] when we actually did the investigation on him and it came to a conclusion, I think he was charged with what they consider a 'no-dope conspiracy'—which is like nothing. It's so minimal. It's like trying to do something when there is nothing there." Blandón's lawyer, Brad Brunon, pointed out that his client had no criminal record, and the DEA had nothing more than some loose talk with criminal informants. There was no evidence of actual drug dealing, Brunon argued.

It made no sense. Why, then, had Blandón so readily agreed to become a government informant? And why had the Justice Department accorded him such a high degree of trust and faith? Blandón was an international criminal, a man who'd brazenly sold drugs and weapons to gang members for more than a decade. Yet here he was jetting in and out of the country at government expense, with no law enforcement supervision whatsoever—free to do as he pleased. Maybe Ricky Ross's suspicions were right, I thought. Perhaps Blandón had worked for the U.S. government before, just as Norwin Meneses had. If he had a track record, it would certainly explain his extraordinary treatment.

I quickly got a taste of how protective the Justice Department was of the Nicaraguan. In October 1995 I received an unsolicited phone call from the big blond man I'd met in the bathroom at the San Francisco federal courthouse a few weeks earlier, Assistant U.S. Attorney David Hall, Rafael Corñejo's prosecutor.

There were some people who wanted to talk to me, Hall said. My activity "has a number of people extremely worried because of an ongoing narcotics investigation that Blandón is working on for the government." Before I printed anything, I needed to know the situation. If I wasn't careful, "there is a distinct possibility that real harm, possibly death, would come to Mr. Blandón and that an investigation we have been working on for a couple of years would be compromised." The DEA wanted to know if some kind of an accommodation could be reached.

Like what? I asked.

Well, Hall said, it had been proposed that if I held off on the story for a couple of months, they might be able to arrange an exclusive interview with Blandón for me.

I told him I didn't think my editors would agree to a delay, but if lives were in danger, I'd certainly be willing to hear them out. On October 19, 1995, I walked into a roomful of DEA agents in the National City regional office, squirreled away in an industrial complex south of San Diego.

Two of the agents I recognized from court and reading their names in the court files: Blandón's handlers, the immaculately coiffed Chuck Jones and his worried-looking sidekick, Judy Gustafson. The other four I didn't know. The agent behind the desk, a tall man with an easy smile, got up and shook my hand warmly. Craig Chretien, he said, special agent in charge.

"This is a little awkward for us," Chretien began. They knew generally the story I was working on, he said, and unfortunately I was getting into some rather sensitive areas. There were undercover operations—more than four of them—that I was in danger of exposing, putting agents and their families at risk. They couldn't give me any details, of course, but I needed to appreciate the seriousness of the situation. "What's your angle here?" Chretien asked. "Is it that the DEA sometimes hires scumbags to go after people?"

"No. It's about Blandón and Norwin Meneses and the Contras," I said. "And their dealings with Ricky Ross."

The agents looked at each other quickly out of the corners of their eyes, but at first said nothing.

"That whole Central American thing," Chretien said dismissively. "I was down there. You heard all sorts of things. There was never any proof that the Contras were dealing drugs. If you're going to get involved in that, you'll never get to the truth. No one ever will."

"I think that's been pretty well established," I said. "Your informant was one of the men who was doing it."

Chretien gave Jones a sidelong glance and Jones came to life. "I can tell you that I have never, *ever* heard anything about Blandón being involved with that," he said firmly. "Not once. His only involvement with the Contras was that his father was a general or something down there."

"And these two have practically lived with the man for two years now," Chretien added, pointing to Jones and Gustafson. "If it had happened they would know about it."

I could not quite believe what I was hearing. What kind of scam was this?

"Have you ever asked him about it?" I asked Jones.

"I've already said more than I should."

"Did you ever ask him about doing it with Norwin Meneses?"

"You'd better go check your sources again," Jones snapped.

"My source is Blandón," I said. "He testified to it under oath, before a grand jury. You're telling me you don't know about that?"

Jones threw up his hands. "Oh, listen, he understands English pretty well, but sometimes he gets confused, and if you ask him a question the wrong way he'll say yes when he means no."

I shook my head. "I've got the transcripts. These weren't yes or no questions. He gave very detailed responses."

Jones's face and forehead grew beet red and his voice rose. "You're telling me that he testified that he sold cocaine for the Contras in *this* country? He sold it in *this* country?"

"That's exactly what I'm telling you. You want to see the transcripts? I've got them right here."

"I cannot believe that those two U.S. attorneys up there, if they had him saying that before a grand jury, that they would ever, ever, ever put him on a witness stand!" Jones fumed. "They'd have to be insane! They'd have to be total idiots!"

"They didn't put him on the witness stand," I reminded him. "They yanked him at the last minute."

"That's because the judge ordered them to turn over all that unredacted material!" Jones blurted. "We're not going to..." He looked quickly at Chretien and clammed up. Just as I suspected. They knew all about this. The DEA had nixed Blandón's appearance because Rafael Corñejo's attorney had discovered the Contra connection and the government had been ordered to turn over the files.

Chretien told me that it would be best for all concerned if I simply left out the fact that Blandón was now working for the DEA. "Your story can just go up to a certain point and stop, can't it? Is it really necessary to mention his current relationship with us? If it comes out that he is in any way connected to DEA, it could seriously compromise some extremely promising investigations."

I said I thought it was important to the story, which prompted another angry outburst from Jones. "Even after what we just told you, you'd still go ahead and put it in the paper? Why? Why would you put a story in the paper that would stop us from keeping drugs out of this country? I don't know if you've got kids or not..."

"I've got three kids," I interrupted, "and I don't know what that has to do with anything."

"So you'll screw up an investigation we've been working on for a long time, just so you can have a story? Is that it?" Jones demanded. "You think this story is more important than what we're doing for this country? How is that more important?"

"I don't buy it," I replied. "You have to put Blandón on the witness stand at Ross's trial. So in five months everyone in the world is going to know he's a DEA informant. Hell, if they want to know now they can just go down to the courthouse and look it up, like I did. So that's one problem I'm having with all this. The other thing is, I think the American public has been lied to for ten years, and I think telling them the truth is a whole lot more important than this investigation of yours."

Jones and I glared at each other, and Chretien stepped in. "I think we're getting off the topic here. Please understand, we're not telling you not to do your story. But your interest is in Meneses primarily and his association with the U.S. government and the Contras, correct?"

That was one of my interests, I said.

"Well, I think we can help him there, can't we?" Chretien asked, glancing around the room at the other agents. "Maybe if we got you that information, you could focus your story more on him and less on Blandón? And maybe you wouldn't have to mention some other things?"

"That all depends," I said, "on what that other information is."

Chretien smiled and stood up. "Okay, then! We're going to have to talk about this among ourselves. I'm not even sure what we have in mind is legal, but we'd at least like to explore it. Could we ask that you please not print anything until we've talked again? Can you give us a week or two?"

I told him I'd wait for his call.

When I returned to Sacramento, I phoned former DEA agent Celerino Castillo III, who had investigated allegations of Contra drug trafficking at Ilopango air base in El Salvador in the mid-1980s. I asked him if he'd ever heard of Craig Chretien.

"Yeah, sure," Castillo said. "I know him. He was one of the people DEA sent to Guatemala to do the internal investigation of me." He said Chretien and another DEA official had ordered him to put the word "alleged" in his reports to Washington about Contra drug shipments from Ilopango. "They said, 'You cannot actually come out and say this shit is going on.' And I told them, 'I'm watching the fucking things fly out of here with my own eyes! Why would I have to say 'alleged'?"

I told him of Chretien's remark that there was no proof the Contras were involved in drugs. He snorted. "Aw, bullshit. Of all people, he knows perfectly well what was going on. He was reading all my reports—looking for grammatical errors."

After two weeks I'd heard nothing back, so I called the San Diego office and asked for Chretien. He no longer works in this office, I was told. He'd been transferred to Washington.

The head of the International Division, Robert J. Nieves—Norwin Meneses's old control agent—had unexpectedly resigned eight days after my meeting with Chretien, I discovered. Chretien had been picked to replace him.

I never spoke to Chretien again, and I suspected that the meeting in San Diego had been set up to find out what I knew and where I was heading. My suspicions on that score were confirmed in early 1998 with the release of a CIA Inspector General's report, which referenced three CIA cables about me, titled "Possible Attempts to Link CIA to Narcotraffickers," written within weeks of my meeting with the DEA agents in San Diego.

"In November 1995, we were informed by DEA that a reporter has been inquiring about activities in Central America and any links with the Contras," a heavily censored December 4, 1995, cable from CIA headquarters in Langley stated. "DEA has been alerted that Meneses will undoubtedly claim that he was trafficking narcotics on behalf of CIA to generate money for the Contras. Query whether Station can clarify or amplify on the above information to better identify Meneses or confirm or refute any claims he may make. HQS trace on (FNU) Meneses reveal *extensive* entries." (Those extensive entries were not revealed in the declassified version of the CIA's 1998 IG report.)

The DEA's public affairs office in Washington later attempted to work out a deal with me to set up an interview with Meneses if I would leave Blandón's DEA ties out of the story, but fortunately my colleague in Nicaragua, freelance journalist Georg Hodel, beat them to the punch. He'd found the massive files of Meneses's 1992 court case in the Nicaraguan Supreme Court and had tracked the drug lord down to a prison outside of Managua.

"The clerk says I am the first journalist ever to ask to see those files, can you imagine?" Hodel asked me. "All the stories written about this case, and not one of those reporters ever looked at the files. I have one of my journalism students, Leonor Delgado, going through and making us an index of all the pages. There are some peculiar things in there, I can tell you."

My tipster, Coral Baca, had told me the truth about Blandón and Meneses, Georg reported. He'd checked it with former Contra commander Edén Pastora, former Contra lawyer Carlos Icaza, and others who knew both men. They were friends and business partners, and their families were very close to Somoza. They were considered to have been among the founders of the Contras. And, he said, Meneses's chief aide, Enrique Miranda, had admitted at trial that Meneses sold cocaine for the Contras, flying it out of an air base in El Salvador into a military airfield in Texas.

"In some of the newspaper stories I'm sending you, you will see that Meneses makes the same claim," Georg said. "It was part of his defense that the Sandinistas persecuted him because of his work for the Contras."

I told him of my conversations with the DEA and suggested that we might want to get to Meneses quickly, before someone else did. He agreed and told me that there was another person we needed to talk to as well: Meneses's chief accuser, Enrique Miranda. According to the files, Miranda was also still in jail, having been moved to a prison in the city of Granada after Meneses had allegedly hired someone to kill him.

He'd already put in a request to the Nicaraguan Ministry of the Interior to arrange an interview, Georg said. "I think we can speak to both of them. How quickly can you come down?"

"As soon as I clear it with my editors," I told him. "I'm not sure if they even know about this story yet. Dawn's been running interference for me with the other editors until I got this somewhat nailed down, but it seems pretty solid to me. We need to get to Meneses before the DEA does, so if you want to go ahead and set up the interviews, do it. I'll start the ball rolling here."

But Georg ran into an inexplicable roadblock. The normally cooperative prison officials in Managua began dodging his calls, offering one excuse and one delay after another. He waited a week, then hopped in his creaky blue Mazda and drove to the prison where Miranda was being held, to see what the problem was.

A nervous prison official informed him that Miranda was not available. Why not? Georg asked. Well, the official stammered, unfortunately, the prisoner had escaped. He'd been out on a weekend furlough, and he'd never come back. It was extremely out of character, Georg was assured, because Miranda had been a model inmate and had only a short time left in his sentence.

Astounded, Georg drove to the police station to see how the manhunt for the notorious trafficker was coming along. The police looked at him blankly. Someone had escaped from prison? Who? When? Miranda had been gone for over a week, and the police had not been notified. Georg's discovery was front-page news in all the Managua papers. Official investigations were launched.

"He supposedly escaped the same day I made my interview request," Georg reported. "My sources tell me he's in Miami and they say the DEA got him out of the country. Do you suppose they don't want us talking to him?"

(Georg's sources would later prove to have been well-informed. Miranda was captured a little over a year later in December 1996 in Miami, where he was living with his wife. It emerged that he had gained entry with the help of a ten-year visa the U.S. embassy in Managua had issued him the day he'd "escaped." State Department officials were at a loss to explain how a convicted cocaine trafficker was able to flee prison and obtain a U.S. visa. The DEA denied arranging his escape but admitted that Miranda had gone to work for the agency in Miami as a paid informant. Apparently, the DEA never bothered to inform the Nicaraguan authorities it was harboring one of their fugitives.)

But Georg had some good news as well. Meneses was willing to talk. George had cleared it through the drug kingpin's wives and lawyers and urged me to come to Nicaragua as soon as possible. We needed to move quickly and carefully, he warned, because there was something about this story that was beginning to give him the creeps.

"I can't say what it is," he said nervously, "but things are moving all around us."

In December I gathered up all my notes and files and wrote a four-page project memo for my editors, outlining the story as I saw it. I proposed to tell the tale of how the infant L.A. crack market had been fueled by tons of cocaine brought in by a Contra drug ring, which helped to spread a deadly new drug habit "through L.A. and from there to the hinterlands."

"This series will show that the dumping of cocaine on L.A.'s street gangs was the back end of a covert effort to arm and equip the CIA's ragtag army of anti-Communist Contra guerrillas," I wrote. "While there has long been solid—if largely ignored—evidence of a CIA-Contra-cocaine connection, no one has ever asked the question: 'Where did all the cocaine go once it got here?' Now we know."

I met with Dawn and managing editor David Yarnold in San Jose, and we spent an hour discussing the progress of the investigation and the proposed series. Yarnold reread the project memo, shook his head, and grinned.

"This is one hell of a story," he said. "How soon do you think you can finish it?"

I told him I needed to go to Miami and Nicaragua to do some interviews with Meneses, some former Contras, and the Nicaraguan police. If that came off, we might be able to have the series ready by March 1996, in time for the Ross trial, which would give it a hard news angle. But, I said, I wanted to get some assurances right up front from both of them.

Because the story had what I called a "high unbelievability factor," I wanted to use the *Mercury*'s Web site, Mercury Center, to help document the series. I wanted us to put our evidence up on the Internet, so readers could see our documents and reports, read the grand jury transcripts, listen to the undercover DEA tapes, check our sources, and make up their own minds about the validity of the story. After seeing the government's reaction to the Contra-cocaine stories of the 1980s, I didn't want to be caught in the old officials-say-there's-no-evidence trap.

The technology now exists for journalists to share our evidence with the world, I told them, and if there was ever a story that needed to be solidly backed up, it was this one. Not only would it help out the story, I wrote in my memo, it would hopefully raise the standards of investigative reporting by forcing the press to play show and tell, rather than hiding behind faceless sources and whisperings from "senior administration officials."

The editors enthusiastically agreed. It would be a good way to showcase the *Mercury*'s cutting-edge Web site, they said, and it was good timing—management directives were coming out to incorporate the Web page into our print stories whenever possible. We were, after all, the newspaper of the Silicon Valley. This would be a chance to use the Internet in a way that had never been done before, they agreed. No problem. What else?

The second point I made was something I was sure they were tired of hearing about. We're going to need space to tell this story, I told them, a lot more space than the paper usually devotes to its investigative projects. It was the one issue that drove me crazy about working for the *Mercury News*.

After writing for the *Plain Dealer* for five years and having as much space as I'd wanted, I'd found the *Mercury's* mania for brevity almost unbearable. My forfeiture series, for example, had been held to two parts, and even those stories had been chopped up into bite-sized bits. I'd had other stories held for weeks and even months because I wouldn't give in to editors' demands to cut them in half.

No one reads long stories, I was told. Our focus groups had shown that readers wanted our stories to be even shorter than they already were—"tighter and brighter" was the answer to dwindling readership.

Details were boring. Readers didn't like having to turn pages to follow jumps. If you couldn't tell a daily story in twelve inches or less, then maybe it was too complicated to tell. For a time, we even had a rule: no stories could be longer than forty-eight inches. Period. And that was for Sundays. Daily stories had an absolute max of thirty-six inches.

"We've got to lay out everything we know," I told Yarnold, "because people are going to come after us on this, and I don't ever want to be in a position where I have to say, 'Oh, yeah, we knew that, but we didn't have the space to put it in the paper.' And I don't think you want to be in that position either."

You'll get as much space as you need, Yarnold assured me. Don't worry about it. Just go out and bring this thing home.

26

"That matter, if true, would be classified"

A few days before Ricky Ross's trial was scheduled to begin, in March 1996, Jesse Katz of the *Los Angeles Times* called me at home, where I had holed up to sketch out the first drafts of the series. Though we worked for competing newspapers, Katz had been a helpful and encouraging source during the months I'd spent wending my way through the rise and fall of Ricky Ross's crack dealing career.

That day, however, he prefaced our conversation with a warning: he was calling me as a reporter, not as a source. He was doing a story about Ross's upcoming trial, and he knew I was investigating Blandón's connections to the CIA and the Contras. He wanted to ask me about that.

I was thunder-struck. I'd never told Katz anything of the sort, precisely for this reason. One of the most devious ways to avoid being scooped was to do a story on the other guy's story first. Though you normally got only a fraction of the tale, it took some of the sting out of getting beat, and some of the wind out of your competitor's sails.

"You must think I'm stupid, Jesse. I'm not telling you anything."

"Well, I already know it, and I'm going to put it in the paper. I'm just offering you a chance to comment," he said. "Look at it this way: as long as I'm going to write about it anyway, it's in your interest to make sure that what goes into the paper is accurate."

I had to laugh. "I haven't heard that line in a long time,"

I said. "Forget it. If you've got the information, print it. You don't need me to comment."

"Look. Alan Fenster filed a motion asking that the case be dismissed because the prosecutors were illegally withholding information from the defense. He filed an affidavit from a private investigator who said he'd spoken to you, and it says you have information that Blandón was involved in the Iran-Contra scandal. So what I'm asking is: is it true?"

I had been double-crossed. A private eye hired by Ross's lawyer had come by my house looking for information on Blandón, but I'd told him very little. He then pulled out a copy of a DEA report Fenster had gotten through discovery, which showed that Blandón clearly knew the cocaine he was selling to Ross was being turned into crack by the Crips and Bloods. It was an important bit of documentation for my story.

He would give me this, he said, if I would simply show him something about Blandón that the government hadn't turned over, so the defense could honestly say there was information being hidden from them. I wouldn't be identified. They didn't need a copy. They just needed to know that such documents existed.

From covering the case, I knew the federal attorneys had been withholding reams of evidence about Blandón's sordid background and his association with the Contras. If Fenster could catch them at it, I thought, maybe the court would order the Justice Department to make all the documents public, which would give me access to records I wanted to see.

I thought it over and agreed to show the PI one of the FBI reports I'd gotten from the Iran-Contra files at the National Archives. The next thing I knew, Fenster had named me and exposed the *Mercury's* investigation in his motion, and now the *L.A. Times* was onto it.

I should have known better. For weeks Ross and Fenster had been badgering me to publish the series before the trial started, figuring that the publicity might give the Justice Department second thoughts about pursuing the case. But after sitting down and roughing out an outline, I saw there was still too much I didn't know—too many unanswered questions. Dawn and I agreed that if Blandón, who was ignoring our interview requests, was going to testify, the story would benefit by waiting.

Several days earlier I'd told Ross that we were holding the story. It would not run before his trial. Angry and desperate, he'd called Katz and told him what little he knew about my investigation, hoping to stampede the *Times* into rushing something into print so they could beat us to the punch. Fenster followed that up by filing the motion and affidavit, giving Katz a court document to hang his story on. But the *Times* still had nothing; it was all secondhand. That's why Katz was fishing for confirmation. I wasn't going to give him my story, I told him. "Well, I had to try," he said. "No hard feelings."

Right after I hung up, Alan Fenster called. The Justice Department, he said, had just filed a motion to prevent him from questioning Blandón about the CIA.

"Why? Have you gotten some information about that?"

"No, but apparently they think I have," he said. "You should read this thing—it's amazing."

The motion, written by Assistant U.S. Attorney L. J. O'Neale, was as bizarre as Fenster had claimed: "The United States believes that at least one defendant will attempt to assert to the effect that the informant in this case sold cocaine to raise money for the Nicaraguan Contras and that he did so in conjunction with, or for, the Central Intelligence Agency."

O'Neale said the government was sure the information was false, but the motion made it clear that he wasn't sure at all. "This matter, if true, would be classified," O'Neale had written, "if false should not be allowed. The only purpose for asking questions in this regard would be as a clumsy attempt to bullyrag the United States into foregoing prosecution."

If the CIA was involved in drug sales, it would be classified? That was a good one. The whole legal basis for O'Neale's motion was tangential; Fenster hadn't filed the required notice to alert the government that he might reveal classified information at trial. Therefore, O'Neale wanted a court order "prohibiting any defendant from making any reference in this case to the United States Central Intelligence Agency, or to any alleged activity of that Agency."

Fenster said there was a hearing on the government's motion scheduled for the next day, and I jumped on a plane to San Diego. I couldn't wait to hear the U.S. Justice Department stand up in court and say that information about CIA involvement in drug trafficking was classified.

When I got there, I noticed that I was the only spectator in the courtroom. Good. I took a seat in the front row.

Shortly before the hearing began, I heard the courtroom door open behind me. It was Jesse Katz, with a big smile on his face. The *Times* had flown him in from his office in Houston just to be here, he told me.

I groaned silently. There goes the ball game. All the connections between Blandón, the Contras, the CIA, and Ricky Ross were going to come out in public, and the *L.A. Times* was going to beat me on my own goddamned story. Nine months worth of work down the crapper. I wanted to tear my hair out.

From a side door, prosecutor L. J. O'Neale strutted in, carrying a boxload of records, followed by DEA agents Jones and Gustafson. O'Neale looked at me; he looked at Jesse Katz; and then he blanched. When federal judge Marilyn Huff called the courtroom to order, O'Neale immediately asked to approach the bench.

He and Fenster huddled with the judge, whispering. Occasionally O'Neale would gesture to Katz and me. The huddle broke up, and Fenster walked back to the defense table, shaking his head.

"I have reviewed the government's request that the court seal, uh, certain portions," Huff announced cryptically. "You may be heard at sidebar. Mr. O'Neale. And defense counsel." The lawyers again trooped up to the judge's bench and began an animated, whispered conversation.

Katz and I strained to catch bits and pieces. I heard "CIA" several times—"murders in Mexico"; "money from the U.S. government"; "Contras."

O'Neale looked at us and turned back to the huddle. He warned defense attorney Juanita Brooks to lower her voice. "The reporters that Mr. Fenster has brought to court today are listening very carefully," he told her.

As with most federal court proceedings, the conversation was recorded and I later obtained a copy of the tape. Brooks, in a low whisper, told the judge that she was very disturbed O'Neale had hidden from the defense the fact that "Blandón was a member of an organization responsible for numerous murders in Mexico." O'Neale denied it. While he admitted that Blandón had gotten into the drug business by selling cocaine for the Contras, he said there was "absolutely no connection between Blandón and the CIA."

"He was never authorized to do that by a CIA agent?" Huff whispered. "Well, look," O'Neale hissed, "that's something I'm not even sure I can say 'Yes' or 'No' to because that comes within the realm of—look, I have no reason to believe he had any contact with the CIA and I would defy counsel to come up with any kind of credible information that he had a connection to the CIA..."

Fenster, struggling to keep his voice low, whispered that the reason he didn't have any information was because the government had refused to turn over "pages and pages of records...that I know for a fact exist!" O'Neale denied there was anything significant in the files.

Ten minutes turned into twenty minutes, and it dawned on us that the entire motion was going to be heard in whispers at the judge's bench. I'd never seen anything like it, and I'd covered many federal trials. Katz was beside himself.

"They can't do this!" he insisted. "How can they do this, just because we're here?" I told him I didn't know and commiserated with him, but inside I was exulting. Thank God for this one instance of government secrecy.

The next morning I ran down to the hotel lobby and grabbed a copy of the *Times*. Katz's story had run, focusing on the relationship between Ross and Blandón. Blandón, Katz wrote, had "taught [Ross] the trade" and oversaw his rise "through the ranks of the Los Angeles underworld, becoming the first crack-dealing millionaire on South Central's streets." The story hinted at "new and surprising dimensions" involving Blandón and some alleged "ties to U.S. intelligence sources," but never said what they were. There was no mention of the Contras. Whew.

When the trial got under way that day, once again I was the only reporter in the courtroom. Katz had apparently gone back to Houston, and no one from the *Times* had been assigned to cover the trial that the paper had previewed that very morning.

Once again, Fenster demanded that the government turn over its records about Blandón, arguing that it was prejudicing Ross's chance to fairly cross-examine his chief accuser. O'Neale calmly assured Fenster that he'd gotten everything the government felt he was entitled to know about Blandón—his prior arrest record and the fact that he'd been paid $40,000 for setting Ross up. What else could he possibly want?

"I don't think my client's life should be up to the government to determine what he should be allowed to know about Blandón's credibility," Fenster told Huff indignantly.

"The system we've set up has the government review all the information in its files to decide whether it complies with the law," Judge Huff replied blandly. "Mr. O'Neale, in good faith, has made that review."

"So we're supposed to trust the government to tell us if the CIA was involved?" Fenster asked. "They say that there's nothing that exists. I don't know if they really know that. I mean, I don't know if they've checked with the CIA to determine if such matters exist."

To my surprise, O'Neale admitted that he hadn't checked. Even though he'd personally assured the court several times that the government had no grounds to believe Blandón had any CIA ties, he'd never actually gotten around to asking the CIA. There was no need, he insisted: "One hopes that whatever the CIA does in the best interests of this country, that it will be concealed from view. And one hopes that if they do something that is in the worst interest or in violation of the laws of this country, that it will come to light. But, no, I haven't checked with the CIA. I've had no cause to check with the CIA."

Huff ignored O'Neale's stunning admission and told Fenster that he should trust her to do the right thing. Why, just that morning, she reminded him, she'd ordered prosecutors to turn over two pages from Sergeant Tom Gordon's long-missing search warrant application for the 1986 raid on Blandón's house.

The rest of it, she'd decided, wasn't relevant. Huff denied Fenster's motions.

There was one other matter the United States wanted to take up, if the court would be so kind, O'Neale said. Huff smiled pleasantly at him and told him to go ahead.

Reaching into his briefcase, O'Neale yanked out a copy of the morning's *L.A. Times* and waved it over his head. It had come to his attention, he announced dramatically, that the defense lawyers were leaking confidential information to the press! Huff appeared shocked and looked angrily at the defense table. O'Neale noted that Katz's story contained a phrase from a Justice Department memo that explained Danilo Blandón's deal with the government.

"I submit to the Court that our reasonable belief is that this document was obtained from one of those four!" O'Neale said, jabbing the offending newspaper in the direction of the four defense attorneys across the courtroom. "And there is no other explanation! It's not a filed document. It's not a public record document...but somehow, somewhere, that letter of February 15th was given to a *journalist!*"

Huff gave the defense lawyers a hard stare.

"I'm not saying that there's any criminal wrongdoing here," O'Neale added. "I'm saying that we have to be very careful in this case about pretrial publicity.... Not only am I concerned about a fair trial, I am also concerned with the safety of the witness and the witness' family. There is a real safety issue here.... We have heard through reliable sources that there are threats of *death* against the witness, and we take those seriously and this is a serious business."

O'Neale stroked his beard and looked reproachfully at the defense lawyers.

"Without ascribing any wrongdoing to any counsel present, it is my opinion, and I state this only as an opinion, that Mr. Ross personally is attempting to manipulate the media, and may be attempting to affect the outcome of the trial *through the media!* As I say, I ascribe this to Mr. Ross personally, and I'm not sure that he is under any obligation—as are attorneys. However, I do again point out that this document comes, there were four copies sent out and here it is in the paper—it *has* to come from one of those four copies! I sure didn't give it to anybody!"

The defense lawyers were shaking their heads and appeared to be chuckling. One of them, Federal Public Defender Maria Forde, slowly got to her feet.

"Ms. Forde?" Huff said icily.

"I find it personally offensive that Mr. O'Neale would take the position that someone had to leak this document to the press," Forde said slowly. "I think with a little review he would have been able to remember that this document became a part of the public record when it was filed as Exhibit A of Mr. Fenster's motion to dismiss because of egregious Brady violations. It is a document of public record."

"Oh," Huff said quickly. "I see."

She looked at O'Neale, who began babbling. "I'm sorry. In that case, Ms. Forde, uh, I will say Ms. Forde is correct, that there may be—uh, that I had forgotten that that was an exhibit and insofar as anyone took personal or otherwise offense, I do apologize for that." Before he sat down, though, he wanted to remind everyone that he was still concerned about the death threats—"wherever *they* came from." I laughed silently. What a clown.

Blandón, wearing tinted aviator glasses and a dark suit, made his grand entry the next day, shielded by U.S. marshals. They led him to a row of chairs directly in front of me, and he sat down stiffly. After chasing him around California and Central America for nine months, seeing him now for the first time sitting only a foot away gave me a strange feeling. "Chanchin" in the flesh. I was sorry Georg wasn't here to see this.

I leaned over the rail and tapped Blandón on the shoulder with one of my business cards.

"I've been calling all over for you," I said. "I'm sure your mother-in-law is tired of hearing my voice." He turned and smiled. "I apologize." I told him I needed to talk to him. He shook his head. "I can't, because of all of this."

"Okay then. How about after the trial?"

"No. Personally, if it was up to me, I would say yes. But they won't let me," he said, nodding toward the prosecution table.

"The prosecutor won't let you talk?"

He shook his head. "DEA."

"So you won't talk to me ever, is that it?"

He nodded and shrugged. "Sorry. What can I do?"

O'Neale called Blandón up to the stand and led him carefully through his testimony. He touched on the Contras, admitting that Meneses had recruited him to sell cocaine for them. He said he'd stopped selling Contra cocaine when he split from Meneses in 1983 and started keeping the money for himself.

That was odd, I thought, flipping through my notebook. When I'd interviewed O'Neale in November, the prosecutor had said that occurred in 1986. The day before the trial, I noticed, O'Neale had said in court that it happened in 1984. By the end of the day, though, Blandón would be insisting that he'd actually quit in 1982—long before he'd met Ross, he said. O'Neale kept going over and over that point.

Then it dawned on me. They were trying to open a window, hoping to put a decent interval between the time Blandón was selling dope for the CIA's army and the time he started selling dope to the L.A. gangs. They were trying to break the chain linking the Contra's cocaine to the Crips and Bloods.

There was one big problem with that tactic. It didn't jibe with all the other facts. Ross said he'd been dealing with Blandón and his minions since 1981. Second, there were government documents out there strongly suggesting that Blandón's testimony was false—records that said he was selling cocaine for Meneses and the Contras all the way through 1986. Of course, Fenster didn't have those records, since the government had refused to turn them over. (Additional records surfaced after the trial was over and Blandón eventually admitted to the Senate Intelligence Committee and the CIA Inspector General that his Contra contributions continued through 1985.)

During the noon break, Fenster approached me in the hallway outside the courtroom. "Can we have lunch?" he asked. We walked to the restaurant of the Doubletree Hotel at Horton Plaza, near the courthouse. Fenster sipped an iced tea and asked me what I thought about Blandón's testimony.

"You got the *Highlights for Children* version of his cocaine dealings with the Contras," I said.

"That's what I thought. How am I supposed to cross-examine this guy? I don't even know what to ask!" He laughed ruefully. "Isn't this just crazy? I mean, here I am, defending a man against a life sentence, and I've got to ask some reporter if the prosecution testimony is accurate. That's justice for you. You know more about the bastard than I do."

"Not as much as I'd like, unfortunately. And he just told me he's never going to talk to me."

A light came on. Wait a minute. What law said I needed to do my interview directly? The solution was right here in front of me. Blandón was up there on a witness stand, under oath, in front of a federal judge. He was a sitting duck. I'd never get a better shot at him than this. For that matter, I doubted he'd ever be seen in public again. It was now or never.

"Tell you what," I said. "I need to make sure this is okay first, but what would you think about me giving you some questions to ask him?"

"You read my mind," Fenster said, getting a notepad out of his briefcase. I excused myself and went to a pay phone. Miraculously, Dawn was at her desk, and I explained the situation. There was no other way, I told her. Could she see any possible harm in giving Fenster some questions about the Contras? "I think it's a great idea," she said. "I wish we could do all of our interviews under oath."

When Fenster began his cross-examination the next day, he came right at Blandón, grilling him about his family's connections to the Somoza dictatorship. "There were certain families in Nicaragua that were part of the ruling cartel of Nicaragua, is that correct?"

O'Neale turned and glared at me and then jumped to his feet.

"Excuse me, I have an objection!" he shouted. "Relevance! Inflammatory language! What is the—the—relevance to—what the—"

He was overruled, and Fenster pushed on, boring in on Blandón's unbelievable claim that he quit dealing cocaine for the Contras when the CIA came through with $19 million in aid.

"Nineteen million dollars isn't even a drop in the bucket when you run that kind of operation, isn't that correct?"

"I didn't...I didn't know we received the $19 million," Blandón confessed. "I cannot tell you."

"Is it your testimony that you decided to keep the profits from the drug dealing because the Contra organization had enough money to fund their own war? Is that your testimony?"

"No sir. Let me explain one thing. When we meet—when we raise money for the Contra revolution, we received orders from the—" He paused and looked at O'Neale. O'Neale stared at him. "From another people." Because of the order prohibiting CIA testimony, Fenster was unable to pursue that line of inquiry.

He quizzed Blandón about his meetings in Honduras with CIA agent Enrique Bermúdez, the FDN organization in Miami, and his connections to the Meneses family. The Nicaraguan looked helplessly at O'Neale, and several times the prosecutor leaped up to object, spluttering that

Fenster's questions were irrelevant and prejudicial. Most of the time he was overruled. Blandón was like a deer caught in the headlights. Every so often DEA agent Jones would turn and give me the evil eye.

He knew where this shit was coming from. So did O'Neale, who actually complained about it to the judge. They'd done their best to keep it bottled up, and it had spilled out anyway. I walked back to my hotel room that night ten feet off the ground.

It was all out in the open now. The FDN had sold drugs to American citizens—mainly black Americans—and the CIA was on the hook for it: a CIA agent had given the goddamned order. I thought back to all the lies that had been told about the Contras' innocence. All the bullshit that had been piled on the reporters, cops, and congressional investigators who'd tried to do an honest job and bring light into the dark swamp where covert operators and criminals colluded. There was no denying it any more.

Now I was ready to write.

27

“A very difficult decision”

Ross and all but one of his codefendants were convicted in the spring of 1996 of conspiring to sell the DEA's cocaine. Considering the facts that were presented, and the evidence that was withheld, there was little else the jurors could do. But in interviews with the Federal Public Defender's Office afterward, several expressed disgust with the government's case.

“Ricky was the hardest one for us to decide,” said juror Norman Brown, a twenty-nine-year-old data entry operator at the San Diego Zoo. “None of us liked Blandón. A few of the jurors were very upset that he is used by law enforcement.” Said another juror, a forty-six-year-old fund-raiser for Scripps Hospital: “Blandón made us all so angry that we would use that kind of sleazeball. We wanted to acquit Ricky Ross just to give the message to the government that we disagreed with the use of Blandón.” (Ross would later receive his sentence: life without parole.)

My story now had an ending, one that seemed to exemplify the hypocrisy of the whole War on Drugs. The crack dealers went to prison while the men who made crack possible—the cocaine importers—walked away whistling. I laid the series out in just those terms, beginning it in the early 1980s with the critical role played by the Nicaraguan “freedom fighters” in founding L.A.'s crack market and ending it in the early 1990s, with the passage of the anticrack laws that were then packing the prisons with thousands of young black dealers—and with Blandón's sudden transformation into an antidrug warrior.

In mid-April I finished the first drafts and sent them up to my editors, with no clue as to how they would be received. They were like nothing I had ever written before, and probably unlike anything my editors had ever grappled with either: a tale spanning more than a decade, that attempted to show how two of the defining issues of the 1980s—the Contra war and the crack explosion, seemingly unconnected social phenomena—were actually intertwined, thanks largely to government meddling.

The four-part series I turned in focused on the relationship between the Contras and the crack king. It mentioned the CIA's role in passing, noting that some of the money had gone to a CIA-run army and that there were federal law enforcement reports suggesting the CIA knew about it. I never believed, and never wrote, that there was a grand CIA conspiracy behind the crack plague. Indeed, the more I learned about the agency, the more certain of that I became. The CIA couldn't even mine a harbor without getting its trenchcoat stuck in its fly.

That the Contras' cocaine ended up being turned into crack was a horrible accident of history, I believed, not someone's evil plan. The Contras just happened to pick the worst possible time ever to begin peddling cheap cocaine in black neighborhoods. That, I believed, was the real danger the CIA has always presented—unbridled criminal stupidity, cloaked in a blanket of national security.

"The fact that a government-connected drug ring was dumping tons of cocaine into the black neighborhoods in L.A.—and to a lesser extent in San Jose, Oakland, San Francisco, Portland, Houston, Oklahoma City, Alabama and New Orleans—goes a long way towards explaining why crack developed such deep roots in the black community," I wrote. "It's where the seed was planted."

Looking back, I can barely believe I was permitted to write such a story, but that was the kind of newspaper the *Mercury News* was at the time. No topic was taboo, or at least if there was one I never discovered it. And I was always looking.

The reason I'd left a much larger paper in Cleveland to work for the *Mercury* was because its editors convinced me that they ran one of the few newspapers in the country with that kind of courage. There were no sacred cows, they pledged; and for nine years they had been true to their word. Not one of my stories was ever spiked or significantly watered down; nearly 300 of them had appeared on the *Merc's* front page, including

Late one night, towards the end of July, the phone rang. "Well, I have some good news and some bad news," Dawn began. "The bad news is that David Yarnold is no longer the editor on this series. He took a new job with Knight-Ridder, and he's out of here. The good news is that Paul Van Slambrouck is the new editor and I showed him the series today and he really likes it and thinks we've got a great story here."

"We've got a brand new editor on this?" I cried. "Now? And he just read it for the first time today? You're shitting me. So what does this mean?"

"Well, unfortunately, it means it's not going to run on the eighteenth. He has some changes he wants to make to it."

I sat up and started laughing. "Really? What kind of changes?"

"He thinks its too long. We need to make it three parts."

I howled. "You can't be serious, Dawn. This is a joke, right?"

"No. I'm sorry. Maybe you should talk to Paul."

Van Slambrouck, the *Mercury*'s national editor and a smart, thoughtful journalist, was apologetic. It wasn't the way he wanted to do things either. But he thought the series was terrific and he wanted very much to get it in the paper and hoped I still felt the same way.

"Dawn said you wanted to make some changes."

It needed to come down in length, he said, and we needed more CIA stuff in the first day. I was back to square one.

I sat down and fired off an angry memo to Dawn. Van Slambrouck had asked me to cut sixty-five inches, I complained. He had suggested that I needed to go through the story myself and be "ruthless" and I'd be able to find sixty-five inches to cut, no problem. If there was sixty-five inches of fat left in those stories, I wrote to Dawn, "we both ought to resign because we obviously aren't doing our jobs right."

An additional problem, I reminded Dawn, was that my family and I were in the midst of moving and were taking our vacation while the new house was being readied. During the next three weeks I rewrote the series on a laptop while on "vacation," first in a beach house on the Outer Banks of North Carolina, then in a motel room in Washington, D.C., and finally in the basement of my in-laws' house in Indiana. It was horrible. I had no way of telling what was being cut back at the *Mercury*, what was being put back in, or what was being rewritten. Five or six different versions were flying around. Don't these people know what they're dealing with here? I wondered. Don't they realize the import of what we're printing?

I eventually realized that for the most part they did not, which may have been the reason the series got in the paper in the first place. It came in under the radar. *Mercury News* executive editor Jerry Ceppos would later tell *Newsweek* that "he read only part of the story" before it appeared in print, an amazing admission if true.

Perhaps my editors thought I was exaggerating the story's significance, trying to gobble up more space than was really justified? It is a common sight in newsrooms to see reporters hype their stories. I knew reporters who worked their editors like PR agents, or lobbyists pimping a bill. But I had never worked that way. I figured my editors knew how to read as well as anyone. My paycheck was the same every week, no matter which page they put my story on. (Legendary investigative reporter I. F. Stone once said that he read every section of the *Washington Post* thoroughly because he never knew where he would find a front-page story.)

But I also knew from my research what kind of backlash would result from a story that dirtied up the CIA, and I stressed it repeatedly to my editors. *New York Times* reporter Seymour Hersh's 1974 exposé of Operation Chaos, a massive illegal CIA domestic spying operation, had brought on attacks in the *Washington Post* (he had no "hard" proof) and *Time* ("There is strong likelihood that Hersh's CIA story is considerably exaggerated"), among many others.

CBS newsman Daniel Schorr was demonized by the CIA and conservative commentators for leaking a copy of a secret Congressional report of CIA abuses to the *Village Voice* in 1976, after CBS had declined to make it public. Eventually, Schorr was dumped by the network and virtually blackballed. A decade later, a similar fate befell Robert Parry and Brian Barger of the Associated Press after they broke several stories on Contra involvement with drug trafficking and Ollie North's secret resupply operation. In both cases, the mainstream journalistic community uttered barely a peep of protest.

At 2:00 A.M.—midnight in San Jose—on August 18, 1996, I was at a party at my best friend's house in Indianapolis. I excused myself, went into a bedroom, plugged in my laptop, and dialed into the *Mercury*'s Web site. A picture of a man smoking crack, superimposed upon the seal of the CIA, drew itself on the screen. After more than a year of work, "Dark Alliance" was finally out. I e-mailed Georg with the news, went back out to the party and got drunk. The next morning I flew back to Sacramento.

Initially, the silence was deafening. Then we realized why. They had unintentionally run the series the week between the Republican and Democratic national conventions. The national media and the nation's politicians were on vacation; nobody was paying much attention to anything, and particularly not a story in a regional northern California newspaper.

By August 21, though, some radio stations began calling. What was this CIA story we've been hearing about on the Web?

That combination—talk radio and the Internet—is what saved "Dark Alliance" from slipping silently below the surface and disappearing without a trace. The Internet wizards at Mercury Center—Mark Hull, Donna Yanish, and Albert Poon—had done a brilliant, eye-popping job on the "Dark Alliance" Web page. It was something right out of the movies: full-color animated maps, one-click access to uncut source documents, unpublished photos, audio clips from undercover DEA tapes and Danilo Blandón's federal court testimony, a bibliography, a timeline—all in far more depth and detail than we were able to get into the newspaper.

For investigative reporting, the Web was a dream come true. No longer did the public have to rely on the word of sources, or the reporter's version of what a document meant. The Web made it possible to share your files directly with your readers. If they cared to, they could read and hear exactly what you had read and heard, and make up their own minds about the story. It was raw interactive journalism, perhaps too interactive for some.

Traditionally, reporters jealously guard their notes and their files. In that sense, journalism has something in common with the cocaine business: You are only as good as your sources. Lousy journalists tend to hide behind unnamed sources, blind quotes, and unrevealed records.

But as far as I was concerned, my best protection was to allow everyone to see what I'd unearthed. I had it on paper—and most of it was public record. We scanned as many of my documents as possible into the computers at Mercury Center and uploaded them onto the Internet. A reader anywhere in the world could now instantly see our supporting documentation.

Cleverly, Mercury Center had sent out advance e-mail alerts to various Usenet newsgroups the day before the series appeared, tipping them off to the unveiling of the page. The cyberjournalists were as proud of their revolutionary handiwork as I was and wanted to make sure the Net world knew what they'd just pulled off: the first major online exposé in newspaper history.

"The unlimited space of the Web allowed the *Mercury News* to move forward into a whole new kind of journalism," Microsoft's *Encarta* encyclopedia would later write of "Dark Alliance." "The *Mercury News* used...the Web to let intelligent readers review the source materials and draw their own conclusions. This step, far beyond the traditional role of newspapers, attracted attention and readers from all over the world."

At the end of that first week I returned to San Diego for Ricky Ross's sentencing. That was where I had my first inkling of the firestorm I'd touched off. Radio stations were blanketing the newspaper with interview requests. Before heading for the courthouse that morning, I'd done radio shows in Washington, D.C., Austin, Texas, and Detroit.

A haggard-looking L. J. O'Neale, the assistant U.S. attorney, spotted me in the hallway outside the courtroom.

"Hey there," I said. "You see the story?"

He scowled and pushed by without saying a word. He'd already fought his way through television camera crews outside the courthouse, and he clearly wasn't pleased with all the attention. Inside the courtroom, reporters jostled for seats.

Fenster asked for a postponement of sentencing, saying the series had raised significant questions about Blandón and his connections to the CIA. O'Neale protested angrily, accusing Ross of dreaming up the whole CIA plot and feeding it to a gullible journalist who was spreading ridiculous conspiracy theories.

But Judge Huff looked troubled and told O'Neale she wanted some answers from the CIA before she passed sentence on Ross and his codefendants. And she also wanted the Justice Department to begin deportation proceedings against Blandón immediately. The news made the wires, and the switchboard at the *Mercury News* lit up. "This place is going crazy!" Dawn reported. "The Web page had something like 500,000 hits on it today!"

The *Mercury News*'s executive editor, Jerry Ceppos, called and congratulated me. The TV networks were calling the paper. We were getting phone calls from all over the world. "Let's stay on top of this," he said. "Anything you need, you let us know. We want to run with this thing." A few days later, I got a $500 bonus check in the mail and a note from Ceppos: "Remarkable series! Thanks for doing this for us."

I was on National Public Radio the following Monday and, as always, gave out the Web site address so people could read the series and see our documents. We had 800,000 hits that day. The synergy was amazing. For the first time, people could hear about a story on the radio—even one that appeared several weeks earlier and thousands of miles away—and immediately read it on their computer screens.

Unlike all the previous stories about the Contras and cocaine, this one couldn't be killed off in the traditional manner, by Big Media ignoring it or relegating it to the news briefs. Millions of people were finding out about "Dark Alliance" anyway—even though not a word had appeared in the so-called national press. That phenomenon was newsworthy by itself.

"The story has serious legs, moving rapidly through the African American community via e-mail and file downloads, and then into living rooms, offices and churches, and onto streets and into more mainstream black papers and radio broadcasts," *HotWired* magazine wrote in October 1996. "For the first time, my grandmother asked to go online and read something. I couldn't believe it. She wouldn't look at a computer before," one black government lawyer e-mailed the magazine. "This story is causing a sensation among blacks. It's all they're talking about. They are enraged about it and they can't believe it isn't on every front page in America."

"Dark Alliance," *HotWired* wrote, "is making digital and media history. The *Mercury News* is demonstrating for perhaps the first time how the Web and the traditional press can fuse to good effect—and that there's still a chance to break modern media's parochial instincts and return some power to journalists outside of Washington and New York.... The story may alter black consciousness about the Net, and further the Web's reputation as a powerful—and serious—information medium." The Associated Press noted that "while no one has been able to track specific numbers of blacks who might have come online because of the *Mercury News* series, many feel it has been a watershed event."

A *Boston Globe* reporter arrived in Los Angeles in early October 1996 and breathlessly reported that the story was "pulsing through [L.A.'s] black neighborhoods like a shockwave, provoking a stunning, growing level of anger and indigation. Talk-radio stations with predominantly black audiences are deluged with calls on the subject. Demonstrations, candle-lighting ceremonies and town-hall meetings are becoming regular affairs. And people on the street are heatedly discussing the topic."

If there was one thing scarier to corporate journalism than the series itself, it was the image of a future where Big Media was unable to control the national agenda. Irrespective of what the series said, "Dark Alliance" proved that the stranglehold a relative few East Coast editors and producers had on what became news could be broken. "This story suddenly raises suspicions that the Internet has changed the equation in support of democracy," author Daniel Brandt ruminated in October 1996 on an Internet e-zine. "Unless regional newspapers agree to mild-mannered, regional interest Web sites, all the resources that the elites have invested in monopolizing the Daily Spin could end up spinning down the drain."

In this case the blend of the Internet and talk radio had made the traditional media irrelevant. The public was marching on without them, and the message got through clearly to California's top politicians. The L.A. City Council unanimously approved a resolution calling for a federal investigation. Both California senators and a half-dozen congressmen wrote letters to CIA director John Deutch and Attorney General Janet Reno demanding an official inquiry. Deutch agreed to conduct one, which infuriated the right-wing *Washington Times*. Deutch was lambasted on the front page by unnamed critics for "his efforts to curry favor with liberal politicians." And on the editorial page, editor-at-large Arnaud de Borchgrave, a "journalist" with a long history of connections to the intelligence community and the Contras, fumed that "the same old pro-Marxist CIA bashers are at it again" and quoted unnamed former colleagues at "another paper" describing me as "an 'activist' journalist who would dearly love to see the CIA scuttle itself."

In his column, de Borchgrave claimed Congress had given the Contras $100 million before the Boland Amendments went into effect, and chided me for being "too young to remember that the CIA had no need for illicit Contra funds in those days." When I appeared on political talk-show host Chris Matthews's live show on CNBC that evening, Matthews eagerly sprung de Borchgrave's crazy timeline on me, demanding to know how I could have written what I did, given the fact that the Contras had plenty of money. After Jack White of *Time* and I pointed out that he had his "facts" backward, Matthews, during a commercial break, began bellowing at his production assistants, loudly accusing them of attempting to "sabotage" his show.

Soon after Deutch ordered an internal investigation, Attorney General Janet Reno—at the urging of Justice Department inspector general Michael Bromwich—followed suit.

Finally, the national news media dipped a toe into the icy waters. *Newsweek* devoted an entire page to the story in late September, calling it "a powerful series" that had some black leaders "ready to carpet-bomb Langley." *Time* that month called it "the hottest topic in black America" and said the Web site "provides a plethora of court documents, recorded interviews and photographs.... This is the first time the Internet has electrified African Americans."

Soon, *60 Minutes* called. "Don't talk to anyone else," a producer told me. "We want this story to ourselves." I got an identical call from *Dateline NBC*. I told both of them I thought it was unethical for a reporter to refuse to talk to the press. The *60 Minutes* producer said that was the most ridiculous thing he'd ever heard. *Dateline* ended up doing the story.

Over the next few weeks, we got interview requests from Jerry Springer, Geraldo Rivera, Tom Snyder, Jesse Jackson, and Montel Williams. I was on CNN, C-SPAN, MSNBC, and CBS Morning News. The *Mercury* printed up 5,000 copies of the series and they were gone in a matter of weeks. An employee from the marketing department was assigned full-time to handle press calls. Each evening she e-mailed a list of interview requests, and by early October the list was three pages long and growing. The *London Times* did a story. *Le Monde* in Paris wrote something. Newspapers in Germany, Belgium, Spain, Colombia, and Nicaragua called for interviews.

It's hard to imagine how many radio stations there are in the United States until they start calling. At home, my phone would begin ringing at 6 A.M. and not stop until 10 PM. Talk radio was burning up the airwaves, spreading the story and the Web site address from coast to coast. One day, the hits on the Web page climbed over 1,000,000. People in Japan, Bosnia, Germany, and Denmark sent me e-mail.

Meanwhile, we continued advancing the story. I teamed up with Pamela Kramer, the *Mercury*'s reporter in Los Angeles, and we wrote several stories about the 1986 police raids on Blandón's house. We came up with the entire Gordon search warrant, which showed that the police had several informants telling them that drug money was going to the Contras. Our sources provided us with the case file number to the supposedly nonexistent investigatory file at the L.A. County Sheriff's Office, and Congresswoman Maxine Waters and her staff marched in and demanded to see it.

"I told them that the only way they were going to get me out of their office was to give me the file or arrest me," she said. She got the file—in it were the police reports about the search of Ronald Lister's house, his claims of CIA involvement, and the inventory of strange items seized at his house.

NBC News did a strong follow-up, finally exposing the drug-related entries in Oliver North's notebooks to a national television audience, but it was the only network attempting to advance the story. The Establishment papers—the *New York Times*, the *Washington Post*, and the *Los Angeles Times*—the same newspapers that had so confidently reported in the 1980s that there was no truth to these claims of Contra drug trafficking, remained largely silent.

"Where is the rebuttal? Why hasn't the media rose in revolt against this story?" an exasperated Bernard Kalb, former spokesman for the Reagan State Department, demanded on CNN's *Reliable Sources*. "It isn't a story that simply got lost. It, in fact, has resonated and echoed and the question is where is the media knocking it down, when that, too, is a journalistic responsibility?"

Kalb's guest, former Reagan Justice Department spokesman Terry Eastland, clucked that he "would expect to see this kind of story in a magazine like *In These Times*, not in a mainstream newspaper such as the *San Jose Mercury News*." No one on Kalb's show bothered to mention that Eastland had a history of trying to cover up the Contra drug link. In May 1986, his office had planted a false story in the *New York Times* stating that the Justice Department had "cleared" the Contras of any involvement in gun running and drug smuggling, a statement the Justice Department was later forced to recant.

One question I was frequently asked during radio appearances was whether I thought the national media reaction would be different if the series had appeared in the *Washington Post* or the *New York Times*. My stock answer was that it hadn't appeared in those newspapers, because they'd decided in 1986 that there was no story here. My feeling was that those newspapers' very familiarity with the story made it more difficult for them to report it. How could they come back ten years later and admit that the Contras had been selling cocaine to Americans, when they'd already assured us it wasn't happening?

In early October, I was in New York City getting ready for an appearance on the *Montel Williams Show*, which was doing a two-day special on the "Dark Alliance" series. About 2:00 AM., Jerry Ceppos called. The *Washington Post* had just moved a story on the wires. It would be in the morning edition and it was highly critical of the series. He asked me to take a look at it and give him my reaction.

"What did they say was wrong?" I asked.

"They don't say any of the facts are wrong," Ceppos said. "They just don't agree with our conclusions."

"And their evidence is what?"

"A lot of unnamed sources, mainly. It's really a strange piece. I'll send you a fax of it, and we can talk in the morning."

The story was headlined "The CIA and Crack: Evidence is Lacking of Alleged Plot." I laughed. What plot?

The reporters, Walter Pincus and Roberto Suro, wrote that their investigation "does not support the conclusion that the CIA-backed Contras—or Nicaraguans in general—played a major role in the emergence of crack as a narcotic in widespread use across the United States. Instead, the available data from arrest records, hospitals, drug treatment centers and drug user surveys point to the rise of crack as a broad-based phenomenon driven in numerous places by players of different nationalities, races and ethnic groups."

Ah ha. The old tidal wave theory. Here it comes again. I wondered what "available data" Pincus and Suro had gathered from the 1982–83 era, the dawn of the L.A. crack market, since the DEA and NIDA had admitted a decade earlier that there was no such data.

The story grudgingly and often backhandedly admitted that the basic facts presented in the series were correct, and it buried key admissions deep inside, such as the fact that "the CIA knew about some of these activities and did little or nothing to stop them." Toward the end Pincus and Suro confirmed that Meneses and Blandón had met with Enrique Bermúdez in Honduras, but without disclosing Bermúdez's relationship with the CIA. CIA agent Adolfo Calero, whom the *Post* euphemistically described as someone "who worked closely with the CIA," also admitted to the *Post* reporters that he had met with Meneses.

Overall, it was a cleverly crafted piece of disinformation that would set the stage for the attacks to follow. It falsely claimed that the series made a "racially charged allegation that the 'CIA's army' of contras deliberately targeted the black community in an effort to expand the market for a cheap form of cocaine." And despite Blandón's testimony that he sold 200 to 300 kilos of cocaine for Meneses in L.A. and that all the profits were sent to the Contras, the *Post* quoted unnamed "law enforcement officials" as saying "Blandón sold $30,000 to $60,000 worth of cocaine in two transactions."

The story also dove right through the "window" that O'Neale had opened at the Ross trial. "If the whole of Blandón's testimony is to be believed," Pincus and Suro wrote, "[then there is no connection] between the Contras and African American drug dealers because Blandón said he had stopped sending money to the Contras by the time he met Ross." No mention was made of the DEA reports and the sheriff's department affidavit that said Blandón was selling Contra cocaine through 1986, nor of the fact that Ross had been buying Blandón's cocaine long before he actually met him. "Moreover," the *Post* declared, "the mere idea that any one person could have played a decisive role in the nationwide crack epidemic is rejected out of hand by academic experts and law enforcement officials." But they identified neither the academic experts nor the law enforcement officials.

I wrote Ceppos a memo pointing out the holes in the *Post's* story. "The Pincus piece," I wrote, "is just silly. It's the kind of story you'd expect from someone who spent three weeks working on a story, as opposed to 16 months." The fact that the *Post*'s unnamed "experts" would reject our scenario "out of hand," I wrote, was the whole problem. "None of them—whoever they are—has ever studied this before."

To his credit, Ceppos fired off a blistering letter to the *Post*, pointing out the factual errors in the piece and calling Pincus's claims of a "racially charged allegation" a "complete and total mischaracterization."

"The most difficult issue is whether a casual reading of our series leads to the conclusion that the CIA is directly responsible for the outbreak of the crack epidemic in Los Angeles. While there is considerable circumstantial evidence of CIA involvement with the leaders of this drug ring, we never reached or reported any definitive conclusion on CIA involvement," Ceppos wrote. "We reported that men selling cocaine in Los Angeles met with people on the CIA payroll. We reported that they received fundraising orders from people on the CIA payroll. We reported that the money raised was sent to a CIA-run operation. But we did not go further and took pains to say that clearly."

Ceppos posted the letter on the staff bulletin board, along with a memo defending the series. "We strongly support the conclusions the series drew and will until someone proves them wrong. What is even more remarkable is that FOUR experienced *Post* reporters, re-reporting our series, could not find a single significant factual error. The *Post*'s conclusions are very different—and I believe, flawed—but the major facts aren't. I'm not sure how many of us could sustain such a microscopic examination of our work and I believe Gary Webb deserves recognition for surviving unscathed."

The *Post* held Ceppos's letter for weeks, ordered him to rewrite it, and then refused to print it.

Shortly afterward I got an e-mail message from a woman in southern California. There was a story in the *Mercury*'s archives that I needed to see, she wrote, and provided a date and a page number. I sent it to our library and got a photocopy of the story in the mail a day later. It had run on February 18, 1967.

"How I Traveled Abroad on CIA Subsidy" was the headline. The author was Walter Pincus of the *Washington Post*.

After disclosures of CIA infiltration of American student associations had exploded that year, Pincus had written a long, smug confessional of how, posing as an American student representative, he'd traveled to several international youth conferences in the late 1950s and early 1960s, secretly gathering information for the CIA and smuggling in anti-Communist propaganda. A CIA recruiter had approached him, he wrote, and he'd agreed to spy not only on the student delegations from other countries but on his American colleagues as well. "I had been briefed in Washington on each of them," Pincus wrote. "None was remotely aware of CIA's interest."

This just cannot be true, I thought. The *Washington Post*'s veteran national security reporter—a former CIA operative and propagandist? Unwilling to believe this piece of information until I dug it up for myself, I went to the state library and got out the microfilm. The story was there. This was the man who was questioning *my* ethics for giving Alan Fenster questions to ask a government witness about the Contras and drugs? Jesus. I'd certainly never spied on American citizens.

Looking into Pincus's background further, I saw that he'd popped up in another situation where the CIA's reputation was under attack. In 1975, he'd been the person the *New York Times* selected to review ex-CIA officer Philip Agee's best-selling exposé about the agency, *CIA Diary*. In an unfavorable review, Pincus strongly suggested that Agee was in league with the Cuban intelligence services in a joint conspiracy to destroy the CIA. (Pincus's previous association with the CIA was not disclosed by the *Times*. He was merely identified as a Washington journalist.)

When the *Post* found itself under rare criticism by the CIA in 1986 for allegedly printing classified information, Pincus went on the *MacNeil/Lehrer NewsHour* and stated that his newspaper wasn't so irresponsible as to pass along government secrets. The *Post* often shielded its readers' eyes from such things, Pincus asserted, frequently in consultation with the government. "We've been dealing with it for a long time and I think we have withheld a great deal of information," Pincus said. "It ought to be made clear to people that we, in determining what we're going to do with a lot of stories, go to the Administration and tell them what we have and listen to what their arguments are and we then do make a decision, but we're not making them in the dark."

Pincus would later play an important role in helping to impede the Iran-Contra investigation, according to Independent Counsel Lawrence Walsh. In his memoirs, *Firewall*, Walsh wrote that at a critical moment in the Iran-Contra probe, Pincus had published a story claiming Walsh was planning to indict Ronald Reagan, a report that made worldwide news and reduced Nancy Reagan to tears. "Of all the sideswipes that we suffered during this period, the false report that we were considering indicting the nation's still admired former president hurt us the most," Walsh wrote. "It infuriated the congressional Republicans, even some of the moderate ones." Walsh suspected that Pincus had been fed the story by Boyden Gray, attorney for then president George Bush.

Gray, Walsh wrote, "had been known to float stories through persons close to the publisher of the *Washington Post;* Pincus had sometimes been asked to write these stories. I suspected Gray or someone else in the White House had played a role in disseminating the misinformation but I had no proof." The *Post*, of couse, never acknowledged what history has proven: Pincus's big scoop was bogus.

The *L.A. Times* and the *New York Times* struck next. On October 20, 1996, both ran long stories attacking my reporting and the series. They took the same tack the *Washington Post* had several weeks earlier: admitting that the basic facts were true and then complaining that the facts didn't mean a thing.

Relying again mostly on unnamed sources, these two newspapers of record claimed Blandón and Meneses hadn't had "official positions" with the Contras. Drug money had been sent, but not millions; it was only tens of thousands, according to unnamed sources. And experts scoffed at the notion that one drug ring could have supplied enough cocaine to feed the tidal wave of crack that engulfed America, a ridiculous claim I'd never made.

The papers found no need to mention the mass of historical evidence that supported the series's findings. Without anything approaching documentation, the papers just flatly declared I was wrong.

"The crack epidemic in Los Angeles followed no blueprint or master plan. It was not orchestrated by the Contras or the CIA. No one trafficker, even kingpins who sold thousands of kilos and pocketed millions of dollars, ever came close to monopolizing the drug trade," the *L.A. Times* assured its readers in the lead paragraphs of a three-day series.

The first part, on the genesis of crack in L.A., was written by Jesse Katz. Though Katz himself, starting in 1994 and continuing through the summer of 1996, had repeatedly referred to Ross as the first and biggest crack dealer in South Central, the master marketer whose activities were "key" to the spread of crack in the city, he now found that Ross was a pygmy who'd had little or nothing to do with the crack explosion. The earlier stories in the *Times*, stating exactly the opposite, were simply ignored.

Instead, Katz trotted out a number of other cocaine dealers he'd apparently missed the first time he'd written about the issue: "Tootie" Reese, who'd gone to jail when the crack market exploded and was never accused of selling a single rock of crack; the Bryant family, which, according to earlier *Times* stories, never sold crack in South Central and was "too small for the department's Major Violators Narcotics Unit in downtown Los Angeles" to bother with. Katz dredged up "Waterhead Bo" Bennett, who didn't start selling crack until 1985, and Elrader Browning, who—again according to the *L.A. Times*—was in jail from 1982 to 1985, making it exceedingly difficult for him to have played any role in the formation of the L.A. crack market.

"This is like reading *Pravda*," I told an L.A. radio station. "History means nothing to these people." Syndicated columnist Norman Solomon described Katz's story as "a show trial recantation."

The next day, the *L.A. Times* absolved the CIA of any involvement with Blandón and Meneses. Its authoritative sources: former CIA director Robert Gates, former CIA official Vincent Cannistraro, and current CIA director John Deutch. "Like good little boys and girls, the *Times*, the *Washington Post* et al., toddled off to the CIA and asked the agency if it had ever done such a thing. When the CIA said 'no' the papers solemnly printed it—just as though the CIA hadn't previously denied any number of illegal operations in which it was later caught red-handed," columnist Molly Ivins observed.

Buried deep within the *L.A. Times* story were admissions by CIA officials that Contra supporters "were involved in drug running, but they bought villas and did not put it into the FDN." And, the story conceded, "the allegation that some elements of the CIA-sponsored Contra army cooperated with drug traffickers has been well documented for years." But the story dismissed the idea that "millions" went to the Contras from the Nicaraguans' drug sales. Unnamed sources said it was around $50,000 or $60,000, which caused former Meneses distributor Rafael Corñejo some mirth.

"Sixty thousand?" he scoffed. "You can raise that in an afternoon."

According to another unnamed source the *Times* quoted, Blandón and Meneses were making only $15,000 a kilo in profits.

Unmentioned was Blandón's testimony that he'd sold 200 to 300 kilos for Meneses during the time they were sending money to the Contras, and his admission that all of the profits were being sent to the rebels. Using the *Times*' own profit figures, that would mean between $3 million and $4.5 million went to the Contras just from Blandón's sales.

And that didn't include the money Meneses's organization—through Cabezas and Renato Peña in San Francisco—was sending. Lost in the debate over whether it was millions or tens of thousands, was the inanity of the idea that a reasonably accurate number could ever be found in a business that deals in cash and eschews written records—it is just as possible that the amounts could have been in the tens of millions.

"No solid evidence has emerged that either Meneses or Blandón contributed any money to the rebels after 1984," the story declared, ignoring the 1986 sheriff's affidavit and the 1986 DEA reports. The story also quoted another unnamed associate who claimed, apparently with a straight face, that the profit margins in the cocaine business in 1982–84—when coke was selling for $60,000 a kilo—were just too slim to allow million-dollar donations to the FDN.

What kind of journalist would unquestioningly accept such a statement, I wondered, looking for a byline. And then I saw it in a box inside: Doyle McManus, the chief of the *L.A. Times*' Washington bureau. That explained it.

In 1984 McManus had played a central role in spreading the CIA's leak about Barry Seal and the Sandinistas dealing cocaine, just in time for the Reagan administration's request to Congress for additional Contra aid. Oliver North's notebooks contain several references to conversations McManus was having with the White House at the time, shortly before and shortly after the details of the CIA-DEA sting were fed to the press.

"McManus talking to W.H." North wrote on July 12, 1984. "Unhappy with negotiations."

On July 17, 1984, the CIA leak appeared in the *Washington Times*, written by Jeremiah O'Leary, a longtime Washington press corps reporter described by investigative reporter Carl Bernstein as having "a valuable personal relationship" with the CIA in the 1960s. O'Leary insisted that "they were more helpful to me than I was to them."

O'Leary's story in the *Washington Times*, which had supported the Contras both editorially and financially, gave McManus the excuse he needed to rush the CIA's leak into the *L.A. Times*. According to North's notebooks, McManus called the White House that morning and informed officials there that the National Security Council would be cited as his official source for the information.

"McManus, *L.A. Times*, says NSC to source claims W.H. has pictures of Borge loading cocaine in Nica," North wrote.

The following morning, on the front page of the *Times*, McManus wrote that "high-ranking members of the Nicaraguan government have been linked to a scheme involving three of Colombia's largest cocaine traffickers, U.S. intelligence sources say." The story declared that Interior Minister Tomas Borge and Defense Minister Humberto Ortega of Nicaragua were "among the officials who the sources said are implicated."

A day later McManus's coauthor, Ronald J. Ostrow, reported that "U.S. intelligence sources have obtained a photograph of Borge standing next to Pablo Escobar Gaviria, one of the two Colombian nationals being sought, as a plane was being loaded June 25 with duffel bags of cocaine at the airport in the Nicaraguan capital of Managua." Unfortunately for the *Times*, no such photograph has ever surfaced, and the DEA later admitted that it had no information implicating high-ranking Sandinista officials in drug trafficking. The story was a hoax, and McManus had been a willing participant or a dupe of embarrassing proportions. So strident in defending U.S. officials against such charges, the *Times* never admitted that it wrongly accused two Nicaraguan government officials of cocaine trafficking—solely on the basis of whispers from U.S. intelligence agents.

McManus and Ostrow later teamed up to refute allegations of Contra cocaine trafficking in early 1987, just as the issue was threatening to go national. In a front-page story bearing the cautionary deck head "No Supporting Evidence, DEA Says," the *Times* reported that a Senate committee "is investigating reports that Nicaraguan rebels and their American supporters have helped smuggle cocaine into the United States, but Drug Enforcement Administration officials say their agents have found no evidence to support any of the charges."

The story went through the litany of accusations—Ilopango, the Frogman case, the Southern Air Transport shipments to Colombia—devoting a sentence or two to each one, and surrounding them with abundant denials from DEA officials and CIA agent Adolfo Calero. The reporters made no attempt at an independent investigation.

In a prison cell in Boron, California, Contra drug courier Carlos Cabezas read McManus's story and couldn't believe his eyes. He banged out a letter to the reporter on February 27, 1987, stating, "I am going to tell you that there was indeed 'supporting evidence,' hidden by the government." The receipt of drug money by the Contras, he wrote, "is absolutely true, at least in my case." Cabezas told McManus of his trip to Costa Rica with $250,000 and noted that the FBI made no attempt to stop him, even though he was traveling with an FBI informant.

He also told McManus the FBI had tape-recorded conversations "between the former Ambassador of Nicaragua in Guatemala, Mr.

Fernando Sánchez and Troilo Sánchez and myself. Both of these gentlemen are brother [sic] of Mr. Adolfo Calero's top aide Mr. Aristides Sánchez. These conversations were related to drug transactions."

McManus replied two months later, asking Cabezas to provide him with names and documents to substantiate his "allegations." And, by the way, he asked, "Can you give me any further information about Sandinista drug trafficking?" Cabezas said he sent McManus the documents about the Contras and never heard another thing.

The unprecedented attacks by three major newspapers alarmed the *Mercury*'s editors. I was called to a meeting with Ceppos and the other editors and told that I should quit trying to advance the story. We needed to start working on a written response to the other newspapers, he said. I vehemently disagreed. "The best way to shut them up is to put the rest of what we know in the paper and keep plowing ahead," I argued. "Let's run a story about Walter Pincus's CIA connections. Let's write about how the *L.A. Times* has been booting this story since 1987." I told them of my discovery that the *L.A. Times*' Washington bureau had been sent a copy of the notes found in Ronald Lister's house in 1990 and had thrown them away. Ceppos disagreed.

"I don't want to get into a war with them," he said.

Fortunately, both Dawn Garcia and Paul Van Slambrouck agreed that we should continue developing the story.

"The best way to answer our critics," Van Slambrouck told Ceppos, "is to advance the story. Let's go out and get some more evidence of drug money being sent to the Contras. Let's get more evidence of this drug ring's dealings with the Contras." Ceppos relented, authorizing another reporting trip to Central America. He also assigned L.A. bureau reporter Pamela Kramer and Pete Carey, an investigative reporter, to gather information about the start of the L.A. crack market. He also made another decision: he was changing the logo that the series had used on the Internet and in the reprints. The CIA's seal was coming off.

"What's the point of doing that?" I asked. "We documented that these traffickers were meeting with CIA agents. If you change the logo, the rest of the media is going to accuse us of backing away from the story."

But Ceppos wouldn't budge. Thousands of reprints with the CIA–crack smoker logo were gathered up and burned and a CD-ROM version of the series—which had been pressed and was ready for distribution—was also destroyed. The *Post* and *L.A. Times* immediately crowed that the *Mercury* was "retreating" from the series.

Georg and I flew to Costa Rica and began interviewing police officials, lawyers, prosecutors, and ex-Contras about Meneses's activities there, fleshing out his role as a DEA informant and his drug operation's connections to Oliver North's resupply network on the Southern Front. In Managua, we interviewed police and Blandón's suspected money launderer, Orlando Murillo. I flew back and started writing the follow-up stories; Georg continued hunting for other members of the Meneses drug ring.

He called me in December 1996, barely able to contain his excitement. He'd found Carlos Cabezas, who admitted that he had in fact delivered millions of dollars in drug money to the Contras. Cabezas had names, dates, and amounts, Georg said, and pages from his drug ledgers. He'd identified a CIA agent, Ivan Gómez, as having had direct knowledge of it all.

"We've got it," Georg cried. "Cabezas is willing to talk on the record."

A week later, Georg called with more good news. Enrique Miranda, the former Meneses aide who'd "escaped" a year earlier, had been found in Miami and tossed on a plane to Nicaragua. Georg had visited him in prison, and Miranda started talking. Meneses's relationship with the CIA and the Contras was deeper than we'd ever realized, Georg said. "We didn't know how right we were," he laughed. "I can't wait to see what the *Washington Post* does with this." I could have kissed him.

In January 1997, I sent first drafts of four follow-up stories to Dawn, written as a two-day series. The first part dealt with Meneses's DEA connections and his Costa Rican operation, along with the interviews Georg had done with Carlos Cabezas and Enrique Miranda. I wrote a sidebar about the drug-dealing Costa Rican shrimp company North and the Cuban CIA operatives were using to funnel aid to the Contras.

The second part was a story about the parallel investigations of Contra drug trafficking done in the summer of 1986 by DEA agent Celerino Castillo at Ilopango and L.A. County Sheriff's deputy Tom Gordon, drawing on recently declassified FBI and CIA records at the National Archives and 3,000 pages of once-secret documents about the Blandón raids that had just been released by the L.A. County Sheriff's Office. I also wrote a sidebar on Joe Kelso's attempts to investigate allegations of DEA drug trafficking in Costa Rica. Altogether the drafts ran 16,000 words.

We'd done it. We had an eyewitness, on the record, who'd delivered the drug money. We had DEA records saying Blandón had sent money to the Contras far longer than we'd previously reported. We had a top CIA official admitting that the agency had reports of drug trafficking at Ilopango. We had evidence Ronald Lister had been meeting with the CIA's former head of covert operations. I expected the editors to be beside themselves with joy.

I heard absolutely nothing. Aside from Dawn, no one called to tell me they'd read the new stories. No one called with questions. No one even suggested that we begin editing them. They sat.

In early February Dawn sent me a copy of the story Pete Carey and Pam Kramer had written on the origins of the L.A. crack market. It was, astonishingly, a virtual repeat of the *L.A. Times* stories. It quoted police and drug experts opining that the Contra drug ring couldn't have supplied enough cocaine to have had a major impact on the crack explosion, because crack had surfaced all over the United States at about the same time. It drew no distinctions between the L.A. crack market in 1982 and the market in 1986. As far as the story was concerned, it had sprung from the ground fully formed. Three men, the story concluded, could not have created a drug epidemic. "The details of the trio's activities—who did what, and when—cannot change the overall story of the crack epidemic, which swept over several U.S. cities in the mid-1980s with the speed and destructiveness of a tidal wave."

I couldn't believe it. I respected Carey as a reporter—he and I had coauthored a story in 1989 that had won a Pulitzer Prize. But here it seemed he'd taken the official government explanation and swallowed it hook, line, and sinker.

Carey, the editors, and I met three times in February to argue about the epidemiology of the L.A. crack market, the amount of money sent to the Contras, and the level of CIA involvement. At the end, Carey informed me that he was canning his crack story. "What I told Ceppos was that we should just continue to work on this and see what the official investigations produced," he said. Kramer said much the same thing. "The problem I had with that story," she told me, "is that no one knows what really happened back in those years because nobody was looking at it." Their crack story never appeared.

With that settled, I plunged back into the investigation. In March I flew to Florida to interview a former CIA pilot, Ronald Lippert, who'd flown drop missions for the Contras in 1986. I spent two days at Lippert's home near Tampa, poring through his voluminous files and picking his brain. My interviews with the Canadian Lippert, jailed for ten years by Fidel Castro for flying explosives into Cuba for the agency, solved one of the final mysteries of the Southern Front: how CIA operative John

Hull—Bill Casey's friend and Oliver North's liaison to the Contras—had escaped from Costa Rica after he was indicted there for drug trafficking in 1989. After being thrown in jail, Hull was let out on bail for health reasons and vanished.

The DEA office in Costa Rica had gotten Hull out, Lippert said. Lippert had flown the mission himself, in a decoy plane hopscotching from Costa Rica to Haiti and then shuttling Hull into Miami, where Hull hid at the apartment of Cuban CIA operative and suspected drug dealer Dagoberto Nuñez, who'd helped North and the CIA in Costa Rica. The DEA officer who'd recruited Lippert for the escape flight, J. J. Perez, was another Cuban anti-Communist, Lippert said. In an interview, Hull confirmed Lippert's story, as did Anthony Ricevuto, the former DEA inspector who'd investigated Perez's role in Hull's escape. Ricevuto believed Perez set up Hull's escape on his own initiative, without official DEA sanction, but Hull disputed that. "Hell, you don't get DEA pilots and DEA planes to fly you around without orders coming down from above," Hull said.

A DEA panel recommended Perez's dismissal, Ricevuto said, but the Justice Department provided Perez with an attorney, and much of the case was dismissed on national security grounds. Perez ended up being suspended for one day.

Perez would not return phone calls, and the files of his disciplinary hearings are sealed as national security secrets. (The United States refused repeated Costa Rican requests to extradite Hull, and the drug charges were eventually dropped. Murder charges that were filed against him shortly after his escape are still pending, however; Hull denied both accusations.)

I was ecstatic. Now we had a story about the DEA aiding and abetting the escape of a CIA agent accused of drug trafficking, with the Justice Department intervening to protect the DEA agent who'd done it. The further I dug, the more amazing the story became.

And then, just like that, it was over.

Executive editor Jerry Ceppos called me at home on March 25, 1997, to inform me that he'd made "a very difficult decision." Mistakes had been made in the series, he said, and the newspaper was going to print a letter to its readers saying so.

"Is this a *fait accompli*?" I asked. "Or do I get a chance to say something?"

"The decision has been made," Ceppos said. "I'll fax you a draft of what we're considering."

According to Ceppos's proposed column, we should have said that Blandón claimed he quit dealing with the Contras in 1983—something that the editors had cut to save space. We had "insufficient proof" to say millions went to the Contras; we should have said it was an estimate. We should have said that we didn't find proof of involvement of "CIA decision-makers," whatever that meant. We should have said Ricky Ross wasn't the only crack supplier in L.A.—but we hadn't said that. And, finally, Ceppos wrote, the experts were unanimous in saying that the Contras had not played a major role in the crack trade and that the series had "oversimplified" how crack had become a problem. Strangely, Ceppos had borrowed his conclusions from Pete Carey's never-published crack story.

I brought a written response to San Jose with me the next day when I met with Ceppos and the other editors in the ornate conference room near the editors' offices. "That 'experts' would disagree with the findings of original research is one of the perils of doing it, as any researcher can tell you," I wrote. "But just because they have a differing opinion—and when you get down to it, that's all it is—is a pretty shoddy reason to take a swan dive on a story.

"Do I think there were no mistakes made in the execution of this story? No. There were," I wrote. "But this draft doesn't mention them. If we want to fully air this issue and be honest with our readers, I request that the following 'failures' be included."

I then described how the editors themselves had requested an increased emphasis on CIA involvement, how cutting the series from four parts to three had damaged it, and how the last-minute assignment of a new editor had weakened it further. Finally, I asked that the paper print my own response to this retraction. I thought it needed to be said that as a reporter, I stood by my story.

Ceppos flushed as he read my memo. "I don't think we should make this personal," he said uneasily.

"That's easy for you to say," I replied. "You're not the one who's being hung out to dry here."

"No one's going to hang you out to dry," insisted Jonathan Krim, the editor who'd been the most strident critic of the series and, in all likelihood, the author of Ceppos's apology. "We all got in this together, and we're all going to get out of this together."

"How can we honestly say that we don't know millions went to the Contras, or that the CIA didn't know about this, when we've got an eyewitness telling us that he personally gave drug money to a CIA agent?

What are we going to do about all that other inconvenient information in the follow-ups? We're going to look awful goddamned stupid running this apology and then printing stories that directly contradict it."

The other editors looked at the table uncomfortably.

"We *are* going to print those other stories, aren't we?"

Ceppos shook his head slightly.

"We're not?" I asked incredulously. "Why not?"

"They're a quarter turn of the screw," he said. "We're not going to print anything else unless it's a major advance."

I exploded. "You think the fact that the head of this Contra drug ring was working for the DEA is a quarter turn of the screw?" I shouted. "You don't think the fact that the DEA helped an accused CIA drug trafficker escape criminal charges is a major advance? You've got to be kidding me. Are we even going to pursue this story any more?"

"No," Ceppos said.

"Let me get this straight," I said. "We're killing the other stories. We're not going to do any more investigation of this topic. And we're going to run this mealymouthed column that pretends we don't know anything else, tuck our tails between our legs, and slink off into the sunset. That's what you've got in mind?"

"You and I have very different views of this situation," he said quietly.

"You got that right."

The result of the stormy meeting was that Ceppos rewrote his column, removing the obvious factual errors but leaving the rest virtually unchanged.

"No matter how many times the words and phrases are tweaked, the end result is still a sham," I responded in a memo. "You're sitting on information that supports what I wrote and pretending to be unaware of it."

Again I objected, and again Ceppos recast it, this time as a personal column and, at Dawn's insistence, disclosing that I disagreed with him. He also inserted some statements that acknowledged that the series was largely accurate and that the basic elements of it were solidly documented. And, to my shock, he reversed his earlier decision to kill the follow-up stories. Dawn asked me to prepare a memo on what we still needed to do to get the stories in shape because Ceppos was now leaning toward running at least part of them.

At a final meeting before the column ran, I predicted that the mainstream press would read the column as a retraction, one that covered everything the series had revealed. "You run this, and all we'll hear is, '*The Mercury News* has admitted it isn't true! The Contras weren't dealing cocaine! The CIA had nothing to do with it!' And you know as well as I do, that's not true."

"Well," shrugged Krim, "you're the one who's always saying that we can't be held responsible for what other people read into things."

There it is, I thought. The truth. They *want* the public to think there was nothing here. They want it all to go away. They're tired of fighting the current of mainstream opinion, tired of being journalistic outcasts for standing by a story that, as Jesse Jackson had put it, "threatened the moral authority of the government."

In nine months, we had gone full circle and crawled into bed with the rest of the apologists who wanted the CIA drug story put back in its grave once and for all.

"Have you got anything else to say?" Ceppos asked.

"Yeah. You're taking a dive on a true story, and one day you're going to find that out."

Ceppos's column ran on May 11, 1997, and if there was ever a chance of getting to the bottom of the CIA's involvement with drug traffickers, it died on that day. The *New York Times*, which hadn't found the original series newsworthy enough to mention, splashed Ceppos's apology on its front page. An editorial lauded Ceppos for his courage and declared that he'd set a brave new standard for dealing with "egregious errors."

Howard Kurtz, the media critic for the *Washington Post*, called for a comment. "It's nauseating," I told him. I had never been more disgusted with my profession in my life. It wasn't because such outrages were unknown in the newspaper business. They weren't. Shortly before I arrived at the *Plain Dealer*, the paper printed a front-page retraction of a story that had appeared more than a year earlier, revealing that former Teamsters Union president Jackie Presser was an FBI informant.

Presser was indeed an informant, as the FBI confirmed years later. But truth had taken a back seat to realpolitik. Court records later revealed that the paper had been pressured into retracting the story by New York mob boss Anthony "Fat Tony" Salerno, who'd asked his attorney, Roy Cohn, to intercede with the Newhouse family, which owned the *Plain Dealer*.

Whether similar pressures were applied to Ceppos from outside the newspaper is something I do not know, nor do I particularly want to. I would prefer to believe the theory advanced by my editor, Dawn Garcia, who suggested that Ceppos's treatment for prostate cancer in the winter of 1996–97 had been a factor. That extended illness, combined with the pressure from other editors, had taken their toll, she believed.

It's a plausible explanation, because there really were only two ways the newspaper could have gone with "Dark Alliance" at that point—forward or backward. The series had created such a superheated controversy that it had become impossible to simply do nothing. Ceppos, who had stood by the story bravely at key moments, simply may not have had the endurance, at that period of his life, to ride the story out.

If the *Mercury* continued pursuing the story and publishing follow-ups, editor Jon Krim worried in a memo, the editors needed to be ready "to deal with the firestorm of criticism that is sure to follow." The other way out was to back out: confess to some "shortcomings," take some quick lumps, and move on, which is the course Ceppos chose. It was certainly the course of least resistance, as the happy reaction of the national media proved.

Had I done what my editors wanted—kept my mouth shut and gone along with the charade—I would probably still be working at the newspaper. But I had no desire to hang around a place that was so easily cowed by the opinions of others. A reporter's job was to pursue the truth, I still believed, no matter how unpopular that pursuit became. And the truth of the matter, as I saw it, was that my editors were trying to rewrite history.

When Howard Kurtz asked me what I intended to do next, I told him about the stories the *Mercury News* was suppressing.

"We've got four more stories sitting in the can, and I intend to try and get them in the newspaper," I said. "I've been told that we're still going to run them."

Kurtz called me back a short time later. "I just got off the phone with Jerry Ceppos, and he says you never turned in any stories. He said the only thing you gave him was a memo and some notes."

"Notes?" I laughed. "I've never given an editor notes in my life. I turned in four stories in January, and I know he's read them because we've discussed them. Maybe you misunderstood."

Kurtz sounded confused. "They're not notes?"

"Of course not. They've got beginnings, middles, and ends."

"Those are stories where I come from," he said.

The controversy raged for another month, and the issue gradually became what Ceppos reportedly had dreaded: he was being accused of suppressing information. He was covering things up. Talk radio had a field day. In Washington, DJ Joe Madison, who'd been making hay with the story for months, urged the listeners of his 50,000-watt station to call Ceppos and demand that he print the stories he was suppressing. Letters and e-mail from outraged readers began pouring in.

Ceppos, who'd not spoken to me since his column ran, called me at home in early June. He was killing the follow-ups, he shouted. I was off the story for good. He couldn't trust me anymore because I'd "aligned myself with one side of the issue."

"Which side is that, Jerry? The side that wants the truth to come out?"

He wasn't getting into a debate, he told me. I was to report to his office in two days "to discuss your future at the *Mercury News*."

It was a very one-sided discussion. Reading from a prepared statement, Ceppos told me that my editors had lost faith in me. I needed closer supervision, which I couldn't get in Sacramento. I needed to regain their faith and their trust, and the only way to do that was to accept a transfer to the main office in San Jose. If I refused, I would be transferred against my will to the West Bureau in Cupertino, the newspaper's version of Siberia—a somnolent training ground for new reporters and a pasture for older ones who'd fallen from favor. It made little sense, because the reporters there had no direct supervision either. Whichever I decided, I had to report in thirty days.

And, by the way, Ceppos said, Pete Carey was going to take over the Contra drug story, and I was to give him all the cooperation he requested.

That night I sat down with my wife, Sue, and my children and gave them the news. In one month, I was going to have to start working in Cupertino, 150 miles away. I'd have to drive there on Mondays and come home on Fridays. In the meantime, I'd fight the transfer through the Newspaper Guild.

My six-year-old daughter looked at me strangely. "Are you still going to sleep here?"

"No, I won't be able to," I told her. "I have to live in another place during the week. But I'll be home on the weekends." She got up, went into her room, and closed the door.

As the deadline approached, I became despondent and told my wife I didn't feel comfortable leaving her and the kids alone. Georg had been getting death threats in Nicaragua, I told her. His wife's law office had been burglarized and ransacked twice; the power lines to his house had been cut, and his brother-in-law had been threatened by armed thugs. He was leaving the country, taking his wife to his native Switzerland.

"It's too dangerous to leave you and the children alone," I told her. "Maybe I should just quit." I didn't want to work there anymore anyway.

"That's just what they want you to do," she said indignantly. "Don't you dare give in to those cowards. I know it's a lousy situation, but we'll just have to put up with it for a while. The Guild says you'll win the arbitration."

Winning the arbitration seemed very likely, because the union contract the newspaper had with the Newspaper Guild, which represented much of the staff, expressly prohibited transfering reporters out of the bureaus against their will. But it would take months for a hearing to occur. And then what? I'd get my old job back working for the same editors? It hardly seemed worth the fight.

On the other hand, going through with it held its own attractions. Every day that I showed up at the Cupertino bureau would be an act of defiance.

Reluctantly I went, spending July and part of August in the Cupertino bureau under protest. I was assigned such pressing matters as the death of a police horse, clothing collections for Polish flood victims, and summer school computer classes. I went on a byline strike, refusing to put my name on any story written while I was working under protest.

To the chagrin of my editors, who were under orders to keep me away from any decent assignments, I turned a press release rewrite about a San Jose landfill into a front-page story. It was the last piece I wrote for the *Mercury*—a page-one story with no one's name on it, which reportedly infuriated Ceppos.

Occasionally, Pete Carey would call with a question or two. He wasn't having much luck corroborating Carlos Cabezas's statements, he told me. He'd been trying to locate the Venezuelan CIA agent Cabezas said he worked with, Ivan Gómez, but couldn't. He'd tried directory assistance in Caracas and complained about how many Ivan Gómezes there were in the phone book. I felt saddened that my two-year investigation had come to this.

I never heard another word from him about it, and none of the follow-up stories ever ran. On November 19, 1997, the *Mercury News* agreed to settle my arbitration but, amusingly, required me to sign a confidentiality agreement swearing that I would never disclose its terms. Nineteen years after becoming a reporter, I quit the newspaper business.

Bob Parry, the AP reporter who first broke the Contra drug story in 1985, sent me a note of condolence. "Like you, I grew up in this business thinking our job really was to tell the public the truth," he wrote. "Maybe that was the mission at one time. Maybe there was that Awakening in the 1970s with Watergate, the Pentagon Papers, the CIA scandals, etc.

"But something very bad happened to the news media in the 1980s. Part of it was the 'public diplomacy' pressures from the outside. But part of it was the smug, snotty, sophomoric crowd that came to dominate the national media from the inside. These characters fell in love with their power to define reality, not their responsibility to uncover the facts. By the 1990s, the media had become the monster.

"I wish it weren't so. All I ever wanted to do was report and write interesting stories—while getting paid for it. But that really isn't possible anymore and there's no use crying over it.

"Hang in there," he concluded. "You're not alone."

"The damage that has been done"

A few days after my resignation was announced, the CIA leaked the conclusion of an internal investigation to the *L.A. Times* and the *Mercury News*. This exhaustive probe, according to unnamed sources, had absolved the CIA of any wrongdoing.

Though the reporters had no idea what the report actually said, since it wasn't released, and none of the officials whispering in their ears was willing to have his name used, they dutifully reported that there was no evidence the CIA knew anything about the dealings of Danilo Blandón, Norwin Meneses, or Freeway Ricky Ross. I tried to imagine what the reaction would have been had those same reporters gone to their editors with unnamed sources citing unobtainable reports claiming the CIA *was* involved in drug trafficking. Journalistic standards can be wonderfully flexible when necessary.

A month later, with the Washington press corps on a scavenger hunt for a dress stained with President Clinton's semen, the declassified version of the CIA report was officially released. It showed that the CIA had known exactly what Norwin Meneses was doing, and had directly intervened in the Frogman case to prevent the public from learning of the relationship between CIA assets and cocaine traffickers. Naturally, those details went largely unreported. But CIA director George Tenet was quoted extensively, lamenting that "the damage to the CIA's reputation may never be fully reversed.

"The allegations made have left an indelible impression in many Americans' minds that the CIA was somehow responsible for the scourge of drugs in our inner cities."

Still, it was hard to avoid that impression after CIA Inspector General Fred P. Hitz appeared before the House Intelligence Committee in March 1998 to update Congress on the progress of his continuing internal investigation.

"Let me be frank about what we are finding," Hitz testified. "There are instances where CIA did not, in an expeditious or consistent fashion, cut off relationships with individuals supporting the Contra program who were alleged to have engaged in drug trafficking activity." The lawmakers fidgeted uneasily. "Did any of these allegations involve trafficking in the United States?" asked Congressman Norman Dicks of Washington. "Yes," Hitz answered. Dicks flushed.

And what, Hitz was asked, had been the CIA's legal responsibility when it learned of this?

That issue, Hitz replied haltingly, had "a rather odd history...the period of 1982 to 1995 was one in which there was no official requirement to report on allegations of drug trafficking with respect to non-employees of the agency, and they were defined to include agents, assets, non-staff employees." There had been a secret agreement to that effect "hammered out" between the CIA and U.S. Attorney General William French Smith in 1982, he testified.

A murmur coursed through the room as Hitz's admission sunk in. No wonder the U.S. government could blithely insist there was "no evidence" of Contra/CIA drug trafficking. For thirteen years—from the time Blandón and Meneses began selling cocaine in L.A. for the Contras—the CIA and Justice had a gentleman's agreement to look the other way.

Why would any sane government strike such a bargain? It was a question that would not be answered that evening. The Intelligence Committee, chaired by a former CIA covert operations officer, quickly changed the subject and adjourned.

Because I find footnotes extraordinarily distracting, I have elected not to use them. The information is sourced in the chapter notes in the order of its appearance in the text; each note is preceded by the page number it refers to, and an identifying phrase.

This book is based primarily upon public record sources: declassified U.S. government documents, mostly from the files of Iran-Contra Independent Counsel Lawrence Walsh at the National Archives; unclassified records released under the Freedom of Information Act (a mere shadow of what it once was); DEA tapes and DEA and FBI reports released to various defense attorneys under pre-trial discovery; congressional reports and hearing transcripts; transcripts and pleadings in state and federal courts (mainly in California and Florida); corporate records from California, Florida, and Nicaragua; records of the Nicaraguan Supreme Court; and reports of the Costa Rican Legislative Assembly and the Costa Rican *Organizacion de Investigacion Judicial* (OIJ), a law enforcement body similar in function to the FBI in the United States.

In the text, when the words "said in an interview" are used, it refers to an interview done by the author and/or his colleague Georg Hodel. Interviews conducted by other journalists, when more than one direct quotation is used, are noted in the text. In other cases, the source of the quotation is listed in the chapter notes.

The use of unidentified sources has been kept to an absolute minimum because I do not trust unsourced information as a general rule. If a source is unidentified, it was at the source's insistence, and I have attempted to identify the source's position as specifically as possible. At times, it may seem as if the sources are unnamed (i.e., "aquaintances say"), but normally their names will be disclosed in the chapter notes.

After the first mention, the following abbreviations are used in the chapter notes:

FBIS—Foreign Broadcast Information Service, a remarkable resource provided by our more useful friends at the CIA. FBIS microfiche is available at federal repository libraries across the country.

LACSO reports—Los Angeles County Sheriff's Office exhibits and interviews, most of them tape-recorded, conducted by investigators for Sheriff Sherman Block in the fall of 1996. In the text, when someone is quoted as having "told police," "told police investigators," or "told L.A. detectives," the quotation or information can safely be assumed to have come from the LACSO reports and appendices. Those reports are summaries of interviews and usually not the subject's verbatim statement. However, I have assumed that the sheriffs accurately reported the spirit of the subject's statement. When possible the accuracy was checked with the subject.

CIA-IG—Cables, interviews, and summaries contained in the Central Intelligence Agency Inspector General Report of Investigation, *Allegations of Connections between CIA and the Contras in Cocaine Trafficking to the United States* (96-0143-IG), vol. 1, *The California Story*, January 29, 1998, Frederick P. Hitz, Inspector General. This is a declassified version of a much longer report released to the House and Senate Intelligence Committees, which has never been released to the public. From my reading of the declassified version, it is obvious that considerable information has been censored. In the text, when a source is quoted as having "told the CIA," "told CIA inspectors," or "told CIA investigators," it is almost always a reference to an interview summarized in this report. Again, I can only assume the CIA related the interviews accurately and fairly, since the actual transcripts have not been made public.

U.S. v. James—The March 1996 criminal trial of Curtis James, Ricky Ross, and Michael McLaurin, 95 CR 353H, U.S. District Court, Southern District of California. If Danilo Blandón is quoted directly in the text, it is a quotation taken from either the court reporter's transcript of his sworn testimony as a government witness or the actual tape of his testimony, as I found there were sometimes substantive differences. In many cases, quotations from Ricky Ross came from his sworn testimony in *U.S. v. James*, though other quotations came from his interviews with the author and/or other journalists. Those other sources are separately noted.

Blandón GJ—The February 1994 testimony of Danilo Blandón before a federal grand jury for the Northern District of California, taken as part of a federal investigation of Norwin Meneses. At the time of this testimony, Blandón was cooperating with the government. In the text, if Blandón is quoted as having "told a grand jury," or "testified secretly," it is this testimony to which the text is referring.

CR Pros—*The Public Prosecutor's Investigation on "La Penca" Case*, San José, Costa Rica, December 26, 1989. This was a report of an investigation by Jorge Chavarria Guzman, then the prosecuting attorney for San José. Chavarria investigated the attempted assassination of Contra commander Edén Pastora at the La Penca rebel camp on May 30, 1984, but he also examined a host of other cases of Costa Rican–based Contras involved in drug trafficking. Included as exhibits are numerous court records from Costa Rican criminal cases. In the text, if information is attributed to "a Costa Rican prosecutor's report," it is a reference to this report.

CR Assy 2—*Segundo Informe de la Comision sobre el Narcotrafico, Asamblea Legislativa*, August 1989. This is the second report of the Costa Rican Legislative Assembly's Commission on Narcotics Trafficking, which examined the explosion of cocaine trafficking in that country during the mid-1980s. After studying the involvement of Contras and U.S. officials with illegal arms running and drug trafficking, the commission recommended that former ambassador Lewis Tambs, CIA station chief Joe Fernández, Lt. Col. Oliver North, former national security adviser John Poindexter, and former air force general Richard Secord be forever denied entry to Costa Rica, a recommendation that was adopted by Costa Rican president Oscar Arias and largely ignored by the U.S. media.

Kerry Report—*Drugs, Law Enforcement and Foreign Policy* (Washington, DC.: Government Printing Office, 1988), 1,166-page report by Sen. John Kerry's Subcommittee on Terrorism, Narcotics and International Operations (Kerry Committee), December 1988.

Prologue: "It was like they didn't want to know"

2 piece…about a convicted cocaine trafficker: Gary Webb, "Blunder Jeopardizes Drug Cases," *San Jose Mercury News*, June 11, 1995.

3 The Forfeiture Racket: Gary Webb, "The Forfeiture Racket," *San*

Jose Mercury News, August 29, 1993; and Webb, "The Money Tree," *San Jose Mercury News*, Aug. 30, 1993.

5 Jim Doyle, "4 Indicted in Prison Breakout Plot," *San Francisco Chronicle*, April 29, 1994.

5 Seth Rosenfeld, "Federal Jailbreak Plot Charged," *San Francisco Examiner*, April 19, 1994.

7 "it is not the first time": Howard Mintz, "Prosecutor's Missteps Place Prison Escape Case in Jeopardy," *San Francisco Daily Recorder*, February 1996.

11 "Ask about the cocaine smuggling": "Protesters Interrupt North with Contra Allegations," *Los Angeles Times*, July 9, 1987. The men, Michael Bardoff and Michael Kreis, were later fined $200 but refused to pay it.

12 People did more time for burglary: In 1992 the average federal prison sentence for burglary was 52 months. For pornography, it was 41 months; for robbery, 101 months; and 43 months for assault (*Sourcebook of Criminal Justice Statistics* [Washington, D.C.: Government Printing Office, 1996], 445).

Though his court files say Blandón was sentenced to 28 months, it's not certain he was in jail all that time. When U.S. Rep. Maxine Waters of Los Angeles asked the Bureau of Prisons in 1996 for his prison records from San Diego, the San Diego facility reported it had no record of him ever being confined there.

13 strongly suggested that Meneses, too, had been dealing: Jonathan Marshall, "Nicaraguans Arrest Ex-Bay Man Linked to Cocaine, Contras," *San Francisco Chronicle*, December 16, 1991; and Seth Rosenfeld, "Nicaraguan Exile's Cocaine-Contra Connections," *San Francisco Examiner*, June 23, 1986.

17 1987 FBI report, 1987 FBI interviews: FBI 302, *Record of Interview with Dennis Ainsworth*, San Francisco, January 21, 1987, file IC 600-1, sub. F-9; Office of Independent Counsel, *Record of Interview, Dennis William Ainsworth*, Berkeley, Calif., March 5, 1987, file IC 600-1, sub. F-18.

1. *"A pretty secret kind of thing"*

21 "let's talk like friends": Anastasio Somoza, *Nicaragua Betrayed* (Boston: Western Islands Publishers, 1980), 333–55; this autobiography also provides a detailed chronology of Somoza's last days in

power. His historical relationship and cooperation with the CIA are explained on 169–75.

Additional conversations between Somoza and Pezzullo in Anthony Lake, *Somoza Falling* (New York: Houghton Mifflin, 1989), 231–36.

23 vaunted National Guard collapsed: Details of the collapse of the National Guard and the final days of the Somoza regime were drawn from the June–July 1979 Central American reports of the Foreign Broadcast Information Service.

23 "Recent developments concerning the state of cocaine": Tennyson Guyer, quoted in House Select Committee on Narcotics Abuse and Control, *Cocaine, a Major Drug Issue of the Seventies: Hearings before the House of Representatives*, 96th Cong., 1st sess.; the hearings took place July 24 and 26 and October 10, 1979.

24 "rediscovery of cocaine in the Seventies": Psychiatrist Ronald Siegel, quoted in Dr. Gabriel Nahas, *Cocaine: The Great White Plague* (Middlebury, Vt.: Paul Eriksson Publisher, 1989), 129.

24 "My first ten years": Jerald Smith, interview by author.

26 And that brought Byck: Dr. Robert Byck, interview by author.

27 Dr. Raul Jeri had been insisting: Jeri reported his conclusions in "Consumption of Dangerous Drugs by Members of the Armed Forces and the Police in Peru," *Rev. Sanid. Minist. Int.* 37 (1976): 104–12; "The Syndrome of Coca Paste," *Rev. Sanid. Minist. Int.* 39 (1978): 1–18; and "Further Experience with the Syndromes Produced by Coca Paste Smoking," in *Cocaine 1980: Proceedings of the Interamerican Seminar on Medical and Sociological Aspects of Coca and Cocaine* (Lima, Peru: Pacific Press, 1980).

27 Dr. Nils Noya...began making similar claims: Noya, "Coca and Cocaine, a Perspective from Bolivia," in *The International Challenge of Drug Abuse*, NIDA research monograph no. 19 (Washington, D.C.: Government Printing Office, 1978), 82–90.

27 some of America's leading researchers: An excellent summary of early research reports can be found in R. K. Siegel, "Cocaine Smoking," *Journal of Psychoactive Drugs*, winter 1982, 301–10.

29 "Immediately after smoking": "Pure Cocaine Proves Devastating," *Journal*, January 1, 1978, 1; cited in Siegel, "Cocaine Smoking," 304.

29 "fairly rudimentary proposal": Dr. David Paly, interview by author. Paly's study was published as "Cocaine Plasma Levels after Cocaine Paste Smoking," in *Cocaine 1980*, 106–10.

31 "a growing trend": Ronald K. Siegel, letter to the editor, *New England Journal of Medicine* 300, no. 7 (February 15, 1979), 373. Siegel was interviewed by the author.

32 "increased happiness and contentment with life": Ronald K. Siegel, "Cocaine: Recreational use and intoxication," in *Cocaine 1977,* NIDA research monograph no. 13 (Washington, D.C.: Government Printing Office, 1977).

33 "most expensive of all mood changers": Dr. Sidney Cohen, "Coca Paste and Freebase: New Fashions in Cocaine Use," *Drug Abuse and Alcoholism Newsletter* (Vista Hill Foundation) 9, no.3 (April 1980).

34 "'I have had to sell even my clothes'": Gregorio Aramayo and Mario Sánchez, in *Cocaine 1980,* 120–26.

34 "impact of these experiences": Siegel, "Cocaine Smoking," 293.

36 California Conference on Cocaine: Details of the Santa Monica conference in Nahas, *Cocaine,* 128–37.

2. "*We were the first*"

38 the world on a platter: Details of Danilo Blandón's life in prerevolutionary Nicaragua came from his testimony in *U.S. v. James,* March 7, 1996. Additional details of Blandón's family history as well as the family history of his wife, Chepita Murillo, were gained from the author's interviews of Blandón's cousin Flor Reyes, his attorney Jose Macario Estrada, his supplier Norwin Meneses, and his wife's uncle Orlando Murillo. More details were gained from Georg Hodel's interviews of Moises Hassan, Edén Pastora, Roger Mayorga, Orlando Murillo, Blanca Margarita Meneses, and Norwin Meneses.

39 Though Somoza's army had beaten them down: The final days of the struggle with the Sandinistas are described in Anthony Lake, *Somoza Falling* (New York: Houghton Mifflin, 1989), 219; and Robert Kagan, *A Twilight Struggle* (New York: Free Press, 1996), 84.

39 "I cannot think of a single thing": Exchange between Ed Koch and Lucy Benson before the Subcommittee on Foreign Operations and Appropropriations of the House Appropriations Committee, March 24, 1977.

40 "Somoza is known to have instructed": Sally Shelton's statements were made before the Subcommittee on International Organizations of the House International Relations Committee, February 16, 1978.

40 Gustavo "El Tigre" Medina: Details of Medina's background and

Sandinista views regarding him were gained during author's interviews with Gustavo Medina, Juan C. Wong, Leonardo Hernandez ,and Jose Macario Estrada; additional information in Oleg Ignatiev and Genrykh Borovik, *The Agony of a Dictatorship* (Moscow: Progress Publishers, 1980), 80.

40 "allegations of cruel, inhuman and degrading treatment": State Department report submitted to the House Committee on International Relations and the Senate Comittee on Foreign Relations, February 3, 1978.

40 Inter-American Commission on Human Rights...did its own inspection: Organization of American States, *Report on the Situation of Human Rights in Nicaragua*, findings of on-site observation in the Republic of Nicaragua, October 3–12, 1978.

41 "Hundred of Nicaraguans struggle daily": Panamanian radio report, in FBIS daily summary for Central America, June 11, 1979, 11.

42 picture of the Blandón family: The photograph was produced during a 1992 detention hearing in *U.S. v. Blandón*, 92 CR 551, U.S. District Court, Southern District of California.

42 Blandón's job was to award grants: Danilo Blandón, testimony in *U.S. v. James*.

43 "I want the U.S. people to help me": Somoza's radio address, in FBIS daily summary for Central America, June 19, 1979, 16.

43 Blandón fell in with a Red Cross convoy: Blandón, testimony in *U.S. v. James*.

43 brothers named Torres: Ibid.

44 cousins of Pablo Escobar: The Torres's relationship with Escobar was obtained from 1996 L.A. County Sheriff's Office (LACSO) interviews of retired Bell police detective Jerry Guzzetta, author's interviews with Guzzetta, and Georg Hodel's interviews with Norwin Meneses.

44 blossoming Miami cocaine market: Description of early Miami cocaine market taken from Kerry Report, 27, and from Guy Gugliotta and Jeff Leen, *Kings of Cocaine* (New York: Harper and Row, 1990): 14–15.

45 "I was the first": Details of Blandón's early involvement with the Contras in L.A. came from his testimony in *U.S. v. James*, and his interviews with the Central Intelligence Agency Inspector General's Office, January 1998, CIA-IG, 69–70.

45 "You Americans have no idea": Jose Macario Estrada, interview by author.

45 Blandón applied for political asylum: Danilo Blandón, *INS Application for Permanent Residence,* December 10, 1986.

45 one of the earliest founders of the FDN: Details of Blandón's pro-Contra activities in L.A. obtained from Georg Hodel's interviews with William Fonseca.

46 Luis Pallais Debayle...began making the rounds: Roy Gutman, *Banana Diplomacy* (New York: Touchstone, 1988), 40–41.

46 "He fit the profile": Sam Dillon, *Comandos* (New York: Henry Holt, 1991), 65. Details of Enrique Bermúdez's background are on p. 62; see also Christopher Dickey, *With the Contras* (New York: Simon and Schuster, 1985), 62, 80.

47 Americans thought so highly of him: U.S. recommendation of Bermúdez to Somoza reported in Anastasio Somoza, *Nicaragua Betrayed* (Boston: Western Islands Publishers, 1980), 383.

47 invited Bermúdez to the Pentagon: Bermúdez's recruitment into CIA reported by Dillon, *Comandos,* 62–63.

47 Legion of September 15: Histories of the legion are in Glenn Garvin, *Everybody Had His Own Gringo* (McLean, Va.: Brassey's, 1992), 22, 26, 31–36; Dickey, *With the Contras,* 82–92; and Dillon, *Comandos,* 635.

48 telephone number of Colonel Ricardo Lau: Dickey, *With the Contras,* 88.

49 "we had to provide some cars": Danilo Blandón, testimony in *U.S. v. James.*

3. *"The brotherhood of military minds"*

50 "He had to talk to me": Danilo Blandón's descriptions of his early involvement with Norwin Meneses are taken from his testimony in *U.S. v. James,* and his testimony before the Grand Jury for the Northern District of California, Grand Jury 93-5, Grand Jury investigation 9301035, February 3, 1994.

51 People who know Barrios describe him: Descriptions of Donald Barrios from author's interviews with Jose Macario Estrada and Ariel Solorzano Jr., and from Georg Hodel's interview with Moises Hassan.

51 a partner of Violeta Chamorro: Norwin Meneses's business partnership with Chamorro was discovered by Georg Hodel in the corporate records of Inversiones Financieras S.A.

51 "I was in the plane": Gustavo Medina, interview by author.

51 a restaurant and an investment company: Barrios and Medina were partners in Los Ranchos de Miami, Inc., and BMS Investments Inc.

51 a career criminal: Details of Norwin Meneses's early career as a trafficker were taken from author's and Georg Hodel's interviews with Roger Mayorga; Mayorga's declarations to the Fifth District Criminal Court, Managua, November 21, 1991; November 16, 1981, affidavit of DEA agent Sandra Smith in *U.S. v. 60 Plymouth Circle, Daly City, California,* 1828-MW, Northern District of California; Eduardo Marenco, "History of a Nicaraguan Godfather," *El Semanario,* August 15, 1996; Roberto Fonseca, "Meneses: King of Drugs," *Barricada,* November 16, 1991; and Eloisa Ibarra, "Arce Refuses to Testify in Cocaine Case," *La Prensa,* November 22, 1991.

52 "one of the most totally corrupt military establishments in the world": Richard Millett, *Guardians of the Dynasty* (Maryknoll, N.Y.: Orbis Books, 1977), 251.

52 another brother, Brigadier General Fermin Meneses, commanded the *Guardia* garrison: Organization of American States, *Report on the Situation of Human Rights in Nicaragua,* findings of on-site observation in the Republic of Nicaragua, October 3–12, 1978, 14; FBIS daily summary for Central America, August 16, 1978, 4; and Juan C. Wong, interview by author.

53 "anti-Sandinista to the death": Marenco, "History of a Nicaraguan Godfather."

53 "Nicaragua is one of the few countries": Sally Shelton, statement before the Subcommittee on International Organizations of the House International Relations Committee, February 16, 1978.

53 "Gambling, alcoholism, drugs, prostitution": Pastoral letter, in exhibits to hearing of House Committee on International Relations, February 16, 1978, 108–10.

53 Edmundo Meneses's background was gathered from testimony before House Committee on International Relations, April 30, 1977, 231; and author's interviews with Jose Macario Estrada, Juan C. Wong, Peter Dale Scott, and Rafael Corñejo.

54 Vivas...said Meneses infiltrated pro-Communist groups: Rene Vivas, interview by author and Georg Hodel.

54 starting up an armed guerrilla group: Marenco, "History of a Nicaraguan Godfather."

54 Norwin appears to have literally gotten away with murder: Ernesto Aburto, "An Old Crime in the History of Norwin," *Barricada,* November 26, 1991; "Arrest Order for Norwin Meneses," *La Prensa,*

June 10, 1977; "Threats to Norwin's family?" *La Prensa*, June 17, 1977; and Rafael Corñejo, interview by author.

56 triggered his heart attack: Don Sinicco, interview by author. Sinicco died of cancer several months after the interview.

56 Ambassador Meneses was machine-gunned: FBIS daily summary for Central America, September 18, 1978, September 19, 1978, and October 2, 1978; and Oleg Ignatiev and Genrykh Borovik, *The Agony of a Dictatorship* (Moscow: Progress Publishers, 1980), 68.

56 "guerillas of Pancasan": Marenco, "History of a Nicaraguan Godfather."

57 Norwin…left Nicaragua in early June 1979: Norwin Meneses, interview by author and Georg Hodel.

57 relatively large Nicaraguan population: James Quesada Jr. and Dennis Ainsworth, interviews by author.

57 posed as a successful businessman: Information about Norwin's businesses in San Francisco from author's interviews of Meneses; Seth Rosenfeld, "Nicaraguan Exile's Cocaine-Contra Connection," *San Francisco Examiner*, June 23, 1986; and Guillermo Fernández, "Nica Resident Here Is Supposed Head of Ring," *La Nacion*, December 1, 1986. Records of Norwin's property purchases were found by author in San Mateo County Clerk's Office.

57 the Mission was home: Roberto Vargas, interview by author.

58 Court records show: Special Agent Ronald J. Kimball, Costa Rican DEA report, DEA file GFR3-76-4001, December 29, 1976.

59 "an interesting combination": Sandra Smith, interview by author.

59 arrested for cocaine sales: Details of Roger Meneses's and Omar Meneses's arrests contained in Smith affidavit, *U.S. v. 60 Plymouth Circle*.

59 Smith got a break: Information about Baldwin Park investigation, Julio Bermúdez's arrest, and Jairo Meneses search was contained in Smith affidavit, *U.S. v. 60 Plymouth Circle*.

61 Blandón accepted Meneses's pitch: Blandón, testimony in *U.S. v. James*. The visit by Bermúdez was contained in his CIA-IG interview.

61 on an FDN fund-raising committee: Meneses explained his role with the Contras in interviews with the author and Georg Hodel. Blandón's description of Meneses's role was contained in Blandón's CIA-IG interview. Additional details in Douglas Farah, "Nicaraguan is Reputed Link between Contras and Cocaine Sales in California,"

Washington Post, October 4, 1996; Tim Golden, "Pivotal Figures of Newspaper Series May Be Only Bit Players," *New York Times*, October 20, 1996; Ricardo Gutierrez, "Show de defensores de narcos," *El Nuevo Diario*, August 15, 1992.

62 Adolfo Calero...denied: Farah, "Nicaraguan is Reputed Link."

62 "brotherhood of military minds": Edgar Chamorro, interview by author.

62 "the ends justify the means": Details of Blandón's meeting with Bermúdez came from Blandón's testimony in *U.S. v. James*, and his CIA-IG interviews.

62 "illicit or dirty business": Senate Intelligence Committee, November 1996.

62 "government-sponsored sting operation": Kerry Report, 759–816.

63 "escorted to Tegucigalpa airport": CIA-IG, 71.

63 "Mr. Meneses explained to me": Blandón's training sessions as a cocaine dealer were detailed in both his testimony in *U.S. v James* and Blandón GJ.

64 "Blandón was introduced": Torres brothers' statements reported by Agents Bruce A. Burroughs and Don A. Allen, FBI-302 report, case file 245B-SF-96287, May 5, 1992.

64 denies traveling with Blandón: Frank Vigil, interview by author and Georg Hodel.

64 "Chepita called me": Orlando Murillo, interview by author and Georg Hodel.

65 "Blandón fled Nicaragua": Chuck Jones's affidavit, filed in *In the Matter of the Search of Premises Commonly Known as Storage Unit L-7, Security First Self Storage, 3089 Main St. Chula Vista, California*, 92-2083-M, Southern District of California, May 18, 1992.

4. *"I never sent cash"*

66 Details of the formation of UDN-FARN in Miami are contained in Shirley Christian, *Nicaragua: Revolution in the Family* (New York: Random House, 1985), 228–29; and Glenn Garvin, *Everybody Had His Own Gringo* (McLean, Va.: Brassey's, 1992), 25–26. The weapons shipments are detailed in Martha Honey, *Hostile Acts* (Gainesville: University of Florida Press, 1994), 224.

67 The generals there had a deal for them: Roy Gutman, *Banana Diplomacy* (New York: Touchstone, 1988), 52–54. The assault on

the radio station is described by Christopher Dickey, *With the Contras* (New York: Simon and Schuster, 1985), 90–92; and Garvin, *His Own Gringo*, 33–34.

68 Reagan...authorized the CIA: Dickey, *With the Contras*, 104.

68 "We were practically official guests": A transcript of William Baltodano Herrera's tape-recorded interview was contained in Dieter Eich and Carlos Rincon, *The Contras: Interviews with Anti-Sandinistas* (San Francisco: Synthesis Publications, 1984), 17–29.

69 "It was in Buenos Aires": Pedro Javier Nuñez Cabezas, cited in Eich and Rincon, *The Contras*, 45–55.

69 tracked fifteen Argentine intelligence operatives: Jack Binns, cited in Gutman, *Banana Diplomacy*, 54.

70 indications that Bermúdez was personally corrupt: Anne Manuel, "Nicaragua: New U.S. Aid Won't End Contra Investigation," Inter Press Service, July 1, 1986.

71 "agree to join efforts": Details of the creation of FDN taken from Peter Kornbluh, *Nicaragua: The Price of Intervention* (Washington, D.C.: Institute for Policy Studies, 1987), 26; Garvin, *His Own Gringo*, 38; and Gutman, *Banana Diplomacy*, 56.

71 "single most detested group of Nicaraguans": Stephen Kinzer, *Blood of Brothers* (New York: Doubleday, 1991).

71 partners in a Miami restaurant: Enrique Sánchez was a partner in Los Ranchos De Miami, Inc.

72 "Calero's hatchet man": Oliver North, notebook entry for January 28, 1986.

72 "Sánchez became one of the Contras' top...strategists": Aminda Marques González, "Aristides Sánchez Dies," *Miami Herald*, September 8, 1993.

72 "$29 million isn't going to buy you much": Bobby Inman, quoted in Bob Woodward, *Veil* (New York: Simon and Schuster, 1987), 192.

73 "role of American mercenary": Alfonso Chardy, "CIA-backed Fighters No Longer Boast of Toppling Sandinistas, Agency Says," *Miami Herald*, May 23, 1983.

73 "deny having met with any U.S. government officials": Edgar Chamorro, *Packaging the Contras* (New York: Institute for Media Analysis, 1987).

74 "just for sitting around at a desk": Hector Frances's statements were published as an appendix to Chamorro, *Packaging the Contras*.

74 "Torres stated": FBI report, 1992.

5. *"God, Fatherland and Freedom"*

76 Details of Carlos Cabezas's background and employment history came from interviews with Cabezas by the author and/or Georg Hodel; his testimony of November 28, 1984, in *U.S. v. Julio Zavala et al.*, 83 CR 0154, U.S. District Court, Northern District of California; and Leo McCarthy, U.S. Department of Probation and Parole, to U.S. Magistrate Owen E. Woodruff, letter, February 18, 1983.

77 Details of Julio Zavala's background came from interviews with Carlos Cabezas, his testimony in *U.S. v. Zavala*, and McCarthy to Woodruff, letter.

80 FBI had joined the chase: Most of the details of the FBI's investigation of Cabezas and Zavala were contained in the Master Affidavit of FBI agent David E. Alba, filed in support of an application for electronic surveillance. Alba's August 1982 affidavit is part of the case file in *U.S. v. Zavala*.

80 recently declassified CIA Inspector General's report: The CIA's early interest in Zavala was disclosed in CIA-IG, 84.

82 Sánchez said he flew for the CIA: Troilo Sánchez, interview by author, Georg Hodel, and Nicaraguan reporter Roberto Orosco, who was later fired by *La Prensa* for investigating the Blandón-Meneses money-laundering operations in Managua.

82 "We are like family": Meneses, interview by Guillermo Fernández R., *La Nacion* (Costa Rica), December 1, 1986. Fernández was forced to flee Costa Rica because of death threats after publishing his extensive 1986 series in Contra-related drug trafficking.

84 FBI teletype shows that by November 1982: Reprinted in Kerry Report, 400–409.

85 "Troilo sold 200 pounds": "Contra Accuses Other Rebels of Corruption, Drug Trafficking," UPI, April 26, 1986. The story was datelined Tegucigalpa, Honduras.

85 agency's "man in Costa Rica": Ivan Gómez's activities in Costa Rica were reported by Martha Honey, *Hostile Acts* (Gainesville: University of Florida Press, 1994), 237, 261, 283, 288, and 306.

85 Three former Costa Rican officials: Edén Pastora and Marcos Aguado, interviews by Georg Hodel. Carol Prado was interviewed by author and Georg Hodel.

86 interview with a British television crew: Dewey Clarridge's comments about Ivan Gómez were made to a film crew from ITV, London, *The Big Story*, which aired in December 1996.

86 "well known to 'The Company'": Agent Sandalio González, DEA-6, *File Opening Report—Debriefing of STF-78-0006 (CI)*, February 6, 1984, file GFTF-84-4004.

87 Pereira was arrested in Miami: Details of Pereira's arrest are contained in a January 10, 1983, application for an extension of a wiretap by FBI special agent David Alba.

88 FBI started taking the operation apart: Details of the surveillance and arrests at Pier 96 are contained in an application for a search warrant dated February 14, 1983, by FBI special agent David Alba, filed as part of the pleadings in *U.S. v. Zavala.* Other details came from a story by Maitland Zane, "Cocaine Seized from Frogmen at S.F. Pier," *San Francisco Chronicle,* January 18, 1983.

89 The very same ship...was found in Houston: The Houston raid on the *Cuidad de Cucuta* was reported by UPI on May 17, 1984. UPI reported three other Gran Colombiana line drug seizures in Los Angeles on May 14, 1986; January 18, 1984; and January 30, 1983; and reported on the Frogman case seizure on January 17, 1983.

89 At 7 a.m. on February 15: Search warrant return was found in case file of *U.S. v. Zavala,* currently on file at the National Archives, San Bruno, Calif.

91 Iverson handed Peckham two letters: Details of Iverson's meetings with Peckham and the court squabble over the depositions were filed in numerous documents, *U.S. v. Zavala*. The conversations between Iverson, Peckham, and Mark Zanides were taken from the trial transcripts in *U.S. v. Zavala.*

94 Costa Rican CIA station fired off a cable: A summary of the CIA cables was contained in CIA-IG.

97 "The government just folded up its tents": Marvin Cahn, interview by author.

6. *"They were doing their patriotic duty"*

100 All of the quotes from Blandón came from either his testimony in *U.S. v. James* or Blandón GJ.

101 "I keeping the books from L.A.": The Q&A was from an exchange between Ricky Ross's defense attorney Alan Fenster and Blandón during *U.S. v. James*.

101 "I went one time": John Lacome, interview by author.

102 nephews all drove flashy new cars: Gloria Lopez, interview by author.

102 "Jaime Sr., I respected him": Rafael Corñejo, interview by author.

102 murdered in 1990: Jaime Meneses's murder was reported by Rodrigo Peralta, "Crimen en asalto a financiera," *La Nacion*, June 27, 1990; and Tomas Zamora, "Aclaran crimen de empresario," *La Nacion*, August 31, 1990.

102 JDM Artwork: Records on file at the Division of Corporations of the California Secretary of State.

102 Edén Pastora said he visited the firm: Edén Pastora, interview by Georg Hodel.

103 Pastora aide Carol Prado claimed: Carol Prado, interview by author and Georg Hodel.

103 former associate of Blandón: Puerto Rican associate, interview by author. He declined to be named because, he says, he was frightened of Blandón. He provided the author with a copy of the photograph of Blandón in the FDN office in L.A.

103 CIA cables filed in federal court: The 1984 CIA cable was filed as an exhibit in *U.S. v. James* and later summarized more thoroughly in CIA-IG.

103 1986 interview: The interview with Meneses was conducted by Seth Rosenfeld of the *San Francisco Examiner.*

103 "appeared like a fund-raiser": Edgar Chamorro, quoted in Seth Rosenfeld, "Nicaraguan Exile's Cocaine-Contra Connection," *San Francisco Examiner*, June 23, 1986.

103 recently declassified CIA cable: CIA-IG, 48. A summary of a CIA interview with Meneses regarding his recruiting appears on 76.

104 "It's true, it was widely spread around": Juan C. Wong, interview by author.

105 "People were being arrested": Bradley Brunon, interview by author.

106 Ronald Jay Lister: Lister's military service records were exhibits to LACSO report, November 1996.

106 "always very successful": Lt. Danielle Adams, interview by author.

106 "You hear lots of things about Ron Lister": Chief Neil Purcell, interview by author.

107 Pyramid International's corporate records are on file at the Division of Corporations, California Secretary of State.

107 "through a Beverly Hills business connection": Ronald Lister was interviewed four separate times by LACSO investigators: November 6, 1996, by Lt. Michael Bornman and Sgt. Axel Anderson; again on November 6, by Bornman; on November 7, 1996, by Bornman; and on November 23, 1996, by Bornman and

Anderson. He was also interviewed in CIA-IG, 55–59. He refused two written interview requests by author.

107 "began working in Central America": Lister's attorney, interview by author.

107 "I think I was actually an officer": Christopher Moore, interview by author.

108 "the 'Reagan Doctrine' may have been born in El Salvador": Robert Kagan, A *Twilight Struggle* (New York: Free Press, 1996), 209.

108 reason…William Casey gave to Congress: Casey's briefing described by Roy Gutman, *Banana Diplomacy* (New York: Touchstone, 1988), p. 85

109 "Under the guise of anti-Communism": Oliver L. North, *Under Fire* (New York: HarperCollins,1991), 224.

109 Colonel Nicholas Carranza: Carranza's role with the death squads and the CIA was reported by Bob Woodward, *Veil* (New York: Simon and Schuster, 1987), 262.

110 "heard rumors of illegal arms trafficking": Gary Shapiro, interview by author.

110 "Lister was in San Salvador": FBI, *Record of Interview, Frederico Cruz,* May 12, 1987, file IC 600-1, sub. M-51. Released to journalist Nick Schou under the FOIA by the National Archives.

111 Lister's company…made a security proposal: A copy of the Pyramid proposal was provided to the author by a member of the raid team, Robert Juarez.

113 "We need the know-how": The Cabazon letters to Tim LaFrance were published by John Connoly, *Spy* magazine, April 1992, as was the quote from the Wackenhut employee. The Cabazon projects were reported by Jonathan Littman in a series in the *San Francisco Chronicle*, September 4, September 6, and September 13, 1991.

113 "spies, arms merchants and others": Casolaro's involvement with the Cabazon investigation is detailed in Michael Taylor and Jonathan Littman, "Death of Conspiracy Investigator Probed," *San Francisco Chronicle,* February 11, 1994.

114 his memoirs, *Compromised:* Terry Reed and John Cummings, *Compromised* (Kew Gardens, N.Y.: Clandestine Publishing, 1995).

114 attempt to portray Reed as a crackpot conspiracy theorist: Howard Schneider, "Clandestination Arkansas," *Washington Post,* July 21, 1994. For a considerably more intelligent look at the goings-on at Mena, see Alexander Cockburn's columns from the *Nation*, March

12, 1992, and March 28, 1992, reprinted in Cockburn, *The Golden Age Is in Us* (New York: Verso, 1995), 264–68.

Reed's book contains transcripts of interviews *Time* magazine reporter Richard Behar did while putting together his appalling hatchet job on Reed. The story, which appeared in *Time*, April 20, 1992, resulted in a libel suit against Behar, during which his interview tapes were produced. To get a flavor of how diligently and open-mindedly the national news media has checked out allegations of government complicity in narcotics trafficking, Behar's obsequious interview with Oliver North (642–44), a pardoned criminal, is illuminating.

The only national media outlets to take Mena seriously have been *Penthouse* and the *Wall Street Journal*. *Penthouse*, in July 1995, published Sally Denton and Roger Morris's heavily documented story, "The Crimes of Mena," after the *Washington Post* once again lost its nerve and sat on it. (For a mealy-mouthed and self-serving explanation of that act of courage, see "Put on Hold," *Washington Post*, February 12, 1995.) The *WSJ* has printed Micah Morrison's reporting on its much-maligned editorial page. See, for example, "Mysterious Mena: CIA Discloses, Leach Disposes," January 29, 1997.

115 "Seal detailed his cocaine-smuggling activities": "IRS Says Smuggler Owes $29 Million, Seizes His Property," *Baton Rouge State Times*, February 5, 1986. The letter to Meese was reported by Denton and Morris, "Crimes of Mena," 60.

115 Hondu Carib Cargo Inc.: Details of Hondu Carib's involvement with Barry Seal and the Contras were in the Kerry Report, 44–45 and 278–97.

115 Another DC-4 Moss controlled: The DC-4 in which Owen's phone number was found was seized by the DEA in March 1987. See Joan Mower, "Owen Criticizes Use of Plane, Crew with Shady Connections," AP, May 19, 1987. North's notebook entry for August 9, 1985, shows Owen's warning about the New Orleans–based DC-6.

116 North was being regularly briefed: North's notebooks, entries for June and July 1984. Copies are on file at the National Security Archive at George Washington University, Washington. North was briefed by CIA official Duane "Dewey" Clarridge, another Iran-Contra indictee, who was then in charge of the Contra project.

Much of the information about North's involvement with the

Seal DEA/CIA sting can be found in *Enforcement of Narcotics, Firearms and Money Laundering Laws*, a record of the oversight hearings of the Subcommittee on Crime of the House Judiciary Committee, July 28, September 23, 29 and October 5, 1988 (Washington, D.C.: Government Printing Office, 1989).

116 "the murder...of a DEA agent": FBI report from the special agent in charge of the Washington FBI field office to the director of the FBI, *Nicaraguan Active Measures Program Directed against Lt. Col. Oliver North*, June 11, 1986. The report was found in the microfiche of the National Security Archive's Iran-Contra compendium, *Making of a Scandal.*

116 "a contract CIA operative": Roger Morris, *Partners in Power* (New York: Henry Holt, 1996), 389–427.

116 "associates of Seal": Kerry Report, 121.

117 "it was a CIA operation": Larry Patterson, cited in Morris, *Partners in Power,* 426.

117 John Bender...swore in a deposition: R. Emmett Tyrell Jr., "The Arkansas Drug Shuttle," *American Spectator*, August 1995; this article also contains Brown's statements about Clinton's knowledge.

117 FBI's description of its investigation: FBI, *National Narcotics Report for 1988*, 254. It is an exhibit to the official report of the June 6 and August 8, 1988, hearings of the Subcommittee on Criminal Justice of the House Committee on the Judiciary.

118 "Whatever the limits": Morris, *Partners in Power,* 425.

118 "darkest backwater": Susan Schmidt, "CIA Probed in Alleged Arms Shipments," *Washington Post*, August 7, 1996.

118 "joint training operation": Kathy Kiely, "CIA Admits 2-Week Training 'Exercise' at Mena," *Arkansas Democrat Gazette*, August 9, 1996.

118 "coded records": Morris, *Partners in Power,* 392.

119 "DIA wanted them to happen": Tim LaFrance, interview by L.A. journalist Nick Schou.

119 "It was kind of touchy": John Vandewerker, interview by Nick Schou.

120 "FDN couldn't collect sufficient funds": Norwin Meneses, interview by Georg Hodel and the author.

120 "contacts with the Contras": Tim Golden, "Pivotal Figures of Newspaper Series May Be Only Bit Players," *New York Times*, October 20, 1996.

120 "led a sales team": Victor Merina and William Rempel, "Ex-

Associates Doubt Onetime Drug Trafficker's Claim of CIA Ties," *Los Angeles Times*, October 21, 1996. (In 1990 Merina was given a copy of some of the evidence seized from Lister's house during a 1986 drug raid and either threw it away, lost it, or gave it to another reporter who lost it. Reporter Jim Newton told the LA County Sheriff's Office in 1996 that the *Times* was "administratively embarassed" that the documents given to Merina for safekeeping could no longer be found.)

121 a federal prosecutor immediately objected: This was Asst. U.S. Attorney L. J. O'Neale, during *U.S. v. James*.

7. *"Something happened to Ivan"*

123 Many of the quotes from Ross in this chapter come from his sworn testimony in *U.S. v. James*. The author also interviewed Ross extensively, but whenever possible his court testimony was used in the text. Information from the interviews was used if his testimony did not address a particular issue, if it expanded upon a point made during the testimony, or was more understandable.

123 "onto something new": Jesse Katz, "Deposed King of Crack," *L.A. Times*, December 20, 1994, A20.

124 "his polyester shirt had melted": *Time*, June 23, 1980, 10. Pryor's explanations for the accident were made to *People Weekly*, June 29, 1981, 74–78; and *Ebony*, October 1980, 42.

124 "When Cocaine Can Kill," *Newsweek*, June 23, 1980, 30.

124 NBA freebase use: "NBA and Cocaine: Nothing to Snort At," *L.A. Times*, August 19, 1980.

124 "pre–Harrison Act yellow journalism": Ronald Siegel, "Cocaine Smoking," *Journal of Psychoactive Drugs*, October–December 1982, 296.

125 "relatively high cost and difficulty": Steven R. Belenko, *Crack and Evolution of Anti-Drug Policy* (Westport, Conn.: Greenwood Press, 1993), 4.

125 Rand Institute study: Jonathan P. Caulkins, *Developing Price Series for Cocaine*, Drug Policy Research Series (Santa Monica, Calif.: Rand Institute, 1994).

125 "You heard Tootie's name": Steven Polak, interview by author.

125 "ain't never been big": Ronald L. Soble, "Drug Dealer Admits: 'I Sold Them,'" *L.A. Times*, June 11, 1984.

126 "amounts of cocaine he allegedly dealt": William Overend,

"Adventures in the Drug Trade," *L.A. Times Magazine*, May 7, 1989.

126 sometime thief, sometime student: Details of Ross's background and childhood came from interviews with Ross, his mother, Annie Ross, and his brother, David Ross, which were conducted by the author.

126 "There exists no information to substantiate your membership": Ross's lack of gang affiliation was reported in a memo from B. Davis, Pima Unit Manager, FCI, Phoenix to Ricky Ross, May 24, 1993, *Subject: Inmate request of staff member*.

127 "culture of a gang member": Jesse Katz, interview by author.

128 "He was a very good player": Pete Brown, interview by author.

131 "There was no evidence": Alan Fenster, interview by author.

8. *"A million hits is not enough"*

136 "one or two keys": All quotes from Blandón in this chapter are taken from his testimony in *U.S. v. James* or Blandón GJ.

137 "Henry was kind of a knucklehead": Ross's quotes in this chapter come either from his interviews with the author, his testimony in *U.S. v. James*, or his 1996 LACSO interview.

139 "a saucer, a glass, a paper towel": Dr. Franklin Sher, testimony from House Select Committee on Narcotics Abuse and Control, *Cocaine, a Major Drug Issue of the Seventies: Hearings before the House of Representatives*, 96th Cong., 1st sess.

139 *The Natural Process:* The information about the 1981 crack pamphlet was contained in Ronald Siegel, "Cocaine Smoking," *Journal of Psychoactive Drugs*, October–December 1982, 309.

140 "what made us start smoking": The interview with Big Shiphead was contained in Yusuf Jah and Sister Shah'Keyah, *Uprising* (New York: Scribner, 1995), 241.

140 1985 study: Malcolm Klein and Cheryl Maxson, "Rock Sales in South Los Angeles," *Sociology and Social Research* 69, no. 4 (July 1985): 561. Their final report was published as National Institute of Justice, *Gang Involvement in Cocaine "Rock" Trafficking*, NIJ #85-IJ-LX-0057, April 1988.

140 "We didn't know what it was": Steve Polak, interview by author.

141 "limited to the Carribean and Haitian communities": James Inciardi, "Beyond Cocaine: Basuco, Crack and Other Coca Products," *Contemporary Drug Problems*, fall 1987, 475–77.

142 "most effective trafficking groups": The information regarding the political roots of the Jamaican crack gangs appeared as U.S. Department of Justice, Drug Enforcement Administration, Intelligence Division, *Crack Cocaine, Drug Intelligence Report*, DEA-94016, 1994, 8.

The Jamaican CIA destabilization program was exposed by Ernest Volkman and John Cummings in "Murder As Usual," *Penthouse*, December 1977. This program was summarized in William Blum, *Killing Hope* (Monroe, Maine: Common Courage Press, 1995), 263–67.

143 "more-or-less standard sizes": David Allen and James Jekel, *Crack: The Broken Promise* (London: MacMillan Press, 1991), 17.

143 "not just a matter of smoking freebase": Byck, interview by author.

146 "first crack millionaire": Jesse Katz, interview; Katz, "Deposed King of Crack," *L.A. Times*, December 20, 1994.

146 "The thing about Rick": James Galipeau, interview by author.

149 visiting one of Ross's "cookhouses": Chico Brown, interview by author.

149 "Wal-Mart of cocaine": *L.A. Times*, December 20, 1994.

149 "rocks hit the streets hard": Leibo, quoted in Jah and Shah'Keyah, *Uprising*, 183.

9. *"He would have had me by the tail"*

151 none other than CIA director William Casey: Casey's leaks to *Newsweek* were reported by Roy Gutman, *Banana Diplomacy* (New York: Touchstone, 1988), 116.

152 "perhaps the most hated group of Nicaraguans": Tom Harkin, cited in Robert Kagan, *A Twilight Struggle* (New York: Free Press, 1996), 242.

152 "hit the roof": Oliver L. North, *Under Fire* (New York: HarperCollins,1991), 237.

152 "to keep the nation's secrets": Edward P. Boland, cited in Kagan, *Twilight Struggle*, 243.

153 "an elegant two-story place": Sam Dillon, *Comandos* (New York: Henry Holt, 1991), 127.

154 "The FDN needed people": Blandón, cited in CIA-IG, 72.

156 "principal group is controlled by Blandón": DEA report, *Debriefing of SRP-86-0018, August 25-27, 1986*, by agent Thomas A. Schrettner of the Riverside, Calif., office. The report is from DEA

file #GFRP-86-4020, titled, *Blandón, Danilo*. The file has never been released to the public. The single report was released as an exhibit to the LACSO report.

157 "As of approximately 1984": The Torres brothers' statements about Blandón and Meneses are contained in an FBI-302 report by Agents Bruce A. Burroughs and Don A. Allen, May 5, 1992, file 245B-SF-96287.

158 "It was going to be a big party": "Examining Charges of CIA Role in Crack Sales," *L.A. Times*, October 21, 1996.

158 "he was with Norwin in '84": Rafael Corñejo, interview by author.

158 "arresting officers also found a small vial": Andy Furillo, *L.A. Herald-Examiner*, "Maury Wills Caught Driving Stolen Car," December 27, 1983.

159 "Norwin was a target": Jerry Smith, interview by author.

159 "the target of unsuccessful investigative attempts": The federal prosecutor was Asst. U.S. Attorney L. J. O'Neale, of San Diego, in a motion for downward reduction of Blandón's sentence, 1993.

160 "totally protected by the U.S. government": Dennis Ainsworth, interview by author.

161 "I got a reputation": Don Sinicco, who died in 1996, was interviewed by the author at his home in Fairfield, Calif., in November 1995. He provided author with numerous documents and photographs.

161 Calero "had been working for the CIA in Nicaragua": Edgar Chamorro, *Packaging the Contras* (New York: Institute for Media Analysis, 1987).

162 "The cocktail party went very smoothly": FBI 302, *Record of Interview with Dennis Ainsworth*, San Francisco, January 22, 1987, file IC 600-1, sub. F-9, released by the National Archives under the Freedom of Information Act.

164 "He assisted the Cuban Legion": Jack Terrell, interview by author.

164 showed the author attendance records: Among other attendees at USACA meetings was Sacramento TV news anchorman Stan Atkinson. Sinicco said Atkinson attended not as a journalist but as a Contra supporter, "but you couldn't tell he was for the Contras from his news reports."

164 "run through an obscure bureau in the Department of State": The House staff report, which is chilling reading, is entitled *State Department and Intelligence Community Involvement in Domestic*

Activities Related to the Iran-Contra Affair. It was written by Spencer Oliver, Bert Hammond, and Vic Zangla of the Committee of Foreign Affairs staff in October 20, 1992. It documents how the CIA and Oliver North ran "highly questionable, improper and illegal" covert propaganda operations against the American public. Naturally, it was ignored by the national media, who were the dupes of this operation.

165 "to affect public opinion favorably": Thomas Dowling's statements were made during the congressional Iran-Contra committees in the once top-secret *Deposition of Father Thomas Dowling,* August 4, 1987. Though ostensibly declassified, huge chunks of Dowling's deposition are still secret. For an excellent article on the bizarre Father Dowling, see Dan Noyes and Ellen Morris, "The Trouble with Father Tom: The Strange Tale of San Francisco's Contra Priest," *San Francisco Examiner "Image" Magazine,* November 8, 1987.

165 "I really did retire": G. James Quesada, interview by author.

166 "there are indications of links": The cables can be found in CIA-IG, 79.

166 Peña was dating Blandón's sister, Leysla: Leysla Balladares, interview by author.

166 "made from six to eight trips": CIA-IG, 78.

167 Renato Peña and Meneses's nephew were arrested: Details taken from the affidavit in support of a search warrant filed November 28, 1984, by DEA agent Sandra Inglese.

169 "I don't know anything": Calero cited in Guillermo Fernández, "Nica Resident Here Is Supposed Head of Ring," *La Nacion,* December 1, 1986.

171 "If Jairo supposedly was my accountant": *La Nacion,* December 1, 1986.

10. "Teach a man a craft and he's liable to practice it"

172 Contra forces were at their lowest ebb: Robert Kagan, *A Twilight Struggle* (New York: Free Press, 1996), 356–57; Glenn Garvin, *Everybody Had His Own Gringo* (McLean, Va.: Brassey's, 1992), 163; Sam Dillon, *Comandos* (New York: Henry Holt, 1991), 140–45; Oliver L. North, *Under Fire* (New York: HarperCollins,1991), 249–50.

173 "cutting both our losses and theirs": Robert McFarland, cited in Kagan, *Twilight Struggle*, 347.
174 "The CIA knows about this guy": Eric Swenson, interview by author.
174 the agency had information tying Meneses: 1984 CIA cable, CIA-IG, 48.
174 1984 had been a terrific year: In *U.S. v. James*, Blandón testified that 1984–85 was when his dealings with Ricky Ross were at their height, a time frame Ross also confirmed.
174 decided to approve his application for political asylum: Blandón testified to his immigration status in *U.S. v. James*, and it was confirmed by author's interview with Jose Macario Estrada, who represented Blandón before the INS in Miami.
175 opened a NADDIS file on Blandón: Danilo's and Chepita's NADDIS reports circa August 1986 were released as exhibits to the LACSO report.
175 "I have some 300 DEA-6 reports": Brunon's comments came during Blandón's detention hearing in *U.S. v. Blandón*, May 30, 1992.
175 "I've had clients deported": The immigration lawyer requested his name not be used because he was revealing information gained as a result of an attorney-client relationship.
175 blanket zero-tolerance policy: The State Department official, Tom Casey, was interviewed by the author.
175 refused to release any information: Both State and INS refused FOIA requests by the author.
176 bought the house under his name: Blandón described the purchase of the home during his testimony in *U.S. v. James*, and it was confirmed by Orlando Murillo during an interview with the author.
177 valued its worth at around $29 million: The DEA had an appraisal done on Guerra's parking lot in 1992—presumably for forfeiture purposes—while he was under investigation for money laundering.
177 $2,000 in drug profits had a legitimate pedigree: The example of money laundering through used car lots was taken from the notes of LACSO Sgt. Ed Huffman, made during a January 1987 meeting with the FBI and DEA regarding Blandón's drug ring. The notes were released as exhibits to the LACSO report.
178 "Blandón became very close to Ricky Ross": The Torres brothers' police interview was conducted by LACSO Sgts. Daniel Cruz and Joseph Hartshorne, November 14, 1996.
179 "the black people": A conversation secretly taped by DEA infor-

mant John P. Arman on July 21, 1990. The tapes were released during discovery in *U.S. v. Blandón*.

180 Jacinto Torres quickly got into trouble: Details of Jacinto Torres's arrest are contained in *People v. Robert Joseph Andreas and Jacinto Jose Torres*, case A590516, Municipal Court of Burbank.

181 "You know your client's guilty": The probation officer's complaints were contained in *Declaration of Alan R. Freedman*, August 6, 1986, part of the case file in *People v. Andreas*.

183 "Police say hundreds": Andy Furillo, "South Central Cocaine Sales Explode into $25 Rocks," *L.A. Times*, November 25, 1984. Furillo was interviewed by the author.

184 "marketing breakthrough": Jay Matthews, "Drug Abuse Takes New Form; Rock Cocaine is Peddled to Poor in Los Angeles," *Washington Post*, December 23, 1984, A15.

184 "Crack first came to the attention": Statement of Robert M. Stutman before the Select Committee on Narcotics Abuse and Control, U.S. House of Representatives, *Crack Situation in New York City*, July 18, 1986.

184 "fewer than fifteen arrests for crack": Ward, testimony before the House Select Committee on Narcotics Abuse and Control.

185 "throughout the Black residential areas": Malcolm Klein and Cheryl Maxson, "Rock Sales in South Los Angeles," *Sociology and Social Research* 69, no. 4 (July 1985): 561.

That South Central L.A. was the nation's first major crack market is fairly well established. Only after I reported in 1996 that much of the cocaine fueling the crack market there came by way of the Contras did the historical record, which had gone unchallenged for years, suddenly become suspect. For the edification of the reader, I am including here some of the many historical references to crack's L.A. roots:

"Sometime during the 1980s rock cocaine was formulated for the first time in South Central Los Angeles. Two or three years passed before it appeared under a different name, crack, on the East Coast" (Robert Conot, "L.A. Gangs: Between a Rock and a Hard Place," *Los Angeles Times*, April 12, 1987).

"L.A. may be the model for other cities around the country: rock cocaine first appeared there nearly three years ago. Houston has been flooded with it for the past two years; Detroit about 18 months; New York police have discovered the crack crisis within the past six months" (*Newsweek*, June 16, 1986).

"In Los Angeles, where the drug was introduced around 1981, more than two-thirds of the 2,500 coke arrests made this year have involved crack" (*Time*, June 2, 1986).

"Rock made its L.A. debut around 1980.... By 1982, Los Angeles hospital emergency rooms reported the nation's greatest increases in cocaine overdoses, a 90 percent rise over the previous year" (*U.S. News and World Report*, August 19, 1991).

"We find that crack came to New York City from Los Angeles, where it made its first appearance in 1981" (Wilhemina E. Holliday, deputy commissioner, New York Police Department, testimony before House Select Committee on Narcotics Abuse and Control, July 15, 1986).

"Rock cocaine, or crack as it is termed on the east coast, was first encountered in the Los Angeles area in 1981" (Ted Hunter, special agent in charge of the Los Angeles DEA office, testimony before House Select Committee on Narcotics Abuse and Control, October 31, 1986).

"It perhaps started here" (L.A. County sheriff Sherman Block, testimony before House Select Committee on Narcotics Abuse, October 31, 1986).

"Crack is thought to have first appeared in the early 1980s on the West Coast" (Rick Hampton, "Crack: Spreading across America," AP, May 25, 1986).

"Crack has been available in southern California now for about five years" (Rep. Mel Levine, California, July 15, 1986, House Select Committee on Narcotics Abuse and Control).

"After crack first became available in Los Angeles in 1981, the lure of huge profits from crack sales attracted local African-American street gangs into the crack trade" (DEA, *Crack Cocaine Drug Intelligence Report*, April 1994).

A handful of researchers, James Inciardi for example, maintain that the crack market in Miami developed simultaneously with that in L.A., but the historical record to support this is much thinner. One of the journalistic advocates of this scenario is Jeff Leen, a self-styled cocaine expert formerly with the *Miami Herald*. If Leen is correct, however, it means he missed the story by about four years. His first article on crack (which he erroneously referred to as "free-base" throughout) didn't appear until December 30, 1985, a month after the *New York Times* announced its presence on the Eastern seaboard. See Jeff Leen, "Freebase Coke Use Sweeping South

Florida," *Miami Herald*, December 30, 1985; and "A New Purified Form of Cocaine Causes Alarm as Abuse Increases," *New York Times*, November 29, 1985.

186 "law enforcement perceptions of gang involvement": Jerome H. Skolnick, *The Social Structure of Street Drug Dealing* (State of California, Office of the Attorney General, 1988); and Skolnick, *Gang Organization and Migration* (State of California, Office of the Attorney General, 1989).

186 "In the early 1980s the gangs began selling crack cocaine": *Nontraditional Organized Crime*, GAO Report #OSI-89-19, 47–49.

187 "came up empty-handed": Nick Kozel's futile crack hunt in Miami was recounted in Dan Baum's excellent book on the drug war, *Smoke and Mirrors* (Boston: Little, Brown, 1996), 213.

187 "By the time the market exploded in 1984": Jesse Katz, "Deposed King of Crack," *L.A. Times*, December 20, 1994.

187 "a cartel": The L.A. detective was Robert Sobel, and the quote comes from his taped administrative interview with LACSO Internal Affairs, June 15, 1988. The transcript was filed as an exhibit to *U.S. v. Polak*, 94 CR 00283, Central District of California.

188 "You name it, you could get it": Leibo, cited in Yusuf Jah and Sister Shah'Keyah, *Uprising* (New York: Scribner, 1995), 183.

189 "'my friends down South'": Lister, in CIA-IG, 56–57.

189 "several top Contra leaders were also in attendance": Blandón, in CIA-IG, 72–73.

189 Montealgre, a CIA-trained Contra pilot: For Mariano Montealgre's background, see Martha Honey, *Hostile Acts* (Gainesville: University of Florida Press, 1994), 262, 355, 371–72.

189 ""loosely associated Nicaraguans...": Thomas Schrettner, DEA report, August 1986.

190 "off the rack": Blandón's Q&A was with defense attorney Alan Fenster during *U.S. v. James*.

190 Mundy Security Group Inc.: Corporate records on file at California Secretary of State's Office, Sacramento.

190 business card found in a drug raid: Inventory of search warrant returns, LACSO, October 27, 1986.

190 "looking down the barrel of a gun": Chris Moore, interview by author.

190 "screaming and yelling": Gary Shapiro, interview by author.

190 Green was prosecuted and disbarred: "Attorney Quits State Bar," *Orange County Register*, March 17, 1987; and "Ex-attorney Given 2-year Sentence," *Orange County Register*, September 3, 1992.

191 "This firm received three DSP-73s": Memorandum from Customs Coordinator Office of Defense Trade Controls to Sgt. Robert Rifkin, Los Angeles County Sheriff's Office, *Subject: Analysis of Flow Chart*, December 2, 1996. The memo was released as an exhibit to the LACSO report.

191 "better equipment than we have": Sobel, cited in "L.A. Law: Gangs and Crack," *Newsweek*, April 27, 1987, 35.

Sobel's description of Ross raid from IA interview cited above.

192 "numerous 9-mm Uzies": Glenn Levant, quoted in LAPD intradepartmental memo from Levant to Detective Steven Polak, *Commendation LASD/LAPD Rock Cocaine Supplier Task Force*, January 13, 1988. Filed as exhibit to *U.S. v. Polak*.

192 "hammered on who I might know": Lister's notes of the FBI encounter were seized during a drug raid on October 27, 1986, and released as exhibit to LACSO report.

192 "my relationship with Soviet agents": LACSO interview with Lister, November 23, 1996.

192 "Lister was attempting to sell classified electronic equipment": Richard Smith, interview by Sgt. Axel Anderson, LACSO, November 13, 1996.

192 "They came down to see me": Neil Purcell, interview by author.

193 "personnel jacket for Ronald J. Lister": Memo from Cruz and Hartshorne, LACSO, to Neal B. Tyler, *Contact with Maywood Police Department Personnel Department*, November 13, 1996.

193 "actual personnel files related to Ronald Lister": Memo from Cruz and Hartshorne, LACSO, to Tyler, *Contact with Laguna Beach P.D. Personnel Department Director*, November 12, 1996.

194 Fluor spokeswoman initially denied: Nick Schou, "Tracks in the Snow," *L.A. Weekly*, May 23–29, 1997.

195 a CIA officer since 1948: Bill Nelson's background came from the Department of State's Biographical Register, 1973, and from CIA-BASE, a computer database operated by former CIA officer Ralph McGehee.

195 "Operation Feature": Nelson's role in Angola was reported by John Prados, *Presidents' Secret Wars* (New York: Morrow and Co., 1986), 338–47.

195 civil suit filed by the widow: The lawsuit against Nelson was reported by Jay Perkins of the Associated Press, June 28, 1978.

196 North…frequently used phony EUCs: "U.S. Government Stipulation on Quid Pro Quos with Other Governments as Part of

Contra Operations," filed April 6, 1989, in *U.S. v. North.* Reprinted in Peter Kornbluh and Malcolm Byrne, *The Iran-Contra Scandal: The Declassified History* (Washington, D.C.: National Security Archives, 1993), 85–97.

196 "Contras can't buy weapons": Alan Fiers, testimony in *U.S. vs. Clair George,* CR91-521, U.S. District Court of the District of Colombia, July 28, 1992, 1120–21.

196 spymaster died of respiratory failure: Details of Nelson's death came from his Certificate of Death, dated April 3, 1995, Orange County, Calif., by coroner James Huang, M.D.

11. *"They were looking in the other direction"*

198 "parried with two journalists": Meneses, interview by author and Georg Hodel.

199 "I'll be right up front": James McGivney, interview by author, December 12, 1995.

199 "Mr. Blandón was considered": Charles Jones's grand jury testimony obtained from "Transcript of Proceedings, San Diego, California, March 15, 1995." Jones appeared before Grand Jury No. 94-4, Southern District of California.

201 "approached the trafficker about becoming an informer": Tim Golden, "Pivotal Figures of Newspaper Series May Be Only Bit Players," *New York Times,* October 20, 1996. Golden's story cites only three named sources, all former Contras, and makes numerous unattributed declarations of "fact," such as "Although Mr. Bermúdez, like other contra leaders, was often paid by the CIA, he was not a CIA agent." Semantics aside, how Golden could possibly have known such a thing with absolute certainty is never explained.

201 they would later persuade a grand jury to file charges: On February 8, 1989, Meneses was secretly indicted on two counts: conspiracy to distribute cocaine and possession with intent to distribute. A copy of the indictment in *U.S. v. Meneses,* 89 CR 0064, and an arrest warrant of the same date were filed as a prosecution exhibit at Meneses's 1992 trial and contained in the pleadings at the Nicaraguan Supreme Court. However, that case file may no longer be public. It was removed from the records room soon after my series appeared in 1996.

201 "They used Meneses": Roger Mayorga, interview by author and Georg Hodel.

202 "Those were very big years": Rafael Corñejo, interview by author.

202 "I went to Costa Rica": John Lacome, interview by author.

202 "Norwin receives political protection": Agent Sandalio González, DEA-6, *File Opening Report—Debriefing of STF-78-0006 (CI)*, February 13, 1984, file GFTF-84-4004.

202 Jose Marti Figueres: Charles Walston, Nancy Nusser, "$6 million lottery ticket scam alleged in Costa Rica," *Orange County Register*, May 11, 1991, A18; "Fraud Charge," *Latin American Weekly Report*, March 16, 1995, 120; "Vesco Political Financing Scandal," *Facts on File*, July 2, 1977, 506.

203 "one of the most important traffickers": The OIJ description of Meneses was contained in a summary of wiretaps compiled during the OIJ's 1985–86 investigation of Horacio Pereira. Provided to author by investigative journalist Douglas Vaughan.

204 "We had the idea in Nicaragua": Troilo Sánchez, interview by author, Georg Hodel, and Nicaraguan reporter Roberto Orosco, who later lost his job at *La Prensa* for pursuing this story.

204 Vigil acknowledged his part ownership: Frank Vigil, interview by author, Georg Hodel, and Hodel's wife, attorney Carmen Maria Santos.

204 "dedicated themselves to international cocaine trafficking": Costa Rican Legislative Assembly, *Special Commission Appointed to Investigate the Acts Reported on Drug Trafficking*, July 10, 1989. English translation by Library of Congress.

204 DEA investigation of Manuel Noriega: Steve Albert, *The Case against the General* (New York: Scribner's, 1993), 5–13.

204 "The people who were flying in the weapons": Lotz's questioning by Jack Blum is attached as an exhibit to the Kerry Committee hearings, on CIS microfiche.

205 told a friend that he was doing it for the CIA: Manfred T. DeRewal, letter to the author, October 29, 1996.

205 "Despite obvious and widespread trafficking": Kerry Report, 122.

206 "looking in the other direction": Chavarria, interview by author and Georg Hodel.

206 "no credible evidence": Jack Lawn, testimony in Kerry Report, 144. Jack Blum confirmed to the author that the DEA officer interviewed by him in Costa Rica was Nieves.

207 OIJ raided the San José home of... Troilo and Isanaqui Sánchez: Guillermo Fernández, "Trafficker Condemned to 12 Years Paid Bail and Escaped," *La Nacion*, November 26, 1986.

207 "pillows full of cocaine": Leonardo Zeledon Rodriguez, cited in

"Contra Accuses other Rebels of Corruption and Drug Trafficking," UPI, April 26, 1986. He was interviewed in Tegucigalpa, Honduras, from his bed at the Military Hospital School, where he wound up after being savagely beaten and paralyzed.

207 "help move drugs to the U.S.": Meneses and Chamorro, CIA-IG, 49.

208 Among those captured on the wiretaps: The list of men captured on the Pereira tapes is from the OIJ summary of wiretapped conversations, which contains a description of each caller.

208 "a personal friend of Manuel Noriega": Pastora's description of González was contained in CR Pros.

208 "drug trafficking activities of Sebastian González": CIA cable summarized at 48, CIA-IG.

209 *CBS Evening News:* The transcript of the CBS broadcast was an exhibit to the Kerry Report, 410.

209 "precisely in that period": CR Assy 2, 70.

209 "there were certainly substantiated cases": Joseph Fernández, testimony to the House Select Committee to Investigate Covert Arms Transactions with Iran and U.S. Senate Select Committee on Secret Military Assistance to Iran and the Nicaraguan Opposition, May 29, 1987, in executive session as declassified, 84.

210 Pastora admits all that: Edén Pastora, interview by Georg Hodel.

210 "The Disruptive Actions of Edén Pastora": CIA cable regarding Pastora introduced as exhibit TC-7 to Fernández's testimony.

210 "We attempted to diminish his influence": Fernández joint testimony, 84.

211 "using his special communications equipment": Arturo Cruz, *Memoirs of a Counter-Revolutionary* (New York: Doubleday, 1989).

211 "they told me they were CIA agents": Morales testified before the Kerry Committee, April 7, 1986, and March 27, 1987.

211 close associate of...John Hull: Marcos Aguado's relationship with John Hull is discussed in a January 12, 1989, report from Jorge Calderon Gómez, Chief of Various Crimes Section; Alfredo Chacon, Judge of Crimes of Transit, and Norman Moya Orrieta, Chief, Department of Criminal Investigation, OIJ, to Jorge Chavarria, No. Info. 052DV-8.

212 Morales later passed a DEA-administered lie detector test: Letter from DEA regarding results of test reprinted in Kerry Report, 382.

212 planeloads of weapons were flown: Fabio Ernesto Carrasco and Gary Wayne Betzner testified as government witnesses in *U.S. v.*

Jose Rafael Abello Silva, 87 CR 140B, Northern District of Oklahoma, 1990. All quotes from Carrasco and Betzner in the text are from a transcript of their sworn testimony.

212 "There is no doubt in Fiers's mind": FBI Special Agent Michael S. Foster, *Record of Interview of Alan D. Fiers*, July 27, 1991, file IC 600-1, 10. Partly declassified and released to author by the National Archives.

212 "it's my own government": Hull, interview by author.

213 "I called our contact at the CIA": Douglas Farah and Walter Pincus, "CIA, Contras and Drugs: Questions in Links Linger," *Washington Post*, October 21, 1996. This story, done in response to my series, reported something that the *Post* had known for a decade.

214 Chamorro identified him in an interview: Chamorro, interview by Georg Hodel.

214 "two individuals who were associated with Pastora": Fernández joint hearing testimony, 84–85.

214 an aged C-47 cargo plane: The C-47 is discussed in the Kerry Report, 51.

214 "repeatedly piloted": Jonathan Kwitny, "Money, Drugs and the Contras," *Nation*, August 29, 1987.

215 when he quit the war: Marcos Aguado, interview by Georg Hodel.

215 "a man who always had money": Pastora testified about Blandón's background to the Senate Intelligence Committee, November 1996.

215 "We reported it": Fiers' testimony was to the Iran-Contra Committees.

216 Saborio was frequently quoted: "Commander Zero Wages Battle for Cash on the Air," *Miami Herald*, February 20, 1985; "Zero Pleads for Army Funds," *Miami Herald*, February 16, 1985; "Sandinista Foes Tentatively Agree on Unity, Rebel Says," *Miami Herald*, February 6, 1985; and "Pastora Secretly Visits Miami, Washington Seeking Aid from US," *Miami Herald*, February 21, 1984.

216 "Saborio was a close friend of Blandón": Carol Prado, interview by author and Georg Hodel.

216 "a Contra member named 'Dr. Sabario'": Ronald Lister's contact with Saborio reported in CIA-IG, 57.

216 posted part of Chepita Blandón's bond: *U.S. v. Chepita Blandón et al.*, "Short Form Deed of Trust and Assignment of Rents Securing a Personal Surety Bond to the United States of America," Trustor, Felix Saborio, July 29, 1992.

216 two Associated Press reporters: The AP story was written by Robert Parry and Brian Barger and moved in the U.S. on December 20, 1985, appearing in several American newspapers in truncated form. It was the first report by an American journalist of Contra involvement in drug trafficking. Interestingly, the AP thought it necessary to add Parry's and Barger's journalism awards and experience to the end of the story, apparently to persuade newspaper editors that the report should be taken seriously.

217 editors sat on the piece for weeks: Robert Parry, interview by author.

217 "diminish Pastora's influence": Fernández testimony to the Senate Select Committee on Secret Military Assistance to Iran and the Nicaraguan Opposition, April 20, 1987, 269.

218 "responsive to the CIA": Lawrence Walsh, *Firewall* (New York: Norton, 1997), 278.

218 "The concern about Chamorro": Owen memo to North, *Subject: Southern Front,* April 1, 1985. Released as an exhibit, RWO7, to Owen's testimony before the Iran-Contra Committees.

218 "most of them were true": Secord's comments to Leslie Cockburn were reported in the U.S. District Court opinion in *Secord v. Cockburn,* Civil Action 88-0727, District of Colombia Federal Court, dismissing Secord's libel suit against Cockburn for suggesting he knew of Contra drug trafficking in her book *Out of Control* (New York: Atlantic Monthly Press, 1989).

219 "They certainly had to get their act together": Fernández Senate testimony, 306.

219 "they wanted them moved out": Owen's testimony regarding UDN-FARN comes from his deposition in *Avirgan v. Hull,* Civil Action 86-1146 and 87-1545, U.S. District Court, Southern District of Florida, February 9, 1988, 607–8.

219 "the last time I remember Negro Chamorro": Fernández Senate tesimony, 307.

12. *"This guy talks to God"*

221 The description of Spadafora's wounds comes from R. M. Koster and Guillermo Sánchez, *In the Time of the Tyrants* (New York: Norton, 1990), 19–31.

222 "reportedly the best known guerrilla fighter": DEA description of Spadafora was contained in a heavily censored DEA-6, file G3-85-0094, September 12, 1986, released to author under FOIA.

222 Telephone intercepts by the U.S. National Security Agency: Koster and Sánchez, *In the Time of the Tyrants*, 28. Noriega's involvement in the murder reported by Steve Albert, *The Case against the General* (New York: Scribner's, 1993), 16, 26. See also testimony of Ambassador Francis McNeil before Kerry Committee, April 4, 1988, 39.

222 story that first exposed Noriega: Seymour Hersh, "Panama Strongman Said to Trade in Drugs, Arms and Illicit Money," *New York Times*, June 12, 1986.

223 "Dr. Spadafora was a very honest man": Floyd Carlton testified before the Kerry Committee on February 10, 1988. His quotes are taken from a transcript of that testimony.

223 had lost $1.8 million in cash: Some of the details of Carlton's operations in Costa Rica were reported by Martha Honey, *Hostile Acts* (Gainesville: University of Florida Press, 1994), 358–63.

224 According to...José Blandón: Blandón testified before the Kerry Committee on February 10, 1988. Most of the quotes from him came from a transcript of that testimony.

224 Spadafora had three meetings with...Nieves: Guillermo Fernández, *La Nacion*, "Political Drug Connection behind Spadafora's Murder," November 25, 1986. Robert Parry and Brian Barger also wrote of meetings between Spadafora and an unnamed "senior American law enforcement official" at which Spadafora discussed the trafficking of "Guachan" González and "a prominent Panamanian official" (AP, December 20, 1985).

224 ordered González arrested: Details of González's alleged involvement in Spadafora's death, his arrest and denials, were contained in interviews conducted with González by investigative reporter Douglas Vaughan during González's imprisonment in Panama in March 1990.

226 North and Noriega struck a very important bargain: North's involvement with Noriega summarized in Kerry Report, 91–97. See also "U.S. Government Stipulation on Quid Pro Quos with Other Government as Part of Contra Operations," filed April 6, 1989, in *U.S. v. North*. Reprinted in Peter Kornbluh and Malcolm Byrne, *The Iran-Contra Scandal: The Declassified History* (Washington, D.C.: National Security Archives, 1993), 85–97.

227 "I took the initiative myself": Norman Bailey testified before the House Select Committee on Narcotics Abuse and Control, March 29, 1988.

228 "he was the top gun": Alan Fiers, testimony at *U.S. v. Clair Elroy George*, 91 CR 521, 92 CR 215, U.S. District Court for the District of Columbia trial, July 28, 1992.

228 "The CIA's strategy determined what North would do": Lawrence Walsh, *Firewall* (New York: Norton, 1997), 275. Walsh was not the only one who believed this. In *Eclipse: The Last Days of the CIA* (New York: William Morrow, 1992), Mark Perry wrote, "While many CIA officers who became entangled in the Iran-contra scandal disagree about many of its details, they are convinced that Casey used Oliver North in order to circumvent the agency's unwillingness to participate in high-risk activities. North became Caseys' unofficial director for operations and the acknowledged inheritor of his activist dream" (48).

228 "turned out to be absolute truth": Fiers, testimony at *U.S. v. George*, July 31, 1992.

228 during one late-night conversation: Ibid., July 28, 1992.

229 "to a GS-15, this guy talks to God": Fernández, testimony to Senate, 505.

229 "Air resupply of the Contras was the key": Fiers, testimony at *U.S. v. George*, October 28, 1992.

230 North simply "hijacked" it: North's plans for controlling NHAO were spelled out in a secret July 29, 1985, memo entitled "Concept for Providing Humanitarian Aid to the Nicaraguan Resistance," on file at National Security Archives.

230 Robert W. Owen: Owen's background came from his immunized testimony to the Iran-Contra committees.

230 "That man has all of the attributes": Fernández on Owen, joint Committee testimony, 62.

230 "I might have gone with the CIA": Owen's plans regarding the CIA were contained in his testimony in *U.S. v. North*, 88 CR 80, U.S. District Court for the District of Columbia, February 24, 1989.

230 "I did ask him to find out about things": Fernández, Senate testimony, 319.

230 "I certainly didn't see the necessity": Deposition of Robert W. Duemling before the Senate Select Committee on Secret Military Assistance to Iran and the Nicaraguan Opposition, August 30, 1987, 68.

231 "what, in fact, Rob Owen could do": Deposition of Chris Arcos, Senate Iran-Contra Committee, 41.

231 "Owen will be expendable": "Highlights of RIG meeting of October

17, 1985," memo by Duemling, reprinted in Kornbluh and Byrne, *Iran-Contra Scandal*, 144–45.

231 "He probably had the most extensive network": Fernández on Owen's contacts, Senate testimony, 447.

231 Frigorificos de Puntarenas: Kerry Report, 43.

232 congressional testimony of former Medellín cartel accountant: Ramon Milian Rodriguez testimony, February 11, 1988, Kerry Report, 260–61.

232 cartel *had* given the Contras $10 million: Carlos Lehder's testimony at Noriega's trial, in Albert, *Case against the General*, 332–34.

233 investigation of a 1983 bombing of a Miami bank: Reprinted in Kerry Report, 371–81.

233 Frigorificos was being used by the Contras: Fabio Ernesto Carrasco testimony from *U.S. v. Jose Rafael Abello Silva*, case 87 CR 140B, Northern District of Oklahoma, 1990.

233 "helpful to the cause": Owen's testimony regarding Frigorificos contained in his deposition in *Avirgan v. Hull*, Civil Action 86-1146 and 87-1545, U.S. District Court, Southern District of Florida, February 8, 1988.

234 Aviles…notarized affidavits: The Aviles notarizations were reprinted in the Kerry Report, 411. Author found additional document in NHAO records on microfiche at National Security Archives.

234 never-explained transfers: The record of the Frigorificos bank account wire transfers was reprinted in the Kerry Report, 364.

The GAO findings regarding the laundered humanitarian aid money were revealed at a May 1, 1986, hearing of the Subcommittee on Western Hemisphere Affairs of the House Committee on Foreign Affairs. When the GAO attempted to find out where the broker accounts had sent the money, the State Department objected on grounds that the information was classified.

235 manager, Moises Nuñez, was a CIA agent: Brian Barger, "CIA Officer Linked to Surveillance on Two Reporters," UPI, February 12, 1988.

235 "small, professionally managed rebel naval force": Vidal, *Projections for a Naval Force in the Atlantic Coast*, memo proposing a Contra maritime operation, February 10, 1986, on file at the National Security Archives.

235 "a problem with drugs": Fernández, cited in Leslie Cockburn, *Out of Control* (New York: Atlantic Monthly Press, 1989), 89.

236 "person who might help with the boats": Owen, memo to North,

Overall Perspective, March 17, 1986, reprinted in Kornbluh and Byrne, *The Iran-Contra Scandal*, 56. Owen updated North on the progress of the operation again on April 7, 1986, in a memo introduced as exhibit TC-15 to Fernández's joint testimony.

236 Fernández admitted to the Iran-Contra committees that he knew Nuñez: Senate testimony, 179–80.

237 "a shell entity": Fiers on NHAO, testimony at *U.S. v. George*, October 28, 1992.

237 DIACSA was run by a Cuban drug dealer: DEA records regarding DIACSA are reprinted in Kerry Report, 342–61.

237 "deposits arranged by...Oliver North": Kerry Report, 47–48.

237 "Caballero was CIA and still is": Carol Prado, interview by author and Georg Hodel.

238 Floyd Carlton testified: "Drug Smuggler Admits Flying Arms to Contras," *San Francisco Chronicle*, October 2, 1991.

238 "largest marijuana business cartel": Testimony regarding Palmer was delivered by U.S. Attorney Roy Hays at a hearing in Detroit on gangs, before a subcommittee of the House Judiciary Committee, August 1, 1988, 279.

238 "Palmer's people got caught": Fiers, FBI interview with Iran-Contra investigators, 10.

238 "Nice group the Boys chose": Owen, memo to North, February 10, 1986.

238 Foley was reportedly overseeing Palmer's operations: Pat Foley's alleged involvement with Palmer came from author's interview with Ronald Lippert, an ex-CIA pilot who flew briefly for Palmer.

238 "A stop at San Andrés Island": Francis McNeil, testimony to Kerry Committee, April 4, 1988.

239 imprisonment...in 1963 for espionage: "Cuban Tribunal Gives Canadian Pilot 30 Years," *Houston Chronicle*, November 24, 1963; and David Weber, "JFK Death Spoils Propaganda Circus," *Dallas Morning News*, December 2, 1963.

239 arranged to buy Lippert's DC-4: Documents regarding the sale of the plane to Insua and Kelley were provided to the author by Lippert.

239 "powerful gang of drug-smugglers": *La Opinion*, January 25, 1987.

240 "Can't we close a bank": Barry Gladden, cited by David Satterfield, "Even Latest Fraud Probe has Contra Tie," *Miami Herald*, September 2, 1987.

240 later exposed as a drug trafficker: José Insua's criminal background

was admitted by him during his cross-examination at *U.S. v. Alfredo Duran*, 89 CR 802, Southern District of Florida, Miami Division, April 13, 1990.

240 "Palmer boasted to prosecutors": Lorraine Adams, "North Didn't Relay Drug Tips," *Washington Post*, October 22, 1994.

240 SETCO, which happened to be owned by…Ballesteros: Noe Leiva, "Contras Established Supply Chain in Honduras," UPI, May 13, 1986; John Dillon and Jon Lee Anderson, "Who's Behind Aid to the Contras," *Nation*, October 6, 1984; and the Kerry Report, 44–45.

240 "One of the policy guidelines": Duemling deposition, 46.

241 "The transportation channel got established": Brunon, interview by author.

241 Meneses's drug-laden planes were flying out: Enrique Miranda, interview by author and Georg Hodel.

241 "practically unfettered": Walsh, *Final Report of the Independent Counsel for Iran/Contra Matters*, August 4, 1993, 1:157.

13. *"The Wrong Kinds of Friends"*

242 Much of the text concerning Celerino Castillo was compiled from three sources: Castillo's memoirs, *Powderburns*, written with Dave Harmon (Buffalo, N.Y.: Mosaic Press, 1994); author's interviews with Castillo; and Castillo's interviews with investigators from Iran-Contra Independent Counsel Lawrence Walsh, most of which were declassified by the National Archives in 1994.

agent-in-charge, Robert Stia, took him aside: Castillo, *Powderburns*, 112–13.

243 Cuban named Socrates Sofi-Perez: Ibid., 126–27.

243 bounced the Cuban's story off…Ramiro Guerra: Ibid., 127–28. Guerra is identified in Castillo's book by a pseudonym, Luis Aparicio.

244 "The woman selling tortillas": FBI agent Michael Foster's interview with assistant regional security officer, name deleted, December 24, 1991, declassified and released to author by National Archives.

244 "We had a capability": Alan Fiers, testimony at *U.S. v. George*, July 31, 1992.

244 "Felix Rodriguez was put into": Ibid., October 28, 1992.

245 "a client who could compromise": Felix Rodriguez and John Weisman, Shadow Warrior (New York: Simon and Schuster, 1989), 220–21.

245 Milian tells a very different story: Milian Rodriguez, testimony before the Kerry Committee, February 11, 1988.

245 "I knew him by his real name: Luis Posada Carriles": Rodriguez, *Shadow Warrior*, 239.

Much of the information on Posada and his connections with the Mob, drugs, and the CIA comes from notes and memos by investigators for the House Select Committee on Assassinations, which examined Posada's CIA files as part of the 1970s reinvestigation of the Kennedy assassination. The files were released by the National Archives.

246 "Posada may have been moonlighting for Rosenthal": Posada's Mob ties appear in a June 26, 1967, memo for record regarding a DOJ investigation of Lefty Rosenthal. Other CIA memos reflecting that information were dated June 28, 1967. The memos make it clear Posada was being controlled by the Miami CIA office, JMWAVE, and at the same time was the subject of numerous investigative reports by the Bureau of Narcotics and Dangerous Drugs, the DEA's predecessor.

247 "get out of Venezuela and relocate in El Salvador": Posada's version of his arrival in El Salvador was contained in his interview by FBI agents Michael Foster and George Kiszynski for the Iran-Contra investigation, February 3, 1992, released to the author by the National Archives. His association with Col. Levia was contained in that and in a subsequent interview on March 16, 1992.

247 "seeking access to Ilopango": Charles Lane, "The Pilot Shark of El Salvador," *New Republic*, September 20, 1990.

248 How Chico Guirola wound up at Ilopango: The section on Chico Guirola was pieced together from several sources: Peter Cary, "Money Smuggling Charges Dropped Against Pilot," *Miami Herald*, June 13, 1985; David Sedeno, "Two Given Probation, Fine in Money-Smuggling Scheme," AP, June 13, 1985; "Boca Man, 2 Others Face Sentencing Today," *Miami Herald*, June 12, 1985; "2 Men Plead to Federal Charges of Trying to Smuggle $6 Million," *Miami Herald*, May 2, 1985; Frank Greve, "Some Latin Politicians Cashing In on Cocaine Smuggling Profits," *Miami Herald*, April 29, 1985; Craig Pyes and Laurie Becklund, "Inside Dope in El Salvador," *New Republic*, April 1985; John MacCormack, "US Hasn't Solved $6 Million Riddle," *Miami Herald*, March 11, 1985; "The Six Million Dollar Man," *Time*, March 4, 1985, 50; Laurie Becklund, "Illicit Money Figure Linked to D'Aubuisson," *L.A.*

Times, February 19, 1985; Joanne Omang, "D'Aubuisson Associate Arrested," *Washington Post*, February 16, 1985; "Bond Set for Smuggling Scheme Suspect," *Miami Herald*, February 12, 1985; and Phil Ward, "Men Nabbed in Money Smuggling Scheme," *Miami Herald*, February 8, 1985.

250 "Norwin was selling drugs": Enrique Miranda's testimony contained in Nicaraguan drug trafficking case against Norwin Meneses, filed in 1991. In addition to his court testimony, Miranda was interviewed extensively by Georg Hodel.

252 "drugs moved in and out": Fiers on Ilopango, interview with Iran-Contra investigators, 1991.

252 "adjoining hangars at Ilopango": Lawrence Walsh, *Firewall* (New York: Norton, 1997), 79.

252 "a very articulate individual": Memorandum from Walter E. Furr, Assistant U.S. Attorney, to Robert W. Merkle, United States Attorney, *Subject: Debriefing of Allen Raul Rudd with Regard to a Conversation with Pablo Escobar and Others regarding a Photograph*, February 18, 1988, released by National Archives.

254 Miami FBI informant, Wanda Palacios: Portions of the Wanda Palacios story reported in "Informant's Smuggling Tale Heart of WPLG Libel Trial," *Miami Herald*, July 22, 1991.

254 meeting with William Weld: The Weld meeting was detailed in Kerry aide Jonathan Winer's "Memorandum to File re: Meeting with William Weld," September 26, 1986.

255 Justice Department admitted there was no evidence: Justice Department memo from Blair Dorminey to Terry Eastland, *Subject: Difficulty in Obtaining Information from Official Sources on Cuban, Nicaraguan and Soviet Involvement in Drug Trafficking*, May 19, 1986, reprinted in the Kerry Report, 869–71.

255 a 1988 congressional investigation raised troubling questions: The hearings regarding the Seal sting were held by the Subcommittee on Crime of the House Judiciary Committee, July 28, September 23, 29, and October 5, 1988.

255 "house belonged to a U.S. Embassy employee": Larry Margasak, "DEA Agent: White House Leaked Cocaine Sting to Implicate Sandinistas," AP, July 28, 1988.

255 In March 1985 the CIA reported: Meneses and Vaughn relationship reported by CIA-IG, 48–49.

256 "no action is being taken": Letter from Stephen S. Trott, Associate Attorney General, to Guy L. Struve, Associate Independent

Counsel, March 29, 1988.

257 "drug trafficking activity would have been 'stumbled on'": CIA-IG, 38.

257 Walsh said he tried to stay away: Lawrence Walsh, interview by author.

257 "very dedicated DEA agent": Corr, interviewed in Dave Harmon "Ex-DEA Man Says US Ran Drugs-for-Guns Operation," *McAllen [Texas] Monitor*, January 24, 1993.

257 "End the Silence": Walsh, *Final Report of the Independent Counsel for Iran/Contra Matters*, August 4, 1993, 1:266.

258 "we're to stay out of it": Fiers testimony regarding Niner from *U.S. v. George*, July 28, 1992.

258 alleged CIA connections to the Camarena murder: "Coverup Alleged in Drug Agent's Death" *L.A. Times*, August 19, 1988; and "Trial in Camarena Case Shows DEA Anger at CIA," *Washington Post*, July 16, 1990.

259 Walter "Wally" Grasheim: Background obtained from December 13, 1990, interview of Grasheim by FBI Agent Michael Foster, for the Iran-Contra Independent Counsel. Grasheim was also interviewed by author.

259 "Some of the rooms in the house": Castillo, interview by FBI Agent Michael Foster on September 20, 1991, for the Iran-Contra Independent Counsel.

259 Grasheim... says that the weapons were legally his: Grasheim, interview by author.

260 "Word of this incident": Joel Brinkley, "Contra Arms Crews Said to Smuggle Drugs," *New York Times*, January 20, 1987. This is the first story ever to deal seriously with the Contra-drug issue; a follow-up was never printed.

261 1994 interview with the Associated Press: "North Knew About Drug Deals, Book Says," AP, August 3, 1994.

14. *"It's bigger than I can handle"*

262 Victor Gill: Details of the Gill investigation obtained during author's interviews with Jerry Guzzetta.

262 glowing piece in the *Los Angeles Times:* Jerry Belcher, "One-Man Narcotics Squad Cracks Major Drug Ring," *Los Angeles Times*, November 7, 1985.

263 loose cannon and a publicity hound: Complaints about Guzzetta

were contained in interviews done with current and former Bell PD officers by LACSO investigators in 1996.

263 "He hated dope dealers": Tom McReynolds, interview by Lt. Michael Bornman, LACSO, November 20, 1996.

263 "did some very good work together": Retired U.S. Customs agent Fred Ghio, interview by Sgt. Axel Anderson, LACSO, November 18, 1996.

264 Guzzetta and the federal agents began debriefing the brothers: During the investigation in which the Torres brothers served as informants, Guzzetta prepared a series of debriefings and progress reports under the code name "Project Sahara." The LACSO detectives found some of the reports, which were released as exhibits to the LACSO report in late 1996 and cited here. But Guzzetta insists that many additional "Project Sahara" reports have been suppressed or destroyed. Indeed, some of the reports that were released reference other, earlier reports that were never released. In addition, it is obvious that some of the released reports once contained additional pages that are missing. Guzzetta said most of the missing reports dealt with the Contras.

266 "reliability of the CI has been substantiated": Ghio's statements were contained in a U.S. Customs Service "Significant Activity Report" dated August 9, 1986, case LA02PR6LA005. It was released as an exhibit to the LACSO report.

267 Roberto Orlando Murillo, the uncle of Blandón's wife: Orlando Murillo's background came from his Uniform Application for Securities Industry Registration dated July 24, 1984, on file with the Florida Comptroller's Office, file 018432, and from interviews with Murillo by the author and Georg Hodel.

268 "cream of the crop": Jay Lichtman's quote appeared in Victor Merina, "Deputies Portrayed as Criminals," *Los Angeles Times*, October 12, 1990.

268 a hard man to impress: Tom Gordon, interview by author.

268 one of the biggest cases he'd ever handled: Lt. Dale Gene (Mike) Fossey, interview by Sgts. David Silversparre and Robert Rifkin, LACSO, October 22, 1996.

269 "We haven't encountered any major network": "New York City Being Swamped by Crack," *Los Angeles Times*, August 1, 1986.

269 Robert Stutman, the head of the DEA office: Robert Stutman and Richard Esposito, *Dead on Delivery* (New York: Warner Books, 1992), 213.

15. *"This thing is a tidal wave"*

271 "fueled with evocative words such as 'epidemic'": Donna M. Hartman and Andrew L. Golub, *The Social Construction of the Crack Epidemic in the Print Media*, monograph, John Jay College of Criminal Justice, March 10, 1997. Other academic studies relied on by the author in describing the media hysteria in the summer of 1986 are Craig Reinarman and Harry G. Levine, "Crack in Context: Politics and Media in the Making of a Drug Scare," *Contemporary Drug Problems*, winter 1989, 535; Steven Belenko, *Crack and the Evolution of Anti-Drug Policy* (Westport, Conn.: Greenwood Press, 1993); and James Inciardi, "Beyond Cocaine: Basuco, Crack and Other Coca Products," *Contemporary Drug Problems*, fall 1987, 461.

271 "a suddenness unprecedented": Sam Nunn's comments were made during a July 15, 1986, hearing of the Permanent Subcommittee on Investigations of the Senate Committee on Governmental Affairs.

271 "never heard of crack": Lawton Chiles's comments were made at the same hearing.

272 "nine months ago, addiction to crack was virtually unheard of": Hamilton Fish, at a Joint Hearing on the Select Committee on Narcotics Abuse and Control and the Select Committee on Children, Youth and Families, July 15, 1986.

272 "We have not had enough time elapse": Charles Schuster testified at the Senate crack hearings, cited above.

272 "crack has emerged": David Westrate testified at the House crack hearings.

272 "We have no current data, is that correct?": The dialogue between Benjamin Gilman and the experts took place at the House crack hearings.

273 "it was going to be the use of free-base cocaine": Robert Byck testified at the Senate crack hearings.

274 "that 50 is the number that got doubled": Robert Byck, interview by author.

274 "real vacuum of knowledge": Belenko, *Crack and the Evolution*, 8.

274 "a hoax": Chicago reseacher quote in Inciardi, "Beyond Cocaine," 484.

274 "phenomenon isolated to the inner cities": Ibid.

275 "least-used drug": Belenko, *Crack and the Evolution*, 13.

275 In Miami…few cocaine customers wanted crack: "94 Arrested in Drug Sting," Miami Herald, April 4, 1986.

275 "growing public outcry": *New York Times*, June 27, 1986. The *Times*'s stories on Reagan and crack appeared July 9, July 11, July 12, July 29, July 31, August 5, and August 7. The "frenzy" comment appeared August 10.

276 "just in time for a crucial election": Reinarman and Levine, "Crack in Context," 563.

276 Robert Stutman, chief of: Robert Stutman and Richard Esposito, *Dead on Delivery* (New York: Warner Books, 1992), 217–19.

277 "those who stand to gain the most": Golub and Hartman, *Social Construction of Crack.*

277 "quietly disbanding": "Police Quietly Disbanding South LA Anti-Drug Unit," *L.A. Times*, October 11, 1986.

278 "They didn't treat it like a major issue": Jack Lawn, cited in *U.S. News and World Report*, August 19, 1991.

280 "obvious intent of Senator Kerry": Memo from Ken Bergquist to Trott, *Subject: Upcoming "Contra" Hearings in the Senate Foreign Relations Committee*, May 13, 1986, reprinted in Kerry Report, 531. Bergquist was also in contact with San Francisco U.S. attorney Joe Russoniello, who'd collaborated with the CIA to keep the details of the Frogman case from becoming public. Bergquist's contacts with Russoniello were reported in an interview of Justice Department official Mark M. Richard, December 31, 1988, by FBI agent Michael Foster of the Walsh investigative team.

280 head off any attempt to obtain certain records: The attempts to discredit Kerry's witnesses and investigators and to stonewall the investigation reported in Kerry Report, 147–67; and in Peter Dale Scott and Jonathan Marshall, *Cocaine Politics* (Berkeley: University of California Press, 1991), 125–64.

280 broke the story of the Frogman case: Seth Rosenfeld, "Big Bay Area Cocaine Ring Tied to Contras," *San Francisco Examiner*, March 16, 1986.

281 "one of the most blatant attempts at contrived news-making": Russoniello's letter reprinted in Kerry Report, 396.

281 White Paper subsequently circulated to Congress: State Department document, July 26, 1986, *Allegations of Drug Trafficking and the Nicaraguan Democratic Resistance*, reprinted in Kerry Report, 266.

281 interview with former Contra official Leonardo Zeledon Rodriguez: United Press International, April 26, 1986, in a 320-word story datelined Tegucigalpa, Honduras. Few, if any, U.S. newspapers carried the UPI report.

282 "We had a terrible, terrible time getting information": Jack Blum, interview by author.

282 "Justice never provided": Page from North's diary on file at National Security Archives, Washington, D.C.

16. *"It's a burn"*

283 Jaime Ramos: Details of the Ramos investigation were contained in Guzzetta's "Project Sahara" reports and in *People v. Ramos et al.*, A789038, L.A. Superior Court.

284 asked the Torres brothers to show him around South Central: Guzzetta's trip to South Central with the Torreses was detailed in "Project Sahara" report, September 11, 1986.

285 Edner confirmed that "Freeway Rick" had a name: John Edner's investigation of Ross was contained in an affidavit for a search warrant filed by Sgt. Robert Tolmaire, March 1987.

285 "Mauldin showed up": The Stubblefield search was discussed by Sgt. Robert Sobel during his June 15, 1988, interrogation by LACSO Internal Affairs Sgt. James Mulay.

285 both specifically denied: Newell's and Ross's denials of a connection to Ramos were contained in "Interview of Ollie Newell" by Sgt. Paul Mondry and Sgt. Susan St. Marie, August 14, 1990, and "Interview of Witness Ricky Donnell Ross," by Sgt. Mondry, November 15, 1990, conducted in connection with an Internal Affairs investigation into the Ramos case, file 490-00057-3010-444. Released as exhibits to LACSO report.

287 The NADDIS reports were released as exhibits to the LACSO report, 1996.

288 "It's a burn": The phone message from González was released as an exhibit to the LACSO report.

289 Schrettner had debriefed a Nicaraguan informant: Thomas Schrettner, DEA-6, *Debriefing of SRP-86-0018, August 25-27, 1986,* file GFRP-86-4020, released as exhibit to LACSO report. The DEA has refused to release any other documents from that file, citing concerns over Blandón's privacy.

291 "his informant had told him": Sgt. Joseph Hartshorne, *Statements from DEA Agent Thomas Schrettner,* November 15, 1996, released as exhibit to LACSO report.

291 "some of the proceeds from the sale of cocaine": by Sgt. Hartshorne, *Interview of FBI Special Agent Douglas Aukland,* November 18, 1996, released as exhibit to LACSO report.

291 "The allegations were": Sgt. David Silversparre and Sgt. Robert Rifkin, *Interview of Retired Lieutenant Dale (Mike) Fossey #029600,* October 22, 1996, released as exhibit to LACSO report.

292 "FBI might 'burn' them": Sgts. Rifkin and Silversparre, *Interview of Retired Captain Robert Wilber,* October 18, 1996, released as exhibit to LACSO report.

17. *"We're going to blow your fucking head off"*

293 Joseph Kelso, an undercover informant: The Kelso case was discussed in *Additional Views of Honorable Peter W. Rodino Jr., Honorable Dante B. Fascell, Vice Chairman, Honorable Jack Brooks and Honorable Louis Stokes: Report of the Congressional Committees Investigating the Iran-Contra Affair* (Washington, D.C.: Government Printing Office, 1987), 643.

Most of the details of Kelso's misadventures in Costa Rica were obtained from his three-volume deposition in the case *Avirgan v. Hull,* Civil Action 86-1146 and 87-1545, U.S. District Court, Southern District of Florida, May 23, 1988. Kelso was also interviewed by the author.

294 German-born arms dealer...named Heinrich Rupp: For a fuller discussion of Rupp's mysterious activities in Colorado, see Stephen Pizzo, Mary Fricker, and Paul Muolo, *Inside Job: The Looting of America's Savings and Loans* (New York: HarperPerennial, 1991),182–86.

294 arrested in 1983 by the U.S. Customs Service: Mark Thomas, "2 Plead Guilty in Try to Sell Missiles to Iraq," *Rocky Mountain News,* March 23, 1983; Sue Lindsay, "2 Fined, Put on Probation for Plan to Sell Arms to Iraq," *Rocky Mountain News,* May 4, 1983.

297 some DEA records concerning Kelso: The existence of DEA records regarding Kelso is evidenced in the footnotes to the Rodino minority report and from an interview the author conducted with former Iran-Contra attorney Pam Naughton, who viewed the records.

297 "both Nieves and Sandy González were connected with the CIA":

Gloria Navas, interview by author and Georg Hodel.

"Sometimes the lines really got blurred": Pam Naughton, interview by author.

The notion of CIA agents using DEA offices as cover is well grounded in recent history. See *Report to the President by the Commission on CIA Activities within the United States*, June 1975, 233–34; Paul Heagen, "CIA 'Using Drug Agency Cover,'" *Long Beach Press Telegram*, March 16, 1975, A3; "53 Ex-CIA Employes Now in Drug Bureau," *Orange County Register*, January 26, 1975, A6; and "Weicker Reports Exhibit of Tools for Assassinations," *L.A. Times*, January 24, 1975.

298 Kelso stole Agent Nieves's briefcase: Customs agent Gary Hilberry reported this allegation during an interview with the author.

298 "Mr. LaDodge had received": All quotes from William Rosenblatt are contained in his once Top Secret deposition to the House Select Committee to Investigate Covert Arms Transactions with Iran, September 25, 1987.

300 "Nieves did not disguise his anger": Guillermo Fernández, "Informants provoke conflict between U.S. agencies," *La Nacion*, December 3, 1986, 8A.

300 Owen, in a deposition, admitted being in Costa Rica": Rob Owen was questioned extensively about the Kelso incident during his deposition in *Avirgan v. Hull*, February 8, 1988. Owen was also questioned about the Kelso case during his deposition to Senate Select Committee to Investigate Covert Arms Transactions with Iran, May 4, 1987.

301 "maps of coke lab locations": John Hull's report on Kelso visit released as an exhibit to the final Iran-Contra congressional report. Hull was interviewed by the author.

304 North knew all about the Kelso affair: North's knowledge of the Kelso affair is documented in his notebook entries for August 26, August 27, and August 28, 1986, in which Kelso's name appears, along with Gary Hilberry's name and phone number.

305 "They were thrown out": Owen's testimony about disposing of the Kelso tapes was contained in his deposition in *Avirgan v. Hull*.

305 charged with violating his probation: Kelso's arrest upon his return to the U.S., his court appearances, and subsequent events are chronicled in Sue Lindsay, "Man Claiming CIA Link Sentenced," *Rocky Mountain News*, February 24, 1987; and Lindsay, "Man Citing Betrayal by CIA Tells Story," *Rocky Mountain News*, March 1, 1987.

306 attempt to help an Italian financier buy MGM studios: Alan Citron and Michael Cieply, "Financing Details Add Bizarre Twist to MGM Saga," *Los Angeles Times*, April 24, 1991.

306 went to work for...Guardian Technologies: Nieves was contacted at the offices of Guardian Technologies by the author but he declined to answer questions.

18. "We bust our ass and the government's involved"

307 Sergeant Tom Gordon...applied for a warrant: Copy of search warrant and affidavit provided to author by source.

308 "'clean pockets'": Alan Fiers's testimony delivered during *U.S. v. George*, July 28, 1992.

310 "a 30 day investigation will culminate": *Background and Operational Plan*, undated, released as exhibit to LACSO report.

310 "pretty bitchin'...doing it anyway": William Wolfbrandt, interview by Sgts. Rifkin and Silversparre, October 28, 1996, exhibit to LACSO report.

310 "there may be a CIA link": Mike Fossey, LACSO interview.

310 "U.S. government backed the operation": Virgil Bartlett, interview by Sgt. Hartshorne and Sgt. Daniel S. Cruz, October 16, 1996, exhibit to LACSO report.

311 "strange that federal agents": Jerry Guzzetta was interviewed on three separate occasions—October 6, November 5, and November 23, 1996—by LACSO investigators.

311 "never seen the likes of it": Blandón's neighbor, who refused to give her name, was interviewed by the author.

311 Descriptions of the raids were based upon the individual reports filed by the raid teams, which were released as exhibits to the LACSO report, and the author's interviews with some of the raid team members. The items seized were listed in inventories, which were also released with the LACSO report.

313 "at least one 1-ton delivery": Blandón's comments regarding Aparicio Moreno in CIA-IG, 69.

313 murder of an American innkeeper: "Panel Says CIA agents in Guatemala Linked to Rights Abuses," AP, June 28, 1996; and "Washington: Guatemala Hid Evidence of Abuse of U.S. Citizens," AP, May 7, 1996.

313 Castillo believes Devine was killed by Guatemalan soldiers: Frank Smyth, "My Enemy's Friends," *New Republic*, June 5, 1995.

313 Castillo reported Moreno's activities in Guatemala: DEA-6, file TG-88-009, May 2, 1988. The DEA released a heavily censored copy of that report to the author. Castillo disclosed its contents to the author in an interview.

313 Juarez and his crew raced over: Juarez's raid report released as exhibit to LACSO report. Juarez was also interviewed about the raid by Sgts. Michael Bornman and Daniel Cruz, October 18, 1996, summary released with LACSO report.

314 "I got power!": Sgt. Art Fransen, interview by Sgts. Rifkin and Silversparre, October 31, 1996, exhibit to LACSO report.

314 "There's a bigger picture here": Richard Love, interview by Sgts. Rifkin and Silversparre on October 17, 1996, LACSO exhibit.

315 Master Narcotics Evidence Control ledger: Released as exhibit to LACSO report.

315 case chronology prepared in late 1986: Released as exhibit to LACSO report.

316 "Blandón simply smiled": Lister's comments to the CIA about the raid are found at 57, CIA-IG.

316 "a clumsy investigation": L. J. O'Neale, interview by Sgts. Rifkin and Silversparre, November 7, 1996, LACSO exhibit.

316 "Department of Defense codes": John Hurtado, interview by Sgts. Cruz and Hartshorne, October 25, 1996, LACSO exhibit.

316 "transporting weapons": Dan Garner, interview by Sgts. Cruz and Hartshorne, October 10, 1996, LACSO exhibit.

317 a sheaf of handwritten papers: Lister's notes had been kept sealed by federal judge Ed Rafeedie from 1990 to 1996, when he released them in response to the "Dark Alliance" series.

318 "Manuel Gómez was found murdered": Sgts. Cruz and Anderson, *Additional Information Regarding Manuel Antonio Gomes*, November 6, 1996, LACSO exhibit; Gómez's Certificate of Death, L.A. County Coroner, February 16, 1993; Sgt. Hartshorne, *Interview with Cynthia Juarez*, October 16, 1996, LACSO exhibit.

For additional information on Salvadoran death squad activities in L.A., see Dennis Bernstein and Connie Blitt, "Death Squad–Style Violence Haunts Salvadoran Organizers in the U.S.," *In These Times*, July 22–August 4, 1987.

318 "vile, vicious son of a bitch": Bradley Brunon, interview by author.

319 "CIA kinda winks at that activity": Brunon's CIA conversation with Huffman was memorialized in a handwritten chronology of events Huffman prepared in November 1986, released as a LACSO exhibit.

Huffman confirmed the conversation in an interview with Sgts. Anderson and Bornman, October 29, 1996, LACSO exhibit; and FBI teletype from SAC, Los Angeles, to Director FBI, *Subject: Front Door, Major Case 90,* December 12, 1986, declassified and released to author by National Archives. After admitting it to the author, Brunon denied the conversation took place when questioned by LACSO.

319 "We bust our ass": Sgts. Rifkin and Silversparre, *Interview of Retired Captain Robert Wilber,* October 18, 1996, released as exhibit to LACSO report.

319 "Three Persons Claiming CIA Affiliation": CIA cable filed in *U.S. v. James.*

321 "If he was a major trafficker": Brian Leighton, interview by author.

322 John M. Garrisi had been charged: Details about Garrisi were found in *In the Matter of John Mark Garrisi, A Member of the State Bar,* 87-E-03-LA, Decision of State Bar Court, Los Angeles, April 13, 1987; "L.A. Lawyer Gets Year in Prison for Visa Fraud," UPI, September 26, 1987; "Lawyer Sentenced for Iranian Immigration Scheme," AP, September 25, 1987.

322 Garrisi had "a pipeline": Roy Koletsky, interview by author.

323 December 8, 1986, teletype: "Re Butelcal SSA [deleted] LA, SSA [deleted] FBIHQ," released by the National Archives to Nick Schou.

323 director of the FBI sent a long teletype: teletype to CIA and DIA dated December 11, 1986, filed in *U.S. v. James,* by the CIA.

323 Douglas Aukland questioned Lister's…real estate agent: "immediate" FBI teletype from LA to FBI headquarters, December 12, 1986.

324 "Scott Weekly is an arms dealer": Huffman's notes, "Mtg @ D.D.A. Susan Deason's office, 1100 hrs, 1-14-87," were released as exhibits to LACSO report.

19. *"He reports to people reporting to Bush"*

325 Scott Weekly: Details of Weekly's background and 1983 POW hunt compiled from following sources: "Thais Vow to Arrest Green Beret POW hunter," UPI, February 21, 1983; "Gritz Says He's on Another Mission to Rescue POWs in Laos," AP, February 21, 1983; untitled story, UPI, a.m. cycle, March 2, 1983; untitled story, UPI, p.m. cycle, March 2, 1983; John Hail, "We Came Because We Believe," UPI, March 4, 1983; John Laird, "Americans Plead Guilty in Thai Court,"

AP, March 11, 1983; "Gritz Receives Suspended Sentence," *Facts on File*, April 8, 1983, 242; "Gritz Leaves Thailand," AP, June 9, 1983.

325 "Scott's kind of a tough little guy": Lynn Ball, interview by author.

325 "combination between John Wayne and Rambo": David Booth, speaking at Weekly's sentencing on April 29, 1987, in *U.S. v. Weekly*, 86 CR 281A, U.S. District Court, Western District of Oklahoma.

325 "large number of demerits": Weekly's statements about the Naval Academy, Weekly's sentencing.

326 "tens of thousands of dollars' worth": Steven Emerson, *Secret Warriors* (New York: G. P. Putnam's Sons, 1988), 79.

326 "Grand Eagle" was officially shelved: James Gritz, testimony at hearing before the Subcommittee on Asian and Pacific Affairs of the House Committee on Foreign Affairs, March 22, 1983.

326 "Department of Defense organization": Paulson, testimony at Subcommittee on Asian and Pacific Affairs hearing.

327 "with at least initial support": Jack Anderson, "Search for POWs in Laos Linked to CIA," *Washington Post*, October 15, 1984.

327 "had some ties to the CIA": CIA involvement with Ronald Ray Rewald reported in Howard Kurtz, "CIA Got IRS to Delay Audit; Intelligence Agency Was Probing Its Ties to Investment Firm," *Washington Post*, December 27, 1984; and Howard Kurtz, "Closed Hearing Set on CIA's Sporkin," *Washington Post*, October 4, 1985.

328 "if he was in the CIA, he wouldn't tell me": Weekly, interview by Lt. Michael Bornman, November 18, 1996, LACSO exhibit.

328 "suddenly exclaimed, 'Whoa!'": Sgt. Daniel Cruz, *Contact with Department of Veteran's Affairs*, November 8, 1996, LACSO exhibit.

328 "international munitions deals": John Kellogg, testimony at Weekly's resentencing, *U.S. v. Weekly*, July 15, 1988. See also John Standefer, "Afghan War Claims Victim in County," *San Diego Union Tribune*, July 26, 1987; Ray Robinson, "Indictment Likely in Case," *Daily Oklahoman*, July 19, 1987; "'Bo' Gritz Trained Rebels in Nevada Desert," UPI, May 1, 1987; Ray Robinson, "Man Pleads Guilty to Shipping Explosives," *Daily Oklahoman*, December 30, 1986; and Ray Robinson, "Sooner Explosives Aided Afghans," *Daily Oklahoman*, April 30, 1987.

329 Gene Wheaton: Wheaton, interview by author.

329 "paramilitary covert action program": Fiers, interview by Walsh's FBI investigator, August 2, 1991; a summary was declassified and released to the author by the National Archives.

329 "keeping in touch with DOD": William Schneider, interview by FBI

agents working for Lawrence Walsh, January 27, 1988; a summary of the interview was declassified and released to the author by the National Archives.

330 "North did refer to going to jail": Nestor Pino Marina, interview by FBI, December 2, 1987, declassified and released to author by the National Archives.

330 Pino...has a history of involvement with the CIA: Record of interview, Nestor Pino Marina, May 20, 1987, by Walsh's investigators, released by National Archives.

330 Pino's relationship with Bustillo reported by FBI Special Agent Michael Foster in a May 20, 1991, report to the Walsh investigation, released by the National Archives.

330 Bode's desk calendars: Released to the author by the National Archives.

330 "I've worked for intelligence agencies": James Gritz, testimony at Weekly's resentencing hearing.

331 "The Afghan program is a covert program": William R. Bode, interviewed in Standefer, "Afghan War Claims Victim."

331 "miscellaneous projects": Albert Hakim, deposition to Iran-Contra committee, May 1987.

331 "She was sitting in her apartment": Stephen Korotash, interview by author.

332 Weld's notes of the briefing: Iran-Contra files of Lawrence Walsh, released by the National Archives.

332 "proceed with such cases?": Bill Price, interview by author.

332 Richard already had some background: Edward Spannaus, "How DOJ Official Mark Richard Won the CIA's Coverup Award," *Executive Intelligence Review*, July 7, 1995, 73–75.

333 Richard was grilled about that briefing: Deposition of Mark Richard before the House and Senate Select Committees, August 19, 1987. The notes of Richard's conversations with Price were attached as exhibits to the deposition.

334 "from Oliver North upwards": Lawrence Walsh, interview by author.

334 federal prisoner, José Bueso Rosa: Information on Bueso Rosa compiled from Warren Fiske, "What did North know?" *Norfolk Virginian Pilot*, October 22, 1994; Jefferson Morley and Murray Waas, "A Favor for a Felon," *Washington Post*, May 29, 1994; Jefferson Morley, "Dealing with Noriega," *Nation*, August 27, 1988; Murray Kempton, "Panama's High Finance," *Newsday*, February 7, 1988; Neil Roland, "North Tried to Hush Honduran," UPI,

November 22, 1987; Susan Rasky, "North Urged Leniency For Honduran Linked to Assassination Plot," *New York Times*, February 23, 1987; "Army Ex-Chief Sentenced in Coup Plot," *Facts on File*, September 5, 1986, 662; "Former General Sentenced in Assassination Plot," UPI, July 24, 1986; "General Arrested in Coup Plot," *Facts on File*, December 20, 1985, 954; "Honduras: Two Former Top Officers Dishonorably Discharged," Inter Press Service, November 5, 1985; Charles Babcock, "Account of Assassination Plot Reads Like TV Script," *Bergen Record*, August 16, 1985; and Oliver North's PROFS notes regarding the case, on file at the National Security Archives.

335 "triumph for the Administration's policy": Francis J. McNeil testified to the Kerry Committee about the Bueso Rosa case, April 4, 1988.

335 "Bueso Rosa…had information": Nestor Pino Marina, interview by FBI agents working for Walsh, May 13, 1987, released by the National Archives.

336 "in from one entrance and out the other": Mark Richard's statements about Weekly and Bueso Rosa were made under oath during in his August 19, 1987 deposition by the Iran-Contra committees.

337 Bode explained his involvement in the case to an FBI agent working for Walsh on November 2, 1987, and that interview was released by the National Archives.

337 CIA had equipped and trained…the 316 Battalion: Bueso Rosa, cited in Gary Cohn and Ginger Thompson, "Unearthed: CIA Secrets," *Baltimore Sun*, reprinted in the *Sacramento Bee*, July 30, 1995.

338 "this investigation would start and stop with me": Weekly testified at length at his resentencing hearing.

338 trekked into the mountains of northern Burma: "Thais: US Adventurer Turned Away," Reuters, September 6, 1986. Gritz's comments regarding Khun Sa were taken from a transcript of his videotape A *Nation Betrayed*, as well as from "Burmese Rebel Links Pentagon Official to Drug Deals," AP, June 5, 1987. His charges of retaliation were reported in an untitled UPI story dated July 19, 1987, datelined Oklahoma City.

340 Gritz was indicted…for misusing a passport: Penny Levin, "LV Grand Jury Indicts Gritz on Passport Misuse," *Las Vegas Sun*, May 21, 1987; Phil LaVelle, "Gritz Surrenders, Alleges U.S. Backing," *Las Vegas Review Journal*, June 4, 1987; and LaVelle, "Gritz Cites Conspiracy in Passport Rap," *Las Vegas Review Journal*, June 6, 1987.

20. *"The Assistant U.S. Attorney was found dead"*

341 Susan Bryant-Deason…told police: Curtis A. Hazell, Head Deputy, Major Narcotics and Forfeiture Division, "Confidential Memorandum to File," Subject: Blandón Investigation," October 16, 1996, LACSO exhibit; and R. Dan Murphy, Assistant District Attorney, to Capt. Neal B. Tyler, confidential letter, October 23, 1996, LACSO exhibit.

342 "We went as far as we could": Ed Huffman, interview by LACSO investigators.

342 "one of the most senior attorneys": Description of Darrell MacIntyre's experience and assignments from untitled UPI report, December 28, 1986; and *Los Angeles Times*, December 30, 1986.

342 he had prosecuted the L.A. end of the Frogman case: Untitled UPI report, April 21, 1984.

343 Darrell MacIntyre's body was found: Untitled AP report, December 29, 1986; two UPI reports, December 28, 1986, one titled "Prosecutor Death Apparent Suicide"; and "Pacific Palisades Death of a Prosecutor a Suicide, US Attorney's Office Says," *L.A. Times*, December 30, 1986. (Amazingly, when Sheriff Sherman Block's investigators heard about the suicide during their 1996 reinvestigation of the Blandón raids, they reported that there was no documentary evidence that it had ever happened, possibly because they had misspelled both the first and last name of the prosecutor.)

343 One of MacIntyre's friends: Curtis Rappe, interview by author.

344 Steven Carr: Kerry Report, 152–53, 158, 161; "Cause Not Found in Contra Case Witness Death," *L.A. Times*, December 16, 1986; UPI story, January 22, 1987; "An American Contra: The Confused Life and Mysterious Death of Steven Carr," *Los Angeles Times Magazine*, May 31, 1987. The latter contained the quote from detective Mel Arnold.

345 Huffman would later say: Huffman interview, LACSO report.

346 "Back then Ricky Ross was a major dealer": Robert Sobel, Internal Affairs interview.

347 "Ross was a vital link": Glenn A. Levant, LAPD intradepartmental memo to Detective Steven Polak, *Commendation LASD/LAPD Rock Cocaine Supplier Task Force*, January 13, 1988.

347 Freeway Rick Task Force: Steve Polak, interview by author; and Polak, "Fact Sheet re: Full Cash Overtime for Major FES Narcotics Div.," January 1987.

347 "All of his locations": LACSO internal affairs interview of Sobel, June 15, 1988.

347 "He's become quite a heavyweight": Sandy Wasson, quoted in "Drug Fugitive Captured in Closet," UPI, November 30, 1989.

347 "He was a *good* bad guy": ABC News, *Day One*, "The Crime Crisis: Freeway," November 29, 1993.

348 "Robin Hood–type guy": James Galipeau, cited in Jesse Katz, "Deposed King of Crack," *L.A. Times*, December 20, 1994.

349 "He kind of fancied himself": Daryl Kelley and Victor Merina, "Query Focuses on Sheriff's Sergeant, Deputies He Led," *Los Angeles Times*, November 16, 1989.

349 "What he did, he poisoned tens of thousands of people": Steve Polak, interview by author.

349 Polak and his men hit the Freeway Motor Inn: "Rock Cocaine Supplier LAPD/LASD Task Force Weekly Activities Report 1-21-87 through 1-27-87."

350 "Going after my mom": Ross, interview by author. Details of the detention of Annie Ross came from Sobel's LACSO internal affairs interview, June 15, 1988.

350 "a cartel": Sobel, LACSO internal affairs interview.

350 "your wife will be in a psychiatric hospital": Blandón, testimony in *U.S. v. James*.

350 "widespread patronage from the Latin community": Bradley Brunon, quoted in transcript of a May 20, 1992, detention hearing, *U.S. v. Blandón.*

351 "Roger Sandino was one of these guys": Brunon, interview by author.

352 Sandino was arrested: Cable from DEA Miami F/O to DEA HQS, October 27, 1980, file G1-81-0002.

352 set up an import-export business: Corporate records of Rosamar International Trading Inc., H26741, on file at Florida Division of Corporation. The attorney who served as Sandino's agent, John Spittler Jr., was also an officer in Inter-America Media Corp. and the agent for Los Ranchos De Miami Inc.

352 busted again in April 1986: The Norfolk, Virginia, bust was described in Dorothy Gast, "700-pound Cocaine Bust Called Largest Ever in Mid-Atlantic," AP, April 8, 1986.

352 DEA issued a fugitive warrant: Sandino's "Fugitive Declaration," filed by DEA on January 12, 1987, DEA file GZ-86-0002.

352 the missing fifty-two pounds: Pete Yost, "DEA Official Says

Cocaine to Panamanian Police was Properly Used," AP, February 18, 1988.

353 "Everywhere you go": Jerome H. Skolnick, *The Social Structure of Street Drug Dealing* (State of California, Office of the Attorney General, 1988); and Skolnick, *Gang Organization and Migration* (State of California, Office of the Attorney General, 1989).

354 "Gang members have flooded the market": Bill Bryan, "Police Fighting a Rising Drug Tide," *St. Louis Post-Dispatch*, March 12, 1989.

354 Brian "Waterhead Bo" Bennett: "Arrests Cut Key Cocaine Link in L.A., Police Say," *Los Angeles Times*, November 30, 1988; Ross, 1996 LACSO interview; and files from *U.S. v. Villabona*, 88 CR 972b, Central District of California, provided to the author by Mario Villabona. In his appeal, Villabona claimed he was set up for arrest by a CIA informant and former Contra, William Guzman.

355 plunged a knife into the doll's head: U.S. Department of Justice's trial memorandum, August 30, 1991, in *U.S. vs. Amers*, 90 CR 111.

355 "jokes about the dope they had ready": Sobel's comments regarding Polak and the planting of cocaine came from "Inquiry into LAPD May Jeopardize Drug Cases," *L.A. Times*, October 3, 1990.

355 "I looked in the rearview mirror": Details of the April 1987 shooting incident were gleaned from Ross's testimony, *U.S. v. James*; Sobel, 1988 interview with the Sheriff's IA investigators; and the 1991 DOJ trial memorandum in *U.S. vs. Amers*.

356 The LAPD issued a press release: "Fact Sheet for Immediate Release," Los Angeles Police Department Narcotics Division, May 18, 1987.

356 dropped by the jail to inspect their prize: U.S. DOJ trial memorandum, August 30, 1991, 24, filed in *U.S. vs. Amers*. Additional details obtained during interviews with Ross and Alan Fenster; and Kelley and Merina, "Query Focuses on Sheriff's Sergeant."

21. *"I could go anywhere in the world and sell dope"*

358 "It was real cool": Quotes from Ross through this chapter came from interviews with the author and his testimony in *U.S. v. James*.

359 Macario was deeply involved with the FDN: José Macario Estrada, interview by author.

360 attorney Carlos Icaza: Information regarding Carlos Icaza was obtained during interviews with Icaza by author and Georg Hodel.

His alleged involvement with the CIA was reported in "Nicaragua Charges CIA Plot, Expels Diplomats; U.S. Retaliates," *Facts on File*, June 10, 1983, 423; and *CIA Conspiracy in Nicaragua*, June 1983, a booklet provided to the press by the Nicarguan government at the press conference announcing the arrests.

His and his wife's involvement with the FDN was reported in "Bomb Explodes Outside Home of Contra Spokeswoman," AP, March 6, 1987; and "Home of Nicaraguan Rebel Spokeswoman Bombed," Reuters, March 6, 1987.

360 Macario was appointed to a blue-ribbon commission by the FDN: Sandra Dibble, "Contras Ask Panel to Audit Funds," *Miami Herald*, August 16, 1986.

361 restaurant became a hangout for Contra leaders: La Parrilla's use as a Contra forum reported in Maria Jose Cartagena, "Nicaraguans Seek to Ease Path for Fellow Exile Professionals," *Miami Herald*, December 20, 1987.

Restaurant reviews included: Lucy Cooper, "La Parrilla: Nicaraguan Food at Its Best," *Miami Herald*, October 24, 1986; Lucy Cooper, "Feast Your Fantasies at South Florida's Finest Restaurants," *Miami Herald*, January 2, 1987; Ivonne Rovira Kelly, "La Parrilla Makes a Name for Itself," *Miami Herald*, August 8, 1985; and Geoffrey Tomb, "The Good News, Part 3," *Miami Herald Tropic Magazine*, June 15, 1986.

361 Alpha II Rent-a-Car: *In re: Alpha II Rent-A-Car*, case 90-13670, Federal Bankruptcy Court, Miami, June 1, 1990.

362 "if the right person paged me, I'd get up": Jesse Katz, "Deposed King of Crack," *L.A. Times*, December 20, 1994.

362 "I knew the recipe": Al Salvato, "The Man Who Brought Crack to Town," *Cincinnati Post*, October 24, 1992. (Salvato was the author's journalism school professor in 1975.) An additional story containing information about Ross's operations in Cincinnati was: George Lecky, "Feds: Gang Leader Built Network in Cincinnati," *Cincinnati Post*, April 16, 1990.

363 "In 1987, we had lots of crack": Robert Enoch, quoted in Salvato, "Man Who Brought Crack."

363 "One day we woke up": D. Michael Crites, ibid.

363 "a guy who could sell Popsicles to an Eskimo": Ernest Halcon, quoted in Katz, "Deposed King of Crack."

363 Cincinnati authorities finally discovered: Details of the police investigation and the affair Ross's girlfriend had in Cincinnati were

contained in the U.S. Probation and Parole Commission's 1991 presentence report prepared for Ross's Cincinnati sentencing.

364 Smith County, Texas...indictment: Evan P. Kirvin, *Presentence Report*, U.S. District Court, Southern District of California, May 6, 1996, 11.

365 barricaded himself inside: "Police Corner Suspected Drug Dealer in Closet," *Los Angeles Times*, November 30, 1989.

366 stories about L.A. gangbangers: Some articles and studies describing the 1988–89 migration of Crips and Bloods from L.A. are Theresa Monsour, "Crip Gangs in St. Paul, Chief Says," *St. Paul Pioneer Press*, May 4, 1988; Lisa Levitt Ryckman, "Crips, Bloods Turn into Traveling Salesmen for Big Drug Money," AP, May 28, 1988; Jerry Nachtigal, "Police: L.A. Drug Gangs More Widespread Than Previously Thought," AP, July 15, 1988; Thom Gross, "L.A. Gangs Are Seen Here," *St. Louis Post Dispatch*, July 17, 1988; Denise Hamilton, "Study Tightly Links Gangs to Trafficking in Cocaine," *Los Angeles Times*, November 15, 1988; Robert C. Unruh, "Gang Problem Grows Deadlier in Denver," AP, December 5, 1988; and Michael J. Ybarra and Paul Leiberman, "U.S. Labels L.A. a Center of Drug Trade, Violence," *Los Angeles Times*, August 4, 1989.

366 "Los Angeles drug gangs are spreading cocaine": Nachtigan, "L.A. Drug Gangs More Widespread."

366 "Los Angeles has become the transshipment area": Jerry Harper, testimony in *Federal Law Enforcement Role in Narcotics Control in Southern California*, hearings of the House Select Committee on Narcotics Abuse and Control, August 23, 1988.

366 "these emerging modern day gangsters": Robert Bonner, testimony in *Organized Criminal Activity by Youth Gangs*, hearings of the Subcommittee on Criminal Justice of the House Judiciary Committee, June 6 and August 8, 1988.

22. *"They can't touch us"*

368 "They didn't ask me nothing about": Ricky Ross, interview by author. Unless otherwise noted, all quotes in this chapter from Ross are either from his interviews with the author, or from his testimony in *U.S. v. James*.

369 "Operation Big Spender": "Jury Views Video of Alleged Money-Skimming by Deputies," UPI, October 16, 1990; and an *L.A. Times* series by Victor Merina, December 1–3, 1993.

369 "This may be a terrible thing to say": "Deputies' Downfall Began with Videotaped Sting" *L.A. Times*, December 3, 1993.

369 an astonishing $33.9 million in cash: The figures from the forfeiture hauls came from LACSO.

370 "My men are all trained to tear flesh": Quote from Sobel in the newsletter reported by *Los Angeles Times*, December 1, 1993.

370 Polak had liposuction performed: The cosmetic surgery done by Polak and his wife was revealed in *U.S. v. Stephen W. Polak and Christina Townly*, 94 CR 283, April 15, 1994, Central District of California.

371 "Dan Garner came in my office": Harland Braun, interview by author.

371 casually asked if the agent knew anything: "Jury Sees Video of Deputies Taking Cash," *L.A. Times*, October 17, 1990; "Drug Cash Tied to Contras, CIA in L.A. Deputies' Trial," *San Diego Union-Tribune*, October 24, 1990; and "Judge Issues Gag Order on Lawyers, Defendants in Sheriff's Drug Case," UPI, October 24, 1990.

372 "publicized matters that are likely to…impair the rights": *Declaration of Thomas Hagemann*, filed in connection with "Government's Motion for Restraining Order Re: Extra-Judicial Statements of Parties and their Agents," filed October 19, 1990, *U.S. v. Amers*, 90 CR 111A, U.S. District Court, Central District of California.

372 "Films of military operations in Central America": Braun's writings from "Defendant Garner's Opposition to Government's Request for Restraining Order," filed October 23, 1990, *U.S. v. Amers*.

373 Justice Department fired back: "Motion in Limine Re: Admissibility of Defendant Garner's Testimony Re: Conversation with Robert Sobel and/or Others About the CIA," filed October 23, 1990, *U.S. v. Amers*.

374 Judge Rafeedie…lashed out at Braun: Transcript of the hearing, filed in *U.S. vs. Amers*.

375 "I didn't pump 500 tons of cocaine into the ghetto": Garner, interview by LACSO investigators..

376 having convinced the Costa Mesa detectives: The details of Lister's deal with Costa Mesa police are contained in a Memorandum of Understanding dated August 26, 1988, between Lister and the Orange County District Attorney's Office, filed in *People v. Ronald Jay Lister*, F13502, Harbor Municipal Court,

376 "Ball indicated that Lister": Meza's comments appeared in CIA-IG, 59–61.

377 "provided the government with a written chronological debriefing": "Appellant's Opening Brief," *U.S. v. Ronald Lister,* 92 CA 50116, U.S. Court of Appeals, Ninth Circuit, June 4, 1992; "Motion for Dismissal of Attorney and Return of Complete Case File," *U.S. v. Lister,* 89 CR 1084, U.S. District Court, Southern District of California, October 13, 1992.

378 "received instructions from Columbia to wire transfer the money": Lister's involvement with the Colombians while a DEA informant is revealed in a series of DEA-6 reports dated April 25, 1991, June 4, 1991, June 6, 1991, and June 10, 1991, filed as exhibits to LACSO case. Additional information is contained in Assistant U.S. Attorney L.J. O'Neale, "Government's Answer to Defendant's Objections to Presentence Report and Sentencing Memorandum," June 22, 1993, *U.S. v. Jose Enrique Urda Jr.,* 92 CR 1308, U.S. District Court, Southern District of California.

378 "'By the way, we want to kill this guy Lister'": Author interviewed the prosecutor who handled the case, who spoke on background.

379 a motion filed to cancel their deal and send Lister to prison: Assistant U.S. Attorney Amalia Meza, "Government's Motion to Seal Motion," July 16, 1991, *U.S. v. Lister.*

380 "Smith waxed at length": Gale Holland, "L.A. Drug Case Becomes Lurid," *San Diego Union Tribune,* October 6, 1991.

23. *"He had the backing of a superpower"*

382 "I did a lot of favors to the Colombians": Blandón GJ, 18.

383 Colombian Humberto Cardona: Blandón identified Cardona as one of his suppliers in two interviews with FBI agents Don Allen and Bruce Burroughs on October 8, 1992, and September 1, 1993, FBI file 245-B-SF-96287.

383 Sergio Guerra, the smooth Mexican millionaire: Guerra's background and holdings detailed in 1992 detention hearing in *U.S. v. Blandón.*

383 reunited with the Meneses family: Blandón's reinvolvement with Meneses and his kin was spelled out in his GJ testimony.

384 secret indictment against Meneses: *U.S. v. Juan Norwin Meneses Cantarero a/k/a Norwin Meneses,* 89 CR 0064, U.S. District Court, Northern District of California, filed February 8, 1989.

384 Neither Meneses's indictment nor the warrant was reported

to...NCIC: Douglass E. Beloof, deputy district attorney for Multnomah County (Oregon) to Cesar A. Aviles Haslam, consul general of Nicaragua, November 21, 1991. The letter, requested by Norwin's daughter, the wife of the governor of Oregon, states that "there is no criminal record of any kind involving this name and date of birth in the United States of America."

384 "it materialized that there was some information": Eric Swenson, interview by author.

385 "For seven years we were used": Tirzo Moreno, quoted in Rogelio Pardo-Maurer, *The Contras, 1980–1989* (New York: **Praeger**, 1990), 116.

385 Meneses...began reclaiming the holdings: The payments to Meneses and the other members of his drug ring were discovered by Georg Hodel, who obtained a November 30, 1996, report of Indemnification for Unjustified Confiscation from the Nicaraguan Ministry of Finance. Listed were convicted trafficker Luis Enrique Meneses ($930,000); Norwin's wife, Maritza, ($53,000), Troilo Sánchez ($353,000) and Horacio Pereira's heirs ($30,000.)

386 Enrique Miranda Jaime: Miranda was interviewed extensively by Georg Hodel and Hodel's wife, Carmen Maria Santos, who became Miranda's attorney upon his return to Nicaragua in 1996.

386 "sending guns to the FMLN in El Salvador": Meneses's statements concerning Miranda were contained in "Declaration to Investigators," November 20, 1991, filed in Nicaraguan Supreme Court.

386 Meneses "had on his payroll": Miranda's statement was handwritten and filed as an exhibit to the drug trafficking case against him in Nicaragua in 1992.

387 "you almost needed flatbed trucks": Rafael Corñejo, interview by author.

388 secretly taped...by DEA informant John Arman: The tapes of Arman's and Blandón's discussions were turned over to defense lawyers during Blandón's criminal case in San Diego in 1992 but never introduced into evidence. The author was permitted to hear and copy the tapes by a source who had access to them.

388 "Blandón is preparing to move back to Nicaragua": Chuck Jones, DEA-6, *Subject: Undercover Negotiations Between [deleted] and Suspect Danilo Blandón*, April 12, 1990.

389 Arman arrived at the Old Bonita Store...wired for sound: Chuck

Jones, DEA-6, *Subject: Undercover Meeting with Sergio Guerra and Oscar Blandón,* July 23, 1990. Author also has tape of the conversation.

391 "going to convert it to crack anyway": Chuck Jones, DEA-6, *Subject: Undercover Negotiations with Danilo Blandón,* June 14, 1991.

391 "They are going to put you in jail": Tapes of Blandón's conversations with Roger Sandino were obtained by author.

392 Sandino had given the DEA the slip: Chuck Jones, DEA-6, *Subject: Ongoing Undercover Negotiations and Surveillance of Danilo Blandón et al.*, September 15, 1991.

392 "He had a big wedding here": Roger Mayorga, interview by author and Georg Hodel.

392 golden opportunity to arrest Blandón: The incident at the border was described in *U.S. v Sergio Guerra-Deguer,* 91 CR 810T, U.S. District Court, Southern District of California, filed Aug 27, 1991.

393 "money orders were on their way to Mexico": O'Neale, comments during a detention hearing for Blandón in 1992, *U.S. v. Blandón,* cited earlier.

393 LAPD strike force arrested him: Described by O'Neale during detention hearing.

394 "I actually had a better case": Ron Hodges, interview by author.

394 Nicaraguan lawmen were after Norwin Meneses: Details of the Meneses investigation came from author's interviews with Mayorga, Rene Vivas, Miranda, Meneses, and Frank Vigil, and a review of the case files at the Nicaraguan Supreme Court.

394 Vivas…was well acquainted with Norwin: Rene Vivas, interview by author and Georg Hodel.

394 "She was something else": Roberto Vargas, interview by author and Georg Hodel.

395 story made several U.S. newspapers: "Record Cocaine Seizure," *L.A. Times*, November 5, 1991; and Jonathan Marshall, "Nicaraguans Arrest Ex-Bay Man Linked to Cocaine, Contras," *San Francisco Chronicle*, December 16, 1991.

395 According to two Nicaraguan prison officials: The prison officials were interviewed by Georg Hodel

399 The DOD and State Department cables concerning Meneses were mentioned in CIA-IG, 50–51.

401 "How do you explain…that Norwin Meneses": The judges' questioning of Mayorga was contained in "Declarcion Testifical,"

November 21, 1991, part of the case file in the Nicaraguan Supreme Court. Mayorga was also hauled before the Nicaraguan National Assembly's Committee on Defense and Government in late 1991 and grilled by Committee Chairman Frank Duarte, a friend and attorney of Meneses

401 paid a deranged inmate…to knife Miranda: The alleged assassination attempt was reported in "He Tried to Murder Miranda," *Barricada*, August 22, 1992; and "Miranda: 'Paragon para asesinarme," *El Nuevo Diario*, August 17, 1992.

401 Chamorro government fired Rene Vivas: Michael Reid, "Chamorro Fires Police Chief to Appease U.S.," *Manchester Guardian*, September 13, 1992; "Sandinista Police Officers Dismissed," *Facts on File*, September 17, 1992, 694; and Shirley Christian, "Managua Seesaw: U.S. vs. Sandinistas," *New York Times*, September 8, 1992.

24. *"They're gonna forget I was a drug dealer"*

402 The identity of the media representatives were contained in media permission requests in Ross's prison files from Phoenix, which Ross made available to the author.

402 "Soft-spoken": Erin J. Aubry, "Ex–Drug Dealer Out to Stage Turnaround," *L.A. Times*, November 14, 1993.

403 "A capitalist": Al Salvato, "The Man Who Brought Crack to Town," *Cincinnati Post*, October 24, 1992.

403 "Standing on the bare stage": Aubry, "Ex-Drug Dealer Out to Stage Turnaround."

404 "Next we have the story of a young man": Forrest Sawyer, correspondent for *Day One*, "Profile: Ex–Drug Dealer 'Freeway' Hopes to Offer Youth Center to South Central Los Angeles," November 29, 1993.

405 "more than 200 people": James Bolden, "Ricky Ross: Ex-Drug Lord Wants to Give Back to S. Central," *Los Angeles Sentinel*, December 9, 1993.

406 "The notorious Los Angeles drug lord": Jesse Katz, "Former L.A. Drug Kingpin Is Set Free," *Los Angeles Times*, September 1, 1994.

407 Compton crack dealer, Leroy "Chico" Brown: Brown, interview by author.

408 "get a little something right now": The tapes and transcripts of some of Ross's conversations with Blandón were introduced into evidence in *U.S. v. James*.

408 According to Blandón's notes: These notes were introduced into evidence in *U.S. v. James*.

408 "This guy won't leave me alone": James Galipeau, interview by author; Galipeau also testified as a defense witness for Ross in *U.S. v. James*.

408 "take care of Tony": The meetings in the restaurant parking lots were taped by Blandón, and the tapes were introduced as evidence in *U.S. v. James*.

409 "saga of Ricky Ross' rise and fall": Jesse Katz, "Deposed King of Crack," *L.A. Times*, December 20, 1994.

409 "Let him pay": Polak, quoted in Katz, "Deposed King of Crack."

412 "They burned rubber": Charles Jones, testimony before Grand Jury No. 94-4, U.S. District Court, Southern District of California, March 15, 1995.

413 Ross told them everything: Judy Gustafson, DEA-6, *Subject: Arrest and Interview of Ricky Ross*, March 7, 1995.

413 "I cussed his Mom out": Norman Tillman, quoted in Jesse Katz, "Sting Snares Drug Lord Who Vowed to Go Straight," *Los Angeles Times*, March 22, 1995.

413 "I caught a lot of shit": Jesse Katz, interview by author.

25. *"Things are moving all around us"*

The quotes in this chapter were largely taken from my interviews with the subjects mentioned, most of which were tape-recorded and later transcribed.

419 I walked into a roomful of agents: The quotes from this session come from a memorandum I prepared immediately following the meeting.

422 three CIA cables about me: CIA-IG, 51–52.

423 Georg's discoveries were front-page news: Roberto Orosco, "Escapo un grande del narcotrafico," *La Prensa*, November 29, 1995; and Heriberto Mercado, "Ex militar narco escapa de prision," *La Tribuna*, November 29, 1995.

424 Miranda was captured: Miranda, whose entry into the States was legal since he had a valid visa, was literally kidnapped by the FBI in Miami and thrown on a plane to Nicaragua at the request of the Nicaraguan police. His kidnapping was covered extensively in the Nicaraguan press. See, for example, Roberto Orosco, "Miranda,

gran jefe de la droga, enviado a Managua," *La Prensa,* December 3, 1996, 1; Lizbeth Garcia, "Recaptura de Miranda Jaime levanta ola de acusactiones," *Barricada,* December 22, 1996; Mario Guevara Somarriba, "Recapturan en Miami al reo Miranda Jaime," *El Nuevo Diario,* December 24, 1996; and Leonardo Coca Palacios, "Miranda Jaime se esfumo?" *El Nuevo Diario,* December 29, 1996. Miranda was finally released from prison in April 1998.

26. *"This matter, if true, would be classified"*

429 "The United States believes": L. J. O'Neale, "Government's Motion in Limine to Preclude Reference to the Central Intelligence Agency and for Reciprocal Discovery," February 26, 1996, filed in *U.S. v. James.*

430 The conversation was recorded: The sidebar discussions, as well as the testimony, in federal criminal trials are tape-recorded, and the tapes are available for purchase by any member of the public at remarkably reasonable rates, a service that court reporters, for obvious reasons, don't advertise. Thanks to federal public defender Maria Forde for this invaluable tip. The public defenders buy the tapes, she said, because they can't afford typed transcripts either.

431 "taught [Ross] the trade": Jesse Katz, "Drug Trial to Focus on Sting; DEA, Former Supplier Offer Glimpse into World of Informants," *Los Angeles Times*, March 5, 1996.

431 "I don't think my client's life": The in-court conversations in this chapter are taken from the tapes of the proceedings in *U.S. v. James*.

27. *"A very difficult decision"*

437 Interviews of the jurors provided to the author by a source.

442 *Mercury News* executive editor: Ceppos's comments to *Newsweek* reported in "Cracks in the Story," November 11, 1996, 65.

442 *New York Times* reporter Seymour Hersh: The reaction of the press to Hersh's story is chronicled in Kathryn S. Olmstead, Challenging the Secret Government (Chapel Hill: University of North Carolina Press, 1996), 33–39.

443 "The unlimited space of the Web": The chapter on online journalism in Encarta's 1997 yearbook was written by Neil Chase of Northwestern University.

445 The Associated Press noted: Elizabeth Weise, "CIA-Crack Story Fueled Interest in Web," AP, **December 5,** 1996.

445 A *Boston Globe* reporter: Adam Pertman, "CIA-Drug Link Stories Outrage Blacks in L.A.," *Boston Globe*, October 6, 1996.

446 infuriated the right-wing *Washington Times*: Bill Gertz, "Deutch's Reaction to Drug Rumor Hit," *Washington Times*, September 24, 1996.

446 And on the editorial page: Arnaud de Borchgrave, "Ritualistic Revival of Assaults on CIA," *Washington Times*, September 24, 1996.

446 *Newsweek* devoted an entire page: Gregory L. Vistica and Vern E. Smith, "Was the CIA Involved in the Crack Epidemic?" *Newsweek*, September 30, 1996, 72.

446 *Time* that month: Jack E. White,"Crack, Contras and Cyberspace," *Time*, September 30, 1996.

447 "Meanwhile, we continued advancing the story…": Gary Webb and Pamela Kramer, "Sealed records may show CIA drug link," *San Jose Mercury News*, Sept. 29, 1996, 1; Gary Webb and Pamela Kramer, "Affadavit: Cops knew of drug ring," *San Jose Mercury News*, Oct. 3, 1996, 1; Gary Webb and Pamela Kramer, "More hints of government involvement," *San Jose Mercury News*, Oct. 6, 1996, 1.

448 Eastland had a history: The Justice Department's role in spreading disinformation about Contra drug investigations in the mid-1980s is detailed in Joel Millman, "Narco-terrorism: A Tale of Two Stories," *Columbia Journalism Review*, September/October 1986, 51; and Peter Dale Scott and Jonathan Marshall, *Cocaine Politics* (Berkeley: University of California Press, 1991), 177.

448 The *Washington Post* had just moved a story: Roberto Suro and Walter Pincus, "The CIA and Crack: Evidence is Lacking of Alleged Plot," *Washington Post*, October 4, 1996.

450 Ceppos fired off a blistering letter: Though the *Post* didn't run it, the *Mercury News* posted the letter on the Internet on the Mercury Center's Dark Alliance Web page (www.sjmercury.com/drugs).

451 a story in the Mercury's archives: Walter Pincus, "How I Traveled Abroad on CIA Subsidy," *San Jose Mercury News*, February 18, 1967.

451 Pincus's previous association with the CIA: Pincus, review of Agee's book, *New York Times Book Review*, August 3, 1975.

451 "we have withheld a great deal of information": Pincus's appearance on the *MacNeil/Lehrer NewsHour* occurred on May 12, 1986.

451 Walsh wrote that at a critical moment: Lawrence Walsh, *Firewall*

(New York: Norton, 1997), 421–22.

452 The *L.A. Times* and the *New York Times* struck next.: The *New Yor Times*'s attack on Dark Alliance appeared on October 20, 1996, headlined "Tale of CIA and Drugs Has Life of Its Own." The *L.A. Times* series ran for three days, beginning on October 20, 1996.

453 Katz trotted out a number of other cocaine dealers: Jesse Katz, "Tracking the Genesis of the Crack Trade," *L.A. Times*, October 20, 1996.

453 the *L.A. Times* absolved the CIA: Doyle McManus, "Examining Charges of CIA Role in Crack Sales," *L.A. Times*, October 21, 1996.

453 "Sixty thousand?": Rafael Corñejo, interview by author.

454 McManus had played a central role: Doyle McManus and Ronald Ostrow, "U.S. Links Top Sandinistas to Drug Trafficking," *L.A. Times*, July 18, 1984.

454 described by investigative reporter Carl Bernstein: Bernstein, "The CIA and the Media," *Rolling Stone*, October 20, 1977, 55.

455 A day later: Ronald Ostrow, "3 Seized in Miami Cocaine Smuggling Linked to Nicaraguan Interior Minister," *L.A. Times*, July 19, 1984.

455 McManus and Ostrow later teamed up: Doyle McManus and Ronald Ostrow, "No Supporting Evidence, DEA Says: Senators Probing Reports of Contra Drug Smuggling," *L.A. Times*, February 18, 1987.

455 He banged out a letter to the reporter: Cabezas provided a copy of his letter to McManus to the author, along with McManus's response of April 9, 1987.

457 "Enrique Miranda, the former Meneses aide…had been found in Miami…": Gary Webb, "U.S. gave visa to Nicaraguan drug trafficker," *San Jose Mercury News*, Dec. 31, 1996, 11A.

458 solved one of the final mysteries of the Southern Front: Hull's escape from Costa Rica and the DEA's suspected involvement in it had been reported previously and ignored by the national media. Brian Donovan of *Newsday* initially reported it in 1991 as part of a retrospective look at the bombing at La Penca in 1984 that killed an American journalist. Martha Honey and David Myers freelanced a piece that appeared in the *San Francisco Chronicle*, August 14, 1991, under the headline "U.S. Probing Drug Agent's Activities in Costa Rica." The information for that story came largely from San Francisco private investigator Josiah Thompson, who was hired by defense lawyer Marvin Cahn to investigate a case involving an accused trafficker named Juan

Merino Noriega. Merino was arrested in 1990 as part of California's biggest cocaine bust, nearly 970 kilos, but despite the size of the case, the Justice Department permitted Merino to plead guilty to a money-laundering count rather than risk having the DEA's involvement in Hull's escape surface publicly in court.

"The United States will not discuss in this memorandum the reason that defendant Merino-Noriega was permitted to plead guilty to the money laundering charge instead of the importation charges other than to remind the Court that the reasons relate in large part to various submissions that were made and remain under seal," Asst. U.S. Attorney Ross W. Nadel wrote in Merino's sentencing memorandum, Dec. 10, 1992, *U.S. v. Merino-Noriega*, 90 CR 0177, Northern District of California.

I believed the story Georg and I had significantly advanced the public knowledge of Hull's escape, since we now had the pilot admitting everything on the record, as well as an on-the-record interview with the investigating agent for DEA internal affairs, who thought Justice had covered up the case. The *Mercury* never ran it.

459 Ricevuto believed Perez: Anthony Ricevuto, interview by author.

462 "Whether similar pressures were applied to Ceppos..." Naturally, rumors swirled that the CIA or other government agencies brought pressure to bear on the *Mercury News*'s owners, Knight-Ridder Newspapers, to torpedo my investigation and kill the follow-up stories but I never put much stock in those suspicions. Subsequently, I learned that Knight-Ridder has a history of collaborating with the CIA, once agreeing to provide journalistic "cover" for CIA agents (see John M. Crewdson and Joseph B. Treaster, "Worldwide Propaganda Network built by the CIA," *New York Times*, Dec. 26, 1977, 1). Additionally, Georg Hodel discovered a CIA cable in a Miami court file suggesting that a longtime editor on the Latin American desk of Knight-Ridder's flagship paper, *The Miami Herald*, had an operational relationship with the CIA during the 1960s. Suffice it to say that I am not quite as dismissive of suspicions of government pressure on the *Mercury*'s owners as I once was.

462 Shortly before I arrived at the *Plain Dealer*: The *Plain Dealer*'s retraction of the Jackie Presser story is discussed in James Neff, *Mobbed Up* (New York: Atlantic Monthly Press, 1989), 337–53. In addition, the author has copies of the debriefings of the Cleveland mobster Angelo "Big Ange" Lonardo, who reported the reasons for the PD's retraction to the authorities.

ARDE (Alizana Revolucionaria Democrática)—Contra faction based in Costa Rica and commanded by Edén Pastora, a former Sandinista.

Bloods—The smaller conglomeration of loosely affiliated L.A. street gangs. Formed in the early 1970s from the combination of the West Coast chapter of the Chicago-based Black Peace Stone Rangers and the L.A.-based Brim Blood Army and Pirus gangs. Blood colors are red.

Brigade 2506—U.S.-based organization made up primarily of Cuban veterans of the CIA-trained Bay of Pigs invasion forces.

CIA (Central Intelligence Agency)—The U.S. government's primary intelligence-gatherers. Its covert action side, the Directorate of Operations, has been the chief culprit behind Agency scandals and outrages.

Crips—The largest group of informally affiliated L.A. street gangs. Started in the late 1960s. Like the Bloods, the Crips are actually a loose confederation of smaller gangs, called "sets," which generally take their names from streets in their neighborhoods (ie. "Grape Street Crips," "Rollin' Forties Crips.") Crip colors are blue.

DEA (Drug Enforcement Administration)—A branch of the U.S. Department of Justice and the principal federal agency responsible for the enforcement of anti-drug laws. Successor to the Bureau of Narcotics and Dangerous Drugs (BNDD).

DIA (Defense Intelligence Agency)—Formed in 1961 as part of the Department of Defense. The primary intelligence service of the U.S. military. The DIA was heavily involved in Central America in the 1980s.

FDN (Fuerza Democrática Nicaragüense)—Contra faction created by the CIA, based in Honduras, and commanded by Enrique Bermúdez, a former National Guardsman. The FDN was the largest, most well-armed and best-trained of all the Contra factions.

FMLN (Frente Farbundo Marti Liberacion Nacional)—Leftist revolutionary group based in El Salvador and supported by the Sandinistas.

Frigorificos de Puntarenas—Costa Rican shrimp fishery set up by the Medellín cartel to launder drug money and transport cocaine shipments. Later purchased by Cuban anti-Communists and suspected drug traffickers and used by Oliver North and the Contras to launder humanitarian aid funds.

Ilopango—Airbase in El Salvador secretly used by the Contras, the CIA, and Oliver North's "Enterprise" to funnel weapons and supplies to the Contra units operating on the Southern Front in Costa Rica. Both the CIA and DEA had reports that Ilopango was used to transship cocaine.

LAPD—Los Angeles Police Department.

Legion of September 15—An early Contra group made up primarily of ex-National Guardsmen. Based in Guatemala where it committed crimes and political kidnappings and assassinations. Commanded by Ricardo (El Chino) Lau and Enrique Bermúdez, it later became the core of the FDN.

M-3 (Movimiento Tercera Via)—Tiny Contra splinter group based in Costa Rica. Commanded by Sebastian "Guachan" González and staffed mainly with Cuban anti-Communist mercenaries.

Majors—The nickname of three elite detective units formed by the Los Angeles County Sheriff's office in the mid-1980s to combat major criminal organizations. Short for Major Violators.

NHAO (Nicaraguan Humanitarian Aid Office)—A State Department operation set up to distribute Congressionally authorized humanitaran aid to the Contras.

NSC (National Security Council)—Ostensibly, the President's advisors on national security matters. Under the Reagan Adminstration, it became an operational intelligence agency based inside the White House.

Nicaraguan National Guard (La Guardia Nacional)—Anastasio Somoza's army, which also ran the national police, state security and intelligence services, the postal service, and customs agency.

OIJ (Organismo de Investigacion Judicial)—Costa Rican law enforcement agency similar in function to the FBI.

OSN (Oficina Seguridad Nacional)—Anastasio Somoza's secret police unit that monitored political dissidents.

Sandinistas (FRS)—Informal name of the Frente Revolucionario de Sandino, the leftist revolutionary guerrilla group that overthrew the U.S.-supported dictatorship of Anastasio Somoza in 1979.

UDN-FARN (Union Democrática Nicaragüense—Fuerzas Armadas Resistencia Nicaragüenses)—Early Contra faction based first in Honduras and then in Costa Rica, commanded by the erratic former Sandinsta Fernando "El Negro" Chamorro. UDN-FARN first joined forces with the FDN, left to link up with Pastora and ARDE, then left Pastora and rejoined the FDN under the umbrella group UNO.

UNO (United Nicaraguan Opposition)—A later CIA-inspired attempt to brush up the Contra's public image and gather all Contra factions under one group. UNO existed mostly as a fa_ade, as the FDN did the bulk of the fighting and retained most of the authority.

Index